THEATRE PROFILES 8

THEATRE PROFILES 8

THE ILLUSTRATED REFERENCE GUIDE TO AMERICA'S NONPROFIT PROFESSIONAL THEATRE

Edited by John Istel

THEATRE COMMUNICATIONS GROUP
NEW YORK · 1988

The publications and programs of Theatre Communications Group, the national organization for the nonprofit professional theatre, are supported by Actors' Equity Foundation, Alcoa Foundation, ARCO Foundation, AT&T Foundation, Citicorp/Citibank, Columbia Pictures Industries, Consolidated Edison Company of New York, Eleanor Naylor Dana Charitable Trust, Dayton Hudson Foundation, Department of Cultural Affairs—City of New York, Exxon Foundation, The William and Mary Greve Foundation, Home Box Office, Inc., The Andrew W. Mellon Foundation, Mobil Foundation, Inc., National Broadcasting Company, National Endowment for the Arts, New York Life Foundation, New York Council on the Arts, The Pew Charitable Trusts, Philip Morris Incorporated, The Rockefeller Foundation, The Scherman Foundation, Shell Oil Company Foundation, The Shubert Foundation, Inc., Consulate General of Spain and the Xerox Foundation.

355 Lexington Ave., New York, NY 10017.

On the cover, Hartford Stage Company's 1987 production of *Pericles* with Darryl Croxton, Angela Bassett, Michelle Ward, Jack Wetherall, Jodi Long, John Wojda and Victoria Gadsden, photograph copyright © 1988 by Jennifer W. Lester.

Design and composition by The Sarabande Press

ISBN 0-930452-77-1

First Edition, April 1988

Frontis. StageWest. *As You Like It.* Photo: Carl Bartels.

CONTENTS

FOREWORD

It seems that practically every other year a new proposal surfaces for a "national theatre" in this country that would rival Great Britain's. However, anyone reading TCG's *Theatre Profiles* series would already be aware of a dynamic "national theatre" in the United States—the sprawling network of nonprofit theatres that mirror the diversity and energy of our citizenry, whether a small Asian-American ensemble, a touring children's theatre or a $10 million institution. While the last volume, the seventh, celebrated the first 25 years of this explosive movement, this eighth edition marches smartly toward a golden anniversary with a new streamlined format that delivers what the title promises: over 220 "theatre profiles."

Theatre Profiles 8's new layout allows more information to fit into less space, including production photographs from each company as well as a statement from each theatre's artistic leader. In addition to articulating the artistic goals of each theatre, these statements could be viewed as brief reports from the front. Many artistic directors give voice to concerns central to every theatre's creative and fiscal health: the frequent inadequacy of rehearsal time, the need for resources devoted to the development of new work, the absence of funding for artists, the use of nontraditional casting and, especially, the need to develop younger audiences who frequently equate comedy with Eddie Murphy's latest movie and drama with a John Hughes coming-of-age flick.

Most of the vital statistics of each theatre remain as in the last volume, with one notable change. To increase the book's usefulness for directors and designers, this edition designates those theatres that are signatories to agreements with the Society of Stage Directors and Choreographers (SSD&C) and United Scenic Artists (USA), as well as listing Actors' Equity Association contracts as in the past.

TCG's *Theatre Profiles* series now encompasses an encyclopedic reference to the last 16 years of regional theatre across America. Whether you're an actor considering a job away from home, a director looking for designers, a theatre history student researching a paper, or a theatre trivia fan wondering if any company has recently mounted a production of *The Duchess of Malfi*, this book and its predecessors should prove invaluable. As each reader thumbs these pages, I have no doubt that *Theatre Profiles 8* will bear witness to the marvelous eclecticism that makes America's "national theatre" so vibrant.

—John Istel

American Repertory Theatre. Diane D'Aquila and John Bottoms in *The Changeling*. Photo: Richard Feldman.

USING THIS BOOK

All the theatres included in *Theatre Profiles 8* are constituents of Theatre Communications Group, the national organization for the nonprofit professional theatre. Information was requested in the spring and summer of 1987. The text of this volume is based on the materials submitted by the 221 theatres included. The following notes provide a guide to the elements of the book.

Personnel

Each theatre's current artistic and managerial leaders are included. This information was updated through December 1, 1987. If there had been a change in the artistic leadership of the theatre within the past two seasons, the former artistic head is noted following the artistic statement, with an indication of the season(s) for which he or she was responsible.

Contact Information

The mailing address of each organization is included, which is not necessarily the address of the theatre. Where two telephone numbers are listed, the first is for the administrative or business "(bus.)" office and the second for the box office "(b.o.)."

Founding Date and Founders

The founding date represents the beginning of public performances, or in a few cases, the conceptual or legal establishment of the organization. The names of all founders are listed under the date in alphabetical order.

Season

The season information is included as a general guide to the annual performance dates of each theatre. The months listed indicate the opening and closing of each theatre's season. "Year-round" designates companies that perform continuously throughout the year; "variable" indicates irregular or varying schedules.

Facilities

The facilities are the theatre space(s) in which each company regularly performs. The seating capacity and type of stage are included for each facility. The name of the space is provided if it differs from the organization's name. The information is current as of July 1987 and doesn't necessarily indicate the performance venues of the seasons highlighted in the book. The following terminology is used in describing each facility:

San Diego Repertory Theatre. Rex Rabold and Michael Lewis in *The Strange Case of Dr. Jekyll and Mr. Hyde*. Photo: Douglas Jacobs.

PROSCENIUM: The traditional, picture-window stage separated from the auditorium by a proscenium arch, so that the audience views the action from a single "fourth wall" perspective.

THRUST: All types of facilities wherein the stage juts into the audience and is thereby surrounded on three sides. A "modified thrust" or "modified proscenium" protrudes less, often utilizing a fan-shaped apron on which action can take place.

ARENA: Also called "theatre-in-the-round." The audience completely surrounds the stage.

FLEXIBLE: All types of theatre space which can be altered or converted from one category to another.

CABARET: A simple performance platform, with the audience usually seated at tables.

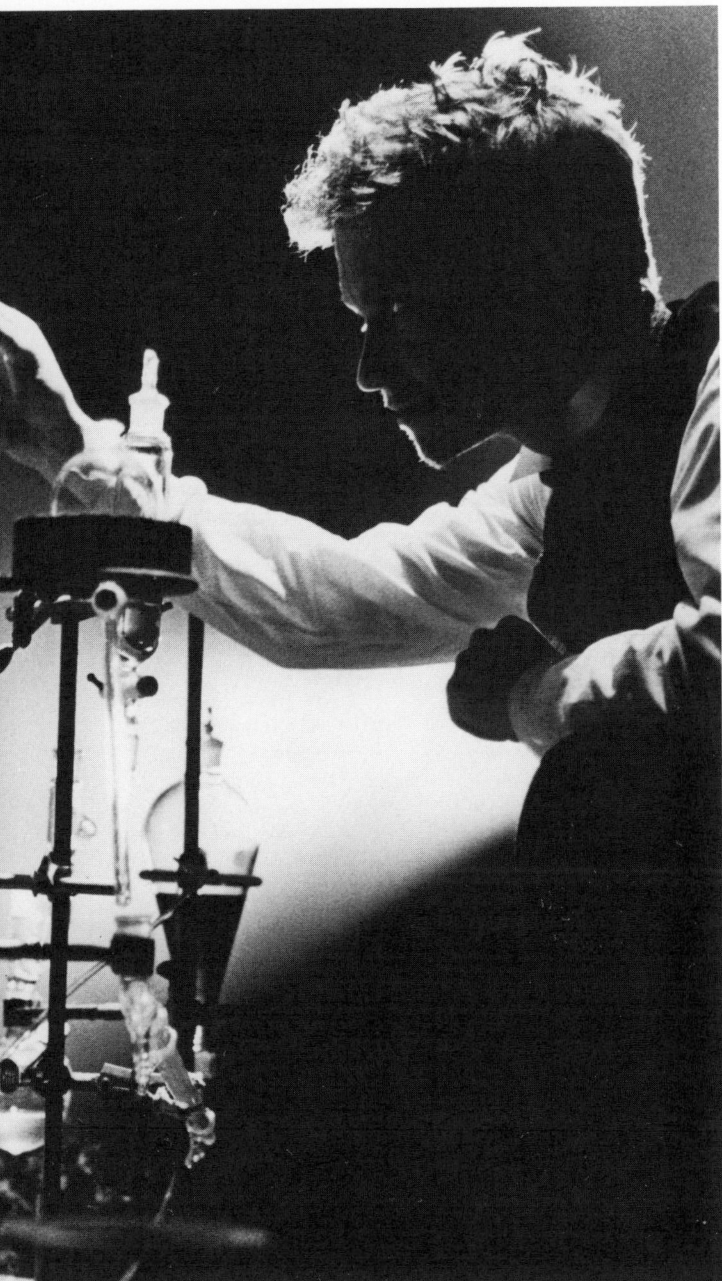

Finances

Operating expenses are included to provide a general sense of the overall size of each theatre's operation. Most often the financial figures are from calendar year 1986 or fiscal year 1986–87, the most recent year available at the time information was gathered for *Theatre Profiles*.

Union Contracts

If a theatre is signatory to agreements with Actors' Equity Association (AEA), the Society of Stage Directors and Choreographers (SSD&C) or United Scenic Artists (USA) the designation is included under the "Contract" heading. Further, the type of AEA contract is also included. The following abbreviations are used:

CAT: Chicago Area Theatre contract

COST: Council on Stock Theatres contract

CORST: Council on Resident Stock Theatres contract

LORT: League of Resident Theatres contract

SPT: Small Professional Theatre contract

TYA: Theatre for Young Audiences contract

U/RTA: University/Resident Theatre Association contract

The letters enclosed in parentheses following the contract abbreviations designate the size of theatre and scale of payment. For more specific information on these contracts, please contact the unions directly.

Artistic Director's Statement

All artistic heads were invited to submit a statement describing the artistic philosophy governing the work at their respective institutions from their personal perspective. While all have been edited for style, every attempt has been made to retain the individuality of each statement.

Production Lists

Productions from the 1985–86 and the 1986–87 seasons (1985 and 1986 for theatres with summer operations) are listed, most often in the chronological order in which they were produced. The title of each production is immediately followed by the name of the playwright, and where applicable the adapter, translator and/or source of literary adaptation if such information was provided by the theatre. In the case of musicals, all composers, librettists and lyricists are included. The director and set, costume and lighting designers follow, designated by a bold-faced letter in parentheses directly preceding the name—(**D**), (**S**), (**C**), (**L**). Choreographers, sound/video designers and musical directors are not included.

Photographs

A photograph from one of each theatre's listed productions accompanies each entry. The photos help convey the range and diversity of production activity and were generally selected for clarity of image from those submitted for possible inclusion by the theatre. Actors' names are included in the caption when there are five or fewer actors pictured.

Regional Index

A geographical, state-by-state listing of every theatre is included to readily identify theatres by region.

Theatre Chronology

The "time line" history of the nonprofit professional theatres included in this volume is intended to demonstrate the growth pattern of the decentralized nonprofit professional theatre movement in the United States.

Name/Title Indices

Playwrights, composers, artistic and management heads, directors, designers and founders appear in the index of names. For convenience, a separate index includes titles of all dramatic works listed in this book.

THEATRES

Academy Theatre
A Contemporary Theatre
The Acting Company
Actors Theatre of Louisville
Actors Theatre of St. Paul
Alabama Shakespeare Festival
Alaska Repertory Theatre
Alley Theatre
Alliance Theatre Company
AMAS Repertory Theatre
American Conservatory Theatre
American Jewish Theatre
The American Place Theatre
American Players Theatre
American Repertory Theatre
The American Stage Company
American Stage Festival
American Theatre Company
Antenna Theater
Arena Stage
Arizona Theatre Company
The Arkansas Arts Center Children's Theatre
Arkansas Repertory Theatre
Asolo Performing Arts Center
A Traveling Jewish Theatre
At the Foot of the Mountain
Attic Theatre
The Back Alley Theatre
Barter Theatre
The Bathhouse Theatre
Berkeley Repertory Theatre
Berkeley Shakespeare Festival
Berkshire Theatre Festival
Bilingual Foundation of the Arts
The Bloomsburg Theatre Ensemble
BoarsHead: Michigan Public Theater
The Body Politic Theatre
Caldwell Theatre Company
California Theatre Center
Capital Repertory Company
The CAST Theatre
Center for Puppetry Arts
Center Stage
Center Theater
The Changing Scene
The Children's Theatre Company
Cincinnati Playhouse in the Park
Circle in the Square Theatre
Circle Repertory Company
City Theatre Company
Clarence Brown Theatre Company
The Cleveland Play House
Coconut Grove Playhouse
Creative Arts Team
The Cricket Theatre
Crossroads Theatre Company
CSC Repertory Ltd.—The Classic Stage Company
Cumberland County Playhouse
Dallas Theater Center
Delaware Theatre Company
Dell'Arte Players Company
Denver Center Theatre Company
Detroit Repertory Theatre
Dorset Theatre Festival
East West Players
Emmy Gifford Children's Theater
Empire State Institute for the Performing Arts
The Empty Space Theatre
The Ensemble Studio Theatre
Eureka Theatre Company
The Fiji Company
Florida Studio Theatre
FMT
Ford's Theatre
Free Street Theater
Fulton Opera House
George Street Playhouse
Germinal Stage Denver
GeVa Theatre
Goodman Theatre
Goodspeed Opera House
Great American Children's Theatre Company
Great Lakes Theater Festival
The Group Theatre Company
Grove Theatre Company
The Guthrie Theater
Hartford Stage Company
Heritage Artists, Ltd.
The Hippodrome State Theatre
Honolulu Theatre for Youth
Horse Cave Theatre
Hudson Guild Theatre
Huntington Theatre Company
Illinois Theatre Center
Illusion Theater
The Independent Eye
Indiana Repertory Theatre
INTAR Hispanic American Arts Center
Interart Theatre
Intiman Theatre Company
Jean Cocteau Repertory
Jewish Repertory Theatre
La Jolla Playhouse
Lamb's Players Theatre
Lamb's Theatre Company
L.A. Theatre Works
Lincoln Center Theater
Living Stage Theatre Company
Long Island Stage
Long Wharf Theatre
Looking Glass Theatre
Los Angeles Theatre Center
Mabou Mines
Magic Theatre
Manhattan Punch Line Theatre
Manhattan Theatre Club
Marin Theatre Company
Mark Taper Forum
McCarter Theatre
Merrimack Repertory Theatre
Milwaukee Repertory Theater
Mirror Repertory Company
Missouri Repertory Theatre
Mixed Blood Theatre Company
Musical Theatre Works
Music-Theatre Group
National Theatre of the Deaf
Nebraska Theatre Caravan
New American Theater
New Dramatists
New Federal Theatre
New Jersey Shakespeare Festival
New Mexico Repertory Theatre
New Playwrights' Theatre
New Stage Theatre
New York Shakespeare Festival
New York Theatre Workshop
Northlight Theatre
Oakland Ensemble Theatre
Odyssey Theatre Ensemble
The Old Creamery Theatre Company
Old Globe Theatre
Omaha Magic Theatre
One Act Theatre Company of San Francisco
O'Neill Theater Center

Alliance Theatre. Michele Shay in *An American Doll's House*. Photo: Charles Rafshoon.

Ontological-Hysteric Theater
The Open Eye: New Stagings
Oregon Shakespearean Festival
Organic Theater Company
Pan Asian Repertory Theatre
Paper Mill Playhouse
PCPA Theaterfest
Pennsylvania Stage Company
The People's Light and Theatre Company
Periwinkle National Theatre for Young Audiences
Perseverance Theatre
Philadelphia Drama Guild
Philadelphia Festival Theatre for New Plays
The Philadelphia Theatre Company
Pioneer Theatre Company
Pittsburgh Public Theater
Playhouse on the Square
The Playmakers
PlayMakers Repertory Company
The Playwrights' Center
Playwrights Horizons
Portland Stage Company
Puerto Rican Traveling Theatre
Remains Theatre
Repertorio Español
The Repertory Theatre of St. Louis
River Arts Repertory
The Road Company
Roadside Theater
Round House Theatre
Sacramento Theatre Company
The Salt Lake Acting Company
San Diego Repertory Theatre
San Francisco Mime Troupe
San Jose Repertory Company
Seattle Children's Theatre
Seattle Repertory Theatre
The Second Stage
Shakespeare Theatre at the Folger
The Snowmass/Aspen Repertory Theatre
Society Hill Playhouse
Soho Repertory Theatre
South Coast Repertory
Stage One: The Louisville Children's Theatre
Stage West
StageWest
Steppenwolf Theatre Company
The Street Theater
Studio Arena Theatre
The Studio Theatre
Syracuse Stage
Tacoma Actors Guild
The Theatre at Monmouth
Theatre de la Jeune Lune
Theatre for a New Audience
Theatre for the New City
Theatre IV
Theatre Project
Theatre Project Company
TheatreVirginia
Theatreworks/USA
Theatre X
Trinity Repertory Company
Unicorn Theatre
Victory Gardens Theater
Vineyard Theatre
Virginia Stage Company
Walnut Street Theatre
Whole Theatre
Williamstown Theatre Festival
The Wilma Theater
Wisdom Bridge Theatre
The Wooster Group
Worcester Foothills Theatre Company
WPA Theatre
Yale Repertory Theatre

THEATRE PROFILES 8

Berkeley Repertory Theatre. Freda Norman in *The Good Person of Szechuan.* Photo: Ken Friedman

Academy Theatre

FRANK WITTOW
Producing Artistic Director

MARGARET FERGUSON
Managing Director

Box 77070
Atlanta, GA 30357
(404) 873-2518 (bus.)
(404) 892-0880 (b.o.)

FOUNDED 1956
Frank Wittow

SEASON
Sept.-June

FACILITIES
The Phoebe Theatre
Seating capacity: 383
Stage: thrust

First Stage
Seating capacity: 200
Stage: flexible

Lab Theatre
Seating capacity: 75
Stage: flexible

FINANCES
July 1, 1986-June 30, 1987
Expenses: $619,318

CONTRACTS
AEA letter of agreement

We are a resident theatre company whose mission is to serve the community through five interdependent programs of performance, education and outreach: the school of performing arts, theatre for youth, mainstage subscription series, First Stage new play series and human service programs. The concept of artist-as-teacher is at the heart of our work, and we provide training for professional and avocational actors. The resident ensemble members serve as the core of our school's faculty, and as facilitators in our outreach programs that work with special populations. From our theatre for youth's issue-oriented, original plays, to the classic, contemporary and sometimes unknown works in our mainstage series, we strive to involve audiences and stimulate them to fresh awareness. This vision is perhaps best realized in our new play series, where audiences, writers and artists join to provide a literal "first stage" for works by our region's best playwrights.

—Frank Wittow

PRODUCTIONS 1985–86

Strider, adapt: Robert Kalfin and Steve Brown, from Leo Tolstoy; book: Mark Rozovsky; lyrics: Uri Riashentsev and Steve Brown; music: Mark Rozovsky, S. Vetkin and Norman Berman; (D) John Stephens; (S) J.A. Benedict; (C) Judy Winograd and P.V.I.; (L) J.A. Benedict

A Christmas Carol, adapt: John Stephens, from Charles Dickens; music and lyrics: Phillip DePoy; (D) John Stephens; (S) J.A. Benedict and Sheila Hullihen; (C) Judy Winograd and P.V.I.; (L) Griff Garmers

Mandragola, Niccolo Machiavelli; adapt: Levi Lee; music: Phillip DePoy; lyrics: Levi Lee, Rebecca Wackler, Chris Kayser and Phillip DePoy; (D) Levi Lee; (S) J.A. Benedict and Sheila Hullihen; (C) Anita Beaty; (L) J.A. Benedict

Wedding Band, Alice Childress; (D) Frank Wittow; (S) J.A. Benedict and Sheila Hullihen; (C) Patricia Munford; (L) J.A. Benedict

A Shayna Maidel, Barbara Lebow; (D) Barbara Lebow; (S) Michael Halpern; (C) Judy Winograd and P.V.I.; (L) S.R. Johnson

La Ronde, Arthur Schnitzler; adapt: John Stephens; (D) John Stephens; (S) Mark Forsythe; (C) Nancy Holloway; (L) Mark Forsythe

The Adventures of Homer McGundy, Barbara Lebow; (D) Barbara Lebow; (S) Michael Halpern and David Pendergraft; (C) Kathleen McManus; (L) David Pendergraft

Pull, Terence Cawley; (D) John Liles; (S) David Pendergraft; (C) Kathleen McManus; (L) David Pendergraft

Mattie Cushman, Ken Anderson; (D) Richard Wesp; (S) Richard Wesp; (C) P.V.I.; (L) David Pendergraft

Doolan's Wake, John Stephens; (D) John Stephens; (S) John Stephens; (C) P.V.I.; (L) J.A. Benedict

The Dream Nibbler, company-developed; (D) John Stephens; (S) John Stephens and Ruth Reid; (C) P.V.I.; (L) J.A. Benedict

The Square Egg of Gratchitt, Barbara Lebow; (D) Holly Stevenson; (S) J.A. Benedict; (C) Celia Hanna; (L) K. Ken Johnston

The Good Life, company-developed; (D) Holly Stevenson; (C) P.V.I.; (L) K. Ken Johnston

Mr. & Mrs. Bach, Dale Dreyfoos; (D) Dale Dreyfoos and Matt Hutchinson; (C) P.V.I.

PRODUCTIONS 1986–87

The Scarecrow, Percy MacKaye; (D) Levi Lee; (S) Steven Seaberg; (C) Laura Paris; (L) Margaret E. Viverito

A Christmas Carol, adapt: John Stephens, from Charles Dickens; music and lyrics: Phillip DePoy; (D) John Stephens; (S) C. Stuart Wolfe; (C) Judy Winograd; (L) Margaret E. Viverito

The Imaginary Invalid, Molière; adapt: Nancy Rhodes; (D) Nancy Rhodes; (S) Gary Jennings; (C) Gary Jennings; (L) Paul R. Ackerman

The Adventures of Homer McGundy, Barbara Lebow; (D) Barbara Lebow; (S) Michael Halpern; (C) Judy Winograd; (L) Paul R. Ackerman

Canterbury Tales!, adapt: Arnold Wengrow, from Geoffrey Chaucer; (D) Frank Wittow; (S) Michael Stauffer; (C) Judy Winograd; (L) Paul R. Ackerman

Elmatha's Apology, Rebecca Ranson; (D) Kerrie Osborne; (S) Kerrie Osborne and Marisa M. Warner; (C) Heather Heath; (L) Kevin Crysler

Headlines!, Frank Wittow; (D) Frank Wittow; (S) Marisa M. Warner; (C) Cindy Reno; (L) Robert Corin

Cyparis, Barbara Lebow; (D) Barbara Lebow; (S) Michael Halpern; (C) Maggi Ewing; (L) Robert Corin

Dance of Apollo, John Forrest Ferguson; (D) John Forrest Ferguson

Teju's Song of Africa, Lolita Woodward and Bill Johns; (D) John Forrest Ferguson; (S) John Forrest Ferguson; (C) Judy Winograd; (L) Robert Corin

Song of Gweneviere, John Stephens; (D) John Stephens; (S) Robert Corin and Ellie Emerick; (C) Harold Ferguson; (L) Robert Corin and Ellie Emerick

"And Now...Back to Our Hero", John Stephens; (D) John Stephens; (C) P.V.I

Doolan's Wake, John Stephens; (D) John Stephens; (C) P.V.I.

Uncle Beethoven, Matt Hutchison; (D) Frank Wittow; (C) P.V.I.

Academy Theatre. Chris Kayser and Kenny Leon in *Cyparis*. Photo: Bernard Cohen.

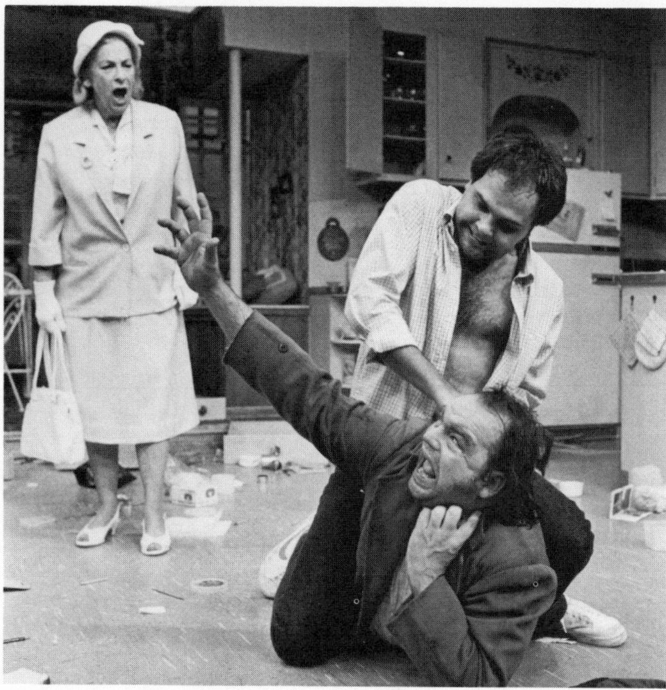

A Contemporary Theatre. Marjorie Nelson, Laurence Ballard and Richard Riehle in *True West.* Photo Chris Bennion

A Contemporary Theatre

GREGORY A. FALLS
Producing Director

PHIL SCHERMER
Producing Manager

SUSAN TRAPNELL MORITZ
Administrative Manager

Box 19400
Seattle, WA 98109
(206) 285-3220 (bus.)
(206) 285-5110 (b.o.)

FOUNDED 1965
Gregory A. Falls

SEASON
May-Nov.

FACILITIES
Mainstage
Seating capacity: 449
Stage: thrust

FINANCES
Jan. 1, 1986-Dec. 31, 1986
Expenses: $2,000,900

CONTRACTS
AEA LORT (C), TYA and SSD&C

With an occasional excursion into other territory, ACT is dedicated to producing the best available contemporary plays. The theatre began in 1965 with a five-play season of works by Arthur Kopit, Tennessee Williams, Peter Shaffer, James Thurber, and Howard Richardson and William Burney. Our professional theatre for young audiences, the Young ACT Company, is one year younger than our mainstage. It has produced more than 30 plays, of which 14 were original scripts. Twice invited to perform at the John F. Kennedy Center in Washington, D.C., the Young ACT Company has won several awards, including the Jennie Heiden Award, and the company's production of *The Odyssey* was included in *Time* magazine's list of 10 best productions in 1985. A new program, Songworks, is devoted to the development and presentation of new musical theatre.

—*Gregory A. Falls*

PRODUCTIONS 1986

Theseus and the Minotaur, adapt: Gregory A. Falls; (D) Gregory A. Falls; (S) Richard J. Harris; (C) Rose Pederson; (L) Donna Grout

A Wrinkle in Time, adapt: Gregory A. Falls, from Madeleine L'Engle; (D) Anne-Denise Ford; (S) Jennifer Lupton; (C) Sarah Campbell; (L) Peter W. Allen

The Navigator, A Story of Micronesia, Michael Cowell; (D) John Kauffman; (S) Joseph Dodd; (C) Laura Crow; (L) Lloyd S. Riford, III

On the Razzle, Tom Stoppard; (D) Jeff Steitzer; (S) Shelley Henze Schermer; (C) Sally Richardson; (L) Phil Schermer

Painting Churches, Tina Howe; (D) Gregory A. Falls; (S) Bill Forrester; (C) Sarah Campbell; (L) Phil Schermer

Tales from Hollywood, Christopher Hampton; (D) Jeff Steitzer; (S) Scott Weldin; (C) Laura Crow; (L) Rick Paulsen

Brighton Beach Memoirs, Neil Simon; (D) Gregory A. Falls; (S) Bill Forrester; (C) Rose Pederson; (L) James Verdery

The Jail Diary of Albie Sachs, David Edgar; (D) Jeff Steitzer; (S) Michael Olich; (C) Celeste Cleveland; (L) Rick Paulsen

Little Shop of Horrors, book and lyrics: Howard Ashman; music: Alan Menken; (D) Anne-Denise Ford; (S) Shelley Henze Schermer; (C) Laura Crow; (L) Jody Briggs

A Christmas Carol, adapt: Gregory A. Falls, from Charles Dickens; (D) Rita Giomi; (S) Bill Forrester; (C) Nanrose Buchman; (L) Jody Briggs

PRODUCTIONS 1987

March of the Falsettos, music and lyrics: William Finn; (D) Jeff Steitzer; (S) Scott Weldin; (C) Sarah Campbell; (L) Rick Paulsen

A Lie of the Mind, Sam Shepard; (D) Gregory A. Falls; (S) Karen Gjelsteen; (C) Sally Richardson; (L) James Verdery

The Diary of a Scoundrel, Alexander Ostrovsky; adapt: Erik Brogger; (D) Jeff Steitzer; (S) Scott Weldin; (C) Michael Olich; (L) Rick Paulsen

The Marriage of Bette and Boo, Christopher Durang; (D) Anne-Denise Ford; (S) Robert Gardiner; (C) Sally Richardson; (L) Jennifer Lupton

Glengarry Glen Ross, David Mamet; (D) David Ira Goldstein; (S) Jerry Hooker; (C) Rose Pederson; (L) Rick Paulsen

Biloxi Blues, Neil Simon; (D) Gregory A. Falls; (S) Bill Forrester; (C) Rose Pederson; (L) Bill Forrester

A Christmas Carol, adapt: Gregory A. Falls, from Charles Dickens; (D) Jeff Steitzer; (S) Bill Forrester; (C) Nanrose Buchman; (L) Jody Briggs

The Acting Company

MICHAEL KAHN
Artistic Director

MARGOT HARLEY
Executive Producer

Box 898, Times Square Station
New York, NY 10108
(212) 564-3510

FOUNDED 1972
Margot Harley, John Houseman

SEASON
Aug.-May

FACILITIES
The John Houseman Theatre
Seating capacity: 289
Stage: proscenium

FINANCES
July 1, 1986-June 30, 1987
Expenses: $2,285,296

CONTRACTS
AEA LORT (B), (C), SSD&C and USA

For 15 years The Acting Company has been committed to the development of young American actors and to the creation of discerning audiences across the nation through our touring company. Now, the New York Ensemble, comprised of alumni from past companies, allows those actors a chance to return to a group of similarly trained and experienced artists and accept the challenges of works such as *The Cradle Will Rock*, *Ten by Tennessee* and *On the Verge or The Geography of Yearning*. We are pleased that three members of the original company, which was formed from Juilliard School graduates, are again working with us: Kevin Kline and David Ogden Stiers have been named artistic associates, and Gerald Gutierrez, who directed last season's *Much Ado About Nothing*, is our associate artistic director. The Acting Company now claims a home base on New York City's Theatre Row—the 280-seat John Houseman Theatre.

—*Michael Kahn*

The Acting Company. Wendy Brennan, Alison Stair Neet and Melissa Gallagher in *Much Ado About Nothing*. Photo: Diane Gorodnitzki.

PRODUCTIONS 1985–86

As You Like It, William Shakespeare; (D) Mervyn Willis; (S) Stephen McCabe; (C) Stephen McCabe; (L) Dennis Parichy

Orchards: Seven American Playwrights Present Stories by Chekhov, Maria Irene Fornes, Spalding Gray, John Guare, David Mamet, Wendy Wasserstein, Michael Weller and Samm-Art Williams; (D) Robert Falls; (S) Adrianne Lobel; (C) Laura Crow; (L) Paul Gallo

Ten by Tennessee: Ten Short One-Act Plays, Tennessee Williams; (D) Michael Kahn; (S) Derek McLane; (C) Ann Hould-Ward; (L) Dennis Parichy

PRODUCTIONS 1986–87

Much Ado About Nothing, William Shakespeare; (D) Gerald Gutierrez; (S) Douglas Stein; (C) Ann Hould-Ward; (L) Pat Collins

The Gilded Age, adapt: Constance Congdon, from Mark Twain and Charles Dudley Warner; (D) Mark Lamos; (S) Marjorie Bradley Kellogg; (C) Jess Goldstein; (L) Pat Collins

On the Verge or The Geography of Yearning, Eric Overmyer; (D) Garland Wright; (S) John Arnone; (C) Ann Hould-Ward; (L) James Ingalls

Actors Theatre of Louisville

JON JORY
Producing Director

ALEXANDER SPEER
Administrative Director

MARILEE HEBERT-SLATER
Associate Director

316-320 West Main St.
Louisville, KY 40202-2916
(502) 584-1265 (bus.)
(502) 584-1205 (b.o.)

FOUNDED 1964
Richard Block, Ewel Cornett

SEASON
Sept.-May

FACILITIES
Pamela Brown Auditorium
Seating capacity: 637
Stage: thrust

Victor Jory Theatre
Seating capacity: 159
Stage: thrust

Downstairs At Actors
Seating capacity: 100
Stage: cabaret

FINANCES
June 1, 1986-May 31, 1987
Expenses: $3,692,000

CONTRACTS
AEA LORT (B), (D), SSD&C and USA

Actors Theatre of Louisville has three primary areas of emphasis which constitute an artistic policy. The first is the discovery and development of a new generation of American playwrights. In the last 15 years Actors Theatre has produced the work of almost 200 new writers. This work, strongly backed by a commissioning program, is central to our aesthetic. Our second area of emphasis is an interdisciplinary approach to the classical theatre combining lectures, discussions, films and plays through the annual Classics in Context Festival. Working under a different umbrella theme each year, this festival provides new insights into the classical repertoire, both for our company and our resident audience. Last year's Pirandello Festival attracted scholars and theatre people from around the world. Finally, ATL is involved in creating a form of documentary drama emphasizing our regional roots. Last season's *Digging In: The Farm Crisis in Kentucky* was developed from 1,400 pages of oral history of the state's small farmer, and a current project is being developed from interviews with the area's homeless.

—Jon Jory

PRODUCTIONS 1985–86

Traveler in the Dark, Marsha Norman; (D) Jon Jory; (S) Paul Owen; (C) Marcia Dixcy; (L) Jeff Hill

Cloud Nine, Caryl Churchill; (D) Ray Fry; (S) Virginia Dancy and Elmon Webb; (C) Marcia Dixcy; (L) Jeff Hill

And a Nightingale Sang, C.P. Taylor; (D) Rob Spera; (S) Jim Sandefur; (C) Marie Anne Chiment; (L) Geoffrey Cunningham

Shorts Festival:

Chicks, Grace McKeaney; (D) Steven D. Albrezzi; (S) Paul Owen; (C) Marcia Dixcy; (L) Jeff Hill

A Narrow Bed, Ellen McLaughlin; (D) Jon Jory; (S) Paul Owen; (C) Marcia Dixcy; (L) Jeff Hill

21A, Kevin Kling; (D) Frazier W. Marsh; (S) Paul Owen; (C) Marcia Dixcy; (L) Jeff Hill

Megs, Stephen Metcalfe; (D) Stephen Metcalfe; (S) Paul Owen; (C) Marcia Dixcy; (L) Jeff Hill

Boaz, Randy Noojin; (D) Larry Deckel; (S) Paul Owen; (C) Marcia Dixcy; (L) Geoff Korf

Isle of Dogs, Larry Larson, Levi Lee and Rebecca Wackler; (D) Jon Jory; (S) Paul Owen; (C) Marcia Dixcy; (L) Geoff Korf

Goodnight Firefly Ravine, Raima Evan; (D) Richard A. Cunningham; (S) Paul Owen; (C) Marcia Dixcy; (L) Jeff Hill

How It Hangs, Grace McKeaney; (D) Rob Spera; (S) Paul Owen; (C) Marcia Dixcy; (L) Jeff Hill

How Gertrude Stormed the Philosopher's Club, Martin Epstein; (D) Frazier W. Marsh; (S) Paul Owen; (C) Marcia Dixcy; (L) Jeff Hill

The Gift of the Magi, adapt, music and lyrics: Peter Ekstrom, from O. Henry; (D) Larry Deckel; (S) Paul Owen; (C) Hollis Jenkins-Evans; (L) Geoff Korf

A Christmas Carol, adapt: Barbara Field, from Charles Dickens; (D) Frazier W. Marsh; (S) Paul Owen; (C) Karen Anderson-Fields; (L) Jeff Hill

Classics in Context Festival:

The Royal Comedians, Mikhail Bulgakov; trans: Ellendea Proffer; (D) Laszlo Morton; (S) Miklos Feher; (C) Marcia Dixcy; (L) Paul Owen

The Misanthrope, Molière; trans: Richard Wilbur; (D) Jon Jory; (S) Paul Owen; (C) Marcia Dixcy; (L) Jeff Hill

Educating Rita, Willy Russell; (D) Larry Deckel; (S) Paul Owen; (C) Marcia Dixcy; (L) Geoff Korf

Actors Theatre of Louisville. Larry Larson and Levi Lee in *Some Things You Need to Know Before the World Ends: A Final Evening with the Illuminati*. Photo: David S. Talbott

Humana Festival:

To Culebra, Jonathan Bolt; (D) Jon Jory and Frazier W. Marsh; (S) Paul Owen; (C) Marcia Dixcy; (L) Paul Owen

Astronauts, Claudia Reilly; (D) Tom Bullard; (S) Paul Owen; (C) Ann Wallace; (L) Paul Owen

No Mercy, Constance Congdon; (D) Jackson Phippin; (S) Paul Owen; (C) Ann Wallace; (L) Geoff Korf

Some Things You Need to Know Before the World Ends: A Final Evening with the Illuminati, Larry Larson and Levi Lee; (D) Jon Jory; (S) Paul Owen; (C) Marcia Dixcy; (L) Paul Owen

How to Say Goodbye, Mary Gallagher; (D) Mary B. Robinson; (S) Paul Owen; (C) Ann Wallace; (L) Jeff Hill

How Gertrude Stormed the Philosopher's Club, Martin Epstein; (D) Frazier W. Marsh; (S) Paul Owen; (C) Marcia Dixcy; (L) Jeff Hill

21A, Kevin Kling; (D) Frazier W. Marsh; (S) Paul Owen; (C) Marcia Dixcy; (L) Jeff Hill

The Shaper, John Steppling; (D) Bob Glaudini; (S) Paul Owen; (C) Ann Wallace; (L) Jeff Hill

Smitty's News, Conrad Bishop and Elizabeth Fuller; (D) Conrad Bishop; (S) Paul Owen; (C) Marcia Dixcy; (L) Jeff Hill

A Streetcar Named Desire, Tennessee Williams; (D) Mladen Kiselov; (S) Paul Owen; (C) Marcia Dixcy; (L) Paul Owen

Master Harold...and the boys, Athol Fugard; (D) Frazier W. Marsh; (S) James Leonard Joy; (C) Marcia Dixcy; (L) Jeff Hill

Tent Meeting, Larry Larson, Levi Lee and Rebecca Wackler; (D) Patrick Tovatt; (S) Paul Owen; (C) Marcia Dixcy

PRODUCTIONS 1986–87

Classics in Context Festival:

Six Characters in Search of an Author, Luigi Pirandello; trans: Paul Avila Mayer; (D) Jon Jory; (S) Paul Owen; (C) Lewis D. Rampino; (L) Jeff Hill

Chee-Chee, Luigi Pirandello; trans: William Murray; (D) Larry Deckel; (S) Paul Owen; (C) Lewis D. Rampino; (L) Jeff Hill

The Man with the Flower in His Mouth, Luigi Pirandello; trans: William Murray; (D) Frazier W. Marsh; (S) Paul Owen; (C) Lewis D. Rampino; (L) Jeff Hill

The Rules of the Game, Luigi Pirandello; trans: William Murray; (D) Tom Bullard; (S) Paul Owen; (C) Lewis D. Rampino; (L) Jeff Hill

The Foreigner, Larry Shue; (D) Ray Fry; (S) John Saari; (C) Lewis D. Rampino; (L) Jeff Hill

The Gift of the Magi, adapt, music and lyrics: Peter Ekstrom, from O. Henry; (D) Larry Deckel; (S) Paul Owen; (C) Hollis Jenkins-Evans; (L) Cliff Berek

A Christmas Carol, adapt: Barbara Field, from Charles Dickens; (D) Jon Jory; (S) Paul Owen; (C) Elizabeth Covey; (L) Paul Owen

Death of a Salesman, Arthur Miller; (D) Tom Bullard; (S) James Leonard Joy; (C) Marcia Dixcy; (L) Jeff Hill

A Moon for the Misbegotten, Eugene O'Neill; (D) Frazier W. Marsh; (S) John Saari; (C) Hollis Jenkins-Evans; (L) Jeff Hill

Quilters, book: Barbara Damashek and Molly Newman; music and lyrics: Barbara Damashek; (D) Larry Deckel; (S) Paul Owen; (C) Lewis D. Rampino; (L) Jeff Hill

Humana Festival:

The Love Talker, Deborah Pryor; (D) Jon Jory; (S) Paul Owen; (C) Colleen Muscha; (L) Ralph Dressler

Fun, Howard Korder; (D) Jon Jory; (S) Paul Owen; (C) Colleen Muscha; (L) Ralph Dressler

Chemical Reactions, Andy Foster; (D) Ray Fry; (S) Paul Owen; (C) Colleen Muscha; (L) Ralph Dressler

Elaine's Daughter, Mayo Simon; (D) Jules Aaron; (S) Paul Owen; (C) Lewis D. Rampino; (L) Ralph Dressler

Gringo Planet, Frederick Bailey; (D) Frederick Bailey; (S) Paul Owen; (C) Frances Kenny; (L) Ralph Dressler

Glimmerglass, Jonathan Bolt; (D) Jonathan Bolt; (S) Paul Owen; (C) Lewis D. Rampino; (L) Jeff Hill

Water Hole, Kendrew Lascelles; (D) Frazier W. Marsh; (S) Paul Owen; (C) Hollis Jenkins-Evans; (L) Jeff Hill

Deadfall, Grace McKeaney; (D) Amy Saltz; (S) Paul Owen; (C) Lewis D. Rampino; (L) Jeff Hill

Digging In: The Farm Crisis in Kentucky, Julie Crutcher and Vaughn McBride; (D) Larry Deckel; (S) Paul Owen; (C) Lewis D. Rampino; (L) Jeff Hill

T Bone N Weasel, Jon Klein; (D) Steven Dietz; (S) Paul Owen; (C) Frances Kenny; (L) Jeff Hill

Murder on the Nile, Agatha Christie; (D) John Going; (S) Lowell Detweiler; (C) Lewis D. Rampino; (L) Jeff Hill

Little Shop of Horrors, book and lyrics: Howard Ashman; music: Alan Menken; (D) Lazslo Morton; (S) Paul Owen; (C) Marie Anne Chiment; (L) Jeff Hill

Actors Theatre of St. Paul

MICHAEL ANDREW MINER
Artistic Director

MARTHA SLOCA RICHARDS
Managing Director

28 West Seventh Pl.
St. Paul, MN 55102
(612) 297-6868 (bus.)
(612) 227-0050 (b.o.)

FOUNDED 1977
Michael Andrew Miner

SEASON
Oct.-Apr.

FACILITIES
Seating capacity: 350
Stage: proscenium

FINANCES
July 1, 1986-June 30, 1987
Expenses: $769,000

CONTRACTS
AEA LORT (D) and SSD&C

Actors Theatre of St. Paul is committed to the cohesive ensemble production of stylistically and thematically varied plays. At the heart of the theatre's aesthetic is an ongoing resident company of actors, playwrights, composers, designers and directors whose collective interests and talents are strong determinants of the direction, change and growth of the theatre from season to season. From its inception, Actors Theatre eagerly embraced responsibility for the generation of new works for the stage. In recent seasons that impulse has manifested itself in more frequent commissions, the inauguration of a developmental workshop series and an increase in new works scheduled in the subscription series. Vital contemporary interpretations of the classics continue to be an important coun-

Actors Theatre of St. Paul. James Craven and Michael Andrew Miner in *The Blood Knot*. Photo: Connie Jerome.

terpoint. Long-term interest in other cultures, demonstrated in the past by exchanges with Surinam, Trinidad and Jamaica, for example, continue next season with our production of a play by Soviet writer Vladlen Dozortsev. Actors Theatre also produces a one-act festival and anticipates a return to touring productions in 1988.

—*Michael Andrew Miner*

PRODUCTIONS 1985–86

Much Ado About Nothing, William Shakespeare; (D) Michael Andrew Miner; (S) Chris Johnson; (C) Nayna Ramey; (L) Chris Johnson

Joyous Noel: A Noel Coward Music Hall, adapt: David Ira Goldstein; music and lyrics: Noel Coward; (D) David Ira Goldstein; (S) Nayna Ramey; (C) Karen Nelson; (L) Jean Montgomery

And a Nightingale Sang, C.P. Taylor; (D) Michael Andrew Miner; (S) Nayna Ramey; (C) Nayna Ramey; (L) Nayna Ramey

More Fun Than Bowling, Steven Dietz; (D) George C. White; (S) Dick Leerhoff; (C) Chris Johnson; (L) Nayna Ramey

The Blood Knot, Athol Fugard; (D) Dawn Renee Jones; (S) Chris Johnson; (C) Chris Johnson; (L) Chris Johnson

Trakker's Tel, Janie Geiser, D. Scott Glasser, Randall Davidson and company; (D) D. Scott Glasser; (S) Janie Geiser; (C) Janie Geiser; (L) Nayna Ramey

The Barber of Seville, Pierre-Augustin Caron de Beaumarchais; trans: Albert Bermel; (D) David Ira Goldstein; (S) Chris Johnson; (C) Chris Johnson; (L) Chris Johnson

PRODUCTIONS 1986–87

The Real Thing, Tom Stoppard; (D) Michael Andrew Miner; (S) Dick Leerhoff; (C) Nayna Ramey; (L) Nayna Ramey

I Love You, I Love You Not, Wendy Kesselman; (D) Michael Andrew Miner; (S) Chris Johnson; (C) Chris Johnson; (L) Chris Johnson

Peg o' My Heart, J. Hartley Manners; (D) David M. Kwait; (S) Nayna Ramey; (C) Rich Hamson; (L) Nayna Ramey

Minnesota One-Act Play Festival:

Minnesota, George Sand; (D) David Ira Goldstein; (S) Dick Leerhoff; (C) Sandra Schulte; (L) Doug Pipan

Bitter Harvest, John Olive; (D) James Cada; (S) Dick Leerhoff; (C) Sandra Schulte; (L) Doug Pipan

An Educated Lady, Ken Jenkins; (D) D. Scott Glasser; (S) Dick Leerhoff; (C) Sandra Schulte; (L) Doug Pipan

Chug, Ken Jenkins; (D) David Ira Goldstein; (S) Dick Leerhoff; (C) Sandra Schulte; (L) Doug Pipan

4:45 AM, Jaime Meyer; (D) David Ira Goldstein; (S) Dick Leerhoff; (C) Sandra Schulte; (L) Doug Pipan

Burning Desire, Steven Dietz; (D) D. Scott Glasser; (S) Dick Leerhoff; (C) Sandra Schulte; (L) Doug Pipan

Blue Mercedes, Elan Garonzik; (D) Louis Schaefer; (S) Dick Leerhoff; (C) Sandra Schulte; (L) Doug Pipan

Bluegrass, Jon Klein; (D) David Ira Goldstein; (S) Dick Leerhoff; (C) Sandra Schulte; (L) Doug Pipan

The Coming of Mr. Pine, Grace McKeaney; (D) James Cada; (S) Dick Leerhoff; (C) Sandra Schulte; (L) Doug Pipan

Photograph, music and lyrics adapt: Paul Boesing, from Gertrude Stein; (D) Martha Boesing; (S) Dick Leerhoff; (C) Sandra Schulte; (L) Doug Pipan

Uncle Vanya, Anton Chekhov; trans: Stark Young; (D) Michael Andrew Miner; (S) Larry Kaushansky; (C) Nayna Ramey; (L) Nayna Ramey

How I Got That Story, Amlin Gray; (D) Michael Andrew Miner; (S) Nayna Ramey; (C) Nayna Ramey; (L) Nayna Ramey

Alabama Shakespeare Festival

MARTIN L. PLATT
Artistic Director

JIM VOLZ
Managing Director

Box 20350
Montgomery, AL 36120-0350
(205) 272-1640 (bus.)
(205) 277-2273 (b.o.)

FOUNDED 1972
Martin L. Platt

SEASON
Dec.-Aug.

FACILITIES
Festival Stage
Seating capacity: 750
Stage: modified thrust

The Octagon
Seating capacity: 225
Stage: flexible

FINANCES
Oct. 1, 1986-Sept. 30, 1987
Expenses: $4,190,193

CONTRACTS
AEA LORT (B), (C), (D), SSD&C and USA

The Alabama Shakespeare Festival is dedicated to producing the classics, with Shakespeare forming the core of our repertoire. We also delve into more contemporary plays when they have a theme and a use of language which parallels our classical work. We believe strongly in three tenets: serving the playwright, maintaining a resident company and performing in rotating repertory. A very important aspect of our work is a commitment to reviving plays that have been neglected and to commissioning translations of European plays that have not been produced in English. Working with a resident body of artists (along with important guest artists) allows us to develop as a company, with a style and vision particular to our theatre. Our ongoing activities include concert presentations, student matinees, humanities programs and touring—all logical outgrowths of our interest in the allied arts and

Alabama Shakespeare Festival. Lisa McMillan and Betty Leighton in *The Royal Family*. Photo: Scarsbrook.

in broadening our audiences. Our MFA/professional actor training program is an important investment both in the future of regional theatre and in the ASF.

—*Martin L. Platt*

PRODUCTIONS 1985–86

A Midsummer Night's Dream, William Shakespeare; (D) Martin L. Platt; (S) Michael Stauffer; (C) Susan Rheaume; (L) Michael Orris Watson

The Glass Menagerie, Tennessee Williams; (D) Russell Treyz; (S) Philipp Jung; (C) Philipp Jung; (L) Paul Ackerman

Death of a Salesman, Arthur Miller; (D) Edward Stern; (S) Michael Stauffer; (C) Susan Rheaume; (L) Michael Stauffer

Pygmalion, George Bernard Shaw; (D) Martin L. Platt; (S) Sam Kirkpatrick; (C) Sam Kirkpatrick; (L) Judy Rasmuson

A Flea in Her Ear, Georges Feydeau; trans: John Mortimer; (D) Martin L. Platt; (S) Mark Marton; (C) Kristine Kearney; (L) Michael Orris Watson

Richard III, William Shakespeare; (D) Edward Stern; (S) Michael Stauffer; (C) Susan Rheaume; (L) Michael Orris Watson

The Merry Wives of Windsor, William Shakespeare; (D) Tony Van Bridge; (S) Michael Stauffer; (C) Alan Armstrong; (L) Michael Orris Watson

The School for Scandal, Richard Brinsley Sheridan; (D) Russell Treyz; (S) Philipp Jung; (C) Philipp Jung; (L) Michael Orris Watson

Betrayal, Harold Pinter; (D) Martin L. Platt; (S) Philipp Jung; (C) Philipp Jung; (L) Paul Ackerman

The Imaginary Heir, Jean-François Regnard; trans: Thomas D'Arfey; (D) Martin L. Platt; (S) Philipp Jung; (C) Philipp Jung; (L) Paul Ackerman

PRODUCTIONS 1986–87

Pump Boys and Dinettes, John Foley, Mark Hardwick, Debra Monk, Cass Morgan, John Schimmel and Jim Wann; (D) Maureen Donley; (S) David Crank; (C) Kristine Kearney; (L) Karen S. Spahn

Rough Crossing, Ferenc Molnar; adapt and lyrics: Tom Stoppard; music: Andre Previn; (D) Martin L. Platt; (S) Sam Kirkpatrick; (C) Sam Kirkpatrick; (L) Judy Rasmuson

Terra Nova, Ted Tally; (D) Martin L. Platt; (S) Michael Stauffer; (C) Kristine Kearney; (L) Judy Rasmuson

Master Harold...and the boys, Athol Fugard; (D) Stephen Hollis; (S) Michael Stauffer; (C) Kristine Kearney; (L) Michael Stauffer

Misalliance, George Bernard Shaw; (D) Tony Van Bridge; (S) Michael Stauffer; (C) Kristine Kearney; (L) Michael Stauffer

The Taming of the Shrew, William Shakespeare; (D) Martin L. Platt; (S) David M. Crank; (C) Alan Armstrong; (L) Judy Rasmuson

The Tempest, William Shakespeare; (D) Martin L. Platt; (S) Michael Stauffer; (C) Alan Armstrong; (L) Michael Stauffer

The Royal Family, George S. Kaufman and Edna Ferber; (D) Edward Stern; (S) John Jensen; (C) Kristine Kearney; (L) Ronald Wallace

Zelda, William Luce; (D) Bill Gregg; (S) Paul K. Looney; (C) Peg Brady; (L) Karen S. Spahn

Othello, William Shakespeare; (D) Edward Stern; (S) John Jensen; (C) Kristine Kearney; (L) Geoffrey Cunningham

Hedda Gabler, Henrik Ibsen; adapt: Christopher Hampton; (D) Martin L. Platt; (S) Michael Stauffer; (C) Lyndall L. Otto; (L) Michael Stauffer

Alaska Repertory Theatre

ANDREW J. TRAISTER
Artistic Director

ALICE CHEBBA
Managing Director

Box 4700
Anchorage, AK 99510-4700
(907) 276-2327 (bus.)
(907) 276-5500 (b.o.)

FOUNDED 1976
Paul Brown, Robert Farley, Alaska State Council of the Arts

SEASON
Nov.-Mar.

FACILITIES
Fourth Avenue Theatre

Alaska Repertory Theatre. David Downing and Robert Ellenstein in *I'm Not Rappaport*. Photo: Chris Arend.

Seating capacity: 604
Stage: proscenium

FINANCES
July 1, 1986-June 30, 1987
Expenses: $1,742,589

CONTRACTS
AEA LORT (B) and SSD&C

Alaska Repertory Theatre, the state's oldest and largest professional performing arts institution, has undergone many changes since my appointment. For the first time in the theatre's history, a majority of the season will be performed with a core company of actors. We have made an artistic choice to make do with less scenery by using minimal sets to evoke our environments. Major plays and playwrights form our season—a conscious decision to fill the theatre by exciting the community with recognizable titles. We are trying to gain momentum as the Rep prepares to move into Anchorage's new performing arts center in the fall of 1988, increasing our audience potential by 25 percent.

—*Andrew J. Traister*

Note: During the 1985-86 and 1986-87 seasons, Robert Farley served as artistic director.

PRODUCTIONS 1985–86

Pump Boys and Dinettes, John Foley, Mark Hardwick, Debra Monk, Cass Morgan, John Schimmel and Jim Wann; (D) Robert J. Farley; (S) Connie Lutz; (C) Jennifer Svenson; (L) Lauren Mackenzie Miller

Twelfth Night, William Shakespeare; (D) Roy Brocksmith; (S) Michael Olich; (C) Carrie Robbins; (L) Spencer Mosse

Watch on the Rhine, Lillian Hellman; (D) Robert J. Farley; (S) Karen Gjelsteen; (C) Jennifer Svenson; (L) Spencer Mosse

Greater Tuna, Jaston Williams, Joe Sears and Ed Howard; (D) Robert J. Farley; (S) Karen Gjelsteen; (C) Jennifer Svenson; (L) Spencer Mosse

Tintypes, Mary Kyte, Mel Marvin and Gary Pearle; (D) Walton Jones; (S) Michael Olich; (C) Deborah Dryden; (L) Spencer Mosse

El Grande de Coca Cola, Ron House, John Neville-Andrews, Alan Sherman, Diz White and Sally Willis; (D) Walton Jones; (S) Connie Lutz; (C) Cathy McFarland; (L) Lauren Mackenzie Miller

PRODUCTIONS 1986–87

El Grande de Coca Cola, Ron House, John Neville-Andrews, Alan Sherman, Diz White and Sally Willis; (D) Walton Jones; (S) Connie Lutz; (C) Cathy McFarland; (L) Lauren Mackenzie Miller

The Rainmaker, N. Richard Nash; (D) Robert J. Farley; (S) Karen

Gjelsteen; (C) Sally Richardson; (L) Lauren Mackenzie Miller
I'm Not Rappaport, Herb Gardner; (D) Andrew J. Traister; (S) William Bloodgood; (C) Jennifer Svenson; (L) Lauren Mackenzie Miller
Sleuth, Anthony Shaffer; (D) Clayton Corzatte; (S) Keith Brumley; (C) Sally Richardson; (L) Lauren Mackenzie Miller
The Foreigner, Larry Shue; (D) David McClendon; (S) Jennifer Lupton; (C) Jayna Orchard; (L) Lauren Mackenzie Miller

Alley Theatre

PAT BROWN
Artistic/Executive Director

V. MICHAEL TIKNIS
Managing Director

615 Texas Ave.
Houston, TX 77002
(713) 228-9341 (bus.)
(713) 228-8421 (b.o.)

FOUNDED 1947
Nina Vance

SEASON
Year-round

FACILITIES
Large Stage
Seating capacity: 824
Stage: thrust

Hugo V. Neuhaus
Seating capacity: 300
Stage: arena

FINANCES
Sept. 1, 1986-Aug. 31, 1987
Expenses: $5,100,000

CONTRACTS
AEA LORT (B+), (C), SSD&C and USA

More and more, the Alley is becoming a theatre for the artists. As our resident acting company has grown, so has the number of resident designers and craftspeople. The 1987-88 season marks the beginning of two new playwrights' programs. Three or more playwrights are invited to spend the season in residence to develop new work, with the advantage of having company actors available to participate in the process. A companion program gives us the funds to produce, to varying degrees, each of the works generated. These new projects bring us closer to our goal of becoming a more comprehensive and self-contained creative entity. In a city the size of Houston, it is important that we keep our programming diversified. Therefore, in addition to the new play program, we will continue to present proven contemporary works to our audience, as well as fresh perspectives on classics. We carry our commitment to the boldest, most challenging theatre into a bright, hopeful future for both the theatre artists and the Alley Theatre alike.

—Pat Brown

PRODUCTIONS 1985–86

Execution of Justice, Emily Mann; (D) Pat Brown; (S) Charles S. Kading; (C) Barbara A. Bell; (L) Greg Sullivan
Kiss Me, Kate, book: Bella and Samuel Spewack; music and lyrics: Cole Porter; (D) Charles Abbott; (S) Charles S. Kading; (C) Lewis Brown; (L) Frances Aronson
The Ice Wolf, Joanna Halpert Kraus; (D) James Martin; (S) Elva Stewart; (C) Howard Tsvi Kaplan; (L) Richard W. Jeter
The Miss Firecracker Contest, Beth Henley; (D) Pat Brown; (S) Richard Ellis; (C) Barbara A. Bell; (L) Richard W. Jeter
Pack of Lies, Hugh Whitemore; (D) Malcolm Morrison; (S) Michael A. Ryan; (C) Sarajane Milligan; (L) Richard W. Jeter
Spring Awakening, Frank Wedekind; trans: Edward Bond; (D) Pat Brown; (S) Charles S. Kading; (C) Howard Tsvi Kaplan; (L) James Sale
The Foreigner, Larry Shue; (D) James Martin; (S) Charles S. Kading; (C) Howard Tsvi Kaplan; (L) Richard W. Jeter
How the Other Half Loves, Alan Ayckbourn; (D) Pat Brown; (S) Michael Olich; (C) Howard Tsvi Kaplan; (L) Barry Griffith
Chocolate Cake, Mary Gallagher; (D) Beth Sanford; (S) Elva Stewart; (C) Patricia E. Doherty; (L) Richard W. Jeter
Painting Churches, Tina Howe; (D) Josephine R. Abady; (S) Richard Ellis; (C) Barbara A. Bell; (L) Richard W. Jeter
Balm in Gilead, Lanford Wilson; (D) George Anderson; (S) Charles S. Kading; (C) Howard Tsvi Kaplan; (L) Pamela A. Gray
The Traveling Lady, Horton Foote; (D) Beth Sanford; (S) Richard Ellis; (C) Patricia E. Doherty; (L) Richard W. Jeter
Orphans, Lyle Kessler; (D) George Anderson; (S) Richard Ellis; (C) Barbara A. Bell; (L) Pamela A. Gray
Losing It, Jon Klein; (D) Beth Sanford; (S) Michael A. Ryan; (C) Patricia E. Doherty; (L) John Ore
What the Butler Saw, Joe Orton; (D) Beth Sanford; (S) Richard Ellis; (C) Barbara A. Bell; (L) Pamela A. Gray
A Christmas Memory, adapt: Beth Sanford and Bettye Fitzpatrick, from Truman Capote; (D) Beth Sanford; (S) Richard Earl Laster; (C) Beth Sanford; (L) John Ore

PRODUCTIONS 1986–87

Another Part of the Forest, Lillian Hellman; (D) Pat Brown; (S) Charles S. Kading; (C) Howard Tsvi Kaplan; (L) James Sale
Trelawny of the "Wells", Arthur Wing Pinero; (D) Robert Bridges; (S) Charles S. Kading; (C) Howard Tsvi Kaplan; (L) Pamela A. Gray
The Adventures of Tom Sawyer, adapt: Timothy Mason, from Mark Twain; (D) James Martin; (S) Elva Stewart; (C) Howard Tsvi Kaplan; (L) John Ore
Glengarry Glen Ross, David Mamet; (D) Pat Brown; (S) Elva Stewart; (C) Patricia E. Doherty; (L) James Sale
The Immigrant: A Hamilton County Album, Mark Harelik; conceived: Randal Myler and Mark Harelik; (D) Beth Sanford; (S) Michael A. Ryan; (C) Patricia E. Doherty; (L) Pamela A. Gray
A Lie of the Mind, Sam Shepard; (D) George Anderson; (S) Charles S. Kading; (C) Howard Tsvi Kaplan; (L) James Sale
The Common Pursuit, Simon Gray; (D) George Anderson; (S) Charles S. Kading; (C) Howard Tsvi Kaplan; (L) James Sale
Shooting Stars, Molly Newman; (D) Pat Brown; (S) Elva Stewart; (C) Howard Tsvi Kaplan; (L) Pamela A. Gray
The Death of Bessie Smith and ***Counting the Ways***, Edward Albee; (D) Edward Albee; (S) Lee Duran; (C) Lee Duran; (L) James Sale
The Marriage of Bette and Boo, Christopher Durang; (D) Beth Sanford; (S) Lee Duran; (C) Patricia E. Doherty; (L) Pamela A. Gray
The Normal Heart, Larry Kramer; (D) George Anderson; (S) Charles S. Kading; (C) Howard Tsvi Kaplan; (L) Pamela A. Gray

Alley Theatre. John Gould Rubin, Jeff Bennett and Donald Berman in *The Normal Heart*. Photo: Carl Davis.

The Middle Ages, A.R. Gurney, Jr.; (D) James Martin; (S) Elva Stewart; (C) Howard Tsvi Kaplan; (L) Pamela A. Gray
The Gin Game, D.L. Coburn; (D) Beth Sanford; (S) Michael A. Ryan; (C) Patricia E. Doherty; (L) Pamela A. Gray
A Christmas Memory, adapt: Beth Sanford and Bettye Fitzpatrick, from Truman Capote; (D) Beth Sanford; (S) Richard Earl Laster; (C) Beth Sanford; (L) John Ore

Alliance Theatre Company

ROBERT J. FARLEY
Artistic Director

EDITH H. LOVE
Managing Director

Robert W. Woodruff Arts Center
1280 Peachtree St., NE
Atlanta, GA 30309
(404) 898-1132 (bus.)
(404) 892-2414 (b.o.)

FOUNDED 1969
Atlanta Arts Alliance

SEASON
Sept.-May

FACILITIES
Alliance Theatre
Seating capacity: 826
Stage: proscenium

Studio Theatre
Seating capacity: 200
Stage: proscenium

FINANCES
Aug. 1, 1986-July 31, 1987
Expenses: $4,793,000

CONTRACTS
AEA LORT (B), (D), TYA, SSD&C and USA

The Alliance Theatre is preparing to celebrate its 20th anniversary in 1988-89. As the theatre's new artistic director, I have come to a city where, culturally and historically, experience is firmly in place, yet idealism is vibrant. This is a community and a theatre reaching its zenith. The Alliance produces 12 plays per year. In addition to the mainstage subscription series and the Studio season, largely devoted to the exploration of new work, the Alliance boasts an outstanding children's theatre program of original adaptations, performed by a seasoned core of adult actors. It is my hope in the years ahead that, through ongoing collaboration among artists inside and outside of the theatre arts, we shall merge our work into a wholeness and unity which establishes a unique voice in the South — for artists and audiences alike.

—Robert J. Farley

Note: During the 1985-86 and 1986-87 seasons, Kent Stephens and Timothy Near, respectively, served as interim directors.

PRODUCTIONS 1985–86

So Long on Lonely Street, Sandra Deer; (D) Kent Stephens; (S) Mark Morton; (C) Joyce Andrulot; (L) Mark B. Weiss
The Importance of Being Earnest, Oscar Wilde; (D) Kent Stephens; (S) Kate Edmunds; (C) Pierre DeRagon; (L) Marilyn Rennagel
Guys and Dolls, book: Jo Swerling and Abe Burrows; music and lyrics: Frank Loesser; (D) Scott Harris; (S) Mark Morton; (C) Susan Hirschfeld; (L) Jason Kantrowitz
Flint and Roses, Jim Peck; (D) Skip Foster; (S) Victor Becker; (C) Susan Mickey; (L) Paulie Jenkins
Great Expectations, adapt: Sandra Deer, from Charles Dickens; (D) Fred Chappell; (S) Charles Caldwell; (C) Kathleen Blake; (L) Marilyn Rennagel
Hamlet, William Shakespeare; (D) Tony Tanner; (S) Kate Edmonds and Robert J. Farley; (C) Susan Hirschfeld; (L) Barry Arnold
'night, Mother, Marsha Norman; (D) Fred Chappell; (S) Lynn Montrey Hiett; (C) Susan Mickey; (L) Peter Shinn
Blue Window, Craig Lucas; (D) William Partlan; (S) Dennis Maudlin; (C) Susan Mickey; (L) Liz Lee
Lady Day at Emerson's Bar and Grill, Lanie Robertson; (D) Woodie King, Jr.; (S) Steve Reardon; (C) Joyce Andrulot; (L) David Brewer
Through Line, Tom Huey; (D) Kent Stephens; (S) Michelle Bellavance; (C) Susan Mickey; (L) William B. Duncan
Pinocchio, adapt: Sandra Deer and Skip Foster, from Carlo Collodi; (D) Skip Foster; (S) Charles Caldwell; (C) Susan Hirschfeld; (L) Marilyn Rennagel
Tales of Edgar Allen Poe, adapt: Tom Huey; (D) Kent Stephens; (S) Dee Wagner; (C) Joyce Andrulot; (L) Paulie Jenkins
Finding Home, Michael Bigelow Dixon and Jerry Patch; (D) Michael Nelson; (S) Mark Edlund; (C) Judy Winograd; (L) Sandra Deer

PRODUCTIONS 1986–87

The Gospel at Colonus, Sophocles; adapt: Lee Breuer and Bob Telson; trans: Robert Fitzgerald; music: Bob Telson; (D) Lee Breuer; (S) Alison Yerxa; (C) Ghretta Hynd; (L) Julie Archer
Our Town, Thornton Wilder; (D) David Kerry Heefner; (S) Paul Wonsek; (C) Patricia Adshead; (L) Marilyn Rennagel
A Funny Thing Happened on the Way to the Forum, music and lyrics: Stephen Sondheim; book: Larry Gelbart and Burt Shevelove; (D) Edward Stone; (S) Mark Morton; (C) Susan Hirschfeld; (L) Jason Kantrowitz

Alliance Theatre. *Guys and Dolls.* Photo: Charles Rafshoon.

The Foreigner, Larry Shue; (D) Ron Lagomarsino; (S) Lowell Detweiler; (C) Pierre DeRagon; (L) Spencer Mosse

An American Doll's House, Henrik Ibsen; adapt: Kathleen Tolan; (D) Timothy Near; (S) Mark Morton; (C) Pierre DeRagon; (L) Paulie Jenkins

The Passion of Dracula, David Richmond and Bob Hall; (D) Skip Foster; (S) Victor Becker; (C) Kathleen Blake; (L) Victor Becker

Annulla, An Autobiography, Emily Mann; (D) Timothy Near; (S) Jeff Struckman; (C) Liz Lee; (L) Jeff Struckman

Orphans, Lyle Kessler; (D) Skip Foster; (S) Michelle Bellevance; (C) Pierre DeRagon; (L) Peter Shinn

Blessé, Cindy Lou Johnson; (D) Paul Lazarus; (S) Bill Barclay; (C) Susan Mickey; (L) Liz Lee

Amazing Grace, Sandra Deer; (D) Dan Bonnell; (S) James Wolk; (C) Pierre DeRagon; (L) William B. Duncan

Don Quixote, adapt: Sandra Deer, from Miguel de Cervantes; (D) Skip Foster; (S) Charles Caldwell; (C) Pierre DeRagon; (L) Marilyn Rennagel

Charlotte's Webb, adapt: Joseph Robinette, from E.B. White; (D) Munson Hicks; (S) Mark Morton; (C) Susan Mickey; (L) Paulie Jenkins

AMAS Repertory Theatre

ROSETTA LeNOIRE
Artistic Director

GARY HALCOTT
Administrator/Business Manager

1 East 104th St.
New York, NY 10029
(212) 369-8000

FOUNDED 1968
Rosetta LeNoire, Gerta Grunen, Mara Kim

SEASON
Oct.-Aug.

FACILITIES
Experimental Theatre
Seating capacity: 99
Stage: thrust

Eubie Blake Children's Theatre
Seating capacity: 75
Stage: proscenium

FINANCES
July 1, 1986-June 30, 1987
Expenses: $275,000

CONTRACTS
AEA Funded Non-Profit Theatre code

AMAS Repertory Theatre is a multiracial theatrical organization dedicated to bringing all people — regardless of race, creed, color, religion or national origin — together through the performing arts. AMAS is devoted exclusively to the creation, development and professional production of original works in the grand tradition of the American musical theatre, and to the encouragement of new musical theatre talent. Since the American musical combines influences from every nationality and culture, spans all age groups and includes within it virtually every other aspect of artistic creativity — drama, music, dance, painting — AMAS's multiracial commitment is embodied in its dedication to this uniquely American art form. AMAS sponsors four major programs: the mainstage musical theatre, the AMAS Eubie Blake Children's Theatre, an adult workshop and a summer tour.

—Rosetta LeNoire

PRODUCTIONS 1985–86

Bingo, music: George Fischoff; book: Ossie Davis and Hy Gilbert; lyrics: Hy Gilbert; (D) Ossie Davis; (S) Tom Barnes; (C) Christina Giannini; (L) Jeffrey Schissler

La Belle Helene, music: Jacques Offenbach; book adapt: John Fearnley, from A.P. Herbert; lyrics: David Baker; (D) John Fearnley; (S) Donald Brooks; (C) Howard Behar; (L) Deborah Matlack

SH-BOOM!, book and lyrics: Eric Tait; music: Willex Brown, Jr. and Eric Tait; (D) Stuart Warmflash; (S) Janice Davis; (C) Candace Warner; (L) Eric Thomann

AMAS Repertory Theatre. Leah Hocking, Tom Flagg and Joie Gallo in *Dazy*. Photo: Stephen Schaffer

My Fair Lady, book and lyrics: Alan Jay Lerner; music: Frederick Loewe; (D) Philip Rosenberg; (S) Donald Brooks; (C) Howard Behar; (L) Deborah Matlack

Carousel, book and lyrics: Oscar Hammerstein, II; music: Richard Rodgers; (D) Frederick Tuso; (S) Donald Brooks; (C) Howard Behar; (L) Deborah Matlack

I Can Still Hear and See Them, book: Rosetta LeNoire; music and lyrics: various; (D) Bob Brooker; (C) Cindy Boyle

PRODUCTIONS 1986–87

Hot Saki...with a Pinch of Salt, book and lyrics: Carol Baker and Lana Stein; music: Jerome Goldstein; (D) William Martin; (S) Frank Boros; (C) Howard Behar; (L) Ken Lapham

Dazy, book: Allan Knee; music: Lowell Mark; lyrics: Norman Simon; (D) Philip Rose; (S) Clarke Dunham; (C) Gail Cooper-Hecht; (L) Ken Billington

Prime Time, music and lyrics: Johnny Brandon; book: R.A. Shiomi; (D) Marvin Gordon; (S) Vicki Davis; (C) Vicki Davis; (L) David Segal

Harold Arlen, That Is, music and lyrics: Harold Arlen; conceived: Bill Hunt; (D) Bob Brooker

Bye Bye Birdie, book: Michael Stewart; lyrics: Lee Adams; music: Charles Strouse; (D) Angela Lockhart; (S) Michael Green; (C) Howard Behar; (L) Deborah Matlack

Kiss Me, Kate, music and lyrics: Cole Porter; book: Samuel and Bella Spewack; (D) Angela Lockhart; (S) Donald Brooks; (C) Emily Allen; (L) Valerie Lau-Kee

American Conservatory Theatre

EDWARD HASTINGS
Artistic Director

JOHN SULLIVAN
Managing Director

450 Geary St.
San Francisco, CA 94102
(415) 771-3880 (bus.)
(415) 673-6440 (b.o.)

FOUNDED 1965
William Ball

SEASON
Oct.-May

FACILITIES
Geary Theatre
Seating capacity: 1,396
Stage: proscenium

American Conservatory Theatre. *The Seagull.* Photo: Larry Merkle

Playroom
Seating capacity: 49
Stage: flexible

FINANCES
June 1, 1986-May 31, 1987
Expenses: $6,500,000

CONTRACTS
AEA LORT (A), SSD&C and USA

The American Conservatory Theatre of San Francisco is a national center for the theatre arts, dedicated to the revelation of the truths of human experience through the exploration of the dramatic literature of all ages and nations. We affirm the principle that the growth of individual creativity is the essential component of cultural progress, and that this growth and its expression in the theatre reach their fullest realization when repertory performance and professional training are concurrent and inseparable. We advocate the inherent right of the company member to participate in the formation of institutional policy, and are committed to the development of artists and audiences from all sectors of the ethnically diverse community that we serve.
—*Edward Hastings*

Note: During the 1985-86 and 1986-87 seasons, William Ball served as general director.

PRODUCTIONS 1985–86

The Majestic Kid, Mark Medoff; (D) Edward Hastings; (S) Jesse Hollis; (C) Jeannie Davidson; (L) Derek Duarte
Opera Comique, Nagle Jackson; (D) Nagle Jackson; (S) Jesse Hollis; (C) Fritha Knudsen; (L) Derek Duarte
A Christmas Carol, adapt: Dennis Powers and Laird Williamson, from Charles Dickens; (D) Laird Williamson; (S) Robert Blackman; (C) Robert Morgan; (L) Richard Devlin
'night, Mother, Marsha Norman; (D) Lawrence Hecht; (S) Oliver C. Olsen; (C) Regina Cate; (L) Derek Duarte
You Never Can Tell, George Bernard Shaw; (D) Janice Hutchins; (S) Jesse Hollis; (C) Fritha Knudsen; (L) Derek Duarte
Private Lives, Noel Coward; (D) Sabin Epstein; (S) Jesse Hollis; (C) Fritha Knudsen; (L) Derek Duarte
The Passion Cycle, anonymous; (D) William Ball; (S) Benicia Martinez; (C) Fritha Knudsen; (L) Derek Duarte
The Lady's Not for Burning, Christopher Fry; (D) Joy Carlin; (S) Warren Travis; (C) Warren Travis; (L) Derek Duarte

PRODUCTIONS 1986–87

Sunday in the Park with George, music and lyrics: Stephen Sondheim; book: James Lapine; (D) Laird Williamson; (S) Richard Seger; (C) Robert Blackman and Hope Hanafin; (L) Derek Duarte
The Doctor's Dilemma, George Bernard Shaw; (D) Joy Carlin; (S) Jesse Hollis; (C) Fritha Knudsen; (L) Derek Duarte
A Christmas Carol, adapt: Dennis Powers and Laird Williamson, from Charles Dickens; (D) Laird Williamson; (S) Robert Blackman; (C) Robert Morgan; (L) Derek Duarte
The Floating Light Bulb, Woody Allen; (D) Albert Takazauckas; (S) Ralph Funicello; (C) Beaver D. Bauer; (L) Derek Duarte
The Real Thing, Tom Stoppard; (D) Edward Hastings; (S) Michael Olich; (C) Robert Fletcher; (L) Derek Duarte
The Seagull, Anton Chekhov; trans: Jean-Claude van Itallie; (D) Jerome Kilty; (S) Richard Seger; (C) Robert Fletcher; (L) Derek Duarte
Ma Rainey's Black Bottom, August Wilson; (D) Claude Purdy; (S) Jesse Hollis; (C) Fritha Knudsen; (L) Derek Duarte
Faustus in Hell, adapt and conceived: Nagle Jackson and ***The Show of the Seven Deadly Sins***, Edward Albee, Christopher Durang, Amlin Gray, John Guare, Romulus Linney, Joyce Carol Oates and Jean-Claude van Itallie; (D) Michael Smuin; (S) Douglas W. Schmidt; (C) Sandra Woodall; (L) Derek Duarte

American Jewish Theatre

STANLEY BRECHNER
Artistic Director

JAN HARTMAN
Associate Artistic Director

15 West 28th St.
New York, NY 10001
(212) 683-7720

FOUNDED 1974
Stanley Brechner

SEASON
Nov.-June

FACILITIES
Theatre Guinevere
Seating capacity: 100
Stage: proscenium

FINANCES
July 1, 1986-June 30, 1987
Expenses: $300,000

CONTRACTS
AEA letter of agreement

American Jewish Theatre. Barbara Eda-Young, Sol Frieder and Peter Riegert in *A Rosen by Any Other Name.* Photo: Gerry Goodstein.

The American Jewish Theatre is dedicated to the presentation of both new plays and revivals that deal with Jewish themes. The theatre also develops its own material in conjunction with its in-house Deborah Project (a group of Jewish women playwrights), and through commissions and play readings of new and promising material. American Jewish Theatre also co-produces new plays with other theatres.

—*Stanley Brechner*

PRODUCTIONS 1985–86

Green Fields, Peretz Hirshbein; (D) Stanley Brechner; (S) Gene Gurlitz; (C) Donna Zakowska; (L) Bob Bessoir

Today I Am a Fountain Pen, Israel Horovitz; (D) Stephen Zuckerman; (S) James Fenhagen; (C) Mimi Maxmen; (L) Curt Ostermann

A Rosen by Any Other Name, Israel Horovitz; (D) Stephen Zuckerman; (S) James Fenhagen; (C) Mimi Maxmen; (L) Curt Ostermann

The Chopin Playoffs, Israel Horovitz; (D) Stephen Zuckerman; (S) James Fenhagen; (C) Mimi Maxmen; (L) Curt Ostermann

PRODUCTIONS 1986–87

Passover, Lloyd Gold; (D) Louis Scheeder; (S) Dan Proett; (C) Don Newcomb; (L) Mitch Bogard

Panache, Ron Mark; (D) Stanley Brechner; (S) Dan Proett; (C) Don Newcomb; (L) Victor En Yu Tan

I Love You, I Love You Not, Wendy Kesselman; (D) Ben Levit; (S) Nancy Thon; (C) Don Newcomb; (L) Beverly Emmons

Bar Mitzvah Boy, book: Jack Rosenthal; music: Jule Styne; lyrics: Don Black; (D) Robert Kalfin; (S) Gene Gurlitz; (C) Gail Hecht; (L) Brian McDevitt

The American Place Theatre

WYNN HANDMAN
Artistic Director

MICKEY ROLFE
General Manager

111 West 46th St.
New York, NY 10036
(212) 246-3730 (bus.)
(212) 247-0393 (b.o.)

FOUNDED 1964
Wynn Handman, Sidney Lanier, Myrna Loy, Michael Tolan

SEASON
Sept.-June

FACILITIES
Mainstage
Seating capacity: 299
Stage: thrust

Subplot Cafe
Seating capacity: 74
Stage: flexible

First Floor Theatre
Seating capacity: 74
Stage: flexible

FINANCES
July 1, 1986-June 30, 1987
Expenses: $900,000

CONTRACTS
AEA Special Production and Mini

The American Place Theatre. Vondie Curtis-Hall and Ben Harney in *Williams & Walker*. Photo: Martha Holmes.

The American Place Theatre is in its 23rd season of producing new works by living Americans. Its continuing purpose is to be a force for the advancement of theatre by actively responding to the contemporary theatre's needs. Toward that end, American Place provides talented writers with a creative environment and facilities free of commercial considerations. Our innovative, original programming opens the way for increased public awareness and enrichment of the mainstream of the nation's theatre. In order to promote and encourage new work of various genres with differing production needs, the American Place has several ongoing programs in addition to its mainstage series. These include: the American Humorists Series, Jubilee! A Black Theatre Festival, and the Women's Project (now a separate corporate entity) specifically designed to encourage, develop and produce women playwrights and directors.

—*Wynn Handman*

PRODUCTIONS 1985–86

Times and Appetites of Toulouse-Lautrec, Jeff Wanshel; lyrics: Michael Feingold; (D) John Ferraro; (S) John Arnone; (C) Edi Giguere; (L) Stephen Strawbridge

Drinking in America, Eric Bogosian; (D) Wynn Handman; (L) Marc D. Malamud

Jubilee! A Black Theatre Festival:

Celebration, Shauneille Perry; (D) Shauneille Perry; (C) Judy Dearing; (L) Marc D. Malamud

Williams & Walker, Vincent D. Smith; (D) Shauneille Perry; (S) Marc D. Malamud; (C) Judy Dearing; (L) Marc D. Malámud

American Humorists Series:

Roy Blount, Jr., Roy Blount, Jr.

Damon Runyon's Broadway, adapt: John Martello, from Damon Runyon; (D) Wynn Handman; (S) Marc D. Malamud; (L) Marc D. Malamud

Women's Project:

Breaking the Prairie Wolf Code, Lavonne Mueller; (D) Liz Diamond; (S) Richard Hoover; (C) Mimi Maxmen; (L) Jane Reisman

Women Heroes: In Praise of Exceptional Women:

Colette in Love, Lavonne Mueller; (D) Mirra Bank; (S) Marc D. Malamud and Ina Mayhew; (C) Judy Dearing; (L) Marc D. Malamud

Personality, Gina Wendkos and Ellen Rattner; (D) Gina

Wendkos and Mickey Rolfe; (s) Marc D. Malamud and Ina Mayhew; (c) Judy Dearing; (l) Marc D. Malamud

Emma Goldman: Love, Anarchy and Other Affairs, Jessica Litwak; (d) Anne Bogart; (s) Marc D. Malamud and Ina Mayhew; (c) Judy Dearing; (l) Marc D. Malamud

Parallax: In Honor of Daisy Bates, Denise Hamilton; (d) Denise Hamilton; (s) Marc D. Malamud and Ina Mayhew; (c) Judy Dearing; (l) Marc D. Malamud

How She Played the Game, Cynthia Cooper; (d) Bryna Wortman; (s) Marc D. Malamud and Ina Mayhew; (c) Judy Dearing; (l) Marc D. Malamud

Millie, Susan J. Kander; (d) Carol Tanzman; (s) Marc D. Malamud and Ina Mayhew; (c) Judy Dearing; (l) Marc D. Malamud

PRODUCTIONS 1986–87

Neon Psalms, Thomas Strelich; (d) Richard Hamburger; (s) Chris Barrecca; (c) Connie Singer; (l) Stephen Strawbridge

American Humorists Series:

A Girl's Guide to Chaos, Cynthia Heimel; (d) Wynn Handman; (s) Brian Martin; (c) Deborah Shaw; (l) Brian MacDevitt

James Thurber Kintypes, James Thurber; (d) Wynn Handman; (s) Marc D. Malamud; (l) Marc D. Malamud

Jubilee! A Black Theatre Festival:

Celebration, Shauneille Perry; (d) Shauneille Perry; (c) Judy Dearing; (l) Brian MacDevitt and Rachel Bickel

Her Talking Drum, various; (d) Lenwood O. Sloan; (s) Brian Martin; (c) Judy Dearing; (l) Steven Jones

Women's Project:

The Snicker Factor, various; (d) Suzanne Bennett and Mickey Rolfe; (l) Nicole Werner

Consequence, Kat Smith; (d) Alma Becker; (s) Robert Perdziola; (c) Judy Dearing; (l) Anne Militello

American Players Theatre

RANDALL DUK KIM
ANNE OCCHIOGROSSO
Co-Artistic Directors

CHARLES J. BRIGHT
Managing Director

Box 819
Spring Green, WI 53588
(608) 588-7401 (bus.)
(608) 588-2361 (b.o.)

FOUNDED 1977
Charles J. Bright, Randall Duk Kim, Anne Occhiogrosso

SEASON
June-Oct.

FACILITIES
Outdoor Theatre
Seating capacity: 704
Stage: thrust

FINANCES
Jan. 1, 1986-Dec. 31, 1986
Expenses: $1,305,809

CONTRACTS
AEA letter of agreement and USA

We seek a theatre that is dedicated to the study and production of classical world drama, while planted in America's heartland and nourished by heaven and earth. We seek to bring together artists and craftsmen of the theatre who understand the collaborative nature of this particular endeavor, and who realize the need for conscientious exploration and disciplined practice while striving to be taught by the poets and guided by the plays themselves, on their own terms, complete and intact. We dream of an astonishingly versatile ensemble bound together by a genuine reverence for the stage, a joyous acceptance of its mortality and humanity, a loving appreciation of its history and those who came before, and a single-mindedness in accomplishing one goal: to embody the world's finest dramatic treasures with clarity and justice in live repertory performance for the recreation and health of the community and the nation.

—Randall Duk Kim

PRODUCTIONS 1986

Hamlet, William Shakespeare; (d) Anne Occhiogrosso and Fred Ollerman; (c) Budd Hill; (l) Daniel Brovarney

The Merchant of Venice, William Shakespeare; (d) Anne Occhiogrosso and Sandra Reigel-Ernst; (c) Kathleen Blake; (l) Daniel Brovarney

The Merry Wives of Windsor, William Shakespeare; (d) Fred Ollerman and Sandra Reigel-Ernst; (c) Ted Boerner; (l) Daniel Brovarney

The Comedy of Errors, William Shakespeare; (d) Theodore Swetz and Fred Ollerman; (c) Budd Hill; (l) Daniel Brovarney

The Harmfulness of Tobacco, Anton Chekhov; trans: John Wyatt; (d) Sandra Reigel-Ernst and Fred Ollerman; (c) Ted Boerner; (l) Daniel Brovarney

The Bear, Anton Chekhov; trans: John Wyatt; (d) Fred Ollerman; (c) Ted Boerner; (l) Daniel Brovarney

The Proposal, Anton Chekhov; trans: John Wyatt; (d) Sandra Reigel-Ernst; (c) Ted Boerner; (l) Daniel Brovarney

The Anniversary, Anton Chekhov; trans: John Wyatt; (d) Sandra Reigel-Ernst and Charles Bright; (c) Pierre DeRagon; (l) Daniel Brovarney

The Wedding, Anton Chekhov; trans: John Wyatt; (d) Sandra Reigel-Ernst and Anne Occhiogrosso; (c) Pierre DeRagon; (l) Daniel Brovarney

Swan Song, Anton Chekhov; trans: John Wyatt; (d) Sandra Reigel-Ernst and Anne Occhiogrosso; (c) Pierre DeRagon; (l) Daniel Brovarney

PRODUCTIONS 1987

Ivanov, Anton Chekhov; trans: John Wyatt; (d) Morris Carnovsky and Phoebe Brand; (s) Chris Johnson; (c) Pierre DeRagon; (l) Daniel Brovarney

The School for Scandal, Richard Brinsley Sheridan; (d) Jewel Walker; (s) Chris Johnson; (c) Budd Hill; (l) Daniel Brovarney

Twelfth Night, William Shakespeare; (d) Sandra Reigel-Ernst and Fred Ollerman; (c) Budd Hill; (l) Daniel Brovarney

Hamlet, William Shakespeare; (d) Anne Occhiogrosso and Theodore Swetz; (c) Budd Hill; (l) Daniel Brovarney

The Comedy of Errors, William Shakespeare; (d) Theodore

American Players Theatre. Randall Duk Kim and Benjamin Reigel-Ernst in *The Merry Wives of Windsor*. Photo: Zane Williams.

Swetz; (C) Budd Hill; (L) Daniel Brovarney

The Merry Wives of Windsor, William Shakespeare; (D) Sandra Reigel-Ernst; (C) Ted Boerner; (L) Daniel Brovarney

American Repertory Theatre

ROBERT BRUSTEIN
Artistic Director

ROBERT J. ORCHARD
Managing Director

64 Brattle St.
Cambridge, MA 02138
(617) 495-2668 (bus.)
(617) 547-8300 (b.o.)

FOUNDED 1979
Robert Brustein

SEASON
Nov.-July

FACILITIES
Loeb Drama Center
Seating capacity: 556
Stage: flexible

ART/New Stages
Seating capacity: 353
Stage: proscenium

FINANCES
July 1, 1986-June 30, 1987
Expenses: $4,459,100

CONTRACTS
AEA LORT (B), SSD&C and USA

The American Repertory Theatre, founded as a professional producing organization and a theatrical training conservatory, is one of a very few companies in this country with a resident acting ensemble performing in rotating repertory. The company has produced 59 premieres, 18 American premieres and 18 new translations. Our productions, which have increasingly involved artists of national and international stature from a wide variety of disciplines, generally fall into three distinct categories: newly interpreted classical productions, new American plays, and neglected works of the past, frequently involving music. ART has toured extensively in this country and abroad, including performances in Avignon, Paris, Venice, Edinburgh, Tel Aviv and Belgrade; at theatres in London and Amsterdam; and at the 1984 Olympic Arts Festival in Los Angeles. In the fall of 1987, following a pilot program, the American Repertory Theatre Institute for Advanced Theatre Training at Harvard began its first year of formal instruction under the direction of Richard Riddell. ART received the 1985 Jujamcyn Theatre Award and a special Tony Award in 1986 for continued excellence in resident theatre.

—Robert Brustein

PRODUCTIONS 1985–86

The Changeling, Thomas Middleton; (D) Robert Brustei (S) Michael H. Yeargan; (C) Michael H. Yeargan; (L) Richard Riddell

The Balcony, Jean Genet; trans: Jean-Claude van Itallie; (D) JoAnne Akalaitis; (S) George Tsypin; (C) Kristi Zea; (L) Jennifer Tipton

Alcestis, Euripides; adapt: Robert Wilson; trans: Dudley Fitts and Robert Fitzgerald; additional text: Heiner Muller; trans: Carl Weber; (D) Robert Wilson; (S) Robert Wilson and Tom Kamm; (C) John Conklin; (L) Jennifer Tipton and Robert Wilson

The Juniper Tree, libretto: Arthur Yorinks; music: Philip Glass and Robert Moran; (D) Andrei Serban; (S) Michael H. Yeargan; (C) Michael H. Yeargan; (L) Jennifer Tipton

Olympian Games, book adapt and lyrics: Barbara Damashek and Kenneth Cavander; music: Barbara Damashek; (D) Barbara Damashek; (S) Alexander Okun; (C) Alexander Okun; (L) Spencer Mosse

The Day Room, Don DeLillo; (D) Michael Bloom; (S) Loy Arcenas; (C) Karen Eister; (L) Richard Riddell

Mistero Buffo (A Comic Mystery), Dario Fo; trans: Stuart Hodd, Ron Jenkins and Walter Valeri; (D) Dario Fo; (S) Lino Avolio; (L) Lino Avolio

Tutta Casa, Letto, e Chiesa (It's All Bed, Board and Church), Dario Fo and Franca Rame; trans: Maria Consagra; (D) Dario Fo; (S) Lino Avolio; (L) Lino Avolio

American Repertory Theatre. *Tonight We Improvise.* Photo: Richard Feldman.

PRODUCTIONS 1986–87

Tonight We Improvise, Luigi Pirandello; adapt: Robert Brustein; (D) Robert Brustein; (S) Michael H. Yeargan; (C) Michael H. Yeargan; (L) Stephen Strawbridge

End of the World with Symposium to Follow, Arthur Kopit; (D) Richard Foreman; (S) Michael H. Yeargan; (C) Lindsay W. Davis; (L) Stephen Strawbridge

Sweet Table at the Richelieu, Ronald Ribman; (D) Andrei Serban; (S) John Conklin; (C) John Conklin; (L) Howell Binkley

The Day Room, Don DeLillo; (D) Michael Bloom and Wheeler David; (S) Loy Arcenas; (C) Karen Eister; (L) Richard Riddell

The Good Woman of Setzuan, Bertolt Brecht; trans: Eric Bentley; (D) Andrei Serban; (S) Jeff Muskovin; (C) Catherine Zuber; (L) Howell Binkley

Archangels Don't Play Pinball, Dario Fo; trans: Ron Jenkins; (D) Dario Fo and Franca Rame; (S) Dario Fo; (C) Dario Fo; (L) Robert M. Wierzel

The Cannibal Masque, Ronald Ribman; (D) David Wheeler; (S) Loy Arcenas; (C) Christine Joly de Lotbiniere; (L) Frank Butler

Mrs. Sorken Presents, Christopher Durang; (D) R.J. Cutler and Savick Wesley; (S) Loy Arcenas; (C) Karen Eister; (L) Frank Butler

The American Stage Company

VICTORIA L. HOLLOWAY
Artistic Director

JOHN A. BERGLUND
Managing Director

Box 1560
St. Petersburg, FL 33731
(813) 823-1600 (bus.)
(813) 822-8814 (b.o.)

FOUNDED 1979
Richard Hopkins, Bobbie Seifer

SEASON
Oct.-June

FACILITIES
Mainstage
Seating capacity: 120
Stage: thrust

FINANCES
July 1, 1986-June 30, 1987
Expenses: $332,000

CONTRACTS
AEA SPT

Our commitment to do large works within the limits of our small budget is dangerous, but we feel the need to explore and give muscle to our artistic discipline. In 1986 we presented audiences in our region with free Shakespeare on the waterfront. Nine thousand patrons experienced the magic of the theatre, under the stars, over a 10-day run. This past season the audience was 16,000 strong. Our evolutionary position within our region, has never forced us to question what was of utmost concern — the work on the stage, for which we live and sacrifice. We direct all available monies to the compensation of our artists, because experience tells us that successful theatre comes from their imagination. We care deeply about the collective of artists in our employ, as well as the ever-growing audience that seems willing to embrace them.

—Victoria L. Holloway

PRODUCTIONS 1985–86

Good, C.P. Taylor; (D) John A. Berglund; (S) Sandy Eppling; (C) Joanne L. Johnson; (L) Michael Newton-Brown

I Love Alice, adapt: Peter Massey and Victoria Holloway, from William Shakespeare; (D) Victoria Holloway; (S) Paul Eppling and Sandy Eppling; (C) Sandy Eppling, Shari Kinney, Joanne L. Johnson and Hugh Slack; (L) Peter Jay

A Weekend Near Madison, Kathleen Tolan; (D) Cathey Crowell Sawyer; (S) Paul Eppling; (C) Hugh Slack; (L) Debbie Adamson

True West, Sam Shepard; (D) Neil DeGroot; (S) Riic Stouder; (C) Joanne L. Johnson; (L) Riic Stouder

The Normal Heart, Larry Kramer; (D) Bruce Siddons; (S) Marshall Oliver; (C) Karen Cardarella; (L) Mark Hendren

Talley's Folly, Lanford Wilson; (D) John A. Berglund; (S) Mark Hendren; (C) Hugh Slack; (L) Mark Hendren

Billy Bishop Goes to War, John Gray and Eric Peterson; (D) Paul Frellick; (S) Paul Eppling; (C) Joanne L. Johnson; (L) Mark Hendren

The Taming of the Shrew, William Shakespeare; (D) Victoria Holloway; (S) Paul Eppling; (C) Joanne L. Johnson; (L) Mark Hendren

PRODUCTIONS 1986–87

Romeo and Juliet, William Shakespeare; adapt: Victoria Holloway; (D) Victoria Holloway; (S) Mark Hendren; (C) Joanne L. Johnson; (L) Mark Hendren

The Hot l Baltimore, Lanford Wilson; (D) Cathey Crowell Sawyer; (S) David Bewley; (C) Mary Beth Sprankle; (L) Mark Hendren

Strange Snow, Stephen Metcalfe; (D) John A. Berglund; (S) Mark Hendren; (C) Mary Beth Sprankle; (L) Mark Hendren

Kiss of the Spider Woman, adapt: Allen Baker, from Manuel Puig; (D) Victoria Holloway; (S) K. Edgar Swados; (C) Mary Beth Sprankle; (L) Michael Newton-Brown

A Midsummer Night's Dream, William Shakespeare; (D) Victoria Holloway; (S) K. Edgar Swados; (C) David Bewley; (L) Michael Newton-Brown

Crimes of the Heart, Beth Henley; (D) Bruce Siddons; (S) David Bewley; (C) Mary Beth Sprankle and Hugh Slack; (L) Cricket

The American Stage Company. Paulo Frediani, Patrick Boyington and Susannah Berryman in *Strange Snow*. Photo: Ken Kinzel.

American Stage Festival

American Stage Festival. William Linton, David Cantor, Darlene Bel Grayson, Betsy Joslyn and Joanne Borts in *Tintypes*. Photo: Jim Witek.

LARRY CARPENTER
Artistic Director

RICHARD ROSE
Managing Director

Box 225
Milford, NH 03055
(603) 673-4005 (bus.)
(603) 673-7515 (b.o.)

FOUNDED 1975
Terry C. Lorden

SEASON
May-Sept.

FACILITIES
Seating capacity: 497
Stage: proscenium

FINANCES
Nov. 1, 1985-Oct. 31, 1986
Expenses: $631,050

CONTRACTS
AEA LORT (C), (D), SSD&C and USA

The artistic mission of the American Stage Festival is to maximize the variety, quality and visibility of our developing regional theatre program. We work to accomplish this mission by combining an aggressive pursuit of theatre art that is stylistically, literarily and politically significant with recent commercially proven popular entertainments. Within this combination we present both significant revivals and premieres and wish to augment this mixture with artistic works and entertainments of greater scope by co-producing with other nonprofit institutions and by forming relationships with commercial producers who seek to develop properties in a well-protected and positive atmosphere.

—Larry Carpenter

PRODUCTIONS 1985–86

The Pirates of Penzance, book: W.S. Gilbert; music: Arthur Sullivan; (D) Larry Carpenter; (S) Gary English; (C) Gary English; (L) John Gisondi

Brighton Beach Memoirs, Neil Simon; (D) Martin Herzer; (S) John Fallabella; (C) Patricia Zipprodt; (L) Ken Farley

A Tale of Two Cities, adapt: Larry Carpenter, from Charles Dickens; (D) Larry Carpenter; (S) John Fallabella; (C) Mark Wendland; (L) David Lockner

Rhymes with Evil, Charles Traeger; (D) Larry Carpenter; (S) Mark Wendland; (C) John Falabella; (L) Marcia Madeira

Tintypes, Mary Kyte, Mel Marvin and Gary Pearle; (D) Pam Hunt; (S) David Lockner; (C) Amanda Aldridge; (L) David Lockner

American Theatre Company

KITTY ROBERTS
Producing Artistic Director

Box 1265
Tulsa, OK 74101
(918) 747-9494 (bus.)
(918) 592-7111 (b.o.)

FOUNDED 1970
Kitty Roberts

SEASON
Sept.-July

FACILITIES
Brook Theatre
Seating capacity: 483
Stage: proscenium

John Williams Theatre
Seating capacity: 429
Stage: proscenium

FINANCES
Jan. 1, 1986-Dec. 31, 1986
Expenses: $300,000

CONTRACTS
AEA Guest Artist

Oklahoma's pioneer spirit arises from a life shared together at the edge of recent American history — the forced resettlement of Native Americans from 1820 on, the land rush by European settlers in 1889, statehood in 1907, the oil boom from 1912 to 1920, the Dustbowl depression of the 1930s, the expansion of military bases during World War II, the energy crisis and oil embargo of 1973. As Oklahoma's only resident professional theatre company, the American Theatre Company can persuade Oklahomans that their frontier viewpoint is mirrored in the traditions of world drama, and that their frontier voices can be expressed in a unique dramatic idiom. Therefore, our goal is to play a leading role in shaping a common public vision for the economic, political, educational, religious and artistic life of Oklahoma. ATC presents six shows a season and conducts an ongoing statewide education program.

—Kitty Roberts

PRODUCTIONS 1985–86

The School for Scandal, Richard Brinsley Sheridan; (D) Scott Rubsam; (S) Richard Ellis; (C) Jo Wimer; (L) Jim Queen
A Christmas Carol, adapt: Robert Odle from Charles Dickens; (D) David Gately; (S) Richard Ellis; (C) Jo Wimer; (L) Jim Queen
Strange Snow, Stephen Metcalfe; (D) Kitty Roberts; (S) Jim French; (C) Jo Wimer; (L) Jim Queen
Greater Tuna, Jaston Williams, Joe Sears and Ed Howard; (D) Kitty Roberts; (S) Richard Ellis; (C) Jo Wimer; (L) Jim Queen
Goodbye Freddie, Elizabeth Diggs; (D) Scott Rubsam; (S) Richard Ellis; (C) Jo Wimer; (L) Jim Queen
The 1940's Radio Hour, Walton Jones; (D) Kitty Roberts; (S) Richard Ellis; (C) Jo Wimer; (L) Jim Queen

PRODUCTIONS 1986–87

Little Shop of Horrors, book and lyrics: Howard Ashman; music: Alan Menken; (D) Kitty Roberts; (S) Richard Ellis; (C) Gene Barnhart; (L) Jim Queen
Painting Churches, Tina Howe; (D) Hank Barrows; (S) Richard Ellis; (C) Gene Barnhart; (L) Jim Queen
A Christmas Carol, adapt: Robert Odle, from Charles Dickens; (D) Jack Eddleman; (S) Richard Ellis; (C) Gene Barnhart and Jo Wimer; (L) Jim Queen
Brighton Beach Memoirs, Neil Simon; (D) Jim Queen; (S) Richard Ellis; (C) Gene Barnhart; (L) Jim Queen
Lone Star and ***Laundry and Bourbon***, James McLure; (D) Jim Queen; (S) Richard Ellis; (C) Gene Barnhart; (L) Melinda Lewis
Blues, Will Bartlett and Randy Wimer; (D) Jim Queen; (S) Richard Ellis; (C) Jo Wimer; (L) Jim Queen

American Theatre Company. Sean P. Harrington and Brennan Brown in *Brighton Beach Memoirs.* Photo: Tom Wachs.

PRODUCTIONS 1986–87

Peg o' My Heart, book adapt: Larry Carpenter, from J. Hartley Manners; book: Ronnie Millar; music: David Heneker; (D) Larry Carpenter; (S) John Falabella; (C) Lowell Detweiler; (L) Marcia Madeira
Sleuth, Anthony Shaffer; (D) Ben Levit; (S) Nancy Thon; (C) Amanda Aldridge; (L) Ann Wrightson
What the Butler Saw, Joe Orton; (D) Larry Carpenter; (S) Mark Wendland; (C) Martha Hally; (L) Ken Smith
Master Harold...and the boys, Athol Fugard; (D) Israel Hicks; (S) Mark Wendland; (C) Mark Wendland; (L) Frances Aronson
Biloxi Blues, Neil Simon; (D) Martin Herzer; (S) Richard Hoover; (C) Barbara Forbes; (L) David Lockner

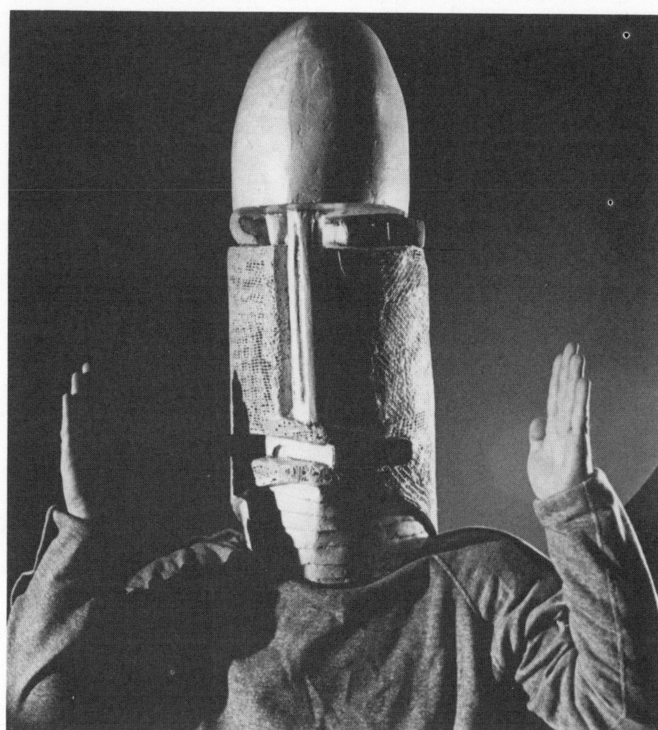
Antenna Theatre. Ed Holmes in *Russia.* Photo: Tom Wachs.

Antenna Theater

CHRIS HARDMAN
Artistic Director

ANNETTE ROSE
Executive Director

Box 176
Sausalito, CA 94966
(415) 332-4862

FOUNDED 1980
Chris Hardman

SEASON
Variable

FINANCES
Jan. 1, 1986-Dec. 31, 1986
Expenses: $229,371

Antenna's goal is to discover, explore and invent new ways in which live theatre can involve the general public in the creation/presentation of live performance. Experimenting with theatrical format has taught us multitudes about the extent to which an audience is willing to be absorbed physically in the development of a play. In *Artery* each audient, wearing a Walkman, walked singly through a 17-room maze following instructions given by the pre-recorded actors in the context of the story. For *Amnesia*, we had an audience of 20 interacting with a cast of 10 while "doing" different stories from the imaginary past of the theatregoer. Antenna's eighth audience-participation piece, *Radio Interference*, used infrared technology so that the audience could have a simultaneous experience not possible with the individual cassette recorder. In putting headphones on the audience we are attempting to speak within each individual's mind — to personalize the experience through this technology while asking for participation not usually required in theatre.

—*Chris Hardman*

PRODUCTIONS 1985–86

Fairplay, Chris Hardman; (D) Chris Hardman; (S) Ronald M. Davis; (L) Jim Schelstrate
Adjusting the Idle, Chris Hardman; (D) Chris Hardman; (S) Ronald M. Davis and Chris Hardman; (L) Jim Schelstrate
Russia, Chris Hardman; music: Jim McKee and Barney Jones; (D) Chris Hardman; (S) Ronald M. Davis; (C) Sherry Charles and Chris Hardman; (L) Jim Schelstrate

PRODUCTIONS 1986–87

Dracula in the Desert, Chris Hardman; music: Bryan Pezzone; (D) Chris Hardman; (S) Ronald M. Davis and Chris Hardman; (C) Sherry Charles and Chris Hardman; (L) Jim Schelstrate
Radio Interference, Chris Hardman; (D) Chris Hardman and Leacock Richard; (S) Ronald M. Davis; (C) Susan Downing; (L) Jim Schelstrate

Arena Stage

ZELDA FICHANDLER
Producing Director

WILLIAM STEWART
Managing Director

6th and Maine Ave., SW
Washington, DC 20024
(202) 554-9066 (bus.)
(202) 488-3300 (b.o.)

FOUNDED 1950
Thomas C. Fichandler, Zelda Fichandler, Edward Mangum

SEASON
Oct.-July

FACILITIES
The Arena
Seating capacity: 827
Stage: arena

The Kreeger Theater
Seating capacity: 514
Stage: thrust

The Old Vat Room
Seating capacity: 180
Stage: cabaret

FINANCES
July 1, 1986-June 30, 1987
Expenses: $7,086,500

CONTRACTS
AEA LORT (B+), (C), (D), SSD&C and USA

Arena Stage embodies the concept of achieving artistic excellence by means of a resident ensemble of actors, directors, technicians, administrators, craftspeople and associate artists who create together in an ongoing, evolving process. Our repertoire is aggressively eclectic, spanning national and international dramatic literature, both classic and modern. We explore subjects that express an involvement with the human condition through a variety of dramatic forms. Most important, the actor stands at the center of our work as the primary embodiment of the art itself, the

Arena Stage. Randall Mell and Kate Fuglei in *Crime and Punishment.* Photo: Joan Marcus.

instrument of highest communication and communion, bringing life to life by means of word, gesture, intelligence, imagination and passion. Arena is a deeply spiritual and spirited artistic home for a family of creative theatre professionals dedicated to enriching the cultural life of our human commmunity.

—*Zelda Fichandler*

PRODUCTIONS 1985–86

The Good Person of Setzuan, Bertolt Brecht; trans: Ralph Manheim; music: John McKinney; (D) Garland Wright; (S) John Arnone; (C) Marjorie Slaiman; (L) Nancy Schertler
Women and Water, John Guare; (D) Douglas C. Wager; (S) Tony Straiges; (C) Marjorie Slaiman; (L) Allen Lee Hughes
'night, Mother, Marsha Norman; (D) James C. Nicola; (S) Russell Metheny; (C) Noel Borden; (L) Frances Aronson
Restoration, Edward Bond; (D) Sharon Ott; (S) Thomas Lynch; (C) Marjorie Slaiman; (L) Paul Gallo
The Philadelphia Story, Philip Barry; (D) Douglas C. Wager; (S) Adrianne Lobel; (C) Ann Hould-Ward; (L) Allen Lee Hughes
The Wild Duck, Henrik Ibsen; trans: David Westerfer; (D) Lucian Pintilie; (S) Radu Boruzescu; (C) Miruna Boruzescu; (L) Beverly Emmons
Old Times, Harold Pinter; (D) Garland Wright; (S) Douglas Stein; (C) Marjorie Slaiman; (L) Nancy Schertler
The Taming of the Shrew, William Shakespeare; (D) Douglas C. Wager; (S) Adrianne Lobel; (C) Martin Pakledinaz; (L) Paul Gallo

PRODUCTIONS 1986–87

The Marriage of Bette and Boo, Christopher Durang; (D) James C. Nicola; (S) Thomas Lynch; (C) Gregg Barnes; (L) Allen Lee Hughes
Measure for Measure, William Shakespeare; (D) Douglas C. Wager; (S) George Tsypin; (C) Marjorie Slaiman; (L) Frances Aronson
The Piggy Bank, Eugene Labiche and A. Delacour; trans: Albert Bermel; (D) Garland Wright; (S) John Arnone; (C) Martin Pakledinaz; (L) Frances Aronson
Crime and Punishment, adapt: Yuri Lyubimov and Yuri Karyakin, from Fyodor Dostoevsky; trans: Michael Henry Heim; (D) Yuri Lyubimov; (S) David Borovsky and David M. Glenn; (C) Marjorie Slaiman; (L) Yuri Lyubimov and Nancy Schertler
Glengarry Glen Ross, David Mamet; (D) Douglas C. Wager; (S) Thomas Lynch; (C) Marjorie Slaiman; (L) Nancy Schertler
Ourselves Alone, Anne Devlin; (D) Les Waters; (S) Annie Smart; (C) Annie Smart; (L) Nancy Schertler
Heartbreak House, George Bernard Shaw; (D) Mel Shapiro; (S) Karl Eigsti; (C) Marjorie Slaiman; (L) Allen Lee Hughes
The Crucible, Arthur Miller; (D) Zelda Fichandler; (S) Douglas Stein; (C) Marjorie Slaiman; (L) Allen Lee Hughes

Arizona Theatre Company

GARY GISSELMAN
Artistic Director

SUSAN GOLDBERG
Managing Director

Box 1631
Tucson, AZ 85702
(602) 884-8210 (bus.)
(602) 622-2823 (b.o.)

1202 West Thomas Road
Phoenix, AZ 85012 (602) 234-2892 (bus.)
(602) 279-0534 (b.o.)

FOUNDED 1966
Sandy Rosenthal

SEASON
Oct.-June

FACILITIES
Tucson Community Center Theatre
Seating capacity: 526
Stage: modified thrust

Phoenix College Theatre
Seating capacity: 305
Stage: thrust

Arizona Theatre Company. Helen Backlin and Patricia Fraser in *A Delicate Balance*. Photo: Tim Fuller.

Scottsdale Center for the Arts
Seating capacity: 785
Stage: modified thrust

FINANCES
July 1, 1986-June 30, 1987
Expenses: $2,489,758

CONTRACTS
AEA LORT (C), SSD&C and USA

The Arizona Theatre Company is in a constant state of rediscovering itself. Tucson and Phoenix are growing and changing so rapidly that ATC is at once a part of, as well as a reflection of, that growth and change. The population moving to Arizona is from all over the U.S., Europe, Central and South America, so the process of discovering our community and our audience is a dynamic one. We are trying to be our own model and discover our own uniqueness as a regional theatre in the Southwest. We try to provide an exciting and nurturing creative atmosphere for all theatre artists. To that end our repertoire is eclectic, drawing from classical and contemporary work, including a strong interest in new plays, adaptations and Latin American literature. All is enhanced by the exotic embrace of the desert which provides an operating metaphor for ATC: not how little grows, but how much grows on so little.

—*Gary Gisselman*

PRODUCTIONS 1985–86

Fool for Love, Sam Shepard; (D) Gary Gisselman; (S) Vicki Smith; (C) Bobbi Culbert; (L) Kent Dorsey
The Real Thing, Tom Stoppard; (D) Ken Ruta; (S) Sam Kirkpatrick and Don Hooper; (C) Diane Fargo; (L) Donald Darnutzer
The Government Inspector, Nikolai Gogol; (D) Walter Schoen; (S) Vicki Smith; (C) David Kay Mickelsen; (L) Donald Darnutzer
Galileo, Bertolt Brecht; trans: Charles Laughton; (D) Gary Gisselman; (S) Vicki Smith; (C) Gene Davis Buck; (L) Donald Darnutzer
Private Lives, Noel Coward; (D) Edward Payson Call; (S) Don Hooper; (C) Christopher Beesley; (L) Don Hooper
My Fair Lady, book and lyrics: Alan Jay Lerner; music: Frederick Loewe; (D) Gary Gisselman; (S) Kent Dorsey and Thomas Buderwitz; (C) Gene Davis Buck; (L) Donald Darnutzer

PRODUCTIONS 1986–87

The House of Blue Leaves, John Guare; (D) John Clark Donahue; (S) Jack Barkla; (C) David Kay Mickelsen; (L) Donald Darnutzer

A Delicate Balance, Edward Albee; (D) Edward Payson Call; (S) Thomas Buderwitz; (C) Gene Davis Buck; (L) Donald Darnutzer
The Marriage of Bette and Boo, Christopher Durang; (D) John Clark Donahue; (S) Vicki Smith; (C) David Kay Mickelsen; (L) Donald Darnutzer
The Matchmaker, Thornton Wilder; (D) Gary Gisselman; (S) Vicki Smith; (C) Lewis Brown; (L) Donald Darnutzer
Glengarry Glen Ross, David Mamet; (D) Edward Payson Call; (S) Kent Dorsey; (C) Bobbi Culbert; (L) Donald Darnutzer
You Can't Take It with You, George S. Kaufman and Moss Hart; (D) Gary Gisselman; (S) Thomas Buderwitz; (C) David Kay Mickelsen; (L) Donald Darnutzer

The Arkansas Arts Center Children's Theatre

BRADLEY D. ANDERSON
Artistic Director

P.J. POWERS
Administrative Manager

Box 2137
Little Rock, AR 72203
(501) 372-4000

FOUNDED 1963
Museum of Fine Arts, The Fine Arts Club, The Junior League of Little Rock

SEASON
Sept.-May

FACILITIES
The Arkansas Arts Center Theatre
Seating capacity: 389
Stage: proscenium

The Arkansas Arts Center Theatre Studio
Seating capacity: 200
Stage: flexible

FINANCES
July 1, 1986-June 30, 1987
Expenses: $196,371

The Arkansas Arts Center Children's Theatre exists to provide high quality theatre experiences for young people and their families. We provide a master/apprentice education where children work alongside professional actors, all sharing in the common goal of excellence. Our best work can be experienced on at least three distinct levels: for the young child there is simply a great story and lots of sensory pleasure; the older child enjoys more of the subtleties in the language and in the art form; adults appreciate the more sophisticated humor or irony and see the symbolism that moves beyond the immediate story itself to the world at large. A dedicated ensemble of actors, directors and designers produce a mainstage season, three touring productions, an experimental lab studio and teach in an intensive summer theatre academy that brings children into direct working contact with the creative process. We attempt to educate young audiences through artistic observations of the human condition, while trying to heighten the quality of theatre experiences for children.

—Bradley D. Anderson

PRODUCTIONS 1985–86

Winnie the Pooh, adapt: Bradley D. Anderson, from A.A. Milne; (D) Bradley D. Anderson; (S) James E. Lyden; (C) Mark Hughes; (L) Alan Keith Smith
The Best Christmas Pageant Ever, Barbara Robinson; (D) Debbie Weber; (S) James E. Lyden; (C) Mark Hughes; (L) Alan Keith Smith
Sherlock Holmes and the Curse of the Sign of the Four, adapt: Dennis Rosa, from Arthur Conan Doyle, Jr.; (D) Bradley D. Anderson; (S) James E. Lyden; (C) Mark Hughes; (L) Alan Keith Smith
A Wrinkle in Time, adapt: Frederick Gaines, from Madeleine L'Engle; (D) Bradley D. Anderson; (S) James E. Lyden; (C) Mark Hughes; (L) Alan Keith Smith
Pinocchio, adapt: Timothy Mason, from Carlo Collodi; (D) Rex Allen; (S) James E. Lyden; (C) Mark Hughes; (L) Alan Keith Smith

Arkansas Arts Center Children's Theatre. Shane Nash, Laura Kirspel, Stephen Mark Hansen, Melanie Ross and Sarah Boss in *Joan of Arc*. Photo: Art Meripol.

PRODUCTIONS 1986–87

The Legend of Sleepy Hollow, adapt: Frederick Gaines, from Washington Irving; (D) Bradley D. Anderson; (S) Alan Keith Smith and Mary Alyce White; (C) Gene Davis Buck; (L) James E. Lyden
Goldilocks and the Three Bears and ***Little Red Riding Hood***, book adapt: Bradley D. Anderson; music: Lori Loree; lyrics: Bradley D. Anderson, Ellen Anderson, Lori Loree and Debbie Weber; (D) Bradley D. Anderson; (S) James E. Lyden; (C) Donna C. Conrad; (L) Alan Keith Smith
Hans Brinker and the Silver Skates, adapt: Marc French; editor: Martin McGeachy; (D) Debbie Weber; (S) Alan Keith Smith; (C) Donna C. Conrad; (L) Alan Keith Smith
Puss 'n' Boots, book adapt: Bradley D. Anderson; music and lyrics: Lori Loree; (D) Ron McIntyre-Fender; (S) James E. Lyden; (C) Donna C. Conrad; (L) Alan Keith Smith
Joan of Arc, Frederick Gaines; (D) Bradley D. Anderson; (S) James E. Lyden; (C) Donna C. Conrad; (L) Alan Keith Smith
The Adventures of Tom Sawyer, adapt: Timothy Mason, from Mark Twain; (D) Ron McIntyre-Fender; (S) James E. Lyden; (C) Donna C. Conrad; (L) Alan Keith Smith

Arkansas Repertory Theatre

CLIFF FANNIN BAKER
Artistic Director

ANDREW C. GAUPP
Managing Director

712 East 11th St.
Little Rock, AR 72202
(501) 378-0445 (bus.)
(501) 378-0405 (b.o.)

FOUNDED 1976
Cliff Fannin Baker

SEASON
Year-round

FACILITIES
Main Stage at 11th St.
Seating capacity: 112
Stage: flexible

Main Stage at 601 Main St.
Seating capacity: 362
Stage: proscenium

Second Stage at 601 Main St.
Seating capacity: 99
Stage: flexible

FINANCES
July 1, 1986-June 30, 1987
Expenses: $610,000

CONTRACTS
AEA letter of agreement

Arkansas Rep's 12th season represents the diversity of our audiences and our outreach goals, while exhibiting a prevailing interest in contemporary scripts and American playwrights. Our mission at the Rep has remained a constant: to provoke, educate and entertain our audiences while providing meaningful experiences for the professional artistic company. The Rep is still best described as "emerging." We moved into a new performing arts center while entering the second year on a new letter of agreement with Actors' Equity Association. Our subscription base has doubled in the past few years, our company is growing and our programming is challenging both artists and audiences. We are proud of the theatre's regional reputation, national support and local impact. Our programs include an eight-play mainstage season, a six-play second stage season, a lunchtime performance series, play readings and "Talkbacks," a professional intern program, a 10-year-old arts-in-education program and a six-state regional tour. Future plans include a film festival, a "Town Hall" humanities series and an outdoor performance series.

—Cliff Fannin Baker

PRODUCTIONS 1985–86

Cloud 9, Caryl Churchill; (D) Terry Sneed; (S) Don Yanik; (C) Don Yanik; (L) Kathy Gray

The Night of the Iguana, Tennessee Williams; (D) Cliff Fannin Baker; (S) Don Yanik; (C) Cathey Crowell Sawyer; (L) Kathy Gray

Agnes of God, John Pielmeier; (D) John Vreeke; (S) Don Yanik; (C) Marcy Bethel; (L) Kathy Gray

2 X 5, music: John Kander; lyrics: Fred Ebb; conceived: Seth Glassman; (D) Cliff Fannin Baker; (S) Don Yanik; (C) Marcy Bethel; (L) Kathy Gray

The Foreigner, Larry Shue; (D) Cliff Fannin Baker; (S) Mike Nichols; (C) Marcy Bethel; (L) Kathy Gray

Quartermaine's Terms, Simon Gray; (D) Cliff Fannin Baker; (S) Mike Nichols; (C) Marcy Bethel; (L) Kathy Gray

Home, Samm-Art Williams; (D) Cathey Crowell Sawyer; (S) Mike Nichols; (C) Marcy Bethel; (L) Kathy Gray

'night, Mother, Marsha Norman; (D) Cliff Fannin Baker; (S) Mike Nichols; (C) Marcy Bethel; (L) Kathy Gray

Quilters, book: Molly Newman and Barbara Damashek; music and lyrics: Barbara Damashek; (D) Terry Sneed; (S) Mike Nichols; (C) Marcy Bethel; (L) Kathy Gray

Arkansas Repertory Theatre. Cathey Crowell Sawyer and Mercedes McCambridge in *'night, Mother.* Photo: Barry Arthur.

PRODUCTIONS 1986–87

Natural Disasters, Jack Heifner; (D) Cliff Fannin Baker; (S) Mike Nichols; (C) Mark Hughes; (L) Kathy Gray

U.S.A., Paul Shyre and John Dos Passos; (D) Terry Sneed; (S) Kathy Gray; (C) Mark Hughes; (L) Kathy Gray

Greater Tuna, Jaston Williams, Joe Sears and Ed Howard; (D) Cliff Fannin Baker; (S) Mike Nichols; (C) Mark Hughes; (L) Robert A. Jones

A...My Name Is Alice, Joan Micklin Silver and Julianne Boyd; (D) Rachel Lampert; (S) Mike Nichols; (C) Mark Hughes; (L) Kathy Gray

Glengarry Glen Ross, David Mamet; (D) Cliff Fannin Baker; (S) Dale Jordan; (C) Mark Hughes; (L) Kathy Gray

The Last Meeting of the Knights of the White Magnolia, Preston Jones; (D) Cathey Crowell Sawyer; (S) Mike Nichols; (C) Mark Hughes; (L) Kathy Gray

Brighton Beach Memoirs, Neil Simon; (D) Cliff Fannin Baker; (S) Mike Nichols; (C) Mark Hughes; (L) Kathy Gray

The Real Thing, Tom Stoppard; (D) Terry Sneed; (S) Keith Belli; (C) Mark Hughes; (L) Kathy Gray

Pump Boys and Dinettes, John Foley, Mark Hardwick, Debra Monk, Cass Morgan, John Schimmel and Jim Wann; (D) Cliff Fannin Baker; (S) Mike Nichols; (C) Mark Hughes; (L) Kathy Gray

Asolo Performing Arts Center

JOHN ULMER
Artistic Director

LEE WARNER
Executive Director

Postal Drawer E
Sarasota, FL 33578
(813) 355-7155 (bus.)
(813) 355-5137 (b.o.)

FOUNDED 1960
Arthur Dorland, Richard G. Fallon, Robert Strane, Eberle Thomas

SEASON
Nov.-July

FACILITIES
Asolo Theater
Seating capacity: 316
Stage: proscenium

Bette Oliver Theater
Seating capacity: 138
Stage: flexible

FINANCES
Sept. 1, 1986-Aug. 31, 1987
Expenses: $2,356,600

CONTRACTS
AEA LORT (C), SSD&C and USA

The Asolo State Theater is one of three units in the new Asolo Performing Arts Center. The other components are the MFA Conservatory for pre-professional theatre artists administered by Florida State University, and extensive film and TV studios, combined with a production and training laboratory. This state-of-the-art plant is presently being constructed to house all three units under one roof. The Asolo is a service institution producing its own local seasons as well as extensive professional school tours and a yearly national tour of one Asolo season offering. We are not in a large metropolitan center and yet we are a major theatre attraction for the state of Florida so Asolo strives for an eclectic play selection with broad audience appeal. Since we are a subsidized theatre, our seasons must add up to theatre art. We strive for a quality of acting and directing which brings the plays to stage life by detailing organic human behavior in all its dazzling variety.

—John Ulmer

PRODUCTIONS 1985–86

A Christmas Carol: Scrooge and Marley, adapt: Israel Horovitz, from Charles Dickens; (D) John Ulmer; (S) Jeffrey Dean; (C) Catherine King; (L) Martin Petlock

Greater Tuna, Jaston Williams, Joe Sears and Ed Howard; (D) Stephen Rothman; (S) Keven Lock; (C) Catherine King; (L) Martin Petlock

A Moon for the Misbegotten, Eugene O'Neill; (D) John Gulley; (S) John Ezell; (C) Catherine King; (L) John Toia

Hamlet, William Shakespeare;

Asolo Performing Arts Center. Alex C. Thayer, Sheridan Crist and Eric Tavares in *Orphans*. Photo: Gary W. Sweetman.

adapt: A.L. Rowse; (D) Porter Van Zandt; (S) Bennet Averyt; (C) Catherine King; (L) Martin Petlock

Sleuth, Anthony Shaffer; (D) Susan Gregg; (S) Holmes Easley; (C) Mitchell Bloom; (L) Martin Petlock

As Is, William M. Hoffman; (D) Jamie Brown; (S) Jeffrey Dean; (C) Catherine King; (L) Martin Petlock

Forgive Me, Evelyn Bunns, Janet Couch; (D) Alan Arkin; (S) Bennett Averyt; (C) Catherine King; (L) Martin Petlock

Tartuffe, Molière; trans: Richard Wilbur; (D) John Ulmer; (S) Kenneth Kurtz; (C) Catherine King; (L) Martin Petlock

How the Other Half Loves, Alan Ayckbourn; (D) Robert Miller; (S) John Ezell; (C) Mitchell Bloom; (L) Martin Petlock

The Foreigner, Larry Shue; (D) John Gulley; (S) Jeffrey Dean; (C) Catherine King; (L) Martin Petlock

A Life in the Theatre, David Mamet; (D) Bill Levis; (S) Charles T. Parsons; (C) Mitchell Bloom; (L) Mark Noble

Orphans, Lyle Kessler; (D) John Gulley; (S) Charles T. Parsons; (C) Catherine King; (L) Mark Noble

Spoon River: An Anthology, adapt: Charles Aidman, from Edgar Lee Masters; (D) John Ulmer; (S) Charles T. Parsons; (C) Marsha Fink; (L) Martin Petlock

PRODUCTIONS 1986–87

A Christmas Carol: Scrooge and Marley, adapt: Israel Horovitz, from Charles Dickens; (D) John Ulmer; (S) Jeffrey Dean; (C) Catherine King; (L) Martin Petlock

The Rainmaker, N. Richard Nash; (D) John Gulley; (S) Joseph Tilford; (C) Catherine King; (L) John Toia

Who's Afraid of Virginia Woolf?, Edward Albee; (D) John Ulmer; (S) Jeffrey Dean; (C) Catherine King; (L) Martin Petlock

Orphans, Lyle Kessler; (D) John Gulley; (S) Keven Lock; (C) Catherine King; (L) Mark Noble

Deathtrap, Ira Levin; (D) Robert Miller; (S) Bennet Averyt; (C) Mitchell Bloom; (L) Martin Petlock

Betrayal, Harold Pinter; (D) John Ulmer; (S) Bennet Averyt; (C) Catherine King; (L) Martin Petlock

Nunsense, Dan Goggin; (D) John Ulmer; (S) Keven Lock; (C) Catherine King; (L) Martin Petlock

Our Town, Thornton Wilder; (D) Robert Miller; (S) Martin Petlock; (C) Catherine King; (L) Martin Petlock

The Perfect Party, A.R. Gurney, Jr.; (D) John Ulmer; (S) Gerry Leahy; (C) Catherine King; (L) Martin Petlock

All My Sons, Arthur Miller; (D) John Gulley; (S) Jeffrey Dean; (C) Mitchell Bloom; (L) Martin Petlock

A Traveling Jewish Theatre

NAOMI NEWMAN
Founding Director

STEVEN KATZ
General Manager

Box 421985
San Francisco, CA 94142
(415) 861-4880

FOUNDED 1978
Corey Fischer, Albert Greenberg, Naomi Newman

SEASON
Variable

FINANCES
July 1, 1986-June 30, 1987
Expenses: $245,000

Like the alchemist, A Traveling Jewish Theatre's key is that which is overlooked, discarded, disowned. The place that is not a place. The dwelling that is built in time rather than space. Diaspora as homeland. Exile as return. Our constant Jewish paradox. Our themes, characters and concerns—Yiddish, Kabbalah, the feminine refugees, lost dreams—all come from a place that is both liminal and transforming. In this, I feel a kinship with the tradition of the Jew outside tradition: the "heretic" poets, mystics, marginal Jews, all searching for their Jewish souls. It is here, in this small community of intention that we call A Traveling Jewish Theatre, that my soul dwells—the intention to give voice to some shared and private vision that can only be expressed in sounds and movements and words and silences passing between us and the audience. This is my soul coming home.

—Naomi Newman

PRODUCTIONS 1985–86

Berlin, Jerusalem and the Moon, company-developed; (D) Michael Posnick; (S) Gene Angell and Ron Pratt; (C) Eliza Chugg and Corey Fischer; (L) David Brune

A Dance of Exile, company-developed; (D) Naomi Newman; (S) Jim Quinn; (C) Jane Pollock and Corey Fischer; (L) David Brune

PRODUCTIONS 1986–87

Berlin, Jerusalem and the Moon, company-developed; (D) Michael Posnick; (S) Gene Angell and Ron Pratt; (C) Eliza Chugg and Corey Fischer; (L) David Brune

A Dance of Exile, company-developed; (D) Naomi Newman; (S) Jim Quinn; (C) Jane Pollock and Corey Fischer; (L) David Brune

The Last Yiddish Poet: An Incantation Against Woe, company-developed; (D) Naomi Newman; (C) Corey Fischer; (L) David Brune

Trotsky and Frida: The Musical, Albert Greenberg and Helen Stoltzfus; (D) David Brune; (S) David Brune; (C) Pat Polen and Eliza Chugg; (L) David Brune

A Traveling Jewish Theatre. Corey Fischer in *Dance of Exile*. Photo. Bernd Uhlig.

Snake Talk, Naomi Newman; (D) Corey Fischer and Hotchkiss Marlow; (S) Colleen Kelly; (C) Michel Henry and Jane Pollack; (L) David Brune
Tales of the Traveler: A Poem for the Theatre, Corey Fischer; (D) Naomi Newman and Hotchkiss Marlow; (S) David Brune; (C) Jane Pollock and Corey Fischer; (L) David Brune
Coma: A Work-in-Progress, Mira Rafalowicz; (D) Joseph Chaikin; (S) David Brune; (C) Gael Russell; (L) David Brune

At the Foot of the Mountain

PHYLLIS JANE ROSE
Artistic Director

NAYO-BARBARA MALCOLM WATKINS
Managing Director

2000 South Fifth St.
Minneapolis, MN 55454-1337
(612) 375-9487

FOUNDED 1974
Martha Boesing, Paul Boesing, Jeff Heller, Jan Magrane, Kathy Rieves, Jeff Woodward

SEASON
Year-round

FACILITIES
Seating capacity: 90
Stage: thrust

FINANCES
July 1, 1986-June 30, 1987
Expenses: $220,000

CONTRACTS
AEA SPT

At the Foot of the Mountain is a theatre of action, transformation, celebration and hope where women of many races, ages, classes and cultures create the magic which makes theatre an awesome catalyst for social change. Our mission is to inspire audience members to generate a just and joyous world. At the heart of our creative process is a full-time performance ensemble working with a playwright and director to create plays about urgent personal, local, national and international concerns. We also produce and commission new scripts; tour our best productions locally, nationally and internationally; provide professional and community workshop opportunities for emergent writers, directors and performers; and adapt appropriate work for film and video markets. We work with new combinations of voices to break the sound barriers of habit, hate and ignorance. We work with new coalitions of minds and hearts to create new contents and new forms.

—*Phyllis Jane Rose*

At the Foot of the Mountain. Dorothy Crabb and Rose Schwartz in *The Ladies Who Lunch*. Photo: Terry Gydesen.

PRODUCTIONS 1985–86

The Ladies Who Lunch, Marilyn Seven; (D) Phyllis Jane Rose; (S) Phyllis Jane Rose; (C) company (L) Bonnie Vaky
Neurotic Erotic Exotics, Spiderwoman; (D) Muriel Miguel; (S) Muriel Miguel; (C) company (L) Bonnie Vaky
Fefu and Her Friends, Maria Irene Fornes; (D) Maria Irene Fornes; (S) Monica Lorca; (C) Monica Lorca; (L) Elisa River Stacy

PRODUCTIONS 1986–87

Funnyhouse of a Negro, Adrienne Kennedy; (D) Shelia Rose Bland; (S) Bonnie Vaky; (C) Cynthia Witzigman; (L) Bonnie Vaky
The Crystal Quilt, Suzanne Lacy; (D) Suzanne Lacy and Phyllis Jane Rose; (S) Miriam Shapiro; (C) Suzanne Lacy; (L) Suzanne Lacy
Just Clowning Around, Jennifer Boesing; (D) Jan Magrane; (S) Bonnie Vaky; (C) Cynthia Witzigman; (L) Bonnie Vaky
Fefu and Her Friends, Maria Irene Fornes; (D) Maria Irene Fornes; (S) Monica Lorca; (C) Monica Lorca; (L) Sue Berger

Attic Theatre

LAVINIA MOYER
Artistic Director

BRUCE MAKOUS
Managing Director

Box 02457
Detroit, MI 48202
(313) 875-8285 (bus.)
(313) 875-8284 (b.o.)

FOUNDED 1975
Curtis Armstrong, Divina Cook, Herbert Ferrer, James Moran, Lavinia Moyer, Nancy Shayne

SEASON
Year-round

FACILITIES
New Center Theatre
Seating capacity: 299
Stage: proscenium

FINANCES
Sept. 30, 1986-Aug. 31, 1987
Expenses: $800,000

CONTRACTS
AEA SPT

The Attic Theatre is best characterized as a body of people striving to provide the best artistic environment possible for artists to create theatre. Now completing its 12th season, the theatre continues to produce primarily regional and world premiere works on its main stage. Additional programs include a writers' unit developed to serve new playwrights; a comprehensive artists-in-schools program; public and master conservatory workshops; American Sign Language interpretation of performances; and a senior citizens touring company called The Oldsters. Our artistic rationale is founded in a professionally trained ensemble approach to productions which recognizes our regional community as a family that nurtures the Attic.

—*Lavinia Moyer*

PRODUCTIONS 1985–86

We Won't Pay! We Won't Pay!, Dario Fo; trans: R.G. Davis; (D) James Moran; (S) Tom Macie; (C) Ann C. Correll; (L) Paul Epton
The 1940's Radio Hour, Walton Jones; (D) Daniel Yurgaitis; (S) Gary Decker; (C) Kristiine Flones-Czeski; (L) Mark Allen Berg
Greater Tuna, Jaston Williams, Joe Sears and Ed Howard; (D) Sharlan Douglas; (S) Gary Decker; (C) Kristiine Flones-Czeski; (L) Paul Epton
Of Mice and Men, John Steinbeck; (D) Lavinia Moyer; (S) Philipp Jung; (C) Philipp Jung; (L) Gary Decker
Monday After the Miracle, William Gibson; (D) Mary F. Bremer; (S) Norm Hamlin; (C) Judith Sheldon; (L) Mark Allen Berg
The Ballad of Conrad and Loretta, book: Christopher Reed and Ronald Martell; music and lyrics: Christopher Reed; (D) Ronald Martell; (S) Gary Decker; (C) Kristiine Flones-Czeski; (L) Paul Brohan

PRODUCTIONS 1986–87

The Real Thing, Tom Stoppard; (D) Kim T. Sharp; (S) T. Andrew Aston; (C) Carmen Cavello; (L) Paul Epton
Vaudeville, Laurence Carr; (D) Laurence Carr; (S) Philipp Jung; (C) Philipp Jung; (L) Gary Decker
Ma Rainey's Black Bottom, August Wilson; (D) Lavinia Moyer; (S) Gary Decker; (C) Laurie Danforth; (L) Paul Epton

Attic Theatre. Earl Van Dyke and Rayse Biggs in *Ma Rainey's Black Bottom.* Photo: Bobbie Hazeltine.

The Miss Firecracker Contest, Beth Henley; (D) Ronald Martell; (S) Melinda Pacha; (C) Anne Saunders; (L) Paul Epton
Back in the World, Stephen Mack Jones; (D) David Regal; (S) Eric M. Johnson; (C) Anne Saunders; (L) Timothy Alvaro
A...My Name Is Alice, Julianne Boyd and Joan Micklin Silver; (D) Jim Corti; (S) Peter W. Hicks; (C) Melinda Pacha; (L) Gary Decker

The Back Alley Theatre

ALLAN MILLER
LAURA ZUCKER
Producing Directors

15231 Burbank Blvd.
Van Nuys, CA 91411-3590
(818) 780-2240

FOUNDED 1979
Allan Miller, Laura Zucker

SEASON
Year-round

FACILITIES
Seating capacity: 93
Stage: proscenium

FINANCES
Jan. 1, 1986-Dec. 31, 1986
Expenses: $262,725

CONTRACTS
AEA 99-seat Waiver, Special Production and Guest Artist

We like good writing, acting and production. We go to the theatre hoping to be surprised, hoping to see something that gets us to think a little differently about life. The subject can be anything, but the expression has to feel original and true. In choosing a project we look for material that makes us feel like explorers, that makes us believe we can help awaken an audience, excite them, move them. When we find and produce such a piece, the only pain we feel is seeing it end.

—Allan Miller

The Back Alley Theatre. Cynthia Carle, Jimmy Hartman and John Dennis Johnston in *Why the Lord Come to Sand Mountain.* Photo: Ed Krieger.

PRODUCTIONS 1985–86

Ringers, Frank X. Hogan; (D) Allan Miller; (S) Rich Rose; (C) Hilary Sloane; (L) Leslie Rose
Danny and the Deep Blue Sea, John Patrick Shanley; (D) June Stein; (S) Leslie McDonald; (L) Oville Doc Ballard
The Greeks, adapt: Kenneth Cavander and John Barton; (D) Allan Miller; (S) Clifton R. Welch; (C) Hilary Sloane; (L) Greg R. McCullough
Found a Peanut, Donald Margulies; (D) Michael Arabian; (S) Rich Rose; (C) Barbara Cox; (L) Leslie Rose

PRODUCTIONS 1986–87

Days and Nights Within, Ellen McLaughlin; (D) Michael Pressman; (S) Rich Rose; (C) Sylvia Moss; (L) Leslie Rose and Ken Lennon
Sand Mountain, Romulus Linney; (D) John Schuck; (S) Jack Forestel; (C) Hilary Sloane; (L) Ken Lennon
Pasta, Dread, and Mazel, John Medici; (D) Allan Miller
Jacques Brel Is Alive and Well and Living in Paris, adapt: Eric Blau and Mort Shuman; music and lyrics: Jacques Brel; (D) Allan Miller; (S) Rich Rose; (C) Sylvia Moss; (L) Leslie Rose

Barter Theatre

REX PARTINGTON
Artistic Director/Producer

Box 867
Abingdon, VA 24210
(703) 628-2281 (bus.)
(703) 628-3991 (b.o.)

FOUNDED 1933
Robert Porterfield

SEASON
Apr.-Oct.

FACILITIES
Barter Theatre
Seating capacity: 391
Stage: proscenium

Barter Playhouse
Seating capacity: 138
Stage: modified thrust

FINANCES
Nov. 1, 1985-Oct. 31, 1986
Expenses: $687,650

CONTRACTS
AEA LORT (D) and SSD&C

Barter is the oldest, longest-running professional repertory theatre in the U.S. It is our desire that the plays we produce, in addition to entertaining our patrons, will give them something to think about. We do not intend that each play must impart a profound message; but we do feel the productions we present, whether they are classical or contemporary or brand new, should be provocative. They should reflect and comment on the times and on the human race. As a pioneer of regional theatre, we are dedicated to quality—whether it's on our mainstage Barter Theatre, in the Playhouse, on our Youth Stage, or in our touring productions. Our diversified audiences can expect to see the finest in classical and contemporary comedy and drama as well as worthwhile new plays.

—Rex Partington

Note: In order to bring Barter Theatre's season information completely up-to-date with this volume, three seasons are included.

PRODUCTIONS 1985

The Dining Room, A.R. Gurney, Jr.; (D) William Van Keyser; (S) John C. Larrance; (C) Sigrid Insull; (L) Al Oster
And a Nightingale Sang..., C.P. Taylor; (D) Judith Haskell; (S) Daniel Ettinger; (C) Sigrid Insull; (L) Al Oster
Billy Bishop Goes to War, John Gray and Eric Peterson; (D) William Van Keyser; (S) Daniel Ettinger; (C) Sigrid Insull; (L) Al Oster
Agnes of God, John Pielmeier; (D) Ken Costigan; (S) Jim Stauder; (C) Lisa C. Micheels; (L) Al Oster
Sea Marks, Gardner McKay; (D) Rex Partington; (S) Gary Aday; (C) Karen Brewster; (L) Al Oster
My Fat Friend, Charles Laurence; (D) Ken Costigan; (S) Daniel Ettinger; (C) Karen Brewster; (L) Al Oster

Barter Theatre. McKee Anderson and Ross Bickell in *The Guardsman.* Photo: Charles Beatty.

Educating Rita, Willy Russell; (D) Ken Costigan; (S) Jim Stauder; (C) Martha Hally; (L) Al Oster

Painting Churches, Tina Howe; (D) William Van Keyser; (S) John C. Larrance; (C) Barbara Forbes; (L) Al Oster

The Guardsman, Ferenc Molnar; (D) Rex Partington; (S) Daniel Ettinger; (C) Martha Hally; (L) Al Oster

Greater Tuna, Jaston Williams, Joe Sears and Ed Howard; (D) Trip Plymale and Partington Rex; (S) Jim Stauder; (C) Karen Brewster; (L) Al Oster

Twice Around the Park, Murray Schisgal; (D) Ken Costigan; (S) Daniel Ettinger; (C) Barbara Forbes; (L) Al Oster

PRODUCTIONS 1986

I Ought to Be in Pictures, Neil Simon; (D) Ken Costigan; (S) Daniel Ettinger; (C) Karen Brewster; (L) Al Oster

Billy Bishop Goes to War, John Gray and Eric Peterson; (D) William Van Keyser; (S) Daniel Ettinger; (C) Sigrid Insull; (L) Al Oster

The Foreigner, Larry Shue; (D) Geoffrey Hitch; (S) Daniel Ettinger; (C) Karen Brewster; (L) Al Oster

I Do! I Do!, book and lyrics: Tom Jones; music: Harvey Schmidt; (D) Byron Grant ; (S) Jim Stauder; (C) Lisa C. Micheels; (L) Al Oster

Morning's at Seven, Paul Osborn; (D) Ken Costigan; (S) Daniel Ettinger; (C) Martha Hally; (L) Al Oster

Vanities, Jack Heifner; (D) Steven Umberger; (S) Jim Stauder; (C) Karen Brewster; (L) Al Oster

Ten Little Indians, Agatha Christie; (D) William Van Keyser; (S) Daniel Ettinger; (C) Dorothy Marshall; (L) Al Oster

Boeing! Boeing!, Marc Camoletti; adapt: Beverly Cross; (D) Frank Lowe; (S) Gary Aday; (C) Karen Brewster; (L) Al Oster

Bedroom Farce, Alan Ayckbourn; (D) Ken Costigan; (S) Jim Stauder; (C) Barbara Forbes; (L) Al Oster

'night, Mother, Marsha Norman; (D) William Van Keyser; (S) Daniel Ettinger; (C) Karen Brewster; (L) Al Oster

PRODUCTIONS 1987

Angel Street, Patrick Hamilton; (D) Ken Costigan; (S) Daniel Ettinger; (C) Lisa C. Micheels; (L) Al Oster

The Odyssey, adapt: Gregory A. Falls and Kurt Beattie, from Homer; (D) Allen Schoer; (S) Shelley Henze Schermer; (C) Sally Richardson; (L) Al Oster

My Fat Friend, Charles Laurence; (D) Ken Costigan; (S) Daniel Ettinger; (C) Lisa C. Micheels; (L) Al Oster

Beyond the Fringe, Allen Bennett, Peter Cook, Jonathan Miller and Dudley Moore; (D) Allen Schoer; (C) Lisa C. Micheels; (L) Al Oster

See How They Run, Phillip King; (D) Rex Partington; (S) Daniel Ettinger; (C) Dorothy Marshall; (L) Al Oster

Village Wooing and ***Augustus Does His Bit***, George Bernard Shaw; (D) Frank Lowe; (S) Jim Stauder; (C) Dorothy Marshall; (L) Al Oster

Children, A.R. Gurney, Jr.; (D) Ken Costigan; (S) Daniel Ettinger; (C) Barbara Forbes; (L) Al Oster

Oh, Coward!, adapt: Roderick Cook; music and lyrics: Noel Coward; (D) William Van Keyser; (S) Jim Stauder; (C) Lisa C. Micheels; (L) Al Oster

Pump Boys and Dinettes, John Foley, Mark Hardwick, Debra Monk, Cass Morgan, John Schimmel and Jim Wann; (D) John Foley; (S) Jim Stauder; (C) Lisa C. Micheels; (L) Al Oster

The Rainmaker, N. Richard Nash; (D) Ken Costigan; (S) Daniel Ettinger; (C) Lisa C. Micheels; (L) Al Oster

The Necklace and Other Stories, Guy de Maupassant; (D) William Van Keyser; (S) M. Lynn Allen; (C) M. Lynn Allen; (L) Al Oster

Relatively Speaking, Alan Ayckbourn; (D) Ken Costigan; (S) Daniel Ettinger; (C) Lisa C. Micheels; (L) Al Oster

The Bathhouse Theatre

ARNE ZASLOVE
Artistic Director

MARY-CLAIRE BURKE
Producer

7312 West Greenlake Dr., North
Seattle, WA 98103
(206) 524-3608 (bus.)
(206) 524-9108 (b.o.)

FOUNDED 1980
Mary-Claire Burke, Arne Zaslove

SEASON
Year-round

FACILITIES
Seating capacity: 130
Stage: thrust

FINANCES
Jan. 1, 1986-Dec. 31, 1986
Expenses: $850,549

CONTRACTS
AEA SPT and letter of agreement

The Bathhouse Theatre. Joyce Mycka-Stettler, Peter Acosta and G. Valmont Thomas in *The Good Person of Szechwan.* Photo: Fred Andrews

Maintaining a permanent resident theatre company with high artistic standards since 1980 has taken some doing—especially given the Bathhouse's 130-seat house and earned income running from 76 to 80 percent of total revenues. Year-round operation has been an economic necessity, as well as a tremendous professional challenge for us. Extensive touring and the mounting of major productions at large downtown theatres tax our resources but, by working together as a team over the years, our core company has developed remarkable strength and versatility. The company system also adds an extra element to play selection: I ask myself not only "Does this script show real dramatic value?" and "Will it appeal to our audience?" but also "How will it stretch the particular talents of individual company members?" We at the Bathhouse take greatest pride in our company's ability to develop new original material such as *The Big Broadcast*, tackle rarely produced scripts like Priestley's *Johnson over Jordan* and create distinctive Shakespeare interpretations.

—*Arne Zaslove*

PRODUCTIONS 1986

The Holiday Big Broadcast, company-developed; (D) Arne Zaslove; (S) Shelley Henze Schermer; (C) Julie James; (L) Judy Wolcott

Lorenzo Pickle in Clown Dreams, Larry Pisoni; (D) Arne Zaslove; (S) Peggy Snider; (C) Peggy Snider; (L) Judy Wolcott

The Glass Menagerie, Tennessee Williams; (D) Jeannie Carson; (S) Jerry S. Hooker; (C) Julie James; (L) Judy Wolcott

A Day in the Life of Vic and Sade, company-adapt, from Paul Rhymer; (D) Arne Zaslove; (C) Julie James and Mary Ellen Walter; (L) Judy Wolcott

Johnson over Jordan, J.B. Priestley; (D) Arne Zaslove; (S) Thomas Fichter; (C) Mary Ellen Walter; (L) Judy Wolcott

Miss Liberty, book: Robert E. Sherwood; music and lyrics: Irving Berlin; (D) Rick Tutor; (S) Robert Gardner; (C) Sarah Campbell; (L) Judy Wolcott

Say It with a Song, company-adapt; music and lyrics: Irving Berlin; (D) Arne Zaslove; (C) Morna McEachern; (L) Judy Wolcott

Puntila, Bertolt Brecht; trans: Ralph Manheim; (D) Arne Zaslove; (S) Shelley Henze Schermer; (C) Julie James; (L) Judy Wolcott

Entertaining Brecht, company-adapt; (D) Arne Zaslove; (S) Shelley Henze Schermer; (C) Jeaudelle Thompson; (L) Judy Wolcott

Cowboy Commedia Capers, company-developed; (D) Arne Zaslove; (S) Shelley Henze Schermer; (C) Mary Ellen Walter

A Midsummer Night's Dream, William Shakespeare; (D) Arne Zaslove; (S) Shelley Henze Schermer; (C) Mary Ellen Walter; (L) Dustin Waln

PRODUCTIONS 1987

The Holiday Big Broadcast, company-developed; (D) Arne Zaslove; (S) Patti Henry; (C) Mary Ellen Walter; (L) Judy Wolcott

Another Day in the Life of Vic and Sade, company-adapt, from Paul Rhymer; (D) Arne Zaslove; (S) Patti Henry; (C) Mary Ellen Walter; (L) Judy Wolcott

The Flowering Peach, Clifford Odets; (D) Arne Zaslove; (S) Patti Henry; (C) Sarah Campbell; (L) Judy Wolcott

Waiting for Godot, Samuel Beckett; (D) Arne Zaslove; (S) Shelley Henze Schermer; (C) Sarah Campbell; (L) Judy Wolcott

Stop the World, I Want to Get Off, book, music and lyrics: Anthony Newley and Leslie Bricusse; (D) Allen Galli; (S) Jerry S. Hooker; (C) Mark Mitchell; (L) Judy Wolcott

The Adventures of Buck Rogers, company-developed; (D) Arne Zaslove; (S) Patti Henry; (C) Mark Mitchell

Othello, William Shakespeare; (D) Arne Zaslove; (S) Jerry S. Hooker; (C) Mark Mitchell; (L) Judy Wolcott

Berkeley Repertory Theatre. Charles Dean and Laurence Ballard in *Twelfth Night*. Photo: Ken Friedman.

Berkeley Repertory Theatre

SHARON OTT
Artistic Director

MITZI SALES
Managing Director

2025 Addison St.
Berkeley, CA 94704
(415) 841-6108 (bus.)
(415) 845-4700 (b.o.)

FOUNDED 1968
Michael W. Leibert

SEASON
Sept.-July

FACILITIES
Mark Taper Mainstage
Seating capacity: 401
Stage: thrust

Addison Stage
Seating capacity: 150
Stage: flexible

FINANCES
Sept. 1, 1986-Aug. 31, 1987
Expenses: $2,618,200

CONTRACTS
AEA (C), (D) and SSD&C

Berkeley Repertory Theatre is dedicated to an ensemble of first-rate artists—including actors, playwrights, directors, artisans and designers. We intend the theatre to be a place where plays are created, not just produced, communicating a distinct attitude about the world of the play and about the world around us. Our repertoire includes plays chosen from the major classical and contemporary dramatic literatures, specifically works that emphasize the cultural richness that makes American art so dynamic and vital. BRT's programming is expanding from the main stage to more flexible local venues in, our concurrent Parallel Season, focusing on adaptations from other sources, collaborations, multimedia pieces and commissioned works. Young artists and artisans are trained through Company Too, an affiliated group of non-Equity actors, and in our production internship program. Each spring we tour two productions to Bay Area schools.

—*Sharon Ott*

PRODUCTIONS 1985–86

The Playboy of the Western World, John Millington Synge; (D) Sharon Ott; (S) Vicki Smith; (C) Jeannie Davidson; (L) Derek Duarte

In the Belly of the Beast, adapt: Adrian Hall and Robert Woodruff, from Jack Henry

Abbott; (D) Richard E.T. White; (S) Michael Olich; (C) Michael Olich; (L) Robert Peterson

The Art of Dining, Tina Howe; (D) Robert Moss; (S) William Bloodgood; (C) Michael Krass; (L) Peter Maradudin

The Sea, Edward Bond; (D) Richard E.T. White; (S) Ralph Funicello; (C) Michael Olich; (L) Robert Peterson

The Diary of a Scoundrel, Alexander Ostrovsky; adapt: Erik Brogger; (D) Jeff Steitzer; (S) Scott Weldin; (C) John Carver Sullivan; (L) Kent Dorsey

The Normal Heart, Larry Kramer; (D) M. Burke Walker; (S) Michael Olich; (C) Michael Olich; (L) Derek Duarte

Twelfth Night, William Shakespeare; (D) Sharon Ott; (S) Kate Edmunds; (C) Susan Hilferty; (L) Dan Kotlowitz

PRODUCTIONS 1986–87

The Revenger, Cyril Tourneur; adapt: Amlin Gray; (D) Sharon Ott; (S) Kate Edmunds; (C) John Carver Sullivan and Kurt Wilhelm; (L) James F. Ingalls

The Night of the Iguana, Tennessee Williams; (D) Tony Amendola; (S) Vicki Smith; (C) John Carver Sullivan; (L) Peter Maradudin

The Servant of Two Masters, Carlo Goldoni; adapt: Tom Cone; (D) Sharon Ott; (S) Kate Edmunds; (C) Michael Olich; (L) Dan Kotlowitz

The Birthday Party, Harold Pinter; (D) Anthony Taccone; (S) John Bonard Wilson; (C) Jeffrey Struckman; (L) Derek Duarte

Blue Window, Craig Lucas; (D) Richard E.T. White; (S) Kent Dorsey; (C) Beaver Bauer; (L) Peter Maradudin

The Good Person of Setzuan, Bertolt Brecht; trans: Ralph Manheim; (D) Sharon Ott and Timothy Near; (S) Ralph Funicello; (C) Carol Oditz; (L) Arden Fingerhut

Hard Times, adapt: Stephen Jeffreys, from Charles Dickens; (D) Richard E.T. White; (S) John Bonard Wilson; (C) Cathleen Edwards; (L) Derek Duarte

Painting It Red, Steven Dietz; music: Gary Rue; lyrics: Leslie Ball; (D) Richard E.T. White; (S) Peggy McDonald; (C) Jane Alois Stein; (L) Kurt Landisman

Berkeley Shakespeare Festival

MICHAEL ADDISON
Artistic Director

ELIZABETH PRICE
Managing Director

Box 969
Berkeley, CA 94701
(415) 548-3422 (bus.)
(415) 525-8844 (b.o.)

FOUNDED 1974
Mikel Clifford, Bay Area actors

SEASON
July-Sept.

FACILITIES
John Hinkel Park (outdoor)
Seating capacity: 350
Stage: thrust

Julia Morgan Theatre
Seating capacity: 350
Stage: thrust

FINANCES
Jan. 1, 1987-Dec. 31, 1987
Expenses: $590,000

CONTRACTS
AEA LORT (D)

The past of the Berkeley Shakespeare Festival informs both present and future. The Festival grew out of the creative energies of Bay Area artists who sought to explore Shakespeare as a living text and has had two driving forces from the outset: a recognition of the primary value of artists banded together in our continuing Festival company; and a commitment to productions based on scholarship but conceived theatrically in vividly contemporary terms. The primary values that have led to 14 seasons and capacity audiences must constantly be rethought and reinvigorated. The idea of "company" must be re-examined, ensuring the infusion of new artistic energies while still building on the contribution of continuing company members. Most important, we now seek to explore our particularly American focus on Shakespeare, and to find theatrical means to reflect the dynamic social and cultural changes that are moving us toward the 21st century.

—Michael Addison

Note: During the 1985-86 season, Dakin Matthews served as artistic director.

PRODUCTIONS 1986

As You Like It, William Shakespeare; (D) Lura Dolas; (S) Warren Travis; (C) Barbara Bush; (L) Theodore Michael Dolas

Coriolanus, William Shakespeare; (D) Julian Lopez-Morillas; (S) Michael Cook; (C) Eliza Chugg; (L) Theodore Michael Dolas

The Tempest, William Shakespeare; (D) Tony Amendola; (S) Peggy McDonald; (C) Warren Travis; (L) Theodore Michael Dolas

PRODUCTIONS 1987

Richard II, William Shakespeare; (D) Kathleen Conlin; (S) Warren Travis; (C) Douglas Russell; (L) Theodore Michael Dolas

Henry IV, Part 1, William Shakespeare; (D) Julian Lopez-Morillas; (S) Ron Pratt and Gene Angell; (C) Eliza Chugg; (L) Theodore Michael Dolas

Henry V, William Shakespeare; (D) Michael Addison; (S) Eric Landisman; (C) Roberta Yuen; (L) Theodore Michael Dolas

Henry IV, Part 2, William Shakespeare; (D) Michael Addison; (S) Michael Cook; (C) Rick Austin; (L) Theodore Michael Dolas

Berkshire Theatre Festival

RICHARD DUNLOP
Artistic Director

STEVEN SIGEL
Managing Director

Box 797
Stockbridge, MA 01262
(413) 298-5536 (bus.)
(413) 298-5576 (b.o.)

FOUNDED 1928
Three Arts Society

SEASON
June-Aug.

FACILITIES
Berkshire Playhouse
Seating capacity: 427
Stage: proscenium

Unicorn Theatre
Seating capacity: 100
Stage: thrust

Children's Theatre
Seating capacity: 100
Stage: arena

FINANCES
Oct. 1, 1985-Sept. 30, 1986
Expenses: $842,435

CONTRACTS
AEA LORT (B), SSD&C and USA

Berkeley Shakespeare Festival. Dakin Matthews and Louis Lotorto in *A Midsummer Night's Dream*. Photo: Allen Nomura.

Berkshire Theatre Festival. George Grizzard and Kim Hunter in *A Delicate Balance*. Photo: Walter Scott

The Berkshire Theatre Festival is one of the oldest theatres in the nation and one of the only theatres in the country dedicated exclusively to producing the American repertoire. In working to achieve national recognition as a center for American drama our challenge is to make BTF a vital home for plays from our past which have something timely to say to today's audiences: by examining our past, we learn about our present and future. We believe it is equally essential to provide strong encouragement and support for new playwrights by presenting their work with the same integrity and conviction that we give to more established pieces. Theatre has been a continuing source of inspiration, enlightenment and joy for people all over the world for centuries—BTF continues this tradition by providing an opportunity for our audiences to explore theatrically the culture, myths and morals that make us unique as a nation.

—Josephine R. Abady

Note: During the 1986 and 1987 seasons, Josephine R. Abady served as artistic director.

PRODUCTIONS 1986

A Little Night Music, music and lyrics: Stephen Sondheim; book: Hugh Wheeler; (D) Josephine R. Abady; (S) David Potts; (C) Linda Fisher and C.L. Hundley; (L) Jeff Davis

A Delicate Balance, Edward Albee; (D) Irene Lewis; (S) David Potts; (C) Robert Wojewodski; (L) Jeff Davis

All the Way Home, adapt: Tad Mosel, from James Agee; (D) Jack Hofsiss; (S) John Lee Beatty; (C) Julie Weiss; (L) Jeff Davis

Visit to a Small Planet, Gore Vidal; (D) Josephine R. Abady; (S) John Lee Beatty; (C) C.L. Hundley; (L) Jeff Davis

PRODUCTIONS 1987

No Time for Comedy, S.N. Behrman; (D) Michael Langham; (S) Desmond Heely; (C) Desmond Heely; (L) Jeff Davis

The Boys Next Door, Tom Griffin; (D) Josephine R. Abady; (S) Brian Martin; (C) C.L. Hundley; (L) Jeff Davis

Portrait of Jennie, book: Dennis Rosa and Enid Futterman; music: Howard Marren; lyrics: Enid Futterman; (D) Gregory Boyd; (S) Dale Jordan; (C) David Toser; (L) Jeff Davis

I Never Sang for My Father, Robert Anderson; (D) Josephine R. Abady; (S) David Potts; (C) Linda Fisher; (L) Jeff Davis

FACILITIES
Little Theatre
Seating capacity: 99
Stage: arena

FINANCES
Jan. 1, 1986-Dec. 31, 1986
Expenses: $448,046

CONTRACTS
AEA 99-seat waiver

Bilingual Foundation of the Arts

MARGARITA GALBAN
Artistic Director

CARMEN ZAPATA
Managing Producer

421 North Ave., 19
Los Angeles, CA 90031
(213) 225-4044

FOUNDED 1973
Margarita Galban, Estela Scarlata, Carmen Zapata

SEASON
Year-round

The Bilingual Foundation of the Arts creates theatre for both the Hispanic and non-Hispanic communities. Each of these communities varies widely. To serve them all, BFA must have an artistic philosophy that can best be characterized by three words: pluralism, diversity and eclecticism. BFA's Theatre/Teatro meets this challenge by presenting a diversity of material drawn from our rich Hispanic heritage in English one night and Spanish the next. We present the classics of the Golden Age of Spain, contemporary Latin American plays and new plays by Hispanic Americans. In 1987 we produced a workshop of a new American musical, *Lorca, Child of the Moon*, based on Lorca's poetry and plays. Touring is integral to BFA, and Theatre/Teatro was recently selected by the Mid-Amer-

Bilingual Foundation of the Arts. Annette Cardona and Maria Bermudez in *Lorca: Child of the Moon*. Photo: Margarita Galban.

ica Arts Alliance to tour six states. Our newest program, Teatro para los ninos (children's theatre), has reached more than 150,000 children, building future theatre audiences.

—*Margarita Galban*

PRODUCTIONS 1986

The Shoemaker's Prodigious Wife, Federico Garcia Lorca; trans: Michael Dewell and Carmen Zapata; music adapt: Ian Krouse; (D) Margarita Galban; (S) Estela Scarlata; (C) Armand Coutu; (L) Magda Gonzalez
The Death of Rosendo, Raul de Cardenas; trans: Mercedes Limon and Lina Montalvo; (D) Margarita Galban; (S) Estela Scarlata; (C) Jackie Bermudez; (L) Magda Gonzalez
Orinoco, Emilio Carballito; trans: Margaret Peden; (D) Margarita Galban; (S) Estela Scarlata; (C) Armand Coutu; (L) Magda Gonzalez

PRODUCTIONS 1987

Villa, Donald Freed; (D) Hector Elizondo; (S) Estela Scarlata; (C) Armand Coutu; (L) Magda Gonzalez
One Hundred Times I Shouldn't, Ricardo Talesnik; trans: Robert Herrera; (D) Hugo Quintana; (S) Estela Scarlata; (C) Estela Scarleta; (L) Magda Gonzalez
Pedro Paramo, Juan Rulfo; trans: Lina Montalvo; (D) Roberto Ramirez; (S) Estela Scarlata; (L) Magda Gonzalez
Lorca: Child of the Moon, adapt: Margarita Galban, from Federico Garcia Lorca; music: Ian Krouse; book: Michael Dewell and Carmen Zapata; (D) Margarita Galban; (S) Estela Scarlata; (L) Bob Fromer
Rainbow Red, Estela Scarlata and Carmen Zapata; music: Dick Hamilton; (D) Jonathon Lucas; (S) Estela Scarlata; (C) Estela Scarlata
Young Moctezuma, Estela Scarlata and Carmen Zapata; music: Dick Hamilton; (D) Jonathon Lucas; (S) Estela Scarlata; (C) Estela Scarlata

The Bloomsburg Theatre Ensemble

LAURIE McCANTS
Ensemble Director

DAN KIRSCH
Administrative Director

Box 66
Bloomsburg, PA 17815
(717) 784-5530 (bus.)
(717) 784-8181 (b.o.)

FOUNDED 1978
The ensemble

SEASON
Oct.-May

FACILITIES
The Alvina Krause Theatre
Seating capacity: 369
Stage: proscenium

FINANCES
Sept. 1, 1986-Aug. 31, 1987
Expenses: $387,275

The Bloomsburg Theatre Ensemble is entering its 10th season with the founding resident collective still at the company's artistic helm. The ensemble as a whole selects its deliberately eclectic seasons of plays with the belief that a rural audience deserves a professional theatre which investigates the privileges and challenges of contemporary American life through the perspective of drama from all cultures and all times. In the face of world events, the ensemble lives and works in a rural region because it needs a home where dialogue with an audience is possible, and the impact of its theatre on the community is positive and demonstrable. The small town of Bloomsburg and its surrounding region has embraced BTE with financial support, dedicated trustees and volunteers, and enthusiastic attendance. The five or six play mainstage season is presented in the Alvina Krause Theatre, named after the acting teacher who was the guiding spirit behind the founding of the ensemble. An annual "Theatre Arts in the Classroom" tour brings original, group-created pieces to schools statewide, and the BTE Theatre School offers classes for children, teens and adults.

—*Laurie McCants*

PRODUCTIONS 1985–86

Thieves' Carnival, Jean Anouilh; (D) Martin Shell; (S) F. Elaine Williams; (C) Michael Krass; (L) Steve Chene
A Christmas Carol, adapt: Whit MacLaughlin, from Charles Dickens; (D) Whit MacLaughlin; (S) Dan Bartlett and Luke Sutherland; (C) Jonathan Bixby; (L) Michael Baumgarten
Bus Stop, William Inge; (D) Gerard Stropnicky; (S) Dan Bartlett; (C) Michael Krass; (L) Tom Sturge
The Birthday Party, Harold Pinter; (D) Bruce Colville; (S) Charles Plummer; (C) Sue Ellen Rohrer; (L) Dan Kinsley
As You Like It, William Shakespeare; (D) Mitchell Ivers; (S) Howard P. Beals, Jr.; (C) David Trimble; (L) Howard P. Beals, Jr.
Trifles, Susan Glaspell; (D) Laurie McCants; (S) Dan Bartlett; (C) Laurie McCants; (L) Gerard Stropnicky
How It Hangs, Grace McKeaney; (D) Gerard Stropnicky; (S) Dan Bartlett; (C) Gerard Stropnicky; (L) Gerard Stropnicky
Ancient Thunder, Tales from Greek Mythology, adapt: Laurie McCants; (D) Laurie McCants; (S) Laurie McCants; (C) Laurie McCants

PRODUCTIONS 1986–87

The Foreigner, Larry Shue; (D) Julia Flood; (S) Dan Bartlett; (C) Karen Anselm Mackes; (L) Dan Kinsley
Master Harold...and the boys, Athol Fugard; (D) Gerard Stropnicky; (S) Sabrina W. Matthews; (C) Gerard Stropnicky; (L) Tom Sturge
A Child's Christmas in Wales, adapt: Adrian Mitchell and Jeremy Brooks, from Dylan Thomas; (D) Sue Atkinson; (S) Dan Bartlett; (C) Karen Anselm Mackes; (L) Gerard Stropnicky
The School for Scandal, Richard Brinsley Sheridan; (D) Martin Shell; (S) Gary Jennings; (C) Karen Anselm Mackes; (L) Dan Kinsley
A Map of the World, David Hare; (D) Martin Shell; (S) John Rodriguez; (C) Nanalee Raphael-Schirmer; (L) Dan Kinsley
The Caucasian Chalk Circle, Bertolt Brecht; trans: Eric Bentley; (D) Whit MacLaughlin; (S) Dan Bartlett; (C) Jonathan Bixby; (L) Kendall Smith
Wait Until Dark, Frederick Knott; (D) Bryan Zocher; (S) Charles Wittreich; (C) James Goode and Betsy Dowd; (L) Dan Bartlett
Dreamscape, Rand Whipple; (D) Rand Whipple; (S) Rand Whipple; (C) Rand Whipple; (L) Rand Whipple and Gerard Stropnicky
Tales of the Roundtable, A. Elizabeth Dowd; (D) A.

The Bloomsburg Theatre Ensemble. Laurie McCants, Martin Shell, Whit McLaughlin and Leigh Strimbeck in *The Birthday Party*. Photo: Marlin Wagner.

Elizabeth Dowd; (s) Dan Bartlett; (c) A. Elizabeth Dowd
The Play's the Thing, Ferenc Molnar; adapt: Rand Whipple; (d) Rand Whipple; (s) Rand Whipple; (c) Rand Whipple

BoarsHead: Michigan Public Theater

JOHN PEAKES
Producing Artistic Director

JUDITH GENTRY
Managing Director

425 South Grand Ave.
Lansing, MI 48933
(517) 484-7800 (bus.)
(517) 484-7805 (b.o.)

FOUNDED 1970
John Peakes, Richard Thomsen

SEASON
Sept.-May

FACILITIES
Lansing Center for the Arts
Seating capacity: 249
Stage: thrust

FINANCES
June 1, 1986-May 31, 1987
Expenses: $500,000

CONTRACTS
AEA SPT

BoarsHead: Michigan Public Theater exists as a center for theatre in our region. Our goal is the presentation of a high-standard professional theatre chosen from the classic and modern repertoires. BoarsHead's commitment to the staging of new plays and support of emerging playwrights is manifest in its special two-month season of all new plays—Winterfare. The resident company remains committed to the idea of an expanding theatre, reaching into both the community and the state. New works tour statewide; new pieces are developed by area writers; designs are commissioned from area artists. The effort to involve new talent and to find new audiences is central. The theatre exists for the company as well, providing time and space for artists' individual growth and development. Our focus remains the audience. Productions must be accessible, must address the concerns of the time and then, hopefully, remain with our audiences beyond the moment.

—*John Peakes*

PRODUCTIONS 1985–86

The General's Daughters, Linda Brumfield; (d) Richard Thomsen; (s) Tim Stapleton; (c) Charlotte Deardorff; (l) Gordon Phetteplace
The Foreigner, Larry Shue; (d) John Peakes; (s) Gordon Phetteplace; (c) Charlotte Deardorff; (l) Rich Bowman
Our Town, Thornton Wilder; (d) Kyle Euckert; (s) Tim Stapleton; (c) Charlotte Deardorff; (l) Gordon Phetteplace

BoarsHead: Michigan Public Theater. Greg Vinkler and Carmen Decker in *Greater Tuna*. Photo: Cathy Ottarson.

Winterfare '86:

The Sonneteer, Larry Atlas; (d) Jim Burton; (s) Tim Stapleton; (c) Charlotte Deardorff; (l) Dennis R. Sherman
Bitter Harvest, John Olive; (d) John Peakes; (s) Gordon Phetteplace; (c) Charlotte Deardorff; (l) Dennis R. Sherman
Niedecker, Kristine Thatcher; (d) Nancy-Elizabeth Kammer; (s) Gordon Phetteplace; (c) Charlotte Deardorff; (l) Dennis R. Sherman
Give the Queen a Dollar, Jeanne Michels and Phyllis Murphy; (d) Kyle Euckert; (s) Tim Stapleton; (c) Charlotte Deardorff; (l) Dennis R. Sherman
The Waterwalker, Stephen Metcalfe; (d) Claude David File; (s) Gordon Phetteplace; (c) Charlotte Deardorff; (l) Dennis R. Sherman
Shards, Richard Thomsen; (d) Gus Kaikkonen; (s) Tim Stapleton; (c) Charlotte Deardorff; (l) Dennis R. Sherman
Potholes, Gus Kaikkonen; (d) Kyle Euckert; (s) Fred Engelgau; (c) Charlotte Deardorff; (l) Dennis R. Sherman
Stagestruck Blues and Waiting Rooms, Andrew Johns and Ariana Johns; (d) Nancy-Elizabeth Kammer; (s) Fred Engelgau; (c) Charlotte Deardorff; (l) Dennis R. Sherman
Power, Sex & Boogie, John Faro PiRoman; (d) Richard Thomsen; (s) Fred Engelgau; (c) Charlotte Deardorff; (l) Dennis R. Sherman

Home, Samm-Art Williams; (d) John Peakes; (s) Gordon Phetteplace; (c) Charlotte Deardorff; (l) Gordon Phetteplace
Jacques Brel Is Alive and Well and Living in Paris, adapt: Eric Blau and Mort Shuman; music: Jacques Brel; (d) Kyle Euckert; (s) Tim Stapleton; (c) Charlotte Deardorff; (l) Dennis R. Sherman

PRODUCTIONS 1986–87

Greater Tuna, Jaston Williams, Joe Sears and Ed Howard; (d) Robert Burpee; (s) Melinda Pacha; (c) Charlotte Deardorff; (l) James E. Peters
In the Sweet Bye and Bye, Donald Driver; (d) Kyle Euckert; (s) Gordon Phetteplace; (c) Charlotte Deardorff; (l) Gordon Phetteplace
The Time of Your Life, William Saroyan; (d) John Peakes; (s) Melinda Pacha; (c) Charlotte Deardorff; (l) James E. Peters

Winterfare '87:

Expensive Tastes, Kent R. Brown; (d) Judy Gentry; (s) James E. Peters; (c) Charlotte Deardorff; (l) James E. Peters
Bullets to the Gun, Justin Peacock; (d) Alan Benson; (s) James E. Peters; (c) Charlotte Deardorff; (l) James E. Peters
The Only Song I Know, John Cameron; (d) Jim Burton; (s) James E. Peters; (c) Charlotte Deardorff; (l) James E. Peters
Two Beers and a Hook Shot, Kent R. Brown; (d) David Edward Jones; (s) James E. Peters; (c) Charlotte Deardorff; (l) James E. Peters
Valentines and Killer Chili, Kent R. Brown; (d) Laural Merlington; (s) James E. Peters; (c) Charlotte Deardorff; (l) James E. Peters
Joe's Friendly, Bruce Gadansky; (d) Judy Gentry; (s) James E. Peters; (c) Charlotte Deardorff; (l) James E. Peters
Photographic Memory, Kim Carney; (d) John Peakes; (s) James E. Peters; (c) Charlotte Deardorff; (l) James E. Peters

Fifth of July, Lanford Wilson; (d) Kyle Euckert; (s) Gary Decker; (c) Charlotte Deardorff; (l) James E. Peters
Pump Boys and Dinettes, John Foley, Mark Hardwick, Debra Monk, Cass Morgan, John Schimmel and Jim Wann; (d) John Peakes; (s) Kyle Euckert; (c) Charlotte Deardorff; (l) James E. Peters
A Picture of Oscar Wilde, Peter Sieruta; (d) John Peakes; (s) James E. Peters; (c) Charlotte Deardorff; (l) James E. Peters

The Body Politic Theatre. Roger Mueller and John Reeger in *Corpse!* Photo: Jennifer Girard.

The Body Politic Theatre

PAULINE BRAILSFORD
Artistic Director

SHARON PHILLIPS
Managing Director

2261 North Lincoln Ave.
Chicago, IL 60614
(312) 348-7901 (bus.)
(312) 871-3000 (b.o.)

FOUNDED 1966
Community Arts Foundation

SEASON
Sept.-June

FACILITIES
Seating capacity: 192
Stage: thrust

FINANCES
Jan. 1, 1986-Dec. 31, 1986
Expenses: $491,700

CONTRACTS
AEA CAT and USA

The work of the Body Politic Theatre is shaped by our professional ensemble of actors, directors and designers. We are dedicated to sharing the works of playwrights who cherish the richness of our language and the resilience of the human spirit. Our work is also shaped by the space itself, which creates an intimate forum for our productions whether classic or contemporary. In addition to our four-play subscription season, we are continuing a Second Series, following the bilingual production of Lorca's *Blood Wedding* in March 1987. We also are expanding our young people's Bible Story Theatre to include myth and legend. To encourage playwrights and the development of new works, we joined forces with Victory Gardens Theater to produce a festival of world premieres by 13 Chicago playwrights in 1987.

—Pauline Brailsford

PRODUCTIONS 1986

Falstaff & Hal, adapt: Arthur Morey, from William Shakespeare; (D) Pauline Brailsford; (S) Jeff Bauer; (C) Kerry Fleming; (L) Michael Rourke

The Hitchhikers, adapt: Larry Ketron, from Eudora Welty; (D) Pauline Brailsford; (S) Jeff Bauer; (C) Kerry Fleming; (L) Michael Rourke

On the Verge or The Geography of Yearning, Eric Overmyer; (D) Tom Mula; (S) Jeff Bauer; (C) Kerry Fleming; (L) Rita Pietraszek

Corpse!, Gerald Moon; (D) Joseph Sadowski; (S) Thomas M. Ryan; (C) Kerry Fleming; (L) Michael Rourke

PRODUCTIONS 1987

Remembrance, Graham Reid; (D) Pauline Brailsford; (S) Jeff Bauer; (C) Kerry Fleming; (L) Michael Rourke

Man and Superman, George Bernard Shaw; (D) Pauline Brailsford; (S) Jeff Bauer; (C) John Hancock Brooks, Jr.; (L) Michael Rourke

Play Expo '87:

Gardinia's 'n' Blum, Nicholas A. Patricca; (D) Dennis Zacek; (S) James Dardenne; (C) John Hancock Brooks, Jr.; (L) Robert Shook

In the Service of Others, Valerie Quinney; (D) James O'Reilly; (S) Jeff Bauer; (C) Kerry Fleming; (L) Michael Rourke

Centipede, Rick Cleveland; (D) Sandy Shinner; (S) Jeff Bauer; (C) Kerry Fleming; (L) Michael Rourke

John Wayne Movies, John Logan; (D) Sandy Shinner; (S) Jeff Bauer; (C) Kerry Fleming; (L) Michael Rourke

Mothers and Sons, Lonnie Carter; (D) Sandy Shinner; (S) Jeff Bauer; (C) Kerry Fleming; (L) Michael Rourke

Takunda, Charles Smith; (D) Nick Faust; (S) Jeff Bauer; (C) Kerry Fleming; (L) Michael Rourke

Roof Top Piper, David Hernandez; (D) Chuck Smith; (S) Jeff Bauer; (C) Maureen Kennedy; (L) Michael Rourke

The News from St. Petersburg, Rich Orloff; (D) Chuck Smith; (S) Jeff Bauer; (C) Maureen Kennedy; (L) Michael Rourke

They Even Got the Rienzi, Claudia Allen; (D) Chuck Smith; (S) Jeff Bauer; (C) Maureen Kennedy; (L) Michael Rourke

Floor Above the Roof, Daniel Therriault; (D) Joseph Sadowski; (S) Jeff Bauer; (C) Maureen Kennedy; (L) Michael Rourke

Before I Wake, William J. Norris; (D) Susan Osborne-Mott; (S) James Dardenne; (C) Glenn Billings; (L) Robert Shook

The Figure, Clifton Campbell; (D) Terry McCabe; (S) James Dardenne; (C) Glenn Billings; (L) Robert Shook

Caldwell Theatre Company

MICHAEL HALL
Artistic/Managing Director

Box 277
Boca Raton, FL 33429
(305) 368-7611 (bus.)
(305) 368-7509 (b.o.)

FOUNDED 1975
Frank Bennett, Michael Hall

SEASON
Nov.-May

Caldwell Theatre Company. Maggie Marshall, Dea Lawrence, Anthony Newfield and Craig Wroe in *Benefactors.* Photo: Mike Bady.

FACILITIES
Seating capacity: 245
Stage: proscenium

FINANCES
Oct. 1, 1985-Sept. 30, 1986
Expenses: $1,000,000

CONTRACTS
AEA LORT (C)

The Caldwell Theatre Company, a state theatre of Florida, was founded as an ensemble group that has two goals: to produce socially relevant contemporary plays, and to revive American and European classics from 1890-1940, while striving to develop the Caldwell as an alternative to the commercial houses in the surrounding Ft. Lauderdale-Palm Beach area. Each spring, Caldwell's annual Mizner Festival highlights plays, musical cabarets and events that relate to the 1920s and '30s—the period when architect Addison Mizner introduced a style of living that made Boca Raton famous. Caldwell's other programs include classes for children and teenagers, a conservatory for professional actors, a touring musical cabaret and special plays and programs for young audiences.

—Michael Hall

PRODUCTIONS 1985–86

The Majestic Kid, Mark Medoff; (D) Michael Hall; (S) James Morgan; (C) Bridget Bartlett; (L) Mary Jo Dondlinger

Murder Among Friends, Bob Barry; (D) Michael Hall; (S) Frank Bennett; (C) Bridget Bartlett; (L) Mary Jo Dondlinger

Fridays, Andrew Johns; (D) Michael Hall; (S) James Morgan; (C) Bridget Bartlett; (L) Mary Jo Dondlinger

The Dark at the Top of the Stairs, William Inge; (D) Michael Hall; (S) Frank Bennett; (C) Bridget Bartlett; (L) Mary Jo Dondlinger

The Boys in the Band, Mart Crowley; (D) Michael Hall; (C) Bridget Bartlett; (L) Mary Jo Dondlinger

The Normal Heart, Larry Kramer; (D) Michael Hall; (C) Bridget Bartlett; (L) Mary Jo Dondlinger

PRODUCTIONS 1986–87

Benefactors, Michael Frayn; (D) Michael Hall; (S) Frank Bennett; (C) Bridget Bartlett; (L) Mary Jo Dondlinger

Beyond Therapy, Christopher Durang; (D) Michael Hall; (S) Frank Bennett; (C) Bridget Bartlett; (L) Mary Jo Dondlinger

The Cherry Orchard, Anton Chekhov; (D) Michael Hall; (S) R.L. Markham; (C) Bridget Bartlett; (L) Mary Jo Dondlinger

The Women, Claire Boothe Luce; (D) Michael Hall; (S) Frank Bennett; (C) Bridget Bartlett; (L) Mary Jo Dondlinger

California Theatre Center

GAYLE CORNELISON
General Director

CHRISTINE SMITH
Managing Director

Box 2007
Sunnyvale, CA 94087
(408) 245-2979 (bus.)
(408) 245-2978 (b.o.)

FOUNDED 1976
Gayle Cornelison

SEASON
Oct.-Aug.

FACILITIES
Sunnyvale Performing Arts Center
Seating capacity: 200
Stage: proscenium

FINANCES
July 1, 1986-June 30, 1987
Expenses: $600,000

CONTRACTS
AEA Guest Artist

The California Theatre Center is a company with three major programs: a resident company that performs primarily for students and families from October to May; a resident company that performs primarily for adults in the summer; and touring companies that perform regionally, nationally and internationally. The performing artist is the focal point of CTC. Since our society fails to recognize the value of performers, it is essential that their worth be fully appreciated in our theatre. We attempt to provide the performing artist with the best possible environment so that he or she can be as creative as possible. At CTC we believe it is important for us to think of excellence as a process rather than a product. Our company strives toward the goal of outstanding theatre. As we grow and mature our concern is with the future, not the past. What we are attempting in the present is always far more exciting than our past successes. We are passionately driven by our search for excellence.

—Gayle Cornelison

California Theatre Center. Dawn Roe and Eva Wu in *The Jungle Book*. Photo: Patrick Short

PRODUCTIONS 1985–86

Most Valuable Player, company-developed; (D) J. Stephen White; (S) Paul Vallerga; (C) Colleen Troy Lewis; (L) Paul Vallerga

The Nightingale, Gayle Cornelison; (D) Mary Hall Surface; (S) Ralph J. Ryan; (C) Colleen Troy Lewis; (L) Michael Cook

The Arkansaw Bear, Aurand Harris; (D) Sydney Walker; (S) Paul Vallerga; (C) Deborah Krahenbuhl; (L) Jon Krahenbuhl

The Frog Prince, Gayle Cornelison; (D) Will Huddleston; (S) Paul Vallerga; (C) Deborah Krahenbuhl; (L) Jon Krahenbuhl

Celebration: An International Holiday, Mary Hall Surface, David Surface and David Nagey Gassner; (D) Mary Hall Surface; (S) Paul Vallerga; (C) Colleen Troy Lewis; (L) John Krahenbuhl

A Christmas Carol, adapt: Mary Hall Surface, from Charles Dickens; (D) Gayle Cornelison; (S) Paul Vallerga; (C) Colleen Troy Lewis; (L) Jon Krahenbuhl

The Princess and the Pea, Gayle Cornelison; (D) Gayle Cornelison; (S) Michael Cook; (C) Colleen Troy Lewis; (L) Jon Krahenbuhl

The Dream of Aladdin, Brian Kral; (D) Gayle Cornelison; (S) Michael Cook; (C) Pam Cornelison; (L) Jon Krahenbuhl

Just So Stories, adapt: Gayle Cornelison, from Rudyard Kipling; (D) Bruce Williams; (S) Paul Vallerga; (C) Colleen Troy Lewis; (L) Jon Krahenbuhl

The Time Odyssey of Jamie 22, Gayle Cornelison; (D) Will Huddleston; (S) Paul Vallerga; (C) Michael Cook; (L) Jon Krahenbuhl

Hansel and Gretel, Gayle Cornelison; (D) Gayle Cornelison; (S) Paul Vallerga; (C) Colleen Troy Lewis; (L) Jon Krahenbuhl

Young Mozart, Mary Hall Surface; (D) Sean Michael Dowse; (S) Michael Cook; (C) Colleen Troy Lewis and Michael Cook; (L) Jon Krahenbuhl

Vasalisa and Baba Yaga, Anne McNaughton; (D) Anne McNaughton; (S) Michael Cook; (C) Colleen Troy Lewis and Deborah Krahenbuhl; (L) Jon Krahenbuhl

Talley's Folly, Lanford Wilson; (D) Moses Goldberg; (S) Michael

Cook; (C) Colleen Troy Lewis; (L) Jon Krahenbuhl

Educating Rita, Willy Russell; (D) Mary Hall Surface; (S) Michael Cook; (C) Colleen Troy Lewis; (L) Jon Krahenbuhl

The Diary of Anne Frank, Frances Goodrich and Albert Hackett; (D) Will Huddleston; (S) Michael Cook; (C) Colleen Troy Lewis; (L) Jon Krahenbuhl

The Day Roosevelt Died, Barry Pritchard; (D) Gayle Cornelison; (S) Michael Cook; (C) Colleen Troy Lewis; (L) Jon Krahenbuhl

PRODUCTIONS 1986–87

Puss in Boots, Gayle Cornelison; (D) Will Huddleston; (S) Paul Vallerga; (C) Jane Lambert; (L) Paul Vallerga

Most Valuable Player, company-developed; (D) Mary Hall Surface; (S) Paul Vallerga; (C) Colleen Troy Lewis; (L) Paul Vallerga

The Emperor's New Clothes, Gayle Cornelison; (D) Gayle Cornelison; (S) Ralph J. Ryan; (C) Colleen Troy Lewis; (L) Ralph J. Ryan

Ancient Memories, Modern Dreams, Gayle Cornelison; (D) Bruce Williams; (S) Ralph J. Ryan; (C) Colleen Troy Lewis; (L) Ralph J. Ryan

Tales of the Holidays, Gayle Cornelison; (D) Tony Haney; (S) Keith Snider; (C) Colleen Troy Lewis; (L) Ralph J. Ryan

Celebration: An International Holiday, Mary Hall Surface, David Surface and David Nagey Gassner; (D) Cheryl Hornstein; (S) Paul Vallerga; (C) Colleen Troy Lewis; (L) Paul Vallerga

A Christmas Carol, adapt: Mary Hall Surface, from Charles Dickens; (D) Will Huddleston; (S) Keith Snider; (C) Jane Lambert; (L) Ralph J. Ryan

The Servant of Two Masters, Carlo Goldoni; (D) Gayle Cornelison; (S) Paul Vallerga; (C) Colleen Troy Lewis; (L) Paul Vallerga

The Jungle Book, adapt: Will Huddleston, from Rudyard Kipling; (D) Will Huddleston; (S) Ralph J. Ryan; (C) Jane Lambert; (L) Ralph J. Ryan

The Miracle Worker, William Gibson; (D) Gayle Cornelison; (S) Tom Dyer; (C) Colleen Troy Lewis; (L) Paul Vallerga

Imagine, Clayton Doherty; (D) Patrick Short; (S) Clayton Doherty; (C) Clayton Doherty; (L) Clayton Doherty

Rumplestiltskin, adapt: Gayle Cornelison; (D) Michael Cook; (S) Ralph J. Ryan; (C) Jane Lambert; (L) Ralph J. Ryan

The Journey of Lewis and Clark, Will Huddleston and company; (D) Will Huddleston; (S) Paul Vallerga; (C) Colleen Troy Lewis; (L) Paul Vallerga

The Frog Prince, Gayle Cornelison; (D) Will Huddleston; (S) Paul Vallerga; (C) Deborah Krahenbuhl; (L) Paul Vallerga

Luv, Murray Schisgal; (D) Paul Gaffney; (S) Ralph J. Ryan; (C) Colleen Troy Lewis; (L) Ralph J. Ryan

The Fantasticks, book and lyrics: Tom Jones; music: Harvey Schmidt; (D) Gayle Cornelison; (S) Ralph J. Ryan; (C) Jane Lambert; (L) Ralph J. Ryan

To Kill a Mockingbird, adapt: Christopher Sergel, from Harper Lee; (D) Bruce Williams; (S) Paul Vallerga; (C) Colleen Troy Lewis; (L) Paul Vallerga

Slow Dance on the Killing Ground, William Hanley; (D) Will Huddleston; (S) Paul Vallerga; (C) Jane Lambert; (L) Paul Vallerga

Capital Repertory Company

PETER CLOUGH
BRUCE BOUCHARD
Producing Directors

Box 399
Albany, NY 12201-0399
(518) 462-4531 (bus.)
(518) 462-4534 (b.o.)

FOUNDED 1980
Oakley Hall, III, Michael Van Landingham

SEASON
Oct.-June

FACILITIES
Market Theatre
Seating capacity: 258
Stage: thrust

FINANCES
July 1, 1986-June 30, 1987
Expenses: $1,100,000

CONTRACTS
AEA LORT (D) and SSD&C

Capital Repertory Company is a theatre in which language is as vital as image or action. Additionally, the characters' survival of their immediate circumstances is framed by the playwright within a particular social, moral or political issue of concern to a broad section of the human community. The majority of Capital Rep's productions are of 20th-century plays and new American works, both principally in the realistic idiom. Production style emphasizes the vision of the playwright and the actor/director relationship rather than production technology. The development of new plays is facilitated by the efforts of a fulltime literary manager and an annual festival of staged readings of new plays is held in late spring. An outreach tour program for secondary schools is also available.

—Peter Clough

PRODUCTIONS 1985–86

The Playboy of the Western World, John Millington Synge; (D) Pamela Berlin; (S) Jeffrey Schneider; (C) Martha Hally; (L) Jackie Manassee

What the Butler Saw, Joe Orton; (D) Michael J. Hume; (S) Rick Dennis; (C) Heidi Hollmann; (L) Lary Opitz

Dreaming Emmett, Toni Morrison; (D) Gilbert Moses; (S) Dale F. Jordan; (C) Lloyd Waiwaiole; (L) Dale F. Jordan

Goodbye Freddy, Elizabeth Diggs; (D) Bruce Bouchard; (S) Leslie Taylor; (C) Catherine Zuber; (L) David Yergan

November, Don Nigro; (D) Gloria Muzio; (S) Rick Dennis; (C) Lloyd Waiwaiole; (L) Lary Opitz

The Phantom of the Opera or The Passage of Christ, book adapt and lyrics: Kathleen Masterson, from Gaston Leroux; music: David Bishop; (D) Peter H. Clough; (S) Dale F. Jordan; (C) Lloyd Waiwaiole; (L) Dale F. Jordan

PRODUCTIONS 1986–87

Dusky Sally, Granville Burgess; (D) Jack Chandler; (S) Jack Chandler; (C) Randy Barcelo; (L) Jane Reisman

Community Property, Dalene Young; (D) Peter H. Clough; (S) Leslie Taylor; (C) Heidi Hollmann; (L) Jackie Manassee

A View from the Bridge, Arthur Miller; (D) Tony Giordano; (S) Hugh Landwehr; (C) Mary Ann Powell; (L) Dennis Parichy

The Mystery of Irma Vep, Charles Ludlam; (D) Bruce Bouchard; (S) Rick Dennis; (C) Martha Hally; (L) Jackie Manassee

Jupiter and Elsewhere, Gram Slaton; (D) Tom Bloom; (S) Robert Thayer; (C) Lynda L. Salsbury; (L) Lary Opitz

Brighton Beach Memoirs, Neil Simon; (D) Lynn Polan; (S) Leslie Taylor; (C) Lynda L. Salsbury; (L) Andi Lyons

Capital Repertory Company. Erica Gimpel in *Dusky Sally*. Photo: Skip Dickstein.

The CAST Theatre

R.T. SCHMITT
Producing Artistic Director

GRETCHEN WEBER
Managing Director

804 North El Centro Ave.
Hollywood, CA 90038
(213) 462-9872 (bus.)
(213) 462-0256 (b.o.)

FOUNDED 1974
Kathleen Johnson, R.T. Schmitt

SEASON
Year-round

FACILITIES
The CAST Theatre
Seating capacity: 65
Stage: proscenium

The CAST-at-The-Circle
Seating capacity: 99
Stage: proscenium

FINANCES
Oct. 1, 1986-Sept. 30, 1987
Expenses: $243,032

CONTRACTS
AEA 99-seat waiver

The CAST Theatre generates new American plays and serves emerging American playwrights by developing their original scripts. CAST plays illuminate the human condition —particularly relationships and the indomitability of the human spirit. The CAST is one of the most playwright-accessible, high-profile, intimate, professional theatres in southern California and is a supportive, embracing, award-winning environment for new works that illustrate the wide variety of experiences in our diverse cultural landscape. Musicals are a theatrical form in which the CAST also excels. In the past 10 years, of the 203 plays presented, 129 were world premieres and 38 were musicals. The CAST uses an intensive three-step process to develop material. First, scripts are screened by the literary staff; some then pass into our Foundry Series of public readings. Selected scripts may then move into the third step, the Safe Harbor—staged, script-in-hand, work-in-progress, non-reviewed presentations that lead ultimately to a mainstage production.

—*R.T. Schmitt*

PRODUCTIONS 1985–86

Wrestlers, Bill C. Davis; (D) Glenn Casale; (S) Larry Fulton; (C) Pauline K. Lecrass; (L) Ilya Mindlin

Request Concert, Franz Xaver Kroetz; (D) Michael Arabian; (S) Michael Devine; (C) Barbara Cox; (L) Ilya Mindlin

Back Home, book: Robert Schrock and Kirby Tepper; music and lyrics: Kirby Tepper; (D) Robert Schrock; (S) Randy Clifton; (C) Eleanor Hedge; (L) Ilya Mindlin

Women's Sexual Fantasies, Andersen Van Hoy, Maureen Murphy, Karin Spritzler, Lyla Graham, Sunja Svensen, Leslie Spencer and Dorene Ludwig; (D) Andersen Van Hoy, Joanne Casey, Karin Spritzler, Audrey Marlyn Singer, Michael Keusch, Shawn Nelson and Dorene Ludwig; (L) Ilya Mindlin

Acme Material, John Pappas; (D) John Pappas; (L) Erika Bradberry

13 Down, Robert Schrock; (D) Robert Schrock; (S) Charles Whetzel; (C) Eleanor Hedge

Pirandello in Singapore, adapt: Ray Holland, from Luigi Pirandello; (D) Ray Holland

Arts & Leisure, Susan Miller; (D) Jules Aaron; (S) Mark Donnelly; (C) Ann Bruice; (L) Pauline Jenkins

Electric Angel, Brad Bailey; (D) Ski Austin; (S) Curtis A. Schnell; (C) Amy Gilbert; (L) Robert Fromer

Forbidden Dreams, Jennifer Smith-Ashley; (D) David Alexander; (S) John Cranham; (C) Ola Hudson; (L) Pauline Jenkins

Buddy Systems, Tim Miller; (D) Tim Miller; (L) George Gizienski

Roadshows, Donald Krieger, Jack Slater, May Sun and Jan Munroe; (D) Donald Krieger, Guy Giarrizo and Steven Keats; (S) Robert Schrock; (C) Robert Schrock; (L) Anthony Battelle and Stephen Bennett

Men's Singles, D.B. Gillis; (D) Jules Aaron; (S) Larry Fulton; (C) Claudia Cordic; (L) Guido Girardi

Roadrunners at the Paradise Drive In, Thomas G. Carter, Raymond Martino and John Del Regno; (D) Andy De Angelo

PRODUCTIONS 1986–87

Early Tennessee, Tennessee Williams; (D) Dan Mason; (S) Renee Hoss; (C) Kevin Ian; (L) J. Kent Inasy

Kiss of the Spider Woman, Manuel Puig; adapt: Alan Baker; (D) Dick Dotterer; (S) Scott Herbertson; (C) Steven Bishop; (L) Anthony Battelle

Behind You, John Pappas; (D) Laurence Braude; (L) Erika Bradberry

A Fine Line, Judy Romberger; (D) Guy Giarrizzo; (S) Steven T. Howell; (C) Paula Higgins; (L) Steven T. Howell

Savage in Limbo, John Patrick Shanley; (D) Roxanne Rogers; (S) Nina Ruscio; (L) Steven T. Howell

Teamster's Basement, Thomas George Carter; (D) Andrew De Angelo; (S) Steve Chase; (L) Erika Bradberry

Stooplife, Louis La Russo; (D) Raymond Martino; (S) Steven T. Howell; (L) Steven T. Howell

Rounds, Sean Michael Rice; (D) John DiFusco; (S) Steven T. Howell; (L) Steven T. Howell

October 22, 4004 B.C.,Saturday, Suzanne Lummis; (D) Robert Schrock; (S) Steven T. Howell; (C) Eleanor Hedge; (L) Steven T. Howell

The CAST Theatre. Enrique Sandino and Javier Grajada in *Kiss of the Spider Woman*. Photo: Jan Deen

Center for Puppetry Arts

VINCENT ANTHONY
Executive Director

1404 Spring St., NW
Atlanta, GA 30309
(404) 873-3089 (bus.)
(404) 873-3391 (b.o.)

FOUNDED 1978
Vincent Anthony

SEASON
Year-round

FACILITIES
Mainstage
Seating capacity: 313
Stage: proscenium

Downstairs Theatre
Seating capacity: 101
Stage: flexible

Experimental Space
Seating capacity: 60
Stage: flexible

FINANCES
July 1, 1986-June 30, 1987
Expenses: $780,000

As the only major arts organization of its kind in North America the Center for Puppetry Arts is dedicated to expanding the public's

Center for Puppetry Arts. Annie Peterle in *Alice in Wonderland.* Photo: Susan Barmon.

awareness of puppetry as a fine art, especially on the adult level; to supporting the work of existing international and American artists through performance residencies at the Center and on tour; to developing new works for the field as well as identifying existing material for adaptation to puppetry; and to serving the general public and the puppeteer through performance, exhibition and educational programming.

—*Vincent Anthony*

PRODUCTIONS 1985–86

Visions of St. Lucy, book: Steve Lindsley, Jon Ludwig, Jim Brook and Ann F. Peterlebook, music: Jim Brooks and Jo Banner; (D) Jon Ludwig; (S) Steve Lindsley; (C) puppets: Jon Ludwig

Puppetry Cabaret, company-developed; (D) Luis Q. Barroso; (S) Luis Q. Barroso; (L) Thomas E. Disbrow

Marie Antoinette Tonight!, Bruce D. Schwartz; (D) Luis Q. Barroso; (S) Johnny Thigpen; (C) Fannie Schubert and Lisa E. Rhodes; (L) Liz Lee and Bruce D. Schwartz, puppets

Jungle Book, adapt: Mitchell Edmonds and Jon Ludwig, from Rudyard Kipling; (D) Luis Q. Barroso; (S) James A. Word,Jr.; (C) Gary Max, puppets; (L) Liz Lee

Hansel and Gretel, Charles Smith and company; (D) Luis Q. Barroso and Bruce D. Schwartz; (S) T. Gary Wetherly; (C) Fannie Schubert and Chimera Productions, Inc., puppets; (L) Liz Lee

Aladdin, company-developed; music: Dennis West; (D) Jon Ludwig; (S) Michael Stauffer; (C) Fannie Schubert and Walton Harris, puppets; (L) Liz Lee

XPT, various; (D) Jon Ludwig

PRODUCTIONS 1986–87

XPT I, various; (D) Jon Ludwig; (S) various; (L) Bill Harrison

XPT II, various; (D) Jon Ludwig; (S) various; (L) Bill Harrison

The Third Bank of the River, Neill Bogan, Chip Epsten and Janie Geiser; (D) Janie Geiser; (S) Janie Geiser; (C) Janie Geiser, puppets; (L) Janie Geiser

Alice, Levi Lee and Rebecca Wackler; (D) Jon Ludwig; (C) Paul Hartis, puppets; (L) Liz Lee

Aesop's Tortoise & the Hare and Other Fables, company-adapted; (D) Luis Q. Barroso; (S) James A. Word, Jr.; (C) Fannie Schubert and Lisa E. Rhodes; (L) Liz Lee and Chimera Productions, Inc., puppets

Alice in Wonderland, adapt: Luis Q. Barroso, from Lewis Carroll; (D) Luis Q. Barroso; (S) Johnny Thigpen; (C) Paul Hartis, puppets; (L) Liz Lee

Around the World in 80 Days, adapt: Nicolas Coppola, from Jules Verne; (D) Luis Q. Barrroso; (S) Bill Harrison; (C) Puppetworks, Inc., puppets; (L) Liz Lee

Center Stage

STAN WOJEWODSKI, JR.
Artistic Director

PETER W. CULMAN
Managing Director

700 North Calvert St.
Baltimore, MD 21202
(301) 685-3200 (bus.)
(301) 332-0033 (b.o.)

FOUNDED 1963
Community Arts Committee

SEASON
Sept.-May

FACILITIES
Seating capacity: 541
Stage: modified thrust

FINANCES
July 1, 1986-June 30, 1987
Expenses: $2,697,500

CONTRACTS
AEA LORT (B), SSD&C and USA

At Center Stage we have grown restless with traditional solutions to a variety of issues: the limited range of producible repertoire, the nature of the subscription audience as a source of subsidy, the level of artist compensation, and the scarcity of working structures tailored to individual projects. On all these fronts we are engaged in vigorous, artistically driven institutional planning. Our scenario for the future demands that we develop a second space and raise a substantial addition to the theatre's endowment. This plan will also create an environment in which the lockstep demands of a traditional "season" do not become de facto artistic policy. It is a vision of one theatre with two stages, and the freedom to suit the project to

Center Stage. Tony Soper, Thomas Hill, Megan Gallagher and Henry Stram in *Major Barbara.* Photo: Richard Anderson.

the venue, the idea to the space. Its profile will be eclectic and bold; its goal to push the stylistic, thematic, formal and temporal frontiers of the American theatre as far outward as possible.

—Stan Wojewodski, Jr.

PRODUCTIONS 1985–86

She Loves Me, book: Joe Masteroff; music: Jerry Bock; lyrics: Sheldon Harnick; (D) Stan Wojewodski, Jr.; (S) Hugh Landwehr; (C) Jess Goldstein; (L) Pat Collins

Boesman and Lena, Athol Fugard; (D) Zakes Mokae; (S) Charles H. McClennahan; (C) Del W. Risberg; (L) Judy Rasmuson

Bedroom Farce, Alan Ayckbourn; (D) Stan Wojewodski, Jr.; (S) Christopher Barreca; (C) Linda Fisher; (L) Stephen Strawbridge

The Normal Heart, Larry Kramer; (D) Michael Engler; (S) Hugh Landwehr; (C) Robert Wojewodski; (L) James F. Ingalls

The School for Wives, Molière; trans: Richard Wilbur; (D) Irene Lewis; (S) Michael H. Yeargan; (C) Jess Goldstein; (L) Robert Wierzel

Buried Child, Sam Shepard; (D) Michael Engler; (S) Hugh Landwehr; (C) Catherine Zuber; (L) James F. Ingalls

In a Pig's Valise, book and lyrics: Eric Overmyer; music: Karl Lundeberg; (D) Mark Harrison; (S) Hugh Landwehr; (C) Jess Goldstein; (L) Pat Collins

Deadfall, Grace McKeaney; (D) Stan Wojewodski, Jr.; (S) Hugh Landwehr; (C) Jess Goldstein; (L) Pat Collins

Reunion, Sybille Pearson; (D) Irene Lewis; (S) Hugh Landwehr; (C) Jess Goldstein; (L) Pat Collins

PRODUCTIONS 1986–87

Present Laughter, Noel Coward; (D) Norman Rene; (S) Andrew Jackness; (C) Walker Hicklin; (L) Debra Kletter

A Map of the World, David Hare; (D) Stan Wojewodski, Jr.; (S) Charles H. McClennahan; (C) Robert Wojewodski; (L) Stephen Strawbridge

Roza, book adapt and lyrics: Julian More, from Romain Gary; music: Gilbert Becaud; (D) Harold Prince; (S) Alexander Okun; (C) Florence Klotz; (L) Ken Billington

Uncle Vanya, Anton Chekhov; adapt: Rick Davis and Irene Lewis; trans: Ronald Hingley; (D) Irene Lewis; (S) Michael Yeargan; (C) Susan Hilferty; (L) Pat Collins

The Marriage of Bette and Boo, Christopher Durang; (D) Richard Hamburger; (S) Hugh Landwehr; (C) Sam Fleming; (L) Stephen Strawbridge

Major Barbara, George Bernard Shaw; (D) Stan Wojewodski, Jr.; (S) Hugh Landwehr; (C) Robert Wojewodski; (L) Pat Collins

Center Theater

DAN LaMORTE
Artistic Director

MARY JANE BLOOMER
Executive Director

1346 West Devon
Chicago, IL 60660
(312) 508-0200 (bus.)
(312) 508-5422 (b.o.)

FOUNDED 1984
Dale Calandra, Carole Gutierrez, Dan LaMorte, Eileen Manganaro

SEASON
Oct.-July

FACILITIES
Playhouse
Seating capacity: 99
Stage: thrust

Studio
Seating capacity: 30
Stage: flexible

FINANCES
Sept. 1, 1986-Aug. 31, 1987
Expenses: $219,619

CONTRACTS
AEA CAT

The Training Center for the Working Actor was developed to create a coherent and unified lifelong approach to the art and science of acting—Center Theater was born out of this dedication. Our repertory company presents both new and established material in a deliberately bold, imaginative manner, and explores all the elements of production to realize the potential of every individual work. Each is dealt with specifically—discovering the play's quality, molding it, designing it with concept and color, bringing it to life for the "first time." Our theatre and training program focus on the actor and the acting process to create exciting and risky theatre. The dream is to build an ensemble of talent—actors, directors, designers, writers—capable of bringing theatre to levels that are truthful and rare, so that risks can be taken to inspire artists and audiences alike.

—Dan LaMorte

PRODUCTIONS 1985–86

Blithe Spirit, Noel Coward; (D) Dale Calandra; (S) Andrew Meyer; (C) Lynn Ziehe; (L) Andrew Meyer

The Lady from Dubuque, Edward Albee; (D) Dan LaMorte; (S) Robert G. Smith; (C) Brigid Brown; (L) Dan LaMorte

Lysistrata, 2411 A.D., adapt: Dale Calandra, from Aristophanes; music and lyrics: Don Coates; (D) Dale Calandra; (S) Rob Hamilton; (C) Rob Hamilton; (L) Dan LaMorte

Mensch Meier, Franz Xaver Kroetz; trans: Roger Downey; (D) Dan LaMorte; (S) John Murbach; (C) John Murbach; (L) Chris Phillips

Anatol, Arthur Schnitzler; trans: Charles Osborne; (D) Dale Calandra; (S) Sheryl Nieman; (C) Erin Quigley; (L) Chris Phillips

PRODUCTIONS 1986–87

Camino Real, Tennessee Williams; (D) Dan LaMorte; (S) John Murbach; (C) John Murbach; (L) Miriam Hack

Lysistrata, 2411 A.D., adapt: Dale Calandra, from Aristophanes; music and lyrics: Don Coates; (D) Dale Calandra; (S) Rob Hamilton; (C) Rob Hamilton; (L) Rob Hamilton

Fen, Caryl Churchill; (D) Dan LaMorte; (S) John Murbach; (C) Margaret Fitzsimmons; (L) Chris Phillips

Blue Window, Craig Lucas; (D) Tracy Friedman and Dan LaMorte; (S) John Murbach; (C) Margaret Fitzsimmons; (L) Chris Phillips

The Village Wooing, George Bernard Shaw; (D) Dan LaMorte; (S) John Murbach; (C) John Murbach; (L) Pam Parker

The Dark Lady of the Sonnets, George Bernard Shaw; (D) Eileen Manganaro; (S) John Murbach; (C) John Murbach; (L) Pam Parker

How He Lied to Her Husband, George Bernard Shaw; (D) Dale Calandra; (S) John Murbach; (C) John Murbach; (L) Pam Parker

Center Theater. Judy Kaplan, Joy Thorbjornsen and Hilary Hammond in *Lysistrata, 2411 A.D.* Photo: Jennifer Girard.

The Changing Scene. Dana Peterson in *Tales of Tiresias.* Photo: Hasi Vogel.

The Changing Scene

ALFRED BROOKS
MAXINE MUNT
Co-Producing Artistic Directors

1527 ½ Champa St.
Denver, CO 80202
(303) 893-5775

FOUNDED 1968
Alfred Brooks, Maxine Munt

SEASON
Year-round

FACILITIES
Seating capacity: 76
Stage: flexible

FINANCES
Jan. 1, 1986-Dec. 31, 1986
Expenses: $107,715

Anticipating the celebration of the start of its 20th-anniversary season during Easter 1988, the Changing Scene is re-evaluating its operating philosophy: Is the policy of producing only world premieres still valid? Our question arises because we are disturbed that the present generation does not have the creative energy in the arts to which we had previously been accustomed. People in their 20s have not discovered the sense of dedication that prevailed earlier. Not that we are receiving fewer manuscripts, but the quality of the writing suggests commercial goals at the expense of the art of drama. Where are the young William Hoffmans, the Martin Shermans, the Jean-Claude van Itallies, the Ernest Joselovitzes among the many writers of our more than 200 new plays? Our reassessment of the importance of our past policy of producing only new works has only resulted in the complete reaffirmation of our theatre's purpose—the development of new writers for the stage.

—*Alfred Brooks*

PRODUCTIONS 1985–86

Hostages, Mary Guzzy; (D) David Quinn; (S) Paul Sehnert; (C) Lisa Mumpton (L) Kevin Bartlett
Alexander, Michael Hulett; (D) Margaret Mancinelli; (S) Van Emden Henson; (C) Jane Nelson Rud; (L) Van Emden Henson
Siamese Twins Face Firing Squad, Richard Dean; (D) Dennis Bontems; (S) Dennis Bontems; (L) Dennis Bontems
The City, J.P. Allen; (D) Dennis Bontems; (S) Dennis Bontems; (L) Dennis Bontems
Tornado Ultra, J.P. Allen; (D) Dennis Bontems; (S) Dennis Bontems; (L) Dennis Bontems
Road, David Earl Jones; (D) Dan Hiester; (S) Dennis Bontems; (L) Dennis Bontems
Portrait of Dora, Helene Cixous; music: Alfred Brooks; trans: Anita Barrows; (D) Dan Hiester; (S) Rod Thompson; (C) Penny Stames (L) Dennis Bontems
Frontiers, M.Z. Ribalow; (D) Dennis Bontems; (S) Dennis Bontems; (C) Dennis Bontems; (L) Dennis Bontems and Peter Nielson
Leaving the Planet Sale, Lisa Williams; (D) Kirby Henderson; (S) Kirby Henderson; (C) Nancy Bassett
Johnny Got His Gun, adapt: Bradley Rand Smith, from Dalton Trumbo; (D) Lue Douthit; (S) Jeffrey Hess; (C) Jeffrey Hess; (L) Peter Nielson
Scatalog, R. Thomas Johnson and Ring Lardner; (D) John Wilson; (S) Bob Schnautz; (C) Candace Pedersen; (L) Mark Davis

PRODUCTIONS 1986–87

Deal with a Dead Man, Tom DeMers; (D) Kirby Henderson; (S) Hugh Graham; (C) Nancy Bassett; (L) Hugh Graham
Foil, Jay Derrah; (D) Dennis Bontems; (S) Dennis Bontems; (C) Dennis Bontems; (L) Dennis Bontems
Tales of Tiresias, company-developed; (D) Hugh Graham; (S) Paul Sehnert; (C) Nancy Bassett; (L) Scott Lewis
American Gothic, Joseph McDonough; (D) Ed Osborn; (S) Ed Osborn; (C) Ed Osborn; (L) Chris Kirchhof
Favorite Sports of the Martyrs, Norman Lock; (D) Dennis Bontems; (S) Dennis Bontems; (C) Dennis Bontems; (L) Dennis Bontems
Descending, David Shawn Klein; (D) Stephen R. Kramer; (S) Paul Sehnert; (C) Stephen R. Kramer; (L) Stephen R. Kramer
Les Mamelles de Tiresias, Guillaume Apollinaire; (D) Dan Hiester; (S) Rod Thompson; (C) Penny Stames; (L) Randy Ornelaz
Shoes, Danny Kerwick; (D) Christine MacDonald; (S) Christine MacDonald; (C) Holly J. Kennedy; (L) Hugh Graham
Muscles of Hands, Bill Gian; (D) Christine MacDonald; (S) Christine MacDonald; (C) Holly J. Kennedy; (L) Hugh Graham
Dust, Danny Kerwick and Bill Gian; (D) Christine MacDonald; (S) Christine MacDonald; (C) Holly J. Kennedy; (L) Hugh Graham
Jog, Kevin Kelly; (D) Tom Rowan; (S) Craig Williamson; (C) Cynthi Voitt; (L) Craig Williamson
The Monkey Man, James Kiefer; (D) Tom Rowan; (S) Craig Williamson; (C) Cynthi Voitt; (L) Craig Williamson
Torture, Lee Patton; (D) Tom Rowan; (S) Craig Williamson; (C) Cynthi Voitt; (L) Craig Williamson

The Children's Theatre Company

JON CRANNEY
Artistic Director

BILL CONNER
Executive Director

2400 Third Ave., South
Minneapolis, MN 55404
(612) 874-0500 (bus.)
(612) 874-0400 (b.o.)

FOUNDED 1961
Beth Linnerson

SEASON
Sept.-June

FACILITIES
Mainstage
Seating capacity: 746
Stage: proscenium

Studio Theatre
Seating capacity: 150
Stage: flexible

Ordway Music Theatre
Seating capacity: 315
Stage: proscenium

FINANCES
July 1, 1986-June 30, 1987
Expenses: $3,304,436

The Children's Theatre Company is a resident repertory theatre comprised of a company of artists and artisans passionately dedicated to the art of theatre for young people and their families. Over the years, our theatre has developed unique technical resources and literary abilities that transform the storybook world into theatrical fantasy. CTC employs a staff of 80 resident artists, technicians and administrators, joined by many guest

The Children's Theatre Company. Patty Donaghue, Michelle Haugen, Gerald Drake and Wendy Lehr in *Cinderella*. Photo: Tom Florey.

artists. The theatre annually produces a seven-play mainstage series at its home in Minneapolis, a younger children's series at the Ordway Music Theatre in St. Paul and a national tour. Within CTC, apprentices and internship programs exist which afford high school and college-age students both theatrical training and performance opportunities. The Children's Theatre Company accepts the responsibility of speaking clearly and directly to children as an exciting artistic challenge, believing only the finest artistic effort will do.

—Jon Cranney

PRODUCTIONS 1985–86

King Arthur and the Magic Sword, adapt: Frederick Gaines; (D) Jon Cranney; (S) Jack Barkla; (C) Pavel Dobrusky; (L) James F. Ingalls

Adventures of a Bear Called Paddington, adapt: Alfred Bradley, from Michael Bond; (D) Myron Johnson; (S) Jack Barkla; (C) Jack Barkla; (L) James F. Ingalls

Goldilocks and the Three Bears and ***Little Red Riding Hood***, adapt: Wendy Lehr; (D) Wendy Lehr; (S) Maggie Belle Calin; (C) Maggie Belle Calin; (L) Barry Browning

Cinderella, adapt: John B. Davidson; music: Diane Cina, Tedd Gillen, Hiram Titus and John Gessner; (D) Myron Johnson; (S) Edward Haynes; (C) Gene Davis Buck; (L) David Karlson

Adventures of Mottel, adapt: Thomas W. Olson and Judith Luck Sher, from Sholom Aleichem; (D) Jon Cranney; (S) James Waters; (C) Sandra Nei Schulte; (L) James F. Ingalls

Harold and the Purple Crayon, adapt: Myron Johnson, from Crockett Johnson; music and lyrics: Roberta Carlson; (D) Myron Johnson; (S) Myron Mortell; (C) Ricia Birturk; (L) Michael Murnane

Little Women, adapt: Marisha Chamberlain, from Louisa May Alcott; (D) Jon Cranney; (S) Don Yunker; (C) Christopher Beesley; (L) Michael Murnane

Peter Pan, James M. Barrie; (D) Stephen Kanee; (S) Jack Barkla; (C) William Schroder; (L) Michael Vennerstrom

The Emperor's New Clothes, adapt: Timothy Mason; (D) Gary Briggle; (S) James Bakkom; (C) James Bakkom; (L) Andrew Sullivan

PRODUCTIONS 1986–87

Little House on the Prairie, adapt: B.J. Forrest, from Laura Ingalls Wilder; (D) Jon Cranney; (S) Maggie Belle Calin; (C) Christopher Beesley; (L) Michael Murnane

Strega Nona, book adapt and lyrics: Dennis Rosa; music: Alan Shorter; (D) Dennis Rosa; (S) Don Yunker; (C) Tomie dePaola; (L) Michael Murnane

Beatrix Potter's Christmas, Thomas W. Olson; (D) Myron Johnson; (S) Jack Barkla; (C) Christopher Beesley; (L) Michael Murnane

Hansel and Gretel, adapt: Thomas W. Olson; music: Roberta Carlson; (D) Richard Russell Ramos; (S) Dahl Delu; (C) David Kay Mickelsen; (L) Jonathan D. Baker

Dracula, adapt: Thomas W. Olson; music: Alan Shorter; (D) Jon Cranney; (S) Pavel Dobrusky; (C) Pavel Dobrusky; (L) Jonathan D. Baker

Little Miss Hollywood, book: Dale Wilson; music: Mel Marvin; lyrics: Mel Marvin and Dale Wilson; conceived: Jon Cranney; (D) Jon Cranney; (S) Marjorie Bradley Kellogg; (C) David Kay Mickelsen; (L) Duane Schuler

Rumpelstiltskin/Kalulu and His Money Farm, adapt: Timothy Mason; (D) Richard D. Thompson; (S) Steven Kennedy and Carey W. Thornton; (C) Ricia Birturk; (L) Barry Browning

Alice in Wonderland, adapt: Sharon Holland, from Lewis Carroll; (D) Bradley D. Anderson; (S) Tom Butsch; (C) Gene Davis Buck; (L) Barry Browning

Cincinnati Playhouse in the Park

WORTH GARDNER
Artistic Director

KATHERINE MOHYLSKY
Managing Director

Box 6537
Cincinnati, OH 45206
(513) 421-5440 (bus.)
(513) 421-3888 (b.o.)

FOUNDED 1960
Community members

SEASON
Sept.-Aug.

FACILITIES
Robert S. Marx Theatre
Seating capacity: 629
Stage: modified thrust

Thompson Shelterhouse Theatre
Seating capacity: 220
Stage: thrust

FINANCES
Sept. 1, 1986-Aug. 31, 1987
Expenses: $2,730,000

CONTRACTS
AEA LORT (B), (D), SSD&C and USA

The Cincinnati Playhouse in the Park is dedicated to expanding the theatrical experience for both artists and audiences through provocative, mysterious works that reawaken the imagination through the language of drama and that recognize theatre's potential to liberate our dreams, reflect our pretenses, celebrate our differences

Cincinnati Playhouse in the Park. Dennis Predovic and Hugh Hodgin in *The Foreigner*. Photo: Sandy Underwood.

and challenge our prejudices. With the recent establishment of a resident ensemble of actors, the personal creative development of all our artists—playwrights, directors, designers and technicians—is nurtured and encouraged to stretch and redefine its limits. One- or two-year acting internships are offered to talented young individuals who become an integral part of the Playhouse productions and receive classroom training and alternate performance opportunities. The Playwright's Fund offers an annual fellowship to an emerging playwright, thus ensuring that the process of playmaking can happen in the most encouraging environment.

—Worth Gardner

PRODUCTIONS 1985–86

The Glass Menagerie, Tennessee Williams; (D) Steven Schachter; (S) Paul Shortt; (C) William Schroder; (L) Jay Depenbrock

Painting Churches, Tina Howe; (D) Mary B. Robinson; (S) Johniene Papandreas; (C) Rebecca Senske; (L) Joseph P. Tilford

Carnival, music and lyrics: Bob Merrill; book: Michael Stewart; (D) Worth Gardner; (S) Paul Shortt; (C) Kurt Wilhelm; (L) Kirk Bookman

Marry Me a Little, music and lyrics: Stephen Sondheim; conceived: Craig Lucas and Norman Rene; (D) Worth Gardner; (S) Joseph P. Tilford; (C) Barbara Kay; (L) Jay Depenbrock

Top Girls, Caryl Churchill; (D) Steven D. Albrezzi; (S) James Leonard Joy; (C) Linda Fisher; (L) Kirk Bookman

Traveler in the Dark, Marsha Norman; (D) D. Lynn Meyers; (S) Joseph P. Tilford; (C) Rebecca Senske; (L) Spencer Mosse

Hamlet, William Shakespeare; (D) Leonard Mozzi; (S) James C. Fenhagen; (C) Kurt Wilhelm; (L) Judy Rasmuson

Rosencrantz and Guildenstern Are Dead, Tom Stoppard; (D) Michael Hankins; (S) James C. Fenhagen; (C) Kurt Wilhelm; (L) Judy Rasmuson

And a Nightingale Sang..., C.P. Taylor; (D) Michael Murray; (S) Karl Eigsti; (C) Mariann S. Verheyen; (L) Spencer Mosse

Sing Hallelujah!, various; (D) Worth Gardner; (S) J. Hinton; (L) Ron Bunt

PRODUCTIONS 1986–87

K2, Patrick Meyers; (D) Michael Hankins; (S) Paul Shortt; (C) D. Bartlett Blair; (L) Spencer Mosse

As Is, William M. Hoffman; (D) Richard Harden; (S) Joseph P. Tilford; (C) Rebecca Senske; (L) Kirk Bookman

Little Shop of Horrors, book and lyrics: Howard Ashman; music: Alan Menken; (D) Worth Gardner; (S) Paul Shortt; (C) Eduardo Sicangco; (L) Kirk Bookman

The Real Thing, Tom Stoppard; (D) D. Lynn Meyers; (S) Joseph P. Tilford; (C) Barbara Kay; (L) Kirk Bookman

Orphans, Lyle Kessler; (D) Sam Blackwell; (S) Richard M. Isackes; (C) D. Bartlett Blair; (L) Kirk Bookman

The Dark at the Top of the Stairs, William Inge; (D) Worth Gardner and D. Lynn Meyers; (S) Richard M. Isackes; (C) James Berton Harris; (L) Kirk Bookman

The Marriage of Bette and Boo, Christopher Durang; (D) Barbara Carlisle; (S) Joseph P. Tilford; (C) James Berton Harris; (L) Kirk Bookman

The Foreigner, Larry Shue; (D) Michael Hankins; (S) Joseph P. Tilford; (C) D. Bartlett Blair; (L) Kirk Bookman

Greater Tuna, Jaston Williams, Joe Sears and Ed Howard; (D) Word Baker; (S) Linda Carmichael Rose; (C) Rebecca Senske; (L) Kirk Bookman

She Stoops to Conquer, Oliver Goldsmith; (D) Worth Gardner; (S) Paul Shortt; (C) James Berton Harris; (L) Kirk Bookman

Sing Hallelujah!, various; (D) Worth Gardner; (S) Joseph P. Tilford; (C) Rebecca Senske; (L) Kirk Bookman

Circle in the Square Theatre

THEODORE MANN
Artistic Director

PAUL LIBIN
Producing Director

1633 Broadway
New York, NY 10019
(212) 307-2700 (bus.)
(212) 307-2704 (b.o.)

FOUNDED 1951
Aileen Cramer, Edward Mann, Theodore Mann, Jose Quintero, Emily Stevens, Jason Wingreen

SEASON
Year-round

FACILITIES
Seating capacity: 682
Stage: arena

FINANCES
July 1, 1986-June 30, 1987
Expenses: $4,510,000

CONTRACTS
AEA LORT (A), SSD&C and USA

Exceptional writing, illuminated by America's best actors, remains the cornerstone of the Circle in the Square Theatre philosophy. We seek to present works that possess a quality of language capable of moving and exciting our audiences. Over the years, these audiences have seen the country's finest actors confront the demands of interpreting material drawn from both classic works and new American plays. We provide the creative environment in which actors are allowed to take on roles which challenge their abilities. We encourage the actors to expand their range by fostering an atmosphere in which each individual involved in our theatre is acknowledged as a collaborator, an essential member of the family. Throughout our history, actors of extraordinary ability have been drawn to the Circle by this process. In the coming years, we will continue to seek overlooked masterworks and new plays of merit, giving both actors and audiences the opportunity to share and participate in our discovery.

—Theodore Mann

PRODUCTIONS 1985–86

The Marriage of Figaro, Pierre-Augustin Caron de Beaumarchais; adapt: Richard Nelson; (D) Andrei Serban; (S) Beni Montresor; (L) Beni Montresor

The Caretaker, Harold Pinter; (D) John Malkovich; (S) Kevin Rigdon; (C) Kevin Rigdon; (L) John Malkovich

The Boys in Autumn, Bernard Sabath; (D) Theodore Mann; (S) Michael Miller; (C) Jennifer von Mayrhauser; (L) Richard Nelson

Circle in the Square Theatre. Anthony Heald, Caitlin Clarke, Christopher Reeve, Mary Elizabeth Mastrantonio and Dana Ivey *The Marriage of Figaro*. Photo: Martha Swope.

PRODUCTIONS 1986–87

You Never Can Tell, George Bernard Shaw; (D) Stephen Porter; (S) Thomas Lynch; (C) Martin Pakledinaz; (L) Richard Nelson
The Widow Claire, Horton Foote; (D) Michael Lindsay-Hogg; (S) Eugene Lee; (C) Van Broughton Ramsey; (L) Natasha Katz
Coastal Disturbances, Tina Howe; (D) Carole Rothman; (S) Bob Shaw; (C) Susan Hilferty; (L) Dennis Parichy

Circle Repertory Company

TANYA BEREZIN
Artistic Director

TIM HAWKINS
Managing Director

161 Ave. of the Americas
New York, NY 10013
(212) 691-3210 (bus.)
(212) 924-7100 (b.o.)

FOUNDED 1969
Tanya Berezin, Marshall W. Mason, Robert Thirkield, Lanford Wilson

SEASON
Sept.-June

FACILITIES
99 Seventh Ave. South
Seating capacity: 160
Stage: flexible

FINANCES
July 1, 1986-June 30, 1987
Expenses: $1,864,469

CONTRACTS
AEA Off Broadway, SSD&C and USA

Circle Repertory Company is a family of over 100 theatre artists who share a common language and a common vision. Grounded in the classics, but with a unique American style, Circle Rep has become a national resource producing more than 100 new works that have been presented at scores of professional theatres in all 50 states and many foreign countries. Circle Rep has led in the rediscovery of lyric realism as the native voice of American theatre, exploring all aspects of this style. The company presents an annual mainstage subscription season which includes new plays, revivals, classics and a staged reading series. The Circle Program, with its playwright, director and actor units, fosters developmental projects. Circle Rep's ensemble of artists—actors, directors, playwrights and designers—works together to create a living play in which the action of the play becomes the experience of the audience. —*Tanya Berezin*

Note: During the 1985-86 and 1986-87 seasons, Marshall W. Mason served as artistic director.

PRODUCTIONS 1985–86

Talley and Son, Lanford Wilson; (D) Marshall W. Mason; (S) John Lee Beatty; (C) Laura Crow; (L) Dennis Parichy
Tomorrow's Monday, Paul Osborn; (D) Kent Paul; (S) John Lee Beatty; (C) Jennifer von Mayrhauser; (L) Dennis Parichy
The Beach House, Nancy Donohue; (D) Melvin Bernhardt; (S) David Potts; (C) Jennifer von Mayrhauser; (L) Dennis Parichy and Mal Sturchio
Caligula, adapt: Marshall W. Mason and Harry Newman, from Albert Camus; trans: Stuart Gilbert; (D) Marshall W. Mason; (S) John Lee Beatty; (C) Jennifer von Mayrhauser; (L) Dennis Parichy
The Mound Builders, Lanford Wilson; (D) Marshall W. Mason; (S) John Lee Beatty; (C) Jennifer von Mayrhauser; (L) Dennis Parichy
Quiet in the Land, Anne Chislett; (D) Daniel Irvine; (S) John Lee Beatty; (C) Jennifer von Mayrhauser; (L) Dennis Parichy

PRODUCTIONS 1986–87

In This Fallen City, Bryan Williams; (D) Marshall W. Mason; (S) David Potts; (C) Jennifer von Mayrhauser; (L) Dennis Parichy
The Early Girl, Caroline Kava; (D) Munson Hicks; (S) John Lee Beatty; (C) Jennifer von Mayrhauser; (L) Dennis Parichy
The Musical Comedy Murders of 1940, John Bishop; (D) John Bishop; (S) David Potts; (C) Jennifer von Mayrhauser; (L) Dennis Parichy and Mal Sturchio

Circle Repertory Company. Ruby Holbrook, Bobo Lewis, Nicholas Wyman, Dorothy Cantwell and Kelly Connell in *The Musical Comedy Murders of 1940*. Photo: Adam Newman.

Burn This, Lanford Wilson; (D) Marshall W. Mason; (S) John Lee Beatty; (C) Laura Crow; (L) Dennis Parichy
As Is, William M. Hoffman; (D) Michael Warren Powell; (S) David Potts; (C) Michael Warren Powell and Susan Lyall; (L) Dennis Parichy
Road Show, Murray Schisgal; (D) Mel Shapiro; (S) David Potts; (C) Laura Crow; (L) Dennis Parichy

City Theatre Company

MARC MASTERSON
Artistic Director

JON BURGE
Managing Director

B-39 Cathedral of Learning
University of Pittsburgh
Pittsburgh, PA 15260
(412) 624-1357 (bus.)
(412) 624-4101 (b.o.)

FOUNDED 1973
City of Pittsburgh

SEASON
Oct.-Apr.

FACILITIES
New City Theatre
Seating capacity: 115
Stage: thrust

FINANCES
July 1, 1986-June 30, 1987
Expenses: $234,336

CONTRACTS
AEA SPT

The City Theatre Company focuses on the development of new American plays and works of the recent past. The company maintains a resident ensemble of actors, designers and directors, supplemented by jobbed-in artists. The objective is to provide actors and audiences with a variety of experience reflecting the diversity of American drama while encouraging the development of new plays. To that end, CTC produces a staged reading series of six new scripts in workshop each season which results in the full production of at least one of these plays on the mainstage. The company also commissions two new plays each year for touring to area schools and community groups. In summer months City Theatre Company produces a free street theatre in conjunction with the city of Pittsburgh and a season at Hartwood Acres park in Allegheny County. —*Marc Masterson*

City Theatre Company. Bob Tracey and David Butler in *Glengarry Glen Ross.* Photo: Kimberly Pasko.

PRODUCTIONS 1985–86

Lovers and Keepers, book and lyrics: Maria Irene Fornes; music: Tito Puente and Fernando Rivas; (D) Maria Irene Fornes; (S) William O'Donnell; (C) Lorraine Venberg; (L) Norman Russell

Glengarry Glen Ross, David Mamet; (D) Jed Harris; (S) Diane Melchitzky; (C) Lorraine Venberg; (L) Norman Russell

PRODUCTIONS 1986–87

On the Verge or The Geography of Yearning, Eric Overmyer; (D) Marc Masterson; (S) Tony Ferrieri; (C) Peter Harrigan; (L) Bob Steineck

The Perfect Party, A.R. Gurney, Jr.; (D) Marc Field; (S) Park Warne; (C) Peter Harrigan; (L) Matt Shaffer

Clarence Brown Theatre Company

WANDALIE HENSHAW
Artistic Director

KEVIN COLMAN
General Manager

UT Box 8450
Knoxville, TN 37996
(615) 974-6011 (bus.)
(615) 974-5161 (b.o.)

FOUNDED 1974
Ralph G. Allen, Anthony Quayle

SEASON
Variable

FACILITIES
Clarence Brown Theatre
Seating capacity: 604
Stage: proscenium

Studio Theatre
Seating capacity: 150
Stage: thrust

Carousel Theatre
Seating capacity: 500
Stage: arena

FINANCES
July 1, 1986-June 30, 1987
Expenses: $410,000

CONTRACTS
AEA LORT (D), TYA, SSD&C and USA

The Clarence Brown Theatre Company, now in its second decade, serves and is well supported by the East Tennessee community, and plays a special role in the theatre program at the University of Tennessee. Its aim and character have been consistent: to do the great plays which are the enduring and inexhaustible heart of the repertoire, and to do them well. As Anthony Quayle, a founding member of the company, observed: "If you do the classics, you must do them justice." The experience that we try to give the audience is of a unified event in which the design as much as the directing and acting is at the service of the play. We are always hearing about "playwrights' theatre" or "actors' theatre" or "directors' theatre." We believe in, and work to achieve, a "Theatre of the Play Itself."

—*Wandalie Henshaw*

PRODUCTIONS 1985–86

The Questions of Hamlet, William Shakespeare; adapt: Peter Garvie; (D) Wandalie Henshaw; (S) Marianne Custer; (C) Pamela Nelson; (L) John R. Horner

The Lion in Winter, James Goldman; (D) Albert Harris; (S) Leonard Harman; (C) Connie Furr; (L) James F. Franklin

The Vinegar Tree, Paul Osborn; (D) Wandalie Henshaw; (S) Robert Cothran; (C) Marianne Custer; (L) G.Scott Corliss

Bus Stop, William Inge; (D) Dennis Erdman; (S) Leonard Harman; (C) Catherine Meacham; (L) Michael J. Garl

PRODUCTIONS 1986–87

The Taming of the Shrew, William Shakespeare; adapt: Wandalie Henshaw; (D) Wandalie Henshaw; (S) Marianne Custer; (C) Sara Irwin; (L) Tim Hester

Present Laughter, Noel Coward; (D) Philip Kerr; (S) Gary Decker; (C) Marianne Custer; (L) Gary Decker

The Harmful Effects of Tobacco...and Other Comedies, Anton Chekhov; (D) Lucien Douglas; (S) Leonard Harman; (C) Bill Black; (L) L. J. DeCuir

Macbeth, William Shakespeare; (D) Wandalie Henshaw; (S) Robert Cothran; (C) Steven Graver; (L) L.J. DeCuir

The Cleveland Play House

JOSEPHINE R. ABADY
Artistic Director

WILLIAM RHYS
Resident Artistic Director

DEAN R. GLADDEN
Managing Director

Box 1989
Cleveland, OH 44106
(216) 795-7010 (bus.)
(216) 795-7000 (b.o.)

FOUNDED 1915
Raymond O'Neill

SEASON
Oct.-June

Clarence Brown Theatre Company. Melissa Gilbert and Teri Copley in *Bus Stop.* Photo: Eric L. Smith.

The Cleveland Play House. Jean Zarzour, Mary Michenfelder, Ann Mortifee, Molly McGrath Cornwell and Robert C. Rhys in *The Arabian Knight*. Photo: Robert C. Ragsdale.

FACILITIES
Kenyon C. Bolton Theatre
Seating capacity: 612
Stage: proscenium

Francis E. Drury Theatre
Seating capacity: 499
Stage: proscenium

Charles S. Brooks Theatre
Seating capacity: 160
Stage: proscenium

FINANCES
July 1, 1986-June 30, 1987
Expenses: $3,700,000

CONTRACTS
AEA LORT (C) and SSD&C

The Cleveland Play House has experienced an aggressive period of growth in both space and style in the past few years. Consolidation into a 555,000-square-foot complex that includes three theatres and complete production support facilities has demanded a vigorous re-evaluation of not only the Play House's responsibility to its audience in terms of programming, but also of the ways in which the complex can be used by Cleveland's entire artistic community. In order to expand the services the Play House offers the community, the complex has become the performance home of the Ohio Chamber Orchestra, the Fairmount Theatre for the Deaf and the Footpath Dance Company. Although 72 years old, the Play House is revitalizing itself by pursuing adventurous works and production values and techniques. The past few seasons have been an opportunity for this theatre to trust its venerable history, while shaking out the comfortableness that may often follow a secure past.

—William Rhys

Note: During the 1985-86 and 1986-87 seasons, William Rhys served as resident artistic director.

PRODUCTIONS 1985–86

Lillian, William Luce; (D) Robert Whitehead; (S) Ben Edwards; (C) Jane Greenwood; (L) Tom Skelton
On the Razzle, Tom Stoppard; (D) William Rhys; (S) Richard Gould; (C) Estelle Painter; (L) Richard Gould
In the Belly of the Beast, adapt: Seymour Morgenstern and Louis Potter, from Jack Henry Abbott; (D) Evie McElroy; (S) James Irwin; (C) Wanda Sue Morain; (L) James Irwin
A...My Name Is Alice, Joan Micklin Silver and Julianne Boyd; (D) Jim Corti; (S) James Irwin; (C) Frances Blau; (L) James Irwin
A Christmas Carol, adapt: Doris Baizley, from Charles Dickens; (D) William Rhys; (S) Charles Berliner; (C) Charles Berliner; (L) Richard Gould
The Portage to San Cristobal of A.H., adapt: Christopher Hampton, from George Steiner; (D) William Rhys; (S) Richard Gould; (C) Frances Blau; (L) Richard Gould
A Streetcar Named Desire, Tennessee Williams; (D) Evie McElroy; (S) Keith Henery; (C) Estelle Painter; (L) Richard Gould
Othello, William Shakespeare; (D) Larry Arrick; (S) Richard Gould; (C) Frances Blau; (L) Richard Gould
Stage Struck, Simon Gray; (D) William Rhys; (S) Keith Henery; (C) Richard Gould; (L) Thomas M. Salzman
Christmas on Mars, Harry Kondoleon; (D) T. Riccio; (S) James Irwin; (C) Edith Drew; (L) James Irwin
Bosoms and Neglect, John Guare; (D) T. Riccio; (S) James Irwin; (C) Melanie Boeman; (L) James Irwin
Candide, adapt: Hugh Wheeler, from Voltaire; music: Leonard Bernstein; lyrics: Stephen Sondheim, Richard Wilbur and John LaTouche; (D) Joseph J. Garry; (S) Richard Gould; (C) Estelle Painter; (L) Eugene Hare

PRODUCTIONS 1986–87

The Praying Mantis, Alejandro Sieveking; trans: Charles Thomas; (D) Evie McElroy; (S) Keith Henery; (C) Estelle Painter; (L) D. Glenn Vanderbilt
Buried Child, Sam Shepard; (D) William Rhys; (S) Richard Gould; (C) Richard Gould; (L) Thomas M. Salzman
To Die for Grenada, Derek Walcott; (D) Kay Matschullat; (S) Charles Berliner; (C) Estelle Painter; (L) Richard Gould
The 1940's Radio Hour, Walton Jones; (D) William Rhys; (S) Keith Henery; (C) Richard Gould; (L) Thomas M. Salzman
A Christmas Carol, adapt: Doris Baizley, from Charles Dickens; (D) William Rhys; (S) Charles Berliner; (C) Charles Berliner; (L) Richard Gould
Orphans, Lyle Kessler; (D) Evie McElroy; (S) Richard Gould; (C) Estelle Painter; (L) Thomas M. Salzman
Mensch Meier, Franz Xaver Kroetz; trans: Roger Downey; (D) George Ferencz; (S) William Stabile; (C) Estelle Painter; (L) Blu
The Three Sisters, Anton Chekhov; trans: Lanford Wilson; (D) Marion Andre; (S) Richard Gould; (C) Estelle Painter; (L) Richard Gould
Cotton Patch Gospel, book: Tom Key and Russell Treyz; music and lyrics: Harry Chapin; (D) William Rhys; (C) Estelle Painter; (L) Richard Gould
Noises Off, Michael Frayn; (D) Donald Ewer; (S) Richard Gould; (C) Dawna Gregory; (L) Richard Gould
The Arabian Knight, book: Joseph J. Garry and David O. Frazier; music and lyrics: Ann Mortifee; (D) Joseph J. Garry; (S) Richard Gould; (C) Estelle Painter; (L) Kirk Bookman

Coconut Grove Playhouse

ARNOLD MITTELMAN
Producing Artistic Director

JORDAN BOCK
General Manager

Box 616
Miami, FL 33133
(305) 442-2662 (bus.)
(305) 442-4000 (b.o.)

FOUNDED 1977
Gerald Pulver, Thomas Spencer

SEASON
Oct.-June

FACILITIES
Main Stage
Seating capacity: 796
Stage: proscenium

Coconut Grove Playhouse. Helen Baldassare, Kaye Ballard and Marcia Lewis in *Nunsense*. Photo: Tom Elliot.

Encore Room
Seating capacity: 117
Stage: flexible

FINANCES
July 1, 1986-June 30, 1987
Expenses: $3,200,000

CONTRACTS
AEA LORT (B), (C), (D), SSD&C and USA

Theatre provides an opportunity for audiences to learn more about the human experience through its power to challenge and enlighten. During the 1985-86 season, my first with the Playhouse, I was able to create, with the Kurt Weill estate, a new adaptation of *Berlin to Broadway with Kurt Weill*. In addition, Edward Albee directed his Pulitzer Prize-winning play *Seascape* with its original Broadway designers. The highlight of our last season was the English-language premiere of *Orchids and Panthers* by Alfonso Vallejo, along with an additional production performed by a separate company in Spanish for the Hispanic community. The creation and fostering of talent is why we exist. We give artists a supportive, professional setting in which to further their work. We have taken productions on tour, created a conservatory and developed programs for youth, seniors and special audiences. All reap the benefits of enrichment, enlightenment and entertainment through theatre.

—*Arnold Mittelman*

PRODUCTIONS 1985–86

Corpse!, Gerald Moon; (D) John Tillinger; (S) Alan Tagg and Dennis Bradford; (C) Lowell Detweiler; (L) Richard Winkler
Cole Porter Requests the Pleasure, adapt: Philip Astor; music and lyrics: Cole Porter; (D) Philip Astor; (S) David Trimble; (C) Jillian Bos; (L) Michael Newton-Brown
I Love My Wife, book adapt and lyrics: Michael Stewart; music: Cy Coleman; (D) Onna White; (S) Neil Price; (C) Ellis Tillman; (L) Marsha Hardy-Grasselli
Berlin to Broadway, adapt: Jack Anderson and Fred Kolo, from Gene Lerner; music: Kurt Weill; (D) Jack Allison; (S) Fred Kolo; (C) Fred Kolo; (L) Fred Kolo
Seascape, Edward Albee; (D) Edward Albee; (S) James Tilton; (C) Fred Voelpel; (L) James Tilton
Rum and Coke, Keith Reddin; (D) James Simpson; (S) Fred Kolo; (C) Ellis Tillman; (L) Fred Kolo

PRODUCTIONS 1986–87

Wait Until Dark, Frederick Knott; (D) George Keathley; (S) David Trimble; (C) Ellis Tillman; (L) David Goodman
Coconuts!, book: William Brown; music and lyrics: Michael Brown and Lesley Davison; (D) Frank Wagner; (S) Howard Beals; (C) Ellis Tillman; (L) Stephen Welsh
Nunsense, Dan Goggin; (D) Dan Goggin; (S) Barry Axtell; (L) Susan A. White
The Hostage, Brendan Behan; (D) Arnold Mittelman; (S) David Trimble; (C) Ellis Tillman; (L) Stephen Welsh
Side by Side by Sondheim, music and lyrics: Stephen Sondheim; music: Leonard Bernstein, Mary Rodgers, Richard Rodgers and Jule Styne; (D) Jack Allison; (S) Fred Kolo; (C) Ellis Tillman; (L) Fred Kolo
Orchids and Panthers, Alfonso Vallejo; (D) Arnold Mittelman; (S) Fred Kolo; (C) Fred Kolo; (L) Fred Kolo
Groucho: A Life in Revue, Arthur Marx and Robert Fisher; (D) Robert Vandergriff; (S) Wade Foy and Michael Hotopp; (C) Ellis Tillman; (L) David Goodman

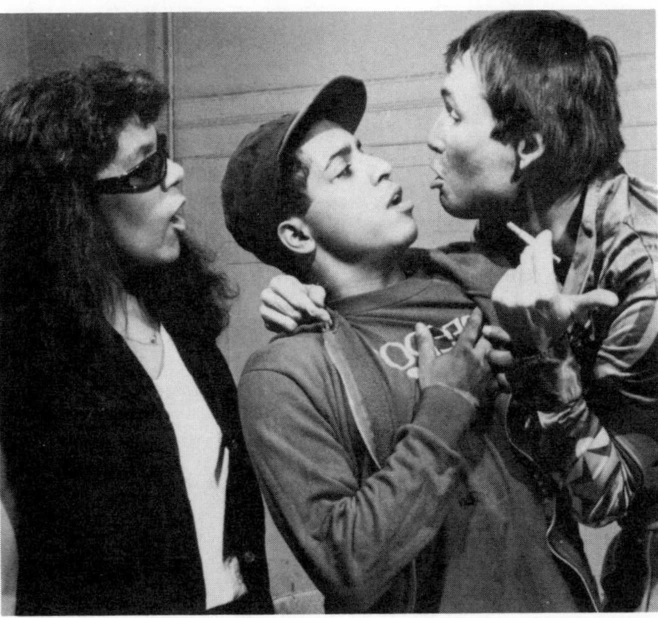

Creative Arts Team. Lillian Adorno, Rhys Green and Michael Littman in *Home Court*. Photo: Lou Mana.

Creative Arts Team

LYNDA ZIMMERMAN
Executive Director

MICHELLE TATUM
Managing Director

New York University
Gallatin Div.
715 Broadway, 5th fl.
New York, NY 10003
(212) 998-7380

FOUNDED 1974
Lynda Zimmerman

SEASON
Year-round

FINANCES
July 1, 1986-June 30, 1987
Expenses: $894,206

The Creative Arts Team is the professional theatre-in-education company in residence at New York University's Gallatin Division. Its pioneering efforts combine original theatre productions and participatory drama workshops designed to address social issues pertinent to adolescents and adults living in an urban society. By presenting compelling, issue-related theatre that confronts audiences with the choices and consequences of decisions, CAT challenges participants to examine topics such as youth employment, pregnancy prevention, illiteracy and ethnic heritage. *I Never Told Anybody*, CAT's production about the cyclical nature of child abuse, and *Home Court*, a drama about the effects of substance abuse on a family, have reached a national audience of over 100,000 young people and adults. As a recent recipient of the New York City "Schools and Culture Award," CAT continues to be recognized for responding to the needs of young people through challenging and provocative theatre.

—*Lynda Zimmerman*

PRODUCTIONS 1985–86

I Never Told Anybody, Dianne Houston and Jim Mirrione; music: Latteta Theresa and Carmen Whip; (D) Dianne Houston; (S) Thurston Reyes and Jeff Pearl; (C) Fontella Boone; (L) Fern Gnesin

PRODUCTIONS 1986–87

I Never Told Anybody, Dianne Houston and Jim Mirrione; music: Latteta Theresa and Carmen Whip; (D) Dianne Houston; (S) Erik Stephenson; (C) Fontella Boone; (L) Ric Rogers
Home Court, Jim Mirrione; music: Eugene, Jahneen, Sam Jacobs; (D) Achim Nowak; (C) Fontella Boone

The Cricket Theatre. Dawn Rene Jones, Karen Esbjornson, Allan Hickle-Edwards, James R. Stowell and Chuck McQuary in *The Angels of Warsaw.* Photo: Chris Johnson.

The Cricket Theatre

WILLIAM PARTLAN
Artistic Director

SEAN MICHAEL DOWSE
General Manager

9 West 14th St.
Minneapolis, MN 55403
(612) 871-3763 (bus.)
(612) 871-2244 (b.o.)

FOUNDED 1971
William Semans

SEASON
variable

FACILITIES
Loring Theatre
Seating capacity: 215
Stage: proscenium

FINANCES
July 1, 1986-June 30, 1987
Expenses: $245,000

CONTRACTS
AEA SPT

The Cricket is a playwright-oriented producing theatre. I believe our playwrights are among our most important visionaries; they create imagined worlds which contain a people, a language and a code of interaction all their own. I look for inventively-peopled theatrical worlds; for intensively interactive plays with muscular language. As theatre artists, we explore the boundaries of these worlds with the writers and together we give them a theatrical life which reaches for resonance in our audiences' lives. The Cricket provides developmental and production resources for a number of local, national and international playwrights in our new, intimate theatre facility. We do not employ a fulltime company but hire the best artists and technicians available to create the world of each project. The Cricket has emerged from economic hard times as a leaner, more flexible organization—attempting to create a vital theatrical proving ground for theatre artists.

—*William Partlan*

Note: During the 1985-86 and 1986-87 seasons, Sean Michael Dowse served as Producing Director.

PRODUCTIONS 1985–86

The Cricket Theatre temporarily suspended operations for this season.

PRODUCTIONS 1986–87

Bring Me Smiles, C.P. Taylor; (D) Howard Dallin; (S) Colin Tugwell; (C) Colin Tugwell; (L) Chris Johnson

Killers, John Olive; (D) Howard Dallin; (S) Chris Johnson; (C) Janet Daverne; (L) Chris Johnson

The Angels of Warsaw, Marisha Chamberlain; (D) George Sand; (S) George Sand; (C) Chris Johnson; (L) Chris Johnson

Crossroads Theatre Company

RICK KHAN
L. KENNETH RICHARDSON
Co-Artistic Directors

ELIZABETH BULLUCK
General Manager

320 Memorial Pkwy.
New Brunswick, NJ 08901
(201) 249-5581 (bus.)
(201) 249-5560 (b.o.)

FOUNDED 1978
Rick Khan, L. Kenneth Richardson

SEASON
Sept.-May

FACILITIES
Seating capacity: 150
Stage: thrust

FINANCES
July 1, 1986-June 30, 1987
Expenses: $774,700

CONTRACTS
AEA letter of agreement

Over the past eight years, Crossroads has done much to redefine the role of black theatre in American culture. We are no longer satisfied with the timeworn definition of black theatre as being "about blacks, for blacks and by blacks." Black theatre, like black life, spans a wide spectrum of emotions and experiences—positive, negative and everything in between. We seek a fuller, more accurate reflection of this life and

Crossroads Theatre Company. Front to rear: Myra Taylor, Vickilyn, Arnold Bankston, Robert Jason and Olivia Virgil Harper in *The Colored Museum.* Photo: Eddie Birch.

culture, rather than emphasizing only one aspect. In addition to presenting the finest classical and contemporary black plays, we have produced the works of David Mamet, Edward Albee and John Pielmeier with black casts. Future plans include Shakespeare, Molière and O'Neill, among others. Black theatre need not and should not be pigeonholed. It is Crossroads' responsibility to present our audience with a more complete and positive experience in black theatre. During the 1985-86 season, we presented three world premieres: one of these, George Wolfe's *The Colored Museum*, received critical praise for its revolutionary style and content, and moved to the New York Shakespeare Festival. We took a great risk in abruptly switching gears, from presenting revivals to producing new works, yet if we seek to secure a place for black theatre in the history books, it is our responsibility to seek out, nurture and develop young writing talent.

—*L. Kenneth Richardson*

PRODUCTIONS 1985–86

One Mo' Time, Vernel Bagneris; (D) Rick Khan; (S) Daniel M. Proett; (C) Judy Dearing; (L) Shirley Prendergast

Tamer of Horses, William Mastrosimone; (D) L. Kenneth Richardson; (S) Daniel M. Proett; (C) Nancy L. Konrardy; (L) Susan A. White

Black Nativity, Langston Hughes; (D) Mike Malone; (S) Daniel M. Proett; (C) Fontella Boone; (L) Shirley Prendergast

Roads of the Mountaintop, Ron Milner; (D) Rick Khan; (S) Daniel M. Proett; (C) Anita Ellis; (L) Shirley Prendergast

The Colored Museum, George C. Wolfe; (D) L. Kenneth Richardson; (S) Brian Martin; (C) Nancy L. Konrardy; (L) William H. Grant, III

Agnes of God, John Pielmeier; (D) Harold Scott; (S) Brian Martin; (C) Judy Dearing; (L) Shirley Prendergast

PRODUCTIONS 1986–87

The River Niger, Joseph Walker; (D) Dean Irby; (S) Daniel M. Proett; (C) Nancy L. Konrardy; (L) William H. Grant, III

Alterations, Michael Abbensetts; (D) Regge Life; (S) Bill Motyka; (C) Alvin Perry; (L) Shirley Prendergast

Eubie, music: Eubie Blake; conceived: Julianne Boyd; (D) Rick Khan; (S) Brian Martin; (C) Nancy L. Konrardy; (L) Susan A. White

Williams & Walker, Vincent D. Smith; (D) Rick Khan; (S) Daniel M. Proett; (C) Judy Dearing; (L) Marc D. Malamud

Hannah Davis, Leslie Lee; (D) L. Kenneth Richardson; (S) Daniel M. Proett; (C) Alvin Perry; (L) Shirley Prendergast

Split Second, Dennis McIntyre; (D) L. Kenneth Richardson; (S) Daniel M. Proett; (C) Nancy L. Konrardy; (L) Victor En Yu Tan

CSC Repertory Ltd.-The Classic Stage Company

CAREY PERLOFF
Artistic Director

CAROL OSTROW
Producing Director

136 East 13th St.
New York, NY 10003
(212) 477-5808 (bus.)
(212) 677-4210 (b.o.)

FOUNDED 1967
Christopher Martin

SEASON
Nov.-May

FACILITIES
Seating capacity: 180
Stage: flexible

FINANCES
July 1, 1986-June 30, 1987
Expenses: $375,000

CONTRACTS
AEA letter of agreement

CSC Repertory Ltd.—The Classic Stage Company. Michael Hammond, Sigourney Weaver, Rocco Sisto and Kristine Nielsen in *The Merchant of Venice*. Photo: Paula Court.

CSC Repertory Ltd.—The Classic Stage Company, exists to rediscover and reinterpret the immensely rich classical repertoire often forgotten in a country voracious for new plays. Located in the East Village, one of the hottest visual and performing arts communities in America, CSC is committed to visually explosive productions of plays from every culture—from Sophocles to Lorca to Chekhov to Ezra Pound—plays that exhibit rich language, theatricality and depth of subject matter. We actively commission new translations and adaptations for our Sneak Previews of New and Undiscovered Classics reading series and for our mainstage productions, and seek out imaginative artists from every race, background, gender and genre to collaborate with us. CSC's conservatory trains young actors in classical theatre, and our City Stages for City Students program brings free productions to New York City students.

—*Carey Perloff*

Note: During the 1985-86 season, Craig D. Kinzer served as artistic director.

PRODUCTIONS 1985–86

Brand, Henrik Ibsen; trans: Michael Meyer; (D) Craig D. Kinzer; (S) Rick Butler; (C) Catherine Zuber; (L) Stephen Strawbridge

Frankenstein, adapt: Laurence Maslon, from Mary Shelley; (D) Craig D. Kinzer; (S) Rick Butler; (C) Catherine Zuber; (L) Whitney Quesenberry

A Country Doctor, adapt: Len Jenkin, from Franz Kafka; (D) Lawrence Sacharow; (S) Marjorie Bradley Kellogg; (C) Marianne Powell-Parker; (L) Arden Fingerhut

The Divine Orlando, William Luce; (D) Paul Lazarus; (S) Rick Butler; (C) Claudia S. Anderson; (L) Curt Ostermann

PRODUCTIONS 1986–87

The Maids, Jean Genet; trans: Bernard Frechtman; (D) David Kaplan; (S) Rick Butler; (C) Marcy Grace Froelich; (L) Ken Tabachnick

The Skin of Our Teeth, Thornton Wilder; (D) Carey Perloff; (S) Loy Arcenas; (C) Candice Donnelly; (L) Anne Militello

The Merchant of Venice, William Shakespeare; (D) James Simpson; (S) Loy Arcenas; (C) Claudia Brown; (L) Anne Militello

Cumberland County Playhouse

JIM CRABTREE
Producing Director

Box 484
Crossville, TN 38555
(615) 484-2300 (bus.)
(615) 484-5000 (b.o.)

FOUNDED 1965
Paul Crabtree, Moses Dorton, Margaret Keyes Harrison

SEASON
Mar.-Dec.

FACILITIES
Cumberland County Playhouse

Cumberland County Playhouse. *Old Hickory.*

Seating capacity: 480
Stage: flexible

Fairfield Dinner Theater
Seating capacity: 165
Stage: proscenium

Theater-in-the-Woods
Seating capacity: 199
Stage: outdoor arena

FINANCES
Jan. 1, 1986-Dec. 31, 1986
Expenses: $539,900

CONTRACTS
AEA Guest Artist

Our home is a town of 6,500 in a rural Appalachian county 75 miles from Knoxville and Chattanooga, and two hours from Nashville. We're committed to the idea that the arts can be an indigenous, homegrown part of rural America, not just an imported commodity. Each year, our Fairfield Living History series presents new work rooted in Tennessee history. Our Playhouse-in-the-Schools project puts staff and company members in area classrooms as the instructional team for the curriculum we are developing with local educators. We advise and direct student productions. Mainstage and young-audience shows tour to rural schools and communities in our audience area. Company and staff, drawn from our community and elsewhere in the Southeast, are joined by guest artists and a strong volunteer corps. We balance our budgets, own and maintain our facility and avoid deficits. Since 1965, over 85 percent of all revenues have come from earned income.

—Jim Crabtree

PRODUCTIONS 1986

The Silver Whistle, Robert McEnroe; (D) Mary Crabtree; (S) Martha Hill; (C) Amelie C. Woods; (L) Jim Crabtree
Second Sons: A Story of Rugby, Tennessee, book and lyrics: Jim Crabtree; music: Dennis Davenport; (D) Jim Crabtree; (S) Leonard Harman; (C) Amelie C. Woods; (L) Ron Fry and Jim Crabtree
Quilters, book: Molly Newman and Barbara Damashek; music and lyrics: Barbara Damashek; (D) Jim Crabtree; (S) Ron Fry and Amelie C. Woods; (C) Don Bolinger; (L) Jim Crabtree
Tennessee, USA, book,music and lyrics: Paul Crabtree; (D) Jim Crabtree; (S) Jim Crabtree and Nathan K. Braun; (C) Mary Crabtree; (L) Jim Crabtree
Annie, book: Thomas Meehan; music: Charles Strouse; lyrics: Martin Charnin; (D) Jim Crabtree; (S) Ron Fry; (C) Amelie C. Woods; (L) Jim Crabtree
The Silver Screen, Jim Crabtree and Herb Bushnell; (D) Mary Crabtree; (S) Ron Fry; (C) Amelie C. Woods and Don Bolinger; (L) Carl Sutton, Jr.
Wiley and the Hairy Man, Susan Zeder; (D) Jan Engelhardt; (S) John Partyka; (L) John Partyka
Fiddler on the Roof, book: Joseph Stein; lyrics: Sheldon Harnick; music: Jerry Bock; (D) Mary Crabtree; (S) Jim Crabtree; (C) Amelie C. Woods; (L) John Partyka
Morning's at Seven, Paul Osborn; (D) Mary Crabtree; (S) Martha Hill; (C) Joyce Carroll; (L) Steve Woods
Cotton Patch Gospel, book: Tom Key and Russell Treyz; music and lyrics: Harry Chapin; (D) Rhonda Wallace; (S) John Partyka; (C) Mary Crabtree; (L) John Partyka
Pump Boys and Dinettes, John Foley, Mark Hardwick, Debra Monk, Cass Morgan, John Schimmel and Jim Wann; (D) Abigail Crabtree; (S) Ron Fry; (C) Amelie C. Woods; (L) Carl Sutton, Jr.

PRODUCTIONS 1987

Old Hickory, book and lyrics: Paul Crabtree and Jim Crabtree; music: Dennis Davenport; (D) Jim Crabtree; (S) John Scheffler; (C) Mary Crabtree; (L) John Partyka
Foxfire, Hume Cronyn and Susan Cooper; (D) Jim Crabtree; (S) Xavier Ironside; (C) Don Bolinger; (L) Steve Woods
The Miracle Worker, William Gibson; (D) Mary Crabtree; (S) John Partyka; (C) Joyce Carroll; (L) John Partyka
Peter Pan, book: James M. Barrie; music: Mark Charlap; lyrics: Carolyn Leigh; (D) Jim Crabtree; (S) Joe Varga; (C) Mary Crabtree; (L) Jim Crabtree
Step on a Crack, Susan Zeder; (D) Jan Engelhardt; (S) John Partyka; (L) John Partyka
1776, book: Peter Stone; music and lyrics: Sherman Edwards; (D) Mary Crabtree; (S) John Partyka; (C) Brenda Schwab; (L) John Partyka
The Foreigner, Larry Shue; (D) Abigail Crabtree; (S) John Partyka; (C) Brenda Schwab; (L) Steve Woods
The Sound of Music, book: Howard Lindsay and Russel Crouse; music: Richard Rodgers; lyrics: Oscar Hammerstein II; (D) Mary Crabtree; (S) Leonard Harman; (C) Mary Crabtree, Brenda Schwab and Terry Schwab; (L) John Partyka
Brand New Beat, Jim Crabtree and Dennis Davenport; (D) Abigail Crabtree; (S) Gary Harris; (C) Brenda Schwab and Terry Schwab; (L) John Partyka
The Diary of Anne Frank, Frances Goodrich and Albert Hackett; (D) Jim Crabtree; (S) Leonard Harman; (C) Brenda Schwab and Terry Schwab; (L) John Partyka
Tennessee Strings, Jim Crabtree and Dennis Davenport; (D) Jim Crabtree; (S) Leonard Harman; (C) Brenda Schwab and Terry Schwab; (L) John Partyka
Peter Pan, book: James M. Barrie; music: Mark Charlap; lyrics: Carolyn Leigh; (D) Carl Sutton, Jr.; (S) Joe Varga; (C) Mary Crabtree; (L) John Partyka

Dallas Theater Center

ADRIAN HALL
Artistic Director

PETER DONNELLY
Executive Managing Director

3636 Turtle Creek Blvd.
Dallas, TX 75219-5598
(214) 526-8210 (bus.)
(214) 526-8857 (b.o.)

Dallas Theater Center. Jack Willis in *All the King's Men.* Photo: Linda Blase.

FOUNDED 1959
Paul Baker, Beatrice Handel, Robert D. Stecker, Sr., Dallas citizens

SEASON
Sept.-May

FACILITIES
Kalita Humphreys Theater
Seating capacity: 466
Stage: modified thrust

In the Basement
Seating capacity: 150
Stage: flexible

Arts District Theater
Seating capacity: 400
Stage: flexible

FINANCES
Sept. 1, 1986-Aug. 31, 1987
Expenses: $3,540,000

CONTRACTS
AEA LORT (C) and SSD&C

I believe that a statement about accomplishment and goals for an institution is usually in conflict with personal artistic goals for identity and acceptance. I don't think this is necessarily wrong. Personally, I would like to continue to explore the relationship between audience and actor—how they interact, come together and confront each other while constantly tightening the screws of the tools at our disposal—space, text and historical connection. At the Dallas Theater Center we are trying to move the artists from the periphery to the center of the institution. The form of government we have agreed on is the troika rule—artists, administrators, trustees. If the artist doesn't produce he fails. If at least one half of the annual budget is not paying the salaries of artists then the balance is wrong. If the grassroot hooks are not being applied then the trustees must be charged. As this theatre begins its 29th consecutive season in Dallas, I begin my fifth as artistic director. I am very optimistic about this institution's future.

—Adrian Hall

PRODUCTIONS 1985–86

The Ups and Downs of Theophilus Maitland, book: Vinnette Carroll; music and lyrics: Micki Grant; (D) Vinnette Carroll; (S) Eugene Lee; (C) Donna M. Kress; (L) Eugene Lee

The Skin of Our Teeth, Thornton Wilder; (D) Peter Gerety; (S) Eugene Lee; (C) Donna M. Kress; (L) Linda Blase

The Marriage of Bette and Boo, Christopher Durang; (D) Adrian Hall; (S) Eugene Lee; (C) Donna M. Kress; (L) Eugene Lee

Kith and Kin, Oliver Hailey; (D) Adrian Hall; (S) Eugene Lee; (C) Donna M. Kress; (L) Linda Blase

The Glass Menagerie, Tennessee Williams; (D) Thomas Hill; (S) William Eckart; (C) Donna M. Kress; (L) Susan Takis

The Tavern, George M. Cohan; (D) Tony Giordano; (S) Eugene Lee; (C) Donna M. Kress; (L) Linda Blase

PRODUCTIONS 1986–87

Noises Off, Michael Frayn; (D) Ken Bryant; (S) Robert D. Soule; (C) Donna M. Kress; (L) Linda Blase

All the King's Men, Robert Penn Warren; (D) Adrian Hall; (S) Eugene Lee; (C) Donna M. Kress; (L) Natasha Katz

The Real Thing, Tom Stoppard; (D) Philip Minor; (S) Eugene Lee; (C) Donna M. Kress; (L) Linda Blase

An Enemy of the People, Henrik Ibsen; adapt: Arthur Miller; (D) Ken Bryant; (S) Eugene Lee; (C) Donna M. Kress; (L) Natasha Katz

The Miser, Molière; (D) Stephen Porter; (S) Robert D. Soule; (C) Donna M. Kress; (L) John F. Custer

A Lie of the Mind, Sam Shepard; (D) Adrian Hall; (S) Eugene Lee; (C) Donna M. Kress; (L) Eugene Lee

Delaware Theatre Company

CLEVELAND MORRIS
Artistic Director

DENNIS LUZAK
Managing Director

200 Water St.
Wilmington, DE 19801
(302) 594-1104 (bus.)
(302) 594-1100 (b.o.)

Delaware Theatre Company. P. J. Benjamin and Laurence Overmire in *Tooth of Crime*. Photo: Richard Carter.

FOUNDED 1979
Peter DeLaurier, Cleveland Morris

SEASON
Oct.-Apr.

FACILITIES
Seating capacity: 300
Stage: proscenium

FINANCES
Sept. 1, 1986-Aug. 31, 1987
Expenses: $527,000

CONTRACTS
AEA letter of agreement

The Delaware Company is the state's only professional theatre. We seek to offer an encompassing, diverse examination of the art of theatre through our annual programs that mix well-known classics with unknown new plays, as well as lesser-known vintage plays with familiar contemporary works. In all cases, we seek plays of lasting social and literary value, worthy of thoughtful consideration by both artist and viewer, and produced in a style designed to strengthen the force of the playwright's language and vision. Our presentations are produced in a boldly modern facility that opened in November 1985, located on Wilmington's historic riverfront. The theatre company offers a wide variety of ancillary and educational programs in an effort to assist the general public in finding in the art of theatre an ongoing and joyful addition to their lives and community.

—Cleveland Morris

PRODUCTIONS 1985–86

Come Back, Little Sheba, William Inge; (D) Cleveland Morris; (S) Eric Schaeffer; (C) E. Lee Florance; (L) Bruce K. Morriss

Fallen Angels, Noel Coward; (D) Kent Thompson; (S) James F. Pyne, Jr.; (C) E. Lee Florance; (L) Bruce K. Morriss

K2, Patrick Meyers; (D) Francis X. Kuhn; (S) David Potts; (L) Bruce K. Morriss

The Majestic Kid, Mark Medoff; (D) Derek Wolshonak; (S) Eric Schaeffer; (C) Barbara Forbes; (L) Bruce K. Morriss

The Grand Duchess of Gerolstein, adapt: Cleveland Morris and Judy Brown; libretto: Ludovic Halevy; music: Jacques Offenbach; (D) Cleveland Morris; (S) Lewis Folden; (C) Catherine Adair; (L) Bruce K. Morriss

PRODUCTIONS 1986–87

Our Town, Thornton Wilder; (D) Cleveland Morris; (C) Marla Jurglanis; (L) Bruce K. Morriss

Why the Lord Come to Sand Mountain, Romulus Linney; and ***The Second Shepherd's Play***, anonymous; (D) Cleveland Morris; (S) Eric Schaeffer; (C) Marla Jurglanis; (L) Bruce K. Morriss

The Tooth of Crime, Sam Shepard; (D) William Woodman; (S) Lewis Folden; (C) Marla Jurglanis; (L) Bruce K. Morriss

The Middle Ages, A.R. Gurney, Jr.; (D) Derek Wolsonak; (S) James F. Pyne, Jr.; (C) Marla Jurglanis; (L) Bruce K. Morriss

Eleemosynary, Lee Blessing; (D) Jamie Brown; (S) Eric Schaeffer; (C) Marla Jurglanis; (L) Bruce K. Morriss

Dell'Arte Players Company. Joan Schirle and Donald Forrest in *The Bacchae*. Photo: Pamela Lyall

Dell'Arte Players Company

MICHAEL FIELDS
DONALD FORREST
JOAN SCHIRLE
Co-Artistic Directors

Box 816
Blue Lake, CA 95525
(707) 668-5411 (bus.)
(707) 668-5782 (b.o.)

FOUNDED 1971
Jon Paul Cook, Michael Fields, Jane Hill, Carlo Mazzone-Clementi, Joan Schirle, Alain Schons, Jael Weisman

SEASON
Year-round

FACILITIES
Dell'Arte Studio
Seating capacity: 100
Stage: flexible

Dell'Arte Amphitheatre
Seating capacity: 200
Stage: thrust

FINANCES
Oct. 1, 1985-Sept. 30, 1986
Expenses: $214,175

CONTRACTS
AEA letter of agreement

The Dell'Arte Players Company is a rurally based touring theatre ensemble skilled in the physical theatre traditions. Our strength derives from a combination of professionalism, attention to craft and our non-urban point of view. Inspiration and themes for most of our major works have come from the region in which we live, where we have assisted in a cultural renaissance as timber resources dwindle and the arts emerge as a key economic component. Our major creative focus remains the creation of original works with strong textual values in a highly physical style. The integration of acting, text, music, movement and content is a primary goal of our ensemble process as we continue to expand the boundaries of physical theatre forms. Our core-company members are also experienced teachers who regularly offer workshops and residencies, as well as serving on the faculty of the Dell'Arte School of Physical Theatre, a fulltime professional training program in physical performance skills. The four core-company artists of Dell'Arte share a decade of collaborative work; it is their dedication to the ensemble process that creates the unique style which brings Dell'Arte world recognition.

—Joan Schirle

PRODUCTIONS 1985–86

Whiteman Meets Bigfoot, company-adapt; music: Tony Heimer; lyrics: Joan Schirle; (D) Jane Hill; (S) Alain Schons; (C) Nancy Betts; (L) Michael Foster

The Road Not Taken: A Scar Tissue Mystery, company-developed; (D) Jael Weisman; (S) Ivan Hess; (C) Nancy Betts; (L) Michael Foster

Malpractice or Love's the Best Doctor, company-adapt, from Molière; (D) Jael Weisman; (S) Andy Stacklin; (C) Mimi Mace; (L) Michael Foster

PRODUCTIONS 1986–87

The Bacchae, Euripides; company-adapt; (D) Jael Weisman; (S) Ivan Hess; (C) Jean Young; (L) Michael Foster

The Road Not Taken: A Scar Tissue Mystery, company-developed; (D) Jael Weisman; (S) Ivan Hess; (C) Nancy Betts; (L) Michael Foster

Malpractice or Love's the Best Doctor, company-adapt, from Molière; (D) Jael Weisman; (S) Andy Stacklin; (C) Mimi Mace; (L) Michael Foster

Denver Center Theatre Company

DONOVAN MARLEY
Artistic Director

SARAH LAWLESS
Executive Director

1050 13th St.
Denver, CO 80204
(303) 893-4200 (bus.)
(303) 893-4100 (b.o.)

FOUNDED 1980
Donald R. Seawell

SEASON
Sept.-June

FACILITIES
The Stage
Seating capacity: 550
Stage: thrust

The Space
Seating capacity: 450
Stage: arena

The Source
Seating capacity: 155
Stage: thrust

FINANCES
July 1, 1986-June 30, 1987
Expenses: $4,600,000

CONTRACTS
AEA LORT (C), (D) and SSD&C

The Denver Center Theatre Company is committed to producing both classic theatre and American plays, as well as to developing new works. The company's ninth season featured 12 plays and two school tours to state high schools and metropolitan-area elementary/middle schools. An integral part of DCTC is the National Theatre Conservatory, headed by Malcolm Morrison; the MFA program allows actors to work, train, develop

Denver Center Theatre Company. Eloise Laws in *House of Flowers*. Photo: Dan Fong.

and learn together in the nurturing atmosphere of a professional theatre, among professional theatre artists. Another important program, PrimaFacie, solicits scripts from playwrights around the country—of the hundreds of plays submitted up to 10 are presented as staged readings. Then, selected plays are fully produced during the next season's subscription series.

—Donovan Marley

PRODUCTIONS 1985–86

The Petrified Forest, Robert E. Sherwood; (D) Peter Hackett; (S) Robert Blackman; (C) Robert Blackman; (L) Michael W. Vennerstrom

Christmas Miracles, Laird Williamson and Dennis Powers; (D) Laird Williamson; (S) Laird Williamson and Andrew V. Yelusich; (C) Andrew V. Yelusich; (L) Wendy Heffner

The Emperor Jones, Eugene O'Neill; (D) Donald McKayle; (S) Richard L. Hay; (C) Andrew V. Yelusich; (L) Michael W. Vennerstrom

The Cherry Orchard, Anton Chekhov; trans: Jean-Claude van Itallie; (D) Garland Wright; (S) Douglas Stein; (C) Ann Hould-Ward; (L) Peter Maradudin

Pygmalion, George Bernard Shaw; (D) James Moll; (S) Richard L. Hay; (C) Andrew V. Yelusich; (L) Wendy Heffner

Purlie, book: Ossie Davis, Philip Rose and Peter Udell; lyrics: Peter Udell; music: Gary Geld; (D) Randal Myler; (S) Richard L. Hay; (C) Andrew V. Yelusich; (L) Michael W. Vennerstrom

The Immigrant: A Hamilton County Album, Mark Harelik; conceived: Randal Myler and Mark Harelik; (D) Randal Myler; (S) Kevin Rupnik; (C) Andrew V. Yelusich; (L) Wendy Heffner

Circe & Bravo, Donald Freed; (D) Laird Williamson; (S) Andrew V. Yelusich; (C) Andrew V. Yelusich; (L) Wendy Heffner

A Woman Without a Name, Romulus Linney; (D) Donovan Marley; (S) Robert Blackman; (C) Robert Blackman; (L) Michael W. Vennerstrom

When the Sun Slides, Stephen Davis Parks; (D) Donovan Marley; (S) Catherine Poppe; (C) Janet S. Morris; (L) Wendy Heffner

Pleasuring Ground, Frank X. Hogan; (D) Peter Hackett; (S) John Dexter; (C) Janet S. Morris; (L) Michael W. Vennerstrom

Hope of the Future, Shannon Keith Kelley; (D) Randal Myler; (S) Pavel Dobrusky; (C) Andrew V. Yelusich; (L) Michael W. Vennerstrom

PRODUCTIONS 1986–87

South Pacific, book and lyrics: Oscar Hammerstein II and Joshua Logan; music: Richard Rodgers; (D) Donovan Marley; (S) Richard L. Hay; (C) Jeannie Davidson; (L) Wendy Heffner

House of Flowers, book: Truman Capote; music: Harold Arlen; lyrics: Truman Capote and Harold Arlen; (D) Donald McKayle; (S) Richard L. Hay; (C) Andrew V. Yelusich; (L) Michael W. Vennerstrom

Shooting Stars, Molly Newman; (D) Randal Myler; (S) Richard L. Hay; (C) Janet S. Morris; (L) Wendy Heffner

Man and Superman, George Bernard Shaw; (D) Dakin Matthews; (S) Ralph Funicello; (C) Andrew V. Yelusich; (L) Michael W. Vennerstrom

Don Juan in Hell, George Bernard Shaw; (D) Anne McNaughton; (S) Ralph Funicello; (C) Andrew V. Yelusich; (L) Michael W. Vennerstrom

The Playboy of the Western World, John Millington Synge; (D) Donovan Marley; (S) Kevin Rupnik; (C) Andrew V. Yelusich; (L) Wendy Heffner

Coriolanus, William Shakespeare; (D) Laird Williamson; (S) Laird Williamson and Andrew V.. Yelusich; (C) Andrew V. Yelusich; (L) Wendy Heffner

Lost Highway: The Music and Legend of Hank Williams, Randal Myler and Mark Harelik; (D) Randal Myler; (S) Richard L. Hay; (C) Andrew V. Yelusich; (L) Charles McLeod

Goodnight, Texas, Terry Dodd; (D) Bruce K. Sevy; (S) Pavel M. Dobrusky; (L) Wendy Heffner

The World of Mirth, Murphy Guyer; (D) Peter Hackett; (S) Pavel M. Dobrusky; (C) Pavel M. Dobrusky; (L) Wendy Heffner

Rachel's Fate, Larry Ketron; (D) Murphy Guyer; (S) John Dexter; (C) John Dexter; (L) Michael W. Vennerstrom

Orphans, Lyle Kessler; (D) Frank Georgianna; (S) Kent Dorsey; (C) Janet S. Morris; (L) Michael W. Vennerstrom

Detroit Repertory Theatre. Henrietta Hermelin and Robert Grossman in *Days and Nights Within.*

Detroit Repertory Theatre

BRUCE E. MILLAN
Artistic Director

ROBERT WILLIAMS
Executive Director

13103 Woodrow Wilson Ave.
Detroit, MI 48238
(313) 868-1347

FOUNDED 1957
T.O. Andrus, Barbara Busby, Bruce E. Millan

SEASON
Nov.-June

FACILITIES
Seating capacity: 196
Stage: proscenium

FINANCES
Jan. 1, 1986-Dec. 31, 1986
Expenses: $260,156

CONTRACTS
AEA SPT

The Detroit Repertory's purpose over the past 29 years has been to build a first-class professional theatre by assembling a resident company of theatre artists recruited from among local professionals in the field; to seed new plays, perform known plays in new ways, and bring worthwhile, forgotten plays back to life; to expand the creative possibilities of theatre by increasing the opportunities for participation of all artists regardless of their ethnic or racial origins or gender; to reach out to initiate the uninitiated; to build a theatre operation that is "close to the people" and to act as a catalyst for the revitalization of the neighborhood in which the theatre resides; and, to attract audiences reflecting the cultural and ethnic diversity of southeastern Michigan. The Repertory received the Governor's Award for outstanding achievement in May 1986.

—Bruce E. Millan

PRODUCTIONS 1985–86

Mendola's Rose, Robert Unger; (D) Von H. Washington; (S) Marylynn Kacir; (C) Anne Saunders; (L) Kenneth R. Hewitt, Jr.

Souvenirs, Sheldon Rosen; (D) Barbara Busby; (S) Bruce E. Millan; (C) Anne Saunders; (L) Kenneth R. Hewitt, Jr.

The Adventures of Stanley Tomorrow, Alan Foster Friedman; (D) Divina Cook; (S) Bruce E. Millan; (C) Anne Saunders; (L) Kenneth R. Hewitt, Jr.

A Touch of the Poet, Eugene O'Neill; (D) Bruce E. Millan; (S) Bruce E. Millan; (C) Anne

Saunders; (L) Kenneth R. Hewitt, Jr.

PRODUCTIONS 1986–87

Heart of a Dog, Mikhail Bulgakov; adapt: Frank Galati; (D) Bruce E. Millan; (S) Bruce E. Millan; (C) Anne Saunders; (L) Kenneth R. Hewitt, Jr.
Days and Nights Within, Ellen McLaughlin; (D) Dee Andrus; (S) Bruce E. Millan; (C) Anne Saunders; (L) Kenneth R. Hewitt, Jr.
Waiting for Godot, Samuel Beckett; (D) Barbara Busby; (S) Peter Knox; (C) Anne Saunders; (L) Kenneth R. Hewitt, Jr.
Time Capsule, Paul Simpson; (D) Bruce E. Millan; (S) Bruce E. Millan; (C) B.J. Essen; (L) Kenneth R. Hewitt, Jr.

Dorset Theatre Festival

JILL CHARLES
Artistic Director

JOHN NASSIVERA
Producing Director

Box 519
Dorset, VT 05251
(802) 867-2223 (bus.)
(802) 867-5777 (b.o.)

FOUNDED 1976
Jill Charles, John Nassivera

SEASON
June-Sept.

FACILITIES
The Dorset Playhouse
Seating capacity: 218
Stage: proscenium

FINANCES
Jan. 1, 1986-Dec. 31, 1987
Expenses: $241,981

CONTRACTS
AEA SPT

The Dorset Theatre Festival produces an annual summer season at the Dorset Playhouse that usually includes five or six contemporary American and British plays as well as revivals of American classics and at least one new play. Over the past 12 seasons, the company has built up a pool of New York-based directors, designers, technicians and actors to draw from, and new talent is added each year. The Festival's educational arm serves the theatre profession in two ways: through its outstanding apprentice program, offering Actors' Equity membership credit and a focus on career development, and through publication of two annual employment resources, *Summer Theatre Directory* and *Regional Theatre Directory*, as well as the *Directory of Theatre Training Programs*. The Dorset Colony House provides living and office space for the Festival from June through September; from September through May it becomes an artists' colony, offering writers (particularly playwrights) a retreat for intensive periods of work.

—Jill Charles

Dorset Theatre Festival. Allan Coates and Frank Anderson in *Down an Alley Filled with Cats*. Photo: William John Aupperlee.

East West Players. Darrell Kunitomi, Benjamin Lum and Timothy Dang in *Rashomon*. Photo: Chris Komura.

PRODUCTIONS 1986

The Only Game in Town, Frank Gilroy; (D) Edgar Lansbury; (S) William John Aupperlee; (C) Deanna Majewski; (L) Timothy Foley
Tintypes, Mary Kyte, Mel Marvin and Gary Pearle; (D) Jill Charles; (S) William John Aupperlee; (C) Deanna Majewski; (L) Timothy Foley
The Orchard, John Nassivera; (D) Jill Charles; (S) William John Aupperlee; (C) Deanna Majewski; (L) Vincent Donvito
The Foreigner, Larry Shue; (D) John Morrison; (S) William John Aupperlee; (C) Deanna Majewski; (L) Timothy Foley
Down an Alley Filled with Cats, Warwick Moss; (D) John Wood; (S) William John Aupperlee; (C) Deanna Majewski; (L) Timothy Foley

PRODUCTIONS 1987

Mass Appeal, Bill C. Davis; (D) Mark S. Ramont; (S) William John Aupperlee; (C) Mary Marsicano; (L) Jeff Bernstein
Without Apologies, Thom Thomas; (D) Edgar Lansbury; (S) William John Aupperlee; (C) Mary Marsicano; (L) Jeff Bernstein
A Thousand Clowns, Herb Gardner; (D) Jill Charles; (S) William John Aupperlee; (C) Mary Marsicano; (L) Jeff Bernstein
Taking Steps, Alan Ayckbourn; (D) John Morrison; (S) William John Aupperlee; (C) Mary Marsicano; (L) Jeff Bernstein
My Three Angels, Bella Spewack and Samuel Spewack; (D) John Morrison; (S) William John Aupperlee; (C) Mary Marsicano; (L) Jeff Bernstein

East West Players

MAKO
Producing Artistic Director

JANET MITSUI
Administrator

4424 Santa Monica Blvd.
Los Angeles, CA 90029
(213) 660-0366

FOUNDED 1965
James Hong, June Kim, Guy Lee, Pat Li, Yet Lock, Mako, Beulah Quo

SEASON
Oct.-July

FACILITIES
Seating capacity: 99
Stage: flexible

FINANCES
July 1, 1985-June 30, 1986
Expenses: $150,000

CONTRACTS
AEA TYA

Asian/Pacific Americans have gone through a period of anger and frustration—feelings springing from the reality that Asian/Pacific Americans have never fully acknowledged their own existence. Because "belonging" is paramount in our modern society, the Asian/Pacific American has exercised a certain amount of self-hatred because of physical differences —the skin is yellow, the eyes are slanted, the hair is straight, and in some cases, English is spoken with an accent. The time has come, however, to stop this self-recrimination. We Asian/Pacific Americans must acknowledge and celebrate our existence. Our goal at East West Players is to preserve and express a language, literature and sound of our own by developing an Asian-American theatre that is vital, truthful and alive.

—Mako

PRODUCTIONS 1985–86

Christmas in Camp II, Dom Magwili and Keone Young; conceived: Mako; (D) Mako and Shizuko Hoshi; (S) Gong Taa; (C) Terence Tam Soon; (L) Rae Creevey

The Memento, Wakako Yamauchi; (D) Mako; (S) Gong Taa; (L) Rae Creevey

Rashomon, adapt: Fay Kanin and Michael Kanin, from Ryunosike Akutagawa; (D) Shizuko Hoshi; (S) Gong Taa; (C) Rodney Kageyama; (L) Rae Creevey

PRODUCTIONS 1986–87

Chikamatsu's Forest, Edward Sakamoto; (D) Shizuko Hoshi; (S) Mako; (C) Terence Tam Soon; (L) Rae Creevey

The Gambling Den, Akemi Kikumura; (D) Mako; (S) Christopher Komuro; (C) Pikke Allen; (L) Rae Creevey

Wong Bow Rides Again, Cherylene Lee; (D) Josie Pepito Kim and Leigh C. Kim; (S) G. Shizuko Herrera; (C) Sylvia Wong; (L) Rae Creevey

The Medium, book and music: Gian Carlo Menotti; (D) Mako; (S) Mako; (C) Rodney Kageyama; (L) Rae Creevey

The Lady of Larkspur, ***Lotion*** and ***Hello from Bertha***, Tennessee Williams; (D) Betty Muramoto; (S) Mako; (C) Rodney Kageyama; (L) Rae Creevey

Hughie, Eugene O'Neill; (D) Alberto Isaac; (S) Mako; (C) Rodney Kageyama; (L) Rae Creevey

The Zoo Story, Edward Albee; (D) Shizuko Hoshi; (S) Mako; (C) Rodney Kageyama; (L) Rae Creevey

Emmy Gifford Children's Theater

JAMES LARSON
Artistic Director

MARK HOEGER
Executive Director

3504 Center St.
Omaha, NE 68105
(402) 345-4852 (bus.)
(402) 345-4849 (b.o.)

FOUNDED 1949
Emmy Gifford, 19 child-advocacy agencies

SEASON
Sept.-May

FACILITIES
Gifford Theater
Seating capacity: 525
Stage: proscenium

FINANCES
June 1, 1986-May 31, 1987
Expenses: $507,000

At the Emmy Gifford Children's Theater we believe that children's theatre is an exciting and suitable performance mode for experimentation. Children have different psychological and aesthetic needs from those of adults, primarily because a child's cerebral design is synaptically more active. For children, fantasy and anti-realism are the *norm*. Thus, artists in children's theatre have startling freedom in the theatrical choices they can make to break out of the straight-jacket of stultifying, ossified realism—the traditional theoretical and formal style out of which most U.S. theatre artists have developed.

—James Larson

Note: During the 1985-86 season, Bill Kirk served as artistic director.

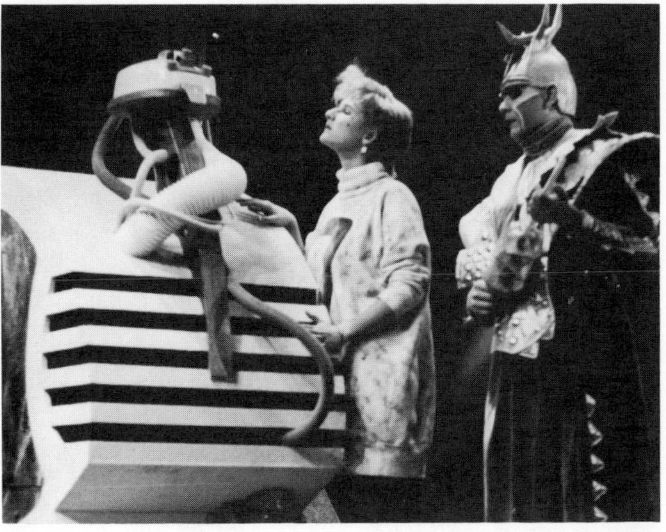

Emmy Gifford's Children's Theater. Debbie Shannon and Wes Bailey in *Jackie Omaha Goes to Mars*. Photo: Cathy Cantor.

PRODUCTIONS 1985–86

The Velveteen Rabbit, adapt: James Still, from Margery Williams; (D) James Larson; (S) Steve Wheeldon; (C) Sherri Geerdes; (L) Steve Wheeldon

Jackie Omaha Goes to Mars, James Larson; (D) Mark Hoeger; (S) Tim Hantula; (C) Sherri Geerdes; (L) Steve Wheeldon

Annie, book: Thomas Meehan; lyrics: Martin Charnin; music: Charles Strouse; (D) Bill Kirk; (S) Steve Wheeldon; (C) Sherri Geerdes; (L) Steve Wheeldon

The Return of Johnny Appleseed, book: James Larson; music and lyrics: Debby Greenblatt and David Seay; (D) Michele Phillips; (S) Tim Hantula; (C) Sherri Geerdes; (L) Laura M. Offerdahl

The Sword of the Stone: The Making of King Arthur, book, music and lyrics: Gail Irwin; (D) James Larson; (S) Tim Hantula; (C) Sherri Geerdes and Mark Lobsinger; (L) Steve Wheeldon

The Adventures of Little Bear, adapt: Bill Kirk, from Else Minarik; (D) Bill Kirk; (S) Tim Hantula; (C) Sherri Geerdes; (L) Laura M. Offerdahl

PRODUCTIONS 1986–87

Where the Wild Things Are, adapt: Bill Kirk, from Maurice Sendak; (D) Bill Kirk; (S) Steve Wheeldon; (C) Sherri Geerdes; (L) Steve Wheeldon

Our Town, Thornton Wilder; (D) Bill Kirk; (S) John Wolf; (C) Sherri Geerdes; (L) John Wolf

The Wizard of Oz, adapt: Frank Gabrielson, from L. Frank Baum; music and lyrics: Harold Arlen and E.Y. Harburg; (D) Mark Hoeger; (S) Steve Wheeldon; (C) Sherri Geerdes; (L) Steve Wheeldon

The Lion, the Witch and the Wardrobe, adapt: Don Quinn, from C.S. Lewis; (D) Roberta Larson; (S) Gregg Hill; (C) Tanya Lee; (L) Steve Wheeldon

Pinocchio, adapt: Nancy Duncan, from Carlo Collodi; (D) James Larson; (S) Mary Lynn Vocelka; (C) Tanya Lee and Sherri Geerdes; (L) Bob Welk

The Adventure of Amelia Bedelia, Ann Triba Dittrick; adapt: Peggy Parish; (D) Bill Kirk; (S) Steve Wheeldon; (C) Sherri Geerdes; (L) Steve Wheeldon

Empire State Institute for the Performing Arts

PATRICIA B. SNYDER
Producing Director

Empire State Plaza
Albany, NY 12223
(518) 443-5222 (bus.)
(518) 443-5111 (b.o.)

Empire State Institute for the Performing Arts. David Bunce and Jeanne Vigliante in *The Mousetrap*. Photo: Tim Raab/Northern Photo.

FOUNDED 1976
Empire State Youth Theatre Institute (State University of New York), Governor Nelson A. Rockefeller Empire State Plaza Performing Arts Center Corporation, Patricia B. Snyder

SEASON
Sept.-June

FACILITIES
Mainstage
Seating capacity: 900
Stage: flexible

Studio Theatre
Seating capacity: 450
Stage: thrust

FINANCES
Apr. 1, 1986-Mar. 31, 1987
Expenses: $2,645,688

CONTRACTS
AEA TYA

The Empire State Institute for the Performing Arts aspires to nurture tomorrow's theatre today. By enriching the lives of our youthful and family audiences through an active blending of professional theatre and education, ESIPA strives to develop its audiences's critical sensibilities through the discovery of the wonder of the human spirit, as expressed by the inner truth of the theatre. A combination of theatre excellence, a "values education" program complementary to the schools' curricula, cultural exchange and a demonstrated commitment to the development of new works are the hallmarks of ESIPA's mission.

—*Patricia B. Snyder*

PRODUCTIONS 1985–86

Rag Dolly, book: William Gibson; music and lyrics: Joe Raposo; (D) Patricia Birch; (S) Gerry Hariton and Vicki Baral; (C) Carrie Robbins; (L) Marc B. Weiss

Verdict, Agatha Christie; (D) John Vreeke; (S) Victor A. Becker; (C) Judy Dearing; (L) Ann G. Wrightson

An Imaginary Report on an American Rock Festival, adapt: Sandor Pos, from Tibor Dery; trans: W.A. Frankonis; music: Gabor Presser; lyrics: Anna Adamis; (D) Rose Deak; (S) Loren Sherman; (C) Karen Kammer; (L) Victor En Yu Tan

A Class "C" Trial in Yokohama, Roger Cornish; (D) Ed Lange; (S) Anne Gibson; (C) Gregg A. Barnes; (L) Victor En Yu Tan

Great Expectations, adapt: Barbara Field, from Charles Dickens; (D) Terence Lamude; (S) Wynn Thomas; (C) Barbara Forbes; (L) Frances Aronson

PRODUCTIONS 1986–87

Possession: The Murder at Cherry Hill, Sidney Michaels; (D) John Going; (S) Stuart Wurtzel; (C) William Schroder; (L) John McLain

A Christmas Carol, adapt: Amlin Gray, from Charles Dickens; (D) Ed Lange; (S) Duke Durfee; (C) Karen Kammer; (L) Ann G. Wrightson

The Mousetrap, Agatha Christie; (D) Terence Lamude; (S) John Wright Stevens; (C) Gregg A. Barnes; (L) Ann G. Wrightson

Amadeus, Peter Shaffer; (D) W.A. Frankonis; (S) Richard Finkelstein; (C) Brent Griffin; (L) Lloyd S. Riford, III

Aladdin, book: Elisabeth Ruthman; music: Dennis Buck; lyrics: Elisabeth Ruthman and Dennis Buck; (D) Peter Webb; (S) Alexander Okun; (C) Alexander Okun; (L) Victor En Yu Tan

The Empty Space Theatre

M. BURKE WALKER
Artistic Director

MELISSA HINES
Managing Director

95 South Jackson
Seattle, WA 98104
(206) 587-3737 (bus.)
(206) 467-6000 (b.o.)

FOUNDED 1970
James Royce, Julian Schembri, M. Burke Walker, Charles Younger

SEASON
Oct.-June

FACILITIES
Seating capacity: 275
Stage: flexible

FINANCES
July 1, 1986-June 30, 1987
Expenses: $824,500

CONTRACTS
AEA letter of agreement

The Empty Space Theatre. Jayne Muirhead, Michael James Smith and Marva Scott in *The Rocky Horror Show*. Photo: Fred Andrews.

The Empty Space Theatre is a home for theatre artists wanting to explore a vigorous, nontraditional mix of new plays, new playwrights, out-of-the-mainstream classics and vulgar (from the Latin *vulgaris*) low comedy. Peter Handke, Henry Fielding and Sam Shepard happily co-existed in our first season, as did *The Rocky Horror Show*, *Don Juan* and *Aunt Dan and Lemon* in our 17th. We continue to dedicate ourselves to the development and presentation of new works on our main stage, such as *Gloria Duplex*, by Rebecca Wells, and the commissioned adaptation of Sabatini's *Scaramouche*, scheduled to open our 1987-88 season. In fall 1984, we began producing in a new, flexible black-box theatre, seating 200-275. Retaining its essential intimacy, the Empty Space is now large enough at 70' x 70' x 20' to allow for dynamic, theatrical staging on an epic scale.

—*M. Burke Walker*

Note: During the 1985-86 season, Richard Allan Edwards served as acting artistic director.

PRODUCTIONS 1985–86

Boesman and Lena, Athol Fugard; (D) Bruce Siddons; (S) Christopher H. Barreca; (C) Anne Thaxter Watson; (L) Richard Devin

Sex Over Easy: The Aerobic Musical, book: Janet Thomas; music: Page Wheeler; lyrics: Jean Burch Falls; (D) Richard Allan Edwards and Susan Glass-Burdick; (S) Thomas M. Fichter; (C) Frances Kenny; (L) Jennifer Lupton

Fen, Caryl Churchill; (D) Rita Giomi; (S) Lynn Graves; (C) Anne Thaxter Watson; (L) Jeff Robbins

Queen of Hearts, Anthony F. Doyle; (D) Stephen Rosenfield; (S) Jennifer Lupton; (C) Rose Pederson; (L) Michael Davidson

American Buffalo, David Mamet; (D) Richard Allan Edwards; (S) Bill Forrester; (C) Celeste Cleveland; (L) Jeff Robbins

On the Verge or The Geography of Yearning, Eric Overmyer; (D) Craig T. Latrell; (S) Karen Gjelsteen; (C) Sally Richardson; (L) Rick Paulsen

PRODUCTIONS 1986–87

The Rocky Horror Show, book, music and lyrics: Richard O'Brien; (D) M. Burke Walker; (S) Michael Olich; (C) Michael Murphy; (L) Michael Davidson

Have You Anything to Declare?, Maurice Hennequin and Pierre Veber; trans: Robert Cogo-Fawcett and Braham Murray; (D) Robert Moss; (S) Scott Weldin; (C) Sally Richardson; (L) Michael Davidson

Don Juan, Molière; trans: Richard Nelson; (D) M. Burke Walker; (S) Scott Weldin; (C) Sally Richardson; (L) Rick Paulsen

Aunt Dan and Lemon, Wallace Shawn; (D) Craig T. Latrell; (S) Karen Gjelsteen; (C) Rose Pederson; (L) Rick Paulsen

Gloria Duplex, Rebecca Wells; (D) M. Burke Walker; (S) Bill Forrester; (C) Nina Moser; (L) Michael Davidson

The Ensemble Studio Theatre

CURT DEMPSTER
Artistic Director

BRIAN BERK
General Manager

549 West 52nd St.
New York, NY 10019
(212) 247-4982 (bus.)
(212) 247-3405 (b.o.)

FOUNDED 1971
Curt Dempster

SEASON
Oct.-June

FACILITIES
Mainstage
Seating capacity: 99
Stage: flexible

Studio
Seating capacity: 60
Stage: flexible

FINANCES
July 1, 1986-June 30, 1987
Expenses: $820,000

CONTRACTS
AEA letter of agreement

Founded in 1971, the Ensemble Studio Theatre remains dedicated to its original mission of nurturing theatre artists, with particular focus on the development and introduction of new American plays by emerging and established playwrights. The Ensemble has been an ecological cause—not just theatre, but a daily challenge to create new plays and keep them alive in an increasingly uncertain environment. The emphasis is on process—whether in the writing of a play or in the creation of a role—rather than product. All the works produced on the Ensemble's main stage are world premieres and have gone through several stages of development including readings, staged readings and workshops. The need of the individual work determines the method and manner of its development. The Ensemble's impact continues to be felt through our annual Marathon festival of new one-act plays and by the more than 360 productions throughout the country of full-length plays first developed at the Ensemble.

—*Curt Dempster*

The Ensemble Studio Theatre. Grace Zabriskie and Bill Cobbs in *Rose Cottages*. Photo: Valerie Brea Ross.

PRODUCTIONS 1985–86

Dennis, James Ryan; (D) Dan Bonnell; (S) James Wolk; (C) Deborah Shaw; (L) Karl Haas

Been Taken, Roger Hedden; (D) Billy Hopkins; (S) Bob Barnett; (C) Isis C. Mussenden; (L) Greg MacPherson

The Tale of Madame Zora, book and lyrics: Aishah Rahman; music: Olu Dara; (D) Glenda Dickerson; (S) Charles H. McClennahan; (C) Sydney Inis; (L) Marshall Williams

Rose Cottages, Bill Bozzone; (D) Risa Bramon; (S) Irene Kaufman; (C) Deborah Shaw; (L) Greg MacPherson

Marathon '86:

Sunday Morning Vivisection, Elise Caitlin; (D) Leslie Ayvazian; (S) Daniel Proett; (C) Deborah Shaw; (L) Greg MacPherson

The Worker's Life, Brandon Cole and John Turturro; (D) Aidan Quinn; (S) Daniel Proett; (C) Deborah Shaw; (L) Greg MacPherson

Blind Date, Horton Foote; (D) Curt Dempster; (S) Daniel Proett; (C) Deborah Shaw; (L) Greg MacPherson

Mink on a Gold Hook, James Ryan; (D) Jack Gelber; (S) Daniel Proett; (C) Deborah Shaw; (L) Greg MacPherson

Vanishing Act, Richard Greenberg; (D) Jeff Perry; (S) Daniel Proett; (C) Isis C. Mussenden; (L) Greg MacPherson

Terry Neal's Future, Roger Hedden; (D) Billy Hopkins; (S) Daniel Proett; (C) Isis C. Mussenden; (L) Greg MacPherson

The West Side Boys Will Rock You Anywhere, Shirley Kaplan; (D) Billy Hopkins; (S) Daniel Proett; (C) Isis C. Mussenden; (L) Greg MacPherson

Comic Dialogue, Alan Zwiebel; (D) Risa Bramon; (S) Daniel Proett; (C) Isis Mussenden; (L) Greg MacPherson

Dolores, Edward Allan Baker; (D) Risa Bramon; (S) Daniel Proett; (C) Martha Hally; (L) Greg MacPherson

Ma Rose, Cassandra Medley; (D) Irving Vincent; (S) Daniel Proett; (C) Martha Hally; (L) Greg MacPherson

Little Feet, Shel Silverstein; (D) Art Wolff; (S) Daniel Proett; (C) Martha Hally; (L) Greg MacPherson

Moonlight Kisses, Stuart Spencer; (D) Barnet Kellman; (S) Daniel Proett; (C) Martha Hally; (L) Greg MacPherson

PRODUCTIONS 1986–87

Dream of a Blacklisted Actor, Conrad Bromberg; (D) Jack Gelber; (S) Steve Saklad; (C) Deborah Shaw; (L) Karl Haas

Cleveland and Half-way Back, Leslie Lyles; (D) James Hammerstein; (S) Richard Harmon; (C) David Woolard; (L) Tina Ann Byers

Mama Drama, Leslie Ayvazian, Donna Daley, Christine Farrell, Marianna Houston, Rita Nachtmann, Anne O'Sullivan and Ann Sachs; (D) Pamela Berlin; (S) Philipp Jung; (C) Lindsay W. Davis; (L) Jackie Manassee

Marathon '87:

The One About the Guy in the Bar, Ernest Thompson; (D) Curt Dempster; (S) Lewis Folden; (C) Deborah Shaw; (L) Greg MacPherson

The Author's Voice, Richard Greenberg; (D) Evan Yionoulis; (S) Lewis Folden; (C) Deborah Shaw; (L) Greg MacPherson

The Last Outpost at the Edge of the World, Stuart Spencer; (D) Shirley Kaplan; (S) Lewis Folden; (C) Deborah Shaw; (L) Greg MacPherson

A Million Dollar Glass of Water, Anthony McKay; (D) Joel Bernstein; (S) Lewis Folden; (C) Deborah Shaw; (L) Greg MacPherson

Lady of Fadima, Edward Allan Baker; (D) Risa Bramon; (S) Lewis Folden; (C) Michael S. Schler; (L) Greg MacPherson

Dinah Washington Is Dead, Kermit Frazier; (D) Fred Tyson; (S) Lewis Folden; (C) Michael S. Schler; (L) Greg MacPherson

A Ripe Banana, Jennifer Lombard; (D) W.H. Macy; (S) Lewis Folden; (C) Michael S. Schler; (L) Greg MacPherson

Afterschool Special, Keith Reddin; (D) Billy Hopkins; (S) Lewis Folden; (C) Michael S. Schler; (L) Greg MacPherson

All for Charity, John Patrick Shanley; (D) Willie Reale; (S) Lewis Folden; (C) Michael S. Schler; (L) Greg MacPherson

Real to Reel, Frank D. Gilroy; (D) Curt Dempster; (S) Lewis Folden; (C) Bruce Goodrich; (L) Greg MacPherson

April Snow, Romulus Linney; (D) David Margulies; (S) Lewis Folden; (C) Bruce Goodrich; (L) Greg MacPherson

Bad Blood, Peter Maloney; (D) Peter Maloney; (S) Lewis Folden; (C) Bruce Goodrich; (L) Greg MacPherson

Waking Women, Cassandra Medley; (D) Irving Vincent; (S) Lewis Folden; (C) Bruce Goodrich; (L) Greg MacPherson

Eureka Theatre Company

ANTHONY TACCONE
Artistic Director

TIMOTHY STEVENSON
Managing Director

2730 16th St.
San Francisco, CA 94103
(415) 558-9811 (bus.)
(415) 558-9898 (b.o.)

FOUNDED 1972
Chris Silva, Robert Woodruff

SEASON
Sept.-June

FACILITIES
Seating capacity: 200
Stage: flexible

FINANCES
July 1, 1986-June 30, 1987
Expenses: $631,000

CONTRACTS
AEA letter of agreement

Eureka Theatre Company. Joe Bellan and Geoff Hoyle in *Ubu Unchained*. Photo: Cristina Taccone.

The Eureka Theatre company is dedicated to producing gutsy plays that deal directly with political and social issues. Artists have the right and responsibility to analyze, criticize and reinvent the world in which we live, and to engage our audience in a critical dialogue about social change. Our focus is moving increasingly toward new work: we have commissioned Amlin Gray's *Ubu Unchained*, Geoff Hoyle's *Boomer!*, Emily Mann's *Execution of Justice* and Ellen McLaughlin's *A Narrow Bed*—developed extensively by our dramaturgical staff. We are also committed to producing work which reflects the cultural and ethnic diversity of San Francisco—Philip Gotanda's *The Wash* and *Roosters* by Milcha Sanchez-Scott address important issues for Asian and Hispanic people, respectively. We also have made a long-term effort to use our stage to tell stories about people of color and to employ multiethnic casts. The remainder of our artistic agenda consists of plays by contemporary political writers—the work of Athol Fugard, Caryl Churchill, David Edgar and Dario Fo is regularly featured on our stage. By pursuing our artistic interests and ideological beliefs we hope to create an exciting and important body of work, one that will have an extended life and serve the larger regional theatre movement in this country.

—*Anthony Taccone*

PRODUCTIONS 1985–86

About Face, Dario Fo; trans: Dale McAdoo and Charles Mann; (D) Richard Seyd; (S) Peggy Snider; (C) Jennifer Q. Smith; (L) Thomas Stocker

Fen, Caryl Churchill; (D) Anthony Taccone; (S) Peggy Snider; (C) Patricia Polen; (L) Jack Carpenter

Gardenia, John Guare; (D) Susan Marsden; (S) Andy Stacklin; (C) Roberta Yuen; (L) Kurt Landisman

The Cherry Orchard, Anton Chekhov; adapt: Trevor Griffiths; (D) Oskar Eustis; (S) William Eddelman; (C) William Eddelman; (L) Barbara Du Bois

Boomer: Geoff Hoyle Meets Geoff Hoyle, Geoff Hoyle and Anthony Taccone; (D) Anthony Taccone; (S) Peggy Snider; (C) Peggy Snider; (L) Kurt Landisman

Every Moment, Oyamo; (D) Richard Seyd; (S) Adam Scher; (C) Paige Philips Cook; (L) Ellen Shireman

The Island, Athol Fugard, John Kani and Winston Ntshona; (D) Richard Seyd; (S) Adam Scher; (C) Paige Philips Cook; (L) Ellen Shireman

PRODUCTIONS 1986–87

Ubu Unchained, Alfred Jarry; adapt: Amlin Gray; (D) Anthony Taccone; (S) Peggy Snider; (C) Lydia Tanji; (L) Jack Carpenter

A Narrow Bed, Ellen McLaughlin; (D) Oskar Eustis; (S) Kate Edmunds; (C) Paige Philips Cook; (L) Ellen Shireman

An Open Couple, Dario Fo; trans: Stuart Hood; adapt: Joan Holden and Ron Jenkins; (D) Susan Marsden; (S) Andy Stacklin; (C) Roberta Yuen; (L) Kurt Landisman

The Wash, Philip Kan Gotanda; (D) Richard Seyd; (S) Barbara Mesney; (C) Roberta Yuen; (L) Ellen Shireman

Danny and the Deep Blue Sea, John Patrick Shanley; (D) Oskar Eustis; (S) Andy Stacklin; (C) Beaver Bauer; (L) Ellen Shireman

The Kathy & Mo Show, Kathy Najimy and Mo Gaffney; (D) Jim Simpson; (S) David Ford; (C) Kathy Najimy; (L) Ellen Shireman

The Fiji Company. *The Angels of Swedenborg.* Photo: Bob Shamus.

The Fiji Company

PING CHONG
Artistic Director

JOE M. JEFCOAT
Managing Director

253 Church St.
New York, NY 10013
(212) 966-0284

FOUNDED 1975
Ping Chong

SEASON
Variable

FINANCES
July 1, 1986-June 30, 1987
Expenses: $133,462

Created out of a desire to address and incorporate the technical means, as well as the global changes that the technological revolution has engendered, the Fiji Company continues to explore the meaning of "contemporary theatre" on the national and international level. In brief, the Fiji Company was established to question the syntax of traditional theatre: If theatre is to survive, instead of competing with the cinema, television and pop concerts, it must paradoxically reinstate the fundamental idea of theatre as a metaphysical place rather than as a poor imitation of the naturalism that film and television can more readily achieve. Yet at the same time, theatre must acknowledge and incorporate this new perceptual syntax into our "brave new world." The Fiji Company has also expanded into the filmmaking and visual arts arenas in our continuing dialogue with the development of art and culture in the late 20th century.

—Ping Chong

PRODUCTIONS 1985–86

Kind Ness, Ping Chong; (D) Ping Chong; (S) Ping Chong; (C) Mel Carpenter; (L) Blu

The Angels of Swedenborg, Ping Chong; (D) Ping Chong; (S) Ping Chong; (C) Mel Carpenter; (L) Blu

The Games, Ping Chong and Meredith Monk; music: Meredith Monk; (D) Meredith Monk and Ping Chong; (S) Yoshio Yabara; (C) Yoshio Yabara; (L) Beverly Emmons

Astonishment and the Twins, Ping Chong and company; text: Louise Smith and Ping Chong; music: Brian Hallas; (D) Ping Chong; (S) Mel Carpenter; (C) Mel Carpenter

A.M./A.M. The Articulated Man, Ping Chong; film score: Meredith Monk; (D) Ping Chong; (S) Paul Krajniak and Ping Chong; (C) Kim Druce and Louise Smith; (L) Blu

Rainer and the Knife, Ping Chong and Rob List; (D) Ping Chong and Rob List; (S) Paul Krajniak

PRODUCTIONS 1986–87

Angels of Swedenborg, Ping Chong; (D) Ping Chong; (S) Ping Chong; (C) Mel Carpenter; (L) Blu

Nosferatu, Ping Chong and company; (D) Ping Chong; (S) Ping Chong; (C) Mel Carpenter

The Travelogue Series, text: Ping Chong; music: Meredith Monk; (D) Ping Chong; (S) Ping Chong; (C) Annemarie Hollander; (L) Beverly Emmons

Astonishment and the Twins, Ping Chong and company; (D) Ping Chong and John Fleming; (S) Ping Chong, Peter Boles and Mel Carpenter; (C) Mel Carpenter; (L) Joe M. Jefcoat

Florida Studio Theatre

RICHARD HOPKINS
Artistic Director

JOHN JACOBSEN
General Manager

1241 North Palm Ave.
Sarasota, FL 34236
(813) 366-9017 (bus.)
(813) 366-9796 (b.o.)

FOUNDED 1973
Jon Spelman

SEASON
Dec.-June

FACILITIES
Seating capacity: 165
Stage: modified thrust

FINANCES
July 1, 1986-June 30, 1987
Expenses: $605,000

CONTRACTS
AEA SPT

Florida Studio Theatre was founded in 1973 by Jon Spelman and toured original and avant-garde works to audiences throughout the southeastern states—in prisons, migrant camps, colleges, hospitals and nontraditional locales. In 1980, Spelman passed me the reins of artistic leadership and the direction of the theatre changed: touring was minimized, and increased focus and energy were placed on building a resident operation in Sarasota. The basic purpose of presenting alternative, thought-provoking theatre remained intact. Today, eight years later, FST has firmly established itself as a "cutting-edge" theatre in the region. FST executes three primary programs: a mainstage season of four plays dedicated to contemporary writers; a new play develop-

Florida Studio Theatre. Scott Burkel and Catherine Campbell in *Little Shop of Horrors.* Photo: J.B. McCortney.

ment program with emphasis on American works and recent translations of Spanish works; and an educational program serving the area's avocational needs, in addition to our training program for theatre students from around the country. The philosophy and driving vision of FST is best summed up in the words of James Joyce, who wrote, "I go for the millionth time to forge in the smithy of my soul the uncreated conscience of the race."

—*Richard Hopkins*

PRODUCTIONS 1985–86

Starry Night, Monte Merrick; (D) Richard Hopkins; (S) John Stone; (C) Robert A. Horek; (L) Paul D. Romance

Sister Mary Ignatius Explains It All for You and ***The Actor's Nightmare***, Christopher Durang; (D) Alkis Papoutsis; (S) John Stone; (C) Robert A. Horek; (L) Paul D. Romance

Painting Churches, Tina Howe; (D) Christian Angermann; (S) Alex Polner; (C) Robert A. Horek; (L) Paul D. Romance

How I Got That Story, Amlin Gray; (D) Jeff Mousseau; (S) Alex Polner; (C) Robert A. Horek; (L) Paul D. Romance

Ain't Misbehavin', music and lyrics: Fats Waller, et al.; book adapt: Richard Maltby, Jr.; (D) Derek Wolshonak; (S) Christopher H. Murray; (C) Robert A. Horek; (L) Paul D. Romance

PRODUCTIONS 1986–87

Little Shop of Horrors, book and lyrics: Howard Ashman; music: Alan Menken; (D) Richard Hopkins; (S) William John Aupperlee; (C) Victoria Pennington; (L) Paul D. Romance

Billy Bishop Goes to War, John Gray and Eric Peterson; (D) Carolyn Michel; (S) William John Aupperlee; (C) Vicki S. Holden; (L) Paul D. Romance

Split Second, Dennis McIntyre; (D) Alkis Papoutsis; (S) William John Aupperlee; (C) Victoria Pennington; (L) Paul D. Romance

Rap Master Ronnie, book and lyrics: Garry Trudeau; music: Elizabeth Swados; (D) Bill Castellino; (S) William John Aupperlee; (C) Randall Ouzts; (L) Paul D. Romance

A Cup of Kindness, Richard S. Burdick; (D) Jeff Mousseau; (L) Paul D. Romance

Warm Bodies, Mark St. Germain; (D) Ann Graham; (L) Paul D. Romance

A Hell of a Town, Monte Merrick; (D) Alkis Papoutsis; (L) Paul D. Romance

FMT

BARBARA LEIGH
MIKE MOYNIHAN
Co-Directors

Box 92127
Milwaukee, WI 53202
(414) 271-8484

FOUNDED 1973
Barbara Leigh, Mike Moynihan

SEASON
Feb.-Dec.

FINANCES
Jan. 1, 1986-Dec. 31, 1986
Expenses: $130,949

The core of FMT is a group of four artists who have worked together from seven to fourteen years. As a traveling company, FMT creates productions that are just as likely to be found in a neighborhood park, library or meeting hall as in a well-appointed theatre. A local/regional company touring the upper Midwest and beyond, and playing to adults and children, FMT has created five to seven new works per year for over a decade. The ensemble has spent the last three seasons reworking, adapting and touring several of these productions, while workshopping new ideas. Like the annual outdoor Cream City Semi-Circus, the present style of our work is "collision theatre": traditions, forms, values, techniques and images collide within a production; the familiar and the strange are integrated, reflecting a common heritage of myths, visions, dreams and stories that provide a re-presentation of a shared culture. FMT strives to created a theatre that is critical, forgiving and hopeful.

—*Mike Moynihan*

FMT. *The Cream City Semi-Circus.* Photo: The Milwaukee Sentinel

PRODUCTIONS 1985–86

The Cream City Semi-Circus, Half Ring Revue and Traveling Theatrical Exposition of 1985!, Ann Melchoir, Mike Moynihan and company; music: Debbie Anderson and Joel Davel; (D) Mike Moynihan; (S) Mike Moynihan; (C) Melinda Boyd

Hands Off/Hands On, Melinda Boyd, Barbara Leigh, Mike Moynihan and Rafael B. Smith; (D) Mike Moynihan; (S) Mike Moynihan; (C) Melinda Boyd and Barbara Leigh; (L) David Drake

The Snow Queen, adapt: Ann Melchior and Mike Moynihan, from Hans Christian Andersen; (D) Mike Moynihan; (S) Mike Moynihan; (C) Barbara Leigh and Melinda Boyd; (L) William Quirmbach

The Gift of the Wind and Other Holiday Stories, Barbara Leigh, Rafael B. Smith and Mike Moynihan; (D) Mike Moynihan; (S) Mike Moynihan; (C) Barbara Leigh; (L) Bo Johnson

Mime Opus '86, company-developed; (D) Barbara Leigh and Boyd Melinda; (C) Melinda Boyd; (L) William Quirmbach

PRODUCTIONS 1986–87

The Cream City Semi-Circus, Half Ring Revue and Traveling Theatrical Exposition of 1986, Ron Anderson, Barbara Chudnow, Mike Moynihan, William Shakespeare and Rafael B. Smith; music: Debbie Anderson and Joel Davel; (D) Ron Anderson; (S) Mike Moynihan and Melinda Boyd; (C) William Wedepohl, Barbara Leigh and Melinda Boyd

The Polowsky Project, company-developed. ***Transformations***, Barbara Leigh, Mike Moynihan and Rafael B. Smith; (D) Melinda Boyd; (S) Mike Moynihan; (C) Melinda Boyd; (L) David Drake

The Snow Queen, adapt: Ann Melchior and Mike Moynihan, from Hans Christian Andersen; (D) Melinda Boyd; (S) Mike Moynihan; (C) Melinda Boyd and Barbara Leigh; (L) Jo Yanish

What's Next..., company-developed; (D) Mike Moynihan

Raf's Show, Rafael B. Smith; (D) Rafael B. Smith

Coloropolis, Mike Moynihan; (D) Mike Moynihan; (S) Mike Moynihan and Melinda Boyd; (C) Melinda Boyd

Ford's Theatre

DAVID H. BELL
Artistic Director

FRANKIE HEWITT
Executive Producer

511 Tenth St., NW
Washington, DC 20004
(202) 638-2941 (bus.)
(202) 347-4833 (b.o.)

FOUNDED 1968
Frankie Hewitt

SEASON
Sept.-July

Ford's Theatre. Robin Baxter, Kathleen Mahoney-Bennett and Val Scott in *Hot Mikado*. Photo: Joan Marcus.

FACILITIES
Seating capacity: 699
Stage: modified proscenium

FINANCES
Oct. 1, 1985-Sept. 30, 1986
Expenses: $3,954,844

CONTRACTS
AEA Special Production and SSD&C

Our intent at Ford's Theatre is to develop and produce more original works, with particular emphasis on the creation of musical theatre, an art currently in a state of crisis. Over the past 20 years new dramatic works have found their home in nonprofit regional theatres; however, the musical has not been as fortunate. Ford's Theatre has made a continuing commitment to the development and preservation of this uniquely American art form. Although Ford's will not forsake presenting nonmusical theatre, the current crisis in musical-theatre production presents a mandate to develop and preserve this honored, indigenous, yet vanishing art form.

—David H. Bell

PRODUCTIONS 1985–86

Little Me, book: Neil Simon; music: Cy Coleman; lyrics: Carolyn Leigh; (D) David H. Bell; (S) Dan Proett; (C) Doug Marmee; (L) Susan White

Hot Mikado, book and lyrics: W.S. Gilbert; music: Arthur Sullivan; book adapt and lyrics: David H. Bell; music: Rob Bowman; (D) David H. Bell; (S) Dan Proett; (C) Carol Oditz; (L) Susan White

PRODUCTIONS 1986–87

Is There Life After High School?, book: Jeffrey Kindley; music and lyrics: Craig Carnelia; (D) David H. Bell; (S) Michael Anania; (C) Bob Beisel; (L) Jeff Davis

Nunsense, book, music and lyrics: Dan Goggin; (D) Dan Goggin; (S) Barry Axtell; (L) Susan White

Free Street Theater

PATRICK HENRY
Producer/Artistic Director

441 West North Ave.
Chicago, IL 60610
(312) 642-1234

FOUNDED 1969
Perry Baer, Patrick Henry

SEASON
Year-round

FINANCES
Apr. 1, 1986-Mar. 31, 1987
Expenses: $305,411

CONTRACTS
AEA CAT and TYA

Free Street Theater is an outreach organization dedicated to developing new audiences and participants for the performing arts. We pursue this goal by creating original performance material based on the experiences of the people we seek to engage. Frequently performers are drawn from the community that has inspired the work—such as an inner city neighborhood (*Project!*), or the community of the elderly (the Free Street Too company). Their experiences are interpreted through music, dance and theatre by Free Street's artistic staff. The resultant performance pieces are unique documentaries of an aspect of the contemporary American condition which speak both to and for the community. Some of our companies operate on Actors' Equity contracts, others do not; but all maintain the highest standards. Although the surroundings and trappings may be low-rent, our endeavor is to make the experience high art.

—Patrick Henry

PRODUCTIONS 1985–86

Chicago!, book: Patrick Henry; music: Doug Lofstrom; lyrics: Tricia Alexander; (D) Patrick Henry; (S) Rob Hamilton; (C) Rob Hamilton; (L) Rob Hamilton

To Life!, Patrick Henry; (D) Patrick Henry; (S) John Aldridge; (L) John Aldridge

What Do You Want to Be When You Grow Old?, Patrick Henry; (D) Patrick Henry; (S) John Aldridge; (L) John Aldridge

Project!, book: Patrick Henry; music: Tricia Alexander and Doug Lofstrom; lyrics: Patrick Henry and Tricia Alexander; (D) Patrick Henry; (S) Rob Hamilton; (L) Rob Hamilton

PRODUCTIONS 1986–87

To Life!, Patrick Henry; (D) Patrick Henry; (S) John Aldridge; (L) John Aldridge

What Do You Want to Be When You Grow Old?, Patrick Henry; (D) Patrick Henry; (S) John Aldridge; (L) John Aldridge

Project!, book: Patrick Henry; music: Tricia Alexander and Doug Lofstrom; lyrics: Patrick Henry and Tricia Alexander; (D) Patrick Henry; (S) Rob Hamilton; (L) Volkmar Gruenert

Kids from Cabrini, adapt: Patrick Hamilton, from African tales; (D) Patrick Henry

Take the Chance, book: Patrick Henry; music: Doug Lofstrom; lyrics: Patrick Henry and Tricia Alexander; (D) Patrick Henry

Free Street Theater. DeAundre Jones in *Kids from Cabrini*. Photo: Dan Rest.

Fulton Opera House. Deidre Warner in *The Codebreaker.* Photo: Ginny Waggoner.

Fulton Opera House

KATHLEEN A. COLLINS
Artistic Director

DEIDRE W. JACOBSON
Executive Director

Box 1865
Lancaster, PA 17603
(717) 394-7133 (bus.)
(717) 397-7425 (b.o.)

FOUNDED 1963
Fulton Opera House Foundation

SEASON
Oct.-Aug.

FACILITIES
Seating capacity: 909
Stage: proscenium

FINANCES
Oct. 1, 1985-Sept. 30, 1986
Expenses: $835,302

CONTRACTS
AEA letter of agreement

The Fulton Opera House, a national historic monument, basked in the glory days of the road house. Today, with the vitality of its own theatre, its legacy still lives and prospers. Working toward full operation on a League of Resident Theatres contract with Actors' Equity Association is the primary goal of our five-year plan. To reach that end, we have consolidated our children's program and our summer program to create one season that includes a Theatre for Young Audiences tour and four mainstage shows for adults. We are moving slowly toward the dream of having an ongoing acting ensemble, as well as a core of designers and technicians who choose to make Lancaster their home. We are committed to new works, having recently commissioned a play, and we are proud of our education program that presents workshops both in the theatre and in schools.

—*Kathleen A. Collins*

PRODUCTIONS 1985–86

A Christmas Carol, adapt: Michael Paller, from Charles Dickens; (D) Kathleen A. Collins; (S) Herbert H. O'Dell; (C) Virginia M. West; (L) Herbert H. O'Dell

The Code Breaker, Pauline C. Conley; (D) Kathleen A. Collins; (S) Charles Walsh; (C) Beth Dunkelberger; (L) Herbert H. O'Dell

Tales of the Arabian Night, Barry Kornhauser; (D) Kathleen A. Collins; (S) Charles Walsh; (C) Virginia M. West; (L) W. Raiford Stout

The Diary of Anne Frank, Frances Goodrich and Albert Hackett; (D) Philip Burton; (S) Charles Walsh; (C) Beth Dunkelberger; (L) James Henke

Dames at Sea, book and lyrics: George Haimsohn and Robin Miller; music: Jim Wise; (D) Kathleen A. Collins; (S) Norman B. Dodge; (C) Virginia M. West; (L) William R. Simmons

The Foreigner, Larry Shue; (D) Michael Nash; (S) Norman B. Dodge; (C) Beth Dunkelberger; (L) William R. Simmons

A Life in the Theatre, David Mamet; (D) Kathleen A. Collins; (S) Norman B. Dodge; (C) Virginia M. West; (L) William R. Simmons

PRODUCTIONS 1986–87

A Christmas Carol, adapt: Barry Kornhauser, from Charles Dickens; (D) Barry Kornhauser; (S) Herbert H. O'Dell; (C) Virginia M. West; (L) James Jackson

To Kill a Mockingbird, adapt: Reginald Rose, from Harper Lee; (D) Kathleen A. Collins; (S) James Henke; (C) Beth Dunkelberger; (L) James Jackson

Color of the Wind, adapt: Kathleen A. Collins; (D) Kathleen A. Collins; (S) James Henke; (C) Virginia M. West; (L) James Jackson

Brighton Beach Memoirs, Neil Simon; (D) Michael Nash; (S) James Henke; (C) Virginia M. West; (L) William R. Simmons

Private Lives, Noel Coward; (D) Michael Nash; (S) James Henke; (C) Virginia M. West; (L) William R. Simmons

I Do! I Do!, book and lyrics: Tom Jones; music: Harvey Schmidt; (D) Kathleen A. Collins; (S) James Henke; (C) Beth Dunkelberger; (L) William R. Simmons

George Street Playhouse

MAUREEN HEFFERNAN
Acting Artistic Director

GEOFFREY MERRILL COHEN
General Manager

9 Livingston Ave.
New Brunswick, NJ 08901
(201) 846-2895 (bus.)
(201) 246-7717 (b.o.)

FOUNDED 1974
John Herochik, Eric Krebs

SEASON
Oct.-May

FACILITIES
Stage I
Seating capacity: 367
Stage: thrust

Stage II
Seating capacity: 90
Stage: flexible

Stage III
Seating capacity: 75
Stage: cabaret

FINANCES
July 1, 1986-June 30, 1987
Expenses: $1,359,060

CONTRACTS
AEA LORT (D), SSD&C, USA

George Street Playhouse is an urban theatre producing work that reflects the diverse population of our region, as well as addressing contemporary issues. During the past 13 years this region has experienced tremendous socioeconomic growth and change, and the theatre has evolved concurrently. We continue to expose and embrace these social and cultural changes in our work. Although we do not employ a resident acting company, we strive to nurture a "home base" atmosphere for a growing family of artists (designers, directors, actors, technicians). The artistic staff is committed to nontraditional casting, and dedicated to the development of playwrights and new works

George Street Playhouse. *Little Ham: The Numbers Musical.* Photo: Suzanne Karp Krebs.

for the main stage, experimental space and theatre for young audiences (both in residence and on tour). We view ourselves not as an autonomous entity but as an active participant in the national regional theatre movement facing the enormous artistic and social challenge of becoming an integral part of the society.

—Maureen Heffernan

Note: During the 1985-86 and 1986-87 seasons, Eric Krebs served as producing director.

PRODUCTIONS 1985–86

The Price, Arthur Miller; (D) Sue Lawless; (S) Daniel Ettinger; (C) Crystal K. Craft; (L) Phil Monat

Cabaret, book: Joe Masteroff; music: John Kander; lyrics: Fred Ebb; (D) Maureen Heffernan; (S) Daniel Proett; (C) Michael J. Cesario; (L) Susan White

Glengarry Glen Ross, David Mamet; (D) Steven Schachter; (S) Steven Schachter; (C) Judith K. Hart; (L) Christina Giannelli

Greater Tuna, Joe Sears, Jaston Williams and Ed Howard; (D) Maureen Heffernan; (S) Daniel Ettinger; (C) Lana Fritz; (L) Rodd McLaughlin

Mrs. Warren's Profession, George Bernard Shaw; (D) Bob Hall; (S) Peter Harrison; (C) Patricia Adshead; (L) Daniel Stratman

The Rise of David Levinsky, book and lyrics: Isaiah Sheffer; music: Bobby Paul; (D) Sue Lawless; (S) Kenneth Foy; (C) Mimi Maxmen; (L) Phil Monat

PRODUCTIONS 1986–87

As Is, William M. Hoffman; (D) Maureen Heffernan; (S) Daniel Ettinger; (C) Nancy Konrardy; (L) Daniel Ettinger

Every Trick in the Book, Georges Feydeau and Maurice Hennequin; trans: Langdon Brown; (D) Peter Bennett; (S) Gary English; (C) Patricia Adshead; (L) Karl Haas

Fool for Love, Sam Shepard; (D) Maureen Heffernan; (S) Daniel Gray; (C) Diane Salmonsen; (L) Jay A. Herzog

Little Ham, Langston Hughes; book adapt: Daniel Owens; music: Judd Woldin; lyrics: Richard Engquist and Judd Woldin; (D) Billie Allen; (S) Daniel Ettinger; (C) Nancy Konrardy; (L) Shirley Prendergast

Man of La Mancha, book: Dale Wasserman; music: Mitch Leigh; lyrics: Joe Darion; (D) Maureen Heffernan; (S) Daniel Proett; (C) Michael J. Cesario; (L) Daniel Stratman

Germinal Stage Denver

ED BAIERLEIN
Director/Manager

2450 West 44th Ave.
Denver, CO 80211
(303) 455-7108

FOUNDED 1974
Ed Baierlein, Sallie Diamond, Jack McKnight, Ginger Valone

SEASON
Oct.-Aug.

FACILITIES
Seating capacity: 132
Stage: thrust

FINANCES
Sept. 1, 1986-Aug. 31, 1987
Expenses: $86,573

Germinal Stage Denver is the runt stepchild of regional theatres, a mom-and-pop store of Thespis, a vestige of the little theatre movement masquerading as an institution. In 13 years, we've gone through several periods of artistic coherence, but these days we're just trying to do the best plays we can, as well as we can, without talking too much about it. We're an actors' theatre, semi-rough, vaguely postmodern, and we have a lot of fun. We just bought our own building, and made sure it was small so we couldn't "grow." We found the place we wanted to live—and made the work happen there. Winning a bunch of awards (including Best Season for a Denver theatre company twice running from the Denver Critics Circle) has strengthened our illusion that we're doing it okay and will be doing it okay for a while more.

—Ed Baierlein

Germinal Stage Denver. Jacob Clark, Ralph Palasek, Evan Mitchell, Ede Lovercheck and David Fenerty in *Quartermaine's Terms*. Photo: Strack Edwards.

PRODUCTIONS 1985–86

The School for Wives, Molière; trans: Richard Wilbur; (D) Ed Baierlein; (S) Ed Baierlein; (C) Sallie Diamond; (L) Ed Baierlein

Quartermaine's Terms, Simon Gray; (D) Ed Baierlein; (S) Ed Baierlein; (C) Margaret Sjoberg; (L) Ed Baierlein

Death of a Salesman, Arthur Miller; (D) Laura Cuetara; (S) Laura Cuetara; (C) Sallie Diamond; (L) Laura Cuetara

The Seagull, Anton Chekhov; adapt: Ed Baierlein; (D) Ed Baierlein; (S) Ed Baierlein; (C) Virginia Rossman; (L) Ed Baierlein

Terra Nova, Ted Tally; (D) Laura Cuetara; (S) Laura Cuetara; (C) Laura Cuetara; (L) Laura Cuetara

PRODUCTIONS 1986–87

The Doctor's Dilemma, George Bernard Shaw; (D) Ed Baierlein; (S) Ed Baierlein; (C) Virginia Rossman; (L) Ed Baierlein

Hurlyburly, David Rabe; (D) Ed Baierlein; (S) Ed Baierlein; (C) Virginia Rossman; (L) Ed Baierlein

Galileo, Bertolt Brecht; trans: Wolfgang Sauerlander and Ralph Manheim; (D) Laura Cuetara; (S) Barbara Craig; (C) Barbara Craig; (L) Laura Cuetara

Who's Afraid of Virginia Woolf?, Edward Albee; (D) Ed Baierlein; (S) Ed Baierlein; (C) Sallie Diamond; (L) Ed Baierlein

Relatively Speaking, Alan Ayckbourn; (D) Laura Cuetara; (S) Laura Cuetara; (C) Sallie Diamond; (L) Laura Cuetara

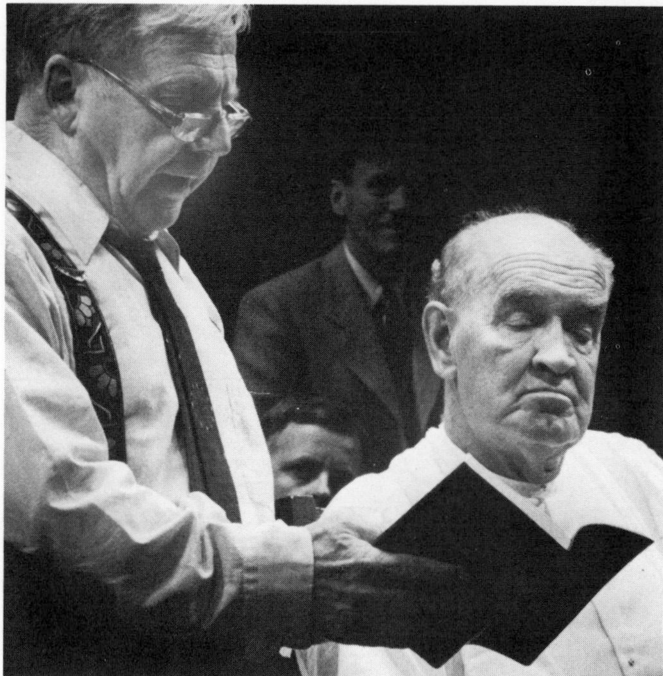

GeVa Theatre. Gerald Richards, Dick St. George and Arch Johnson in *Inherit the Wind.* Photo: Wayne Calabrese.

GeVa Theatre

HOWARD J. MILLMAN
Producing Director

THOMAS PECHAR
Managing Director

75 Woodbury Blvd.
Rochester, NY 14607
(716) 232-1366 (bus.)
(716) 232-1363 (b.o.)

FOUNDED 1972
Cynthia Selden, William Selden

SEASON
Year-round

FACILITIES
Seating capacity: 550
Stage: thrust

FINANCES
July 1, 1986-June 30, 1987
Expenses: $2,629,000

CONTRACTS
AEA LORT (C) and SSD&C

In the past two years GeVa Theatre has experienced unprecedented growth, beginning with the opening of the theatre's new facility in downtown Rochester, that virtually doubled the seating capacity and operating budget overnight. The new facility, a renovated historic landmark, has allowed GeVa the flexibility to expand its production capabilities. Committed to the cultivation of relationships with playwrights, GeVa's play development series, Plays in Progress, gives readings of works in their early stages. In addition to this emphasis on new work, GeVa maintains a broad-based production philosophy that includes the staging of the world's theatrical literature. The seasons are chosen with balance in mind, selected from the classics of literary history, as well as contemporary works previously performed by theatres around the country. Summer and Christmas presentations have been added so that the theatre is now open year-round. GeVa Theatre has become a vital force in the Rochester community; an emphasis on education and cultivation of young audiences has strengthened that artistic relationship.

—Howard J. Millman

PRODUCTIONS 1985–86

Ain't Misbehavin', adapt: Murray Horwitz and Richard Maltby, Jr.; music and lyrics: Fats Waller, et al.; (D) Arthur Faria; (S) John Lee Beatty; (C) Eaves Brooks; (L) Barry Arnold

A Christmas Carol, adapt: Eberle Thomas, from Charles Dickens; (D) Howard J. Millman; (S) William Barclay; (C) Pamela Scofield; (L) Phil Monat

Isn't It Romantic?, Wendy Wasserstein; (D) Terence Lamude; (S) Duke Durfee; (C) Barbara Forbes; (L) Ann G. Wrightson

Fences, August Wilson; (D) Claude Purdy; (S) David Potts; (C) Thom Coates; (L) Phil Monat

The Importance of Being Earnest, Oscar Wilde; (D) Thomas Gruenewald; (S) Charles Cosler; (C) Thom Coates; (L) Craig Miller

Diminished Capacity, Tom Dulack; (D) Allen R. Belknap; (S) James Fenhagen; (C) Pamela Scofield; (L) Curt Ostermann

The Lion in Winter, James Goldman; (D) Howard J. Millman; (S) Bob Barnett; (C) Pamela Scofield; (L) Phil Monat

PRODUCTIONS 1986–87

Pump Boys and Dinettes, John Foley, Mark Hardwick, Debra Monk, Cass Morgan, John Schimmel and Jim Wann; (D) Peter Glazer; (S) Christopher Shriver; (C) Dana Harnish Tinsley; (L) Phil Monat

Inherit the Wind, Jerome Lawrence and Robert E. Lee; (D) Howard J. Millman; (S) Bob Barnett; (C) Pamela Scofield; (L) Phil Monat

What the Butler Saw, Joe Orton; (D) Allen R. Belknap; (S) Michael Rizzo; (C) April Parke; (L) Jeffrey Schissler

A Christmas Carol, adapt: Eberle Thomas, from Charles Dickens; (D) Eberle Thomas; (S) Bob Barnett; (C) Pamela Scofield; (L) Phil Monat

National Anthems, Dennis McIntyre; (D) Allen R. Belknap; (S) David Potts; (C) Dana Harnish Tinsley; (L) Richard Winkler

A View from the Bridge, Arthur Miller; (D) Tony Giordano; (S) Hugh Landwehr; (C) Mary Ann Powell; (L) Dennis Parichy

The Misanthrope, Molière; trans: Richard Wilbur; (D) Allen R. Belknap; (S) David Potts; (C) Pamela Scofield; (L) Richard Winkler

The Immigrant: A Hamilton County Album, Mark Harelik; conceived: Randal Myler and Mark Harelik; (D) Howard J. Millman; (S) Kevin Rupnik; (C) Mimi Maxmen; (L) Phil Monat

Goodman Theatre

ROBERT FALLS
Artistic Director

ROCHE SCHULFER
Producing Director

200 South Columbus Dr.
Chicago, IL 60603

Goodman Theatre. Barbara Robertson, Peter Amster and Paula Scrofano in *She Always Said, Pablo.* Photo: Kevin Horan.

(312) 443-3811 (bus.)
(312) 443-3800 (b.o.)

FOUNDED 1925
Art Institute of Chicago

SEASON
Sept.-July

FACILITIES
Mainstage
Seating capacity: 683
Stage: proscenium

Studio
Seating capacity: 137
Stage: proscenium

FINANCES
July 1, 1986-June 30, 1987
Expenses: $4,457,500

CONTRACTS
AEA LORT (B+), SSD&C and USA

The Goodman is Chicago's largest and oldest nonprofit theatre, and we mean to use its great resources to produce classic and contemporary works of size—large in both imagination and physical scale. We mean to infuse the classics with the energy usually reserved for new works and we aim to treat new plays with the care and reverence usually given to the classics. Working with associate director Frank Galati and resident director Michael Maggio, I intend to concentrate our efforts on the Goodman's five-play series and to expand the artistic scope of our audience by introducing them to the work of leading theatre artists and companies whose work is rarely seen in Chicago. We will continue to expand auxiliary programming that accompanies each production, encouraging our audience into active participation in the theatrical process. We will also continue to develop younger audiences through our program of free student matinees and close collaboration with the public school system.

—*Robert Falls*

PRODUCTIONS 1985–86

The Government Inspector, Nikolai Gogol; trans: Milton Ehre and Fruma Gottschalk; (D) Frank Galati; (S) Michael Merritt; (C) Virgil Johnson; (L) Kevin Rigdon

A Christmas Carol, adapt: Larry Sloan, from Charles Dickens; (D) Sandra Grand; (S) Joseph Nieminski; (C) Christa Scholtz; (L) Robert Christen

Fences, August Wilson; (D) Lloyd Richards; (S) James D. Sandefur; (C) Candice Donnelly; (L) Danianne Mizzy

Happy Days, Samuel Beckett; (D) Andrei Belgrader; (S) Douglas Stein; (C) Candice Donnelly; (L) Frances Aronson

PRODUCTIONS 1986–87

Galileo, Bertolt Brecht; trans: James Schevill and Adrian Hall; (D) Robert Falls; (S) George Tsypin; (C) Jessica Hahn; (L) James F. Ingalls

A Christmas Carol, adapt: Larry Sloan, from Charles Dickens; (D) Sandra Grand; (S) Joseph Nieminski; (C) Christa Scholtz; (L) Robert Christen

Ghost on Fire, Michael Weller; (D) Les Waters; (S) Loren Sherman; (C) Martin Pakledinaz; (L) Stephen Strawbridge

She Always Said, Pablo, words: Gertrude Stein; music: Virgil Thompson and Igor Stravinsky; conceived: Frank Galati; (D) Frank Galati; (S) Mary Griswold; (C) John Paoletti; (L) Geoffrey Bushor

The Tempest, William Shakespeare; (D) Robert Falls; (S) Adrianne Lobel; (C) Jessica Hahn; (L) James F. Ingalls

Sunday in the Park with George, music and lyrics: Stephen Sondheim; book: James Lapine; (D) Michael Maggio; (S) John Lee Beatty; (C) Nan Cibula; (L) Robert Christen

Goodspeed Opera House

MICHAEL P. PRICE
Executive Director

Goodspeed Landing
East Haddam, CT 06423
(203) 873-8664 (bus.)
(203) 873-8668 (b.o.)

FOUNDED 1963
Goodspeed Opera House Foundation

SEASON
Apr.-Dec.

FACILITIES
Goodspeed Opera House
Seating capacity: 398
Stage: proscenium

Goodspeed-at-Chester/The Norma Terris Theatre
Seating capacity: 200
Stage: proscenium

CONTRACTS
AEA LORT (B+), (D) and SSD&C

Goodspeed Opera House. *Irma La Douce.* Photo: Norman Glasband.

The Goodspeed Opera House is one of the theatres in the United States dedicated to the heritage, preservation and development of the American musical. Devoted to both classic and contemporary musicals, the Opera House has sent 12 productions to Broadway, including *Annie*, *Shenandoah* and *Man of La Mancha*. The Goodspeed was awarded a special Tony in 1980 for its contributions to this uniquely American art form. Goodspeed's second stage, Goodspeed-at-Chester/The Norman Terris Theatre, provides an intimate performing space exclusively for new works of musical theatre. Here, writers and creative staff have a rare opportunity to develop a "musical-in-progress" before an audience.

—*Michael P. Price*

PRODUCTIONS 1985–86

You Never Know, book adapt: Rowland Leigh and Paul Lazarus, from Siegfried Geyer, Karl Farkas and Robert Katscher; music and lyrics: Cole Porter; (D) Paul Lazarus; (S) James Leonard Joy; (C) John Falabella; (L) Curt Ostermann

Fiorello!, book: Jerome Weidman and George Abbott; music: Jerry Bock; lyrics: Sheldon Harnick; (D) Gerald Gutierrez; (S) Douglas Stein; (C) Ann Hould-Ward; (L) Pat Collins

Leave It to Jane, music: Jerome Kern; book and lyrics: Guy Bolton and P.G. Wodehouse; (D) Thomas Gruenewald; (S) James Leonard Joy; (C) John Carver Sullivan; (L) Craig Miller

Georgia Avenue, book adapt: Joe Masteroff, from Fannie Hurst; music: Howard Marren; (D) Fran Soeder; (S) James Leonard Joy; (C) Andrew B. Marlay; (L) Curt Ostermann

PRODUCTIONS 1986–87

Irma La Douce, book and lyrics: Alexandre Breffort; trans: Julian More, David Heneker and Monty Norman; music: Marguerite Monnot; (D) Fran Soeder; (S) James Leonard Joy; (C) Mariann Verheyen; (L) Craig Miller

Fanny, book adapt: S.N. Behrman and Joshua Logan, from Marcel Pagnol; music and lyrics: Harold Rome; (D) Thomas Gruenewald; (S) James Leonard Joy; (C) John Carver Sullivan; (L) Curt Ostermann

Carnival!, book: Michael Stewart; music and lyrics: Bob Merrill; (D) Thomas Gruenewald;

(S) James Leonard Joy; (C) Oleksa; (L) Craig Miller

Jokers, book, music and lyrics: Hugo Peretti, Luigi Creatore and George David Weiss; (D) Martin Charnin; (S) James Leonard Joy; (C) Ann Hould-Ward; (L) Judy Rasmuson

A House in the Woods, book and lyrics: Ellen Weston; music: Marvin Laird; (D) Michael Leeds; (S) Evelyn Sakash; (C) John Carver Sullivan; (L) Curt Ostermann

The Great American Children's Theatre Company

TERI SOLOMON MITZE
Artistic Director

MICHAEL DUNCAN
Managing Director

Box 92123
Milwaukee, WI 53202
(414) 276-4230

FOUNDED 1976
Teri Solomon Mitze, Thomas C. Mitze

SEASON
Oct.-May

FACILITIES
Pabst Theater
Seating capacity: 1,432
Stage: proscenium

Madison Civic Center, Madison, WI
Seating capacity: 2,185
Stage: proscenium

West High Auditorium, Green Bay, WI
Seating capacity: 1,527
Stage: proscenium

Marshall Field's Forum
Seating capacity: 550
Stage: arena

FINANCES
July 1, 1986-June 30, 1987
Expenses: $301,165

The future of theatre in America is largely dependent on the development of the young audience. Children's theatre is no longer a puppet show and a clown, designed to keep the kids' attention. When produced with creative energy and the highest professional standards, children's theatre can shape the future of the performing arts. The thrust of the Great American Children's Theatre Company's work is, indeed, for children and teenagers. The plays are selected or commissioned to be of interest to a young audience, but they often require the audience to reach beyond their limited experience. Since 1975, more than 900,000 children and adults have attended GACT productions, and an entire generation has been introduced to the infinite possibilities of theatre. In addition to the mainstage productions, GACT presents "A Peek Behind the Scenes," an in-school program designed to link the classroom and theatre experiences, as well as an annual holiday musical in a "breakfast theatre" arrangement, which includes five identical productions being performed simultaneously in five locations. In 1987, when construction on Milwaukee's new theatre district is complete, including the renovation of the Pabst Theater, the Great American Children's Theatre plans to expand its season there.

—Teri Solomon Mitze

PRODUCTIONS 1985–86

Bring on the Clowns, book and music: Bill Solly; (D) Monty Davis; (S) Allen H. Jones; (C) William Wedepohl; (L) Curt Crain

Toby Tyler, book: Dan Stein; music: Ricky Gordon; lyrics: Bill Solly; (D) Leslie Reidel; (S) Allen H. Jones; (C) Susan Tsu; (L) Spencer Mosse

PRODUCTIONS 1986–87

All Ready for Christmas, book and music: Bill Solly; (D) Monty Davis; (S) Allen Jones; (C) Ted Boerner; (L) Curt Crane, Jr.

Legend of Sleepy Hollow, adapt: Frederick Gaines, from Washington Irving; (D) Leslie Reidel; (S) Allen Jones and Al Tucci; (C) Ellen Kozak; (L) Spencer Mosse

The Great American Children's Theatre Company. Marc Cohen and Richard Gabriel in *Toby Tyler*.

Great Lakes Theater Festival

GERALD FREEDMAN
Artistic Director

MARY BILL
Managing Director

1501 Euclid Ave., Suite 250
Cleveland, OH 44115
(216) 241-5490 (bus.)
(216) 241-6000 (b.o.)

Great Lakes Theater Festival. Jean Stapleton and Gwyllum Evans in *Arsenic and Old Lace*. Photo: Mary Beth Camp.

FOUNDED 1962
Community members

SEASON
May-Oct.

FACILITIES
Ohio Theatre
Seating capacity: 643
Stage: proscenium

Alma Theater
Seating capacity: 300
Stage: thrust

FINANCES
Feb. 1, 1986-Jan. 31, 1987
Expenses: $1,212,000

CONTRACTS
AEA LORT (B), (D) and SSD&C

Though the Great Lakes Theater Festival continues to uphold the classical theatre mandate that launched it, we have been challenging our perception of what that responsibility means. We are interested in the whole spectrum of American plays—not only the acknowledged great works, but the culturally significant plays and musicals that placed Broadway in the mainstream of American entertainment from the 1920s through the 1950s. And we are interested in pursuing the special resonance that comes from seeing world classics side by side with new plays. With regard to performance style, I am drawn to actors adept at both classic drama and musicals. I find a kinship between doing Shakespeare, for example, and musical theatre. The presentational styles—the soliloquies in one form, the songs in the other—each require a high-energy performance level that forms a visceral relationship with an audience that is very much my signature.

—Gerald Freedman

PRODUCTIONS 1986

Arsenic and Old Lace, Joseph Kesselring; (D) Brian Murray; (S) Marjorie Bradley Kellogg; (C) Jeanne Button; (L) Pat Collins

Ghosts, Henrik Ibsen; trans: Christopher Hampton; (D) Gerald Freedman; (S) John Ezell; (C) Jeanne Button; (L) Martin Aronstein

The Show-Off, George Kelly; (D) Richard Hamburger; (S) John Ezell; (C) Jeanne Button; (L) Stephen Strawbridge

Macbeth, William Shakespeare; (D) Gerald Freedman; (S) John Ezell; (C) Lawrence Casey; (L) Thomas Skelton

PRODUCTIONS 1987

The Boys from Syracuse, book: George Abbott; lyrics: Lorenz Hart; music: Richard Rodgers; (D) Gerald Freedman; (S) John Ezell; (C) Stanley Simmons; (L) Martin Aronstein

Broadway, Philip Dunning and George Abbott; (D) George Abbott; (S) John Ezell; (C) Jeanne Button; (L) Martin Aronstein

Absent Forever, John Hopkins; (D) Gerald Freedman; (S) Jim Morgan; (L) Mary Jo Dondlinger

Up from Paradise, Arthur Miller; (D) Kent Paul; (S) Jane Clark; (C) Gene K. Lakin; (L) Mary Jo Dondlinger

Hedda Gabler, Henrik Ibsen; (D) Richard Hamburger; (S) Christopher Barreca; (C) Jeanne Button; (L) Craig Miller

Romeo and Juliet, William Shakespeare; (D) Gerald Freedman; (S) John Ezell; (C) Jamie Scott; (L) Thomas Skelton

The Group Theatre Company

RUBEN SIERRA
Artistic Director

MARLA MILLER-HECK
Managing Director

3940 Brooklyn Ave., NE
Seattle, WA 98105
(206) 545-4969 (bus.)
(206) 543-4327 (b.o.)

FOUNDED 1978
Scott Caldwell, Ruben Sierra, Gilbert Wong

SEASON
Sept.-July

FACILITIES
Ethnic Theatre
Seating capacity: 195
Stage: modified thrust

Seattle Center House Theatre
Seating capacity: 285
Stage: modified thrust

FINANCES
July 1, 1986-June 30, 1987
Expenses: $1,115,500

CONTRACTS
AEA SPT

The Group Theatre has a strong aesthetic base that speaks directly to our community about what is happening around us. We are committed to socially provocative and relevant themes—delayed stress syndrome, South Africa, English as a second language, the disabled—that reveal who we are and where we are as a society. We want our audiences to ask questions and to re-examine how they view the world and their community. We seek to enhance the opportunities of all artists—black, white, Hispanic, Asian, Native American, disabled—to realize their visions. As a theatre company we want to be a negotiator and a catalyst for playwrights, actors and designers. One of our programs, the Minority Playwrights Festival, focuses solely on new scripts by American minority playwrights, allowing them a forum to develop new work. We have toured to high schools with the Apartheid Project, a program involving workshops and a dramatic presentation dealing with South Africa. We have also toured nationally with the one-man show *I Am Celso*, a collaboration between poet Leo Romero, educator Jorge Huerta and me. Finally, we are a theatre that attempts to transform and transcend circumstances, limitations and obstacles—theatre that reflects the melting pot which is America.

—Ruben Sierra

The Group Theatre Company. Brent B. Fraser and Alvin Sanders in *Tamer of Horses*. Photo: Fred Andrews

PRODUCTIONS 1985–86

Jacques Brel Is Alive and Well and Living in Paris, adapt: Eric Blau and Mort Shuman; music and lyrics: Jacques Brel; (D) Rita Giomi; (S) Alex Hutton; (C) Marilyn Erly; (L) Rex Carleton

Staring Back, Lawrence Perkins and Susan Nussbaum; (D) Tim Bond; (S) Gilbert Wong; (C) Anne Thaxter Watson; (L) Peter Allen

Voices of Christmas, Ruben Sierra; (D) Ruben Sierra; (S) Gilbert Wong; (C) Gilbert Wong; (L) Rex Carleton

Nappy Edges, Tanya Pettiford-Wates; (D) Anne-Denise Ford; (S) Anna Schlobohm; (C) Frances Kenny; (L) Collier Woods

Fifth Sun, Nicholas Patricca; (D) Tim Bond; (S) Karen Gjelsteen; (C) Josie Gardner; (L) Rex Carleton

A...My Name Is Alice, Joan Micklin Silver and Julianne Boyd; (D) John Kauffman; (S) Gilbert Wong; (C) Josie Gardner; (L) Rex Carleton

PRODUCTIONS 1986–87

Rap Master Ronnie, book and lyrics: Garry Trudeau; music: Elizabeth Swados; (D) Frank Condon; (S) Gilbert Wong; (C) Josie Gardner; (L) Rex Carleton

Voices of Christmas, Ruben Sierra; (D) Paul O'Connell; (S) Rex Carleton; (C) Leslie McGovern; (L) Darren McCroom

Two Can Play, Trevor Rhone; (D) Tim Bond; (S) Karen Gjelsteen; (C) Josie Gardner; (L) Rex Carleton

Idioglossia, Mark Handley; (D) Ruben Sierra; (S) Gilbert Wong; (C) Nina Moser; (L) Jennifer Lupton

Tamer of Horses, William Mastrosimone; (D) Ruben Sierra; (S) Patti Henry; (C) Kathleen Maki; (L) Darren McCroom

Orphans, Lyle Kessler; (D) John Kazanjian; (S) Jennifer Lupton; (C) Nina Moser; (L) Rex Carleton

Grove Theatre Company

THOMAS F. BRADAC
Executive Director

RICHARD STEIN
Managing Director

12852 Main St.
Garden Grove, CA 92640

Grove Theatre Company. Wayne Watkins and John-David Keller in *A Life in the Theater.*

(714) 636-7214 (bus.)
(714) 636-7213 (b.o.)

FOUNDED 1979
Thomas F. Bradac

SEASON
Year-round

FACILITIES
Gem Theatre
Seating capacity: 172
Stage: proscenium

Festival Amphitheatre
Seating capacity: 550
Stage: thrust

FINANCES
July 1, 1986-June 30, 1987
Expenses: $415,000

CONTRACTS
AEA Guest Artist and U/RTA

The Grove Theatre Company is dedicated to producing the finest examples of theatre art. Utilizing the plays of Shakespeare as a cornerstone for our program, the theatre presents works that challenge both artists and audience by addressing our mutual experiences, beliefs and concerns. In our theatre, whose inspiration is launched by the playwright, the text becomes the principal source for artistic exploration and fulfillment. In short, the Grove Theatre Company strives to pay tribute to the art form and to be a resource for our community.

—*Thomas F. Bradac*

PRODUCTIONS 1985–86

The Tempest, William Shakespeare; (D) John C. Fletcher; (S) Cliff Faulkner; (C) Shigeru Yaji; (L) Greg Sullivan
The Taming of the Shrew, William Shakespeare; (D) Thomas F. Bradac; (S) Gil Morales; (C) Karen Weller; (L) Pamela Rank
The Rivals, Richard Brinsley Sheridan; (D) Richard Rossi; (S) Cliff Faulkner; (C) Shigeru Yaji; (L) Pamela Rank
Going to See the Elephant, Karen Hensel, Elana Kent, Patti Johns, Sylvia Meredith, Laura Toffenetti and Elizabeth Shaw; (D) Carl Reggiardo; (S) Gil Morales; (C) Karen Weller; (L) David Palmer
Some Enchanted Evening, music: Richard Rodgers; lyrics: Oscar Hammerstein, II; conceived: Jeffrey B. Moss; (D) Denise Dell Reiss; (S) Gil Morales; (C) Mary Morales; (L) Kevin Cook
Crimes of the Heart, Beth Henley; (D) Daniel Bryan Cartmell; (S) Gil Morales; (C) Karen Weller; (L) David Palmer
The Dresser, Ronald Harwood; (D) Thomas F. Bradac; (S) Gil Morales; (C) Karen Weller; (L) David Palmer
A Moon for the Misbegotten, Eugene O'Neill; (D) Thomas F. Bradac; (S) Gil Morales; (C) Karen Weller; (L) Kevin Cook
What the Butler Saw, Joe Orton; (D) Phillip Beck; (S) Gil Morales; (C) Mary Morales; (L) David Palmer

PRODUCTIONS 1986–87

Henry IV, Part 1, William Shakespeare; (D) Richard E.T. White; (S) Cliff Faulkner; (C) Shigeru Yaji; (L) Peter Maradudin
The Merry Wives of Windsor, William Shakespeare; (D) Thomas F. Bradac; (S) Stanley Meyer; (C) Karen Weller; (L) Pamela Rank
Love's Labour's Lost, William Shakespeare; (D) Phillip Beck; (S) Cliff Faulkner; (C) Shigeru Yaji; (L) Pamela Rank
Quilters, book and lyrics: Molly Newman and Barbara Damashek; music: Barbara Damashek; (D) Thomas F. Bradac; (S) Gil Morales; (C) Karen Weller; (L) David Palmer
A Child's Christmas in Wales, adapt: Adrian Mitchell and Jeremy Brooks, from Dylan Thomas; (D) Daniel Bryan Cartmell; (S) Gil Morales; (C) Clarice Bessey; (L) Bob Cady
True West, Sam Shepard; (D) Frank Condon; (S) Gil Morales; (C) Karen Weller; (L) David Palmer
Devour the Snow, Abe Polsky; (D) Thomas F. Bradac; (S) Gil Morales; (C) Karen Weller; (L) David Palmer
The Show-Off, George Kelly; (D) David Herman; (S) Gil Morales; (C) Karen Weller; (L) Kevin Cook
A Life in the Theatre, David Mamet; (D) Daniel Bryan Cartmell; (S) Gil Morales; (C) Mary Morales; (L) David Palmer

The Guthrie Theater

GARLAND WRIGHT
Artistic Director

EDWARD A. MARTENSON
Executive Director

725 Vineland Pl.
Minneapolis, MN 55403
(612) 347-1100 (bus.)
(612) 377-2224 (b.o.)

FOUNDED 1963
Tyrone Guthrie, Oliver Rea, Peter Zeisler

SEASON
June-Apr.

FACILITIES
Seating capacity: 1,441
Stage: thrust

FINANCES
Apr. 1, 1986-Mar. 31, 1987
Expenses: $8,284,935

CONTRACTS
AEA LORT (A), SSD&C and USA

The Guthrie Theater. *A Midsummer Night's Dream.*

Theatre is not a place or thing, but an act—an interchange that has consequence. It is the means by which actors and audiences choose together to examine and participate in the world—to recognize it, to experience it and, ultimately, to understand it. Theatre reflects the complexity of our reality and, although it is perhaps better at illuminating questions than providing answers, its questioning spirit gives testimony to the seriousness with which it seeks to contribute to the human endeavor. We at the Guthrie firmly commit our efforts to artistic excellence at every level, to the greatest plays of the world repertoire, to the actor as the central communicator of the ideas and poetry within those plays, and to the imagination and its transforming power.

—Garland Wright

Note: During the 1985-86 season, Liviu Cuilei served as artistic director.

PRODUCTIONS 1985–86

Great Expectations, adapt: Barbara Field, from Charles Dickens; (D) Stephen Kanee; (S) Jack Barkla; (C) Jack Edwards; (L) Dawn Chiang

Cyrano de Bergerac, Edmond Rostand; trans: Brian Hooker; (D) Edward Gilbert; (S) Jack Barkla; (C) Jack Edwards; (L) Judy Rasmuson

A Midsummer Night's Dream, William Shakespeare; (D) Liviu Ciulei; (S) Beni Montresor; (C) Beni Montresor; (L) Beni Montresor

Candida, George Bernard Shaw; (D) William Gaskill; (S) Deidre Clancy; (C) Deidre Clancy; (L) Dawn Chiang

Execution of Justice, Emily Mann; (D) Emily Mann; (S) Ming Cho Lee; (C) Jennifer von Mayrhauser; (L) Pat Collins

A Christmas Carol, adapt: Barbara Field, from Charles Dickens; (D) Howard Dallin; (S) Jack Barkla; (C) Jack Edwards; (L) Marcus Dilliard

On the Razzle, Tom Stoppard; (D) Stephen Kanee; (S) John Conklin; (C) John Conklin; (L) Craig Miller

The Rainmaker, N. Richard Nash; (D) Timothy Near; (S) Kate Edmunds; (C) Jeff Struckman; (L) John Gisondi

PRODUCTIONS 1986–87

Saint Joan, George Bernard Shaw; (D) Patrick Mason; (S) Eugene Lee; (C) Donna M. Kress; (L) Duane Schuler

The Merry Wives of Windsor, William Shakespeare; (D) Derek Goldby; (S) Eugene Lee; (C) John Pennoyer; (L) John Custer

The Birthday Party, Harold Pinter; (D) Stephen Kanee; (S) Andrei Both; (C) Andrei Both; (L) Marcus Dilliard

On the Verge or The Geography of Yearning, Eric Overmyer; (D) Stan Wojewodski, Jr.; (S) Hugh Landwehr; (C) Jack Edwards; (L) Pat Collins

Rhinoceros, Eugene Ionesco; trans: Derek Prouse; (D) Kazimierz Braun; (S) John Conklin; (C) Jack Edwards; (L) Marcus Dilliard

A Christmas Carol, adapt: Barbara Field, from Charles Dickens; (D) Richard Ooms; (S) Jack Barkla; (C) Jack Edwards; (L) Marcus Dilliard

Double Infidelities, Pierre Marivaux; trans and adapt: William Gaskill; (D) William Gaskill; (S) John Conklin; (C) John Conklin; (L) James F. Ingalls

The Gospel at Colonus, Sophocles; adapt: Lee Breuer; trans: Robert Fitzgerald; music: Bob Telson; lyrics: Lee Breuer and Bob Telson; (D) Lee Breuer; (S) Alison Yerxa; (C) Ghretta Hynd; (L) Julie Archer

Candida, George Bernard Shaw; (D) Howard Dallin; (S) Deidre Clancy; (C) Deidre Clancy; (L) Dawn Chiang

Hartford Stage Company

MARK LAMOS
Artistic Director

DAVID HAWKANSON
Managing Director

50 Church St.
Hartford, CT 06103
(203) 525-5601 (bus.)
(203) 527-5151 (b.o.)

FOUNDED 1964
Jacques Cartier

Hartford Stage Company. Earl Hindeman and Lois Smith in *The Stick Wife*. Photo: T. Charles Erickson.

SEASON
Oct.-June

FACILITIES
John W. Huntington Theatre
Seating capacity: 489
Stage: thrust

FINANCES
July 1, 1986-June 30, 1987
Expenses: $2,500,000

CONTRACTS
AEA LORT (B) and SSD&C

The work at Hartford Stage reflects the desire to explore every possible kind of theatrical style: new plays, commissioned translations of old plays and adaptations of nontheatrical works. The center of our work is the production of texts from the past—primarily works by Shakespeare, but also plays by Schnitzler, Shaw, Molière and Ibsen—pieces that are modern, that draw parallels, chart paths and create possibilities. Occasionally, plays from the recent past are also revived, and fully half of each season is devoted to world premieres or to second productions of new plays by U.S. writers. All works, whether written B.C., in the Middle Ages, during the Renaissance, at the turn of the century or yesterday, are presented on a single stage. I believe that the theatre is a place meant for the exploration of dreams; the presentation of mysteries; the seeking of guidance, coherencies, lessons, laughter and wonder. Wonder most of all.

—Mark Lamos

PRODUCTIONS 1985–86

Twelfth Night, William Shakespeare; (D) Mark Lamos; (S) Michael H. Yeargan; (C) Jess Goldstein; (L) Stephen Strawbridge

A Shayna Maidel, Barbara Lebow; (D) Robert Kalfin; (S) Wolfgang Roth; (C) Eduardo Sicangco; (L) Curt Ostermann

Androcles and the Lion, George Bernard Shaw; (D) Jerome Kilty; (S) Lowell Detweiler; (C) Jess Goldstein; (L) John McLain

The Tooth of Crime, Sam Shepard; (D) David Petrarca; (S) John Conklin; (C) Eduardo Sicangco; (L) Vivien Leone

Distant Fires, Kevin Heelan; (D) Mark Lamos; (S) Marjorie Bradley Kellogg; (C) G.W. Mercier; (L) Stephen Strawbridge

On the Verge or The Geography of Yearning; Eric Overmeyer; (D) Mark Lamos; (S) Derek McLane; (C) Dunya Ramicova; (L) Robert Wierzel

PRODUCTIONS 1986–87

The Gilded Age, adapt: Constance Congdon, from Mark Twain and Charles Dudley Warner; (D) Mark Lamos; (S) Marjorie Bradley Kellogg; (C) Jess Goldstein; (L) Pat Collins

A Doll House, Henrik Ibsen; adapt: Gerry Bamman; trans: Irene B. Berman; (D) Emily Mann; (S) Andrew Jackness; (C) Dunya Ramicova; (L) Pat Collins

Children, A.R. Gurney, Jr.; (D) Jackson Phippin; (S) Hugh

Landwehr; (C) Sam Fleming; (L) Pat Collins

The Painful Adventures of Pericles, Prince of Tyre, William Shakespeare; adapt: George Wilkins; (D) Mark Lamos; (S) John Conklin; (C) John Conklin; (L) Robert Wierzel

The Stick Wife, Darrah Cloud; (D) Roberta Levitow; (S) Michael H. Yeargan; (C) Michael H. Yeargan; (L) Robert Wierzel

Morocco, Allan Havis; (D) Mark Lamos; (S) Michael H. Yeargan; (C) Michael H. Yeargan; (L) Robert Wierzel

Heritage Artists, Ltd.

ROBERT W. TOLAN
Producing Director

Box 586
Cohoes, NY 12047
(518) 235-7909 (bus.)
(518) 235-7969 (b.o.)

FOUNDED 1982
John P. Ryan, Jr.

SEASON
Oct.-May

FACILITIES
Cohoes Music Hall
Seating capacity: 250
Stage: proscenium

FINANCES
July 1, 1986-June 30, 1987
Expenses: $350,000

CONTRACTS
AEA SPT

Heritage Artists is committed to the development and production of music theatre works, with emphasis on small, ensemble, non-chorus musicals. The company blends revivals of the classics of the genre—*The Fantasticks*, *Godspell*—with remountings of rarely produced works of merit—*Strider*, *Billy Bishop Goes to War*—and new or unproduced works—*The Wonder Years*, *Yours, Anne*—as well as such recent hit shows as *Baby* and *Little Shop of Horrors*. While the historic Cohoes Music Hall, built in 1874, is the performing home base for Heritage Artists, the company was seen at Empire State Institute for the Performing Arts in Albany and Off-Off Broadway at the York Theatre Company during 1987. The company believes in mounting productions whose physical scale retains the focus on the performers and the materials. A vigorous Equity membership candidate program provides training for preprofessionals throughout the season.

—*Robert W. Tolan*

Heritage Artists, Ltd. Robin Haynes and T.O. Sterret in *Billy Bishop Goes to War*. Photo: Ed Schultz.

PRODUCTIONS 1985–86

The Wonder Years, music and lyrics: David Levy; book: David Levy, Steve Liebman, David Holdgrive and Terry La Bolt; (D) David Holdgrive; (S) Duke Durfree; (C) Duke Durfee; (L) Duke Durfree

Billy Bishop Goes to War, John Gray and Eric Peterson; (D) William Morris; (S) James M. Youmans; (L) Rachel Bickel

Baby, book: Sybille Pearson; music: David Shire; lyrics: Richard Maltby, Jr.; (D) Robert W. Tolan; (S) James M. Youmans; (C) Nancy Palmatier; (L) James Parsons

Godspell, music and lyrics: Stephen Schwartz; book: John-Michael Tebelak; (D) Vincent Telesco; (S) David Finley; (C) Chelsea Harriman; (L) Rachel Bickel

Something's Afoot, book, music and lyrics: James McDonald, David Vox and Robert Gerlach; (D) Gary Gage and Robert W. Tolan; (S) Gary English; (C) Amanda Aldridge; (L) Debra Dumas

The Drunkard, W.H.W. Smith; adapt: Bro Herrod; music and lyrics: Barry Manilow; (D) David Holdgrive; (S) Nancy Thun; (C) Amanda Aldridge; (L) Rachel Bickel

The Fantasticks, book and lyrics: Tom Jones; music: Harvey Schmidt; (D) David Holdgrive; (S) Nancy Thun; (C) Nancy Thun; (L) Rachel Bickel

PRODUCTIONS 1986–87

Strider, adapt: Steve Brown and Robert Kalfin, from Leo Tolstoy; book: Mark Rozovsky; music: S. Vetkin, Norman L. Berman and Mark Rozovsky; lyrics: Uri Riashentsev and Steve Brown; trans: Tamara Bering Sunguroff. (D) Robert W. Tolan; (S) Michael E. Daughtry; (C) Mary Marsicano; (L) Rachel Bickel

Little Shop of Horrors, book and lyrics: Howard Ashman; music: Alan Menken; (D) David Holdgrive; (S) James M. Youmans; (C) Mary Marsicano; (L) Rachel Bickel

I'm Getting My Act Together and Taking It on the Road, book and lyrics: Gretchen Cryer; music: Nancy Ford; (D) Robert W. Tolan; (S) James M. Youmans; (C) Mary Marsicano; (L) Rachel Bickel

Yours, Anne, book and lyrics: Enid Futterman; music: Michael Cohen; (D) Robert W. Tolan; (S) James Morgan; (C) Mary Marsicano; (L) David Lockner

Working, book adapt: Stephen Schwartz and Nina Faso, from Studs Terkel; music and lyrics: Stephen Schwartz, et al.; (D) David Holdgrive; (S) James M. Youmans; (C) Mary Marsicano; (L) Rachel Bickel

The Hippodrome State Theatre

MARY HAUSCH
GREGORY VON HAUSCH
Producing Directors

TEE LEE BEISTLE
Business Manager

25 Southeast Second Pl.
Gainesville, FL 32601
(904) 373-5968 (bus.)
(904) 375-4477 (b.o.)

FOUNDED 1973
Bruce Cornwell, Mary Hausch, Kerry McKenney, Gregory von Hausch, Marilyn Wall-Asse, Orin Wechsberg

SEASON
Year-round

FACILITIES
Mainstage
Seating capacity: 266
Stage: proscenium

Second Stage
Seating capacity: 86
Stage: flexible

FINANCES
June 1, 1986-May 31, 1987
Expenses: $1,100,000

CONTRACTS
AEA LORT (D)

The Hippodrome State Theatre has been nationally recognized for its imaginative theatre that spans contemporary, classic and international boundaries. Founded as an artistic cooperative 15 years ago, the Hippodrome still retains three of its

Hippodrome State Theatre. Malcolm Gets in *Little Shop of Horrors.* Photo: Gary Wolfson.

five original members. Their collective artistic input, intensely individual visions and stylistic variety create the theatre's unique eclectic style. The Hippodrome has produced world premieres, new works, Southeastern premieres, translations, original adaptations of screenplays and classical works. Internationally recognized playwrights like Tennessee Williams, Adrian Mitchell, Eric Bentley, Lee Breuer, Mario Vargas Llosa and Brian Thomson have collaborated with the company. Other programs include touring; an intern/conservatory program; an artistic residency program; and a Theatre for Young Audiences that has created 12 original plays, toured to 14 states and performed for over one million children. The Hippodrome is also part of a 25-theatre network addressing such problems as drug addiction, sexual abuse, suicide, pregnancy and discrimination through improvisational performances and discussion groups.

—*Mary Hausch*

PRODUCTIONS 1985–86

Ain't Misbehavin', music and lyrics: Fats Waller, et al.; book: Richard Maltby, Jr. and Murray Horwitz; (D) Malcolm Gets; (S) Carlos Francisco Asse; (C) Marilyn Wall-Asse; (L) Robert Robins

The Real Thing, Tom Stoppard; (D) Mary Hausch; (S) Carlos Francisco Asse; (C) Marilyn Wall-Asse; (L) Robert Robins

A Christmas Carol, adapt: Gregory von Hausch, from Charles Dickens; (D) Jim Wren; (S) Carlos Francisco Asse; (C) Marilyn Wall-Asse; (L) Robert Robins

Season's Greetings, Alan Ayckbourn; (D) Gregory von Hausch; (S) Carlos Francisco Asse; (C) Marilyn Wall-Asse; (L) Robert Robins

Romeo and Juliet, William Shakespeare; (D) Gregory von Hausch; (S) Carlos Francisco Asse; (C) Marilyn Wall-Asse; (L) Robert Robins

Little Shop of Horrors, book and lyrics: Howard Ashman; music: Alan Menken; (D) Mary Hausch; (S) Carlos Francisco Asse; (C) Marilyn Wall-Asse; (L) Robert Robins

The Middle Ages, A.R. Gurney, Jr.; (D) Gregory von Hausch; (S) Carlos Francisco Asse; (C) Marilyn Wall-Asse; (L) Robert Robins

The Energy Carnival, Margaret Bachus and Kevin Rainsberger; (D) Margaret Bachus; (S) Carlos Francisco Asse; (C) Marilyn Wall-Asse; (L) Robert Robins

The Water Log, Margaret Bachus and Kevin Rainsberger; (D) Margaret Bachus; (S) Carlos Francisco Asse; (C) Marilyn Wall-Asse; (L) Robert Robins

Vaudeville Jazz, Margaret Bachus and Kevin Rainsberger; (D) Margaret Bachus; (S) Carlos Francisco Asse; (C) Marilyn Wall-Asse; (L) Robert Robins

Captain Jim's Fire Safety Review Revue, Margaret Bachus and Kevin Rainsberger; (D) Margaret Bachus; (S) Carlos Francisco Asse; (C) Marilyn Wall-Asse; (L) Robert Robins

PRODUCTIONS 1986–87

...Cause Baby Look at You Now, Gregory von Hausch; (D) Gregory von Hausch; (S) Carlos Francisco Asse; (C) Marilyn Wall-Asse; (L) Robert Robins

Ain't Misbehavin', music and lyrics: Fats Waller, et al.; book: Richard Maltby, Jr. and Murray Horowitz; (D) Malcolm Gets; (S) Carlos Francisco Asse; (C) Marilyn Wall-Asse; (L) Robert Robins

A Chorus Line, book: James Kirkwood and Nicholas Dante; music: Marvin Hamlisch; lyrics: Edward Kleban; (D) Carole Brandt; (S) Carlos Francisco Asse; (C) Marilyn Wall-Asse; (L) Robert Robins

Noises Off, Michael Frayn; (D) Gregory von Hausch; (S) Carlos Francisco Asse; (C) Marilyn Wall-Asse; (L) Robert Robins

Orphans, Lyle Kessler; (D) Mary Hausch; (S) Carlos Francisco Asse; (C) Marilyn Wall-Asse; (L) Robert Robins

Cyrano de Bergerac, Edmond Rostand; (D) Gregory von Hausch; (S) Carlos Francisco Asse; (C) Lisa Martin; (L) Robert Robins

Brighton Beach Memoirs, Neil Simon; (D) David Shelton; (S) Carlos Francisco Asse; (C) Marilyn Wall-Asse; (L) Robert Robins

The Energy Carnival, Margaret Bachus and Kevin Rainsberger; (D) Margaret Bachus; (S) Carlos Francisco Asse; (C) Marilyn Wall-Asse; (L) Robert Robins

Portraits, Margaret Bachus and Kevin Rainsberger; (D) Margaret Bachus; (S) Carlos Francisco Asse; (C) Marilyn Wall-Asse; (L) Robert Robins

Just Florida, Margaret Bachus and Kevin Rainsberger; (D) Margaret Bachus; (S) Carlos Francisco Asse; (C) Marilyn Wall-Asse; (L) Robert Robins

Honolulu Theatre for Youth

JOHN KAUFFMAN
Artistic Director

JANE CAMPBELL
Managing Director

Box 3257
Honolulu, HI 96801
(808) 521-3487

FOUNDED 1955
Nancy Corbett

SEASON
Year-round

FINANCES
June 1, 1986-May 31, 1987
Expenses: $562,700

Honolulu Theatre for Youth is Hawaii's only professional theatre company. Dedicated to producing high-quality theatre for young audiences, each season offers a broad spectrum of performances adapted from fairy tales, literary classics, contemporary issues and plays celebrating Pacific Rim Cultures. HTY annually tours statewide with one major production. Our education program provides materials, workshops and classes to teachers and students. Additionally, HTY provides assistance to projects such as Very Special Arts Hawaii. We actively encourage the development of new American plays and playwrights by commissioning works and hosting playwrights-in-residence. HTY has provided international outreach programs and has toured to American Samoa, Micronesia and Australia. The ethnic mix of the HTY company is as diverse as the people of Hawaii: nontraditional casting is the norm. The exploration of cultures, values and theatre forms is what HTY is all about.

—*John Kauffman*

PRODUCTIONS 1985–86

Rashomon, adapt: Fay Kanin and Michael Kanin, from Ryunosuke Akutagawa; (D) John Kauffman; (S) Joseph Dodd; (C) Ann Asakura Kimura; (L) Lloyd S. Riford, III

Honolulu Theatre for Youth. James Pestana, James Rabauliman, Don Nahaku and Ray Bumatai in *Song for the Navigator.* Photo: Keoni Wagner.

Cinderella, adapt: Gayle L. Cornelison; (D) John Kauffman; (S) Shelley Henze Schermer; (C) Nicole Thibadeaux; (L) Lloyd S. Riford, III

Song for the Navigator, Michael Cowell; (D) John Kauffman; (S) Joseph Dodd; (C) Laura Crow; (L) Lloyd S. Riford, III

F.O.B., David Hwang; (D) Phyllis S.K. Look; (S) Joseph Dodd; (C) Ann Asakura Kimura; (L) Chris Markiewicz

Charlotte's Webb, adapt: Joseph Robinette, from E.B. White; (D) Clayton Corzatte; (S) Karen Gjelsteen; (C) Maurice Palinski; (L) Lloyd S. Riford, III

The Story of Buck Buck Buh Deek, book: Cal Turlock; music and lyrics: Richard Roblee; (D) John Kauffman; (S) Maurice Palinski; (C) Maurice Palinski; (L) Alan Will

PRODUCTIONS 1986–87

Song for the Navigator, Michael Cowell; (D) John Kauffman; (S) Joseph Dodd; (C) Laura Crow; (L) Lloyd S. Riford, III

Our Town, Thornton Wilder; (D) John Kauffman; (S) Lloyd S. Riford, III; (C) Ann Asakura Kimura; (L) Lloyd S. Riford, III

The Island, Athol Fugard; (D) Tim Bond; (S) Don Yanik; (C) Ann Asakura Kimura

The Flying Prince, Aurand Harris; (D) John Kauffman; (S) Don Yanik; (C) Ann Asakura Kimura; (L) Chris Markiewicz

The Story of Perseus, Will Huddleston; (D) John Kauffman; (S) Mary E. Lewis; (C) Julie James; (L) Lloyd S. Riford, III

Puss in Boots, adapt: Max Bush, from Charles Perrault; (D) Anne-Denise Ford; (S) Charles Walsh; (C) Ann Asakura Kimura; (L) Chris Markiewicz

The Original Absurd Musical Revue for Children, Arne Zaslove; (D) John Kauffman; (S) Gerald Kawaoka; (C) Trudi Vetter; (L) Gerald Kawaoka

Horse Cave Theatre

WARREN HAMMACK
Director

PAMELA WHITE
Administrative Director

Box 215
Horse Cave, KY 42749
(502) 786-1200 (bus.)
(502) 786-2177 (b.o.)

FOUNDED 1977
Horse Cave citizens

SEASON
July-Sept.

FACILITIES
Seating capacity: 355
Stage: thrust

FINANCES
Oct. 1, 1985-Sept. 30, 1986
Expenses: $227,875

CONTRACTS
AEA letter of agreement

Horse Cave Theatre provides professional theatre for the citizens of southern Kentucky by presenting works from the best of our dramatic heritage. The theatre has demonstrated a commitment to Kentucky's artists; provides a wide range of educational programs; and produces a mixture of contemporary plays, new scripts and popular classics in rotating repertory each summer. Under the prestigious Kentucky Voices program, the theatre presents works which combine the unique cultural resources of the region with its own professional resources; a televised production in this series has recently won two national awards. The theatre makes the plays of Shakespeare available to Kentucky's students, supplementing live performances with study guides, discussions, artist residencies and in-service training for teachers. Student theatre workshops allow young people to explore the creative process with resident teaching artists. The touring program brings small-cast plays to students and arts groups statewide.

—*Warren Hammack*

PRODUCTIONS 1986

Painting Churches, Tina Howe; (D) Laura Fine; (S) Sam Hunt; (C) Rebecca Shouse; (L) Gregory Etter

Gas Light, Patrick Hamilton; (D) William Groth; (S) John Partyka; (C) Rebecca Shouse; (L) Gregory Etter

Marching to Zion, Jim Peyton; (D) Warren Hammack; (S) John Partyka; (C) Rebecca Shouse; (L) Gregory Etter

The Taming of the Shrew, William Shakespeare; (D) Warren Hammack; (S) John Partyka; (C) Rebecca Shouse; (L) Gregory Etter

PRODUCTIONS 1987

A Flea in Her Ear, Georges Feydeau; trans: Barnett Shaw; (D) Warren Hammack; (S) Sam Hunt; (C) Rebecca Shouse; (L) Gregory Etter

The Dining Room, A.R. Gurney, Jr.; (D) Laura Fine; (S) John Partyka; (C) Rebecca Shouse; (L) Gregory Etter

Mossie and the Strippers, Billy Edd Wheeler; (D) Warren Hammack; (S) Sam Hunt; (C) Rebecca Shouse; (L) Gregory Etter

Horse Cave Theatre. Scott Edmunds in *The Taming of the Shrew.* Photo: Warren Hammack.

The Merchant of Venice, William Shakespeare; (D) David Shookhoff; (S) John Partyka; (C) Rebecca Shouse; (L) Gregory Etter

Hudson Guild Theatre

GEOFFREY SHERMAN
Producing Director

JAMES ABAR
Associate Director

441 West 26th St.
New York, NY 10001
(212) 760-9839 (bus.)
(212) 760-9810 (b.o.)

FOUNDED 1896
John Lovejoy Elliott

SEASON
Sept.-June

FACILITIES
Arthur Strasser Auditorium
Seating capacity: 135
Stage: proscenium

FINANCES
Oct. 1, 1986-Sept. 30, 1987
Expenses: $365,000

CONTRACTS
AEA letter of agreement and USA

Located in the Chelsea district, in Manhattan's second-oldest settlement house, the Hudson Guild Theatre has grown from a community-based playhouse to one of the leading Off-Broadway theatres in New York City. HGT has been a pioneering force in the introduction of new American and European playwrights, as well as previously unknown actors and directors, to the New York theatre world. The theatre is dedicated to the development of a socially and politically challenging artistic vision that encompasses the finest and most innovative American and international drama. This commitment is implemented through premieres of works by both new and established playwrights; readings and workshops; and an annual festival of new plays by and about minorities.

—Geoffrey Sherman

Note: During the 1985-86 season, David Kerry Heefner served as producing director.

PRODUCTIONS 1985–86

Seascape with Sharks and Dancer, Don Nigro; (D) David Kerry Heefner; (S) Daniel Conway; (C) Mary L. Hayes; (L) Phil Monat

And They Dance Real Slow in Jackson, Jim Leonard, Jr.; (D) David Kerry Heefner; (S) Paul Wonsek; (C) Pamela Scofield; (L) Paul Wonsek

The Second Man, S.N. Behrman; (D) Thomas Gruenewald; (S) Paul Wonsek; (C) Pamela Scofield; (L) Paul Wonsek

Wrestlers, Bill C. Davis; (D) Geraldine Fitzgerald; (S) Paul Wonsek; (C) Mary L. Hayes; (L) Paul Wonsek

Writer's Cramp, John Byrne; (D) David Kerry Heefner; (S) Richard Harmon; (C) Patricia Adshead; (L) Richard Harmon

PRODUCTIONS 1986–87

Insignificance, Terry Johnson; (D) Geoffrey Sherman; (S) Paul Wonsek; (C) Pamela Scofield; (L) Paul Wonsek

Pantomime, Derek Walcott; (D) Kay Matschullat; (S) Rosario Provenza; (C) Pamela Peterson; (L) Robert Wierzel

Moms, Alice Childress; (D) Walter Dallas; (S) Rosario Provenza; (C) Judy E. Dearing; (L) Robert Wierzel

Crackwalker, Judith Thompson; (D) James Abar; (S) Paul Wonsek; (C) Karen Hummel; (L) Paul Wonsek

No Way to Treat a Lady, book adapt, music and lyrics: Douglas J. Cohen, from William Goldman; (D) Jack Hofsiss; (S) David Jenkins; (C) Michael Kaplan; (L) Beverly Emmons

Hudson Guild Theatre. Elizabeth Berridge and Joe Mantello in *Crackwalker*. Photo: Bob Marshak.

Huntington Theatre Company. Maryann Plunkett in *Saint Joan*. Photo: Gerry Goodstein.

Huntington Theatre Company

PETER ALTMAN
Producing Director

MICHAEL MASO
Managing Director

264 Huntington Ave.
Boston, MA 02115
(617) 353-3320 (bus.)
(617) 266-3913 (b.o.)

FOUNDED 1982
Boston University

SEASON
Sept.-June

FACILITIES
Boston University Theatre
Seating capacity: 855
Stage: proscenium

Studio 210
Seating capacity: 99
Stage: flexible

FINANCES
July 1, 1986-June 30, 1987
Expenses: $2,200,000

CONTRACTS
AEA LORT (B), SSD&C and USA

The Huntington Theatre Company's aim is to produce annual seasons of classics and superior contemporary plays that are acted, directed and designed at a standard of excellence comparable to that of the nation's leading professional companies. We continually seek to devote ourselves to the great masterpieces of dramatic literature; to respond to today's issues and emotions by presenting literate, trenchant contemporary plays new to Boston; and to be enterprising and cosmopolitan in choosing worthy writing from varied countries and periods. Because we honor the theatre's heritage, we strive to present classic works in their true spirit. In producing plays of any era or style, we enjoy and admire truthful situations, vivid characters, sound dramatic construction, eloquent language, imaginative staging with well-balanced casts and the finest possible level of craftsmanship. We believe that a flexible, allied family of professionals who share this vision will best extend, fulfill and serve our theatre's vision.

—Peter Altman

PRODUCTIONS 1985–86

Sullivan and Gilbert, book: Kenneth Ludwig; music: Arthur Sullivan; lyrics: W.S. Gilbert; (D) Larry Carpenter; (S) John Falabella; (C) David Murin; (L) Marcia Madeira
The Misanthrope, Molière; trans: Richard Wilbur; (D) Edward Gilbert; (S) John Conklin; (C) John Conklin; (L) Beverly Emmons
The Birthday Party, Harold Pinter; (D) Ben Levit; (S) James Leonard Joy; (C) Mariann Verheyen; (L) Frances Aronson
Saint Joan, George Bernard Shaw; (D) Jacques Cartier; (S) Karl Eigsti; (C) Robert Morgan; (L) Roger Meeker
On the Verge or The Geography of Yearning, Eric Overmyer; (D) Pamela Berlin; (S) Franco Colavecchia; (C) Lindsay Davis; (L) Jackie Manassee

PRODUCTIONS 1986–87

Joe Turner's Come and Gone, August Wilson; (D) Lloyd Richards; (S) Scott Bradley; (C) Pamela Peterson; (L) Michael Giannitti
Heartbreak House, George Bernard Shaw; (D) Edward Gilbert; (S) John Conklin; (C) Robert Morgan; (L) Nicholas Cernovich
Awake and Sing!, Clifford Odets; (D) Ben Levit; (S) James Leonard Joy; (C) Mariann Verheyen; (L) Frances Aronson
Jumpers, Tom Stoppard; (D) Jacques Cartier; (S) Karl Eigsti; (C) John Falabella; (L) Toshiro Ogawa
The Diary of a Scoundrel, Alexander Ostrovsky; adapt: Larry Carpenter; trans: Roberta Reeder; (D) Larry Carpenter; (S) James Leonard Joy; (C) Lindsay Davis; (L) Marcia Madeira

Illinois Theatre Center

STEVE S. BILLIG
Artistic Director

ETEL BILLIG
Managing Director

400A Lakewood Blvd.
Park Forest, IL 60466
(312) 481-3510

FOUNDED 1976
Etel Billig, Steve S. Billig

SEASON
Year-round

FACILITIES
Seating capacity: 187
Stage: thrust

FINANCES
Sept. 1, 1986-Aug. 31, 1987
Expenses: $224,000

CONTRACTS
AEA CAT

The Illinois Theatre Center was founded in 1976 with the belief that a vigorous artistic and cultural life should be part of all communities. It is through theatre that we hope to enrich the quality of life for all area residents. Through the world of theatre we want our audiences to appreciate man's infinite diversity of expression and the vast range of human invention. Along with our seven-play mainstage season, we have an active outreach program which provides special programming for the elderly, the handicapped and the economically disadvantaged. We also hold an annual free outdoor Shakespeare Festival.

—Steve S. Billig

PRODUCTIONS 1985–86

Quilters, book and lyrics: Molly Newman and Barbara Damashek; music: Barbara Damashek; (D) Steve S. Billig; (S) Kevin Ervick and Nancy Eads; (C) Henriette Swearingen; (L) Richard Peterson
Messiah, Martin Sherman; (D) Etel Billig; (S) Jonathan Roark; (C) Henriette Swearingen; (L) Richard Peterson
110 in the Shade, book: N. Richard Nash; music: Harvey Schmidt; lyrics: Tom Jones; (D) Etel Billig; (S) Jonathan Roark; (C) Henriette Swearingen; (L) Richard Peterson
Painting Churches, Tina Howe; (D) Travis Stockley; (S) Jonathan Roark; (L) Jonathan Roark
Greater Tuna, Jaston Williams, Joe Sears and Ed Howard; (D) Jonathan Roark; (S) Nancy Eads; (C) Henriette Swearingen; (L) Jonathan Roark
Sherlock's Last Case, Charles Marowitz; (D) Steve S. Billig; (S) Jonathan Roark; (C) Henriette Swearingen; (L) Jonathan Roark
Hangin' Round, Steve S. Billig; (D) Steve S. Billig; (S) Jonathan Roark; (L) Jonathan Roark

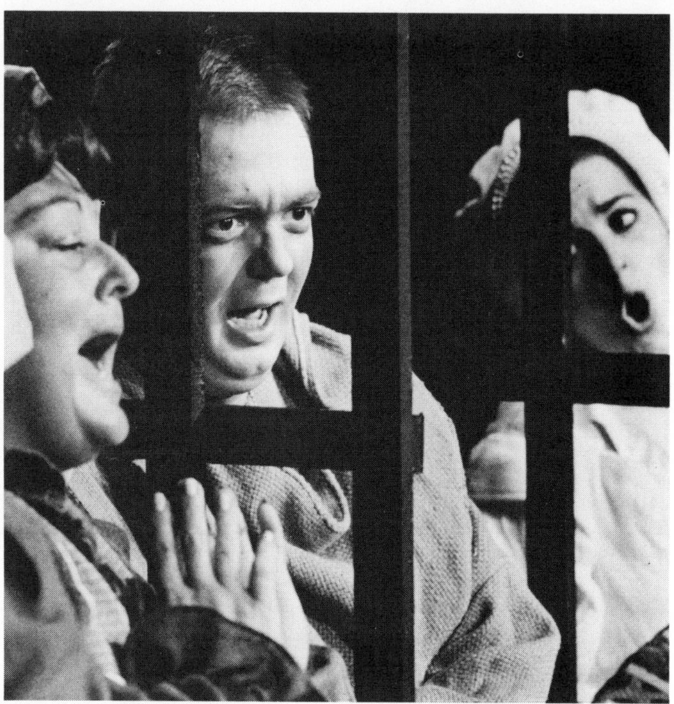

Illinois Theatre Center. Cinda Moak-Forsythe, Herb Nottlemann and Rosalind Hurwitz in *Man of La Mancha*. Photo: Lloyd De Grane.

PRODUCTIONS 1986–87

Nuts, Tom Topor; (D) Steve S. Billig; (S) Jonathan Roark; (L) Jonathan Roark
A Day in the Death of Joe Egg, Peter Nichols; (D) Pete Forster; (S) Jonathan Roark; (L) Jonathan Roark
Man of La Mancha, book: Dale Wasserman; lyrics: Joe Darion; music: Mitchell Leigh; (D) Steve S. Billig; (S) Archway Scenic; (C) Henriette Swearingen; (L) Richard Peterson
A Sense of Humor, Ernest Thompson; (D) Steve S. Billig; (S) Jonathan Roark; (L) Jonathan Roark
Kuni-Leml, book: Nahma Sandrow; music: Raphael Crystal; lyrics: Richard Engquist; (D) Maureen Kelly; (S) Archway Scenic; (C) A & J Designs; (L) Richard Peterson
Little Footsteps, Ted Tally; (D) Steve S. Billig; (S) Jonathan Roark; (L) Jonathan Roark
High Kickers, Steve S. Billig; (D) Steve S. Billig; (S) Archway Scenic; (S) GWTW Enterprises; (L) Jonathan Roark

Illusion Theater

BONNIE MORRIS
MICHAEL ROBINS
Producing Directors

JOHN MONTILINO
Managing Director

528 Hennepin Ave., Suite 704
Minneapolis, MN 55403
(612) 339-4944 (bus.)
(612) 338-8371 (b.o.)

FOUNDED 1974
Carole Harris Lipschultz, Michael Robins

SEASON
Feb.-July

FACILITIES
Hennepin Center for the Arts
Seating capacity: 224
Stage: thrust

FINANCES
July 1, 1985-June 30, 1986
Expenses: $799,000

CONTRACTS
AEA SPT

We live in a time when much art is involved in self-examination, postmodern analysis and the practice of distancing ourselves from our lives by intellectualizing the human condition. Illusion Theater's aesthetic uses the power of theatre to do the opposite—to reflect the times we live in by exposing the emotional underside of that same human condition. We do this by consistently producing world and area premieres of new work, and rarely produced classics. We maintain a resident company of actors and create new plays collaboratively with writer, director and actor. Encompassed in our aesthetic is also a belief that theatre can effect sound change. We demonstrate this belief through our repertoire of plays dedicated to the prevention of sexual abuse and interpersonal violence, which we tour across the country. We will continue to invest in the talent of emerging and established artists as we create a body of plays for the American theatre.

—Bonnie Morris, Michael Robins

PRODUCTIONS 1985–86

Becoming Memories, Arthur Giron and company; (D) Michael Robins; (S) David Krchelich; (C) Sonya Berlovitz; (L) Jeff Bartlett
Biography: A Game, Max Frisch; trans: Michael Bullock; (D) Ben Kreilkamp; (S) Lori Sullivan; (C) Mona Toft; (L) Jeff Bartlett
Overnight, Michael Smith and company; (D) David Ira Goldstein; (S) Michael Sommers; (C) Nayna Ramey; (L) Michael Murnane
White House Wives, Chris Cinque and company; (D) Michael Robins and Gail Turner; (S) Dean Holzman; (C) Sonya Berlovitz; (L) Michael Murnane
Andersen: Dream Lover, Kenneth Cavander and company; (D) David Shookhoff; (S) Lori Sullivan; (C) Linda Cassone; (L) Jeff Bartlett

PRODUCTIONS 1986–87

Nosferatu, Ping Chong; (D) Ping Chong; (S) Ping Chong; (C) Mel Carpenter and Sonya Berlovitz; (L) Jeff Bartlett
The Sea, Edward Bond; (D) Michael Robins; (S) Michael Sommers; (C) Cheryl Horne; (L) Michael Vennerstrom
Family, Cordelia Anderson, Bonnie Morris, Michael Robins and company; (D) Michael Robins; (S) Dean Holzman; (C) Linda Cameron; (L) David Vogel
No Place to Park, Eric Anderson and company; (D) David Ira Goldstein; (S) Linda Cassone; (C) Sonya Berlovitz; (L) Jeff Bartlett
The Einstein Project, Jon Klein, Paul D'Andrea and company; (D) Steven Dietz; (S) Dean Holzman; (C) Janet Groenert and Sonya Bervolitz; (L) Michael Murnane

Illusion Theater. Ben Kreilkamp and company in *The Einstein Project.* Photo: Walker Arts Center.

The Independent Eye. Conrad Bishop and Elizabeth Fuller in *Marie Antoinette.* Photo: C. Bishop.

The Independent Eye

CONRAD BISHOP
Producing Director

LINDA BISHOP
Associate Producing Director

208 East King St.
Lancaster, PA 17602
(717) 393-9088

FOUNDED 1974
Conrad Bishop, Linda Bishop

SEASON
Sept.-May

FACILITIES
Eye Theatre Works
Seating capacity: 100
Stage: proscenium

FINANCES
July 1, 1986-June 30, 1987
Expenses: $174,180

The Independent Eye is devoted to new work and new visions of classics, using many dramatic forms to examine deeply felt, commonly shared experiences. Founded in 1974, the Eye has presented more than 2,000 performances in 33 states for every sort of audience. The Eye focuses on human incongruity, incorporating the unsettling mood-swings of real experience, in many styles: horror melodrama in *Goners*; a mask-puppet-actor *Macbeth*; shadow puppetry in the documentary *Marie Antoinette* and the contemporary comic-book adaptation *American Splendor*; cabaret in *Black Dog* and *Le Cabaret de Camille*. The performers' personal stake and the clarity of storytelling are primary in each. In 1977, the Eye moved from Chicago to Lancaster, Pa. and began growing local roots, opening the Eye Theatre Works in 1981. Today, we present a resident season, create radio and video works, tour, and host guest artists who share our vision.

—Conrad Bishop

PRODUCTIONS 1985–86

American Splendor, adapt: Conrad Bishop, from Harvey Pekar; (D) Conrad Bishop; (S) Herbert O'Dell; (C) Nancy Whiting; (L) Dean Novosat
True West, Sam Shepard; (D) Stephen Patterson and Barry Kornhauser; (S) Herbert O'Dell; (C) Beth Dunkelberger; (L) Dean Novosat
Hedda Gabler, Henrik Ibsen; trans: Conrad Bishop; (D) Conrad Bishop; (S) Conrad Bishop; (C) Beth Dunkelberger; (L) Conrad Bishop
Spaces, Camilla Schade and company; (D) Camilla Schade; (S) Herbert O'Dell; (C) Nancy Whiting; (L) John Whiting

Song Stories, Conrad Bishop and Elizabeth Fuller; (D) Conrad Bishop

PRODUCTIONS 1986–87

Valentines and Killer Chili, Kent Brown; (D) Conrad Bishop; (S) Dan Gluibizzi; (C) Nancy Whiting; (L) Conrad Bishop
Jacques Brel Is Alive and Well and Living in Paris, adapt: Eric Blau and Mort Shuman; music and lyrics: Jacques Brel; (D) Pat Lemay; (S) Neil Dreibelbis; (L) Conrad Bishop
The Eye Comedy Works, Camilla Schade; (D) Camilla Schade; (S) Louise Schintz; (L) Conrad Bishop
No More to Prophesy, Sidney Sulkin; (D) Gary Smith; (S) Richard Whitson; (C) Bernie Keller; (L) Conrad Bishop
Marie Antoinette, Conrad Bishop and Elizabeth Fuller; (D) Conrad Bishop; (S) Linda Cunningham; (C) Beth Dunkelberger; (L) Conrad Bishop

FINANCES
July 1, 1986-June 30, 1987
Expenses: $2,278,457

CONTRACTS
AEA LORT (B), (D), SSD&C and USA

Indiana Repertory Theatre

TOM HAAS
Artistic Director

140 West Washington St.
Indianapolis, IN 46204
(317) 635-5277 (bus.)
(317) 635-5252 (b.o.)

FOUNDED 1972
Benjamin Mordecai, Gregory Poggi, Edward Stern

SEASON
Oct.-May

FACILITIES
Mainstage
Seating capacity: 607
Stage: proscenium

Upperstage
Seating capacity: 269
Stage: proscenium

Cabaret Club
Seating capacity: 150
Stage: modified thrust

In 1987, the Indiana Repertory Theatre celebrated the 15th anniversary of its founding by launching a new programming initiative: America in Performance will focus our work over the next few years on a combination of American classics, new American works and neglected works of the American repertoire, interspersed with a small number of contrasting works from non-American repertoires. With our resident acting company, we have developed a festival staging approach designed specifically to meet the needs of American plays. The Cabaret Club, our nightclub space, produces musical satires, providing a popular entertainment venue to contrast with the in-depth exploration of the mainstage production series. As the only resident professional theatre in the state, we provide extensive community services, the most significant of which is an educational outreach program aimed at developing the audiences of the future.

—Tom Haas

PRODUCTIONS 1985–86

The Front Page, Ben Hecht and Charles MacArthur; (D) Tom Haas; (S) Christopher Barreca; (C) Nancy Pope; (L) Stuart Duke
Peter Pan, James M. Barrie; (D) Tom Haas; (S) Christopher Barreca; (C) Bobbi Owen; (L) Rachel Budin
Dracula, Bram Stoker; (D) Gavin Cameron-Webb; (S) Alison Ford; (C) Gail Brassard; (L) Rachel Budin
Dial "M" for Murder, Frederick Knott; (D) Paul Moser; (S) Russ Metheny; (C) Gail Brassard; (L) Michael Lincoln
The Boys in Autumn, Bernard Sabath; (D) Paul Moser; (S) Russ Metheny; (C) Gail Brassard; (L) Stuart Duke
Romeo and Juliet, William Shakespeare; (D) Tom Haas; (S) G.W. Mercier; (C) William Walker; (L) Stephen Strawbridge
Virginia, Edna O'Brien; (D) Paul Moser; (S) Christopher Barreca; (C) Connie Singer; (L) Stuart Duke

Indiana Repertory Theatre. David Williams and Michael Lipton in *The Front Page*. Photo: Tod Martens.

Sister Mary Ignatius Explains It All for You and ***The Actor's Nightmare***, Christopher Durang; (D) Ben Cameron; (S) Christopher Barreca; (C) Connie Singer; (L) Stuart Duke
Mourning Becomes Electra, Eugene O'Neill; (D) Tom Haas; (S) Christopher Barreca; (C) Gail Brassard; (L) Rachel Budin
Torch Song Trilogy, Harvey Fierstein; (D) Paul Moser; (S) Christopher Barreca; (C) Connie Singer; (L) Stuart Duke

PRODUCTIONS 1986–87

The Skin of Our Teeth, Thornton Wilder; (D) Tom Haas; (S) Christopher Barreca; (C) Gail Brassard; (L) Stuart Duke
The Mousetrap, Agatha Christie; (D) Tom Haas; (S) Steven Rubin; (C) William Walker; (L) Michael Lincoln
The Crucible, Arthur Miller; (D) Paul Moser; (S) Christopher Barreca; (C) Connie Singer; (L) Stuart Duke
To Culebra, Jonathan Bolt; (D) Tom Haas; (S) Christopher Barreca; (C) William Walker; (L) Stuart Duke
Tobacco Road, adapt: Jack Kirkland, from Erskine Caldwell; (D) Paul Moser; (S) Christopher Barreca; (C) Connie Singer; (L) Stuart Duke
Hay Fever, Noel Coward; (D) Tom Haas; (S) G.W. Mercier; (C) G.W. Mercier; (L) Stephen Strawbridge

INTAR Hispanic American Arts Center

MAX FERRA
Artistic Director

DENNIS FERGUSON-ACOSTA
Managing Director

Box 788
New York, NY 10108
(212) 695-6134

FOUNDED 1966
Max Ferra, Oscar Garcia, Antonio Gonzalez-Jaen, Benjamin Lopez, Gladys Ortiz, Elsa Ortiz Robles, Frank Robles

SEASON
Sept.-July

FACILITIES
Mainstage
Seating capacity: 99
Stage: proscenium

Second Stage
Seating capacity: 99
Stage: proscenium

FINANCES
July 1, 1986-June 30, 1987
Expenses: $547,000

CONTRACTS
AEA letter of agreement

INTAR Hispanic American Arts Center identifies, presents and develops contemporary Latin and Hispanic artists living in the U.S. and throughout the world. The INTAR Theatre season is designed to highlight plays that have local and universal appeal. Included in each season is at least one new American work, one musical and the participation of an internationally known artist. INTAR Gallery, one of the most important alternative spaces in New York City for the Latin visual artist, mounts 7 to 10 exhibitions per year, featuring emerging as well as established minority artists. The INTAR Playwrights-in-Residence Laboratory is designed to encourage and support the creative forces that impel talented Hispanic artists from all over the country to write for the stage. INTAR Music Theatre Laboratory, also national in scope, was created to develop new music theatre pieces drawing from the richness and variety of Latin music. Through all its programs, INTAR serves the social and cultural needs of the community and country by nurturing the expressive voices and visions of the Hispanic peoples.

—Max Ferra

PRODUCTIONS 1985–86

La Chunga, Mario Vargas Llosa; trans: Joanne Pottlitzer; (D) Max Ferra; (S) Ricardo Morin; (C) David Velasquez; (L) Beverly Emmons

Lovers and Keepers, book and lyrics: Maria Irene Fornes; music: Tito Puente and Fernando Rivas; (D) Maria Irene Fornes; (S) Ricardo Morin; (C) Gabriel Berry; (L) Anne Militello

Burning Patience, Antonio Skarmeta; trans: Marion Peter Holt; (D) Paul Zimet; (S) Christopher Barreca; (C) David Velasquez; (L) Arden Fingerhut

PRODUCTIONS 1986–87

The Red Madonna or A Damsel for a Gorilla, Fernando Arrabal; trans: Lynne Alvarez; (D) Fernando Arrabal; (S) David Peterson; (C) David Zakowska; (L) John Gisondi

Roosters, Milcha Sanchez-Scott; (D) Jackson Phippin; (S) Loy Arcenas; (C) C. Hundley; (L) John Gisondi

Our Lady of the Tortilla, Luis Santiero; (D) Max Ferra; (S) James Sandefur; (C) Arnall Downs; (L) Michael Chybowski

INTAR Hispanic American Arts Center. Albert Farrar, Jonathan del Arco and Joaquim de Almeida in *Roosters.* Photo: Chris Montagna.

Interart Theatre

MARGOT LEWITIN
Artistic Director

ANNE L. PETERS
Managing Director

549 West 52nd St.
New York, NY 10019
(212) 246-1050

Interart Theatre. Peggy Shaw and Lois Weaver in *Patience and Sarah.* Photo: Eva Weiss.

FOUNDED 1971
Jane Chambers, Marjorie De Fazio, Margot Lewitin, Alice Rubenstein

SEASON
Year-round

FACILITIES
Interart Theatre
Seating capacity: 74
Stage: flexible

Annex I
Seating capacity: 50
Stage: flexible

Annex II
Seating capacity: 35
Stage: flexible

FINANCES
July 1, 1986-June 30, 1987
Expenses: $110,325

CONTRACTS
AEA Mini

Interart Theatre is committed to exploring all areas of theatrical expression, while emphasizing the presentation of new plays and playwrights. Interart undertakes projects with an established text as well as experimental material designed to encourage the development of directors and designers. We also support the long-term development of playwrights and new works outside the confines of a standard rehearsal-production period. Interart Theatre is a program of the Women's Interart Center, a nonprofit, multiarts organization that produces work by artists (primarily, but not exclusively, women) in varying disciplines. The Center provides space and facilities for artists to explore the full gamut of the arts through workshops, colloquia and productions. By encouraging artists and audiences to venture into various media and by stressing the interactive exchanges inherent in the concept "interart," the Center aims to expand its vision and enliven its idea of what art is and can be. To achieve these goals, we support the C&L Collective, a group of over 75 playwrights, directors, actors and designers that presents a developmental workshop reading series; and we maintain an Integrated Media Arts program that provides training in acting and directing, and offers artistic apprenticeships.

—Margot Lewitin

PRODUCTIONS 1985–86

Trilogy: Seventeen; At That Time I Was Studying Carole Lombard; The Father, Beatrice Roth; (D) Valeria Waslilewski; (S) Valeria Wasilewski; (C) Beatrice Roth; (L) Rocky Greenberg

Walking Through, Bernett Belgraier; (D) Melody Brooks; (S) Daniel Kenney; (C) Melody Brooks; (L) Paula Gordon

...About Anne, adapt: Salome Jens, from Anne Sexton; (D) Salome Jens; (S) Seth Price; (C) Salome Jens; (L) Jackie Manassee

Solo Voyages, Adrienne Kennedy; (D) Joseph Chaikin; (S) Jun Maeda; (C) Gwen Fabricant; (L) Beverly Emmons

Is This Real?, Ronnie Gilbert and Mira Rafalowicz; (D) Ronnie Gilbert and Dianne Houston; (S) Jun Maeda; (C) Gwen Fabricant; (L) Rachel Budin

The Hour Before My Brother Dies and ***Echoes of Ruby Da***, Daniel Keene; (D) Lindzee Smith and Rhonda Wilson; (S) Robert Cooney and Jay Johnson; (C) Rhonda Wilson; (L) Jay Johnson and Robert Cooney

PRODUCTIONS 1986–87

Womantalk, Sandra Fae Dietrick; (D) Olivia Negron; (S) Todd Lewey; (C) Ernest Mossiah; (L) Larry G. Decle

The Depot, Eve Ensler; (D) Joanne Woodward; (S) Nina Jordan; (C) Laura Ensler; (L) Larry G. Decle

Patience and Sarah, Isabel Miller; (D) Lois Weaver and Salome Jens; (S) Joni Wong; (C) Susan Young; (L) Joni Wong

Dress Suits to Hire, Holly Hughes, Lois Weaver and Peggy Shaw; (D) Lois Weaver; (S) Joni Wong; (C) Susan Young; (L) Joni Wong

Bedroom Farce, Alan Ayckbourn; (D) Caymichael Patten; (S) Wendy J. Ponte; (C) Ileane Meltzer; (L) Larry G. Decle

Intiman Theatre Company

ELIZABETH HUDDLE
Artistic Director

PETER DAVIS
Managing Director

Box 19645
Seattle, WA 98109-6645
(206) 624-4541 (bus.)
(206) 624-2992 (b.o.)

FOUNDED 1972
Margaret Booker

SEASON
June-Oct.

FACILITIES
Intiman Playhouse at Seattle Center
Seating capacity: 424
Stage: modified thrust

FINANCES
Jan. 1, 1986-Dec. 31, 1986
Expenses: $700,214

CONTRACTS
AEA LORT (D) and SSD&C

Intiman's mission is grounded in the classics, but regardless of whether the play is classic or contemporary, our production emphasis is on the actor and the word. Intiman produces the classics because they are exciting, relevant and of tremendous value. People reach to the classics from a fragmented society—for order, for meaning and for spiritual nourishment. At Intiman we work with an ensemble of actors, designers and directors in an intimate setting, and we try to find what a play is saying and to help that meaning resonate with our contemporary audiences.

—*Elizabeth Huddle*

PRODUCTIONS 1986

The Doctor in Spite of Himself and ***Rehearsal at Versailles***, Molière; adapt: Elizabeth Huddle; (D) Elizabeth Huddle; (S) Jerry S. Hooker; (C) Frances Kenny; (L) Peter W. Allen

The Second Mrs. Tanqueray, Arthur Wing Pinero; (D) Elizabeth Huddle; (S) Jerry S. Hooker; (C) Sarah Nash Gates; (L) Peter W. Allen

The Play's the Thing, Ferenc Molnar; adapt: P.G. Wodehouse; (D) Laird Williamson; (S) Andrew Yelusich; (C) Andrew Yelusich; (L) Rick Paulsen

Mrs. Warren's Profession, George Bernard Shaw; (D) Elizabeth Huddle; (S) Jerry S. Hooker; (C) Laura Crow; (L) Collier Woods

Vikings, Stephen Metcalfe; (D) Warner Shook; (S) Michael Olich; (C) Michael Olich; (L) Rick Paulsen

PRODUCTIONS 1987

Man and Superman, George Bernard Shaw; (D) Elizabeth Huddle; (S) William Forrester; (C) Frances Kenny; (L) Rick Paulsen

Intiman Theatre Company. John Alyward and John Procaccino in *The Doctor in Spite of Himself*. Photo: Chris Bennion.

Little Foxes, Lillian Hellman; (D) Richard Allen Edwards; (S) William Forrester; (C) Sally Richardson; (L) Rick Paulsen

The Sea Horse, Edward J. Moore; (D) Elizabeth Huddle; (S) Jerry Hooker; (C) Frances Kenny; (L) Richard Devin

A Doll's House, Henrik Ibsen; (D) Elizabeth Huddle; (S) William Forrester; (C) Sarah Nash Gates; (L) Collier Woods

Private Lives, Noel Coward; (D) Warner Shook; (S) Jennifer Lupton; (C) Sally Richardson; (L) Peter W. Allen

Jean Cocteau Repertory

EVE ADAMSON
Artistic Director

ROBERT M. HUPP
Managing Director

330 Bowery
New York, NY 10012
(212) 677-0060

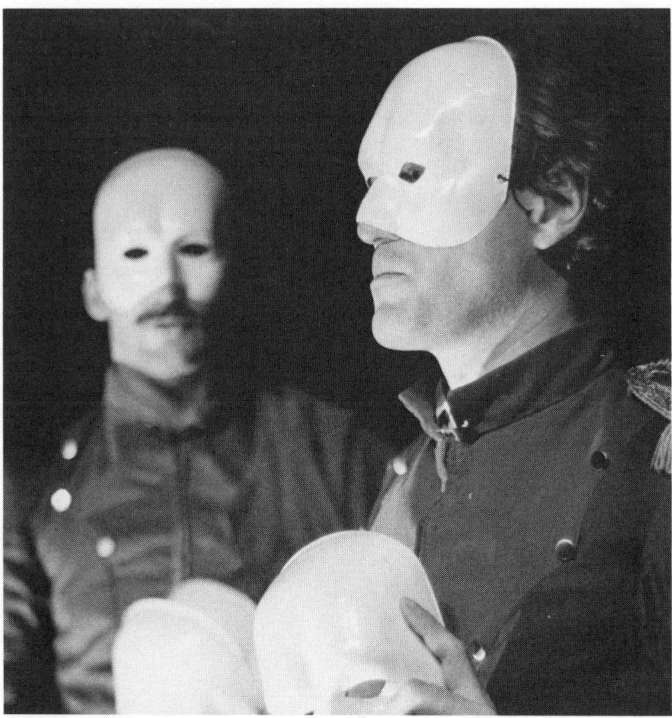

Jean Cocteau Repertory. William Dante and Craig Cook in *Lunin: Theatre of Death*. Photo: Gerry Goodstein.

FOUNDED 1971
Eve Adamson

SEASON
Sept.-May

FACILITIES
Bouwerie Lane Theatre
Seating capacity: 140
Stage: proscenium

FINANCES
July 1, 1986-June 30, 1987
Expenses: $250,000

The Cocteau is a resident company of artists performing in rotating repertory those works of world theatre which by their very nature demand to live on a stage. The company is committed to Jean Cocteau's "poetry of the theatre" in which all elements of production—performance, design, music—fuse into a whole that illuminates the heart of the play and elevates it into a "dramatic poem." Whether approaching a classic or a contemporary work of provocative content and structure, the Cocteau strives to create that unique production style appropriate to each play which will engage the audience intellectually and emotionally. Meeting this artistic challenge in rotating repertory requires a disciplined and flexible resident acting company, as well as bold and imaginative designers and directors. Towards that end, the Cocteau has developed and continued to nurture a growing community of repertory-oriented theatre artists.

—Eve Adamson

PRODUCTIONS 1985–86

Lunin: Theatre of Death, Edward Radzinsky; trans: Alma Law; (D) Eve Adamson; (S) G. Spelvin; (C) G. Spelvin; (L) Giles Hogya
King Lear, William Shakespeare; (D) Eve Adamson; (S) Robert Joel Schwartz; (C) Bill Layton; (L) Craig Smith
Six Characters in Search of an Author, Luigi Pirandello; adapt: David Caldwell; (D) Daniel Irvine; (S) Tom Reynolds; (C) Susan Lyle; (L) Giles Hogya
The Miser, Molière; (D) Giles Hogya; (S) Giles Hogya; (C) Barbara Beccio; (L) Giles Hogya
Rosencrantz and Guildenstern Are Dead, Tom Stoppard; (D) Eve Adamson; (S) Bill Layton; (C) Bill Layton; (L) Craig Smith
Under Milk Wood, Dylan Thomas; (D) Anthony Naylor; (L) Craig Smith

PRODUCTIONS 1986–87

Socrates: Theatre of Life, Edward Radzinsky; trans: Alma Law; (D) Eve Adamson; (S) Robert Joel Schwartz; (C) Bill Layton; (L) Giles Hogya
The Duchess of Malfi, John Webster; (D) Anthony Naylor; (S) Peter Riesenberg; (C) Barbara Bell; (L) Peter Riesenberg
Of Mice and Men, John Steinbeck; (D) Eve Adamson; (S) Bill Layton; (C) Bill Layton; (L) Craig Smith
The Rivals, Richard Brinsley Sheridan; (D) Giles Hogya; (S) Giles Hogya and Bridget McGuire; (C) Barbara Bell; (L) Peter Riesenberg
The Shoemakers, Stanislaw Witkiewicz; adapt: Wlodimierz Herman and Daniel Gerould; trans: C.S. Durer; (D) Wlodimierz Herman; (S) Jan Sawka; (C) Teresa Seda and Ella Skwarska; (L) Peter Riesenberg

Jewish Repertory Theatre

RAN AVNI
Artistic Director

DONALD GELLER
Executive Director

344 East 14th St.
New York, NY 10003
(212) 674-7200 (bus.)
(212) 505-2667 (b.o.)

FOUNDED 1974
Ran Avni

SEASON
Oct.-June

FACILITIES
Seating capacity: 99
Stage: flexible

FINANCES
September 1, 1986-Aug. 31, 1987
Expenses: $232,570

CONTRACTS
AEA Mini

Jewish Repertory Theatre. Braden Danner, Chris Ceraso and Mark Zeller in *Lies My Father Told Me*. Photo: Adam Newman.

The Jewish Repertory Theatre is now in its 13th season. JRT has revived such treasured classics as *Awake and Sing!*, *Green Fields*, and *Incident at Vichy*; has rediscovered forgotten American works such as *Me and Molly*, *Unlikely Heroes* and *Success Story*; has shed new light on the plays of Chekhov, Pinter, Sartre and de Ghelderode; has produced a series of new musicals including *Vagabond Stars*, *Up from Paradise*, *Kuni-Leml*, which won four Outer Critics' Awards, including Best Off Broadway Musical, *Pearls*, *The Special*, and *The Shop on Main Street*. The JRT Writers' Lab, led by associate director Edward M. Cohen, does readings, workshops and mini-productions aimed at developing the works of young writers. This program has resulted in JRT productions of *Taking Steam*, *Benya the King*, *36*, *Crossing Delancey* and other plays which are now being produced throughout the country.

—Ran Avni

PRODUCTIONS 1985–86

The Special, book and lyrics: Mike Guttwillig; music: Galt MacDermot; (D) Ran Avni; (S) Jeffrey Schneider; (C) Karen Hummel; (L) Dan Kinsley
The Shop on Main Street, book and lyrics: Bernard Spiro; music: Saul Honigman; (D) Fran Soeder; (S) James Leonard Joy; (C) Mardi Philips; (L) Phil Monat
I, Shaw, Irwin Shaw and William Kramer; (D) Edward M. Cohen; (S) Joel Fontaine; (C) Edi Giguere; (L) Dan Kinsley
Light Up the Sky, Moss Hart; (D) Robert Bridges; (S) Carl A. Baldasso; (C) Edi Giguere; (L) Tom Hennes
Lies My Father Told Me, Ted Allan; (D) Lynn Polan; (S) Ray Recht; (C) Debra Stein; (L) Dan Kinsley

PRODUCTIONS 1986–87

Roots, Arnold Wesker; (D) Edward M. Cohen; (S) Geoffrey Hall; (C) Karen Hummel; (L) Dan Kinsley
The Square Root of Three, Michael Golder; (D) Steven Robman; (S) Marjorie Bradley Kellogg; (C) Jennifer von Mayrhauser; (L) Donald Holder

Our Own Family, Four One-Act Plays:

Zimmer, Donald Margulies; (D) Michael Arabian; (S) Ray Recht; (C) Edi Giguere; (L) Dan Kinsley
The Renovation, Susan Sandler; (D) Susan Einhorn; (S) Ray Recht; (C) Edi Giguere; (L) Dan Kinsley
The Converts, Michael Taav; (D) William Partlan; (S) Ray Recht; (C) Edi Giguere; (L) Dan Kinsley

Scrabble, David Rush; (D) Lynn Polan; (S) Ray Recht; (C) Edi Giguere; (L) Dan Kinsley

Waving Goodbye, Bob Morris; (D) Robin Saex; (S) Jeffrey Schneider; (C) Karen Hummel; (L) Dan Kinsley

Half a World Away, book: Murray Horwitz; lyrics: Richard Engquist; music: Raphael Crystal; (D) Ran Avni; (S) Ray Recht; (C) Laura Drawbaugh; (L) Donald Holder

La Jolla Playhouse

DES McANUFF
Artistic Director

ALAN LEVEY
Managing Director

Box 12039
La Jolla, CA 92037
(619) 534-6760 (bus.)
(619) 534-3960 (b.o.)

FOUNDED 1947
Mel Ferrer, Dorothy McGuire, Gregory Peck

SEASON
May-Oct.

FACILITIES
Mandell Weiss Center for the Performing Arts
Seating capacity: 492
Stage: proscenium

Warren Theatre
Seating capacity: 248
Stage: thrust

FINANCES
Nov. 1, 1986-Oct. 31, 1987
Expenses: $2,279,367

CONTRACTS
AEA LORT (B), (C), SSD&C and USA

The La Jolla Playhouse provides a summer home for theatre artists to gather, share ideas and extend themselves in a state-of-the-art facility. At the heart of each project we produce is a director, playwright or performer who we feel can impact the development of our art form and thereby help define the course of American theatre. We have no prejudice against genre or style and believe that the vitality of the American theatre is bound to our rich and varied theatrical and cultural heritages. We produce new work and classics side by side, because we believe that they inform each other —that contemporary artists, including writers, can expand their ideas about theatre by working on play forms from other eras, and that new works keep classics honest by reminding us that they must be pertinent. This juxtaposition allows artists and audiences alike to examine contemporary problems in an historical context.

—Des McAnuff

La Jolla Playhouse. Kenneth McMillan and Linda Hunt in *The Matchmaker*. Photo: Micha Langer.

PRODUCTIONS 1986

Shout Up a Morning, book adapt: Paul Avila Mayer and George W. George, from Peter Farrow; music: Julian Adderley and Nathaniel Adderley; lyrics: Diane Charlotte Lampert; (D) Des McAnuff; (S) John Arnone; (C) Susan Denison-Geller; (L) Richard Riddell

The Three Cuckolds, Leon Katz; adapt: Bill Irwin and Michael Greif; (D) Bill Irwin and Michael Greif; (S) Jill Moon; (C) Deborah Dryden; (L) Richard Riddell

Figaro Gets a Divorce, Odon von Horvath; trans: Roger Downey; (D) Robert Woodruff; (S) Douglas Stein; (C) Susan Hilferty; (L) Stephen Strawbridge

Gillette, William Hauptman; (D) Des McAnuff; (S) John Arnone; (C) Susan Hilferty; (L) Richard Riddell

Ajax, Sophocles; adapt: Robert Auletta; (D) Peter Sellars; (S) George Tsypin; (C) Dunya Ramicova; (L) James F. Ingalls

PRODUCTIONS 1987

The Matchmaker, Thornton Wilder; (D) Des McAnuff; (S) Michael H. Yeargan; (C) Susan Hilferty; (L) Richard Riddell

Hedda Gabler, Henrik Ibsen; trans: Gerry Bamman and Irene B. Berman; (D) Emily Mann; (S) Thomas Lynch; (C) Jennifer von Mayrhauser; (L) Pat Collins

A Walk in the Woods, Lee Blessing; (D) Des McAnuff; (S) Bill Clarke; (C) Ellen McCartney; (L) Richard Riddell

School for Wives, Molière; trans: Richard Wilbur; (D) Mark Lamos; (S) John Arnone; (C) Martin Pakledinaz; (L) Pat Collins

The Tempest, William Shakespeare; (D) Robert Woodruff; (S) Douglas Stein; (C) Susan Hilferty; (L) Stephen Strawbridge

Lamb's Players Theatre. Vanda Eggington, Tess Card, Don Lonsbrough and Pamela Turner in *Once Upon a Mattress*. Photo: Christian Turner.

Lamb's Players Theatre

ROBERT SMYTH
Producing Artistic Director

RICHARD PARKER
Administrative Director

Box 26
National City, CA 92050
(619) 474-3385 (bus.)
(619) 474-4542 (b.o.)

FOUNDED 1978
Robert Smyth, Steve Terrell

SEASON
Feb.-Dec.

FACILITIES
Seating capacity: 175
Stage: arena

FINANCES
Dec. 1, 1985-Nov. 30, 1986
Expenses: $774,824

Lamb's Players Theatre is a year-round ensemble of artists—actors, designers, directors, writers and administrators—working in collaboration over an extended period of time, pushing each other toward our best work, seeking to integrate faith and art. While not a "religious" theatre, we are a company that holds the Christian faith as the basis of its artistic vision and its philosophical world view. In addition to our resident theatre we maintain a touring company which performs nationwide on campuses and in prisons as well as in schools with productions dealing with adolescent chemical dependency.

—*Robert Smyth*

PRODUCTIONS 1986

1776, book: Peter Stone; music and lyrics: Sherman Edwards; (D) Deborah Gilmour Smyth; (S) Michael Buckley; (C) Margaret Neuhoff-Vida; (L) David Thayer

The Diviners, Jim Leonard, Jr.; (D) Robert Smyth; (S) Michael Buckley; (C) Veronica Murphy Smith; (L) David Thayer

The Tavern, George M. Cohan; (D) Kerry Cederberg; (S) David Thayer; (C) Norman Miller; (L) David Carminito

The Miser, Molière; trans: A.R. Waller; (D) David McFadzean; (S) Michael Buckley; (C) Margaret Neuhoff-Vida; (L) Michael Buckley

Spoon River Anthology, adapt: Charles Aidman, from Edgar Lee Masters; (D) Deborah Gilmour Smyth; (S) Michael Buckley; (C) Michael Buckley; (L) David Thayer

Oklahoma Rigs, David McFadzean; (D) Robert Smyth; (S) David Thayer; (C) Margaret Neuhoff-Vida; (L) Michael Buckley

Lamb's Players Festival of Christmas, Kerry Cederberg; (D) Robert Smyth; (S) Michael Buckley; (C) Margaret Neuhoff-Vida; (L) David Carminito

PRODUCTIONS 1987

A Man for All Seasons, Robert Bolt; (D) Deborah Gilmour Smyth; (S) Michael Buckley; (C) Margaret Neuhoff-Vida; (L) David Thayer

Talley's Folly, Lanford Wilson; (D) Kerry Cederberg; (S) Michael Buckley; (C) Veronica Murphy Smith; (L) David Thayer

Rhinoceros, Eugene Ionesco; (D) Robert Smyth; (S) Michael Buckley; (C) Veronica Murphy Smith; (L) David Thayer

Dames at Sea, book and lyrics: George Haimsohn and Robin Miller; music: Jim Wise; (D) Rick Meads; (S) David Thayer; (C) Veronica Murphy Smith; (L) Michael Buckley

The Passion of Dracula, adapt: Kerry Cederberg and Robert Smyth, from Bram Stoker; (D) Robert Smyth; (S) Michael Buckley; (C) Kristin Allen; (L) Michael Buckley

Godspell, book: John-Michael Tabelak; music and lyrics: Stephen Schwartz; (D) Robert Smyth; (S) Michael Buckley; (C) Veronica Murphy Smith; (L) Michael Buckley

Lamb's Players Festival of Christmas, Kerry Cederberg; (D) Kerry Cederberg; (S) Michael Buckley; (C) Margaret Neuhoff-Vida; (L) David Carminito

Lamb's Theatre Company

CAROLYN ROSSI COPELAND
Producing Director

JOEL RUARK
General Manager

130 West 44th St.
New York, NY 10036
(212) 575-0300 (bus.)
(212) 997-1780 (b.o.)

FOUNDED 1984
Carolyn Rossi Copeland

SEASON
Sept.-June

FACILITIES
Lamb's Theatre
Seating capacity: 365
Stage: proscenium

Lamb's Little Theatre
Seating capacity: 100
Stage: flexible

CONTRACTS
AEA letter of agreement

The Lamb's Theatre Company was established out of an idealistic and compelling conviction: that theatre offers special opportunities for people to look empathetically at other peoples' lives while nurturing respect for the courage and intelligence required for individuals and groups to survive and surmount inter- and intra-cultural challenges and tests. That conviction has shaped this theatre company's commitment to bringing the lives of minorities and disenfranchised people to the stage, and in turn, to bringing a cross-section of these people and the population at large to this theatre for entertainment, reflection and greater understanding. From the Lamb's Theatre Company's earliest days, there has been a conscious effort to link the resources of this company—our Broadway location, the audiences at our doorstep, the historical significance of our building and our talents—with the work of new American playwrights.

—*Carolyn Rossi Copeland*

Lamb's Theatre Company. Blanca Camacho and Trini Alvarado in *Maggie Magalita*. Photo: Martha Swope Associates/Carol Rosegg.

PRODUCTIONS 1985–86

The Gift of the Magi, book adapt and lyrics: Mark St. Germain and Randy Courts, from O. Henry; music: Randy Courts; (D) Christopher Catt; (S) Michael C. Smith; (C) Hope Hannafin; (L) Heather Carson

Big Time, Steven Braunstein; (D) Tony Lo Bianco; (S) Bob Phillips; (C) Eiko Yamaguchi; (L) John McLean

Maggie Magalita, Wendy Kesselman; (D) Julianne Boyd; (S) Michael C. Smith; (C) Nan Cibula; (L) James F. Ingalls

PRODUCTIONS 1986–87

The China Fish, David McFadzean; (D) Susan Gregg; (S) Dale Jordan; (C) Ellen Ryba; (L) Dale Jordan

The Gift of the Magi, book adapt and lyrics: Mark St. Germain and Randy Courts, from O. Henry; music: Randy Courts; (D) Carolyn Rossi Copeland; (S) Michael C. Smith; (C) Hope Hannafin; (L) Heather Carson

The Wonderful Ice Cream Suit, Ray Bradbury; (D) Sonja Baehr; (S) Bob Phillips; (C) Susan Branch; (L) Jean Redman

L.A. Theatre Works

SUSAN ALBERT LOEWENBERG
Producing Director

SARA MAULTSBY
Associate Producing Director

681 Venice Blvd.
Venice, CA 90291
(213) 827-0808

FOUNDED 1974
Jeremy Blahnik, Robert Greenwald, Susan Albert Loewenberg

SEASON
Oct.-Aug.

FINANCES
Oct. 1, 1985-Sept. 30, 1986
Expenses: $245,943

CONTRACTS
AEA LORT (D)

L.A. Theatre Works. Jack Coleman, Andrew Stevens, Dan Gerrity and Gerrit Graham in *Bouncers.* Photo: Stephen Paley.

As producing director of L.A. Theatre Works my task has been to guide the evolution of our company—from its beginning as an informally organized group of theatre artists exploring ways to make theatre in unorthodox settings such as prisons and community workshops, to a formal producing organization that develops and presents the new work of emerging and established playwrights from the U.S. and abroad. Our commitment is exclusively to new work, new forms and the explication of a particular vision. As a post-Brechtian theatre that truly mirrors the "unease" of modern culture, we want our audiences to experience the exhilaration of change, as opposed to the emotional release that comes from artifice. We support and nurture our theatrical vision through our new play reading series; long-term collaborations involving conceptual directors, playwrights and designers; and a new venture—the L.A. Classic Theatre Works Company, an ensemble of distinguished, classically trained actors who share our ideas about theatre. We are currently working to bring our original obsession with work that is new, startling and controversial into sharper focus through joint projects with orchestras, opera and dance companies in bold ventures that will reach wider audiences.

—*Susan Albert Loewenberg*

PRODUCTIONS 1985–86

Bouncers, John Godber; (D) Ron Link; (S) Cliff Faulkner; (L) Peter Maradudin

Danny and the Deep Blue Sea, John Patrick Shanley; (D) June Stein; (S) Leslie McDonald; (L) Orville Doc Ballard

Tracers, conceived: John DiFusco; (D) John DiFusco; (S) John Falabella; (C) David Navarro Velasquez; (L) Terry Wuthrich

PRODUCTIONS 1986–87

Bouncers, John Godber; (D) Ron Link; (S) Cliff Faulkner; (L) Peter Maradudin

Lincoln Center Theater

GREGORY MOSHER
Director

BERNARD GERSTEN
Executive Producer

150 West 65th St.
New York, NY 10023
(212) 362-7600 (bus.)
(212) 239-6200 (b.o.)

FOUNDED 1985
Lincoln Center for the Performing Arts

SEASON
Year-round

FACILITIES
Vivian Beaumont Theater
Seating capacity: 1,108
Stage: thrust

Mitzi Newhouse Theater
Seating capacity: 299
Stage: thrust

FINANCES
July 1, 1986-June 30, 1987
Expenses: $9,579,000

CONTRACTS
AEA LORT (A), (B), SSD&C and USA

PRODUCTIONS 1985–86

Prairie Du Chien and ***The Shawl***, David Mamet; (D) Gregory Mosher; (S) Michael Merritt; (C) Nan Cibula; (L) Kevin Rigdon

The House of Blue Leaves, John Guare; (D) Jerry Zaks; (S) Tony Walton; (C) Ann Roth; (L) Paul Gallo

The Flying Karamazov Brothers, company-developed; (S) Tony Walton

Terrors of Pleasure,Sex and Death to the Age of 14 and ***Swimming to Cambodia***, Spalding Gray; (D) Spalding Gray

PRODUCTIONS 1986–87

Woza Afrika! A Festival of Plays from South Africa:

Asinamali, Mbongeni Ngema; (D) Mbongeni Ngema; (L) Mannie Manim

Bopha!, Percy Mtwa; (D) Percy Mtwa; (L) Mannie Manim

Children of Asazi, Matsemela Manaka; (D) Matsemela Manaka; (L) Ali Hlogwane and Paul Abrams

Gangsters, Maishe Maponya; (D) Maishe Maponya; (L) Simon Modikidi

Born in the RSA—A Living Newspaper, Barney Simon and company; (D) Barney Simon; (S) Sarah Roberts; (L) Mannie Manim

The Transposed Heads, adapt: Julie Taymor and Sidney Goldfarb, from Thomas Mann; music: Elliot Goldenthal; (D) Julie Taymor; (S) Alexander Okun; (C) Carol Oditz and Julie Taymor; (L) Marcia Madeira and Caterina Bertolotto

The Front Page, Ben Hecht and Charles MacArthur; (D) Jerry Zaks; (S) Tony Walton; (C) Willa Kim; (L) Paul Gallo

Bodies, Rest and Motion, Roger Hedden; (D) Billy Hopkins; (S) Thomas Lynch; (C) Isis Mussenden; (L) James F. Ingalls

Clara and ***I Can't Remember Anything***, Arthur Miller; (D) Gregory Mosher; (S) Michael Merritt; (C) Nan Cibula; (L) Kevin Rigdon

Death and the King's Horseman, Wole Soyinka; (D) Wole Soyinka; (S) David Gropman; (C) Judy Dearing; (L) Pat Collins

The Comedy of Errors, William Shakespeare; (D) Robert Woodruff; (S) David Gropman; (C) Susan Hilferty; (L) Paul Gallo

Lincoln Center Theater. Jeff Raz and Ethyl Eichelberger in *The Comedy of Errors.* Photo: Brigitte Lacombe.

Living Stage Theatre Company. Brenda Woolley-Gonzales and Ezra Knight in *Things Have Got to Get Better.* Photo: Kelly Jerome.

Living Stage Theatre Company

ROBERT A. ALEXANDER
Director

CATHERINE IRWIN
Managing Director

6th and Maine Aves., SW
Washington, DC 20024
(202) 554-9066

FOUNDED 1966
Robert A. Alexander

SEASON
Sept.-June

FACILITIES
Seating capacity: 124
Stage: flexible

FINANCES
July 1, 1986-June 30, 1987
Expenses: $552,500

CONTRACTS
AEA LORT (C)

Our work is, and always has been, intended to impact on the lives of our forgotten young who have been thrown away by society. We turn our audiences on to their own magnificence as artists—their irresistible urge to communicate their deepest feelings and most profound thoughts. The theme of racism runs constant thorughout our work—the causes, the results and the possible means of annihilating this disease which is an intrinsic part of the soil of our land. We have recently been increasing our residencies in other cities and creating larger scripted plays for adult audiences. Our company intends to strengthen our American Sign Language skills and learn to speak Spanish so we can continue to work with deaf audiences and extend our work to Spanish-speaking children and teens. We need to create a school where young actors can be trained in our philosophies and techniques in order to ensure the strength of our ensemble acting company in the future.

—Robert A. Alexander

PRODUCTIONS 1985–87

All performances are company-developed from improvisations; dir: Robert A. Alexander.

Long Island Stage

CLINTON J. ATKINSON
Artistic Director

RALPH J. STALTER, JR.
Managing Director

Hays Theatre, Box 9001
Rockville Centre, NY
11571-9001
(516) 867-3090 (bus.)
(516) 546-4600 (b.o.)

FOUNDED 1975
Susan E. Barclay

SEASON
Oct.-June

FACILITIES
Hays Theatre, Molloy College
Seating capacity: 298
Stage: proscenium

FINANCES
Sept. 1, 1986-Aug. 31, 1987
Expenses: $680,000

CONTRACTS
AEA LORT (D)

Long Island Stage expects its audience to be changed by what it experiences in our theatre. Believing in the primacy of the written word, we also trust in the co-equal power of the visual to create emotional impact. We are interested in works seen to have relevance to the lives of our audience: for example, each season we produce a work by our contemporary, George Bernard Shaw. In any year our repertoire might range from the revival of important classics to the examination of lesser-known works by the major writers to more lightweight fare. We produce one original script a season, alloting it equal weight with more established selections. Working with fine creative talents, we explore the art of theatre, and our play selections acknowledge the drama's power to affect the moral, political and social fabric. Words and ideas are honored at Long Island Stage: as written, interpreted, spoken, visualized, comprehended and absorbed.

—Clinton J. Atkinson

PRODUCTIONS 1985–86

The Play's the Thing, Ferenc Molnar; adapt: P.G. Wodehouse; (D) Clinton J. Atkinson; (S) James Singelis; (C) Jose Lengson; (L) John Hickey

Long Island Stage. Jim Hillgartner and Dennis Helfend in *Tartuffe.* Photo: Brian Ballweg.

A Funny Thing Happened on the Way to the Forum, music and lyrics: Stephen Sondheim; book: Larry Gelbart and Burt Shevelove; (D) Clinton J. Atkinson; (S) Dan Conway; (C) David Navarro Velasquez; (L) John Hickey
Re-Viewing Saroyan, William Saroyan; (D) Clinton J. Atkinson; (S) Charles Cosler; (C) Don Newcomb; (L) John Hickey
Wars of Attrition, Patricia Goldstone; (D) Clinton J. Atkinson; (S) Dan Conway; (C) David Navarro Velasquez; (L) John Hickey
A Lesson from Aloes, Athol Fugard; (D) Norman Hall; (S) Mark Fitzgibbons; (C) Don Newcomb; (L) John Hickey and Vivian Leone
You Never Can Tell, George Bernard Shaw; (D) Clinton J. Atkinson; (S) Dan Ettinger; (C) Don Newcomb; (L) John Hickey

PRODUCTIONS 1986–87

Tartuffe, Molière; trans: Richard Wilbur; (D) Clinton J. Atkinson; (S) Dan Conway; (C) Sharon Sobel; (L) John Hickey
Painting Churches, Tina Howe; (D) Norman Hall; (S) Dan Ettinger; (C) Don Newcomb; (L) John Hickey
Death Defying Acts, Doug Haverty; (D) Clinton J. Atkinson; (S) Dale F. Jordan; (C) Don Newcomb; (L) John Hickey
Arms and the Man, George Bernard Shaw; (D) Clinton J. Atkinson; (S) Dan Conway; (C) Claudia Stephens; (L) John Hickey
True West, Sam Shepard; (D) Michael Breault; (S) Dan Ettinger; (C) Don Newcomb; (L) John Hickey
Peg o' My Heart, J. Hartley Manners; (D) Clinton J. Atkinson; (S) Dan Conway; (C) Don Newcomb; (L) John Hickey

Long Wharf Theatre

ARVIN BROWN
Artistic Director

M. EDGAR ROSENBLUM
Executive Director

222 Sargent Dr.
New Haven, CT 06511
(203) 787-4284 (bus.)
(203) 787-4282 (b.o.)

FOUNDED 1965
Jon Jory, Harlan Kleiman

SEASON
Oct.-June

FACILITIES
Mainstage
Seating capacity: 484
Stage: thrust

Stage II
Seating capacity: 199
Stage: flexible

FINANCES
July 1, 1986-June 30, 1987
Expenses: $3,600,000

CONTRACTS
AEA LORT (B), (C), SSD&C and USA

Long Wharf Theatre. Ralph Waite and Joyce Ebert in *All My Sons*. Photo: T. Charles Erickson.

Long Wharf Theatre approaches the end of its first quarter-century with a renewed sense of its future goals and responsibilities. We continue to offer imaginative revivals of classic and modern plays, rediscoveries of little-known works from the past, and a variety of world and American premieres. Additionally, we have directed attention to a critical aspect of American theatre today—the fostering of the creative voices that are the theatre's greatest future resource. Long Wharf Theatre has established a series of works-in-process that explore the development of each script rather than the finished products. This project allows emerging playwrights to shape their ideas, while working closely with a director and actors, before an audience. Our productions and workshops represent our continued commitment to maintaining the quality and diversity of the theatrical experience while fulfilling our artistic goal—the presentation of plays of character that examine the human condition and spirit.

—*Arvin Brown*

PRODUCTIONS 1985–86

Paris Bound, Philip Barry; (D) John Tillinger; (S) Steven Rubin; (C) Bill Walker; (L) Judy Rasmuson
Pride and Prejudice, adapt: David Pownall, from Jane Austen; (D) Kenneth Frankel; (S) John Conklin; (C) Dunya Ramicova; (L) Pat Collins
Crystal Clear, Phil Young; (D) Phil Young; (S) Hugh Landwehr; (C) Linda Fisher; (L) Ronald Wallace
The Normal Heart, Larry Kramer; (D) Arvin Brown; (S) D. Martyn Bookwalter; (C) Bill Walker; (L) Ronald Wallace
The Glass Menagerie, Tennessee Williams; (D) Nikos Psacharopoulos; (S) Andrew Jackness; (C) Jess Goldstein; (L) Pat Collins
Fugue, Leonora Thuna; (D) Kenneth Frankel; (S) David Jenkins; (C) Jess Goldstein; (L) Judy Rasmuson
Lost in the Stars, book: Maxwell Anderson; music: Kurt Weill; (D) Arvin Brown; (S) Michael H. Yeargan; (C) Jennifer von Mayrhauser; (L) Ronald Wallace

PRODUCTIONS 1986–87

All My Sons, Arthur Miller; (D) Arvin Brown; (S) Hugh Landwehr; (C) Bill Walker; (L) Ronald Wallace
Progress, Doug Lucie; (D) John Tillinger; (S) David Jenkins; (C) Jess Goldstein; (L) Ronald Wallace
Camille, Pam Gems; (D) Ron Daniels; (S) Ming Cho Lee; (C) Jess Goldstein; (L) Ronald Wallace
Self Defense, Joe Cacaci; (D) Arvin Brown; (S) Marjorie Bradley Kellogg; (C) Bill Walker; (L) Ronald Wallace
Dalliance, Arthur Schnitzler; adapt: Tom Stoppard; (D) Kenneth Frankel; (S) John Conklin; (C) David Murin; (L) Pat Collins
Painting Churches, Tina Howe; (D) David Trainer; (S) James Noone; (C) David Murin; (L) Mimi Jordan Sherin
The Tender Land, music: Aaron Copland; libretto: Horace Everett; (D) Arvin Brown; (S) Michael H. Yeargan; (C) David Murin; (L) Ronald Wallace

Looking Glass Theatre

DIANE POSTOIAN
Artistic Director

LINDA D'AMBRA
Producing Director

175 Mathewson St.
Providence, RI 02903
(401) 331-9080

FOUNDED 1965
Elaine Ostroff, Arthur Torg

SEASON
Variable

FINANCES
July 1, 1986-June 30, 1987
Expenses: $85,000

A theatre that excites and inspires children, a theatre they can feel part of, and one that gives both form to their imaginings and importance to their strivings—these were the goals set forth for the Looking Glass Theatre by a group of Rhode Island actors, artists, writers, dancers, educators, parents and children. Their efforts led them to develop an approach to theatre for children that has affected all subsequent work. This approach is based on a belief that the depth of involvement of young audiences is directly proportional to their proximity to the performance, and to the opportunity for them to invest themselves physically, verbally and emphatically in the dramatic action. We feel we do this best by going to where the children are—primarily schools and libraries.

—Linda D'Ambra

PRODUCTIONS 1985–86

Through the Looking Glass, adapt: Eileen Boarman, from Lewis Carroll; (D) Jeannie Walker; (S) Kathy Fillion; (C) Ray Lanoway

The Bremen-Town Musicians, adapt: Jeannie Walker; (D) Jeannie Walker; (S) Kathy Fillion; (C) Ray Lanoway

Touch, Illusion Theater company; (D) Wrenn Goodrum; (S) Kathy Fillion; (C) company

PRODUCTIONS 1986–87

Leap into Literature, C.V. Richardson; (D) Wrenn Goodrum; (S) Kathy Fillion; (C) Marilyn Salvatore

New Reader's Theatre, adapt: Diane Postoian; (D) Diane Postoian; (S) company; (C) company

Wizard's Brew, book: Nola Rocco and Jeannie Walker; music: Bruce Murray; (D) Nola Rocco; (S) Steve Wall; (C) Elsie Collins

Looking Glass Theatre. Donna Meierdiercks in *Wizard's Brew*. Photo: Gordon Rowley.

Los Angeles Theatre Center. Bill Pullman and Anthony Geary in *Barabbas*. Photo: Chris Gulker.

Los Angeles Theatre Center

BILL BUSHNELL
Artistic Producing Director

DIANE WHITE
Producer

CAROL BAKER THARP
General Manager

514 South Spring St.
Los Angeles, CA 90013
(213) 627-6500 (bus.)
(213) 627-5599 (b.o.)

FOUNDED 1985
Bill Bushnell, Diane White

SEASON
Year-round

FACILITIES
Tom Bradley Theatre
Seating capacity: 503
Stage: flexible

Theatre #2
Seating capacity: 296
Stage: proscenium

Theatre #3
Seating capacity: 323
Stage: thrust

Theatre #4
Seating capacity: 99
Stage: flexible

FINANCES
May 5, 1986-May 4, 1987
Expenses: $6,015,169

CONTRACTS
AEA LORT (D)

Los Angeles Theatre Center's artistic mission springs from my own cares and concerns: to make theatre which, in its excellence, passion, truth and cultural diversity, reflects and improves the community and the world. The city of Los Angeles—a city of diverse cultures that personifies the social, ethnic and political future—is our inspiration. LATC's four stages and year-round programming serve as "a gathering place" where talented artists from various cultures can propagate brilliant artistic truth that is joyful, beautiful and passionate, while reflecting the toughness and vitality of contemporary life for a dedicated, enthusiastic and constructively critical multicultural audience. At the heart of LATC's philosophy is the belief that theatre is the synthesizer of all the arts, that all theatre is political in the universal sense and that our role as artists is to agitate, to propagate and to disseminate our perception of the truth.

—Bill Bushnell

PRODUCTIONS 1985–86

Nanawatai, William Mastrosimone; (D) Lamont Johnson; (S) Timian Alsaker; (C) Timian Alsaker; (L) Timian Alsaker

Rich Full Life, Mayo Simon; (D) Alan Mandell; (S) Russell Pyle; (C) Nicole Morin; (L) Kathy Perkins

The Quartered Man, Donald Freed; (D) Mark W. Travis; (S) Russell Pyle; (C) Armand Coutu; (L) Lawrence Metzler

Tumbleweed, Adele Shank; (D) Ted Shank; (S) Karl Eigsti; (C) Nicole Morin; (L) Karl Eigsti

I Don't Have to Show You No Stinking Badges, Luis Valdez; (D) Luis Valdez; (S) Russell Pyle; (C) Nicole Morin; (L) Russell Pyle

The Three Sisters, Anton Chekhov; trans: Michael Frayn; (D) Stein Winge; (S) Timian Alsaker; (C) Timian Alsaker; (L) Timian Alsaker

The Petrified Forest, Robert Sherwood; (D) Charles Marowitz; (S) D. Martyn Bookwalter; (C) Marianna Elliot; (L) Martin Aronstein

Boesman and Lena, Athol Fugard; (D) Bill Bushnell; (S) Timian Alsaker; (C) Timian Alsaker; (L) Timian Alsaker

The Birthday Party, Harold Pinter; (D) Alan Mandell; (S) D. Martyn Bookwalter; (C) Nicole Morin; (L) Kathy Perkins

The Fair Penitent, Nicolas Rowe; (D) Charles Marowitz; (S) Karl Eigsti; (C) Noel Taylor; (L) Martin Aronstein

Fool for Love, Sam Shepard; (D) Julie Hebert; (S) Andy Stacklin; (C) Ardyss T. Golden; (L) Kurt Landisman

It's a Man's World, Greg Mehrten; (D) David Schweizer; (S) Simon Doonen; (C) Michael Kaplan; (L) Barbara Ling

Triumph of the Spider Monkey, Joyce Carol Oates; (D) Al Rossi; (S) Doug Smith; (C) Susan Ninninger; (L) Kathy Perkins

Help Wanted, Franz Xaver Kroetz; trans: Gitta Honegger; (D) Robert Harders; (S) Nicole Morin; (C) Nicole Morin; (L) Kathy Perkins

As the Crow Flies and ***Sound of a Voice***, David Hwang; (D) Reza Abdoh; (S) Timian Alsaker; (C) Timian Alsaker; (L) Timian Alsaker

Diary of a Hunger Strike, Peter Sheridan; (D) Peter Sheridan; (S) Russell Pyle; (C) Heidi Kaczenski; (L) Todd Jared

PRODUCTIONS 1986–87

All My Sons, Arthur Miller; (D) Bill Bushnell; (S) D. Martyn Bookwalter; (C) Marianna Elliot; (L) Tom Ruzika

Spain '36, book: Joan Holden; music and lyrics: Bruce Barthol and Edward Barnes; (D) Daniel Chumley; (S) Timian Alsaker; (C) Timian Alsaker; (L) Timian Alsaker

Company, Samuel Beckett; (D) S.E. Gontarski; (S) Timian Alsaker; (C) Timian Alsaker; (L) Timian Alsaker

Barabbas, Michel de Ghelderode; trans: George Hauger; (D) Stein Winge; (S) Timian Alsaker; (C) Timian Alsaker; (L) Timian Alsaker

Eyes of the American, Samm-Art Williams; (D) Edmund J. Cambridge; (S) Russell Pyle; (C) Nicole Morin; (L) Russell Pyle

Tartuffe, Molière; trans: Richard Wilbur; (D) Robert Goldsby; (S) Karl Eigsti; (C) Nicole Morin; (L) Toshiro Ogawa

Alpha, Slawomir Mrozek; trans: Jacęk Laskowski; (D) Robert Goldsby; (S) Timian Alsaker; (C) Timian Alsaker; (L) Timian Alsaker

Alfred and Victoria, Donald Freed; (D) Gerald Hiken; (S) Cliff Welch; (C) Jill Brousard; (L) Doug Smith

Happy Days, Samuel Beckett; (D) Alan Mandell; (S) Timian Alsaker; (C) Timian Alsaker; (L) Todd Jared

Tamer of Horses, William Mastrosimone; (D) Bill Bushnell; (S) D. Martyn Bookwalter; (C) Christine Hover; (L) D. Martyn Bookwalter

Beyond the Fringe, Alan Bennett, Peter Cook, Jonathan Miller and Dudley Moore; (D) Paxton Whitehead; (S) Cliff Welch; (C) Jill Brousard; (L) Kathy Perkins

The Film Society, Jon Robin Baitz; (D) Robert Eagan; (S) D. Martyn Bookwalter; (C) Robert Blackman; (L) Martin Aronstein

The Glass Menagerie, Tennessee Williams; (D) Stein Winge; (S) Timian Alsaker; (C) Noel Taylor; (L) Stephen Bennett

The Stick Wife, Darrah Cloud; (D) Roberta Levitow; (S) Pavel Dobrusky; (C) Pavel Dobrusky; (L) Pavel Dobrusky

La Victima, El Teatro de la Esperanza; (D) Jose Luis Valenzuela; (S) Jose de Santiago; (C) Jose de Santiago; (L) Jose de Santiago and Doug Smith

Mabou Mines. Fred Neumann in *Worstward Ho*. Photo: Tom Victor.

Mabou Mines

JOANNE AKALAITIS, LEE BREUER, L.B. DALLAS, RUTH MALECZECH, ELLEN McELDUFF, GREG MEHRTEN, FREDERICK NEUMANN, TERRY O'REILLY, BILL RAYMOND
Company Members

ANN EAKLUND
Company Manager

150 First Ave.
New York, NY 10009
(212) 473-0559

FOUNDED 1970
JoAnne Akalaitis, Lee Breuer, Philip Glass, Ruth Maleczech, David Warrilow

SEASON
Variable

FINANCES
July 1, 1986-June 30, 1987
Expenses: $580,000

CONTRACTS
AEA Guest Artist

Mabou Mines is an ensemble of nine artists who create original theatre, film, video and radio works, as well as new interpretations of existing texts. The company's approach to the engagement and development of artists has been rooted in its deep commitment to a shared aesthetic, support of one another's artistic evolution and long-term collaboration. Company members have chosen to work together because of this commitment, and new artists have gravitated to Mabou Mines to share in this ideology. In 18 years, Mabou Mines has produced 35 projects, incorporating multi-disciplinary elements in many works and challenging concepts in all. For their artistry, Mabou Mines has received 41 awards including a 1986 Obie Award for Sustained Achievement. In its history, the company has become an inspiration to numerous theatres around the world. Its enduring commitment to artistic excellence ensures that Mabou Mines will continue to play a major role in this country's theatrical life for many years to come.

—*Ellen McElduff, for the members*

PRODUCTIONS 1985–86

Starcock, Apple Vail; (D) Fred Neumann; (S) Sabrina Hamilton and Tom Andrews; (L) Sabrina Hamilton and Tom Andrews

Help Wanted, Franz Xaver Kroetz, trans: Gitta Honegger; (D) JoAnne Akalaitis; (C) Greg Mehrten and Anne Herzog; (L) Jennifer Tipton

Hajj, Lee Breuer; (D) Lee Breuer; (S) Julie Archer; (L) Julie Archer

A Prelude to Death in Venice, Lee Breuer; (D) Lee Breuer; (S) Alison Yerxa and L.B. Dallas; (L) Julie Archer

PRODUCTIONS 1986–87

Worstward Ho, Samuel Beckett; adapt: Frederick Neumann; (D) Frederick Neumann; (S) John Arnone; (C) Gabriel Berry; (L) Jennifer Tipton
Cold Harbor, Dale Worsley; (D) William Raymond and Dale Worsley; (S) Linda Hartinian; (C) Greg Mehrten; (L) B. St. John Schofield
A Prelude to Death in Venice, Lee Breuer; (D) Lee Breuer; (S) Alison Yerxa and L.B. Dallas; (C) Greg Mehrten; (L) Julie Archer
It's a Man's World, Greg Mehrten; (D) David Schweizer; (S) Philip Jung; (C) Michael Kaplan; (L) Pat Dignan

Magic Theatre

JOHN LION
General Director

MARCIA O'DEA
Managing Director

Fort Mason Center, Bldg. D
San Francisco, CA 94123
(415) 441-8001 (bus.)
(415) 441-8822 (b.o.)

FOUNDED 1967
John Lion

SEASON
Oct.-June

FACILITIES
Northside Theatre
Seating capacity: 150
Stage: thrust

Southside Theatre
Seating capacity: 150
Stage: proscenium

FINANCES
Sept. 1, 1985-Aug. 31, 1986
Expenses: $780,000

CONTRACTS
AEA letter of agreement

The Magic Theatre has grown up around its writers. At various times our work has been known as "surrealistic," "gritty realism," "fantasy" and "dark-comedic"—all after-the-fact labels that indicate only that we have developed a wide range of interests. I'm often asked what I look for in a script; the answer is what does not entirely appear on the page. It's more a feeling, a subject-object sense, that emerges from the work, a little like developing a new language, both unique and universal. Work we've premiered has been readily embraced here and abroad, both published and produced, maybe because it exemplifies a kind of world-view of America, a bit brazen and unpredictable. But the important thing for me is that the work has been up to my professional—as well as the public's—standards and that there's still the requisite amount of mystery in each new work we mount.

—John Lion

Magic Theatre. Robert A. Behling, Gregory Pace and Kathleen Cramer in *Honeymoon*. Photo: Allen Nomura.

PRODUCTIONS 1985–86

Buried Child, Sam Shepard; (D) Andrew Doe; (S) Shevra Tait; (C) Frances Kenny; (L) Joseph Dignan
Scar, Murray Mednick; (D) Murray Mednick; (S) John Bonard Wilson; (C) Beaver Bauer; (L) Margaret Anne Dunn
Wild Indian, Theodore Shank; (D) Simon L. Levy; (S) Barbara J. Mesney; (C) Walter Watson and Catherine Verdier; (L) Glenn A. Wade
The Detective, Vaudeville Noveau company; (D) Joseph Chaikin; (S) Andy Stacklin; (C) Regina Cate; (L) Margaret Anne Dunn
Bully, Paul D'Andrea; (D) Dennis Lowry; (S) Jeff Hunt; (C) Gael Russell; (L) Maurice Vercoutere
Sharon and Billy, Alan Bowne; (D) Albert Takazauckas; (S) Barbara J. Mesney; (C) Beaver Bauer; (L) Alan Baron
Honeymoon, Susan Champagne; (D) Julie Hebert; (S) Sandra Howell; (C) Lydia Tanji; (L) Novella T. Smith

PRODUCTIONS 1986–87

Aunt Dan and Lemon, Wallace Shawn; (D) John Lion; (S) John Bonard Wilson; (C) Regina Cate; (L) Joe Dignan
Visions of Beckett: A Quartet of One-Acts, Samuel Beckett; (D) S.E. Gontarski; (S) Andy Stacklin; (C) Bill Brewer; (L) Joe Dignan
Roshi, Lynne Kaufman; (D) Simon L. Levy; (S) Tim Bird, Jeff Hunt and Andy Stacklin; (C) Lydia Tanji; (L) Margaret Anne Dunn
True Beauties, Julie Hebert; (D) Julie Hebert; (S) John Mayne; (C) Lydia Tanji; (L) Novella T. Smith
Spider Rabbit and ***The Beard***, Michael McClure; (D) John Lion; (S) John Bonard Wilson; (C) Regina Cate; (L) David Welle
Between East and West, Richard Nelson; (D) Carl Weber; (S) William Eddelman; (C) William Eddelman; (L) Kurt Landisman

DoublePlay: Two Soon 3 productions:

The Man in the Nile at Night: A Proxy Romance and ***A Wall in Venice/3 Women/Wet Shadows***, Alan Finnernan; (D) Alan Finnernan; (S) Alan Finnernan; (C) Alan Finnernan; (L) Jim Quinn

Manhattan Punch Line Theatre

STEVE KAPLAN
Artistic Director

CRAIG BOWLEY
Executive Director

410 West 42nd St., 3rd fl.
New York, NY 10036
(212) 239-0827 (bus.)
(212) 279-4200 (b.o.)

FOUNDED 1979
Faith Caitlan, Steve Kaplan, Mitch McGuire

SEASON
Oct.-June

FACILITIES
Judith Anderson Theatre
Seating capacity: 94
Stage: proscenium

INTAR Theatre
Seating capacity: 94
Stage: proscenium

Samuel Beckett Theatre
Seating capacity: 99
Stage: proscenium

FINANCES
July 1, 1986-June 30, 1987
Expenses: $313,500

CONTRACTS
AEA Showcase code

Manhattan Punch Line is a theatre dedicated to the spirit of the clown, the gadfly, the satirist. We see laughter as both a curative and a cauterizing agent. We recognize that the ability to laugh at the amazing irrationality of life may be what ultimately makes us most human; in an absurd universe, comedy may be the only rational stance. MPL is a place where actors, directors, designers, comics and playwrights can concentrate on the art of comedy. We are creating the foundation for a vital artistic future through programs such as Comedyworks, our script-development program; Comedy Corps, our in-house script-development acting ensemble; Late Nite Punch Line; and the Comedy Institute. Our mainstage productions introduce

Manhattan Punch Line Theatre. Toby Wherry, Mary Testa and Christina Haag in *Child's Play*. Photo: Martha Swope Associates/Carol Rosegg.

new comic voices and performers, and the Festival of One-Act Comedies is the single largest presentation of new comic work in the country. At MPL artists share their comic vision in a creative environment dedicated to excellence, innovation and an appreciation of our comic past.

—*Steve Kaplan*

PRODUCTIONS 1985–86

Goodbye Freddy, Elizabeth Diggs; (D) Barbara Rosoff; (S) Johniene Papandreas; (C) Martha Hally; (L) Jackie Manassee

Love As We Know It, Gil Schwartz; (D) Josh Mostel; (S) Randy Benjamin; (C) Mimi Maxmen; (L) Greg MacPherson

Second Annual Festival of One-Act Comedies:

Alone at Last, Gina Barnett; (D) Melodie Somers; (S) Brian Martin; (C) David C. Woolard; (L) Scott Pinckney

The Middle Kingdom, Howard Korder; (D) Robert S. Johnson; (S) Brian Martin; (C) David C. Woolard; (L) Scott Pinckney

Powder, Judy Engles; (D) Peter Glazer; (S) Brian Martin; (C) David C. Woolard; (L) Scott Pinckney

Square One, Richard Aellen; (D) Robert S. Johnson; (S) Brian Martin; (C) David C. Woolard; (L) Scott Pinckney

Lip Service, Howard Korder; (D) Robin Saex; (S) Brian Martin; (C) David C. Woolard; (L) Scott Pinckney

Smoke, Laurence Klavan; (D) Steve Kaplan; (S) Brian Martin; (C) Marcy Grace Froelich; (L) Scott Pinckney

The Interrogation, Murphy Guyer; (D) Pamela Singer; (S) Brian Martin; (C) Marcy Grace Froelich; (L) Scott Pinckney

The Art of Conversation, Mark Malone; (D) Gavin Cameron-Webb; (S) Brian Martin; (C) Marcy Grace Froelich; (L) Scott Pinckney

The Job Search, Brandon Toropov; (D) Jason Buzas; (S) Brian Martin; (C) Marcy Grace Froelich; (L) Scott Pinckney

Uncle Lumpy Comes to Visit, Laurence Klavan; (D) Steve Kaplan; (S) Brian Martin; (C) Marcy Gracy Froelich; (L) Scott Pinckney

PRODUCTIONS 1986–87

Epic Proportions, Larry Coen and David Crane; (D) Paul Lazarus; (S) William Barclay; (C) Mary L. Hayes; (L) Curt Ostermann

Third Annual Festival of One-Act Comedies:

Words, Words, Words, David Ives; (D) Fred Sanders; (S) Jane Clark; (C) Michael S. Schler (L) Mark Di Quinzio

The Moaner, Susan Sandler; (D) Pamela Berlin; (S) Jane Clark and Christopher Stapleton; (C) Michael S. Schler; (L) Mark Di Quinzio

The Deep End, Neil Cuthbert; (D) Charles Karchmer; (S) Jane Clark; (C) Michael S. Schler; (L) Mark Di Quinzio

Child's Play, Peter Manos; (D) Lee Costello; (S) Kurt Rauchenberger; (C) Michael S. Schler; (L) Mark Di Quinzio

Almost Romance, Howard Morris; (D) Robin Saex; (S) Kurt Rauchenberger; (C) Michael S. Schler; (L) Mark Di Quinzio

In the Park, M.B. Valle; (D) Jason Buzas; (S) Jane Clark and Christopher Stapleton; (C) Lillian Pan; (L) Mark Di Quinzio

The Greenhouse Keeper Died Over the Weekend, Terri Wagener; (D) Gavin Cameron-Webb; (S) Jane Clark; (C) Lillian Pan; (L) Mark Di Quinzio

The Tablecloth of Turin, Ron Carlson; (D) Jason Buzas; (S) Jane Clark; (C) Lillian Pan; (L) Mark Di Quinzio

If Walls Could Talk, Laurence Klavan; (D) Steve Kaplan; (S) Jane Clark; (C) Lillian Pan; (L) Mark Di Quinzio

Second Avenue, Allan Knee; (D) Steve Kaplan; (S) Richard Harmon; (C) David Loveless; (L) Mark Di Quinzio

Bigfoot Stole My Wife, Ron Carlson; (D) Jason Buzas; (S) Bobby Berg; (C) Mimi Maxmen; (L) Brian MacDevitt

Manhattan Theatre Club

LYNNE MEADOW
Artistic Director

BARRY GROVE
Managing Director

453 West 16th St., 2nd fl.
New York, NY 10011
(212) 645-5590 (bus.)
(212) 246-8989 (b.o.)

FOUNDED 1970
Philip Barber, Gene Frankel,, William Gibson, Barbara Hirschl, A.E. Jeffcoat, Margaret Kennedy, Gerard L. Spencer, George Tabori, A. Joseph Tandet, Peregrine Whittlesey

SEASON
Oct.-June

FACILITIES
City Center Stage I
Seating capacity: 299
Stage: proscenium

City Center Stage II
Seating capacity: 150
Stage: flexible

FINANCES
July 1, 1986-June 30, 1987
Expenses: $2,159,161

CONTRACTS
AEA Off Broadway (A) and (C) contracts, SSD&C

The Manhattan Theatre Club has grown from a showcase theatre to one of America's most dynamic and productive cultural centers. A staff of top professionals dedicated to quality work is at the core of MTC's producing activities. A theatre of national and international scope, MTC's primary goals are to

Manhattan Theatre Club. Zeljko Ivanek and Joseph Maher in *Loot*. Photo: Gerry Goodstein.

encourage, develop and present challenging new theatrical work by the world's best writers, demonstrating the infinite variety of theatrical expression through their insights into the life, culture and conflicts of our times. We aim to bring to the stage the finest performers, directors and designers; support and enrich the art of playwriting; develop a committed, discriminating audience for the theatre; and give opportunities for the development of new talents for all areas of the theatre. Our Stage I theatre features five productions annually, while our new Stage II will focus on the development of new plays and musicals. Now in its 15th year, our Writers-in-Performance series features readings by well-known authors of prose and poetry, emphasizing the range, diversity and excitement of contemporary writing. Our subscription audience numbers close to 10,000. MTC is made accessible to the broadest community through student, senior citizen and group discounts; free ticket distribution; and frequent post-performance discussions.

—Lynne Meadow

PRODUCTIONS 1985–86

Oliver Oliver, Paul Osborn; (D) Vivian Matalon; (S) Tom Schwinn; (C) Albert Wolsky; (L) Richard Nelson

It's Only a Play, Terrence McNally; (D) John Tillinger; (S) John Lee Beatty; (C) Rita Ryack; (L) Pat Collins

Loot, Joe Orton; (D) John Tillinger; (S) John Lee Beatty; (C) Bill Walker; (L) Richard Nelson

Principia Scriptoriae, Richard Nelson; (D) Lynne Meadow; (S) John Lee Beatty; (C) William Ivey Long; (L) Jennifer Tipton

Women of Manhattan, John Patrick Shanley; (D) Ron Lagomarsino; (S) Adrianne Lobel; (C) Ann Emonts; (L) James F. Ingalls

PRODUCTIONS 1986–87

The Hands of Its Enemy, Mark Medoff; (D) Kenneth Frankel; (S) John Lee Beatty; (C) Jennifer von Mayrhauser; (L) Pat Collins

Bloody Poetry, Howard Brenton; (D) Lynne Meadow; (S) John Lee Beatty; (C) Dunya Ramicova; (L) Dennis Parichy

Hunting Cockroaches, Janusz Glowacki; trans: Jadwiga Kosicka; (D) Arthur Penn; (S) Heidi Landesman; (C) Rita Ryack; (L) Richard Nelson

The Lucky Spot, Beth Henley; (D) Stephen Tobolowsky; (S) John Lee Beatty; (C) Jennifer von Mayrhauser; (L) Dennis Parichy

Claptrap, Ken Friedman; (D) David Trainer; (S) David Potts; (C) David Murin; (L) Ken Billington

Death of a Buick, John Bunzel; (D) Jonathan Alper; (S) Philipp Jung; (C) C.L. Hundley; (L) Arden Fingerhut

Frankie and Johnny in the Clair De Lune, Terrence McNally; (D) Paul Benedict; (S) Jim Noone; (C) David Woolard; (L) David Noling

Marin Theatre Company

WILLIAM MARCHETTI
Artistic Director

ANDREW ZARRILLO
Executive Director

Box 1439
Mill Valley, CA 94942
(415) 388-5200 (bus.)
(415) 388-5208 (b.o.)

FOUNDED 1966
Sali Lieberman

SEASON
Sept.-June

FACILITIES
Mainstage
Seating capacity: 250
Stage: proscenium

Second Stage
Seating capacity: 99
Stage: flexible

FINANCES
July 1, 1986-June 31, 1987
Expenses: $367,500

CONTRACTS
AEA SPT

Marin Theatre Company, founded in 1966, provides the community with a regional theatre encompassing two working stages and a school for theatre arts. Our seasons are designed to create innovative and provocative productions. Our repertoire is chosen to lead as well as to serve the community. Plays are selected from the world's theatre literature: plays with universal themes, as well as new works which reach toward fresh dimensions. We are committed to the development of an ensemble working together with guest artists, while our Playwrights' Forum recognizes the importance of the playwright to the future of the art form. The company's School for Theatre Arts reflects our commitment to the participation of youth—the American theatre's future artists and audiences. As the owner and operator of our own facilities, we also provide other artists with rehearsal and performance opportunities.

—William Marchetti

Note: During the 1985-86 and 1986-87 seasons, Karl Rawicz served as artistic director.

Marin Theatre Company. Mack Owen and Nellie Cravens in *Foxfire*. Photo: Joseph Greco.

PRODUCTIONS 1985–86

Foxfire, Susan Cooper and Hume Cronyn; (D) Karl Rawicz; (S) Andy Stacklin; (C) Don Lev; (L) Joseph R. Morley

Starting Here, Starting Now, Richard Maltby, Jr. and David Shire; (D) Marilyn Izdebski; (S) Karl Rawicz; (C) Lynn Osborn; (L) Timothy Welch

K2, Patrick Meyers; (D) Karl Rawicz; (S) Karl Rawicz; (C) Karla Renee; (L) Joseph R. Morley

The Night of the Tribades, Per Olov Enquist; trans: Ross Shideler; (D) Julian Lopez-Morillas; (S) Jasper Meerheimb; (C) Christopher Thomsen; (L) Michael Jayson

Crimes of the Heart, Beth Henley; (D) Ben Dickson; (S) Jasper Meerheimb; (C) Karla Renee; (L) Ron Litz

The Unseen Hand, Sam Shepard; (D) Karl Rawicz; (S) Karl Rawicz; (C) Anita Walden; (L) William Simonds

PRODUCTIONS 1986–87

Homesteaders, Nina Shengold; (D) J.D. Trow; (S) John Terpening; (C) Gayle Howard; (L) Ron Litz

The Abdication, Ruth Wolff; (D) Andrea Gordon; (S) Barbara Henley; (C) Leone Calvert; (L) Jim Schelstrate

Two for the Seesaw, William Gibson; (D) Ben Dickson; (S) Kenneth Rowland; (C) Cynthia Beckley; (L) R.D. Marsan

The Guardsman, Ferenc Molnar; adapt: James Keller; (D) Albert Takazauckas; (S) Jesse Hollis; (C) Julia Lazar; (L) Kurt Landisman

Wings, Arthur Kopit; (D) Ken Grantham; (S) Gene Angel and Ron Pratt; (C) Dhyanis; (L) Barbara Du Bois

We Won't Pay! We Won't Pay!, Dario Fo; trans: R.G. Davis; (D) Will Marchetti; (S) Jane Robbins; (C) Magrita Klassen; (L) William Simonds

Mark Taper Forum

GORDON DAVIDSON
Artistic Director/Producer

WILLIAM P. WINGATE
Executive Managing Director

STEVEN J. ALBERT
General Manager

135 North Grand Ave.
Los Angeles, CA 90012
(213) 972-7353 (bus.)
(213) 972-7392 (b.o.)

FOUNDED 1967
Gordon Davidson

SEASON
Year-round

FACILITIES
Mark Taper Forum
Seating capacity: 767
Stage: thrust

Taper, Too
Seating capacity: 99
Stage: flexible

Itchey Foot
Seating capacity: 99
Stage: cabaret

James A. Doolittle Theatre
Seating Capacity: 1,049
Stage: proscenium

FINANCES
June 30, 1986-June 28, 1987
Expenses: $8,059,000

CONTRACTS
AEA LORT (A), SSD&C and USA

This year's commemoration of 20 years of work for me, and for my theatre, the Mark Taper Forum, has given me perspective on the identities of us both. Reviewing our many activities, I realize that breadth of programming is essential to our artistic profile. We do a wide range of work—adventurous new material, classics in repertory, outreach and special-access programming, laboratory and special events, media and cross-disciplinary projects—working in as many venues as we can, serving as many artists as we can, and creating the most fertile environment that we can. We're working hard to think nontraditionally, creating opportunities for artists of all backgrounds and colors while finding ways of creating a rainbow audience that can respond to this new work. The Taper must always be more than its "plays." It must be a fruitful environment where we continue to experiment. If we are a theatre with another 20 years of history to be written, we must create a new age of theatre—theatre that continues to make contributions to a changing way of life.

—Gordon Davidson

Mark Taper Forum. John Malkovich and Joan Allen in *Burn This*. Photo: Jay Thompson.

PRODUCTIONS 1985–86

The Beautiful Lady, book: Elizabeth Swados and Paul Schmidt; music and lyrics: Elizabeth Swados; (D) Elizabeth Swados; (S) Karl Eigsti; (C) Marianna Elliot; (L) Arden Fingerhut

Romance Language, Peter Parnell; (D) Sheldon Larry; (S) Loren Sherman; (C) Sheila McLamb-Wilcox; (L) Martin Aronstein

'night, Mother, Marsha Norman; (D) Tom Moore; (S) Richard Seger; (C) Heidi Landesman; (L) Martin Aronstein

Green Card, JoAnne Akalaitis; (D) JoAnne Akalaitis; (S) Douglas Stein; (C) Marianna Elliot; (L) Frances Aronson

The Real Thing, Tom Stoppard; (D) Gordon Davidson; (S) David Jenkins; (C) Robert Blackman; (L) Martin Aronstein

Hedda Gabler, Henrik Ibsen; trans: Christopher Hampton; (D) Robert Egan; (S) David Jenkins; (C) Robert Blackman; (L) Martin Aronstein

On the Verge or The Geography of Yearning, Eric Overmyer; (D) Jackson Phippin; (S) Larry Fulton; (C) Susan Denison-Geller; (L) Liz Stillwell

See Below Middle Sea, Mimi Seton; (D) Mimi Seton; (S) Nancy Seruto; (C) Sylvia Moss; (L) Liz Stillwell

Rat in the Skull, Ron Hutchinson; (D) Dana Elcar; (S) Claire Scarpulla; (C) Durinda Wood; (L) Peter Maradudin

Newcomer, Janet Thomas; (D) Peter C. Brosius; (S) Rob Murphy; (C) Armand Coutu

The Dream Coast, John Steppling; (D) John Steppling; (S) John Ivo Gilles; (C) Terry Soon; (L) Paulie Jenkins

Mrs. California, Doris Baizley; (D) Warner Shook; (S) John Ivo Gilles; (C) Deborah Dryden; (L) Paulie Jenkins

Planet Fires, Thomas Babe; (D) John Henry Davis; (S) Dan Dryden; (C) Susan Denison-Geller; (L) Paulie Jenkins

Sleeping Dogs, Neal Bell; (D) Jody McAuliffe; (S) Dan Dryden; (C) Ann Bruice; (L) Paulie Jenkins

An Evening of Micro Operas:

For Under the Volcano, music: Carla Bley; text: Malcolm Lowry; (D) John Cunning; (S) Mark W. Morton; (L) Paulie Jenkins

A Madrigal Opera Parts III, IV and Closing, music: Philip Glass; text: Len Jenkin; (D) Robert Woodruff; (S) Mark W. Morton; (L) Paulie Jenkins

Slow Fire, music: Paul Dresher and Rinde Eckert; (D) Richard E.T. White; (S) Mark W. Morton; (L) Paulie Jenkins

Legends, Kendrew Lascelles; (D) Robert Egan; (S) Michael Devine; (C) Grania O'Connor; (L) Paulie Jenkins

The Wash, Philip Kan Gotanda; (D) Barbara Damashek; (S) Michael Devine; (C) Elizabeth Palmer; (L) Paulie Jenkins

PRODUCTIONS 1986–87

The Immigrant: A Hamilton County Album, Mark Harelik; conceived: Mark Harelik and Randal Myler; (D) Randal Myler; (S) Kevin Rupnik; (C) Andrew V. Yelusich; (L) Martin Aronstein

Ghetto, Joshua Sobol; trans: Jack Viertel; (D) Gordon Davidson; (S) Douglas Stein; (C) Julie Weiss; (L) Paulie Jenkins

Burn This, Lanford Wilson; (D) Marshall W. Mason; (S) John Lee Beatty; (C) Laura Crow; (L) Dennis Parichy

The Traveler, Jean-Claude van Itallie; (D) Steven Kent; (S) Douglas W. Schmidt and Jerome Sirlin; (C) Carol Brolaski; (L) Beverly Emmons

Roza, book adapt and lyrics: Julian More, from Romain Gary; music: Gilbert Becaud; (D) Harold Prince; (S) Alexander Okun; (C) Florence Klotz; (L) Ken Billington

Loot, Joe Orton; (D) John Tillinger; (S) John Lee Beatty; (C) Bill Walker; (L) Martin Aronstein

Entertaining Mr. Sloane, Joe Orton; (D) John Tillinger; (S) John Lee Beatty; (C) Bill Walker; (L) Martin Aronstein

The Dream Coast, John Steppling; (D) John Steppling and Robert Egan; (S) John Iacovelli; (C) Nicole Morin; (L) Paulie Jenkins

The Game of Love and Chance, Pierre Marivaux; trans: Adrienne Schizzano Mandel and Oscar Mandel; (D) Brian Kulick; (S) Mark Wendland; (C) Mark Wendland; (L) Liz Stillwell

Largo Desolato, Vaclav Havel; trans: Tom Stoppard; (D) Richard Jordan; (S) John Iacovelli; (C) Shigeru Yaji; (L) Brian Gale

Aunt Dan and Lemon, Wallace Shawn; (D) Robert Egan;

McCarter Theatre. Richard Leighton and Wanda Bimson in *Napoleon Nightdreams.* Photo: Andrea Kane.

(s) Mark Wendland; (c) Mark Wendland; (l) Paulie Jenkins
One Thousand Cranes, Colin Thomas; (d) Peter C. Brosius; (s) Richard Hoover; (c) Nicole Morin

McCarter Theatre

NAGLE JACKSON
Artistic Director

ROBERT ALTMAN
Managing Director

91 University Pl.
Princeton, NJ 08540
(609) 683-9100 (bus.)
(609) 683-8000 (b.o.)

FOUNDED 1972
Daniel Seltzer

SEASON
Oct.-May

FACILITIES
Mainstage
Seating capacity: 1,078
Stage: flexible

Forbes College Theatre
Seating capacity: 200
Stage: flexible

Richardson Auditorium
Seating capacity: 882
Stage: thrust

FINANCES
July 1, 1986-June 30, 1987
Expenses: $3,781,000

CONTRACTS
AEA LORT (B+), SSD&C and USA

My wish for the McCarter Theatre is to provide an alternative theatre experience for a region which is steeped in and accustomed to the commercial theatre, and to provide a company feeling and company home for the weary New York- and New Jersey-based actors looking for a place to do meaningful work, both classical and experimental. We are proud of what I call our "resident company of commuters" who flee Manhattan and Hoboken for a few months of creative peace and who give a burgeoning audience of transplanted New Yorkers—corporations are moving here in droves—a fresh experience as well. In our newly renovated theatre, we look for an equivalent renovation of the creative spirit.

—Nagle Jackson

PRODUCTIONS 1985–86

Christmas Gifts, adapt: Robert Lanchester; (d) Robert Lanchester; (s) Robert Little; (c) Barb Taylorr; (l) Don Ehman
As You Like It, William Shakespeare; (d) Robert Lanchester; (s) Peter Harrison; (c) Elizabeth Covey; (l) Don Ehman
The Boys Next Door, Tom Griffin; (d) Nagle Jackson; (s) John Jensen; (c) Marie Miller; (l) F. Mitchell Dana

PRODUCTIONS 1986–87

Our Town, Thornton Wilder; (d) Nagle Jackson; (s) Daniel Boylen; (c) Elizabeth Covey; (l) F. Mitchell Dana
Little Murders, Jules Feiffer; (d) Paul Weidner; (s) Daniel Boylen; (c) Elizabeth Covey; (l) F. Mitchell Dana
A Christmas Carol, adapt: Nagle Jackson, from Charles Dickens; (d) Nagle Jackson; (s) Brian Martin; (c) Elizabeth Covey; (l) Richard Moore
Don't Trifle with Love, Alfred de Musset; trans: Nagle Jackson; (d) Nagle Jackson; (s) Pavel Dobrusky; (c) Elizabeth Covey; (l) F. Mitchell Dana
Napoleon Nightdreams, James McLure; (d) Nagle Jackson; (s) Pavel Dobrusky; (c) Pavel Dobrusky; (l) F. Mitchell Dana
Uncle Vanya, Anton Chekhov; trans: Michael Henry Heim; (d) Georgi Tovstonogov; (s) Eduard Kochergin; (c) Eduard Kochergin; (l) F. Mitchell Dana
Debut..., Bruce E. Rodgers; (d) Robert Lanchester; (s) Don Ehman; (c) Barb Taylorr; (l) Don Ehman

Merrimack Repertory Theatre

DANIEL L. SCHAY
Producing Director

Box 228
Lowell, MA 01853
(617) 454-6324 (bus.)
(617) 454-3926 (b.o.)

FOUNDED 1979
John R. Briggs, Mark Kaufman

SEASON
Nov.-May

FACILITIES
Liberty Hall
Seating Capacity: 402
Stage: thrust

FINANCES
July 1, 1986-June 30, 1987
Expenses: $596,500

CONTRACTS
AEA LORT (D) and SSD&C

The Merrimack Repertory Theatre has come into its own as a theatrical presence and independent cultural resource in a community that had not known such for many years. Our season has always been chosen for its potential resonance in a New England mill town in the midst of revitalization. Now, productions like *Working*, *Educating Rita* and Lowell playwright Jack

Merrimack Repertory Theatre. Leslie Bennett, Dorothy Gallagher, Ed Peed and Kevin Fennessy in *The Hostage.* Photo: Kevin Harkins.

Neary's *First Night* have given voice to the particular concerns of our demographically varied audience, while productions like the expressionistic *The Adding Machine* or the classical *The School for Wives* have brought them experiences that reveal the breadth of the theatrical form. What sets theatre apart from other media is that it exists in real time for a specific body politic, not just in the context of its own history or aesthetic, or the current fashion within the field. The Merrimack works in such a context, on its main stage and in ongoing programs with young people and with Lowell's Hispanic and Cambodian communities. We seek to expand the range and impact of our work, while keeping it vital to this time and place.

—Daniel L. Schay

PRODUCTIONS 1985–86

The School for Wives, Molière; trans: Richard Wilbur; (D) Daniel L. Schay; (s) Leslie Taylor; (c) Barbara Forbes; (L) Sid Bennett

A Christmas Carol, adapt: Larry Carpenter, from Charles Dickens; (D) Thomas Clewell; (s) Leslie Taylor; (c) Amanda Aldridge; (L) David Lockner

Educating Rita, Willy Russell; (D) Richard Rose; (s) Leslie Taylor; (c) Amanda Aldridge; (L) Kendall Smith

Requiem for a Heavyweight, Ro Serling; (D) Daniel L. Schay; (s) Gary English; (c) Amanda Aldridge; (L) Kendall Smith

Crimes of the Heart, Beth Henley; (D) Judy Braha; (s) Leslie Taylor; (c) Joan St. Germain; (L) Kendall Smith

Something's Afoot, book, music and lyrics: James McDonald, David Vos and Robert Gerlach; (D) Richard Rose; (s) Gary English; (c) Amanda Aldridge; (L) Kendall Smith

PRODUCTIONS 1986–87

The Foreigner, Larry Shue; (D) Daniel L. Schay; (s) Alison Ford; (c) Amanda Aldridge; (L) John Ambrosone

A Christmas Carol, adapt: Larry Carpenter, from Charles Dickens; (D) Thomas Clewell; (s) Leslie Taylor; (c) Amanda Aldridge; (L) David Lockner

The Adding Machine, Elmer L. Rice; (D) Richard Rose; (s) Jeff Schneider; (c) Gary English; (L) Kendall Smith

First Night, Jack Neary; (D) Joan Courtney Murray; (s) Leslie Taylor; (c) Amanda Aldridge; (L) John Abrosone

The Hostage, Brendan Behan; (D) Daniel L. Schay; (s) Gary English; (c) Joan St. Germain; (L) Sid Bennett

The Importance of Being Earnest, Oscar Wilde; (D) Richard Rose; (s) Dale F. Jordan; (c) Amanda Aldridge; (L) John Ambrosone

Milwaukee Repertory Theater

JOHN DILLON
Artistic Director

SARA O'CONNOR
Managing Director

108 East Wells St.
Milwaukee, WI 53202
(414) 224-1761 (bus.)
(414) 224-9490 (b.o.)

FOUNDED 1954
Mary John

SEASON
Oct.-June

FACILITIES
Mainstage
Seating capacity: 720
Stage: flexible

Stiemke Theater
Seating capacity: 200
Stage: flexible

Stackner Cabaret
Seating capacity: 100
Stage: flexible

FINANCES
July 1, 1986-June 30, 1987
Expenses: $2,400,000

CONTRACTS
AEA LORT (A), (C), (D), SSD&C and USA

Virtually from its inception, the resident acting company has been at the core of Milwaukee Repertory Theater's identity. Over the years we've enlarged this multiracial troupe to include resident writers, directors, composers and dramaturgs. To challenge the company, we maintain an active program of exchange with theatres in Japan, Mexico, Ireland and Chile. And to deepen the bonds between the company and the community, we've commissioned works that explore the social and spiritual past and present of our region. Our acting interns work with company members in the Lab, our in-house research and development wing that seeks to develop new works and explore unusual acting styles, while innovative artists like Maria Irene Fornes. Tadashi Suzuki and Ping Chong help us try to keep our artistry on the cutting edge.

—John Dillon

PRODUCTIONS 1985–86

Henry IV, Part 1, William Shakespeare; (D) Gregory Boyd; (s) Peter D. Gould; (c) Sam Fleming; (L) Robert Jared

Two Brothers, Felipe Santander; trans: Amlin Gray; (D) John Dillon; (s) Laura Maurer and Tim Thomas; (c) Sam Fleming; (L) Derek Duarte

The Art of Dining, Tina Howe; (D) Dilys Hamlett; (s) Michael Merritt; (c) Sam Fleming; (L) Dawn Chiang

The Crucible, Arthur Miller; (D) M. Burke Walker; (s) Scott Weldin; (c) Sally Richardson; (L) Rick Paulsen

A Flea in Her Ear, Georges Feydeau; trans: Sara O'Connor; (D) Kenneth Albers; (s) Bil Mikulewicz; (c) Sam Fleming; (L) Dan Kotlowitz

Glengarry Glen Ross, David Mamet; (D) John Dillon; (s) Michael Olich; (c) Michael Olich; (L) Spencer Mosse

A Christmas Carol, adapt: Amlin Gray, from Charles Dickens; (D) Richard E.T. White; (s) Stuart Wurtzel; (c) Carol Oditz; (L) Derek Duarte

PRODUCTIONS 1986–87

The Black Cross, Mikhail Bulgakov; trans: Barbara Field; (D) John Dillon; (s) Scott Weldin; (c) Sam Fleming; (L) Dan Kotlowitz

Tartuffe, Molière; trans: Richard Wilbur; (D) Kenneth Albers; (s) Scott Weldin; (c) Sam Fleming; (L) Dan Kotlowitz

Hay Fever, Noel Coward; (D) Dilys Hamlett; (s) Michael Merritt; (c) Sam Fleming; (L) Dawn Chiang

An American Journey, Kermit Frazier and John Leicht; (D) John Dillon; (s) Laura Maurer and Tim Thomas; (c) Carol Oditz; (L) Victor En Yu Tan

Hedda Gabler, Henrik Ibsen; adapt: Maria Irene Fornes;

Milwaukee Repertory Theater. Peter Silbert, Tamu Gray, Rose Pickering and Tom Blair in *Twelfth Night*. Photo: Mark Avery.

(D) Maria Irene Fornes; (S) Donald Eastman; (C) Gabriel Berry; (L) Anne Militello

Twelfth Night, William Shakespeare; (D) Kenneth Albers; (S) Victor Becker; (C) Sam Fleming; (L) Robert Jared

A Christmas Carol, adapt: Amlin Gray, from Charles Dickens; (D) Kristine Thatcher; (S) Stuart Wurtzel; (C) Carol Oditz; (L) Spencer Mosse

The Caretaker, Harold Pinter; (D) Daniel Mooney; (S) Pat Doty; (C) Cecelia Mason; (L) Kenneth Kloth

Niedecker, Kristine Thatcher; (D) Kristine Thatcher; (S) John Story; (C) Therese Donarski; (L) Nancy A. Brunswick

Mirror Repertory Company

SABRA JONES
Artistic Director

WEILER/MILLER ASSOCIATES
General Managers

352 East 50th St.
New York, NY 10022
(212) 888-6087 (bus.)
(212) 223-6440 (b.o.)

FOUNDED 1983
Sabra Jones

SEASON
Variable

FACILITIES
Theatre at St. Peter's Church
Seating capacity: 199
Stage: proscenium

FINANCES
July 1, 1986-June 30, 1987
Expenses: $73,000

CONTRACTS
AEA letter of agreement, SSD&C and USA

The Mirror Repertory Company has been in operation for four years and is an alternating repertory company run by the actors and headed by an actor/manager. The Mirror intends to fill the gap left by the demise of the APA/Phoenix Repertory company in the late '60s and, with the late Geraldine Page as artist-in-residence, produced 15 plays in three years, growing from a company of 16 actors with a $150,000 budget to one with 70 actors and a budget well in excess of $1.3 million. Following the company's rapid, inorganic growth, we have been in hiatus this year. Believing that art must serve the public it reflects, we have concentrated our efforts this season on New York State's Arts in Education initiative, and we are extremely proud of our three-play collaboration with the Julia Richman High School. We hope to find a place in New York City beyond conventional competition: though we strive for excellence, we most of all wish to create a theatre of loving communion that becomes a satisfying and joyful place for us all. Most important, we hope to provide audiences with opportunities to feel—to be an active part of the creative process, as we mirror each other.

—Sabra Jones

Mirror Repertory Company. Brian Clark and Geraldine Page in *Paradise Lost*. Photo: Martha Swope.

PRODUCTIONS 1985–86

The Madwoman of Chaillot, Jean Giraudoux; adapt: Maurice Valency; (D) Stephen Porter; (S) James Tilton; (C) Gail Cooper-Hecht; (L) James Tilton

The Time of Your Life, William Saroyan; (D) Peter Mark Schifter; (S) James Tilton; (C) Gail Cooper-Hecht; (L) James Tilton

Children of the Sun, Maxim Gorky; trans: Ariadne Nicolaeff; (D) Tom Brennan; (S) James Tilton; (C) Gail Cooper-Hecht; (L) James Tilton

The Circle, W. Somerset Maugham; (D) Stephen Porter; (S) James Tilton; (C) Gail Cooper-Hecht; (L) James Tilton

PRODUCTIONS 1986–87

The Elephant Man, Bernard Pomerance; (D) Thomas McAteer

Hatful of Rain, Michael Gazzo; (D) Thomas McAteer

Born Yesterday, Garson Kanin; (D) John Strasberg

Missouri Repertory Theatre. Jim Birdsall and Peter Byger in *A Christmas Carol*. Photo: Larry Pape.

Missouri Repertory Theatre

GEORGE KEATHLEY
Artistic Director

JAMES D. COSTIN
Executive Director

4949 Cherry St.
Kansas City, MO 64110
(816) 276-2727 (bus.)
(816) 276-2700 (b.o.)

FOUNDED 1964
James D. Costin, Patricia McIlrath

SEASON
July-Mar.

FACILITIES
Helen F. Spencer Theatre
Seating capacity: 730
Stage: flexible

Studio 116
Seating capacity: 99
Stage: thrust

FINANCES
May 1, 1986-April 30, 1987
Expenses: $2,204,215

CONTRACTS
AEA LORT (B), SSD&C and USA

Theatre has always been a medium through which we can see ourselves and therefore a medium through which we can influence behavior and alter perceptions. This influence is, hopefully, in the upward direction of taste, of morality, of ideas. Since theatre both instructs and entertains, the material and style of production must be carefully chosen. The Missouri Repertory Theatre expends a grea deal of energy in both of these areas. New plays continue to be a high priority for us. We also consider touring to be a vital part of what we do. Last year our tour covered 12,000 miles and we played in states as far afield as Florida. In addition to performing, while on tour we conducted dozens of workshops and master classes.

—George Keathley

PRODUCTIONS 1985–86

Agammenon, Aeschylus; adapt: John Lewis; (D) Erik Vos; (S) Niels Hamel; (C) Niels Hamel; (L) Joseph Appelt
Foxfire, Susan Cooper and Hume Cronyn; (D) Jerome Kilty; (S) John Ezell; (C) J. Henry Kester; (L) Joseph Appelt
Side by Side by Sondheim, music and lyrics: Stephen Sondheim, et al.; (D) Francis Cullinan; (S) Jack Ballance; (C) Vincent Scassellati; (L) Jackie Manassee
A Christmas Carol, adapt: Barbara Field, from Charles Dickens; (D) Francis Cullinan; (S) John Ezell; (C) Baker S. Smith; (L) Joseph Appelt
Fallen Angels, Noel Coward; (D) Francis Cullinan; (S) John Ezell; (C) Vincent Scassellati; (L) Joseph Appelt
Master Harold...and the boys, Athol Fugard; (D) George Keathley; (S) Harry Feiner; (C) Vincent Scassellati; (L) Joseph Appelt
Othello, William Shakespeare; (D) Peter Bennett; (S) Carolyn L. Ross; (C) Virgil Johnson; (L) Robert Jared

PRODUCTIONS 1986–87

Brighton Beach Memoirs, Neil Simon; (D) George Keathley; (S) Harry Feiner; (C) Baker S. Smith; (L) Joseph Appelt
Equus, Peter Shaffer; (D) George Keathley; (S) Harry Feiner; (C) Vincent Scassellati; (L) James F. Ingalls
Fool for Love, Sam Shepard; (D) Peter Bennett; (S) David Wallace; (C) Gwen Walters; (L) Joseph Appelt
A Christmas Carol, adapt: Barbara Field, from Charles Dickens; (D) Beverly Shatto; (S) John Ezell; (C) Baker S. Smith; (L) Joseph Appelt
A Class "C" Trial in Yokohama, Roger Cornish; (D) George Keathley; (S) Herbert L. Camburn; (C) Vincent Scassellati; (L) Joseph Appelt
And Miss Reardon Drinks a Little, Paul Zindel; (D) George Keathley; (S) James Leonard Joy; (C) Vincent Scassellati; (L) Joseph Appelt
The Glass Menagerie, Tennessee Williams; (D) George Keathley; (S) John Ezell; (C) John Carver Sullivan; (L) Curt Ostermann

Mixed Blood Theatre Company

JACK REULER
Managing/Artistic Director

1501 South Fourth St.
Minneapolis, MN 55454
(612) 338-0937 (bus.)
(612) 338-6131 (b.o.)

FOUNDED 1976
Jack Reuler

SEASON
Sept.-May

FACILITIES
Seating capacity: 220
Stage: flexible

FINANCES
July 1, 1986-June 30, 1987
Expenses: $393,995

CONTRACTS
AEA SPT

Mixed Blood Theatre Company. Joe Keyes, Lia Rivamonte and James Williams in *Rebel Without a Cause*. Photo: Mike Paul.

The Mixed Blood Theatre Company is a prototype of a multiracial company and has become a national resource because of its colorblind approach. Just as current headlines expose the continuing state of racism in baseball, recent forums on nontraditional casting have exposed the sad state of casting and race in the theatre. Stalwarts of the American theatre have now begun to discuss in theory what Mixed Blood has been doing in practice for 11 years. That theoretical discussion has centered on audience reaction, box office risk, aesthetic integrity, critical reaction and playwrights' rights. At Mixed Blood we have proved that colorblind casting works. It isn't "affirmative action." It expands a casting director's horizons in the search for extraordinary talent within a pool brimming with brilliance. Above all, it is the right thing to do. If we all were to cast in a color-blind mode, no one would notice. Nontraditional would become traditional. In such a world, rather than being known as a "mission theatre," or "the place that does colorblind casting," the Mixed Blood Theatre Company would be known to the American theatre, as indeed it is in the Twin Cities, simply as the theatre that does new work with an aggressive cinematic style.

—Jack Reuler

PRODUCTIONS 1985–86

Rebel Without a Cause, Jack Reuler; (D) Jack Reuler; (S) Lori Sullivan; (C) Lori Sullivan; (L) Scott Peters
Beyond Therapy, Christopher Durang; (D) David Ira Goldstein; (S) Robert Fuecker; (C) Lia Rivamonte; (L) Scott Peters
In the Belly of the Beast, adapt: Jack Henry Abbott and Seymour Morganstern; (D) John Clark Donahue; (S) Robert Fuecker; (C) Deian Miller; (L) Scott Peters
A...My Name Is Alice, Joan Micklin Silver and Julianne Boyd; (D) Sharon Walton; (S) Robert Fuecker; (C) Jane Thompson; (L) Scott Peters
Glengarry Glen Ross, David Mamet; (D) Michael Arndt; (S) Robert Fuecker; (C) Leisa Luis

PRODUCTIONS 1986–87

Rap Master Ronnie, book and lyrics: Garry Trudeau; music: Elizabeth Swados; (D) Ron Peluso; (S) Robert Fuecker; (C) Anne Ruben; (L) Scott Peters
A...My Name Is Alice, Joan Micklin Silver and Julianne Boyd; (D) Sharon Walton; (S) Robert Fuecker; (C) Jane Thomson; (L) Scott Peters
A Map of the World, David Hare; (D) David Ira Goldstein; (S) Lori Sullivan; (C) Anne Ruben; (L) Scott Peters
How to Improve Your Golf Game, David Babcock; (D) Mark Sieve; (S) Colin Tugwell; (C) Anne Ruben; (L) Scott Peters

Musical Theatre Works

ANTHONY J. STIMAC
Executive Director

MARK HERKO
Associate Artistic Director

440 Lafayette St., 3rd fl.
New York, NY 10003
(212) 677-0040

FOUNDED 1983
Anthony J. Stimac

SEASON
Sept.-May

FACILITIES
CSC Repertory Theatre
Seating capacity: 152
Stage: flexible

MTW Studio Lab
Seating capacity: 50
Stage: flexible

FINANCES
July 1, 1986-June 30, 1987
Expenses: $367,500

CONTRACTS
AEA letter of agreement

Musical Theatre Works is a nonprofit producing organization located in New York City. It is devoted exclusively to developing new musicals and new writers for the musical theatre. Each year MTW presents 10 informal readings of new musicals, 10 staged readings and four full productions. Since its inception MTW has presented 78 readings and 17 full productions, of which six have gone on to production in other venues. With the cost of a Broadway musical regularly exceeding $5 million MTW was created as a place where composers, lyricists, librettists, directors, choreographers and actors can learn and develop their craft by going through the whole process. During the run of each production revisions are made daily and tested on the audience at each performance. Essentially MTW is seeking to develop a process for creating new works for the American musical theatre in today's inflated economic environment.

—*Anthony J. Stimac*

PRODUCTIONS 1985–86

Legs, book and lyrics: Robert Satuloff; music: Mel Marvin; (D) Stephen Zuckerman; (S) James Fenhagen; (C) Bruce Goodrich; (L) Richard Winkler

Señor Discretion, Himself, music and lyrics: Frank Loesser; book: Budd Schulberg, Frank Loesser and Anthony J. Stimac; (D) Anthony J. Stimac; (S) Michael Keith; (C) Bruce Goodrich; (L) Victor En Yu Tan

Charley's Tale, book and lyrics: Tricia Tunstall; music: Donald Johnston; (D) Gideon Y. Schein; (S) James Wolk; (C) Pamela Scofield; (L) Victor En Yu Tan

The House in the Woods, book and lyrics: Ellen Weston; music: Marvin Laird; (D) Michael Leeds; (S) Evelyn Sakash; (C) Bruce Goodrich; (L) Victor En Yu Tan

PRODUCTIONS 1986–87

A Romantic Detachment, music and lyrics: John Clifton; book: Russell Treyz; (D) Russell Treyz; (S) John Falabella; (C) John Falabella; (L) Clarke W. Thornton

Abyssinia, book: Ted Kociolek and James Racheff; lyrics: James Racheff; music: Ted Kociolek; (D) Tazewell Thompson; (S) Evelyn Sakash; (C) Amanda J. Klein; (L) Clarke W. Thornton

Starmites, music and lyrics: Barry Keating; book: Stuart Ross and Barry Keating; (D) Mark S. Herko; (S) Evelyn Sakash; (C) Amanda J. Klein; (L) Clarke W. Thornton

(212), book and lyrics: Victor Joseph; music: Donald Siegal; (D) Maggie L. Harrer; (S) Evelyn Sakash; (C) Amanda J. Klein; (L) Clarke W. Thornton

Musical Theatre Works. Ellen Foley, Carolyn Mignini and Karen Ziemba in *Legs*. Photo: Rita Katz.

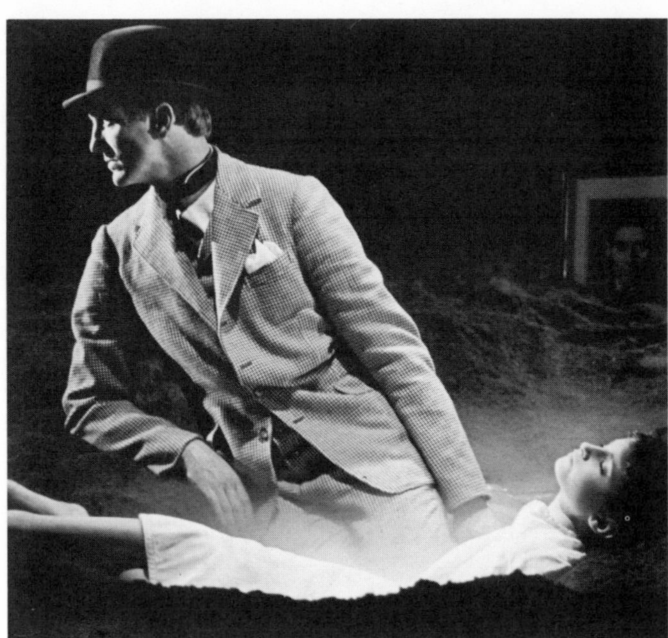

Music-Theatre Group. Rob Besserer and David Jon in *The Hunger Artist*. Photo: Tom Brazil.

Music-Theatre Group

LYN AUSTIN
Producing Director

DIANE WONDISFORD
Managing Director

735 Washington St.
New York, NY 10014
(212) 924-3108 (bus.)
(212) 265-4375 (b.o.)

Lenox Arts Center
Box 128
Stockbridge, MA 01262
(413) 298-3460 (bus.)
(413) 298-4963 (b.o.)

FOUNDED 1971
Lyn Austin

SEASON
Year-round

FACILITIES
St. Clement's, New York, NY
Seating capacity: 99
Stage: flexible

Citizens Hall, Stockbridge, MA
Seating capacity: 75
Stage: flexible

FINANCES
July 1, 1986-June 30, 1987
Expenses: $969,419

CONTRACTS
AEA letter of agreement

Music-Theatre Group is a leading pioneer in the development of new works in which theatre, music, dance and the visual arts are combined to create new forms. Music-Theatre Group's work is deliberately eclectic and has been variously termed theatre with music, dance-theatre, opera and musical theatre. Most of the work is developed from an idea rather than a completed score or script. MTG brings together a carefully selected combination of director, composer, writer/lyricist and choreographer and places them in a supportive, collaborative environment. Long-term developmental periods and careful nurturing of the artists are key elements in the organization's artistic approach. We seek to create an atmosphere in which artists can set new sights and take risks, while receiving supporting insight and meaningful critical feedback. The work is fully produced both Off Broadway and in Stockbridge, Mass., and often tours nationally and internationally.

—*Lyn Austin*

PRODUCTIONS 1985–86

The Making of Americans, book and lyrics adapt: Leon Katz; music: Al Carmines; (D) Anne Bogart; (S) Jim Buff and Nancy Winters; (C) Jim Buff and Nancy Winters; (L) Carol Mullins

Alliances, book and music: Edward Flower; (D) Susan Landau; (S) Nancy Winters; (L) Steven Ehrenberg

Africanis Instructus, book and lyrics: Richard Foreman; music: Stanley Silverman; (D) Richard Foreman; (S) Richard Foreman and Nancy Winters; (C) Jim Buff; (L) William Armstrong

Chacona, adapt: Susan Landau and Edward Flower, from Gabriele Mistral; trans: Doris Dana; music: Edward Flower; (D) Susan Landau; (S) Carl Sprague; (C) Jim Buff; (L) Carol Mullins

Vienna: Lusthaus, conceived: Martha Clarke; music: Richard Peaslee; text: Charles Mee, Jr.; (D) Martha Clarke; (S) Robert Israel; (C) Robert Israel; (L) Paul Gallo

PRODUCTIONS 1986–87

Between Wind, conceived: Anne Bogart; text: Jessica Litwak; music: Seth Cooper; (D) Anne Bogart; (S) Sarah Bonnemaison; (C) Jim Buff; (L) Carol Mullins

Black Sea Follies, conceived and music adapt: Stanley Silverman, from Dmitri Shostakovich; book: Paul Schmidt; (D) Stanley Silverman; (S) James Noone; (C) Jim Buff; (L) Ken Tabachnick

The Hunger Artist, conceived: Martha Clarke; text adapt: Richard Greenberg, from Franz Kafka; music: Richard Peaslee; (D) Martha Clarke; (S) Robert Israel; (C) Robert Israel; (L) Paul Gallo

National Theatre of the Deaf

DAVID HAYS
Artistic Director

DAVID RELYEA
General Manager

The Hazel E. Stark Center
Chester, CT 06412
(203) 526-4971

FOUNDED 1967
David Hays

SEASON
Sept.-June

FINANCES
Jan. 1, 1986-Dec. 31, 1986
Expenses: $1,197,347

CONTRACTS
AEA Guest Artist and USA

The guiding artistic purpose of The National Theatre of the Deaf has been, and continues to be, the creation and development of a unique theatrical form which combines sign language and the spoken word. We endeavor to present the finest productions to as broad an audience as possible (26 countries and 50 states to date) with a fully professional company of deaf and hearing actors. Our artistic aims will always be based on the development of our own theatrical form, with its infinite capabilities of extension, growth, application. Our greatest achievement to date has been our compelling style which strives to deepen the content of our work. Our professional theatre school enables us to train deaf actors from all over the world and has resulted in the creation of theatres of the deaf in England, Sweden, Australia, Japan, India and, soon, in the People's Republic of China.

—*David Hays*

National Theatre of the Deaf. Shanny Mow in *Farewell, My Lovely!*. Photo: David Hays.

PRODUCTIONS 1985–86

Farewell, My Lovely, company-adapt, from E.B. White; (D) Will Rhys; (S) Chuck Baird; (C) Fred Voelpel; (L) David Hays

In a Grove, company-adapt, from Ryunosuke Akutagawa; trans: Tadashi Yokoyama; (D) Arvin Brown; (S) David Hays; (C) Fred Voelpel; (L) David Hays

PRODUCTIONS 1986–87

The Heart Is a Lonely Hunter, adapt: Glenn Berenbeim, from Carson McCullers; (D) J Ranelli; (S) David Hays; (C) Lana Fritz; (L) David Hays

Nebraska Theatre Caravan

CHARLES JONES
Artistic Director

CAROLYN RUTHERFORD
Managing Director

6915 Cass St.
Omaha, NE 68132
(402) 553-4890 (bus.)
(402) 553-0800 (b.o.)

FOUNDED 1976
Charles Jones, Omaha Community Playhouse

SEASON
Sept.-May

FACILITIES
Omaha Community Playhouse
Seating capacity: 600
Stage: proscenium

Omaha Playhouse Fonda-McGuire Series
Seating capacity: 300
Stage: flexible

FINANCES
July 1, 1986-June 30, 1987
Expenses: $568,912

The Nebraska Theatre Caravan is the professional touring wing of the Omaha Community Playhouse, the largest community theatre in the nation and the only community theatre to sponsor a national professional touring company. The original mission of the Caravan is to provide high-quality entertainment and educational opportunities to communities where distance, financial limitations or lack of appropriate resources has hindered or prevented such activities. However, we are finding that the company is now providing performances and workshops to all sizes of cities across the U.S. and Canada, as well as in our home state. The 15-member resident company now works together eight months each year. Our dream is to have year-round employment for the professional company that not only performs in our home theatre's Fonda-McGuire Series, but also tours nationally and internationally.

—*Charles Jones*

PRODUCTIONS 1985–86

Pump Boys and Dinettes, John Foley, Mark Hardwick, Debra Monk, Cass Morgan, John Schimmel and Jim Wann; (D) Carl Beck; (S) James Othuse; (C) Susan Snowden; (L) James Othuse

Monkey and the Golden Sunrise, Charles Jones; (D) Charles Jones; (S) James Othuse; (C) Denise Ervin; (L) James Othuse

The Taming of the Shrew, William Shakespeare; adapt: Carl Beck and Chris Kliesen; (D) Carl Beck; (S) James Othuse; (C) Denise Ervin; (L) James Othuse

Cyrano!, Edmond Rostand; adapt: John Foley; (D) Carl Beck; (S) James Othuse; (C) Denise Ervin; (L) James Othuse

A Christmas Carol, adapt: Charles Jones, from Charles Dickens; (D) Charles Jones, Carl Beck, John Bennett and Joanne Cady; (S) James Othuse; (C) Tom Crisp, Denise Ervin and Kathryn Wilson; (L) James Othuse

PRODUCTIONS 1986–87

The Hunchback of Notre Dame, adapt: Carl Beck and Chris Kliesen, from Victor Hugo; (D) Carl Beck; (S) James Othuse; (C) Denise Ervin; (L) James Othuse

Man of La Mancha, book: Dale Wasserman; music: Mitch Leigh; lyrics: Joe Darion; (D) Carl Beck; (S) James Othuse; (C) Denise Ervin; (L) James Othuse

Beauty and the Beast, Michael Elliot Brill; (D) Chris Kliesen; (S) James Othuse; (C) Denise Ervin; (L) James Othuse

A Christmas Carol, adapt: Charles Jones, from Charles Dickens; (D) Carl Beck, Charles Jones, John Bennett and Joanne Cady; (S) James Othuse; (C) Tom Crisp, Denise Ervin and Kathryn Wilson; (L) James Othuse

Nebraska Theatre Caravan. Bridget Juline Wiley and Joel Stevenor in *The Hunchback of Notre Dame*. Photo: Joan McIntyre.

New American Theater

J.R. SULLIVAN
Producing Director

SHARON L. HENSLEY
Managing Director

118 North Main St.
Rockford, IL 61101
(815) 963-9454 (bus.)
(815) 964-8023 (b.o.)

New American Theater. Matt K. Miller in *Luther*. Photo: Chris Welsh.

FOUNDED 1972
J.R. Sullivan

SEASON
Sept.-June

FACILITIES
Mainstage
Seating capacity: 282
Stage: thrust

Cabaret
Seating capacity: 90
Stage: flexible

FINANCES
July 1, 1986-June 30, 1987
Expenses: $715,000

CONTRACTS
AEA SPT

New American Theater's mission is to produce classical, contemporary and new works in a manner consistent with the high standards of the contemporary American theatre: innovative productions that foster lasting audience and ensemble growth. When New American Theater was founded, its aim was the production of new plays. NAT is now poised to achieve the pursuit of this oft-stated mission with a modern, fully equipped mainstage thrust space designed to feature classic as well as contemporary plays, and a second stage providing workshop and performance space for new work. With a two-season planning process in place, NAT can now pursue workshops of new plays and transfer them to the main stage, while maintaining an ensemble. Energizing audiences with this mix of theatre has been central to NAT's concept of itself. With our new quarters offering workshops, classes and spaces for affiliate artists and attention to special populations within our community, the promise of consistent and high-quality new work seems on the threshold of fulfillment. To perform with dynamism and to perform with truth, while making every play a new play, remains New American Theater's greatest goal.

—*J.R. Sullivan*

PRODUCTIONS 1985–86

Sly Fox, Larry Gelbart; (D) J.R. Sullivan; (S) James Wolk; (C) Jon R. Accardo; (L) James Wolk

Painting Churches, Tina Howe; (D) J.R. Sullivan; (S) Michael S. Philippi; (C) Jon R. Accardo; (L) Michael S. Philippi

Great Expectations, adapt: J.R. Sullivan, from Charles Dickens; (D) J.R. Sullivan; (S) Michael S. Philippi; (C) Jon R. Accardo; (L) Michael S. Philippi

As You Like It, William Shakespeare; (D) J.R. Sullivan; (S) Michael S. Philippi; (C) Jon R. Accardo; (L) Michael S. Philippi

The Foreigner, Larry Shue; (D) Allan Carlsen; (S) Kenneth Kloth; (C) Jon R. Accardo; (L) David L. Radunsky

And a Nightingale Sang..., C.P. Taylor; (D) J.R. Sullivan; (S) Michael S. Philippi; (C) Jon R. Accardo; (L) Michael S. Philippi

Strange Snow, Stephen Metcalfe; (D) John Going; (S) James Wolk; (C) Jon R. Accardo; (L) James Wolk

PRODUCTIONS 1986–87

Luther, John Osborne; (D) J.R. Sullivan; (S) James Wolk; (C) Jon R. Accardo; (L) James Wolk

Inherit the Wind, Jerome Lawrence and Robert E. Lee; (D) J.R. Sullivan; (S) Chuck Drury; (C) Laura Cunningham; (L) Chuck Drury

A Christmas Carol, adapt: Amlin Gray, from Charles Dickens; (D) Francis X. Kuhn; (S) James Wolk; (C) Jon R. Accardo; (L) James Wolk
Brighton Beach Memoirs, Neil Simon; (D) J.R. Sullivan; (S) Laura Cunningham; (C) Laura Cunningham; (L) Daniel Eastman
The Real Thing, Tom Stoppard; (D) Tom Mula; (S) Michael S. Philippi; (C) Jon R. Accardo; (L) Miriam Hack
Kingdom Come, Amlin Gray; (D) J.R. Sullivan; (S) Jon R. Accardo; (C) Jon R. Accardo; (L) David L. Radunsky
The Voice of the Prairie, John Olive; (D) J.R. Sullivan; (S) Michael S. Philippi; (C) Barbara Niederer; (L) David L. Radunsky

New Dramatists

THOMAS G. DUNN
Executive Director

BEVERLY KNOX
General Manager

424 West 44th St.
New York, NY 10036
(212) 757-6960

FOUNDED 1949
John Golden, Oscar Hammerstein, II, Moss Hart, Howard Lindsay, Michaela O'Hara, Richard Rodgers, John Wharton

SEASON
Sept.-May

FACILITIES
Mainstage
Seating capacity: 90
Stage: flexible

Lindsay/Crouse Studio
Seating capacity: 60
Stage: flexible

FINANCES
July 1, 1986-June 30, 1987
Expenses: $458,506

CONTRACTS
AEA Workshop

New Dramatists is the oldest non-profit service organization for the theatre in the country. The fact that we were founded to help playwrights and that we have been serving them continually for 39 years says a great deal about the orientation of the American theatre. We are a playwrights' theatre, and in recent years New Dramatists has expanded its vision of the word, "services." Chosen by a panel of their peers, our writers are members for five to six years. Some 45 playwrights are currently engaged in one or more of the 120 projects we do each season.

—Thomas G. Dunn

PRODUCTIONS 1985–86

The Knife's Edge, Bryan Oliver; (D) Alma Becker
Bombs on the Halfshell, Stephen Levi; (D) Tom Gruenewald
Opera Presentation, Ben Krywosz; (D) Ben Krywosz
Bodacious Flapdoodle, Mac Wellman; (D) James Simpson
Panic in Longueuil, Rene-Daniel Dubois; (D) Gideon Y. Schein
Lucian's Woods, David Hill; (D) Susan Gregg
Poetry Reading, Pedro Juan Pietri; (D) Lynne Alvarez
And Howl at the Moon, James Nicholson; (D) Susan Gregg
Between the Acts, Joan Schenkar; (D) Joan Schenkar
Free Fall, Laura Harrington; (D) Alma Becker
Cherry Soda Water, Stephen Levi; (D) Robert Moss
The Tattler, Terri Wagener; (D) Casey Childs
Souvenirs, Sheldon Rosen; (D) Steven Katz
The Memory Theatre of Guilio Camillo, Matthew MacGuire; (D) Matthew MacGuire
Timothy's Nuclear Strategy, Russell Davis; (D) John Pynchon Holmes
Nights and Days, Emily Mann; (D) Emily Mann
Beautiful Bodies, Laura Cunningham; (D) Laura Cunningham
Paven for the Princess of Clevs, Romulus Linney; (D) Romulus Linney
Energumen, Mac Wellman; (D) Mac Wellman
Carrie and Nell, Thomas G. Dunn; (D) Susan Gregg
Eat Rocks, Pedro Juan Pietri; (D) Lynne Alvarez
Primary Colors, Steve Carter; (D) Alma Becker
Private Assumptions, Richard Toscan; (D) Will MacAdam
The Bad Infinity, Mac Wellman; (D) Mac Wellman

PRODUCTIONS 1986–87

Love in the Third Degree, book: O-Lan Jones and Kathleen Cramer; music: O-Lan Jones; (D) Chris Silva
Sweetness, Glenn Lumsden; (D) Alma Becker
The Perfect Light, Geraldine Sherman and Eduardo Machado; (D) Joel Bishoff
Getting the Message Across, Pedro Juan Pietri; (D) Livia Perez
Nightmare #9, Mark Handley; (D) Nick Flynn
Finding Your Way, book: Eduardo Machado; music: Greg Pliska; (D) Mark Lutwak
No Passengers, Pedro Juan Pietri; (D) Paul Ellis
Inside Out, Willy Holtzman; (D) John Pynchon Holms
Bargains, Jack Heifner; (D) Diane Kamp
Paradise Re-Lost, book: OyamO; (D) Thomas Gruenewald
Dobbs Is Dead, Sebastian Barry; (D) Rhea Gaisner
Three Views of Mt. Fuji, Ntozake Shange; (D) Laurie Carlos
Albanian Softshoe, Mac Wellman; (D) Gordon Edelstein
Alone at the Beach, Richard Dresser; (D) John Pynchon Holms
Visit from the Wild, Anne Legault; trans: Jill MacDougall; (D) Alma Becker

New Dramatists. Deborah Hedwall and David Straithairn in a reading of *The Last Good Moment of Lily Baker*. Photo: Christie Mullen.

New Federal Theatre

WOODIE KING, JR.
Producer

LINDA HERRING
Company Manager

466 Grand St.
New York, NY 10002
(212) 598-0400

FOUNDED 1970
Woodie King, Jr.

SEASON
Sept.-June

FACILITIES
Playhouse
Seating capacity: 350
Stage: proscenium

Experimental Theatre
Seating capacity: 150
Stage: arena

Recital Hall
Seating capacity: 100
Stage: thrust

FINANCES
July 1, 1986-June 30, 1987
Expenses: $350,000

CONTRACTS
AEA letter of agreement

Growing out of the New York State Council on the Arts' Ghetto Arts Program, the New Federal Theatre was officially founded by Woodie King, Jr. at Henry Street Settlement. Now in its 18th season, the New Federal Theatre has carved a much admired special niche for itself in the New York and national theatre worlds. Specializing in minority drama, it has brought the joy of the living stage to the many

New Federal Theatre. Mark Lienthal, Kobie Powell, Crist Swann and Lia Alexi in *The Second Hurricane*. Photo: Bert Andrews.

minority audience members who live in the surrounding Lower East Side community and the greater metropolitan area. It has brought minority playwrights, actors and directors to national attention, and has sponsored a variety of ethnic theatre groups and events.

—Woodie King, Jr.

PRODUCTIONS 1985–86

Long Time Since Yesterday, P.J. Gibson; (D) Bette Howard; (S) Charles H. McClennahan; (C) Judy Dearing; (L) William H. Grant

Once Upon the Present Time, Geri Lipschultz; (D) Lawrence Butch Morris; (L) Richard Leu

Non Sectarian Conversations with the Dead, Laurie Carlos; (D) Laurie Carlos and La Tanya Richardson

Second Hurricane, libretto: Edwin Denby; music: Aaron Copland; (D) Tazewell Thompson; (S) Steve Saklad; (C) Laura Drawbaugh; (L) Dan Kotlowitz

Appear and Show Cause, Stephen Taylor and Leon Gildin; (D) Woodie King, Jr.; (S) Richard Harmon; (C) Judy Dearing; (L) Leo Gambacorta

In the House of Blues, David Charles; (D) Buddy Butler; (S) Lew Harrison; (C) Judy Dearing; (L) Buddy Butler

I Have a Dream, Josh Greenfeld; (D) Woodie King, Jr.; (S) Ina Mayhew; (C) Judy Dearing

December Seventh, George Rattner; (D) Gordon Edelstein; (S) James Wolk; (C) David C. Woolard; (L) Leo Gambacorta

Williams & Walker, Vincent Smith; (D) Shauneille Perry; (S) Marc Malamud; (C) Judy Dearing; (L) Marc Malamud

Ma Maw Blacksheep, Stafford Harrison; (D) Stafford Ashani; (L) Edgar Gordon

PRODUCTIONS 1986–87

Sovereign State of Boogedy Boogedy, Lonnie Carter; (D) Dennis Zacek; (S) Bob Edmonds; (C) Judy Dearing; (L) William H. Grant, III

Lillian Wald: At Home on Henry St., Clare Coss; (D) Bryna Wortman; (S) Richard Harmon; (C) Gail Cooper-Hecht; (L) Jackie Manassee

Time Out of Time, Cliff Mason; (D) Al Freeman, Jr.; (S) Charles McClennahan; (C) Judy Dearing; (L) James Worley

Boogie Woogie and Booker T., Wesley Brown; (D) Dean Irby; (S) Charles McClennahan; (C) Judy Dearing; (L) Victor En Yu Tan

The Meeting, Jeff Stetson; (D) Judyann Elder; (S) Virgil Woodford; (C) Violette Fasion; (L) Leroy Meadows

New Jersey Shakespeare Festival

PAUL BARRY
Artistic Director

ELLEN BARRY
Producing Director

Drew University
Route 24
Madison, NJ 07940
(201) 377-5330 (bus.)
(201) 377-4487 (b.o.)

FOUNDED 1963
Paul Barry

SEASON
June-Jan.

FACILITIES
Bowne Theatre
Seating capacity: 238
Stage: thrust

FINANCES
Jan. 1, 1986-Dec. 31, 1986
Expenses: $639,046

CONTRACTS
AEA LORT (D) and SSD&C

The New Jersey Shakespeare Festival's vision is best explained by the plays produced through 1987, our 25th anniversary: 179 productions from Sophocles to Fugard, including 56 mountings of 34 of Shakespeare's plays (we'll soon become one of the few theatres anywhere to complete the canon). The list is justified by our own aesthetic values, which include a commitment to the preservation of the American classical theatre and to the development of artists for it; a firm preference for proven excellence over newness for its own sake; and devotion to the challenges and resonances of repertory, where related works are juxtaposed for added insights (e.g. the complete War of the Roses, *Henry VIII* and *A Man for All Seasons* or *Julius Caesar* and *Antony and Cleopatra*). If we have accomplished anything, it is this: we are able to choose plays because we believe in them, not because they will turn a dollar—plays of great value that may heal and excite, teach and console. And this brings rare fulfillment to us.

—Paul Barry

PRODUCTIONS 1986

Julius Caesar, William Shakespeare; (D) Paul Barry; (S) Mark Evancho; (C) Bruce Goodrich; (L) Richard Dorfman

Antony and Cleopatra, William Shakespeare; (D) Paul Barry; (S) Mark Evancho; (C) Bruce Goodrich; (L) Richard Dorfman

Two Noble Kinsmen, William Shakespeare and John Fletcher; (D) Paul Barry; (S) Mark

New Jersey Shakespeare Festival. Jonathan Smoots and David S. Howard in *Julius Caesar*. Photo: Specialized Photodesign.

Evancho; (C) Heidi Hollmann; (L) Richard Dorfman

Noises Off, Michael Frayn; (D) Davey Marlin-Jones; (S) Mark Evancho; (C) Mitchell Bloom; (L) Terry Kaye

Terra Nova, Ted Tally; (D) Paul Barry; (S) Mark Evancho; (C) Nanalee Raphael-Schirmer; (L) Terry Kaye

Hurlyburly, David Rabe; (D) Paul Barry; (S) Mark Evancho; (C) Julie Abels; (L) Terry Kaye

A Child's Christmas in Wales, adapt: Adrian Mitchell and Jeremy Brooks, from Dylan Thomas; (D) Paul Barry; (S) Mark Evancho; (C) Heidi Hollmann; (L) Terry Kaye

PRODUCTIONS 1987

The Taming of the Shrew, William Shakespeare; (D) Paul Barry; (S) Mark Evancho; (C) Heidi Hollmann; (L) Terry Kaye

Coriolanus, William Shakespeare; (D) Paul Barry; (S) Mark Evancho; (C) Nanalee Raphael-Schirmer; (L) Terry Kaye

The Winter's Tale, William Shakespeare; (D) Paul Barry; (S) Mark Evancho; (C) Heidi Hollmann; (L) Terry Kaye

Present Laughter, Noel Coward; (D) Sam Maupin; (S) Mark Evancho; (C) Mitchell Bloom; (L) Terry Kaye

A Streetcar Named Desire, Tennessee Williams; (D) Davey Marlin-Jones; (S) Mark Evancho; (C) Mitchell Bloom; (L) Terry Kaye

Translations, Brian Friel; (D) Paul Barry; (S) Mark Evancho; (L) Terry Kaye

The Diary of Anne Frank, Frances Goodrich and Albert Hackett; (D) Ken Costigan; (S) Mark Evancho; (C) Julie Abels; (L) Terry Kaye

A Christmas Carol, adapt: Paul Barry, from Charles Dickens; (D) Paul Barry; (S) Mark Evancho; (C) Kathleen Brown; (L) Terry Kaye

New Mexico Repertory Theatre

ANDREW SHEA
Artistic Director

LISA R. JAMES
Managing Director

Box 789
Albuquerque, NM 87103
(505) 243-4577 (bus.)
(505) 243-4500 (b.o.)

Box 9279
Sante Fe, NM 87504
(505) 983-2382 (bus.)
(505) 982-1192 (b.o.)

FOUNDED 1983
Clayton Karkosh, Steven Schwartz-Hartley, Andrew Shea

SEASON
Oct.-May

FACILITIES
KiMo Theatre, Albuquerque
Seating capacity: 755
Stage: proscenium

Johnson St. Theatre, Santa Fe
Seating capacity: 228
Stage: proscenium

FINANCES
July 1, 1986-June 30, 1987
Expenses: $856,440

CONTRACTS
AEA LORT (D) and SSD&C

New Mexico Repertory Theatre is in residence in both Albuquerque, an emerging city of 500,000 and the focus of the state's population and business growth, and Santa Fe, the cultural center of the Southwest. NMRT's success in its first three years has been due not only to the high quality of its varied mainstage seasons, but also to its commitment to community and outreach programs that include classes and workshop productions for nonprofessional children and adults, student matinees, statewide tours, school visits and postperformance discussions. In future seasons, NMRT will continue to concentrate on the works of the best contemporary playwrights, with special attention paid to writers of a regional significance. There will be less emphasis, however, on recent New York commercial successes, and greater emphasis on addressing our Hispanic communities, and on developing and producing new material.

—*Andrew Shea*

New Mexico Repertory Theatre. Howard Witt and Shelly Lipkin in *Glengarry Glen Ross*. Photo: Paul Jeremias.

PRODUCTIONS 1985–86

Master Harold...and the boys, Athol Fugard; (D) Andrew Shea; (S) Brian Jeffries; (C) Gwendolyn Nagle; (L) John Malolepsy

Twelfth Night, William Shakespeare; (D) Andrew Shea; (S) John Malolepsy; (C) David Kay Mickelsen; (L) John Malolepsy

Happy End, book: Bertolt Brecht; adapt: Michael Feingold; music: Kurt Weill; (D) Jim Holmes; (S) Thomas C. Umfrid; (C) Gwendolyn Nagle; (L) Jason Sturm

Orphans, Lyle Kessler; (D) Roxanne Rogers; (S) Cheryl Dee Odom; (C) Joan Catanzariti; (L) Dante Cordone

The Rainmaker, N. Richard Nash; (D) Andrew Shea; (S) John Malolepsy; (C) Stephanie Ogden; (L) John Malolepsy

The Heart Outright, Mark Medoff; (D) Mark Medoff; (S) Jim Billings; (C) Kathi Perkowski Mills; (L) Jason Sturm

PRODUCTIONS 1986–87

Fool for Love, Sam Shepard; (D) Phil Killian; (S) Howard Wellman; (C) Joan Catanzariti; (L) Jason Sturm

A Christmas Carol, adapt: Barbara Field, from Charles Dickens; (D) Andrew Shea; (S) Tim Papienski; (C) David Kay Mickelsen; (L) John Lassiter

The Taming of the Shrew, William Shakespeare; (D) Jules Aaron; (S) John Malolepsy; (C) Claremarie Verheyen; (L) John Malolepsy

Who's Afraid of Virginia Woolf?, Edward Albee; (D) Andrew Shea; (S) Brian Jeffries; (C) Gwendolyn Nagle; (L) John Malolepsy

The Real Thing, Tom Stoppard; (D) Tom Prewitt; (S) John Malolepsy; (C) Gwendolyn Nagle; (L) John Malolepsy

Glengarry Glen Ross, David Mamet; (D) Phil Killian; (S) John Malolepsy; (C) Christine K.A. Boyce; (L) Jason Sturm

New Playwrights' Theatre

PETER FRISCH
Artistic Director

CATHERINE WILSON
Managing Director

1742 Church St., NW
Washington, DC 20036
(202) 232-4527 (bus.)
(202) 232-1122 (b.o.)

FOUNDED 1972
Harry M. Bagdasian

SEASON
Sept.-May

FACILITIES
Seating capacity: 140
Stage: flexible

FINANCES
July 1, 1986-June 30, 1987
Expenses: $322,000

CONTRACTS
AEA SPT and Guest Artist

Marking our 15th anniversary in 1987-88, the New Playwrights' Theatre remains dedicated to the solicitation, development and presentation of new work for the stage. Washington audiences have witnessed the nurturing of a generation of playwrights through the production of 100 plays and musicals; nearly 200 staged readings; and numerous labs, workshops, seminars and classes. The fruits of our labor have been produced commercially Off Broadway and at many other nonprofit theatres, including the New York Shakespeare Festival, Actors Theatre of Louisville, Circle Repertory Company, the Mark Taper Forum and Arena Stage. As the recently appointed artistic director, I have created National Affiliates, a network of writers, agents, literary managers and producers who help NPT with solicitation, exchanges and coproduction ideas. Together, they form a strong new play organization giving New Playwrights' national exposure, and provide information, talent and production access. NPT is dedicated to the playwright and the play, with a special emphasis on lively, visceral energy in writing and performance. We try to promote a theatre of content with a humanist perspective focusing on the personal and public issues of our time.

—Peter Frisch

Note: During the 1985-86 season, Arthur Bartow served as artistic director. During the transitional 1986-87 season, NPT produced five staged readings and presented three outside productions.

PRODUCTIONS 1985–86

Thin Wall, Phoef Sutton; (D) Arthur Bartow; (S) Lewis Folden; (C) Jane Schloss Phelan; (L) Daniel M. Wagner

Secret Honor, Donald Freed and Arnold M. Stone; (D) Robert Harders; (S) Russell Pyle; (L) Russell Pyle

Brotherhood, John Richardson; (D) William Partlan; (S) Michael Franklin-White; (C) Jane Schloss Phelan; (L) Daniel M. Wagner

Earth and Water, J.R. Dalton; (D) Arthur Bartow; (S) Lewis Folden; (C) Jane Schloss Phelan; (L) Daniel M. Wagner

Something Blue, Peg Sheldrick; (D) Ron Ross; (S) Gary Eckhart; (C) Jane Schloss Phelan; (L) Steve Summers

PRODUCTIONS 1986–87

You're Gonna Love Tomorrow, music and lyrics: Stephen Sondheim; (D) Peter Frisch; (S) Russell Metheny; (C) Jane Schloss Phelan; (L) Daniel M. Wagner

New Playwrights' Theatre. Gregory J. Ford and Kathryn L. Jones in *Earth and Water*. Photo: Doc Dougherty.

New Stage Theatre. Nancy Munger, Karen Rice and Shari Schneider in *Lydie Breeze*. Photo: Chuck Allen.

New Stage Theatre

JANE REID-PETTY
Producing Artistic Director

MAC GROVES
Managing Director

1100 Carlisle St.
Jackson, MS 39202
(601) 948-3533 (bus.)
(601) 948-3531 (b.o.)

FOUNDED 1966
Jane Reid-Petty

SEASON
Sept.-May

FACILITIES
Meyer Crystal Auditorium
Seating capacity: 364
Stage: proscenium

Jimmy Hewes Room
Seating capacity: 100
Stage: flexible

FINANCES
July 1, 1986-June 30, 1987
Expenses: $440,000

CONTRACTS
AEA letter of agreement and USA

The artist comes first at New Stage Theatre, and our energies are directed toward sustaining a vital environment in which artists can work together to achieve their finest moments on stage. Mississippi audiences are bred on the rich literary heritage of the state that produced William Faulkner, Eudora Welty and Richard Wright, and they respond to the dramatic event that is rooted in the playwright's word and vision. Our emphasis on new work evolves from this heritage; our special programming of the Eudora Welty New Plays Series, for example, provides the creative meeting of playwright and performing artists that nurtures both the art of the dramatist, and the present and future vitality of the American theatre.

—Jane Reid-Petty

PRODUCTIONS 1985–86

Cat on a Hot Tin Roof, Tennessee Williams; (D) Peter DeLaurier; (S) Sandy McNeal and Jimmy Robertson; (C) Mark Horton; (L) Morgan Billingsley

'night, Mother, Marsha Norman; (D) Tom Irwin; (S) Sandy McNeal and Jimmy Robertson; (C) Mark Horton; (L) Morgan Billingsley

A Christmas Carol, adapt: Peter DeLaurier, from Charles Dickens; (D) Peter DeLaurier; (S) Sandy McNeal and Jimmy Robertson; (C) Mark Horton; (L) Morgan Billingsley

Greater Tuna, Jaston Williams, Joe Sears and Ed Howard; (D) Ivan Rider; (S) Jimmy Robertson; (C) Nana Kratochvil; (L) Morgan Billingsley

A Midsummer Night's Dream, William Shakespeare; (D) Peter DeLaurier; (S) John Wylie; (C) Christine R. Turbitt; (L) Morgan Billingsley

Blithe Spirit, Noel Coward; (D) Peter DeLaurier; (S) Tom Schraeder; (C) Nana Kratochvil; (L) Tom Schraeder

PRODUCTIONS 1986–87

Oh, Mr. Faulkner, Do You Write?, John Maxwell; (D) William Partlan; (S) Jimmy Robertson; (C) Martha Wood; (L) Bill McCarty, III

The Foreigner, Larry Shue; (D) Ivan Rider; (S) Jimmy Robertson and Sonny White; (C) Janet Gray; (L) Morgan Billingsley

Dear Liar, Jerome Kilty; (D) Ivan Rider; (S) Roger Farkash; (C) Janet Gray; (L) Morgan Billingsley and Bill McCarty, III

The Gift of the Magi, music and lyrics adapt: Peter Ekstrom, from O. Henry; (D) Annie Chadwick; (S) Kenneth J. Lewis; (C) Janet Gray; (L) Bill McCarty, III

Lydie Breeze, John Guare; (D) Jane Reid-Petty; (S) Roger Farkash; (C) Janet Gray; (L) Morgan Billingsley

Mass Appeal, Bill C. Davis; (D) Cynthia White; (S) Janet Gray; (C) Janet Gray; (L) Morgan Billingsley

The Fantasticks, book and lyrics: Tom Jones; music: Harvey Schmidt; (D) Ivan Rider; (S) Jimmy Robertson and Sonny White; (C) Janet Gray; (L) Morgan Billingsley

New York Shakespeare Festival

JOSEPH PAPP
Producer

JASON STEVEN COHEN
Associate Producer

BOB MacDONALD
General Manager

425 Lafayette St.
New York, NY 10003
(212) 598-7100 (bus.)
(212) 598-7150 (b.o.)

FOUNDED 1954
Joseph Papp

SEASON
Year-round

FACILITIES
Newman Theater
Seating capacity: 299
Stage: proscenium

Martinson Hall
Seating capacity: 190
Stage: flexible

LuEsther Hall
Seating capacity: 150
Stage: flexible

Susan Stein Shiva Theater
Seating capacity: 100
Stage: flexible

Anspacher Theater
Seating capacity: 275
Stage: ¾ arena

Delacorte Theater
Seating capacity: 1,932
Stage: thrust

FINANCES
Sept. 1, 1986-Aug. 31, 1987
Expenses: $12,000,000

CONTRACTS
AEA Off Broadway and LORT (B)

Since 1954, the New York Shakespeare Festival has operated in the belief that a theatre with the highest professional standards can attract, and should be made available to, a broadly based public. From this guiding principle a contemporary theatre of extraordinary range and quality has emerged, rooted in the classics but with new American plays as its primary focus. Each summer for the past 30 years, NYSF has presented free outdoor productions of the classics, usually Shakespeare, throughout the five boroughs of New York City, and for the past 25 years at the Delacorte Theater in Central Park. NYSF's permanent home is the Public Theater, the landmark Astor Library building. There, a repertoire of new American plays and a generation of American actors, directors and designers have been developed through the Festival's working process. Three programs fully integrated into NYSF's activities are Playwriting in the Schools, which teaches elementary and junior high school students playwriting while introducing them to the world of professional theatre; Shakespeare on Broadway, which offers free Shakespeare to New York's high school students; and Festival Latino, a three-week international series of theatre, film, music and dance events. In order to make our productions available to an even larger audience, the lives of a number of shows have been extended on Broadway, network and cable T.V., on film and through national tours.

—*Joseph Papp*

New York Shakespeare Festival. Ralph Macchio and Robert DeNiro in *Cuba and His Teddy Bear*. Photo: Martha Swope.

PRODUCTIONS 1985–86

A Chorus Line, book: James Kirkwood and Nicholas Dante; music: Marvin Hamlisch; lyrics: Edward Kleban; (D) Michael Bennett; (S) Robin Wagner; (C) Theoni V. Aldredge; (L) Tharon Musser

Drood, book adapt, music and lyrics: Rupert Holmes, from Charles Dickens; (D) Wilford Leach; (S) Bob Shaw; (C) Lindsay W. Davis; (L) Paul Gallo

Aunt Dan and Lemon, Wallace Shawn; (D) Max Stafford-Clark; (S) Peter Hartwell; (C) Jennifer Cook; (L) Christopher Toulmin and Gerard P. Bourcier

Hamlet, William Shakespeare; (D) Liviu Ciulei; (S) Bob Shaw; (C) William Ivey Long; (L) Jennifer Tipton

Largo Desolato, Vaclav Havel; trans: Marie Winn; (D) Richard Foreman; (S) Richard Foreman and Nancy Winters; (C) Lindsay W. Davis; (L) Heather Carson

A Map of the World, David Hare; (D) David Hare; (S) Hayden Griffin; (C) Jane Greenwood; (L) Rory Dempster

Rum and Coke, Keith Reddin; (D) Les Waters; (S) John Arnone; (C) Kurt Wilhelm; (L) Stephen Strawbridge

Twelfth Night, William Shakespeare; (D) Wilford Leach; (S) Bob Shaw; (C) Lindsay W. Davis; (L) Stephen Strawbridge

Jonin', Gerard Brown; (D) Andre Robinson, Jr.; (S) Wynn P. Thomas; (C) Karen Perry; (L) Ric Rogers

The Normal Heart, Larry Kramer; (D) Michael Lindsay-Hogg; (S) Eugene Lee and Keith Raywood; (C) Bill Walker; (L) Natasha Katz

PRODUCTIONS 1986–87

A Chorus Line, book: James Kirkwood and Nicholas Dante; music: Marvin Hamlisch; lyrics: Edward Kleban; (D) Michael Bennett; (S) Robin Wagner; (C) Theoni V. Aldredge; (L) Tharon Musser

Drood, book adapt, music and lyrics: Rupert Holmes, from Charles Dickens; (D) Wilford Leach; (S) Bob Shaw; (C) Lindsay W. Davis; (L) Paul Gallo

Cuba and His Teddy Bear, Reinaldo Povod; (D) Bill Hart; (S) Donald Eastman; (C) Gabriel Berry; (L) Anne E. Militello

The Knife, book: David Hare; music: Nick Bicat; lyrics: Tim Rose Price; (D) David Hare; (S) Hayden Griffin; (C) Jane Greenwood; (L) Tharon Musser

My Gene, Barbara Gelb; (D) Andre Ernotte; (S) William Barclay; (C) Muriel Stockdale; (L) Phil Monat

Shakespeare on Broadway:
MacBeth*, *As You Like It* and *Romeo and Juliet, William Shakespeare; (D) Estelle Parsons; (S) Loren Sherman; (C) Ruth Morley; (L) Victor En Yu Tan

The Colored Museum, George C. Wolfe; (D) L. Kenneth Richardson; (S) Brian Martin; (C) Nancy L. Konrardy; (L) Victor En Yu Tan and William H. Grant, III
Richard II, William Shakespeare; (D) Joseph Papp; (S) Loren Sherman; (C) Theoni V. Aldredge; (L) Jules Fisher
Two Gentlemen of Verona, William Shakespeare; (D) Stuart Vaughn; (S) Bob Shaw; (C) Lindsay W. Davis; (L) Jules Fisher and Peggy Eisenhauer
Henry IV, Part 1, William Shakespeare; (D) Joseph Papp; (S) David Mitchell; (C) Theoni V. Aldredge; (L) Jules Fisher
Talk Radio, Eric Bogosian; conceived: Ted Savinar; (D) Frederick Zollo; (S) David Jenkins; (C) Pilar Limosner; (L) Jan Kroeze

New York Theatre Workshop

JAMES C. NICOLA
Artistic Director

NANCY KASSAK DIEKMANN
Managing Director

220 West 42nd St., 18th fl.
New York, NY 10036
(212) 302-7737 (bus.)
(212) 279-4200 (b.o.)

FOUNDED 1979
Stephen Graham

SEASON
Oct.-May

FACILITIES
Perry Street Theatre
Seating capacity: 95
Stage: proscenium

FINANCES
July 1, 1986-June 30, 1987
Expenses: $563,000

CONTRACTS
AEA letter of agreement

At New York Theatre Workshop we are committed to presenting the public with works of intelligence and conscience. In an era obsessed with form, we look to content first. We hold fast to the belief that theatre can provide society with a perspective on our history, and on the events and institutions that shape our lives. To that end, we apply our resources to the nurturing of artists who can grapple with ideas and transform them into theatrical events. We do this through two programs: the New Directors Project provides an early professional production opportunity for the most promising directors of this country's next generation; our multifaceted Play Development Program consists of a range of processes created to serve the playwright in the development of new work. Each season, both programs culminate in fully mounted productions of literate, unconventional plays.

—Jean Passanante

Note: During the 1985-86 and 1986-87 seasons, Jean Passanante served as artistic director.

PRODUCTIONS 1985–86

On the Verge or The Geography of Yearning, Eric Overmyer; (D) Michael Engler; (S) Loy Arcenas; (C) Catherine Zuber; (L) David N. Weiss
Mud, Maria Irene Fornes; (D) Mark Lutwak; (S) Loy Arcenas; (C) Catherine Zuber; (L) David N. Weiss
Sore Throats, Howard Brenton; (D) Rosey Hay; (S) Loy Arcenas; (C) Jeffrey Ullman; (L) David N. Weiss
Battery, Daniel Therriault; (D) R.J. Cutler; (S) Loy Arcenas; (C) Jeffrey Ullman; (L) David N. Weiss
Bosoms and Neglect, John Guare; (D) Larry Arrick; (S) Loy Arcenas; (C) Jeffrey Ullman; (L) David N. Weiss
1951, conceived: Anne Bogart; text: Mac Wellman; music: Michael S. Roth; (D) Anne Bogart; (S) Sarah Bonnemaison; (C) Walker Hicklin; (L) Carol Mullins

PRODUCTIONS 1986–87

The Dispute, Pierre Marivaux; trans: Daniel Gerould; (D) David Warren; (S) Loy Arcenas; (C) David Woolard; (L) David N. Weiss
Farmyard, Franz Xaver Kroetz; trans: Michael Roloff and Jack Gelber; (D) David Esbjornson; (S) Loy Arcenas; (C) Walker Hicklin; (L) David N. Weiss
Burrhead, Deborah Pryor; (D) Valerie Knight; (S) Loy Arcenas; (C) Catherine Zuber; (L) David N. Weiss
Seventy Scenes of Halloween, Jeffrey Jones; (D) Michael Greif; (S) Loy Arcenas; (C) Jeffrey Ulllman; (L) David N. Weiss
As It Is in Heaven, Joe Sutton; (D) Mark Lutwak; (S) Richard Hoover; (C) Walker Hicklin; (L) John Gisondi
Three Ways Home, Casey Kurtti; (D) Chris Silva; (S) Norbert Kolb; (C) Jeffrey Ullman; (L) Tracy Eck
A Narrow Bed, Ellen McLaughlin; (D) Sarah Ream; (S) Kate Edmunds; (C) Michael Krass; (L) John Gisondi

New York Theatre Workshop. Thomas Kopache and Terres Unsoeld in *Farmyard*. Photo: Bob Marshak.

Northlight Theatre

RUSSELL VANDENBROUCKE
Artistic Director

SUSAN MEDAK
Managing Director

2300 Green Bay Rd.
Evanston, IL 60201
(312) 869-7732 (bus.)
(312) 869-7278 (b.o.)

FOUNDED 1974
Gregory Kandel

SEASON
Sept.-May

FACILITIES
Seating capacity: 298
Stage: proscenium

FINANCES
July 1, 1986-June 30, 1987
Expenses: $1,040,000

CONTRACTS
AEA LORT (D), SSD&C and USA

Northlight Theatre is committed to ambitious plays of heightened theatricality that stimulate the imagination and intelligence of artist and audience alike. Eager to explore and expand the allied arts of the theatre, Northlight relies on both local and national artists. The repertoire is composed of contemporary work (including Chicago subjects), fresh interpretations of classics, adaptations and forgotten plays of the recent or distant past. Northlight is especially interested in out-of-the-ordinary language, characters, settings and ideas. A strong sense of Northlight's role in this community at this time informs all choices. The theatre also develops new work through workshops, staged readings and commissions. Each year, more than 300 performances are seen by an audience exceeding 70,000. Many patrons discover theatre through

Northlight Theatre. Trazana Beverly and Robert Curry in *Boesman and Lena*. Photo: Jennifer Girard.

Northlight's extensive outreach programs which provide special access for older adults, students, veterans and handicapped persons.

—*Russell Vandenbroucke*

Note: During the 1985-86 and 1986-87 seasons, Michael Maggio served as artistic director.

PRODUCTIONS 1985–86

The Real Thing, Tom Stoppard; (D) Michael Maggio; (S) Gary Baugh; (C) Kaye Nottbusch; (L) Robert Shook

Quilters, book: Molly Newman and Barbara Damashek; music and lyrics: Barbara Damashek; (D) Kyle Donnelly; (S) Linda Buchanan; (C) Jessica Hahn; (L) Rita Pietraszek

Boesman and Lena, Athol Fugard; (D) Woodie King, Jr.; (S) Michael Philippi; (C) Colleen Muscha; (L) Robert Christen

West Memphis Mojo, Martin Jones; (D) Michael Maggio; (S) Gary Baugh; (C) Kaye Nottbusch; (L) Robert Shook

Sister and Miss Lexie, adapt: David Kaplan and Brenda Currin, from Eudora Welty; (D) David Kaplan; (S) Susan Hilferty; (C) Susan Hilferty; (L) Ken Tabachnick

PRODUCTIONS 1986–87

Angels Fall, Lanford Wilson; (D) Tom Mula; (S) Gary Baugh; (C) Kerry Fleming; (L) Rita Pietraszek

Free Advice from Prague, Vaclav Havel; trans: Jan Novak; (D) Kyle Donnelly; (S) Eve Cauley; (C) Jessica Hahn; (L) Rita Pietraszek

Dealing, Richard Fire and June Shellene; (D) Michael Maggio; (S) Linda Buchanan; (C) Kaye Nottbusch; (L) Robert Shook

Benefactors, Michael Frayn; (D) J.R. Sullivan; (S) Gary Baugh; (C) Kaye Nottbusch; (L) Robert Shook

The Perfect Party, A.R. Gurney, Jr.; (D) Nick Faust; (S) Bil Mikulewicz; (C) Virgil Johnson; (L) Dan Kotlowitz

Oakland Ensemble Theatre

BENNY SATO AMBUSH
Producing Director

KERYL E. MCCORD
Managing Director

1428 Alice St., Suite 289
Oakland, CA 94612
(415) 763-7774 (bus.)
(415) 839-5510 (b.o.)

FOUNDED 1974
Ron Stacker Thompson

SEASON
Sept.-June

FACILITIES
Seating capacity: 600
Stage: flexible

FINANCES
July 1, 1986-June 30, 1987
Expenses: $299,100

CONTRACTS
AEA SPT

Oakland Ensemble Theatre is committed to producing—through the sensibilities and world view of black Americans—insightful, engaging and substantive works of contemporary theatre that explore and illuminate the diverse issues, themes and human dilemmas of the New World experience called America. Steeped in the cultural expressions of black Americans, our voice speaks to an ethnically and culturally diverse audience reflective of Bay Area demographics. Our particular interest is to offer commentary and provide responsible points of view about both the achievements and the problems that emanate from the plural nature of America's national life, as seen from the perspective of black people. We believe in uplifting entertainment, with challenging, relevant ideas, that affirms and celebrates the beauty, strength, dignity and truth about black people and their struggles. We strive to provide theatre that enlightens the conditions and complexities of contemporary living, while conveying a useful understanding of ourselves for the shaping of a more informed, humane world.

—*Benny Sato Ambush*

PRODUCTIONS 1985–86

Alterations, Michael Abbensetts; (D) Benny Sato Ambush; (S) Alan Curreri; (C) Roberta Yuen; (L) Leslie Siegel

Letters from a New England Negro, Sherley Anne Williams; (D) Benny Sato Ambush; (S) Ken Ellis; (C) Sheradi Cannon; (L) Leslie Siegel

Dunbar, adapt: Ayanna and Ron Stacker Thompson; lyrics: Quitman Fludd, III; music: Lonnie Hewitt, Quitman Fludd, III and Paul E. Smith; (D) Ron Stacker Thompson; (S) Ken Ellis; (C) Suzan Anderson; (L) Ken Ellis

Mr. Dingo's Show, Derique L. McGee; (D) Derique L. McGee; (S) Ken Ellis; (C) Derique L. McGee; (L) Ken Ellis

PRODUCTIONS 1986–87

Stops Along the Way, Jeffrey Sweet; (D) Keryl E. McCord; (S) Ken Ellis; (C) Ken Ellis; (L) Ken Ellis

Open Admissions, Shirley Lauro; (D) Keryl E. McCord; (S) Ken Ellis; (C) Ken Ellis; (L) Leslie Siegel

Division Street, Steve Tesich; (D) Benny Sato Ambush; (S) Ken Ellis; (C) Suzanne Raferty; (L) Jack Carpenter

Boesman and Lena, Athol Fugard; (D) Floyd Gaffney; (S) Richard Battle; (C) Odessa McDuffie; (L) Stephanie Johnson

Oakland Ensemble Theatre. Jesse Moore, Curtis Whitener Sims, James P. Phillips and Kathleen McCormick in *Alterations*. Photo: Fred Spieser.

Odyssey Theatre Ensemble. Mitch Kreindel, Kurt Fuller and Laura Esterman in *Kvetch*. Photo: Ron Sossi.

Odyssey Theatre Ensemble

RON SOSSI
Artistic Director

LUCY POLLAK
Production Manager

12111 Ohio Ave.
Los Angeles, CA 90025
(213) 826-1626

FOUNDED 1969
Ron Sossi

SEASON
Year-round

FACILITIES
Odyssey I
Seating capacity: 99
Stage: proscenium

Odyssey II
Seating capacity: 95
Stage: thrust

Odyssey III
Seating capacity: 91
Stage: thrust

FINANCES
July 1, 1986-June 30, 1987
Expenses: $625,000

CONTRACTS
AEA 99-seat waiver

The Odyssey Theatre Ensemble's prime *raison d'être* is the production of a six-play mainstage season and a three-play Lab Season of exploration-oriented works drawn from contemporary, classical and original sources. Every Odyssey production is, in some important sense, an adventure in form—an attempt to push outward the boundaries of theatrical possibility. Year-by-year, more Odyssey-evolved work moves out into the larger theatre world. This past year marked the Off Broadway opening of OTE's long-running world premiere production of Steven Berkoff's *Kvetch*; the production for HBO of a special program based on the Odyssey-created *The Chicago Conspiracy Trial*; and enormously successful nationwide productions of Odyssey's version of Elizabeth Swados and Gary Trudeau's *Rap Master Ronnie*. Additionally, 1987 culminated over two years worth of American and European runs of the highly honored Odyssey-evolved *Tracers* by John DiFusco. All in all, the Odyssey Theatre Ensemble retains and builds upon its reputation as one of Southern California's leading experimental and process-oriented theatre institutions.

—Ron Sossi

PRODUCTIONS 1985–86

Bashville, music: Dennis King; lyrics: Benny Green; (D) John Allison; (S) Dan Dryden; (C) Sherry Linnell; (L) Nancy Hood
Crossing Niagara, Alonso Alegria; (D) Albert Paulsen; (S) Mitra Emadian; (C) Bonnie Stauch; (L) Lowell Richard
Blood Moon, Nick Kazan; (D) Frank Condon; (S) Mitra Emadian; (C) Lisa Lovaas; (L) Pam Rank
Wings, Arthur Kopit; (D) Mark Travis; (S) Brad R. Loman; (C) Brad R. Loman; (L) William Strom
Four Corners, Gina Wendkos and Donna Bond; (D) Gina Wendkos; (S) Gina Wendkos; (L) David Hoyt
Personality, Gina Wendkos and Ellen Ratner; conceived: Gina Wendkos; (D) Richard Press and Gina Wendkos; (S) Gina Wendkos; (L) David Hoyt
A Voyage to Arcturus, adapt: David Wolpe, from David Lindsay; (D) Ron Sossi; (S) Don Llewellyn; (C) Jean Blanchette; (L) Greg McCullough
The Jail Diary of Albie Sachs, David Edgar; (D) Deborah LaVine; (S) Melody Boyd; (C) Valeria Watkins; (L) Terri Gens
Bosoms and Neglect, John Guare; (D) Ron Sossi; (S) Eric Warren; (C) Kim Simons; (L) Patrick Pankhurst
Confessions of an Irish Rebel, adapt: Shay Duffin, from Brendan Behan; (D) Shay Duffin; (L) Carol Brainard
Kvetch, Steven Berkoff; (D) Steven Berkoff; (S) Don Llewellyn; (C) Ruth A. Brown

PRODUCTIONS 1986–87

Johnny Johnson, book and lyrics: Paul Green; music: Kurt Weill; (D) Ron Sossi; (S) Chez Cherry; (C) Gayle Susan Baizer; (L) R. Craig Wolf
Tom and Viv, Michael Hastings; (D) Robert W. Goldsby; (S) Ariel; (C) Ruth A. Brown; (L) Ken Lennon
The Woods, David Mamet; (D) Frank Condon; (S) Christa Bartels; (C) Martha Ferrara; (L) Doc Ballard
Master Class, David Pownall; (D) Ron Sossi; (S) Susan Lane; (C) Jackie Dalley; (L) Dawn Hollingsworth
A Provincial Episode, Lali Roseba; trans: Robert Daglish; (D) Melanie Jones; (S) Sergei Ponomarov; (C) Valerie T. O'Brien; (L) David A. Taylor
Early Tennessee, Tennessee Williams; (D) Dan Mason; (S) Renee Hoss; (C) Kevin Ian; (L) J. Kent Inasy

The Old Creamery Theatre Company

THOMAS PETER JOHNSON
Producing Director

BETTY WINSOR
General Manager

Box 160
Garrison, IA 52229
(319) 477-3925 (bus.)
(319) 477-3165 (b.o.)

FOUNDED 1971
David Berendes, Rita Berendes, Mick Denniston, Judy Johnson, Thomas Peter Johnson, Steve Koch, Merritt Olsen, Ann Olson, David Olson, Erica Zaffarano

SEASON
May-Oct.

FACILITIES
Mainstage
Seating capacity: 259
Stage: thrust

Brenton Stage
Seating capacity: 134
Stage: flexible

FINANCES
Jan. 1, 1986-Dec. 31, 1986
Expenses: $320,000

CONTRACTS
AEA SPT

The simple mission of the Old Creamery Theatre Company is to bring theatre of the highest possible quality to the largest possible audience in the rural Midwest. In pursuing this goal the company produces a 156-performance resident season in Garrison, maintains an extensive touring program to rural communities, and has established performance centers on four

The Old Creamery Theatre Company. Mary Graham, John Stortz and Marquetta Senters in *Pump Boys and Dinettes.* Photo: Robert Lippert.

college campuses in various parts of Iowa. A major objective is the encouragement of developing artists through various internship programs in performance, playwriting and technical theatre. The main element of our artistic vision is to find ways of making all types of theatre palatable to an inexperienced theatre audience by offering a "menu" of theatrical choices. By providing various kinds of fare, the company hopes to broaden its audience base while broadening the tastes of that audience.

—*Thomas Peter Johnson*

PRODUCTIONS 1986

The Gingerbread Lady, Neil Simon; (D) Anne Oberbroeckling; (S) Thomas Peter Johnson; (C) Marquetta Senters; (L) Jason Hoover

Noises Off, Michael Frayn; (D) Thomas Peter Johnson; (S) Jan Czechowski; (C) Marquetta Senters; (L) Jan Czechowski

A Midsummer Night's Dream, William Shakespeare; adapt: Thomas Peter Johnson; (D) Thomas Peter Johnson; (S) Thomas Peter Johnson; (C) Marquetta Senters; (L) David Berendes

Move Over, Mrs. Markham, Ray Cooney and John Chapman; (D) Tom Atha; (S) Jan Czechowski; (C) Julia Yurista; (L) Jan Czechowski

A Night With Marquetta, Thomas Peter Johnson and Marquetta Senters; (D) Thomas Peter Johnson; (S) Thomas Peter Johnson; (C) Marquetta Senters; (L) Beth Johns

The Foreigner, Larry Shue; (D) Ron Peluso

PRODUCTIONS 1987

Twice Around the Park, Murray Schisgal; (D) Thomas Peter Johnson; (S) Thomas Peter Johnson; (C) Julie McLaughlin; (L) Beth Johns

The Murder Room, Jack Sharkey; (D) Steve Shaffer; (S) Thomas Peter Johnson; (C) Julie McLaughlin; (L) Eric Bench

Pump Boys and Dinettes, John Foley, Mark Hardwick, Debra Monk, Cass Morgan, John Schimmel and Jim Wann; (D) Ron Peluso; (S) Paul Sannerud; (C) Julie McLaughlin; (L) Steve Engel

The Imposter, Molière; adapt: Warren G. Green; (D) Ron Peluso; (S) Thomas Peter Johnson; (C) Julie McLaughlin; (L) Steve Engel

A Funny Thing Happened on the Way to the Forum, book: Burt Shevelove and Larry Gelbart; music and lyrics: Stephen Sondheim; (D) Thomas Peter Johnson; (S) Jan Czechowski; (C) Julie McLaughlin; (L) Steve Engel

Educating Rita, Willy Russell; (D) Ron Peluso; (S) Jan Czechowski; (C) Julie McLaughlin; (L) Steve Engel

Old Globe Theatre

JACK O'BRIEN
Artistic Director

THOMAS HALL
Managing Director

Box 2171
San Diego, CA 92112
(619) 231-1941 (bus.)
(619) 239-2255 (b.o.)

FOUNDED 1937
Community members

SEASON
Dec.-Oct.

FACILITIES
Old Globe Theatre
Seating capacity: 581
Stage: flexible

Lowell Davies Festival Theatre
Seating capacity: 612
Stage: thrust

Cassius Carter Centre Stage
Seating capacity: 225
Stage: arena

FINANCES
Nov. 1, 1985-Oct. 31, 1986
Expenses: $6,700,000

CONTRACTS
AEA LORT (B+), (C), SSD&C and USA

I believe the network of regional theatres is in transition, moving toward its inevitable emergence as the American National Theatre. The Old Globe Theatre, a bastion of craft, skill and technique, has kept the classical tradition flourishing in Southern California for 52 years. From the vantage point of this tradition, we offer remarkable venues to writers and artists who formerly flocked to New York for exposure and artistic freedom. Across this country, over the last decade or so, our ability to articulate the classics has shrunk in direct proportion to the influence of film and television, but the Globe still offers an opportunity to actors, directors and designers to stretch their talents and add to their skills in a healthy, competitive market alongside the literature that has sustained theatre for hundreds of years. By juxtaposing the contemporary and the classical we offer audiences the most vigorous, comprehensive theatre experience possible, and we have a wonderful time doing it.

—*Jack O'Brien*

Old Globe Theatre. Joanna Gleason, Chip Zien and Ellen Foley in *Into the Woods.* Photo: John Peter Weiss.

PRODUCTIONS 1985–86

Bert and Maisy, Robert Lord; (D) Robert Berlinger; (S) Kent Dorsey; (C) Christina Haatainen; (L) Kent Dorsey

Pygmalion, George Bernard Shaw; (D) Jack O'Brien; (S) Richard Seger; (C) Robert Morgan; (L) Robert Peterson

On the Verge or The Geography of Yearning, Eric Overmyer; (D) Craig Noel; (S) Kent Dorsey; (C) Dianne Holly; (L) Kent Dorsey

Spokesong, book and lyrics: Stewart Parker; music: Jimmy Kennedy; (D) Warner Shook; (S) Robert Blackman; (C) Robert Blackman; (L) John B. Forbes

Cat's Paw, William Mastrosimone; (D) Daniel Sullivan; (S) Thomas Fichter; (C) Sally Richardson; (L) Wendy Heffner

Pump Boys and Dinettes, John Foley, Mark Hardwick, Debra Monk, Cass Morgan, John Schimmel and Jim Wann; (D) Matt Casella; (S) Fred M. Duer; (C) Virginia Gadzala; (L) John B. Forbes

Beyond the Fringe, Alan Bennett, Peter Cook, Jonathan Miller and Dudley Moore; (D) Paxton Whitehead; (S) Alan K. Okazaki; (C) Steven Rubin; (L) John B. Forbes

Tartuffe, Molière; trans and adapt: Robert Strane and Eberle Thomas; (D) Craig Noel; (S) Richard Seger; (C) Lewis Brown; (L) Kent Dorsey

Richard II, William Shakespeare; (D) Joseph Hardy; (S) Douglas W. Schmidt; (C) Steven Rubin; (L) David F. Segal

Julius Caesar, William Shakespeare; adapt: Dakin Matthews; (D) Dakin Matthews and Anne McNaughton; (S) Fred M. Duer; (C) Lewis Brown; (L) John B. Forbes

Much Ado About Nothing, William Shakespeare; (D) Brian Bedford; (S) Richard Seger; (C) Lewis Brown; (L) Kent Dorsey

Emily, Stephen Metcalfe; (D) Jack O'Brien; (S) Douglas W. Schmidt; (C) Steven Rubin; (L) David F. Segal

PRODUCTIONS 1986–87

Orphans, Lyle Kessler; (D) Robert Berlinger; (S) Alan K. Okazaki; (C) Christina Haatainen; (L) John B. Forbes

The Petition, Brian Clark; (D) David Hay; (S) Fred M. Duer; (C) Clare Henkel; (L) John B. Forbes

Into the Woods, book: James Lapine; music and lyrics: Stephen Sondheim; (D) James Lapine; (S) Tony Straiges; (C) Ann Hould-Ward and Patricia Zipprodt; (L) Richard Nelson

The Incredibly Famous Willy Rivers, Stephen Metcalfe; (D) Jack O'Brien; (S) Douglas W. Schmidt; (C) Robert Blackman; (L) David F. Segal

Another Antigone, A.R. Gurney, Jr.; (D) John Tillinger; (S) Steven Rubin; (C) Steven Rubin; (L) Kent Dorsey

Intimate Exchanges, Alan Ayckbourn; (D) Craig Noel; (S) Richard Seger; (C) Lewis Brown; (L) John B. Forbes

The Night of the Iguana, Tennessee Williams; (D) Craig Noel; (S) Richard Seger; (C) Robert Blackman; (L) Kent Dorsey

Antony and Cleopatra, William Shakespeare; (D) Jack O'Brien; (S) Richard Seger; (C) Lewis Brown; (L) David F. Segal

Benefactors, Michael Frayn; (D) Thomas Bullard; (S) Fred M. Duer; (C) Christina Haatainen; (L) Wendy Heffner

The Comedy of Errors, William Shakespeare; (D) David McClendon; (S) Douglas W. Schmidt; (C) Robert Blackman; (L) Kent Dorsey

There's One in Every Marriage, Georges Feydeau; trans and adapt: Suzanne Grossman and Paxton Whitehead; (D) Stan Wojewodski, Jr.; (S) Douglas W. Schmidt; (C) Lewis Brown; (L) David F. Segal

Marry Me a Little, music and lyrics: Stephen Sondheim; conceived: Craig Lucas and Norman Rene; (D) Tom Gardner; (S) Alan K. Okazaki; (C) Lewis Brown; (L) Wendy Heffner

Omaha Magic Theatre

JO ANN SCHMIDMAN
Producing Artistic Director

2309 Hanscom Blvd.
Omaha, NE 68105
(402) 346-1227

FOUNDED 1968
Jo Ann Schmidman

SEASON
Year-round

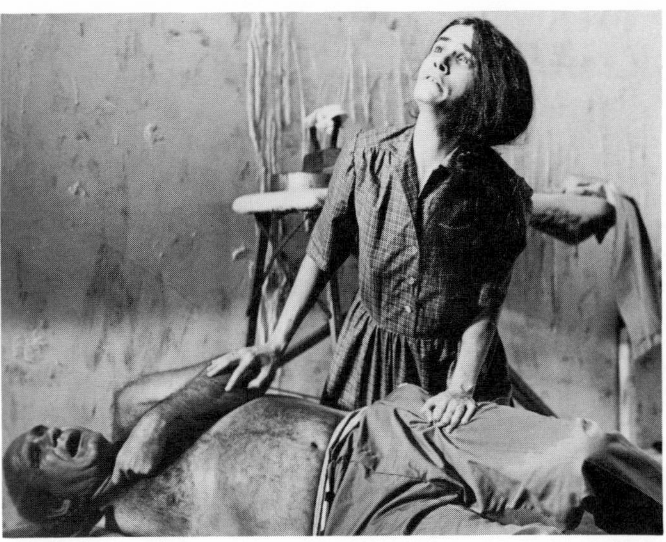

Omaha Magic Theatre. Don Fiedler and Jo Ann Schmidman in *Mud*. Photo: Megan Terry.

FACILITIES
Seating capacity: 93
Stage: flexible

FINANCES
June 1, 1986-May 31, 1987
Expenses: $177,919

One of the longest-lived alternative theatres, the Omaha Magic Theatre has produced more than 78 new plays. We take a joyful, adventurous, zany, yet philosophical approach to all our new work. Our plays deal with social and ethical considerations—human responsibility, autonomy, communication. Our main objective is to present the most vital, compelling, new American performance theatre for our audiences. We work to stretch play structure and image, explore new modes of presentation, promote interplay among the creative team so that the artist may grow within the creative process. We've toured a seven-state area extensively since 1974, focusing on Midwest audiences. National highlights include: commission of *Running Gag* performances for the 1980 Winter Olympics; a performance of *Kegger* in Washington, D.C. for the National Conference for Youth on Drinking and Driving; and a presentation of *Mud* at the 1986 International Theatre Festival in Boston. To meet the demand for our new works, the production editions of our plays are distributed by Broadway Play Publishing in New York City.

—Jo Ann Schmidman

PRODUCTIONS 1985–86

No Heroes, book, music and lyrics: Mark Blackman; (D) Mark Blackman; (S) company; (C) company; (L) Jo Ann Schmidman

Mud, Maria Irene Fornes; (D) Maria Irene Fornes; (S) Maria Irene Fornes; (C) Maria Irene Fornes and Meg Flamer; (L) Maria Irene Fornes and Jo Ann Schmidman

Cellophane Ceiling, book, music and lyrics: John Wolf; (D) John Wolf; (S) company; (C) company; (L) Jo Ann Schmidman

Soul Grinders, book, music and lyrics: Jerry Smith; (D) Jerry Smith; (S) company; (C) company; (L) Jo Ann Schmidman

Troubadour, Kermit Dunkelberg; (D) Kermit Dunkelberg; (S) Kermit Dunkelberg; (C) Kermit Dunkelberg; (L) Kermit Dunkelberg

Kegger, book and lyrics: Megan Terry; music: Marianne de Pury and Joe Budenholzer; (D) Jo Ann Schmidman; (S) company; (C) Kermit Dunkelberg; (L) Jo Ann Schmidman

Family Talk, book and lyrics: Megan Terry; music: Joe Budenholzer and John J. Sheehan; (D) Jo Ann Schmidman; (S) Diane Ostdiek; (C) Megan Terry; (L) Jo Ann Schmidman

PRODUCTIONS 1986–87

Sleazing Toward Athens, book and lyrics: Megan Terry; music: Joe Budenholzer and John J. Sheehan; (D) Michelle Hensley; (S) Colin Smith; (C) company; (L) Frank Xavier Kosmicki

Sea of Forms, book and lyrics: Jo Ann Schmidman and Megan Terry; music: John J. Sheehan, Mark Nelson and Ivy Dow; (D) Jo Ann Schmidman; (S) Bill Farmer; (C) Kenda Slavin; (L) Jo Ann Schmidman

Family Talk, book and lyrics: Megan Terry; music: Joe Budenholzer and John J. Sheehan; (D) Jo Ann Schmidman; (S) Diane Ostdiek; (C) Megan Terry; (L) Jo Ann Schmidman

Masque of Dionysos, book and lyrics: Clarinda Karpov; music: John J. Sheehan; (D) John J. Sheehan; (S) Brian Murphy; (C) Theresa Cervantes; (L) Ron Pursley

The Line of Least Existence, book and lyrics: Rosalyn Drexler; music: Mark Nelson, Bill Farber, Frank Fong and Eric Goolsby; (D) Mike Hitzelberger; (S) Bill Farmer; (C) Kenda Slavin; (L) Jim Schumacher

Future Soap, book and lyrics: Megan Terry; music: Mark Nelson, Bill Farber, Frank Fong and Eric Goolsby; (D) Gerald Ostdiek; (S) Dan Shepard and Judith Shepard; (C) Kenda Slavin; (L) Jim Schumacher

Astro°Bride, book: Jo Ann Schmidman; lyrics: Megan Terry, Jo Ann Schmidman and Sora Kim; music: John J. Sheehan, Joe Budenholzer and Jerry Kazakevicius; (D) Jo Ann Schmidman; (S) Sora Kim; (C) Dorothy Oleson; (L) Linda Erhard

One Act Theatre Company of San Francisco

SIMON L. LEVY
Artistic Director

LAUREN BROWN
General Manager

430 Mason St.
San Francisco, CA 94102
(415) 421-5355 (bus.)
(415) 421-6162 (b.o.)

FOUNDED 1976
Jean Schiffman, Peter Tripp, Laurellee Westaway

SEASON
Year-round

FACILITIES
Seating capacity: 140
Stage: thrust

FINANCES
Aug. 1, 1986-July 31, 1987
Expenses: $320,000

CONTRACTS
AEA SPT

For 11 years the One Act Theatre Company of San Francisco has remained the only theatre in America solely dedicated to the development and presentation of the one-act play. Exploration of that form and our commitment to new voices in world drama continue to be our dual artistic mission. Together with a core company of dedicated theatre professionals and the finest talents in the San Francisco Bay Area, the One Act Theatre presents unique programs of new and established one-acts that focus on sociopolitical issues and contemporary playwrights.

—*Simon L. Levy*

One Act Theatre Company of San Francisco. Robert Elross and Tony Haney in *Pantomime*. Photo: Allen Nomura.

PRODUCTIONS 1985–86

Playing for Time, Arthur Miller; (D) Simon L. Levy; (S) Stephen Elspas; (C) Diane Harrell; (L) William Simonds

Lone Star and *Laundry and Bourbon*, James McLure; (D) Ellery Edwards and Carla Sarvis; (S) Gene Angell and Ron Pratt; (C) Judy Boraas; (L) James McCracken

Purgatory, William Butler Yeats; adapt: Julie Hebert; (D) Julie Hebert; (S) Jamie Chipman and Ken Short; (C) Laura Hazlett; (L) Novella Smith

Table for One, Merle Kessler and J. Raoul Brody; (D) Mark Petrakis and Merle Kessler; (S) John Mayne; (C) Laura Hazlett; (L) Novella Smith

She-Who-Looks-Up, Michael Lynch; (D) Simon L. Levy; (S) Andrew De Shong; (C) Judy Boraas; (L) Rhonda Birnbaum

A Perfect Analysis Given By a Parrot, Tennessee Williams; (D) Simon L. Levy and Michael Allen; (S) Michael Allen; (C) Judy Boraas; (L) Tom Hansen

Lemonade, James Prideaux; (D) Simon L. Levy; (S) Michael Allen; (C) Judy Boraas; (L) Tom Hansen

Save Me a Place at Forest Lawn, Lorees Yerby; (D) Simon L. Levy and Michael Allen; (S) Michael Allen; (C) Judy Boraas; (L) Tom Hansen

The Inca of Perusalem and *The Man of Destiny*, George Bernard Shaw; (D) Andrea Gordon; (S) Susan Jackson; (C) Gael Russell; (L) Tom Hansen

The Case of the Purloined Sterling, Anita Merzell; (D) Anita Merzell; (S) Stephen Elspas; (C) Anita Merzell; (L) William Simonds

A Need for Brussels Sprouts, Murray Schisgal; (D) Bruce Ducat; (S) Susan Jackson; (C) Gael Russell; (L) Tom Hansen

The White Liars, Peter Shaffer; (D) Wanda McCaddon; (S) Jeff Hunt; (C) Laura Hazlett; (L) Tom Hansen

Today a Little Extra, Michael Kassin; (D) Hal Gelb; (S) Susan Jackson; (C) Judy Boraas; (L) Tom Hansen

Dark Lady of the Sonnets, George Bernard Shaw; (D) Wanda McCaddon; (S) Susan Jackson; (C) Gael Russell; (L) Tom Hansen

PRODUCTIONS 1986–87

The Dreamer and the Runner, book, music and lyrics: James J. Mellon; (D) Simon L. Levy; (S) Eric Sinkkonen and Joe Watson; (C) Margaret Dunn; (L) Kurt Landisman

Squirrels and *The Shawl*, David Mamet; (D) Ellery Edwards; (S) John Wilson; (C) Judy Boraas; (L) Tom Hansen

Chicks, Grace McKeaney; (D) Wanda McCaddon; (S) Jeff Hunt; (C) Judy Boraas; (L) Joe Dignan

Off the Hook, Terry Hunter and Nat Fast; (D) Carla Sarvis; (S) Jeff Hunt; (C) Judy Boraas; (L) Joe Dignan

A Woman Alone, Dario Fo and Franca Rame; (D) Jael Weisman; (S) Jeff Hunt; (C) Judy Boraas; (L) Joe Dignan

Pantomime, Derek Walcott; (D) Simon L. Levy; (S) Barbara Mesney; (C) Judy Boraas; (L) Novella Smith

Orchards: Seven American Playwrights Present Stories by Chekhov, adapt: Maria Irene Fornes, Spalding Gray, John Guare, David Mamet, Wendy Wasserstein, Michael Weller and Samm-Art Williams, from Anton Chekhov; (D) Andrea Gordon; (S) John Mayne; (C) Gael Russell; (L) Ellen Shireman

O'Neill Theater Center

GEORGE C. WHITE
President

LLOYD RICHARDS
Artistic Director, National Playwrights Conference

PAULETTE HAUPT
Artistic Director, National Opera/Music Theater Conference

SYLVIA S. TRAEGER
General Manager

234 West 44th St., Suite 901
New York, NY 10036
(212) 382-2790

305 Great Neck Rd.
Waterford, CT 06385
(203) 443-5378 (bus.)
(203) 443-1238 (b.o.)

FOUNDED 1964
George C. White

SEASON
July-Aug.

FACILITIES
Margo and Rufus Rose Barn
Seating capacity: 200
Stage: flexible

Instant Theater
Seating capacity: 200
Stage: arena

Amphitheater
Seating capacity: 300
Stage: thrust

FINANCES
Sept. 1, 1986-Aug. 31, 1987
Expenses: $2,268,596

CONTRACTS
AEA LORT (C) and SSD&C

The Eugene O'Neill Memorial Theater Center is a collection of allied programs including Creative Arts in Education, Institute of Professional Puppetry Arts, Monte Cristo Cottage Museum and Library, National Critics Institute, National Opera/Music Theater Conference, National Playwrights Conference, National Theater Institute, and Special International Programs, united to foster theatre via exploration, development, training, promotion, conservation and utilization of all aspects of the art form. Named for America's only Nobel Prize-winning playwright, the O'Neill Center pays homage to his memory by initiating and harboring projects of value to the theatre; challenging existing theatrical "truths"; creating an environment for experimentation, deliberation and examination; providing a venue for national and international theatrical interaction, discussion and exchange; and protecting and preserving our native theatrical heritage.

—*George C. White*

O'Neill Theater Center. Robert Gossett, Courtney Vance and Ed Hall in a reading of *The Piano Lesson*. Photo: A. Vincent Scarano.

PRODUCTIONS 1986

National Playwrights Conference:

A Walk in the Woods, Lee Blessing; (D) Steve Robman
Abandoned in Queens, Laura Maria Censabella; (D) Dennis Scott
Banner, Kathleen Clark; (D) Amy Saltz
Piano for Sale, Barbara Davenport; (D) Dennis Scott
The Last Good Moment of Lilly Baker, Russell Davis; (D) William Partlan
Bait and Switch, Richard Dresser; (D) Barnet Kellman
Blood Brothers, Nancy Grome; (D) Amy Saltz
The Emigration of Adam Kurtzik, Theodore Herstand; (D) Gitta Honegger
Blesse, Cindy Lou Johnson; (D) Gitta Honegger
The Lost Colony, Wendy MacLeod; (D) Andrew Weyman
Blood in the Straw and ***The Fighting Party***, Christopher Moore; (D) Gordon Rigsby
The Squeeze, Stephen Davis Parks; (D) Gordon Rigsby
Overnight Lows, Susan Rivers; (D) William Partlan
Italian American Reconciliation, John Patrick Shanley; (D) Ron Lagomarsino
The Piano Lesson, August Wilson; (D) Steve Robman
Provincial Episode, Lali Rostova; (D) B. Rodney Marriott
The Wedding Portrait, Gudmunder Steinsson; (D) Stefan Baldursson

National Opera/Music Theater Conference:

Six Wives, book: Joe Masteroff; music: Edward Thomas; (D) Fran Soeder
A Vision, book adapt, music and lyrics: Thomas F. Megan; (D) Leon Major
Farenheit 451, book: Ray Bradbury; lyrics: Georgia Bogardus Holof; music: David Mattee; (D) Maggie L. Harrer

PRODUCTIONS 1987

National Playwrights Conference:

Southern Comforts, Kathleen Clark; (D) Dennis Scott
Drawing Down the Moon, McCarthy Coyle; (D) Gitta Honegger
Saintly Mother, Donald Drake; (D) Gordon Rigsby
Soulful Scream of a Chosen Son, Ned Eisenberg; (D) Amy Saltz
Reclaimed, Judy GeBauer; (D) Margaret Booker
Amnesia, Richard Dresser; (D) Luis Soto
Neddy, Jeffrey Hatcher; (D) Amy Saltz
The Holy Note, Nancy Grome; (D) Dennis Scott
Nobody, Howard Korder; (D) Gitta Honegger
The My House Play, Wendy MacLeod; (D) William Partlan
Slippers on the Street, Paul Minx; (D) Dennis Scott
Chute Roosters, Craig Volk; (D) Margaret Booker
Angela, E.A. Wyatt; (D) William Partlan

National Opera/Music Theater Conference:

A Fine and Private Place, book: Erik Haagensen; music: Richard Isen
Lucy's Lapses, book: Laura Harrington; music: Christopher Drobny
Punch and Judy, Judy and Punch, music: Gary Fagin

Ontological-Hysteric Theater

RICHARD FOREMAN
Artistic Director

GEORGE ASHLEY
Managing Director

c/o Performing Artservices
325 Spring St., Suite 225
New York, NY 10013
(212) 243-6153

FOUNDED 1968
Richard Foreman

Ontological-Hysteric Theater. *Film Is Evil: Radio Is Good.* Photo: Martha Swope.

SEASON
Variable

FINANCES
July 1, 1986-June 30, 1987
Expenses: $100,000

Since 1968 I have evolved my own, idiosyncratic theatre language, which is nevertheless applicable to many different moods, subjects and settings. I attempt to stretch the employment of that language further each year, which in itself seems self-evident. But, more important, I try to build into my plays secret reflections upon the inevitable failure involved in pursuing such a goal.

—Richard Foreman

PRODUCTIONS 1985–86

Africanis Instructus, book and lyrics: Richard Foreman; music: Stanley Silverman; (D) Richard Foreman; (S) Richard Foreman and Nancy Winters; (C) Jim Buff; (L) William Armstrong

The Cure, Richard Foreman; (D) Richard Foreman; (S) Richard Foreman; (C) Jim Buff; (L) Richard Foreman

PRODUCTIONS 1986–87

Film Is Evil: Radio Is Good, Richard Foreman; (D) Richard Foreman; (S) Richard Foreman; (C) Richard Foreman; (L) Heather Carson

The Open Eye: New Stagings

AMIE BROCKWAY
Artistic Director

ADRIENNE J. BROCKWAY
Production/Business Manager

270 West 89th St.
New York, NY 10024
(212) 769-4141 (bus.)
(212) 769-4142 (b.o.)

FOUNDED 1972
Joseph Campbell, Jean Erdman

SEASON
Variable

FACILITIES
Seating capacity: 104
Stage: proscenium

FINANCES
July 1, 1986-June 30, 1987
Expenses: $245,000

CONTRACTS
AEA letter of agreement

In 1986 we changed our name to The Open Eye: New Stagings to reflect the work we do with new plays and adaptations from classical literature. New Stagings continues the Theatre of the Open Eye's commitment to a more theatrical—rather than naturalistic—production style that emphasizes the actor-audience relationship. Many plays selected have a mythological quality and incorporate live music and dance. In 1987 we inaugurated New Stagings for Youth, a multiethnic ensemble which develops and performs new plays and adaptations from the classics, specifically for young people and their families. These productions are designed for touring as well as performance in our own space. Another vital program is the New Stagings Lab, which offers opportunities for development of new theatre pieces through a program of rehearsed readings and workshop productions.

—Amie Brockway

PRODUCTIONS 1985–86

The Legend of Sleepy Hollow, adapt: Alice Hale, from Washington Irving; (D) Amie Brockway; (S) Adrienne J. Brockway; (C) David Kay Mickelsen; (L) Adrienne J. Brockway

The Cricket on the Hearth, adapt: Amie Brockway, from Charles Dickens; (D) Amie Brockway; (S) Adrienne J. Brockway; (C) Adrienne J. Brockway; (L) Adrienne J. Brockway

The Bone Ring, Donald Hall; (D) Kent Paul; (S) Jennifer Gallagher; (C) Judith Ruskin Wong; (L) Karl E. Haas

Festival: The Eye on Directors:

Equals, Patricia Ryan; (D) John Genke

The Raven, Richard Atkins; (D) Rawleigh Moreland

Spurts and His Desire, Liz Sedlack; (D) Cynthia S. Stokes

Sphere of Heaven, Owen M. McGehee; (D) James S. Sweeney

Landscape with Waitress, Robert Pine; (D) Gary Pollard

Property of Wanda Payne, Lucas Walker; (D) Neil Larson

Gilgamesh, adapt: Tina Landau; (D) Tina Landau

Johnny Star on the Corner, William Robert Nave; (D) Joe Ferrell

The Sixteen Appropriate Steps for Viewing Your Grandfather in an Open Coffin, Billy Aronson; (D) Carol Elliott

The Hobbit, adapt: Patricia Gray, from J.R.R. Tolkien; (D) Laurie Eliscu

Armistice, Ed Musto; (D) Richard Galgano

Last Rites, John Rawlins; (D) Rose Bonczek

(All sets, costumes and lights in the Festival were designed by Adrienne J. Brockway.)

A.K.A. Marleen, Carol K. Mack; (D) Arnold Willens; (S) Arnold Willens; (C) Arnold Willens; (L) Arnold Willens

Exchange, William DiCanzio; (D) Diane Wynter; (S) Diane Wynter; (C) Diane Wynter; (L) Diane Wynter

Zero, Philip Kan Gotanda; (D) James H. Sweeney; (S) James

The Open Eye: New Stagings. Hugh Hodgin in *The Legend of Sleepy Hollow.* Photo: Martha Swope Associates/Carol Rosegg.

H. Sweeney; (C) James H. Sweeney; (L) James H. Sweeney
What Comes After Ohio?, Daniel Meltzer. ; (D) Denise Hamilton; (S) Denise Hamilton; (C) Denise Hamilton; (L) Denise Hamilton
And Next to Nature, Art and March, Olwen Wymark and Alberto Adellach; (D) Rob Bundy; (S) Rob Bundy; (C) Rob Bundy; (L) Rob Bundy
Equals, Patricia Ryan; (D) John Genke; (S) John Genke; (C) John Genke; (L) John Genke
Subject to Change, F.J. Hartland; (D) Peter M. Gordon; (S) Peter M. Gordon; (C) Peter M. Gordon; (L) Peter M. Gordon
The Alchemist, Ben Jonson; adapt: Amie Brockway; (D) Amie Brockway; (S) Adrienne J. Brockway; (C) Adrienne J. Brockway; (L) Adrienne J. Brockway

PRODUCTIONS 1986–87

The Nightingale, adapt: William Electric Black, from Hans Christian Andersen; music: Elliot Sokolov; (D) Gary Pollard; (S) Adrienne J. Brockway; (C) Adrienne J. Brockway; (L) Adrienne J. Brockway
The Odyssey, adapt: Amie Brockway, from Homer; music: Elliot Sokolov; (D) Amie Brockway; (S) Adrienne J. Brockway; (C) Adrienne J. Brockway; (L) Adrienne J. Brockway
A Taste of Honey, Shelagh Delaney; (D) Betsy Shevey; (S) Adrienne J. Brockway; (C) Adrienne J. Brockway; (L) Adrienne J. Brockway
The Dream of Kitamura, Philip Kan Gotanda; (D) Jean Erdman and Philip Kan Gotanda; (S) Adrienne J. Brockway; (C) Eiko Yamaguchi; (L) Victor En Yu Tan

Oregon Shakespearean Festival

JERRY TURNER
Artistic Director

WILLIAM W. PATTON
Executive Director

Box 158
Ashland, OR 97520
(503) 482-2111 (bus.)
(503) 482-4331 (b.o.)

FOUNDED 1935
Angus Bowmer

SEASON
Feb.-Nov.

FACILITIES
Angus Bowmer Theatre
Seating capacity: 600
Stage: modified thrust

Elizabethan Theatre
Seating capacity: 1,200
Stage: outdoor

Black Swan Theatre
Seating capacity: 140
Stage: arena

FINANCES
Jan. 1, 1986-Dec. 31, 1986
Expenses: $5,766,850

CONTRACTS
AEA Special Production based on LORT (B)

The Oregon Shakespearean Festival was founded in 1935 to present Shakespeare's works on a stage roughly equivalent to those of Elizabethan playhouses. Today, the Festival operates a large outdoor playhouse modeled after the historic Fortune Theatre; a modern indoor theatre known as the Angus Bowmer; and the Black Swan, an intimate "black box" space. Production style is dictated first and foremost by the demands of the text and vision of the author; second, by the talent and sensibilities of the company; and finally by contemporary taste and the experience of the audience. Our task is to select and perform plays of dramatic stature—ancient and contemporary, classical and modern—that speak to the human condition; and to present them as vividly, clearly and boldly as resources permit, making demands on the audience as well as the company in pursuit of an impossible vision: the definitive production. Almost as important as the repertoire is the selection, nurturing and care of the company. Both continuity and freshness are assured by the systematic welcoming and training of new talent. The Festival accepts new members in order to fulfill its obligation to train artists for classical work, and as a necessary protection against staleness and complacency.

—Jerry Turner

Oregon Shakespearean Festival. *Macbeth*. Photo: Hank Kranzler.

PRODUCTIONS 1986

The Tempest, William Shakespeare; (D) Edward Hastings; (S) Richard L. Hay; (C) Sarah Nash Gates; (L) Robert Peterson
The Threepenny Opera, book: Bertolt Brecht; music: Kurt Weill; (D) Andrew Traister; (S) William Bloodgood; (C) Jeannie Davidson; (L) Robert Peterson
On the Verge or The Geography of Yearning, Eric Overmyer; (D) Jerry Turner; (S) William Bloodgood; (C) Jeannie Davidson; (L) James Sale
An Enemy of the People, Henrik Ibsen; trans and adapt: Jerry Turner; (D) Jerry Turner; (S) Richard L. Hay; (C) Claudia Everett; (L) James Sale
Strange Snow, Stephen Metcalfe; (D) Andrew Traister; (S) William Bloodgood; (C) Frances Kenny; (L) Robert Peterson
Sea Marks, Gardner McKay; (D) Henry Woronicz; (S) Scott Weldin; (C) Jeannie Davidson; (L) James Sale
Broadway, Philip Dunning and George Abbott; (D) Pat Patton; (S) William Bloodgood; (C) Michael Olich; (L) Robert Peterson
As You Like It, William Shakespeare; (D) Anne-Denise Ford; (S) Richard L. Hay; (C) Claudia Everett; (L) Robert Peterson
Titus Andronicus, William Shakespeare; (D) Pat Patton; (S) William Bloodgood; (C) Jeannie Davidson; (L) Robert Peterson
Measure for Measure, William Shakespeare; (D) James Edmondson; (S) Jesse Hollis; (C) Deborah M. Dryden; (L) Robert Peterson
Cold Storage, Ronald Ribman; (D) Denis Arndt; (S) William Bloodgood; (C) Carole Wheeldon; (L) James Sale

PRODUCTIONS 1987

Richard II, William Shakespeare; (D) Jerry Turner; (S) William Bloodgood; (C) Michael Olich; (L) James Sale
She Stoops to Conquer, Oliver Goldsmith; (D) Walter Schoen; (S) Richard L. Hay; (C) Jeannie Davidson; (L) James Sale
The Hostage, Brendan Behan; (D) Michael Kevin; (S) William Bloodgood; (C) Jeannie Davidson; (L) Robert Peterson
Curse of the Starving Class, Sam Shepard; (D) Andrew Traister; (S) William Bloodgood; (C) Frances Kenny; (L) Robert Peterson
The Member of the Wedding, Carson McCullers; (D) Robert Loper; (S) Jesse Hollis; (C) Sarah Nash Gates; (L) James Sale
Taking Steps, Alan Ayckbourn; (D) Pat Patton; (S) Richard L. Hay; (C) Deborah Trout; (L) Robert Peterson
Master Harold...and the boys, Athol Fugard; (D) Henry Woronicz; (S) Vicki Smith; (C) Michael Chapman; (L) James Sale

Ballerina, Arne Skouen; (D) Cynthia White; (S) Richard L. Hay; (C) Candice Cain; (L) James Sale
A Midsummer Night's Dream, William Shakespeare; (D) Pat Patton; (S) Jesse Hollis; (C) Michael Olich; (L) Robert Peterson
The Shoemaker's Holiday, Thomas Dekker; (D) Jerry Turner; (S) Richard L. Hay; (C) Claudia Everett; (L) Robert Peterson
Macbeth, William Shakespeare; (D) James Edmondson; (S) William Bloodgood; (C) Deborah M. Dryden; (L) Robert Peterson

SEASON
Year-round

FACILITIES
Buckingham Theater
Seating capacity: 250
Stage: flexible

Organic Lab
Seating capacity: 65
Stage: proscenium

FINANCES
July 1, 1986-June 30, 1987
Expenses: $276,000

CONTRACTS
AEA CAT

Organic Theater Company

THOMAS RICCIO
Artistic Director

RICHARD FRIEDMAN
General Manager

3319 North Clark St.
Chicago, IL 60657
(312) 327-5507 (bus.)
(312) 327-5588 (b.o.)

FOUNDED 1969
Stuart Gordon, Carolyn Purdy-Gordon

The Organic Theater Company is devoted to both the development of new plays and the reinterpretation of existing works of dramatic literature, guided by a commitment to research for the means, methods and vocabulary of new performance expression. To achieve this vision the Organic is developing an artistic community of similarly minded artists from a variety of divergent disciplines who collaborate on the development of new work. Over the past two years composers, musicians, instrument builders, visual artists, video and performance artists have worked at the Organic in collaboration with theatre-trained professionals. The Organic believes that it is only through the commitment to interdisciplinary exploration that a meaningful, responsive and vital theatre experience can be forged. The Organic believes that the tools of many art forms will be brought to theatre's awareness and advantage in this way. Theatre must reinvent itself.

—Thomas Riccio

Organic Theater Company. Richard Duslack and Kathryn Hill in *The Stranger in Stanley's Room*. Photo: Lolita Lorre.

PRODUCTIONS 1985–86

Dope, S. Rohmer and Stuart Gordon; (D) Stuart Gordon; (S) Mary Margaret Bartley; (C) Mary Margaret Bartley; (L) Larry Schoeneman
Kiss It Goodbye, Michael Andrew Miner; (D) Thomas Riccio; (S) Mary Margaret Bartley; (C) Mary Margaret Bartley; (L) Larry Schoeneman
Akron, Thomas Riccio; (D) Thomas Riccio; (S) Mary Margaret Bartley; (C) Mary Margaret Bartley; (L) Larry Schoeneman
Rubber City, Thomas Riccio; (D) Thomas Riccio; (S) Mary Margaret Bartley; (C) Mary Margaret Bartley; (L) Larry Schoeneman

Seed Show #1 (A Short New Works Series):
Eine Kleine Theatricale, Alan Gross
El Scene, Sherry Narens
The Piece, Deb Lacusta and Dan Castellaneta
Canis Lupis Loop De Loo, Judy Morgan
An Immigrant's Dream, Rick Cleveland
The Pursuit of Happiness, Nicholas A. Patricca
On the Rack, Steven Ivcich
Roof, Rick Cleveland
Park Gardens, Chris Barnes and Barbara Thomas
(All Seed Show works were directed by Michael J. Gellman and had sets, costumes and lights designed by Michael Paxton, Ellen Gross and Peter Gottlieb, respectively.)

Late Night with David Mamula, David Mamula; (D) Warren Baumgart; (S) David Mamula; (C) David Mamula; (L) Linda Rodriguez

PRODUCTIONS 1986–87

The Stranger in Stanley's Room, George Freek; (D) Thomas Riccio; (S) Watt King and Michael Paxton; (C) Claudia Boddy; (L) Peter Gottlieb

Seed Show #2 (A Short New Works Series):
Omnioptics, Deb Lacusta and Dan Castellaneta
The Dollmaker, Jean Howard
Private Dancing, Michael Andrew Miner
(All Seed Show works were directed by Michael J. Gellman and had sets, costumes and lights designed by Judith Austin Essex, Sarah Stauderman and Peter Gottlieb, respectively.)

Betawulf, Lisa Barns, Ray Miller, Thomas Riccio and Bob Hoftetter; (D) Thomas Riccio; (S) Watt King and Michael Paxton; (C) Claudia Boddy; (L) Peter Gottlieb
Candyland, Sharon Evans; (D) Judy Morgan; (S) David Csicsko; (C) David Csicsko; (L) James Card
Reconstructing (The Temple) from Memory, Michael Meyers; (D) Michael Meyers; (S) Michael Meyers; (C) Vickie Hoch; (L) Lou Mallozzi
Fits and Parts, P. Martin and company; (D) Watt King; (S) Watt King, James Card and Michael Paxton; (C) Jeanne Nemcek; (L) Peter Gottlieb
Mukluk, Carl Aniel and Patrick Penney; (D) Michael Paxton; (S) Watt King, Michael Paxton and James Card; (C) Jeanne Nemcek; (L) Peter Gottlieb

Pan Asian Repertory Theatre

TISA CHANG
Artistic Producing Director

BONNIE HYSLOP
Managing Director

47 Great Jones St.
New York, NY 10012
(212) 505-5655 (bus.)
(212) 245-2660 (b.o.)

FOUNDED 1977
Tisa Chang

SEASON
Oct.-June

FACILITIES
Playhouse 46
Seating capacity: 102
Stage: arena

FINANCES
Sept. 1, 1986-Aug. 31, 1987
Expenses: $370,536

Pan Asian Repertory Theatre. Donald Li and Mary Lee-Aranas in *The Man Who Turned into a Stick.* Photo: Corky Lee.

CONTRACTS
AEA letter of agreement

Pan Asian Repertory Theatre has plucked up the courage to take on our greatest challenge to date—that of designating Senior Artists who will form the initial core of a permanent resident acting ensemble. By working on nontypical roles, by devloping new projects, by having plays commissioned for them, by being able to make acting a primary priority in their existence—financially and spiritually—our actors will help set new standards of dedication and artistic risk-taking. For the Asian-American actor, it will be especially fulfilling to be able to work regularly on nontypical roles, *tout ensemble*, from plays in the classical repertoire of world drama to our regular premieres of contemporary Asian and Asian-American works. As we embark on our 11th season, I reflect on the awesome sacrifices made in order for Pan Asian Rep's work to endure, and I do not regret one moment. We can proudly say Pan Asian Rep is a professional Asian-American resident ensemble.

—*Tisa Chang*

PRODUCTIONS 1985–86

Once Is Never Enough, R.A. Shiomi, Marc Hayashi and Lane Kiyomi Nishikawa; (D) Raul Aranas; (S) Christopher Stapleton; (C) Eiko Yamaguchi; (L) Victor En Yu Tan

Ghashiram Kotwal, Vijay Tendulkar; trans: Eleanor Zelliot and Jayant Karve; (D) Tisa Chang; (S) Atsushi Moriyasu; (C) Eiko Yamaguchi; (L) Victor En Yu Tan

Medea, Euripides; trans and adapt: Claire Bush and Alkis Papoutsis; (D) Alkis Papoutsis; (S) Alex Polner; (C) Eiko Yamaguchi; (L) Richard Dorfman

The Man Who Turned into a Stick, Kobo Abe; trans: Donald Keene; (D) Ron Nakahara; (S) Bob Phillips; (C) Eiko Yamaguchi; (L) Tina Charney

PRODUCTIONS 1986–87

The Impostor (If I Were Real), Sha Yexin, Li Shoucheng and Yao Mingde; trans: Daniel Kane; (D) Ron Nakahara; (C) Linda Taoka; (L) Victor En Yu Tan

Shogun Macbeth, William Shakespeare; adapt: John R. Briggs; (D) John R. Briggs; (S) Atsushi Moriyasu; (C) Eiko Yamaguchi; (L) Tina Charney

Wha...I, Whai, a Long Long Time Ago, Che Inhoon; trans: Hui-jin Pak and Oh-kon Cho; (D) Tisa Chang; (S) Alex Polner; (C) Eiko Yamaguchi; (L) Victor En Yu Tan

The Life of the Land, Edward Sakamoto; (D) Kati Kuroda; (S) Bob Phillips; (C) Eiko Yamaguchi; (L) Richard Dorfman

Paper Mill Playhouse

ANGELO DEL ROSSI
Executive Producer

ROBERT JOHANSON
Artistic Director

WADE MILLER
General Manager

Brookside Dr.
Millburn, NJ 07041
(201) 379-3636 (bus.)
(201) 376-4343 (b.o.)

FOUNDED 1934
Frank Carrington, Antoinette Scudder

SEASON
Sept.-July

FACILITIES
Playhouse
Seating capacity: 1,192
Stage: proscenium

Musical Theatre Project Laboratory
Seating capacity: 80
Stage: flexible

FINANCES
July 1, 1986-June 30, 1987
Expenses: $7,261,200

CONTRACTS
AEA COST, SSD&C and USA

Paper Mill Playhouse produces a wide range of performing arts. Our particular mission is the creation, preservation and production of musical theatre works. In addition to our full-scale productions from the musical repertoire, including American operettas, we give special effort to the creation of new works through our ongoing development program, the Paper Mill Musical Theatre Project. Four musicals and two plays make up our mainstage season for a total of 272 performances. Our productions have been toured, transferred to the Kennedy Center in Washington, D.C. and to Broadway, and broadcast on cable and public television. In 1986, we were named "most outstanding" in a nationwide "Search for Excellence in American Theatre" competition, encompassing over 280 nonprofit theatres. With our diverse schedule of productions and presented events, we serve more than 400,000 theatregoers annually, attracting a season subscription audience of over 39,000.

—*Angelo Del Rossi*

PRODUCTIONS 1985–86

Windy City, book and lyrics: Dick Vosburgh; music: Tony Macaulay; (D) David H. Bell; (S) Michael Anania; (C) Guy Geoly; (L) Jeff Davis

Carousel, book and lyrics: Oscar Hammerstein, II; music: Richard Rodgers; (D) Robert Johanson; (S) Michael Anania; (C) Guy Geoly; (L) Brian MacDevitt

Paper Mill Playhouse. *Damn Yankees.* Photo: Gerry Goodstein.

Run for Your Wife, Ray Cooney; (D) Chris Johnston; (S) Michael Anania; (C) Alice S. Hughes; (L) David Kissel

The Foreigner, Larry Shue; (D) David Saint; (S) Michael Anania; (C) Alice S. Hughes; (L) David Kissel

The 1940's Radio Hour, Walton Jones; (D) Robert Johanson; (S) Michael Anania; (C) Guy Geoly; (L) David Kissel

Candide, book adapt: Hugh Wheeler, from Voltaire; music: Leonard Bernstein; lyrics: Richard Wilbur, John LaTouche and Stephen Sondheim; (D) Robert Johanson; (S) Michael Anania; (C) Guy Geoly; (L) Brian MacDevitt

PRODUCTIONS 1986–87

Damn Yankees, book: George Abbott and Douglass Wallop; music and lyrics: Richard Adler and Jerry Ross; (D) George Abbott; (S) Michael Anania; (C) Guy Geoly and Alice S. Hughes; (L) Mimi Jordan Sherin

Barnum, book: Mark Bramble; music: Cy Coleman; lyrics: Michael Stewart; (D) Neal Kenyon; (S) David Mitchell; (C) Guy Geoly and Alice S. Hughes; (L) Brian MacDevitt

Brighton Beach Memoirs, Neil Simon; (D) John Going; (S) David Mitchell; (C) Alice S. Hughes; (L) David Kissel

Sunrise at Campobello, Dore Schary; (D) John Going; (S) Michael Anania; (C) Guy Geoly; (L) David Kissel

Naughty Marietta, music: Victor Herbert; adapt: Robert Johanson; book and lyrics: Rida Johanson Young; (D) Robert Johanson; (S) Michael Anania; (C) Alice S. Hughes; (L) Brian MacDevitt

Annie Get Your Gun, book: Herbert Fields and Dorothy Fields; music and lyrics: Irving Berlin; (D) Robert Johanson; (S) Robert O'Hearn; (C) Guy Geoly; (L) David Kissel

PCPA Theaterfest

JACK SHOUSE
Artistic Director

JOHN S. CARTER
Managing Director

Box 1700
Santa Maria, CA 93456
(805) 928-7731 (bus.)
(805) 922-8313 (b.o.)

FOUNDED 1964
Donovan Marley

SEASON
Oct.-Sept.

FACILITIES
Marian Theatre
Seating capacity: 508
Stage: thrust

Interim Theatre
Seating capacity: 175
Stage: flexible

Festival Theatre
Seating capacity: 772
Stage: thrust

FINANCES
Oct. 1, 1985-Sept. 30, 1986
Expenses: $2,464,140

CONTRACTS
AEA U/RTA

We, as theatre artists, performers and craftsmen, share our product with our audience in an attempt to entertain and create a heightened awareness of the human condition, and to promote a better understanding of what our roles are as individuals and contributors to society. This collaboration is the essence of the theatre. It is the artist who initiates the creative process and the audience who responds, thus maintaining a cycle of realization and growth for both. At PCPA Theaterfest we create an environment for those artists dedicated to taking that creative initiative. We strive to protect and nurture a theatrical process we feel is vital to our development as individuals and our growth as a civilization. As a performing company and conservatory, we commit ourselves to serving the community, professional staff and students by producing an even wider variety of theatrical works of excellence, while preserving our tradition of offering the classics of world theatre, new plays, contemporary plays, and the new and classic in American musical theatre.

—Jack Shouse

Note: During the 1985-86 season, Vincent Dowling served as artistic director

PCPA Theaterfest. Kristine Lowry and Phil Brotherton in *The Rainmaker*. Photo: Tom Smith/Images.

PRODUCTIONS 1985–86

Funny Girl, book: Isobel Lennart; music: Jule Styne; lyrics: Bob Merrill; (D) George Maguire; (S) Jack Shouse; (C) Lewis D. Rampino; (L) Robert Jared

Annie Get Your Gun, music and lyrics: Irving Berlin; book: Herbert Fields and Dorothy Fields; (D) Jack Shouse; (S) John Dexter; (C) Lewis D. Rampino; (L) Robert Jared

All My Sons, Arthur Miller; (D) Michael Winters; (S) John Dexter; (C) Kevin McLeod; (L) Michael Peterson

They're Playing Our Song, book: Neil Simon; music: Marvin Hamlisch; lyrics: Carol Bayer Sager; (D) Jack Shouse; (S) Craig Edelblut; (C) Susan Snowden; (L) Michael Peterson

The Crucifer of Blood, adapt: Paul Giovanni, from Arthur Conan Doyle; (D) John C. Fletcher; (S) Everett Chase; (C) Lewis D. Rampino; (L) Greg Sullivan

Dopes on a Rope, John C. Fletcher; (D) John C. Fletcher; (S) Everett Chase; (C) Kevin McLeod; (L) Michael Peterson

Richard II, William Shakespeare; (D) John C. Fletcher; (S) Everett Chase; (C) Lewis D. Rampino; (L) Greg Sullivan

PRODUCTIONS 1986–87

The Rainmaker, N. Richard Nash; (D) Ben Cooper; (S) Carol Russell; (C) Kevin McLeod; (L) Michael Peterson

Cinderella, book and lyrics: Oscar Hammerstein, II; music: Richard Rodgers; (D) Brad Carroll; (S) Jack Shouse; (C) Claremarie Verheyen; (L) Michael Peterson

The Foreigner, Larry Shue; (D) Sandy McCallum; (S) John Dexter; (C) April Guttierrez; (L) Michael Peterson

The Ghost and Mrs. Muir, book adapt: Arthur Marx and Robert Fisher; music and lyrics: Scott DeTurk and Bill Francoeur; (D) Jack Shouse; (S) John Dexter; (C) Susan Snowden; (L) Michael Peterson

Our Town, Thornton Wilder; (D) John C. Fletcher; (S) Craig Edelblut; (C) Susan Snowden; (L) Jeff Sharp

Pennsylvania Stage Company

GREGORY S. HURST
Producing Director

DANIEL B. FALLON
Managing Director

837 Linden St.
Allentown, PA 18101
(215) 434-6110 (bus.)
(215) 433-3394 (b.o.)

FOUNDED 1977
Anna Rodale

SEASON
Oct.-July

FACILITIES
J.I. Rodale Theatre
Seating capacity: 274
Stage: proscenium

FINANCES
July 1, 1986-June 30, 1987
Expenses: $1,170,756

CONTRACTS
AEA LORT (C) and SSD&C

Pennsylvania Stage Company's artistic purpose is clear: to present and develop plays and musicals, by playwrights and composers who transcend their own time and remain contemporary through sheer force of form and character or through artistic interpretation and ambition. Every fourth play we present is new. In eight seasons, we have presented 14 premieres; classics by Miller, Williams and O'Neill; 12 musicals; and a variety of plays that ignite the senses—from Shakespeare to Athol Fugard to Sam Shepard. PSC premieres have been produced subsequently in New York, London, on public television and in other regional theatres. We strive to shape, and be shaped by, the character and values of our community. Our goal is to interact with our audience—to inform, surprise, astonish and delight. Our Scenes from Theatre Classics program annually visits 20,000 students at 80 schools, while our matinee series (with study guides and discussion sessions) brings 12,000 students to our productions.

—Gregory S. Hurst

PRODUCTIONS 1985–86

Pump Boys and Dinettes, John Foley, Mark Hardwick, Debra Monk, Cass Morgan, John Schimmel and Jim Wann; (D) Debra Monk; (S) Christopher J. Shriver; (C) Deborah Shippee O'Brien; (L) John Gisondi
The Crucible, Arthur Miller; (D) Gregory S. Hurst; (S) Bennet Averyt; (C) Barbara Forbes; (L) Bennet Averyt
Painting Churches, Tina Howe; (D) Pam Pepper; (S) Curtis Dretsch; (C) Marianne Faust; (L) Curtis Dretsch
Quality Time, Barbara Field; (D) Gregory S. Hurst; (S) Atkin Pace; (C) Karen Gerson; (L) Curtis Dretsch
The Club, Eve Merriam; music and lyrics: Alexandra Ivanoff; (D) Bick Goss; (S) Harry Feiner; (C) Susan Hirschfeld; (L) Quentin Thomas
Greater Tuna, Jaston Williams, Joe Sears and Ed Howard; (D) Stephen Rothman; (S) Keven Lock; (C) Catherine King; (L) Linda Sechrist
Billy Bishop Goes to War, John Gray and Eric Peterson; (D) Mitchell Ivers; (S) Patricia Woodbridge; (C) Myra Bumgarner; (L) Jackie Manassee

PRODUCTIONS 1986–87

Brighton Beach Memoirs, Neil Simon; (D) Gregory S. Hurst; (S) Atkin Pace; (C) Barbara Forbes; (L) Curtis Dretsch
Dames at Sea, book and lyrics: George Haimsohn and Robin Miller; music: Jim Wise; (D) Sue Lawless; (S) Curtis Dretsch; (C) Marcy Grace Froelich; (L) Donald Holder
The Housekeepr, James Prideaux; (D) Wendy Liscow; (S) Linda Sechrist; (C) Marianne Faust; (L) Linda Sechrist
Cat on a Hot Tin Roof, Tennessee Williams; (D) Gregory S. Hurst; (S) Atkin Pace; (C) Barbara Forbes; (L) Curtis Dretsch
More Fun Than Bowling, Steven Dietz; (D) Gregory S. Hurst; (S) Clarke Dunham; (C) Kathleen Egan; (L) Clarke Dunham
A Lesson from Aloes, Athol Fugard; (D) Allen R. Belknap; (S) Linda Sechrist; (C) Marianne Faust; (L) Linda Sechrist
The Foreigner, Larry Shue; (D) Thomas Bullard; (S) Bennet Averyt; (C) Barbara Forbes; (L) Bennet Averyt

Pennsylvania Stage Company. Joanne Camp in *Quality Time*. Photo: Gregory M. Fota.

The People's Light and Theatre Company. Susan Wilder, Daniel Oreskes and Jarlath Conroy in *Kabuki Othello*. Photo: Kenneth Kaufman.

The People's Light and Theatre Company

DANNY S. FRUCHTER
Producing Director

GREGORY T. ROWE
General Manager

39 Conestoga Rd.
Malvern, PA 19355
(215) 647-1900 (bus.)
(215) 644-3500 (b.o.)

FOUNDED 1974
Danny S. Fruchter, Margaret E. Fruchter, Richard L. Keeler, Ken Marini

SEASON
Apr.-Jan.

FACILITIES
Mainstage
Seating capacity: 400
Stage: flexible

Second Stage
Seating capacity: 180
Stage: modified thrust

FINANCES
Feb. 1, 1986-Jan. 31, 1987
Expenses: $1,301,573

CONTRACTS
AEA LORT (D) and SSD&C

Can a regional theatre be of service to its community without being both very good, and popular well beyond currently accepted levels of attendance? I think not. Therefore, we at the People's Light and Theatre Company are planning to attend to those elements in our work which keep us from accomplishing both aims. I hope we can identify those attitudes and structures within our organization which, although they make minimal economic survival possible, have condemned us to the demoralizing limitations of short rehearsals, woefully little planning time and lack of continuous training. Further, I believe there is a sophistry in proclaiming the theatre vitally connected to those we serve, without a commitment from theatre workers to be bound to each other and to our community over sufficient time to become unified in our collective and civic purposes. Beyond that, a further question persists: How, in a society which truly fears and actively denegrates collectivism, can theatre, the quintessence of collective activity, prosper and mature? Having no pat answers, we are trying to find enough time to address ourselves to fundamental change.

—*Danny S. Fruchter*

PRODUCTIONS 1985–86

The Diviners, Jim Leonard, Jr.; (D) Ken Marini; (S) James F. Pyne, Jr.; (C) Lynn Fox; (L) Joe Ragey

Summerfolk, Maxim Gorky; adapt: Lee Devin; trans: Margaret Wettlin; (D) Abigail Adams; (S) Joe Ragey; (C) Colleen Muscha; (L) Joe Ragey

Inherit the Wind, Jerome Lawrence and Robert E. Lee; (D) Danny S. Fruchter; (S) Joe Ragey; (C) Barbara Forbes; (L) Joe Ragey

Kabuki Othello, conceived: Shozo Sato; text: Karen Sunde; (D) Shozo Sato; (S) Joe Ragey and Shozo Sato; (C) Shozo Sato; (L) James F. Pyne, Jr.

Waiting for Godot, Samuel Beckett; (D) Ken Marini; (S) Joe Ragey; (C) Susan Pratt; (L) Joe Ragey

The Chalk Garden, Enid Bagnold; (D) Abigail Adams; (S) Joe Ragey; (C) Barbara Forbes; (L) James F. Pyne, Jr.

PRODUCTIONS 1986–87

What the Butler Saw, Joe Orton; (D) Abigail Adams; (S) James F. Pyne, Jr.; (C) Barbara Forbes; (L) Joe Ragey

American Buffalo, David Mamet; (D) Ken Marini; (S) Joe Ragey; (C) P. Chelsea Harriman; (L) James F. Pyne, Jr.

The Stone House, Louis Lippa; (D) Jackson Phippin; (S) James F. Pyne, Jr.; (C) P. Chelsea Harriman; (L) Joe Ragey

Ah, Wilderness!, Eugene O'Neill; (D) Abigail Adams; (S) Joe Ragey; (C) Colleen Muscha; (L) Joe Ragey

A Lovely Sunday for Creve Coeur, Tennessee Williams; (D) Abigail Adams; (S) Joe Ragey; (C) P. Chelsea Harriman; (L) James F. Pyne, Jr.

Hamlet, William Shakespeare; (D) Danny S. Fruchter; (S) James F. Pyne, Jr.; (C) Lindsay W. Davis; (L) Arden Fingerhut

Periwinkle National Theatre for Young Audiences

SUNNA RASCH
Artistic Director

KEN UY
Business Manager

19 Clinton Ave.
Monticello, NY 12701
(914) 794-1666

FOUNDED 1963
Sunna Rasch

SEASON
Year-round

FINANCES
Aug. 1, 1986-July 31, 1987
Expenses: $215,000

The premise—and promise—of Periwinkle National Theatre for Young Audiences has been to develop theatre programs that communicate with youth, with which young audiences can identify and through which they can expand themselves creatively, intellectually, artistically and emotionally. Periwinkle has developed 25 original productions for every age level, and has toured them to schools and communities nationwide, reaching over two million young people. Programs available for touring reflect our diversity: *The Magic Work*, a play-with-music for primary grades; *The Fabulous Dream of Andrew H. Lupone*, a musical for elementary shools; *Hooray for Me*, a satire for middle schools; and *Halfway There*, a drama for high schools. Periwinkle's productions can stand alone as theatre, but they go beyond, because we believe that theatre is a vital educational tool as well. Periwinkle is committed to the arts in education, and looks forward to reaching even more young people everywhere.

—*Sunna Rasch*

PRODUCTIONS 1985–86

Halfway There, Sunna Rasch and company; (D) Jack Sims and Michael Dacunto; (S) Michael Daughtry; (C) Marcie Miller; (L) Ronald Selke

America, Yes!, Sunna Rasch; (D) Scott Laughead; (S) Maude DeAngelis; (C) Marlu Costumes

The Fabulous Dream of Andrew H. Lupone, book, music and lyrics: Scott Laughead; (D) Scott Laughead; (S) Earl Wertheim; (C) Mary Alice Orito

The Pooh Show, Scott Laughead; (D) Scott Laughead; (S) David Cooper; (C) Susan Scherer

PRODUCTIONS 1986–87

Halfway There, Sunna Rasch and company; (D) Michael Dacunto; (S) Michael Daughtry; (C) Marcie Miller; (L) Ron Selke

The Mad Poet Strikes—Again!, Sunna Rasch; (D) Scott Laughead; (S) David Cooper; (C) Scott Laughead

The Fabulous Dream of Andrew H. Lupone, book, music and lyrics: Scott Laughead; (D) Scott Laughead; (S) Earl Wertheim; (C) Mary Alice Orito

Hooray for Me!, Scott Laughead; (D) Scott Laughead; (S) Sunna Rasch; (C) Scott Laughead

The Frog Prince, Scott Laughead; (D) Scott Laughead; (S) Michael Daughtry; (C) Stephanie Liebowitz

America, Yes!, Sunna Rasch; (D) Scott Laughead; (S) Maude DeAngelis; (C) Marlu Costumes

Periwinkle National Theatre for Young Audiences. *Halfway There*. Photo: Diana Henry.

Perseverance Theatre. Mike Peterson, Gregg W. Brevoort and Lynette Turner in *The Birds*. Photo: Susan Kaufman.

Perseverance Theatre

MOLLY D. SMITH
Artistic Director

DEBORAH B. BALEY
Producing Director

914 Third St.
Douglas, AK 99824
(907) 364-2151 (bus.)
(907) 364-2421 (b.o.)

FOUNDED 1979
Kate Bowns, Jack Cannon, Susie Fowler, Bill C. Ray, Joe Ross, Kay Smith, Molly D. Smith

SEASON
Year-round

FACILITIES
Mainstage
Seating capacity: 150
Stage: flexible

Second Stage
Seating capacity: 50
Stage: flexible

Elk's Hall
Seating capacity: 200
Stage: proscenium

FINANCES
July 1, 1986-June 30, 1987
Expenses: $605,538

Perseverance Theatre is located just outside Juneau, the capital of Alaska, in Douglas, a community of 25,000 situated in an area inaccessible by road. Alaska's rich cultural heritage and its environmental and social background contribute profoundly to the artistic direction and scope of Perseverance Theatre. The complex personality of the state encompasses and draws many kinds of people: winners and losers, people out to get rich quick, Aleuts, Tlingits, Eskimos and whites, gold rush families, oil tycoons and environmentalists looking for the "last frontier." Our major artistic goal is to wrestle with this spirit, this uniquely Alaskan experience, and to develop a voice for it. We produce a full season of classical and contemporary theatre (including at least one new play by an Alaskan playwright), a second stage series and the Great Alaskan Playrush (a statewide playwriting competition). We also tour around the state and offer extensive training programs.

—*Molly D. Smith*

PRODUCTIONS 1985–86

The Cherry Orchard, Anton Chekhov; trans: Helen Rapapport; adapt: Trevor Griffiths; (D) Molly D. Smith; (S) Bill C. Ray and Molly D. Smith; (C) Deborah Trout; (L) Jim Sale

The Lady That's Known as Lou, book and lyrics: Gordon Duffey; music: Alan Chapman; (D) Jamieson McLean; (S) Bill C. Ray; (C) Barbara Casement; (L) Lee Riggs

We Won't Pay! We Won't Pay!, Dario Fo; trans: R.G. Davis; (D) Kate Bowns; (S) Mary Ellen Frank; (C) Deborah Smith; (L) Louanne Jensen

You Can't Take It with You, Moss Hart and George S. Kaufman; (D) Molly D. Smith; (S) Billy Hudson; (C) Barbara Casement; (L) Vikki Benner

The Birds, Aristophanes; adapt: Dave Hunsaker; (D) Bob Ernst; (S) Bill C. Ray; (C) Bill C. Ray; (L) Lee Riggs

Talking With..., Jane Martin; (D) Molly D. Smith; (S) Bill C. Ray; (C) Barbara Casement; (L) Lee Riggs

The Lady Lou Revue, book and lyrics: Gordon Duffey; music: Alan Chapman; (D) Kate Bowns and Jamieson McLean; (S) Bill C. Ray; (C) Barbara Casement; (L) Lee Riggs

PRODUCTIONS 1986–87

Macbeth, William Shakespeare; (D) Molly D. Smith; (S) Pavel M. Dobrusky; (C) Pavel M. Dobrusky; (L) Pavel M. Dobrusky

Sea Marks, Gardner McKay; (D) Kate Bowns; (S) Billy Hudson; (C) Barbara Casement; (L) Vikki Benner

Water of Life, Bill C. Ray; (D) Molly D. Smith; (S) Bill C. Ray; (C) Bill C. Ray; (L) Lee Riggs

Birds of Passage, Mary Lou Spartz; (D) Dave Hunsaker; (S) Billy Hudson; (C) Barbara Casement; (L) Joe Ross

The Majestic Kid, Mark Medoff; (D) Jamieson McLean; (S) Dan De Roux; (C) Natalee Rothaus; (L) Vikki Benner

Ringers, Frank X. Hogan; (D) Tim Wilson; (S) Jane Terzis and Doug Larson; (C) Deborah Smith; (L) Brendan Wallace

The Lady Lou Revue, book and lyrics: Gordon Duffey; music: Alan Chapman; (D) Kate Bowns and Marty Clements; (S) Bill C. Ray; (C) Barbara Casement and Norma Sardeson; (L) Brendan Wallace

Philadelphia Drama Guild

GREGORY POGGI
Producing Director

KATHLEEN KUND NOLAN
Business Manager

112 South 16th St., Suite 802
Philadelphia, PA 19102
(215) 563-7530 (bus.)
(215) 898-6791 (b.o.)

FOUNDED 1956
Sidney S. Bloom

SEASON
Oct.-May

FACILITIES
Zellerbach Theatre
Seating capacity: 944
Stage: thrust

Harold Prince Theatre
Seating capacity: 166
Stage: flexible

Studio Theatre
Seating capacity: 120
Stage: proscenium

FINANCES
June 1, 1986-May 31, 1987
Expenses: $2,025,000

CONTRACTS
AEA LORT (B+), SSD&C and USA

Great theatre keeps us in touch with a common denominator—the human soul. It compels our imagination and perception and leads us to the unique pleasures of emotional discovery and intellectual revelation. I am attracted to writers who provoke a confrontation and understanding of those distinctly human qualities in which we all share to create a "theatre of involvement"—producing works that are provocative, imaginative and strong on the human condition. Three touchstones inform my

Philadelphia Drama Guild. S. Epatha Merkerson and David Downing in *A Raisin in the Sun*. Photo: Kenneth Kauffman.

play selection at the Philadelphia Drama Guild and motivate their production style: the originality of each writer's world and point of view; the vigor of his or her moral concern for the way we live; and the inherent theatricality of each work, particularly the expressiveness of the playwriting "voice" in filling the playing area of our large Zellerbach Theatre space. Our programming also reflects a conscious effort to attract, entertain and inform young minds. In fulfilling my artistic objectives, this audience of the future remains of paramount importance.

—*Gregory Poggi*

PRODUCTIONS 1985–86

Tent Meeting, Larry Larson, Levi Lee and Rebecca Wackler; (D) Patrick Tovatt; (S) Kevin Rupnik; (C) Kevin Rupnik; (L) James L. Leitner

A Raisin in the Sun, Lorraine Hansberry; (D) Edmund J. Cambridge; (S) Daniel P. Boylen; (C) Frankie Fehr; (L) William H. Grant, III

Absurd Person Singular, Alan Ayckbourn; (D) Charles Karchmer; (S) John Falabella; (C) Jess Goldstein; (L) Jeff Davis

A Delicate Balance, Edward Albee; (D) Michael Murray; (S) John Jensen; (C) Frankie Fehr; (L) F. Mitchell Dana

The Hot l Baltimore, Lanford Wilson; (D) Charles Karchmer; (S) John Falabella; (C) Jess Goldstein; (L) Jeff Davis

PRODUCTIONS 1986–87

A Shayna Maidel, Barbara Lebow; (D) Robert Kalfin; (S) Fred Kolo; (C) Eduardo Sicangco; (L) Fred Kolo

The Amen Corner, James Baldwin; (D) Edmund J. Cambridge; (S) Daniel P. Boylen; (C) Frankie Fehr; (L) William H. Grant, III

The Foreigner, Larry Shue; (D) Art Wolff; (S) John Jensen; (C) Frankie Fehr; (L) James Leitner

The Crucible, Arthur Miller; (D) Michael Murray; (S) Neil Peter Jampolis; (C) Karen Roston; (L) Neil Peter Jampolis

The Middle Ages, A.R. Gurney, Jr.; (D) Charles Karchmer; (S) John Falabella; (C) Jess Goldstein; (L) Jeff Davis

Playwrights of Philadelphia Play Festival:

Mother, Claude Koch; (D) Charles Conwell; (S) Edward Worthington; (C) Edward Worthington; (L) Jerald R. Forsyth

Mean Harvest, John Erlanger; (D) Lon Winston; (S) Edward Worthington; (C) Edward Worthington; (L) Jerald R. Forsyth

The Vigil, Charles J. Jenkins; (D) Clay Goss; (S) Christopher Nestor; (C) Christopher Nestor; (L) Jerald R. Forsyth

Philadelphia Festival Theatre for New Plays

CAROL ROCAMORA
Artistic/Producing Director

GRACE E. GRILLET
Administrative Director

3900 Chestnut St.
Philadelphia, PA 19104
(215) 222-5000 (bus.)
(215) 898-6791 (b.o.)

FOUNDED 1981
Carol Rocamora

SEASON
Year-round

FACILITIES
Harold Prince Theatre
Seating capacity: 200
Stage: thrust

FINANCES
July 1, 1986-June 30, 1987
Expenses: $430,000

CONTRACTS
AEA LORT (D)

The Philadelphia Festival Theatre for New Plays is one of the few independent, nonprofit professional theatres in the country dedicated exclusively to the production of new plays by American playwrights. The theatre's mission is twofold: to foster a commitment to new play development and production for the local and national theatre audience, and to make a lasting contribution to American dramatic literature by discovering new plays by established and new writers. In its first six years the theatre has produced 45 world premieres from more than 7,500 script submissions. Three-quarters of these premieres have gone on to additional productions or publication. Playwrights' residencies, Curtain Call discussions for playwrights, directors, actors and audiences, new play development seminars, and the Play-Offs reading series are among the programs offered by PFT. We will expand to a year-round schedule in 1987-88.

—*Carol Rocamora*

PRODUCTIONS 1986

Advice to the Players, Bruce Bonafede; (D) David Rotenberg

Eleemosynary, Lee Blessing; (D) Gloria Muzio

When the Bough Breaks, Robert Clyman; (D) Jan Silverman

Philadelphia Festival Theatre for New Plays. Helen-Jean Arthur and Peter Zapp in *Penguin Blues*. Photo: Liselotte Riva.

In Celebration (An Evening of One-Act Plays and Monologues):

Just Good Honest Food, Bill Bozzone; (D) Steve Kaplan
Breakdown, Bill Bozzone; (D) Steve Kaplan
No Time, Laurence Klavan; (D) Steve Kaplan
Montana, David Kranes; (D) Gloria Muzio
Four A.M., David Mamet; (D) Jason Buzas
I Am Bigfoot, Ron Carlson; (D) Jason Buzas
Bigfoot Stole My Wife, Ron Carlson; (D) Jason Buzas
I Ate My Best Friend's Brain, Ron Carlson; (D) Jason Buzas
Baby Born with a 2,000 Year Old Bracelet, Ron Carlson; (D) Jason Buzas
The Tablecloth of Turin, Ron Carlson; (D) Jason Buzas

PRODUCTIONS 1986–87

Early One Evening at the Rainbow Bar & Grille, Bruce Graham; (D) Gloria Muzio
Better Days, Richard Dresser; (D) Gloria Muzio
The Deal, Matthew Witten; (D) William Partlan
Heathen Valley, Romulus Linney; (D) Romulus Linney

Two x 2 (Two One-act Plays):

Penguin Blues, Ethan Phillips; and ***Abandoned in Queens***, Laura Maria Censabella; (D) Gloria Muzio
(All the above productions had sets, costumes and lights designed by Eric Schaeffer, Vicki Esposito and Curt Senie, respectively.)

The Philadelphia Theatre Company

SARA GARONZIK
Artistic Director

IRA SCHLOSSER
Managing Director

The Bourse Bldg., Suite 735
21 South 5th St.
Philadelphia, PA 19106
(215) 592-8333

FOUNDED 1974
Jean Harrison, Robert Headley

SEASON
Sept.-June

FACILITIES
Plays & Players Theatre
Seating capacity: 324
Stage: proscenium

FINANCES
Sept. 1, 1986-Aug. 31, 1987
Expenses: $613,000

CONTRACTS
AEA letter of agreement

The Philadelphia Theatre Company retains a strong commitment to producing the emerging, as well as the established, contemporary American voice. Within this mission we are able to achieve tremendous thematic and visual variety. At our heart we are an urban theatre with a strong social and humanitarian conscience—always in service to Philadelphia where we have become one of the prime producers of American drama. We have built our reputation by consistently striving for high-quality work—superior acting and sharp, well-interpreted directing have become the cornerstones of our aesthetic goals. Equally important is our wish to create a sane and supportive environment where playwrights and artists can accomplish their best work. We pride ourselves on our collaborative nature, often seeking coproducing opportunities, as our last two seasons reflect. The next five years will see an increasing emphasis on initiating new work through our Stages program.

—*Sara Garonzik*

PRODUCTIONS 1985–86

Painting Churches, Tina Howe; (D) Sara Garonzik; (S) Robert Little; (C) Pierre Deragon; (L) John Senter
Split Second, Dennis McIntyre; (D) John E. Allen, Jr.; (S) Daniel P. Boylen; (C) Frankie Fehr; (L) James L. Leitner

The Great American Sideshow:

Goodbye, Howard and ***Tennessee***, Romulus Linney; ***Landscape with Waitress***, Robert Pine; ***Between Cars***, Alan Zweibel; (D) Lynn M. Thomson; (S) M.R. Daniels; (C) Vickie Esposito; (L) James L. Leitner

The Philadelphia Theatre Company. Richard Thomas and Zach Grenier in *Citizen Tom Paine*. Photo: Joan Marcus.

Extremities, William Mastrosimone; (D) Sara Garonzik; (S) Robert Little; (C) Susan Trimble; (L) Don Ehman

Stages New Play Festival:

Bovver Boys, Willy Holtzman; (D) Lynn M. Thomson; (S) M.R. Daniels; (L) James L. Leitner
The Traveling Squirrel, Robert Lord; (D) Peter Webb; (S) M.R. Daniels; (L) James L. Leitner
Starry Night, Monte Merrick; (D) Richard Hopkins; (S) M.R. Daniels; (L) James L. Leitner
Warm Bodies, Mark St. Germain; (D) Jan Silverman; (S) M.R. Daniels; (L) James L. Leitner

PRODUCTIONS 1986–87

Williams & Walker, Vincent D. Smith; (D) Shauneille Perry; (S) Marc D. Malamud; (C) Judy Dearing; (L) Marc D. Malamud
Citizen Tom Paine, Howard Fast; (D) James Simpson; (S) James Sandefur; (C) Dunya Ramicova; (L) James F. Ingalls
Days and Nights Within, Ellen McLaughlin; (D) Lynn M. Thomson; (S) Kate Edmunds; (C) Kate Edmunds; (L) James F. Ingalls
As Is, William M. Hoffman; (D) Anita Khanzadian; (S) Joseph P. Flauto; (C) Vickie Esposito; (L) James L. Leitner

Stages New Play Festival:

Isolate, Jule Selbo; (D) Peg Denithorne; (S) M.R. Daniels; (L) James L. Leitner
Old Sins, Long Shadows, Ellen Byron; (D) Jan Silverman; (S) M.R. Daniels; (L) James L. Leitner
The Lost Colony, Wendy MacLeod; (D) Sara Garonzik; (S) M.R. Daniels; (L) James L. Leitner
Where She Went, What She Did, Laura Cunningham; (D) Sue Lawless; (S) M.R. Daniels; (L) James L. Leitner

Pioneer Theatre Company. Michelle Farr in *Macbeth*. Photo: Robert Clayton.

Pioneer Theatre Company

CHARLES MOREY
Artistic Director

KEITH ENGAR
Executive Producer

University of Utah
Salt Lake City, UT 84112
(801) 581-7118 (bus.)
(801) 581-6961 (b.o.)

FOUNDED 1962
C. Lowell Lees, University of Utah, local citizens

SEASON
Sept.-May

FACILITIES
Lees Main Stage
Seating capacity: 1,000
Stage: proscenium

FINANCES
July 1, 1986-June 30, 1987
Expenses: $1,602,326

CONTRACTS
AEA LORT (B) and U/RTA

Pioneer Theatre Company is the resident professional theatre of the University of Utah. It has the largest subscription audience of any arts organization in Utah and draws audiences from four western states. The company's primary concern is to provide our community with an ongoing theatre of the highest professional standards. Secondarily, the company serves an educational purpose as both a cultural resource to the university community, and as a training ground for aspiring professionals. The educational purpose cannot be fulfilled without first satisfying the primary concern of artistic excellence. The company recently implemented a long-range plan which mandates refocusing the repertoire upon the classics, developing a resident acting ensemble, operating under a League of Resident Theatres contract with Actors' Equity Association, and developing mutually beneficial ongoing intern programs with the university theatre department.

—Charles Morey

PRODUCTIONS 1985–86

Hello, Dolly!, book: Michael Stewart; music and lyrics: Jerry Herman; (D) Milton Lyon; (S) Ronald Crosby; (C) Doug Marmee; (L) Peter L. Willardson

The Tempest, William Shakespeare; (D) Charles Morey; (S) Ariel Balliff; (C) Elizabeth Novak; (L) Peter L. Willardson

Our Town, Thornton Wilder; (D) Charles Morey; (S) John W. Holman; (C) Elizabeth Novak; (L) Karl E. Haas

The Importance of Being Earnest, Oscar Wilde; (D) Geoffrey Sherman; (S) George Maxwell; (C) Elizabeth Novak; (L) Michael Clifford

The Pirates of Penzance, book: W.S. Gilbert; music: Arthur Sullivan; (D) Larry Carpenter; (S) Ariel Ballif; (C) Ariel Balliff; (L) Peter L. Willardson and Hugh Hitchens

Talley's Folly, Lanford Wilson; (D) Charles Morey; (S) George Maxwell; (C) George Maxwell; (L) Spencer Brown

A Chorus Line, book: James Kirkwood and Nicholas Dante; music: Marvin Hamlisch; lyrics: Edward Kleban; (D) Patti D'Beck; (S) George Maxwell; (C) David C. Paulin; (L) Peter L. Willardson

PRODUCTIONS 1986–87

Kiss Me, Kate, book: Samuel Spewack and Bella Spewack; music and lyrics: Cole Porter; (D) Larry Carpenter; (S) George Maxwell; (C) Elizabeth Novak; (L) Peter L. Willardson

Macbeth, William Shakespeare; (D) Charles Morey; (S) Ariel Balliff; (C) Elizabeth Novak; (L) Peter L. Willardson

The Man Who Came to Dinner, Moss Hart and George S. Kaufman; (D) Richard Russell Ramos; (S) Ariel Balliff; (C) Elizabeth Novak; (L) Gary P. Jung

Noises Off, Michael Frayn; (D) Charles Morey; (S) George Maxwell; (C) Elizabeth Novak; (L) Spencer Brown

Arms and the Man, George Bernard Shaw; (D) Charles Morey; (S) Mark Haack; (C) David C. Paulin; (L) Peter L. Willardson

Of Mice and Men, John Steinbeck; (D) Charles Morey; (S) Ariel Balliff; (C) Elizabeth Novak; (L) Karl E. Haas

On Your Toes, book: George Abbott; music: Richard Rodgers; lyrics: Lorenz Hart; (D) Patti D'Beck; (S) Ronald Crosby; (C) Elizabeth Novak; (L) Peter L. Willardson

Pittsburgh Public Theater

WILLIAM T. GARDNER
Producing Director

Allegheny Square
Pittsburgh, PA 15212-5362
(412) 323-8200 (bus.)
(412) 321-9800 (b.o.)

FOUNDED 1975
Joan Apt, Margaret Rieck, Ben Shaktman

SEASON
Sept.-June

FACILITIES
Theodore L. Hazlett, Jr. Theatre
Seating capacity: 449
Stage: flexible

FINANCES
Sept. 1, 1986-Aug. 31, 1987
Expenses: $2,725,163

CONTRACTS
AEA LORT (C), SSD&C and USA

The Pittsburgh Public Theater seeks to present the finest plays of the American and world repertoire to the widest possible audience in a city noted for its cultural diversity. We are also committed to the development of new works by such playwrights as Arthur Giron, Corinne Jacker and Marc Alan Zagoren. During the next few years we will devote much of the repertoire to the centennial celebrations of Eugene O'Neill in 1988, and Pittsburgh native George S. Kaufman in 1989. The 1987-88 season begins with a revival of *The Hairy Ape* and we plan two other O'Neill productions during the next three seasons, as well as three Kaufman comedies written with various collaborators. Our community outreach programs include performances for student, senior citizen and handicapped constituencies; professional internships; a speakers' bureau; programs in schools; and a developing professional affiliation with the Carnegie Mellon University drama department.

—William T. Gardner

Pittsburgh Public Theater. Catherine Butterfield and Thomas A. Stewart in *Serenading Louie*. Photo: Mark Portland.

PRODUCTIONS 1985–86

The Real Thing, Tom Stoppard; (D) Lee Sankowich; (S) Ray Recht; (C) Mary Mease Warren; (L) Kirk Bookman

Life with Father, Howard Lindsay and Russel Crouse; (D) Susan Einhorn; (S) Frank Boros; (C) David Murin; (L) Ann Wrightson

Master Harold...and the boys, Athol Fugard; (D) Larry Arrick; (S) Ursula Belden; (C) Flozanne John; (L) Kristine Bick

She Stoops to Conquer, Oliver Goldsmith; (D) Philip Minor; (S) John Jensen; (C) David Toser; (L) Kristine Bick

Gardenia, John Guare; (D) Stephen McCorkle; (S) Ray Recht; (C) David Murin; (L) Kirk Bookman

The Show Off, George Kelly; (D) Philip Minor; (S) Allen Cornell; (C) Ann Wrightson; (L) Jeffrey Ullman

PRODUCTIONS 1986–87

Serenading Louie, Lanford Wilson; (D) Lee Sankowich; (S) Ursula Belden; (C) Flozanne John; (L) Kirk Bookman

She Loves Me, book: Joe Masteroff; music: Jerry Bock; lyrics: Sheldon Harnick; (D) Peter Bennett; (S) Harry Feiner; (C) David Toser; (L) Kirk Bookman

Orphans, Lyle Kessler; (D) Mel Shapiro; (S) Karl Eigsti; (C) Karl Eigsti; (L) Kirk Bookman

The Play's the Thing, Ferenc Molnar; adapt: P.G. Wodehouse; (D) George Sherman; (S) Cletus Anderson; (C) David Murin; (L) Kristine Bick

Vikings, Stephen Metcalfe; (D) Lee Sankowich; (S) Eldon Elder; (C) Flozanne John; (L) Kirk Bookman

Princess Grace and the Fazzaris, Marc Alan Zagoren; (D) Peter Bennett; (S) Gary English; (C) Laura Crow; (L) Phil Monat

Playhouse on the Square

JACKIE NICHOLS
Executive Producer

ELIZABETH HOWARD
Administrative Director

51 South Cooper St.
Memphis, TN 38104
(901) 725-0776 (bus.)
(901) 726-4656 (b.o.)

FOUNDED 1968
Jackie Nichols

SEASON
Year-round

FACILITIES
Playhouse on the Square
Seating capacity: 260
Stage: proscenium

Circuit Playhouse
Seating capacity: 150
Stage: proscenium

FINANCES
July 1, 1986-June 30, 1987
Expenses: $454,000

Playhouse on the Square is completing its first season in a newly acquired and renovated old movie theatre. The move has enabled us to greatly expand our programming for young audiences, which we feel is essential for any theatre's growth. Our programming enables us to present morning matinees aimed at high school students for three of our regular full-length season productions, and two one-hour matinees for the elementary student. We feel it is extremely important that the event of "going to the theatre" is established at an early age and that we do not just 'take free theatre to the schools. Through our outreach company, A Show of Hands, we have also been performing a production of *Touch*, which deals with child abuse. The regular subscription season offers a wide range of themes and an opportunity for the family to experience theatre together.

—*Jackie Nichols*

PRODUCTIONS 1985–86

Evita, book and lyrics: Tim Rice; music: Andrew Lloyd Webber; (D) Terry Sneed; (S) Jackie Nichols; (C) Mauny Mesecher; (L) Steve Forsyth

Of Mice and Men, John Steinbeck; (D) Gene Crain; (S) Joe Ragey; (C) Mauny Mesecher; (L) Joe Ragey

Gypsy, book: Arthur Laurents; music: Jule Styne; lyrics: Stephen Sondheim; (D) Lester Malizia; (S) Susan Christensen; (C) Mauny Mesecher; (L) Tim Osteen

Spider's Web, Agatha Christie; (D) Ken Zimmerman; (S) Joe Ragey; (C) Renee Weiss; (L) Joe Ragey

A Midsummer Night's Dream, William Shakespeare; (D) Ken Zimmerman; (S) Steve Pair; (C) Renee Weiss; (L) Joe Ragey

Purlie, book: Ossie Davis; music: Gary Geld; lyrics: Peter Udell; (D) Vera Walker; (S) Kathy Haaga; (C) Renee Weiss; (L) Peter Bowman

'night, Mother, Marsha Norman; (D) Gene Crain; (S) Jim Manning; (C) Renee Weiss; (L) Steve Forsyth

Extremities, William Mastrosimone; (D) Julia Ewing; (S) Joe Ragey; (C) Renee Weiss; (L) Peter Bowman

K2, Patrick Meyers; (D) Brent Blair; (S) Alex Jankowski; (C) Renee Weiss; (L) Alex Jankowski

Baby with the Bathwater, Christopher Durang; (D) Gene

Playhouse on the Square. Archie Grinalds, Linda Brinkerhoff and Bates Brooks in *A Spider's Web*. Photo: Saul Rown.

Crain; (s) Kermit Medsker; (c) Mauny Mesecher; (l) Ray Fuller
Cloud 9, Caryl Churchill; (d) Barry Fuller; (s) Steve Pair; (c) Renee Weiss; (l) Peter Bowman

PRODUCTIONS 1986–87

A Chorus Line, book: James Kirkwood and Nicholas Dante; music: Marvin Hamlisch; lyrics: Edward Kleban; (d) Lester Malizia; (s) Kathy Haaga; (c) Renee Weiss; (l) Steve Forsyth
A Raisin in the Sun, Lorraine Hansberry; (d) Ken Zimmerman; (s) Kathy Haaga; (c) Renee Weiss; (l) Kathy Haaga
Peter Pan, book: James M. Barrie; lyrics: Carolyn Leigh; music: Mark Charlap; (d) Ken Zimmerman; (s) Joe Ragey; (c) Renee Weiss; (l) Joe Ragey
Auntie Mame, Jerome Lawrence and Robert E. Lee; (d) Ken Zimmerman; (s) Joe Ragey; (c) Renee Weiss; (l) Joe Ragey
Hamlet, William Shakespeare; (d) Ken Zimmerman; (s) Joe Ragey; (c) Renee Weiss; (l) Kathy Haaga
Nine, adapt: Mario Fratti; book: Arthur Kopit; music and lyrics: Maury Yeston; (d) Lester Malizia; (s) Kathy Haaga; (c) Renee Weiss; (l) Peter Bowman
Torch Song Trilogy, Harvey Fierstein; (d) Lester Malizia; (s) Kathy Haaga; (c) Kevin Pothier; (l) Peter Bowman
Quilters, book: Molly Newman and Barbara Damashek; music and lyrics: Barbara Damashek; (d) Vivian Morrison; (s) Mike Nichols; (c) Kevin Pothier; (l) Rick Moncrief
Top Girls, Caryl Churchill; (d) Carol Ries; (s) Gregory D. Boyd; (c) Renee Weiss; (l) Michael Cimbalo

The Playmakers

MARK HUNTER
Producing Artistic Director

SUSAN PAUL
Executive Director

Box 5745
Tampa, FL 33675
(813) 248-6933

FOUNDED 1981
Robert Hatch, Mark Hunter

SEASON
Oct.-May

FACILITIES
Cuban Club Theatre
Seating capacity: 304
Stage: proscenium

FINANCES
July 1, 1986-June 30, 1987
Expenses: $400,000

CONTRACTS
AEA SPT

The Playmakers have come together because we believe that the theatre represents a historically proven means to unite a diverse assortment of creative impulses emanating from a universal desire to narrate experience and celebrate mysteries. Theatre has always been a social phenomenon—a venue not only for the communion of artists but also for the communion of spectators who merge into a collective identity we call an audience. Only when these two elements interact dynamically do we experience the wonderful immediacy, electricity and creative energy that is the essence of live theatre. All good theatre entertains the senses as well as the mind. For Playmakers, it is the method by which we examine the human condition, explore ideas, acknowledge our confusion, rejoice in humanity and seek common truths.

—Mark Hunter

PRODUCTIONS 1985–86

Album, David Rimmer; (d) James Rayfiled; (s) Eric Veenstra; (c) Loren Bracewell; (l) Richard Sharkey
Short Eyes, Miguel Pinero; (d) Mark Hunter; (s) Charles Parsons; (c) Floy Carroll; (l) Richard Sharkey
Sherlock's Last Case, Charles Marowitz; (d) Richard Sharkey; (s) Barton Lee; (c) Bambi-Jeanne Stoll; (l) Charles Parsons
The Diary of Anne Frank, Frances Goodrich and Albert Hackett; (d) Robert Hatch; (s) Charles Parsons; (c) Floy Carroll; (l) Dan Gordon
Passion, Peter Nichols; (d) Mark Hunter; (s) Charles Parsons; (c) Loren Bracewell; (l) Charles Parsons
The Miss Firecracker Contest, Beth Henley; (d) Monica Bishop; (s) Charles Parsons; (c) Abby Lillethun; (l) Karl Schmitt
Torch Song Trilogy, Harvey Fierstein; (d) Robert Hatch; (s) Robert T. Williams; (c) Diane Keith; (l) Charles Parsons

The Playmakers. Candace Clark, Susan Alexander and Robin O'Dell in *The Miss Firecracker Contest*. Photo: Charles T. Parsons.

PRODUCTIONS 1986–87

Stop the World—I Want to Get Off, book, music and lyrics: Anthony Newley and Leslie Bricusse; (d) Mark Hunter; (s) Charles Parsons; (c) Loren Bracewell; (l) G.B. Stephens
Brighton Beach Memoirs, Neil Simon; (d) Robert Hatch; (s) Charles Parsons; (c) Loren Bracewell; (l) A.J. Sutton
On the Verge or The Geography of Yearning, Eric Overmyer; (d) Mark Hunter; (s) Charles Parsons; (c) Abby Lillethun; (l) Charles Parsons
Isn't It Romantic, Wendy Wasserstein; (d) Robert Hatch; (s) Robert Barnes; (c) Loren Bracewell; (l) Herbert Schmoll
Cat's Paw, William Mastrosimone; (d) Mark Hunter; (s) Charles Parsons; (c) Loren Bracewell; (l) A.J. Sutton
Loot, Joe Orton; (d) Paul Frellick; (s) Gerry Leahy; (c) Joanne L. Johnson; (l) Charles Parsons
The Rocky Horror Show, book, music and lyrics: Richard O'Brien; (d) Paul Hughes; (s) Alan S. Reynolds; (c) Loren Bracewell; (l) Charles Parsons

PlayMakers Repertory Company

DAVID HAMMOND
Artistic Director

MILLY S. BARRANGER
Executive Producer

MARGARET HAHN
Managing Director

203 Graham Memorial 052A
Chapel Hill, NC 27514
(919) 962-1122 (bus.)
(919) 962-1121 (b.o.)

FOUNDED 1976
Arthur L. Housman

SEASON
Sept.-May

FACILITIES
Paul Green Theatre
Seating capacity: 499
Stage: thrust

Playmakers Theatre
Seating capacity: 285
Stage: proscenium

PlayMakers Repertory Company. John Feltch, Steven Hendrickson and Tandy Cronyn in *Waiting for Godot*. Photo: Kevin Keister.

FINANCES
July 1, 1986-June 30, 1987
Expenses: $618,359

CONTRACTS
AEA LORT (D), SSD&C and USA

PlayMakers Repertory Company is dedicated to the actor as the center of the performance event. We are committed to the revelation of each play, not by the application of visual metaphor or directorially imposed thematic statement, but through the varying processes applied by the actor in the investigation of the material. Our repertoire is eclectic, and we hope that audiences are unable to anticipate our production "style" from play to play. We aspire to bring to classic and standard works the sense of excitement and discovery too often reserved only for new scripts, and to approach new texts with the discipline, skill and theatrical perceptions of a classically trained company. The interaction of our professional company with students in our training program is a vital aspect of our work: our students carry the results of our efforts to other stages throughout the country.

—*David Hammond*

PRODUCTIONS 1985–86

She Stoops to Conquer, Oliver Goldsmith; (D) Douglas Johnson; (S) Linwood Taylor; (C) Bobbi Owen; (L) Robert Wierzel
The Storm, Alexander Ostrovsky; adapt: David Hammond; (D) David Hammond; (S) Linwood Taylor; (C) Bobbi Owen; (L) Robert Wierzel

PlayFest '86, Three Plays in Rep:

The Dining Room, A.R. Gurney, Jr.; (D) Ben Cameron; (S) Linwood Taylor; (C) Suzanne Y. Wilkins; (L) Robert Wierzel
The Guiteau Burlesque, Dick Beebe; (D) Evan Yionoulis; (S) Linwood Taylor; (C) Bobbi Owen; (L) Robert Wierzel
Clarence Darrow: A One-Man Play, David W. Rintels; (D) John C. Fletcher; (S) Linwood Taylor; (C) John Owen Franklin; (L) Robert Wierzel

Much Ado About Nothing, William Shakespeare; (D) David Hammond; (S) Linwood Taylor; (C) Bobbi Owen; (L) Robert Wierzel

PRODUCTIONS 1986–87

Look Homeward, Angel, Ketti Frings; (D) David Hammond; (S) Linwood Taylor; (C) Bobbi Owen; (L) Robert Wierzel
Waiting for Godot, Samuel Beckett; (D) David Hammond; (S) Linwood Taylor; (C) Laurel Clayson; (L) Robert Wierzel
The Matchmaker, Thornton Wilder; (D) Evan Yionoulis; (S) Mark Pirolo; (C) Mark Pirolo; (L) Robert Wierzel

PlayFest '87, Three Plays in Rep:

A Doll's House, Henrik Ibsen; trans: Eva Le Gallienne; (D) Christian Angermann; (S) Linwood Taylor; (C) Bobbi Owen; (L) Robert Wierzel
The Human Voice, Jean Cocteau; trans: Anthony Wood; (D) Arthur Housman; (S) Linwood Taylor; (C) Marianne Custer; (L) Robert Wierzel
Lu Ann Hampton Laverty Oberlander, Preston Jones; (D) Craig Turner; (S) Linwood Taylor; (C) Laurel Clayson; (L) Robert Wierzel

A Midsummer Night's Dream, William Shakespeare; (D) David Hammond; (S) Rusty Smith; (C) Bobbi Owen; (L) Robert Wierzel

The Playwrights' Center

DAVID MOORE, JR.
Executive Director

2301 Franklin Ave., East
Minneapolis, MN 55406
(612) 332-7481

FOUNDED 1971
Gregg Almquist, Erik Brogger, Thomas G. Dunn, Barbara Field, Jon Jackoway, John Olive

SEASON
Year-round

FACILITIES
Seating capacity: 150
Stage: flexible

FINANCES
July 1, 1986-June 30, 1987
Expenses: $389,000

CONTRACTS
AEA letter of agreement

The Playwrights' Center is dedicated to providing playwrights at all levels with services that develop their skills while serving as an advocate for production of their work. To participate in Center programs a playwright can apply for core membership through a script submission process or become a general member by paying yearly dues. The Center provides space, professional actors, directors and dramaturgs for "cold" readings, non-performance workshops, staged readings and script critiques. Midwest Playlabs is a two-week development conference for six scripts. The Center awards fellowships annually to 12 writers, ranging in size from $5,000 to $10,000. Jones Awards are one-act play commissions for six Center writers. The Center provides information on playwright opportunities

The Playwrights' Center. James Williams in Storytalers' *Rainbow Wrapped Around My Shoulders*. Photo: John Cross.

and various services to playwrights. A Young Playwrights unit offers three-week summer writing conferences as well as a national contest and festival. Storytalers is a professional touring company that performs original works in schools and community centers. The Artist-in-Education program places playwrights in public school residencies. The goal of all Center programs is to provide playwrights with a place to develop their work without the pressure of production.

—Joan Patchen

Note: During the 1985-86 and 1986-87 seasons, Joan Patchen served as executive director. The listings below are the summer Midwest Playlab's workshops.

PRODUCTIONS 1986

Adagio West, L. Ray Wheeler; (D) Steven Dietz
The Deal, Matthew Witten; (D) William Partlan
The Monkees Come Out at Night, Tom Williams; (D) Susan Gregg
The Breathtaking Night Trains of Werner Schmidt, August Baker; (D) Susan Gregg
Retribution Rag, Buffy Sedlachek; (D) William Partlan
T Bone N Weasel, Jon Klein; (D) Steven Dietz

PRODUCTIONS 1987

The First Light Home, Rosemarie Caruso; (D) Oscar Eustis
Salvation, Buffy Sedlachek; (D) Alma Becker
Shooting Shiva, Shelley Berc; (D) Alma Becker
Little Trip to Venus, Gram Slaton; (D) Steven Dietz
The Wall of Water, Sherry Kramer; (D) Steven Dietz
What Jojo Wants, Ben Kreilkamp; (D) Ben Kreilkamp

Playwrights Horizons

ANDRE BISHOP
Artistic Director

PAUL S. DANIELS
Executive Director

416 West 42nd St.
New York, NY 10036
(212) 564-1237 (bus.)
(212) 279-4200 (b.o.)

FOUNDED 1971
Robert Moss

SEASON
Sept.-June

FACILITIES
Mainstage
Seating capacity: 156
Stage: proscenium

Studio
Seating capacity: 74
Stage: flexible

FINANCES
Sept. 1, 1985-Aug. 31, 1986
Expenses: $2,500,000

CONTRACTS
AEA Off Broadway and SSD&C

Playwrights Horizons is dedicated to the support and development of contemporary American playwrights, composers and lyricists, and to the production of their work. Playwrights Horizons seeks to provide its writers with skilled and talented collaborators, and with the time and freedom to take risks during the development of their work. Playwrights Horizons aims to provide affordable, challenging theatre to an audience of dedicated and informed theatregoers.

—Andre Bishop

PRODUCTIONS 1985–86

Paradise!, book and lyrics: George C. Wolfe; music: Robert Forrest; (D) Theodore Pappas; (S) James Noone; (C) David C. Woolard; (L) Frances Aronson
Anteroom, Harry Kondoleon; (D) Garland Wright; (S) Adrianne Lobel; (C) Rita Ryack; (L) James F. Ingalls
Miami, book: Wendy Kesselman; music: Jack Feldman; lyrics: Bruce Sussman and Jack Feldman; (D) Gerald Gutierrez; (S) Heidi Landesman; (C) Ann Hould-Ward; (L) Richard Nelson
Little Footsteps, Ted Tally; (D) Gary Pearle; (S) Thomas Lynch; (C) Ann Hould-Ward; (L) Nancy Schertler
The Perfect Party, A.R. Gurney, Jr.; (D) John Tillinger; (S) Steven Rubin; (C) Jane Greenwood; (L) Dan Kotlowitz
The Nice and the Nasty, Mark O'Donnell; (D) Douglas Hughes; (S) Loren Sherman; (C) Andrew B. Marlay; (L) Stephen Strawbridge

Playwrights Horizons. Dana Ivey and Morgan Freeman in *Driving Miss Daisy*. Photo: Bob Marshak.

PRODUCTIONS 1986–87

5th Annual Young Playwrights Festival:
Coup D'Etat, Carolyn Jones; (D) Art Wolff; (S) Rick Dennis; (C) Michael Krass; (L) Ann G. Wrightson
A Delicate Situation, Eve Goldfarb; (D) Mary B. Robinson; (S) Rick Dennis; (C) Michael Krass; (L) Ann G. Wrightson
Remedial English, Evan Smith; (D) Ron Lagomarsino; (S) Rick Dennis; (C) Michael Krass; (L) Ann G. Wrightson

Highest Standard of Living, Keith Reddin; (D) Don Scardino; (S) John Arnone; (C) David C. Woolard; (L) Joshua Dachs
Black Sea Follies, conceived and musical adapt: Stanley Silverman, from Dmitri Shostakovich; book: Paul Schmidt; (D) Stanley Silverman; (S) James Noone; (C) Stanley Silverman; (L) Ken Tabachnick
The Maderati, Richard Greenberg; (D) Michael Engler; (S) Philipp Jung; (C) Candice Donnelly; (L) Michael Orris Watson
Driving Miss Daisy, Alfred Uhry; (D) Ron Lagomarsino; (S) Thomas Lynch; (C) Michael Krass; (L) Ken Tabachnick
Three Postcards, Craig Lucas and Craig Carnelia; (D) Norman Rene; (S) Loy Arcenas; (C) Walker Hicklin; (L) Debra J. Kletter

Portland Stage Company

BARBARA ROSOFF
Artistic Director

RICHARD HAMBURGER
Acting Artistic Director

MARK SOMERS
Managing Director

Box 1458
Portland, ME 04104
(207) 774-1043 (bus.)
(207) 774-0465 (b.o.)

FOUNDED 1974
Ted Davis

SEASON
Nov.-May

FACILITIES
Portland Performing Arts Center
Seating capacity: 290
Stage: proscenium

FINANCES
June 1, 1986-May 31, 1987
Expenses: $730,784

CONTRACTS
AEA LORT (D) and SSD&C

Portland Stage Company serves a broad-based constituency through productions, artistic development projects and educational outreach programs. In selecting mainstage productions I focus on works that explore issues and themes relevant to the community through a variety of theatrical periods and styles. Our programs focus on the development of young artists through an intern program, and mature artists through providing new artistic opportunities. A network of programs has been developed to provide both adult and student audiences with further insights into the plays presented. These include humanities lectures, scholarly articles published in a company newsletter and a cable television series. Through in-school workshops we assist in the theatre education of elementary and high school students throughout the state.

—Barbara Rosoff

PRODUCTIONS 1985–86

Billy Bishop Goes to War, John Gray and Eric Peterson; (D) Mitchell Ivers; (S) Patricia Woodbridge; (C) Deborah Shippee O'Brien; (L) Jackie Manassee

Holiday, Philip Barry; (D) Barbara Rosoff; (S) John Falabella; (C) David Murin; (L) Jeff Davis

Master Harold...and the boys, Athol Fugard; (D) Alma Becker; (S) Tim Thomas and Laura Maurer; (C) Martha Hally; (L) Arden Fingerhut

Levitation, Timothy Mason; (D) Munson Hicks; (S) John Doepp; (C) Deborah Shippee O'Brien; (L) Jackie Manassee

Curse of the Starving Class, Sam Shepard; (D) Mel Marvin; (S) John Jensen; (C) Martha Hally; (L) Frances Aronson

The Cherry Orchard, Anton Chekhov; trans: Trevor Griffiths; (D) Barbara Rosoff; (S) George Tsypin and Byron Taylor; (C) Martha Hally; (L) Arden Fingerhut

PRODUCTIONS 1986–87

Handy Dandy, William Gibson; (D) Barbara Rosoff; (S) Jennifer Gallagher; (C) Susan Hirschfeld; (L) Jackie Manassee

The Real Thing, Tom Stoppard; (D) Mel Marvin; (S) Marjorie Bradley Kellogg; (C) Martha Hally; (L) Donald Holder

Stuff as Dreams Are Made On, Fred Curchack; (D) Fred Curchack

Long Day's Journey into Night, Eugene O'Neill; (D) Barbara Rosoff; (S) Arden Fingerhut; (C) Susan Tsu; (L) Arden Fingerhut

Year of the Duck, Israel Horovitz; (D) Barbara Rosoff; (S) Patricia Woodbridge; (C) Mimi Maxmen; (L) Jackie Manassee

Fifth of July, Lanford Wilson; (D) Barbara Rosoff; (S) John Doepp; (C) Martha Hally; (L) Donald Holder

Portland Stage Company. Jordan Roberts and Michael Murphy in *Curse of the Starving Class.* Photo: Stephen B. Nichols.

Puerto Rican Traveling Theatre. Ilka Tanya Payan and Jeannette Mirabal in *The Bitter Tears of Petra Von Kant.* Photo: Martha Swope.

Puerto Rican Traveling Theatre

MIRIAM COLON VALLE
Executive Director

PATRICIA BALDWIN
Managing Director

141 West 94th St.
New York, NY 10025
(212) 354-1293

FOUNDED 1967
Miriam Colon Valle

SEASON
Jan.-Sept.

FACILITIES
Seating capacity: 194
Stage: proscenium

FINANCES
Oct. 1, 1985-Sept. 30, 1986
Expenses: $472,307

CONTRACTS
AEA letter of agreement

For 20 years the Puerto Rican Traveling Theatre's two objectives have been to establish a bilingual theatre emphasizing Hispanic dramatists, both international- and U.S.-based, and to make these presentations accessible to the widest possible range of people. Our four programs continue to further these goals: a free, bilingual summer tour production travels throughout New York City annually; a training unit provides free, professional-level classes in the arts to minority students; our playwrights unit offers a free-of-charge page-to-stage play development program, including a staged reading series; our mainstage season has presented more than 50 bilingual productions, 46 of which have been English-language premieres. We perform in Spanish to reaffirm our proud Hispanic heritage while gaining a fuller understanding of the American way of life. We perform in English to provide a bridge which will enhance communication, not only with ourselves, but with a broader segment of the world around us.

—Miriam Colon Valle

PRODUCTIONS 1986

Bodega, Federico Fragauda; trans: Freddy Valle and Dennis Calandra; (D) Alba Oms; (S) Carl Baldasso; (C) Sue Ellen Rohrer; (L) Rachel Budin

The Bitter Tears of Petra Von Kant, Rainer Werner Fassbinder; trans: Fernando Masllorens and Federico Gonzalez del Pino; (D) Andre Ernotte; (S) Carl Baldasso; (C) Betsy Gonzalez; (L) Rachel Budin

The Birds Fly Out with Death, Edilio Pena; trans: Asa Zatz; (D) Vicente Castro; (S) Rafael Mirabal; (C) Rafael Mirabal; (L) Craig Kennedy

Lady with a View, Eduardo Ivan Lopez; trans: Manuel Ramos Otero; music and lyrics: Fernando Rivas; (D) Max Ferra; (S) James D. Sandefur; (C) David Navarro Velazquez

PRODUCTIONS 1987

A Little Something to Ease the Pain, Rene R. Aloma; trans: Alberto Sarrain; (D) Mario Ernesto Sanchez; (S) Rolando Moreno; (C) Kay Panthaky; (L) Rachel Budin

A Rose of Two Aromas, Emilio Carballido; trans: Margaret Peden; (D) Vicente Castro; (S) Janice Davis; (C) Gail Brassard; (L) Rachel Budin

Bodega, Federico Fraguada; trans: Freddy Valle and Dennis Calandra; (D) Alba Oms; (S) Carl Baldasso; (C) Sue Ellen Rohrer; (L) Rachel Budin

Remains Theatre

LARRY SLOAN
Artistic Director

JENNIFER BOZNOS
Producing Director

3319 North Clark St.
Chicago, IL 60657
(312) 549-7725 (bus.)
(312) 327-5588 (b.o.)

FOUNDED 1979
Lindsay McGee, D.W. Moffett, David Alan Novak, Earl Pastko, Jim Roach

SEASON
Sept.-June

FACILITIES
Organic Performance Center
Seating capacity: 232
Stage: flexible

FINANCES
July 1, 1986-June 30, 1987
Expenses: $354,840

CONTRACTS
AEA CAT

Remains Theatre is a group of actors, a stage manager, a small staff, a copier, a fight song and a table at the local bar. In its first seven years Remains explored the work of writers mostly outside the mainstream, such as Franz Xaver Kroetz, Richard Foreman, Spalding Gray, Herman Melville and others. The years were marked by much acclaim and the emergence of exceptional acting, both as an ensemble and individually. I joined Remains as its first artistic director in 1986 to lead the theatre into the next generation. We maintain a strong devotion to new works with writers-in-residence and also look to explore more eclectic programming—large but lesser-known plays such as Brecht's *Puntila*, ensemble-developed pieces and collaborations with artists from the other arts. We continue to challenge ourselves as a group, learn from our growing audiences and take an active role in Chicago's strong theatre community.

—Larry Sloan

PRODUCTIONS 1985–86

The Nest, Franz Xaver Kroetz; (D) Ted Levine; (S) Patrick Kerwin; (C) Natalie West; (L) Kevin Rigdon

Seventy Scenes of Halloween, Jeffrey M. Jones; (D) James Roach; (S) Patrick Kerwin; (C) Kathryn Kerch; (L) Mary McAuliffe

Days and Nights Within, Ellen McLaughlin; (D) Dennis Zacek; (S) Patrick Kerwin; (C) Mick Levine and Brenda McMahon; (L) Robert Shook

Puntila and His Hired Man, Bertolt Brecht; trans: Gerhard Nellhaus; (D) Larry Sloan; (S) Rob Hamilton; (C) Rob Hamilton; (L) Michael S. Philippi

PRODUCTIONS 1986–87

Highest Standard of Living, Keith Reddin; (D) Michael Maggio; (S) Michael S. Philippi; (C) Erin Quigley; (L) Michael S. Philippi

The Mystery of Irma Vep, Charles Ludlam; (D) Larry Sloan; (S) David Tennenbaum; (C) Jeffrey Kelly; (L) Mary McAuliffe

Road, Jim Cartwright; (D) Robert Falls; (S) Michael S. Philippi; (C) Kaye Nottbusch; (L) Michael S. Philippi

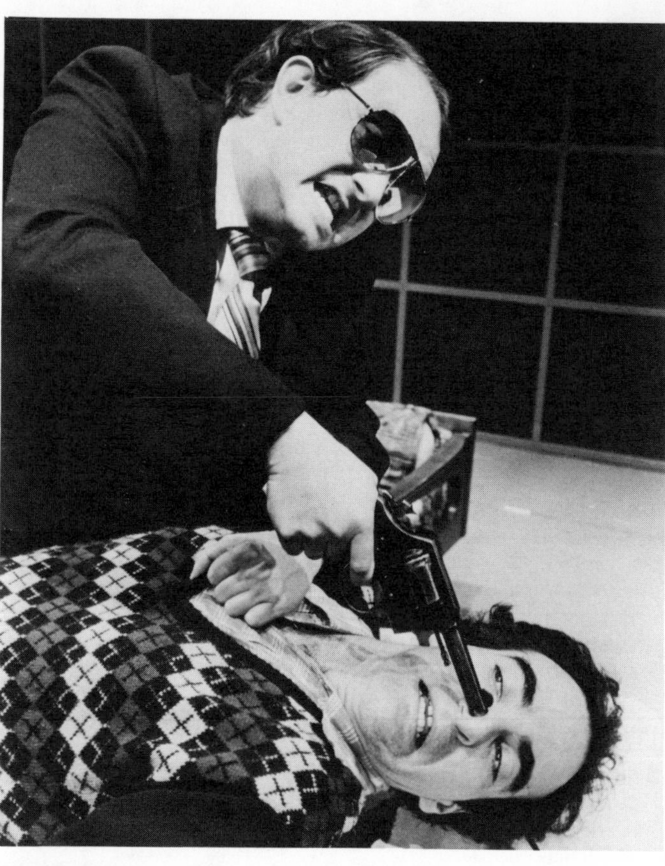

Remains Theatre. Alan Wilder and Alan Novak in *Highest Standard of Living*. Photo: Lisa Ebright.

Repertorio Español

RENE BUCH
Artistic Director

GILBERTO ZALDIVAR
Producer

138 East 27th St.
New York, NY 10016
(212) 889-2850

FOUNDED 1968
Rene Buch, Gilberto Zaldivar

SEASON
Year-round

FACILITIES
Gramercy Arts Theatre
Seating capacity: 150
Stage: proscenium

Equitable Tower
Seating capacity: 485
Stage: proscenium

FINANCES
Sept. 1, 1986-Aug. 31, 1987
Expenses: $1,014,000

Artistically, the past two years have brought us great satisfaction, with many advances made possible by our National Endowment for the Arts Ongoing Ensemble grant. It has given Repertorio Español the ability to do several important productions in repertory. A new, young breed of actor has joined our core group, challenging us by

Repertorio Español. Adriana Sananes and Rene Sanchez in *Fuente Ovejuna*. Photo: Gerry Goodstein.

their presence, bringing different training, experiences and philosophies to the company. I have been able to delve more deeply into projects I wanted to do while the productions by our new guest directors have been exemplary. A grant from the Wallace Funds has made possible the commission of new plays and the Mellon Foundation has provided funding for classic works. Touring appearances have expanded, and the musical company has developed into a real ensemble. The company is now presenting two eight-week seasons yearly at the new Equitable Tower. Our audience grows steadily in its size and diversity, so the future seems to hold great promise.

—*Rene Buch*

PRODUCTIONS 1985–86

Puerto Rico: Encanto y Cancion, various; (D) Rene Buch
Habana: Antologia Musical, various; (D) Rene Buch
Cafe con Leche, Gloria Gonzalez; trans: Rene Buch; (D) Rene Buch
Las Damas Modernas de Guanabacoa, Eduardo Machado; trans: Rene Buch; (D) Rene Buch
Fuente Ovejuna, Lope de Vega; (D) Rene Buch
La Fiaca, Ricardo Talesnik; (D) Delfor Peralta; (C) Robert Weber Federico
Yerma, Federico Garcia Lorca; (D) Christopher Martin; (S) Christopher Martin; (C) Christopher Martin; (L) Christopher Martin
Luisa Fernanda, Federico Moreno Torreba; libretto: G. Fernandez Shaw; (D) Rene Buch
Bodas de Sangre, Federico Garcia Lorca; (D) Rene Buch
Acto Cultural o Colon/Cristobal El Genoves Alucinado, Jose Ignacio Cabrujas; (D) Rene Buch

PRODUCTIONS 1986–87

Puerto Rico: Encanto y Cancion, various; (D) Rene Buch
Habana: Antologia Musical, various; (D) Rene Buch
Cafe con Leche, Gloria Gonzalez; trans: Rene Buch; (D) Rene Buch
Las Damas Modernas de Guanabacoa, Eduardo Machado; trans: Rene Buch; (D) Rene Buch
Fuente Ovejuna, Lope de Vega; (D) Rene Buch
La Fiaca, Ricardo Talesnik; (D) Delfor Peralta
La Zarzuela, various; (D) Rene Buch
Yerma, Federico Garcia Lorca; (D) Christopher Martin; (S) Christopher Martin; (C) Christopher Martin; (L) Christopher Martin
Luisa Fernanda, Federico Moreno Torroba; libretto: G. Fernandez Shaw; (D) Rene Buch
El Burlador de Sevilla y El Convidado de Piedra, Tirso de Molina; trans: Robert Weber Federico and Rene Buch; (D) Rene Buch
Prohibido Suicidarse en Primavera, Alejandro Casona; (D) Delfor Peralta

All productions, except Yerma, *had sets, costumes and lights designed by Robert Weber Federico.*

The Repertory Theatre of St. Louis

STEVEN WOOLF
Artistic Director

MARK D. BERNSTEIN
Managing Director

Box 28030
St. Louis, MO 63119
(314) 968-7340 (bus.)
(314) 968-4925 (b.o.)

FOUNDED 1966
Webster College

SEASON
Sept.-Apr.

FACILITIES
Mainstage
Seating capacity: 733
Stage: thrust

Studio
Seating capacity: 125
Stage: flexible

FINANCES
June 1, 1986-May 31, 1987
Expenses: $2,748,000

CONTRACTS
AEA LORT (B), (D), SSD&C and USA

Through its three performance venues—the main stage, the studio theatre and the Imaginary Theatre Company—the Repertory Theatre of St. Louis presents more services than any other performing group in the state of Missouri. The mainstage season offers the most accessible work to the public. Performing in a thrust theatre, our artists fill the space with work from varied sources—contemporary, classical, musical, American and world dramatic literature—presenting a mix of styles for our widest audience to experience. Our studio theatre explores the new, the old seen in new ways, poetry, music and sometimes season-long themes. The Imaginary Theatre Company is spreading the word about the Rep throughout the state—going into communities where people may have never seen live theatre before. Using literature as a base, this company is the mainstay of our outreach program. Our overall goal is to create a partnership with our audiences that infuses all of us with the vitality of live performance.

—*Steven Woolf*

Note: During the 1985-86 season, David Chambers served as artistic director.

The Repertory Theatre of St. Louis. John Cothran, Jr. and McKinley Henderson in *Sizwi Bansi Is Dead*. Photo: Judy Andrews.

PRODUCTIONS 1985–86

Twelfth Night, William Shakespeare; (D) David Chambers; (S) Oliver Smith; (C) Marie Anne Chiment; (L) Max De Volder
Under Statements, Susan Rivers; (D) Irene Lewis; (S) Kevin Rupnik; (C) Marie Anne Chiment; (L) Jennifer Tipton
Little Shop of Horrors, book and lyrics: Howard Ashman; music: Alan Menken; (D) M. Burke Walker; (S) Carolyn L. Ross; (C) Carolyn L. Ross; (L) Peter E. Sargent
The Mighty Gents, Richard Wesley; (D) Hal Scott; (S) Charles H. McClennahan; (C) Judy Dearing; (L) Allen Lee Hughes
Golden Boy, Clifford Odets; (D) Tony Kushner; (S) Jim Sandefur; (C) Jim Buff; (L) Max De Volder
A Streetcar Named Desire, Tennessee Williams; (D) David Chambers; (S) Carolyn L. Ross; (C) Marie Anne Chiment; (L) Max De Volder
The Marriage of Bette and Boo, Christopher Durang; (D) Jackson Phippin; (S) William Schmiel;

(C) Elizabeth Eisloeffel; (L) Max De Volder

Tom and Viv, Michael Hastings; (D) Peter Farago; (S) John Roslevich, Jr.; (C) Elizabeth Eisloeffel; (L) Max De Volder

Miss Julie Bodiford, James Nicholson; (D) Susan Gregg; (S) John Roslevich, Jr.; (C) Dorothy L. Marshall; (L) Glenn Dunn

Yes Yes No No, Tony Kushner; (D) Tony Kushner; (S) Tony Kushner; (C) Susan Hoffman

The Baseball Show, James Nicholson; (D) Wayne Salomon; (S) Larry Biedenstein; (C) Susan Hoffman

Actors on Acting, Tony Kushner; (D) Wayne Salomon; (S) Larry Biedenstein; (C) Susan Hoffman

Crossroads, Rhonnie Washington; (D) Rhonnie Washington; (S) Larry Biedenstein; (C) Susan Hoffman

PRODUCTIONS 1986–87

All My Sons, Arthur Miller; (D) Timothy Near; (S) Carolyn L. Ross; (C) Jeffrey Struckman; (L) Max De Volder

The Rainmaker, N. Richard Nash; (D) Jackson Phippin; (S) Timothy Jozwick; (C) Del W. Risberg; (L) Steven G. Rosen

The Foreigner, Larry Shue; (D) Edward Stern; (S) John Ezell; (C) Dorothy L. Marshall; (L) Peter E. Sargent

Sizwe Bansi Is Dead, Athol Fugard, John Kani and Winston Ntshona; (D) Jim O'Connor; (S) Arthur Ridley; (C) Arthur Ridley; (L) Peter E. Sargent

The Phantom of the Opera, adapt: Ken Hill, from Gaston Leroux; (D) Peter Farago; (S) Joe Vanek; (C) Jim Buff; (L) Max De Volder

Billy Bishop Goes to War, John Gray and Eric Peterson; (D) William van Keyser; (S) Dorothy L. Marshall; (C) Teri McConnell; (L) Peter E. Sargent

Lucky Lindy, Dick D. Zigun; (D) Russell Vandenbroucke; (S) Richard Tollkuhn; (C) Holly Poe Durbin; (L) Glenn Dunn

Beyond Here Are Monsters, James Nicholson; (D) Susan Gregg; (S) Dale F. Jordan; (C) Dorothy L. Marshall; (L) Dale F. Jordan

In Great Eliza's Golden Time, Tony Kushner; (D) Tony Kushner; (S) Tony Kushner; (C) Michele Friedman

The Protozoa Revue, Tony Kushner; (D) Kari Ely; (S) Larry Biedenstein; (C) Michele Friedman

Gendervision, Kimberly Flynn and Michael Mayer; (D) Wayne Salomon; (S) Larry Biedenstein; (C) Michele Friedman

Tales of South Africa, Charles Smith; (D) Wayne Salomon; (S) Larry Biedenstein; (C) Michele Friedman

River Arts Repertory

LAWRENCE SACHAROW
Artistic Director

BRUCE ALLARDICE
Managing Director

Box 1166
Woodstock, NY 12498
(914) 679-2493 (bus.)
(914) 679-2100 (b.o.)

FOUNDED 1979
Lawrence Sacharow, Mrs. Lawrence Webster

SEASON
June-Sept.

FACILITIES
Byrdcliffe Theatre
Seating capacity: 150
Stage: flexible

FINANCES
Apr. 1, 1986-Mar. 31, 1987
Expenses: $150,000

CONTRACTS
AEA SPT

River Arts Repertory is in summer residence at the Byrdcliffe Theatre in Woodstock, N.Y. Founded in 1908 by Ralph Radcliffe Whitehead as the first socialist utopian artist colony in America, the original artists and craftsmen came together to create a life away from the encroaching industrialization and technology in order to live in harmony closer to nature. River Arts Repertory presents a season of three plays on its main stage while hosting five writers-in-residence. The emphasis is on process and the collaboration among writers, directors, actors and designers. The resident writers present staged readings of their plays at whatever level or length their play reaches when the residency ends. The experience of developmental work going on in the same environment as fully mounted productions creates a context of work that nourishes the artists and puts the focus on striving for excellence in each person's work. When presenting a classic, we try to create an experience of being rooted in a here-and-now reality even while working in the period of Chekhov or Shakespeare. New work is presented that has been nurtured the summer before, or developed with the writer during the winter. Many of our plays go on to feed the mainstream of American theatre, both Off Broadway and in regional theatres. River Arts will soon present work during the winter in New York.

—*Lawrence Sacharow*

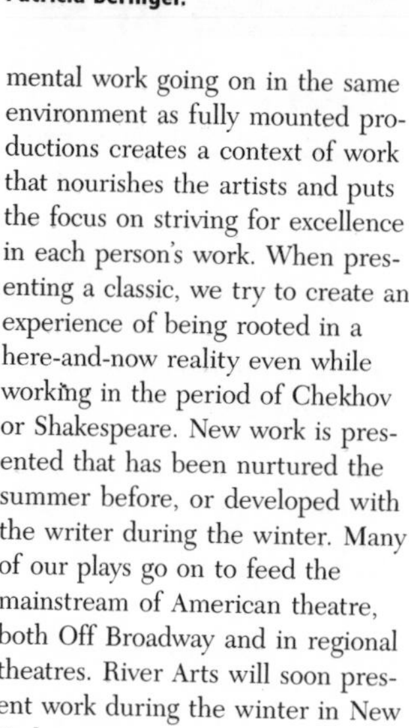

River Arts Repertory. Joanne Woodward and Edmond Genest in *The Seagull*. Photo: Patricia Beringer.

PRODUCTIONS 1986

The Concept, text: Casey Kurtti and company; conceived: Lawrence Sacharow; (D) Lawrence Sacharow; (C) Marianne Powell-Parker; (L) Frances Aronson

Insignificance, Terry Johnson; (D) Lawrence Sacharow; (S) Tom Kamm; (C) Marianne Powell-Parker; (L) Frances Aronson

Breaking Up, Michael Cristofer; (D) Michael Cristofer; (S) Marjorie Bradley Kellogg; (C) Marianne Powell-Parker; (L) Frances Aronson

PRODUCTIONS 1987

Dracula, Mac Wellman; (D) Len Jenkin; (S) Stephen Quinn; (C) Marianne Powell-Parker; (L) Frances Aronson

Casablanca, adapt: Michael Christofer, from Howard Koch, Julius Epstein and Philip Epstein; (D) Lawrence Sacharow; (S) Pepper Ross; (C) Marianne Powell-Parker; (L) Frances Aronson

Tea with Mommy and Jack, Sheila Walsh; (D) Lawrence Sacharow; (S) Tom Kamm; (C) Marianne Powell-Parker; (L) Frances Aronson

The Road Company

ROBERT H. LEONARD
Producing Director

Box 5278 EKS
Johnson City, TN 37603
(615) 926-7726

FOUNDED 1975
Robert H. Leonard

SEASON
Sept.-June

FACILITIES
The Down Home
Seating capacity: 175
Stage: flexible

Gilbreath Theater
Seating capacity: 375
Stage: thrust

Memorial Theater
Seating capacity: 650
Stage: proscenium

FINANCES
July 1, 1986-June 30, 1987
Expenses: $110,000

I believe theatre is a community event. The Road Company is a working environment for artists who want to apply their skills to the investigation and expression of our community in Upper East Tennessee. The ensemble works on the premise that theatre is a compact between the artists and the audience—artistically and organizationally. The successful theatre event happens when the audience joins the imagination of the production during performance. This belief assumes the enjoyment of theatre is active not passive. It also assumes a long-term relationship between the ensemble and the community. These concepts do not define or restrict subject matter, form or style. These are matters of constant investigation. What subjects are actually of concern? To whom? What style or form is effective within the framework of content and audience aesthetic? These issues and the artistic growth of the ensemble constitute the basis of our dramaturgy. We tour our own works to communities all over Tennessee and the nation.

—Robert H. Leonard

The Road Company. Eugene Wolf and Christine Murdock in *The Lovliest Afternoon of the Year.* Photo: June Manzer.

PRODUCTIONS 1985–86

Blind Desire, company-developed; (D) Robert H. Leonard; (S) Robert H. Leonard; (C) Kelly R. Hill, Jr.; (L) Robert H. Leonard

Echoes and Postcards, company-developed; (D) Robert H. Leonard; (S) company; (C) company; (L) Robert H. Leonard

Greater Tuna, Jaston Williams, Joe Sears and Ed Howard; (D) Robert H. Leonard; (S) George McAtee; (C) Cissy Sanders; (L) Robert H. Leonard

PRODUCTIONS 1986–87

Blind Desire, company-developed; (D) Robert H. Leonard; (S) Robert H. Leonard; (C) Kelly R. Hill, Jr.; (L) Robert H. Leonard

Echoes and Postcards, company-developed; (D) Robert H. Leonard; (S) company; (C) company; (L) Robert H. Leonard

Rupert's Birthday, Ken Jenkins; (D) Robert H. Leonard; (S) Margaret Gregg; (C) Margaret Gregg; (L) Robert H. Leonard

Chug, Ken Jenkins; (D) Robert H. Leonard; (S) Margaret Gregg; (C) Margaret Gregg; (L) Robert H. Leonard

An Educated Lady, Ken Jenkins; (D) Robert H. Leonard; (S) Margaret Gregg; (C) Margaret Gregg; (L) Robert H. Leonard

The Loveliest Afternoon of the Year, John Guare; (D) Robert H. Leonard; (S) Margaret Gregg; (C) Margaret Gregg; (L) Robert H. Leonard

Tartuffe, Molière; trans: Richard Wilbur; (D) Robert H. Leonard; (S) Margaret Gregg; (C) Margaret Gregg; (L) Robert H. Leonard

The Last Good Moment of Lilly Baker, Russell Davis; (D) Robert H. Leonard; (S) Robert H. Leonard; (C) Karen Brewster; (L) Robert H. Leonard

Roadside Theater

DUDLEY COCKE
Director

DONNA PORTERFIELD
Administrative Director

Box 743
Whitesburg, KY 41858
(606) 633-0108

FOUNDED 1974
Appalshop, Inc.

SEASON
Year-round

FACILITIES
Appalshop Theater
Seating capacity: 165
Stage: thrust

FINANCES
Jan. 1, 1986-Dec. 31, 1986
Expenses: $238,311

Roadside is an ensemble of actors, musicians, designers, writers, directors and managers, most of whom grew up in the Appalachian mountains. Appalachia is the subject of the theatre's original plays, and the company has developed its theatrical style from its local heritage of storytelling, mountain music and oral history. In making indigenous theatre and creating a body of native dramatic literature, Roadside sees itself as continuing this cultural tradition. Roadside's hometown has 1,200 people and its region's main work is coal mining. The theatre tours year-round, both within and outside the region, most often performing for folks who are not in the habit of attending theatre. Roadside is an integral part of the multimedia organization Appalshop, which also produces work about Appalachia through the media of film, television, radio, photography, music and sound recording, and visual art.

—Dudley Cocke

PRODUCTIONS 1985–86

Mountain Tales and Music, company-adapt; (D) company

Red Fox/Second Hangin', Don Baker and Dudley Cocke; (D) Don Baker and Dudley Cocke; (L) Don Baker

Brother Jack, book: Don Baker and Ron Short; music: Ron Short; (D) Don Baker and Dudley Cocke; (L) Ron Short

South of the Mountain, Ron Short; (D) Dudley Cocke and Ron Short; (L) Ron Short

Pretty Polly, book: Don Baker Ron Short; music: Ron Short; (D) Dudley Cocke and Ron Short; (L) Jerry McColgan

PRODUCTIONS 1986–87

Mountain Tales and Music, company-adapt; (D) company

Red Fox/Second Hangin', Don Baker and Dudley Cocke; (D) Don Baker and Dudley Cocke; (L) Don Baker

Brother Jack, book: Don Baker and Ron Short; music: Ron Short; (D) Don Baker and Dudley Cocke; (L) Ron Short

Roadside Theater. Kim Cole and Tommy Bledsoe in *Leaving Egypt*. Photo: Pastime Photo.

reacquaint ourselves with that actor's "impulse" toward theatre. Why theatre is needed becomes, simply and wonderfully, obvious. That joy comes full circle in the darkened room where the actor tells a story.

—*Jerry Whiddon*

PRODUCTIONS 1985–86

Fool for Love, Sam Shepard; (D) Susann Brinkley; (S) Richard H. Young; (C) Rosemary Pardee-Holz; (L) Scott Bethke
The Man Who Killed the Buddha, Martin Epstein; (D) Jerry Whiddon; (S) Richard H. Young; (C) Ric Thomas Rice; (L) Jane Williams
Sally and Marsha, Sybille Pearson; (D) Gillian Drake; (S) Jane Williams; (C) Rosemary Pardee-Holz; (L) Susan Munson
What the Butler Saw, Joe Orton; (D) Max Mayer; (S) Richard H. Young; (C) Rosemary Pardee-Holz; (L) Scott Bethke
Two Gentlemen of Verona, William Shakespeare; (D) Jerry Whiddon; (S) Richard H. Young; (C) Rosemary Pardee-Holz; (L) Jane Williams Flank

PRODUCTIONS 1986–87

The Water Engine, David Mamet; (D) Gillian Drake; (S) Richard H. Young; (C) Rosemary Pardee-Holz; (L) Jane Williams Flank
American Dreams, adapt: Peter Frisch, from Studs Terkel; (D) Kim Rubinstein; (S) Richard H. Young; (C) Rosemary Pardee-Holz; (L) Richard H. Young
Filthy Rich, George F. Walker; (D) James C. Nicola; (S) Jane Williams Flank; (C) Rosemary Pardee-Holz; (L) Richard H. Young
The Nest, Franz Xaver Kroetz; (D) Max Mayer; (S) Richard H. Young; (C) Marsha M. LeBoeuf; (L) Jane Williams Flank
Little Victories, Lavonne Mueller; (D) Gillian Drake; (S) Jane Williams Flank; (C) Catherine Adair; (L) Richard H. Young

South of the Mountain, Ron Short; (D) Ron Short and Dudley Cocke; (L) Ron Short
Pretty Polly, book: Don Baker and Ron Short; music: Ron Short; (D) Dudley Cocke and Ron Short; (L) Jerry McColgan
Leaving Egypt, Ron Short; (D) Dudley Cocke; (L) Jerry McColgan

FACILITIES
Seating capacity: 218
Stage: thrust

FINANCES
July 1, 1986-June 30, 1987
Expenses: $495,000

CONTRACTS
AEA Guest Artist

Round House Theatre

JERRY WHIDDON
Artistic Director

LINDA YOST
Producing Director

12210 Bushey Dr.
Silver Spring, MD 20902
(301) 468-4172 (bus.)
(301) 468-4234 (b.o.)

FOUNDED 1978
June Allen, Montgomery County Department of Recreation

SEASON
Oct.-June

Looking at music videos, one can get chills seeing how fast our perceptions of this world are changing, even down to the way linear thought is being broken into fragments—prisms that multiply angles and colors. Round House Theatre, though still devoted to the concept of developing and encouraging a company of actors, directors, designers and staff, is beginning to reflect these changes. The past two seasons have been devoted to sharing newer works, newer thoughts, newer voices with our audience. It is that dynamic —a newer challenging and rewarding adventure with the theatregoer—that drives us and that is at work for us on all levels, in all our programs. Indeed it imbues our programs with purpose. We welcome the commitment to make our art accessible through classes and performances in schools and senior citizen centers, and through these programs

Round House Theatre. Mark Jaster and Jim Wilder in *The Man Who Killed the Buddha*. Photo: Brian Eggleston.

Sacramento Theatre Company. David DiFrancesco and Janice Akers Wagner in *A Streetcar Named Desire*. Photo: John Kenneth Wagner.

Sacramento Theatre Company

DENNIS BIGELOW
Producing Director

1419 H St.
Sacramento, CA 95814
(916) 446-7501 (bus.)
(916) 443-6722 (b.o.)

FOUNDED 1949
Eleanor McClatchy

SEASON
Sept.-May

FACILITIES
McClatchy Mainstage
Seating capacity: 297
Stage: proscenium

Stage Two
Seating capacity: 80
Stage: flexible

FINANCES
Sept. 1, 1986-Aug. 31, 1987
Expenses: $723,650

CONTRACTS
AEA Guest Artist

Simple as it seems, our name—Sacramento Theatre Company—provides the best springboard for artistic definition. Sacramento is where we've chosen to live and work, its population is our audience. Our work is intended to entertain, provoke, please, stretch and occasionally jolt them. We work for their trust, secure in the knowledge that their dedication buys a future for the theatre. We recognize as our responsibility and privilege the presentation of a balanced season of the best classic and contemporary works, striving to make each and every one resonate to this Central Valley audience. All the while we see a greater responsibility: to discover the new voices in the American theatre. That's what the word "company" is all about. Our art is collaborative, and it's our goal to embrace the artists—living or dead, tried or untried—and give them a fulfilled present, and hopefully a more glorious future. We're small, yet our goals are great. Success comes only in small steps but we've survived this far.

—Dennis Bigelow

PRODUCTIONS 1985–86

The Time of Your Life, William Saroyan; (D) Dennis Bigelow; (S) William Bloodgood; (C) Debra Bruneaux; (L) Kathryn Burleson

Sisters: A Legend, Stuart Duckworth and Dennis Bigelow; (D) Dennis Bigelow and Stuart Duckworth; (S) Noel Uzemack; (C) Debra Bruneaux; (L) Kathryn Burleson

Night Must Fall, Emlyn Williams; (D) Dennis Bigelow; (S) Edward Duffy, Susie Owens, Dorothy Wictum and company; (C) Michael Chapman; (L) Kathryn Burleson

Billy Bishop Goes to War, John Gray and Eric Peterson; (D) Jacqueline Schultz; (S) Jerry Reynolds; (C) Ellen Sedor; (L) Jeff Sharp

Twelfth Night, William Shakespeare; (D) Dennis Bigelow; (S) Jesse Hollis; (C) Debra Bruneaux; (L) Maurice Vercoutere

Ashes, David Rudkin; (D) Larry Russell; (S) Jerry Reynolds; (C) Debra Bruneaux; (L) Maurice Vercoutere

A Streetcar Named Desire, Tennessee Williams; (D) Dennis Bigelow; (S) Paul Waldo; (C) Debra Bruneaux; (L) Kathryn Burleson

Master Harold...and the boys, Athol Fugard; (D) Mark Cuddy; (S) Jesse Hollis; (C) Debra Bruneaux; (L) Glenn A. Wade

Joy Solution, Stuart Duckworth; (D) Dennis Bigelow; (S) Jesse Hollis; (C) Debra Bruneaux; (L) Kathryn Burleson

What the Butler Saw, Joe Orton; (D) Dennis Bigelow; (S) Jesse Hollis; (C) Debra Bruneaux; (L) Kathryn Burleson

PRODUCTIONS 1986–87

Brighton Beach Memoirs, Neil Simon; (D) Dennis Bigelow; (S) William Bloodgood; (C) Debra Bruneaux; (L) Kathryn Burleson

Marry Me a Little, music: Stephen Sondheim; conceived by: Craig Lucas and Norman Rene; (D) Jacqueline Schultz; (S) Jerry Reynolds; (C) Michael Fitzpatrick; (L) Kathryn Burleson

Translations, Brian Friel; (D) Mark Cuddy; (S) Jeff Hunt; (C) Michael Chapman; (L) Maurice Vercoutere

The Gift of the Magi, book adapt, music and lyrics: Peter Ekstrom, from O. Henry; (D) Dennis Bigelow; (S) Ralph Fetterly; (C) Debra Bruneaux; (L) Keith Underwood

The Taming of the Shrew, William Shakespeare; (D) Dennis Bigelow; (S) Jeff Hunt; (C) Debra Bruneaux; (L) Kathryn Burleson

Noises Off, Michael Frayn; (D) Andrew Traister; (S) Jenny Guthrie; (C) Debra Bruneaux; (L) Kathryn Burleson

Crossings: One-Acts by Sacramento Playwright's Workshop:

Garlic and Sex, Sandra Rockman; (D) Jacqueline Schultz

The Bargain, Joyce Lander; (D) Jacqueline Schultz

Hot Stick and the Iceman, Steve Mackenroth; (D) Sandra Rockman

Bitchin' in the Kitchen, John Arnold; (D) Susie Owens

Civil Disobedience, Judith Piper; (D) Jacqueline Schultz

A Fine Romance, Marianne Crawford; (D) Sandra Rockman

You're Getting Warmer, Vicki L. Davis; (D) Susie Owens

Couvade, Richard Hellesen; (D) Tom Elliott

(All sets, costumes and lights for Crossings... were designed by Jenny Guthrie, Debra Bruneaux and Kathryn Burleson, respectively.)

Moonshadow, Richard Helleson; (D) Dennis Bigelow; (S) Jenny Guthrie, (C) Debra Bruneaux; (L) Kathryn Burleson

'night, Mother, Marsha Norman; (D) Jacqueline Schultz; (S) Jerry Reynolds; (C) Debra Bruneaux; (L) Geoff Korf

Orphans, Lyle Kessler; (D) Dennis Bigelow; (S) Jerry Reynolds; (C) Debra Bruneaux; (L) Kathryn Burleson

Little Shop of Horrors, book and lyrics: Howard Ashman; music: Alan Menken; (D) Dennis Bigelow; (S) Ralph Fetterly; (C) Debra Bruneaux; (L) Kathryn Burleson

The Salt Lake Acting Company. Tom Cramer and Leslie Rohland in *Out of Gas on Lover's Leap.* Photo: Jess Allen.

The Salt Lake Acting Company

EDWARD J. GRYSKA
Artistic Director

168 West 500 North
Salt Lake City, UT 84103
(801) 363-0526 (bus.)
(801) 363-0525 (b.o.)

FOUNDED 1970
Edward J. Gryska

SEASON
Sept.-June

FACILITIES
Seating capacity: 150
Stage: flexible

FINANCES
July 1, 1986-June 30, 1987
Expenses: $385,082

The Salt Lake Acting Company is dedicated to increasing the public's awareness of theatre. By producing a season of regional premieres and introducing new plays and new playwrights, the public is given a chance to see current national trends. We offer regular new play readings and tour regionally in an effort to develop new works and encourage new writers. The growing support of our community confirms the vital need of a theatrical experience here. We are indebted and attached to a community of artists. And we are committed to producing theatre with the highest artistic integrity, and to making a vital contribution to the cultural life of our city.

—*Edward J. Gryska*

PRODUCTIONS 1985–86

Danny and the Deep Blue Sea, John Patrick Shanley; (D) Edward J. Gryska; (S) Ladd Lambert; (L) Rory Maxwell

Saturday's Voyeur: Christmas '85, Nancy Borgenicht and Michael Buttars; add'l material: Edward J. Gryska; (D) Edward J. Gryska; (S) Ladd Lambert; (L) Shaun Elam, Cory Dangerfield and Ladd Lambert

Standing on My Knees, John Olive; (D) Nancy Borgenicht; (S) George Maxwell; (C) Sandra Sharp; (L) Spencer Brown

Idle Wheels, James Morrison; (D) David Kirk Chambers; (S) Cory Dangerfield; (L) Jack Vetterli

Angry Housewives, A.M. Collins and Chad Henry; (D) John Ogden; (S) Cory Dangerfield; (C) Susan Crotts; (L) Shaun Elam

PRODUCTIONS 1986–87

Little Shop of Horrors, book and lyrics: Howard Ashman; music: Alan Menken; (D) Edward J. Gryska; (S) Ladd Lambert; (C) Susan Crotts; (L) Jack Vetterli

Montana, David Kranes; (D) Kenneth Washington; (S) Kevin Myhre; (C) Susan Crotts; (L) Tom Pavich

Bigfoot Stole My Wife and Other Monologues, Ron Carlson; (D) Edward J. Gryska; (S) Kevin Myhre; (C) Susan Crotts; (L) Tom Pavich

Saturday's Voyeur: Christmas '86, Nancy Borgenicht and Michael Buttars; add'l material: Edward J. Gryska; (D) Edward J. Gryska; (S) Ladd Lambert; (L) Tom Pavich

The Foreigner, Larry Shue; (D) James Morrison; (S) Cory Dangerfield; (C) Doug Hansen; (L) Megan McCormick

Out of Gas on Lover's Leap, Mark St. Germain; (D) Edward J. Gryska; (S) Cory Dangerfield; (L) Tom Pavich

Brighton Beach Memoirs, Neil Simon; (D) Anne Cullimore Decker; (S) George Maxwell; (C) Doug Hansen; (L) Peter L. Willardson

San Diego Repertory Theatre

DOUGLAS JACOBS
Artistic Director

SAM WOODHOUSE
Producing Director

79 Horton Plaza
San Diego, CA 92101
(619) 231-3586 (bus.)
(619) 235-8025 (b.o.)

FOUNDED 1976
Douglas Jacobs, Sam Woodhouse

SEASON
Apr.-Dec.

FACILITIES
Lyceum Stage
Seating capacity: 550
Stage: flexible

Lyceum Space
Seating capacity: 250
Stage: flexible

Sixth Avenue Playhouse
Seating capacity: 190
Stage: thrust

FINANCES
Jan. 1, 1986-Dec. 31, 1986
Expenses: $2,112,863

CONTRACTS
AEA LORT (D)

San Diego Repertory Theatre. *Holy Ghosts.* Photo: Douglas Jacobs.

Based on the conviction that theatre continually reinvents itself through an ongoing blending of all the arts, the San Diego Repertory Theatre operates its three theatres as a multidisciplinary, multicultural arts complex. We produce our own season for nine months of the year; during the other three months we book, present or rent our theatre to other artists. Our eclectic programming is based on the belief that the arts should reflect the diversity of the world around and within us, and that the theatre is a uniquely appropriate place to explore the boundaries and borders of life and art. Our seasons emphasize contemporary plays, seldom-seen classics and revivals of well-known classics. We are committed to ensemble development, non-traditional casting, lifelong training for professionals, and to explorations of music, dance, visual arts and poetry, in order to expand and deepen the range of theatrical expression.

—Douglas Jacobs

PRODUCTIONS 1985–86

To Gillian on Her 37th Birthday, Michael Brady; (D) Joseph Hanreddy; (S) Mark Donnelly; (C) Clare Henkel; (L) Don Childs

Rap Master Ronnie, book and lyrics: Garry Trudeau; music: Elizabeth Swados; (D) Frank Condon; (S) Don Llewllyn; (C) Lisa Lovaas; (L) Rob Murphy

Quilters, book: Molly Newman and Barbara Damashek; music and lyrics: Barbara Damashek; (D) Sam Woodhouse; (S) Don Childs; (C) Mary Gibson; (L) Rob Murphy

Holy Ghosts, Romulus Linney; (D) Douglas Jacobs; (S) D. Martyn Bookwalter; (C) Ray C. Naylor; (L) D. Martyn Bookwalter

Top Girls, Caryl Churchill; (D) Meg Wilbur; (S) Dan Dryden; (C) Clare Henkel; (L) John B. Forbes

Little Shop of Horrors, book and lyrics: Howard Ashman; music: Alan Menken; (D) Sam Woodhouse; (S) Mark Donnelly; (C) Mary Gibson; (L) Peter Maradudin

Fool for Love, Sam Shepard; (D) Sam Woodhouse; (S) D. Martyn Bookwalter; (C) Ingrid Helton; (L) D. Martyn Bookwalter

The Strange Case of Dr. Jekyll and Mr. Hyde, adapt: Douglas Jacobs, from Robert Louis Stevenson; (D) Douglas Jacobs; (S) Ladislav Vychodil; (C) Mary Gibson; (L) Don Childs

Master Harold...and the boys, Athol Fugard; (D) Michael Addison; (S) Eric Sinkkonen; (C) Ingrid Helton; (L) Eric Sinkkonen

A Christmas Carol, adapt: Douglas Jacobs, from Charles Dickens; (D) Sabin Epstein; (S) Kent Dorsey; (C) Nancy Jo Smith; (L) Peter Maradudin

PRODUCTIONS 1986–87

I Don't Have to Show You No Stinking Badges, Luis Valdez; (D) Tony Curiel; (S) Russell Pyle; (C) Nicole Morin; (L) Russell Pyle

Hard Times, adapt: Stephen Jeffreys, from Charles Dickens; (D) Sabin Epstein; (S) D. Martyn Bookwalter; (C) Ray C. Naylor; (L) D. Martyn Bookwalter

Blue Window, Craig Lucas; (D) Sam Woodhouse; (S) Jill Moon; (C) Juli Bohn; (L) Peter Maradudin

Warren's Story, Kedric Robin Wolfe; (D) Scott Kelman; (S) Kedric Robin Wolfe and Alex Wright; (L) R.S. Hoyes

A Midsummer Night's Dream, William Shakespeare; (D) George Ferencz; (S) Rob Murphy; (C) Sally Lesser; (L) Peter Maradudin

Six Women with Brain Death or Expiring Minds Want to Know, Cheryl Benge, Christy Brandt, Rosanna E. Coppedge, Valerie Fagan, Ross Freese, Mark Houston, Sandee Johnson and Peggy Pharr-Wilson; music and lyrics: Mark Houston; (D) Sam Woodhouse; (S) Rob Murphy; (C) Sally Cleveland; (L) Peter Nordyke

The Genius, Howard Brenton; (D) Douglas Jacobs; (S) Mark Donnelly; (C) Nancy Jo Smith; (L) Kent Dorsey

A Christmas Carol, adapt: Douglas Jacobs, from Charles Dickens; (D) Sabin Epstein; (S) Kent Dorsey; (C) Nancy Jo Smith; (L) Peter Maradudin

San Francisco Mime Troupe. Sigrid Wurschmidt and Jesse Moore in *The Mozamgola Caper*. Photo: Cristina Taccone.

San Francisco Mime Troupe

COLLECTIVE LEADERSHIP

PATRICK L. OSBON
General Manager

855 Treat St.
San Francisco, CA 94110
(415) 285-1717

FOUNDED 1959
R.G. Davis

SEASON
Year-round

FINANCES
Jan. 1, 1986-Dec. 31, 1986
Expenses: $590,000

CONTRACTS
AEA Guest Artist

We are mimics not pantomimics. Believing that all art is political, that art that does not challenge the status quo supports it, we create plays and perform them to raise hell, to make people mad enough so that someday they will throw the bastards out. Our chosen form is comedy, because laughter lowers people's defenses against unwelcome truths, combined with music, because music has the power to raise their hopes. All our comedies are serious—they dramatize the conflict between the presently powerful and the presently powerless. We work collectively and across racial lines to prove the possibility of the future we present; we exist as a challenge to despair.

—Joan Holden,
Resident Playwright

PRODUCTIONS 1985–86

Crossing Borders, Michelle L'Enfant and Stephen Most; (D) Brian Freeman; (S) David Brune and Rinaldo Iturrino; (C) Jennifer Telford

Hotel Universe, Joan Holden and company; (D) Dan Chumley; (S) Paty Silver and Spain; (C) Jennifer Telford

Spain '36, Joan Holden; (D) Dan Chumley; (S) Timian Alsaker; (C) Timian Alsaker; (L) Timian Alsaker

The Mozamgola Caper, John O'Neal, Joan Holden and Robert Alexander; (D) Dan Chumley; (S) David Brune; (C) Jennifer Telford

PRODUCTIONS 1986–87

The Mozamgola Caper, John O'Neal, Joan Holden and Robert Alexander; (D) Dan Chumley; (S) David Brune; (C) Jennifer Telford

The Dragon Lady's Revenge, Joan Holden and company; (D) Arthur Holden; (S) Peggy Snider; (C) Jennifer Telford; (L) Stephanie Johnson

San Jose Repertory Company

JAMES P. REBER
Executive Producer

TIMOTHY NEAR
Interim Artistic Director

SHANNON LESKIN
General Manager

Box 2399
San Jose, CA 95109
(408) 294-7595 (bus.)
(408) 294-7572 (b.o.)

FOUNDED 1980
James P. Reber

SEASON
Nov.-July

FACILITIES
Montgomery Theatre
Seating capacity: 500
Stage: proscenium

FINANCES
July 1, 1986-June 30, 1987
Expenses: $1,770,000

CONTRACTS
AEA LORT (C) and SSD&C

San Jose Repertory Company is specifically dedicated to providing professional theatre for the people who reside in the San Jose area, often referred to as "Silicon Valley." The inhabitants of this region have lives that are filled with fast-paced, computerized, impersonal encounters and relationships. More and more our audience members live in separate, individual worlds apart from each other and from the rest of the world. San Jose Repertory Company attempts to provide these people not only with access to the ideas of contemporary and classical playwrights, but with a "humanizing" experience. It is the constant desire of San Jose Rep to produce plays that address our humanity and interpersonal relationships while emphasizing the actor, as opposed to the technological or mechanical aspects of theatre. What makes San Jose Rep a unique force in the community is our ability to gather people together to experience theatre. The actors, creating their version of a playwright's vision, interpreted by a creative director, supported by designers and technicians, offer San Jose an enriching, entertaining and often penetrating view into themselves.

—*James P. Reber*

San Jose Repertory Company. *Godspell.* Photo: Charles I. Savadelis.

Note: During the 1985-86 and 1986-87 seasons, David Lemos served as artistic director.

PRODUCTIONS 1985–86

Quilters, book: Molly Newman and Barbara Damashek; music and lyrics: Barbara Damashek; (D) David Lemos; (S) Barbara J. Mesney; (C) Marcia Frederick; (L) Barbara Du Bois

Passion Play, Peter Nichols; (D) Joy Carlin; (S) Michael Olich; (C) Warren Travis; (L) Peter Maradudin

A Man for All Seasons, Robert Bolt; (D) Kenneth Kelleher; (S) John Bonard Wilson; (C) Marcia Frederick; (L) Derek Duarte

Strange Snow, Stephen Metcalfe; (D) James Edmondson; (S) Ken Holamon; (C) Karen Mitchell; (L) Barbara Du Bois

007 Crossfire, Ken Jenkins; (D) Edward Hastings; (S) John Bonard Wilson; (C) Eliza Chugg; (L) Barbara Du Bois

Cyrano de Bergerac, Edmond Rostand; trans: Brian Hooker; (D) Kenneth Kelleher and David Lemos; (S) Vicki Smith; (C) Marcia Frederick; (L) Barbara Du Bois

Yup It Up, Roy Zimmerman; (D) David Lemos; (S) Steve Snyder; (C) Karen Mitchell; (L) Marc Cooper

PRODUCTIONS 1986–87

Godspell, book: John-Michael Tebelak; music and lyrics: Stephen Schwartz; (D) David Lemos; (S) David Lemos; (C) Ray C. Naylor; (L) Peter Maradudin

Vikings, Stephen Metcalfe; (D) Kenneth Kelleher; (S) William Bloodgood; (C) Cassandra M. Carpenter; (L) John G. Rathman

Translations, Brian Friel; (D) James Edmondson; (S) Richard R. Goodwin; (C) Frances Kenny; (L) Peter Maradudin

The Very Last Lover of the River Cane, James McLure; (D) David Lemos; (S) Ken Holamon; (C) Kate Irvine; (L) John G. Rathman

Master Harold...and the boys, Athol Fugard; (D) Kenneth Kelleher; (S) Vicki Smith; (C) Cassandra M. Carpenter; (L) Peter Maradudin

Tintypes, Mary Kyte, Mel Marvin and Gary Pearle; (D) Paul Barnes; (S) Ray C. Naylor; (C) Ray C. Naylor; (L) Peter Maradudin

Seattle Children's Theatre

LINDA HARTZELL
Artistic Director

MICHAEL R. PENDLETON
Managing Director

305 Harrison
Seattle, WA 98109
(206) 443-0807 (bus.)
(206) 633-4567 (b.o.)

FOUNDED 1975

SEASON
Sept.-June

FACILITIES
PONCHO Theatre
Seating capacity: 280
Stage: proscenium

FINANCES
July 1, 1986-June 31, 1987
Expenses: $700,000

CONTRACTS
AEA TYA

Seattle Children's Theatre is a leading provider of professional arts experiences for young people and their families. The mission of SCT is: to produce professional theatre for the young with appeal to people of all ages; to provide theatre education and theatre arts training, taught by professional artists, that ensure participatory experiences for young people; and to develop new scripts and musical scores for new theatre works for young audiences. To facilitate this mission, SCT offers a wide variety of programs to make the theatre accessible to as many children and their families as possible. In addition to the five mainstage productions performed annually at PONCHO Theatre, SCT offers year-round education for grades K-12. Classroom workshops, study guides and post-play discussions further enhance the educational experience of the main stage. SCT is most proud of its achievements in commissioning new works and adaptations. Of the 60 productions staged at PONCHO Theatre, 40 have been new works or new adaptations.

—*Linda Hartzell*

Seattle Children's Theatre. George Catalano, John Pribyl and Gordon Carpenter in *The Strange Case of Dr. Jekyll and Mr. Hyde*. Photo: Fred Andrews.

PRODUCTIONS 1985–86

The Former One-on-One Basketball Champion, Israel Horovitz; (D) Linda Hartzell; (S) William Forrester; (C) Sheryl Collins; (L) Claudia Gallagher

Puss in Boots, book adapt: Greg Palmer; music and lyrics: Chad Henry; (D) R. Hamilton Wright; (S) Jennifer Lupton; (C) Guy Beuttler; (L) Lee A. DeLorme

The Best Christmas Pageant Ever, Barbara Robinson; (D) Mark Sheppard; (S) William Forrester; (C) Rose Pederson; (L) Richard Devin

Robin Hood, adapt: Roger Downey; (D) Rex E. Allen; (S) Shelley Henze Schermer; (C) Sheryl Collins; (L) Lee A. DeLorme

The Strange Case of Dr. Jekyll and Mr. Hyde, adapt: Bruce Hurlbut, from Robert Louis Stevenson; (D) Linda Hartzell; (S) William Forrester; (C) Guy Beuttler; (L) Jennifer Lupton

Little Lulu, Chad Henry; (D) Linda Hartzell; (S) William Bloodgood; (C) Guy Beuttler; (L) Michael Davidson

PRODUCTIONS 1986–87

The Curse of Castle Mongrew, Roger Downey; (D) Linda Hartzell; (S) William Forrester; (C) Sarah Campbell; (L) Jennifer Lupton

Snow White and the Seven Dwarfs, book adapt: Greg Palmer; music and lyrics: Chad Henry; (D) Linda Hartzell; (S) Jennifer Lupton; (C) Guy Beuttler; (L) Patty Mathieu

Follow the Drinking Gourd: A Play about Harriet Tubman, Colleen J. McElroy; (D) Linda Hartzell; (S) William Forrester; (C) Sarah Campbell; (L) Jennifer Lupton

Tales of a Fourth Grade Nothing, book adapt: Bruce Mason, from Judy Blume; (D) Rita Giomi; (S) Janet Snyder Neil; (C) Guy Beuttler; (L) Collier Woods

The Three Musketeers, adapt: Bruce Hurlbut, from Alexander Dumas; (D) Rex E. Allen; (S) Jennifer Lupton; (C) Michael Murphy; (L) Richard Devin

Little Lulu, Chad Henry; (D) Linda Hartzell; (S) William Bloodgood; (C) Guy Beuttler; (L) Michael Davidson

Seattle Repertory Theatre

DANIEL SULLIVAN
Artistic Director

BENJAMIN MOORE
Managing Director

155 Mercer St.
Seattle, WA 98109
(206) 443-2210 (bus.)
(206) 443-2222 (b.o.)

FOUNDED 1963
Bagley Wright

SEASON
Oct.-May

FACILITIES
Bagley Wright Theatre
Seating capacity: 856
Stage: proscenium

PONCHO Forum
Seating capacity: 142
Stage: flexible

FINANCES
July 1, 1986-June 30, 1987
Expenses: $3,966,400

CONTRACTS
AEA LORT (B+), (D), SSD&C and USA

After 25 years Seattle Repertory Theatre has returned to practices that characterized its early years. A resident acting company is provided long-term employment, with each member performing four or five roles across a season of six mainstage and three Stage 2 productions. Two of the mainstage plays are presented in rotating repertory followed by a tour of both productions through the northwestern states and California. Plays selected for both stages blend the classics and contemporary work and usually include a premiere as the final production for each series. The commitment to new work is also reflected in workshop productions of four new scripts every spring. The schedule for the resident company often affords an opportunity to include major work on the main stage from such other nonprofit theatres as Yale Repertory Theatre and Music-Theatre Group.

—Daniel Sullivan

PRODUCTIONS 1985–86

The Merry Wives of Windsor, William Shakespeare; (D) Daniel Sullivan; (S) Ralph Funicello; (C) Laura Crow; (L) Pat Collins

All My Sons, Arthur Miller; (D) Edward Hastings; (S) Hugh Landwehr; (C) Robert Wojewodski; (L) Dennis Parichy

The Real Thing, Tom Stoppard; (D) Paxton Whitehead; (S) Robert A. Dahlstrom;

Seattle Repertory Theatre. *Richard III*. Photo: Chris Bennion.

(C) Laura Crow; (L) Neil Peter Jampolis

The Forest, Alexander Ostrovsky; adapt: Douglas Hughes; trans: Marina Coachman-Tarlinskaja and Vicki Yehling; (D) Douglas Hughes; (S) Loren Sherman; (C) Kurt Wilhelm; (L) James F. Ingalls

Fences, August Wilson; (D) Lloyd Richards; (S) Jim Sandefur; (C) Candice Donnelly; (L) Danianne Mizzy

Girl Crazy, book: Guy Bolton and John McGowen; music: George Gershwin; lyrics: Ira Gershwin; (D) Daniel Sullivan; (S) Ralph Funicello; (C) Laura Crow; (L) Pat Collins

Endgame, Samuel Beckett; (D) Douglas Hughes; (S) Ralph Funicello; (C) Laura Crow; (L) Dennis Parichy

Cat's-Paw, William Mastrosimone; (D) Daniel Sullivan; (S) Thomas Fichter; (C) Sally Richardson; (L) Rick Paulsen

PRODUCTIONS 1986–87

Richard III, William Shakespeare; (D) Daniel Sullivan; (S) Ralph Funicello; (C) Robert Morgan; (L) Pat Collins

You Can't Take It with You, Moss Hart and George S. Kaufman; (D) Douglas Hughes; (S) Hugh Landwehr; (C) Robert Wojewodski; (L) Dennis Parichy

Joe Turner's Come and Gone, August Wilson; (D) Lloyd Richards; (S) Scott Bradley; (C) Pamela Peterson; (L) Michael Giannitti

Noises Off, Michael Frayn; (D) Ron Lagomarsino; (S) Ralph Funicello; (C) Robert Wojewodski; (L) Craig Miller

A Moon for the Misbegotten, Eugene O'Neill; (D) Irene Lewis; (S) Ralph Funicello; (C) Robert Blackman; (L) James F. Ingalls

Red Square, Theodore Faro Gross; (D) Daniel Sullivan; (S) Richard Seger; (C) Robert Wojewodski; (L) Pat Collins

Landscape of the Body, John Guare; (D) Douglas Hughes; (S) Scott Weldin; (C) Rose Pederson; (L) Rick Paulsen

Curse of the Starving Class, Sam Shepard; (D) Denis Arndt; (S) Randy Richards; (C) Sally Richardson; (L) Robert R. Scales

The Understanding, William Mastrosimone; (D) Douglas Hughes; (S) Thomas Fichter; (C) Rose Pederson; (L) Robert R. Scales

The Second Stage

CAROLE ROTHMAN
ROBYN GOODMAN
Artistic Directors

ROSA I. VEGA
Managing Director

Box 1807, Ansonia Station
New York, NY 10023
(212) 787-8302 (bus.)
(212) 873-6103 (b.o.)

FOUNDED 1979
Robyn Goodman, Carole Rothman

SEASON
Nov.-June

FACILITIES
McGinn/Cazale Theatre
Seating capacity: 108
Stage: proscenium

FINANCES
July 1, 1986-June 30, 1987
Expenses: $712,000

CONTRACTS
AEA letter of agreement

The Second Stage was incorporated in July 1979. Our purpose is to produce plays of the recent past that we believe deserve another chance—including plays that were ahead of their time, not accessible to a wide audience, poorly publicized or obscured by inferior productions. The ability to rewrite is a skill that most playwrights have not had an opportunity to develop. In fostering this talent, the Second Stage is helping them to grow as artists. Thanks to our leadership, the concept of presenting previously produced contemporary plays has become an accepted and frequently imitated part of the theatre scene. At the same time, we have discovered it is difficult to insist that a playwright have a play produced elsewhere before we can consider it. Therefore, in 1982, we made a commitment to present new plays by our developing corps of writers.

—Robyn Goodman

The Second Stage. Wayne Tippit and Jeff Daniels in *Lemon Sky*. Photo: Stephanie Saia.

PRODUCTIONS 1985–86

Lemon Sky, Lanford Wilson; (D) Mary B. Robinson; (S) G.W. Mercier; (C) Connie Singer; (L) Stephen Strawbridge

Black Girl, J.e. Franklin; (D) Glenda Dickerson; (S) Charles H. McClennahan; (C) Ellen Ellis Lee; (L) Marshall Williams

Rich Relations, David Hwang; (D) Harry Kondoleon; (S) Kevin Rupnik; (C) Candice Donnelly; (L) Pat Collins

The Further Adventures of Kathy and Mo, Kathy Najimy and Mo Gaffney; (D) Don Scardino; (S) Andrew Jackness; (C) Gregg Barnes; (L) Joshua Dachs

PRODUCTIONS 1986–87

Coastal Disturbances, Tina Howe; (D) Carole Rothman; (S) Tony Straiges; (C) Susan Hilferty; (L) Dennis Parichy

Division Street, Steve Tesich; (D) Risa Bramon; (S) Bill Stabile; (C) Deborah Shaw; (L) Greg MacPherson

The Redthroats, David Cale

Little Murders, Jules Feiffer; (D) John Tillinger; (S) Andrew Jackness; (C) Candice Donnelly; (L) Natasha Katz

Shakespeare Theatre at the Folger

MICHAEL KAHN
Artistic Director

MARY ANN DE BARBIERI
Managing Director

301 East Capitol St., SE
Washington, DC 20003
(202) 547-3230 (bus.)
(202) 546-4000 (b.o.)

FOUNDED 1969
Richmond Crinkley, Folger Shakespeare Library, O.B. Hardison

SEASON
Oct.-June

FACILITIES
Seating capacity: 253
Stage: modified proscenium

FINANCES
July 1, 1986-June 30, 1987
Expenses: $2,395,910

CONTRACTS
AEA LORT (C), SSD&C and USA

The central issue of the Shakespeare Theatre at the Folger is the development of an American classical style for the 1980s and beyond. Our true challenge is to connect the technical demands made on the classical actor (vocal range, articulation of the text, etc.) and the necessary emotional life (including the larger-than-real-life feelings that Shakespearean characters experience in connecting themselves to the cosmos) to the full use of an actor's intellectual powers and a highly physical acting style. Our other concerns include the need to merge multigenerational artists in all areas of the theatre in a true collaboration; to continue our policy of color-blind casting; to expand our educational outreach programs; to address major social issues as the plays illuminate them; and to connect productively with the complex community in which we work and live.

—Michael Kahn

Note: During the 1985-86 season, John Neville-Andrews served as artistic producer.

PRODUCTIONS 1985–86

Othello, William Shakespeare; (D) Mikel Lambert; (S) Russell Metheny; (C) Ann Hould-Ward; (L) Stuart Duke

The Merry Wives of Windsor, William Shakespeare; (D) John Neville-Andrews; (S) Michael Layton; (C) Holly Cole; (L) Daniel M. Wagner

The Cherry Orchard, Anton Chekhov; trans: John Faro PiRoman; (D) John Neville-Andrews; (S) Ursula Belden; (C) Mark Pirolo; (L) Stuart Duke

The Miser, Molière; trans: Miles Malleson; (D) John Going; (S) William Schroder; (C) William Schroder; (L) F. Mitchell Dana

Twelfth Night, William Shakespeare; (D) Gavin Cameron-Webb; (S) Russell Metheny; (C) Gail Brassard; (L) Allen Lee Hughes

PRODUCTIONS 1986–87

Romeo and Juliet, William Shakespeare; (D) Michael Kahn; (S) Derek McLane; (C) Ann Hould-Ward; (L) Nancy Schertler

Mandragola, Niccolo Machiavelli; adapt: Peter Maloney; (D) Peter Maloney; (S) Joel Fontaine; (C) Martha Kelly; (L) James Irwin

The Winter's Tale, William Shakespeare; (D) Michael Kahn; (S) Robert Edward Darling; (C) Jane Greenwood; (L) Nancy Schertler

Love's Labour's Lost, William Shakespeare; (D) Paul Giovanni; (S) Robert Klingelhoefer; (C) Jess Goldstein; (L) Dawn Chiang

Shakespeare Theatre at the Folger. Mikel Lambert and John Wylie in *The Miser*. Photo: Joan Marcus.

The Snowmass/Aspen Repertory Theatre. Casey Kizziah and Steve Hunt in *Cyrano de Bergerac*. Photo: Frank Martin.

The Snowmass/Aspen Repertory Theatre

MICHAEL T. YEAGER
Producing and Artistic Director

Box 6275
Snowmass Village, CO 81615
(303) 923-2618 (bus.)
(303) 923-3773 (b.o.)

FOUNDED 1984
Ruth Kevan, Michael T. Yeager

SEASON
Jan.-Mar./June-Aug.

FACILITIES
The Snowmass Festival Theatre
Seating capacity: 253
Stage: thrust

The Wheeler Opera House in Aspen
Seating capacity: 488
Stage: proscenium

FINANCES
Sept. 1, 1986-Aug. 31, 1987
Expenses: $234,883

CONTRACTS
AEA letter of agreement

The Snowmass/Aspen Repertory Theatre is organized and operated as a true repertory company with one set of actors and one set of designers and directors for all of the plays in each season. Our seasonal repertoire is selected to present a wide range of theatrical experiences, and it is not unusual to find a popular modern farce playing side by side with a classical tragedy. The artistic focus of the company is on exploring the creative potential of the artform and ourselves as artists. Actors and staff are hired for their commitment to craft and imagination, and for their ability to collaborate creatively. Actors have to be capable of sincere character transformations; designers and directors must be capable of moving deftly from one style and genre to another. S/ART's goal, no matter what the play, is to make the production unique to both the artists who create it and the community within which it is created.

—*Michael T. Yeager*

PRODUCTIONS 1986

The Foreigner, Larry Shue; (D) Michael T. Yeager; (S) Steve Peterson; (C) David Robinson; (L) Steve Peterson
Misalliance, George Bernard Shaw; (D) Peter Syvertsen; (S) Steve Peterson; (C) David Robinson; (L) Steve Peterson
And a Nightingale Sang, C.P. Taylor; (D) Michael T. Yeager; (S) Steve Peterson; (C) David Robinson; (L) Steve Peterson
Androcles and the Lion, Aurand Harris; (D) Jane Page; (S) Steve Peterson; (C) David Robinson; (L) Steve Peterson
Brighton Beach Memoirs, Neil Simon; (D) Michael T. Yeager; (S) Steve Peterson; (C) Erin Quigley; (L) Steve Peterson
The Foreigner, Larry Shue; (D) Jane Page; (S) Steve Peterson; (C) Erin Quigley; (L) Steve Peterson
Rosencrantz and Guildenstern Are Dead, Tom Stoppard; (D) Michael T. Yeager; (S) Steve Peterson; (C) Erin Quigley; (L) Steve Peterson

PRODUCTIONS 1987

Little Shop of Horrors, book and lyrics: Howard Ashman; music: Alan Menken; (D) Michael T. Yeager; (S) Jack D.L. Ballance; (C) Diane Rininsland; (L) Steve Peterson
Baby, book: Sybille Pearson; music: David Shire; lyrics: Richard Maltby, Jr.; (D) Michael T. Yeager; (S) Jack D.L. Ballance; (C) Diane Rininsland; (L) Steve Peterson
Cyrano de Bergerac, Edmund Rostand; trans and adapt: Anthony Burgess; (D) Michael T. Yeager; (S) Donato Moreno; (C) Erin Quigley; (L) Steve Peterson
Noises Off, Michael Frayn; (D) Casey Kizziah; (S) Donato Moreno; (C) Erin Quigley; (L) Steve Peterson
Biloxi Blues, Neil Simon; (D) Michael T. Yeager; (S) Donato Moreno; (C) Erin Quigley; (L) Steve Peterson
Macbeth, William Shakespeare; (D) Michael T. Yeager; (S) Donato Moreno; (C) Erin Quigley; (L) Steve Peterson
Scapino, Jim Dale and Frank Dunlop; (D) Michael T. Yeager; (S) Donato Moreno; (C) Erin Quigley; (L) Steve Peterson

Society Hill Playhouse

JAY KOGAN
Artistic Director

DEEN KOGAN
Managing Director

507 South 8th St.
Philadelphia, PA 19147
(215) 923-0211 (bus.)
(215) 923-0210 (b.o.)

FOUNDED 1959
Deen Kogan, Jay Kogan

SEASON
Year-round

FACILITIES
Mainstage
Seating capacity: 223
Stage: proscenium

Second Space
Seating capacity: 60
Stage: flexible

FINANCES
July 1, 1986-June 30, 1987
Expenses: $415,862

CONTRACTS
AEA SPT

The primary goal of Society Hill Playhouse was and is to present great contemporary plays to Philadelphians who might not otherwise see them. For years we produced the Philadelphia premieres of such playwrights as Brecht, Genet, Sartre, Frisch, Beckett. England's Arden, Wesker and Pinter first played here. American playwrights like Arthur Kopit and LeRoi Jones were first seen in Philadalphia at this theatre. During the years, many experiments also done by other theatres of the world, were done by us in Philadelphia: public script-in-hand readings, playwrights' workshops, one-act play marathons, street theatre, youth theatre. Our interaction with Philadelphians, not just as spectators but in every aspect of making theatre, produced an expanding commitment and role in the community, affecting many people as an arts institution functioning well beyond just presenting plays. Our continued dedication to our original goals still leads us into new paths of community involvement.

—*Jay Kogan*

Society Hill Playhouse. James J. Mellon and Denice Hicks in *Careless Love*. Photo: Ray Buffington.

PRODUCTIONS 1985–86

Careless Love, John Olive; (D) John Albano; (S) Frederick D. Wright; (C) Thelma Peake; (L) Jeff Goldstein
Over My Dead Body, Michael Sutton and Anthony Fingelton; (D) Will Stutts; (S) Michael Powers; (C) Debbie Pokallus; (L) Jeff Goldstein
Quilters, book: Molly Newman and Barbara Damashek; music and lyrics: Barbara Damashek; (D) Deen Kogan; (S) Frederick D. Wright; (C) Thelma Peake; (L) Jeff Goldstein
Nunsense, Dan Goggin; (D) Dan Goggin; (S) Barry Axtell; (C) Debbie Pokallus; (L) Morris Cooperman

PRODUCTIONS 1986–87

Nunsense, Dan Goggin; (D) Dan Goggin; (S) Barry Axtell; (C) Debbie Pokallus; (L) Morris Cooperman
Handy Dandy, William Gibson; (D) John Albano; (S) Wynn P. Thomas; (C) Ralph Wilson; (L) Terry L. Franceschi
Begat, James L. Rosenberg; (D) Will Stutts; (S) John Ignarri; (C) Jacqueline Royle; (L) Liz Polanski
Kiss of the Spider Woman, Manuel Puig; trans: Allan Baker; (D) Randal Hoey; (S) Michael J. Hotopp; (C) Ralph Wilson; (L) Michael J. Hotopp

Soho Repertory Theatre

JERRY ENGLEBACH
MARLENE SWARTZ
Artistic Directors

80 Varick St.
New York, NY 10013
(212) 925-2588

FOUNDED 1975
Jerry Engelbach, Marlene Swartz

SEASON
Nov.-June

FACILITIES
Seating capacity: 100
Stage: flexible

FINANCES
July 1, 1986-June 30, 1987
Expenses: $150,000

CONTRACTS
AEA Non-Profit Funded Theatre code

Soho Repertory Theatre. Scott Whitehurst, Gerald Gilmore, LaDonna Mabry and Jaison Walker in *One Fine Day*. Photo: Gerry Goodstein.

Those who care about art in the 20th century are forced to worry about its relevance, a problem that did not exist before technology demystified much of the artistic process. Our colleagues who ignore the problem wind up producers not of theatres but museums. There is room for re-creation, but that ought not to be our main function. The creation of a relevant, live, three-dimensional aesthetic in the age of instant video can be a breathtaking challenge, if we regard it, as artists should, as a process more important than box office, community acceptance, and product, and if we refuse to be seduced into mistaking an economically or politically successful diversion for our real purpose. Soho Rep's goals are to re-create the rare dramatic literature of the past without becoming a museum, and to try to develop a theatrical aesthetic with risk-taking new material—maintaining at all times the right to fail.

—Marlene Swartz

PRODUCTIONS 1986

The Two Orphans, Adolphe D'Ennery and Eugene Cormon; trans: John Oxenford; add'l text: Julian Webber; (D) Julian Webber; (S) Daniel Conway; (C) Patricia Adshead; (L) David Noling

One Fine Day, Nicholas Wright; (D) Tazewell Thompson; (S) Joseph A. Varga; (C) Laura Drawbaugh; (L) David Noling

The Grub-Street Opera, book and lyrics: Henry Fielding; music: Anthony Bowles; (D) Anthony Bowles; (S) Alison Ford; (C) Gabriel Berry; (L) David Noling

PRODUCTIONS 1986–87

The Ragged Trousered Philanthropists, adapt: Stephen Lowe, from Robert Tressell; (D) Julian Webber; (S) David Nelson; (C) Patricia Adshead; (L) Nancy Collings

Sergeant Ola and His Followers, David Lan; (D) Tazewell Thompson; (S) Dale F. Jordan; (C) Eiko Yamaguchi; (L) David Noling

The Mock Doctor or The Dumb Lady Cured/Eurydice, book and lyrics: Henry Fielding; music: Anthony Bowles; (D) Anthony Bowles; (S) Joseph A. Varga; (C) Michael S. Schler; (L) David Noling

South Coast Repertory

DAVID EMMES
Producing Artistic Director

MARTIN BENSON
Artistic Director

Box 2197
Costa Mesa, CA 92628-1197
(714) 957-2602 (bus.)
(714) 957-4033 (b.o.)

FOUNDED 1964
David Emmes, Martin Benson

SEASON
Sept.-July

FACILITIES
Mainstage
Seating capacity: 507
Stage: modified thrust

Second Stage
Seating capacity: 161
Stage: thrust

SCR Amphitheatre
Seating capacity: 200
Stage: flexible

FINANCES
Sept. 1, 1986-Aug. 31, 1987
Expenses: $4,257,000

CONTRACTS
AEA LORT (B), (D), SSD&C and USA

South Coast Repertory commits itself to exploring the most important human and social issues of our time and to testing the bounds of theatre's possibilities. While valuing all elements of theatrical production, we give primacy to the text and its creators. Through premiere productions and an array of developmental programs we serve, nurture and establish long-term relationships with America's most promising playwrights. Around our core company of actors we have built a large and dynamic ensemble of artists, constantly infusing their work with the fresh perspective of artists new to our collaboration. We devote our financial resources to making theatre a viable and rewarding profession for all our artists. While striving to advance the art of theatre, we also serve our community with a variety of educational, multicultural and outreach programs designed to support our artistic mission.

—Martin Benson

PRODUCTIONS 1985–86

Galileo, Bertolt Brecht; (D) Martin Benson; (S) Susan Tuohy; (C) Robert Blackman; (L) Tom Ruzika

Before I Got My Eye Put Out, Timothy Mason; (D) David Emmes; (S) Cliff Faulkner; (C) Barbara Cox; (L) Cameron Harvey

The Foreigner, Larry Shue; (D) Ron Lagomarsino; (S) Robert Blackman; (C) Susan Denison-Geller; (L) Peter Maradudin

As You Like It, William Shakespeare; (D) Lee Shallat; (S) Cliff Faulkner; (C) Shigeru Yaji; (L) Peter Maradudin

Buried Child, Sam Shepard; (D) Sam Weisman; (S) Ralph Funicello; (C) Dwight Richard Odle; (L) Tom Ruzika

Jitters, David French; (D) Martin Benson; (S) Michael Devine; (C) Sylvia Moss; (L) Paulie Jenkins

A Christmas Carol, adapt: Jerry Patch, from Charles Dickens; (D) John-David Keller; (S) Cliff Faulkner; (C) Dwight Richard Odle; (L) Donna Ruzika and Tom Ruzika

Blue Window, Craig Lucas; (D) Norman Rene; (S) Cliff Faulkner; (C) Shigeru Yaji; (L) Paulie Jenkins

Painting Churches, Tina Howe; (D) Lee Shallat; (S) Mark Donnelly; (C) Shigeru Yaji; (L) Peter Maradudin

Driving Around the House, Patrick Smith; (D) Martin Benson; (S) John Ivo Gilles; (C) Charles Tomlinson; (L) Brian Gale

Unsuitable for Adults, Terry Johnson; (D) David Emmes; (S) Michael Devine; (C) Susan Denison-Geller; (L) Cameron Harvey

Virginia, Edna O'Brien; (D) Robert Berlinger; (S) Cliff

South Coast Repertory. John C. Moskoff and Tony Plana in *Charley Bacon and His Family*. Photo: Ron M. Stone.

Faulkner; (c) Sally Cleveland; (L) Paulie Jenkins

Tomfoolery, Tom Lehrer; (D) John-David Keller; (s) Charles Tomlinson; (c) Charles Tomlinson; (L) Donna Ruzika

PRODUCTIONS 1986–87

Highest Standard of Living, Keith Reddin; (D) David Emmes; (s) Ralph Funicello; (c) Susan Denison-Geller; (L) Peter Maradudin

All the Way Home, Tad Mosel; (D) Martin Benson; (s) Cliff Faulkner; (c) Shigeru Yaji; (L) Tom Ruzika

Three Postcards, Craig Lucas and Craig Carnelia; (D) Norman Rene; (s) Loy Arcenas; (c) Walker Hicklin; (L) Debra Kletter

Romeo and Juliet, William Shakespeare; (D) Edward Payson Call; (s) Cliff Faulkner; (c) Susan Denison-Geller; (L) Tom Ruzika

Charley Bacon and His Family, Arthur Giron; (D) Martin Benson; (s) Karl Eigsti; (c) Susan Denison-Geller; (L) Peter Maradudin

The Real Thing, Tom Stoppard; (D) Lee Shallat; (s) Cliff Faulkner; (c) Shigeru Yaji; (L) Paulie Jenkins

A Christmas Carol, adapt: Jerry Patch, from Charles Dickens; (D) John-David Keller; (s) Cliff Faulkner; (c) Dwight Richard Odle; (L) Donna Ruzika and Tom Ruzika

Cloud Nine, Caryl Churchill; (D) Jules Aaron; (s) Cliff Faulkner; (c) Shigeru Yaji; (L) Paulie Jenkins

Birds, Lisa Loomer; (D) Ron Lagomarsino; (s) Kent Dorsey; (c) Charles Tomlinson; (L) Cameron Harvey

Fool for Love, Sam Shepard; (D) Martin Benson; (s) Michael Devine; (c) Dwight Richard Odle; (L) Paulie Jenkins

Cold Sweat, Neal Bell; (D) David Emmes; (s) Michael Devine; (c) Nicole Morin; (L) Peter Maradudin

Beyond Therapy, Christopher Durang; (D) Warner Shook; (s) Robert Blackman; (c) Robert Blackman; (L) Tom Ruzika

Stage One: The Louisville Children's Theatre

MOSES GOLDBERG
Producing Director

DEBRA HUMES
Managing Director

425 West Market St.
Louisville, KY 40202
(502) 589-5946 (bus.)
(502) 584-7777 (b.o.)

FOUNDED 1946
Ming Dick, Sara Spencer

SEASON
Sept.-May

FACILITIES
Kentucky Center for the Arts: Bomhard Theater
Seating capacity: 626
Stage: modified thrust

Kentucky Center for the Arts: Large Rehearsal Hall
Seating capacity: 250
Stage: arena

Macauley Theatre
Seating capacity: 1,453
Stage: proscenium

FINANCES
June 1, 1986-May 31, 1987
Expenses: $723,030

CONTRACTS
AEA TYA

Stage One: The Louisville Children's Theatre provides theatre experiences for young people and families. Choosing plays for specific age groupings, we attempt to develop the aesthetic sensitivity of our audience, step by step, until they emerge from our program as committed adult theatregoers. We play to both school groups and weekend family audiences. Stage One is also committed to developing professionalism in theatre for young audiences, including upgrading compensation to the level of adult theatres our size. We perform an eclectic repertoire, including traditional children's plays, company-created pieces, commissioned plays, plays translated from other cultures and carefully selected works from the adult repertoire. Stage One operates in the belief that the classics (both ancient and modern) of folk and children's literature contain archetypal human relationships which make them compelling subjects for dramatization. We hope to preserve the complexities of these tales, while introducing new audiences to the power of living theatre.

—*Moses Goldberg*

Stage One: The Louisville Children's Theatre. Geoffrey Hobin, Deborah Rhodes, Thomas James O'Leary, William Groth and Jill Susan Meyers in *Hey, There - Hello!*. Photo: Kenneth Hayden.

PRODUCTIONS 1985–86

The Tale of Peter Rabbit, Beatrix Potter; (D) Ingrid Gunderson; (s) Randal R. Cochran; (c) Doug Watts; (L) H. Charles Schmidt

Everyone Is Good for Something, Beatrice Schenk de Regniers; (D) Curt L. Tofteland; (s) John Michael Roberts; (c) Doug Watts; (L) H. Charles Schmidt

Cinderella, adapt: Moses Goldberg; (D) Moses Goldberg; (s) Randal R. Cochran; (c) Doug Watts; (L) H. Charles Schmidt

Jungalbook, adapt: Edward Mast, from Rudyard Kipling; (D) Moses Goldberg; (s) Randal R. Cochran; (c) Doug Watts; (L) H. Charles Schmidt

The Miracle Worker, William Gibson; (D) Mary Hall Surface; (s) Randal R. Cochran; (c) Doug Watts; (L) H. Charles Schmidt

Johnny Tremain, book adapt: Moses Goldberg, from Esther Forbes; music and lyrics: David Humphrey; (D) Moses Goldberg; (s) Randal R. Cochran; (c) Doug Watts; (L) H. Charles Schmidt

Hansel and Gretel, adapt: Moses Goldberg; (D) Curt L. Tofteland; (s) Randal R. Cochran; (c) Doug Watts; (L) H. Charles Schmidt

PRODUCTIONS 1986–87

Rumplestiltskin, adapt: Moses Goldberg, from Brothers Grimm; (D) Moses Goldberg; (s) H. Charles Schmidt; (c) Connie Furr; (L) H. Charles Schmidt

The Legend of Sleepy Hollow, adapt: Frederick Gaines, from Washington Irving; (D) Bain Boehlke; (s) Michael Cottom; (c) Daniel Fedie; (L) H. Charles Schmidt

The Snow Queen, adapt: Suria Saint-Denis and Rudolf Weil, from Hans Christian Andersen; (D) Moses Goldberg; (s) John Saari; (c) Connie Furr; (L) H. Charles Schmidt

Little Red Riding Hood and ***The Three Little Pigs***, adapt: Curt L. Tofteland; (D) Curt L. Tofteland; (s) Karen Kay Kinkor and Michael Cottom; (c) Daniel Fedie

The Death and Life of Sherlock Holmes, Susan Zeder; (D) Moses Goldberg; (s) Gary C. Eckhart; (c) Connie Furr; (L) H. Charles Schmidt

Charlotte's Web, adapt: Joseph Robinette, from E.B. White; (D) Moses Goldberg; (s) Sharon Perlmutter; (c) Connie Furr; (L) H. Charles Schmidt

Hey, There—Hello!, Gennadi Mamlin; trans: Miriam Morton; (D) Moses Goldberg and Geoffrey Hobin; (s) Michael Cottom; (c) Connie Furr; (L) H. Charles Schmidt

Stage West

JERRY RUSSELL
Artistic/Managing Director

Box 2587
Fort Worth, TX 76113
(817) 332-6265 (bus.)
(817) 332-6238 (b.o.)

FOUNDED 1979
Jerry Russell

SEASON
Year-round

FACILITIES
Seating capacity: 167
Stage: proscenium

FINANCES
Sept. 1, 1986-Aug. 31, 1987
Expenses: $402,000

CONTRACTS
AEA SPT

Stage West has established the only professional theatre that Fort Worth has ever known. From a beginning with no outside support and only the commitment of our founders, we have grown to over 1,500 subscribers, the second highest annual attendance among the city's performing arts groups, and have gained an enviable reputation in the Dallas-Fort Worth area. Our play selection philosophy is broad-based, with each season containing a mix of contemporary and period pieces, musicals, classical adaptations and original works. We are committed to producing one new work each season. Future objectives include the building of a new 350-seat theatre, the redevelopment of our experimental performing space and advancement to LORT contract status with Actors' Equity Association. To date, budgets have allowed only local casting. The next five years should see an expansion in our casting policies, and possibly a small resident company.

—*Jerry Russell*

Stage West. Gail Cronauer and James Tasse in *A Midsummer Night's Dream*. Photo: Buddy Myers.

PRODUCTIONS 1985–86

Loot, Joe Orton; (D) Jerry Russell; (S) Mark Walker; (C) Jim Covault; (L) Michael O'Brien

Breakfast with Les and Bess, Lee Kalcheim; (D) Jim Covault; (S) Mark Walker; (C) Jim Covault; (L) Michael O'Brien

Greater Tuna, Joe Sears, Jaston Williams and Ed Howard; (D) Jerry Russell; (S) Jim Covault; (C) Jim Covault; (L) Michael O'Brien

Foxcodd, Ted Enik and Kip Rosser; (D) J. Center; (S) Mark Walker; (C) Jim Covault; (L) Michael O'Brien

Piaf, Pam Gems; (D) Jerry Russell; (S) Mark Walker; (C) Jim Covault; (L) Michael O'Brien

The Miser, Molière; (D) Jim Covault; (S) Mark Walker; (C) Jim Covault; (L) Michael O'Brien

Fool for Love, Sam Shepard; (D) Jerry Russell; (S) Jim Covault; (C) Jim Covault; (L) Michael O'Brien

StageWest. William Meisle and Kathryn Meisle in *As You Like It*. Photo: Carl Bartels.

Waiting for Godot, Samuel Beckett; (D) Jim Covault; (S) Jim Covault; (C) Jim Covault; (L) Michael O'Brien

Brighton Beach Memoirs, Neil Simon; (D) Jerry Russell; (S) Jim Covault; (C) Jim Covault; (L) Michael O'Brien

PRODUCTIONS 1986–87

A Man for All Seasons, Robert Bolt; (D) Pam McDaniel; (S) Dale Domm; (C) Jim Covault; (L) Michael O'Brien

Season's Greetings, Alan Ayckbourn; (D) Jerry Russell; (S) Matt Aston; (C) Jim Covault; (L) Michael O'Brien

Perfectly Frank, conceived: Kenny Solms; music and lyrics: Frank Loesser; (D) Jerry Russell; (S) Jim Covault; (C) Jim Covault; (L) Michael O'Brien

Starry Night, Monte Merrick; (D) Jerry Russell; (S) Dale Domm; (C) Jim Covault; (L) Michael O'Brien

Orphans, Lyle Kessler; (D) Jim Covault; (S) Matt Aston; (C) Jim Covault; (L) Michael O'Brien

A Midsummer Night's Dream, William Shakespeare; (D) Jim Covault; (S) Dale Domm; (C) Jim Covault; (L) Michael O'Brien

Holiday, Philip Barry; (D) Jerry Russell; (S) Jim Covault; (C) Jim Covault; (L) Michael O'Brien

Heroes Left Behind, Mark Oristano and R. Brent Keis; (D) Jerry Russell; (S) Jim Covault; (C) Jim Covault; (L) Michael O'Brien

Cabaret, book: Joe Masteroff; music: John Kander; lyrics: Fred Ebb; (D) Jim Covault; (S) Dale Domm; (C) Jim Covault; (L) Michael O'Brien

StageWest

GREGORY BOYD
Artistic Director

MARVIN WEAVER
Managing Director

One Columbus Center
Springfield, MA 01103
(413) 781-4470 (bus.)
(413) 781-2340 (b.o.)

FOUNDED 1967
Stephen E. Hays

SEASON
Oct.-June

FACILITIES
S. Prestley Blake Theatre
Seating capacity: 447
Stage: thrust

Winnifred Arms Studio Theatre
Seating capacity: 99
Stage: flexible

FINANCES
July 1, 1986-June 30, 1987
Expenses: $1,700,000

CONTRACTS
AEA LORT (C), (D) and SSD&C

StageWest's artistic identity is reflected in its commitment to a company of artists whose ongoing collaboration in a varied and expanding repertoire forms the central condition of our work. The goals of the theatre are to develop and cultivate the artists; to revitalize "classic" texts and produce important neglected plays; to produce new work and new writing (especially that of American theatre artists); to train and develop young talent; and to continue to collaborate with other theatre companies. Ongoing classes for students and special projects in research and development continue throughout the season. An intern acting company works alongside the Equity company all season long, and daily classes in the Suzuki method of actor training are offered to every company member throughout the season.

—Gregory Boyd

PRODUCTIONS 1985–86

As You Like It, William Shakespeare; (D) Gregory Boyd; (S) Peter David Gould; (C) V. Jane Suttell; (L) Robert Jared
Peter Pan, J.M. Barrie; (D) Gregory Boyd; (S) Peter David Gould; (C) V. Jane Suttell; (L) Robert Jared
Painting Churches, Tina Howe; (D) Eric Hill; (S) Jeffrey Struckman; (C) Jeffrey Struckman; (L) Robert Jared
Happy Days, Samuel Beckett; (D) Gregory Boyd; (S) Peter David Gould; (C) V. Jane Suttell; (L) Robert Jared
U.S.A., Paul Shyre and John Dos Passos; (D) Gregory Boyd; (S) Peter David Gould; (C) V. Jane Suttell; (L) Robert Jared
A Flea in Her Ear, Georges Feydeau; trans: Douglas Johnson; (D) Douglas Johnson; (S) Jeffrey Struckman; (C) Sam Fleming; (L) Robert Jared
Courage, John Pielmeier; (D) Nancy Niles Sexton; (S) Jeffrey Struckman; (C) Jeffrey Struckman; (L) Robert Jared

PRODUCTIONS 1986–87

The Novelist, Howard Fast; (D) Gregory Boyd; (S) Peter David Gould; (C) V. Jane Suttell; (L) Robert Jared
Guys and Dolls, book: Jo Swerling and Abe Burrows; music and lyrics: Frank Loesser; (D) Gregory Boyd; (S) Rusty Smith; (C) Rusty Smith; (L) Robert Jared
The Crucible, Arthur Miller; (D) Jean-Bernard Bucky; (S) Hugh Landwehr; (C) Frances Blau; (L) Arden Fingerhut
A Midsummer Night's Dream, William Shakespeare; (D) Gregory Boyd; (S) Hugh Landwehr; (C) Sam Fleming; (L) Robert Jared
Cat's-Paw, William Mastrosimone; (D) Eric Hill; (S) Jennifer Gallagher; (C) Douglas Fisher; (L) Robert Jared
The Foreigner, Larry Shue; (D) Gregory Boyd; (S) Jennifer Gallagher; (C) Frances Blau; (L) Robert W. Rosentel

Steppenwolf Theatre Company

Steppenwolf Theatre Company. Francis Guinan, Danny Glover and Joan Allen in *A Lesson from Aloes*. Photo: Lisa Ebright.

RANDALL ARNEY
JEFF PERRY
Artistic Directors

STEPHEN B. EICH
Managing Director

2851 North Halsted St.
Chicago, IL 60657
(312) 472-4515 (bus.)
(312) 472-4141 (b.o.)

FOUNDED 1976
Terry Kinney, Jeff Perry, Gary Sinise

SEASON
Sept.-July

FACILITIES
Seating capacity: 211
Stage: thrust

FINANCES
Oct. 1, 1985-Sept. 30, 1986
Expenses: $1,382,003

CONTRACTS
AEA CAT

Steppenwolf Theatre is committed to the concept of a community of actors, directors and designers working closely together with a common artistic vision. With a 21-member ensemble of actor-directors producing a wide-ranging repertoire, Steppenwolf aims to provide great theatre through a collective approach to dramatic art—an approach conducive to artistic growth and thus challenging to audience and actor alike. Each artist's commitment to the ensemble approach testifies to its worth: seven of nine original members are still with the group after 11 years. Steppenwolf strives to achieve that rare combination: talented individuals who put the group effort first and simultaneously develop their own individual potential. Steppenwolf now possesses the desire and ability to tackle new challenges—the commissioning of new works, ensemble/playwright residencies, local and national productions, and production exchange. The theatre remains committed to maintaining a permanent resident company in Chicago and to promoting the goals of the ensemble by the presentation of its work to new audiences.

—Randall Arney, Jeff Perry

Note: During the 1985-86 season, Gary Sinise served as artistic director.

PRODUCTIONS 1985–86

The Caretaker, Harold Pinter; (D) John Malkovich; (S) Kevin Rigdon; (C) John Malkovich; (L) Kevin Rigdon
You Can't Take It with You, George S. Kaufman and Moss Hart; (D) Frank Galati; (S) Kevin Rigdon; (C) Kaye Nottbusch; (L) Kevin Rigdon
A Lesson from Aloes, Athol Fugard; (D) Suzanne Shepherd; (S) Kevin Rigdon; (C) Nan Cibula; (L) Kevin Rigdon
Lydie Breeze, John Guare; (D) Rondi Reed; (S) Kevin Rigdon; (C) Nan Cibula; (L) Kevin Rigdon
Frank's Wild Years, book: Kathleen Brennan; music and lyrics: Tom Waits; (D) Gary Sinise; (S) Kevin Rigdon; (C) Erin Quigley; (L) Kevin Rigdon

PRODUCTIONS 1986–87

Bang, Laura Cunningham; (D) Randall Arney; (S) Kevin Rigdon; (C) Erin Quigley; (L) Kevin Rigdon
Cat on a Hot Tin Roof, Tennessee Williams; (D) Austin Pendleton; (S) Kevin Rigdon; (C) Nan Cibula; (L) Kevin Rigdon
Educating Rita, Willy Russell; (D) Jeff Perry; (S) Kevin Rigdon; (C) Erin Quigley; (L) Kevin Rigdon
A Lie of the Mind, Sam Shepard; (D) Julie Hebert; (S) Kevin Rigdon; (C) Erin Quigley; (L) Kevin Rigdon
Aunt Dan and Lemon, Wallace Shawn; (D) Frank Galati; (S) Kevin Rigdon; (C) Nan Cibula; (L) Kevin Rigdon

The Street Theater

GRAY SMITH
Executive Director

228 Fisher Ave., Room 226
White Plains, NY 10606
(914) 761-3307

FOUNDED 1970
Gray Smith

SEASON
Year-round

FINANCES
June 1, 1986-May 31, 1987
Expenses: $233,233

CONTRACTS
AEA TYA

All Street Theater audience members—whether in parks, blocked-off streets, day camps, schools or other institutions —are viewed as potential actors. If they see themselves on stage our work is validated; if not, we have more work to do. We try to eliminate spectacle and to provide little support for "spectators"; whenever possible our performances lead to their performances—of pieces developed with our directors through training and collaboration. Some of these pieces go on tour, usually within the school districts where they originate. All of our work is original, growing either out of actor-director collaboration or the development of commissioned scripts. Most members of our audience are also "originals": they are eager to challenge, celebrate and renew our capacity to tell their story.

—Gray Smith

PRODUCTIONS 1985–86

Turned Around Tales, Sara Rubin and company; (D) Sara Rubin
Too Good to Be True, Sara Rubin and company; (D) Sara Rubin

PRODUCTIONS 1986–87

The Question of Tomorrow, Sara Rubin and company; (D) Sara Rubin
The Way Out, Sara Rubin and company; (D) Sara Rubin

The Street Theater. Greg Berlanti, David Boyce, Michael Givens and Laura Dorivall in *Turned Around Tales*. Photo: Loren Maron.

Studio Arena Theatre

DAVID FRANK
Artistic Director

RAYMOND BONNARD
Managing Director

710 Main St.
Buffalo, NY 14202-1990
(716) 856-8025 (bus.)
(716) 856-5650 (b.o.)

FOUNDED 1965
Neal DuBrock

SEASON
Sept.-May

FACILITIES
Seating capacity: 637
Stage: thrust

FINANCES
July 1, 1986-June 30, 1987
Expenses: $2,379,500

Studio Arena Theatre. Herb Downer, James Hartman and Michael Butler in *T Bone N Weasel*. Photo: K.C. Kratt.

CONTRACTS
AEA LORT (B), SSD&C and USA

Studio Arena Theatre's artistic policy is based on the premise that the challenge of running a major theatre in a community with unusually limited resources can lead to satisfying and distinctive work that enthusiastically accepts the pragmatic necessity of being a popular theatre with high earned income. To this end, Studio Arena's programming is eclectic; new work, American premieres and works from the standard repertoire are selected, not to fulfill programming policy, but in the belief that we have some exciting insight, idea or concept to share with our audience. After a period of major economic difficulty and subsequent retrenchment, which necessitated small casts and lowered artistic goals, we are rapidly returning to a more ambitious schedule of productions in fulfillment of our fundamental goal—a "popular theatre" accessible to a large audience, based on the intuitive work of the artist and tailored to the specific needs of the community.

—David Frank

PRODUCTIONS 1985–86

The Foreigner, Larry Shue; (D) Nick Faust; (S) Gary C. Eckhart; (C) John Carver Sullivan; (L) Dan Kotlowitz
Children of a Lesser God, Mark Medoff; (D) Kathyrn Long; (S) Victor Becker; (C) Mary Ann Powell; (L) Victor Becker
Sleuth, Anthony Shaffer; (D) David Frank; (S) Lewis Folden; (C) Mary Ann Powell; (L) Curt Ostermann
Ain't Misbehavin', music and lyrics: Fats Waller, et.al.; book adapt: Richard Maltby, Jr.; (D) Arthur Faria; (S) John Lee Beatty; (L) Barry Arnold
The Importance of Being Earnest, Oscar Wilde; (D) David Frank; (S) Robert Morgan; (C) Mary Ann Powell; (L) Curt Ostermann
Greater Tuna, Jaston Williams, Joe Sears and Ed Howard; (D) Kathryn Long; (S) Curtis Trout; (C) Mary Ann Powell; (L) Michael Orris Watson
Arsenals, Jeremy Lawrence; (D) Gwen Arner; (S) D. Martyn Bookwalter; (C) Bill Walker; (L) Brett Thomas

PRODUCTIONS 1986–87

A View from the Bridge, Arthur Miller; (D) Tony Giordano; (S) Hugh Landwehr; (C) Mary Ann Powell; (L) Dennis Parichy
The Value of Names, Jeffrey Sweet; (D) John Monteith; (S) Michael C. Smith; (C) Mary Ann Powell; (L) Curt Ostermann
Quilters, book: Molly Newman and Barbara Damashek; music and lyrics: Barbara Damashek; (D) Kyle Donnelly; (S) Jeff Bauer; (C) Mary Ann Powell; (L) Judy Rasmuson
The Real Thing, Tom Stoppard; (D) Kathryn Long; (S) Loy Arcenas; (C) Robert Morgan; (L) Curt Ostermann
A Little Night Music, book: Hugh Wheeler; music and lyrics: Stephen Sondheim; (D) David

Frank; (S) Robert Morgan; (C) Mary Ann Powell; (L) Pat Collins

T Bone N Weasel, Jon Klein; (D) Kathryn Long; (S) Rick Dennis; (C) Bill Walker; (L) Anne Militello

Hay Fever, Noel Coward; (D) Robert Morgan; (S) Steven Perry; (C) Mariann Verheyen; (L) Curt Ostermann

The Studio Theatre

JOY ZINOMAN
Artistic/Managing Director

RUSSELL METHENY
Associate Artistic Director

VIRGINIA CRAWFORD
Associate Managing Director

1401 Church St., NW
Washington , DC 20005
(202) 232-7267 (bus.)
(202) 265-7412 (b.o.)

FOUNDED 1978
Joy Zinoman

SEASON
Sept.-June

FACILITIES
Seating capacity: 110
Stage: thrust

FINANCES
Sept. 1, 1986-Aug. 31, 1987
Expenses: $424,500

CONTRACTS
AEA SPT and USA

Because the Studio Theatre grew out of an acting conservatory, our primary focus is to present theatre that is performance-oriented, suited to an intimate space, and with strict attention paid to the highest quality in design and production values. We believe that in nurturing and challenging actors, directors, designers and technical staff, we can provide our audiences with a theatrical experience that is immediate, personal and dynamic. We present a wide range of plays—from August Wilson's *Ma Rainey's Black Bottom* and William Hoffman's *As Is* to *The Birthday Party* by Harold Pinter; from Tennessee Williams' *Camino Real* to John Byrne's *The Slab Boys Trilogy*—plays that speak to contemporary society and that are important to the artistic aesthetics of our time.

—*Joy Zinoman*

PRODUCTIONS 1985–86

Playing for Time, Arthur Miller; (D) Joy Zinoman; (S) Russell Metheny; (C) Ric Thomas Rice; (L) Daniel MacLean Wagner

A Walk Out of Water, Donald Driver; (D) Donald Driver; (S) Russell Metheny; (C) Ric Thomas Rice; (L) Stuart Duke

Landscape of the Body, John Guare; (D) James C. Nicola; (S) Russell Metheny; (C) Nancy Konrardy; (L) Daniel Maclean Wagner

The Birthday Party, Harold Pinter; (D) Joy Zinoman; (S) Michael Layton; (C) Jane Schloss Phelan; (L) Daniel MacLean Wagner

Ma Rainey's Black Bottom, August Wilson; (D) Samuel P. Barton; (S) Michael Layton; (C) Ric Thomas Rice; (L) Daniel MacLean Wagner

The Studio Theatre. Simon Brooking in ***The Slab Boys***. Photo: Joan Marcus.

Syracuse Stage. Noel Craig, Christopher Wells and William Fichtner in ***Bent***. Photo: Susan Piper Kublick.

PRODUCTIONS 1986–87

Slab Boys, Cuttin' a Rug and ***Still Life***, John Byrne; (D) Joy Zinoman; (S) Russell Metheny; (C) Ric Thomas Rice; (L) Daniel MacLean Wagner

Under Milk Wood, Dylan Thomas; (D) Joy Zinoman; (S) Russell Metheny; (C) Ric Thomas Rice; (L) Daniel MacLean Wagner

Lemon Sky, Lanford Wilson; (D) Samuel P. Barton; (S) Michael Layton; (C) Ric Thomas Rice; (L) Daniel MacLean Wagner

The Entertainer, John Osborne; (D) Joy Zinoman; (S) Russell Metheny; (C) Jane Schloss Phelan; (L) Daniel MacLean Wagner

As Is, William M. Hoffman; (D) Cynthia Levin; (S) Atif Rome; (C) Atif Rome; (L) Art Kent

Syracuse Stage

ARTHUR STORCH
Producing Artistic Director

JAMES A. CLARK
Managing Director

820 East Genesee St.
Syracuse, NY 13210
(315) 423-4008 (bus.)
(315) 423-3275 (b.o.)

FOUNDED 1974
Arthur Storch

SEASON
Oct.-Apr.

FACILITIES
John D. Archbold Theatre
Seating capacity: 510
Stage: proscenium

Experimental Theatre
Seating capacity: 202
Stage: proscenium

Daniel C. Sutton Pavillion
Seating capacity: 100
Stage: flexible

FINANCES
July 1, 1986-June 30, 1987
Expenses: $1,684,374

CONTRACTS
AEA LORT (C), SSD&C and USA

The principal purpose of Syracuse Stage is to present central New York state residents with a variety of plays selected from the world's dramatic literature as well as American and foreign contemporary playwriting; each season, the theatre strives to present at least one new play. Commitment to the actor in all aspects of his or her stay in Syracuse is a cornerstone of this theatre's policy, and giving the actor the supportive environment to encourage the highest degree of creativity is our goal. Because of the relationship between Syracuse Stage and the Syracuse University drama department, both headed by the same person, there is a mutual commitment to excellence and creativity.

—Arthur Storch

PRODUCTIONS 1985–86

The Foreigner, Larry Shue; (D) Charles Karchmer; (S) Timothy Galvin; (C) Maria Marrero; (L) Ann G. Wrightson
Glengarry Glen Ross, David Mamet; (D) Tony Giordano; (S) Hugh Landwehr; (C) Maria Marrero; (L) Dennis Parichy
Ain't Misbehavin', music and lyrics: Fats Waller, et al.; book adapt: Richard Maltby, Jr.; (D) Arthur Faria; (S) John Lee Beatty; (C) Brooks Company; (L) Barry Arnold
Romeo and Juliet, William Shakespeare; (D) Arthur Storch; (S) Victor A. Becker; (C) Nanzi Adzima; (L) Ralph Dressler
Luv, Murray Schisgal; (D) Terry Schreiber; (S) Michael Miller; (C) Gregg Barnes; (L) Victor A. Becker
Bent, Martin Sherman; (D) Tom Walsh; (S) Victor A. Becker; (C) Victor A. Becker; (L) Victor A. Becker

PRODUCTIONS 1986–87

Little Shop of Horrors, book and lyrics: Howard Ashman; music: Alan Menken; (D) Carl Schurr; (S) Michael Miller; (C) Patricia M. Risser; (L) Michael Newton-Brown
A View from the Bridge, Arthur Miller; (D) Tony Giordano; (S) Hugh Landwehr; (C) Mary Ann Powell; (L) Dennis Parichy
Pygmalion, George Bernard Shaw; (D) John Going; (S) Charles A. Cosler; (C) Maria Marrero; (L) Marcia Madeira
Of Mice and Men, John Steinbeck; (D) Arthur Storch; (S) Victor A. Becker; (C) Maria Marrero; (L) Judy Rasmuson
Stage Struck, Simon Gray; (D) Tom Walsh; (S) Gary May; (C) Mary Zihal; (L) Sandra Schilling
On the Verge or The Geography of Yearning, Eric Overmyer; (D) Robert Berlinger; (S) Michael Miller; (C) Maria Marrero; (L) Marc B. Weiss

Tacoma Actors Guild

WILLIAM BECVAR
Artistic Director

KATE HAAS
Managing Director

1323 South Yakima Ave.
Tacoma, WA 98405
(206) 272-3107 (bus.)
(206) 272-2145 (b.o.)

FOUNDED 1978
William Becvar, Rick Tutor

SEASON
Sept.-Apr.

FACILITIES
Seating capacity: 299
Stage: proscenium

FINANCES
July 1, 1986-June 30, 1987
Expenses: $681,799

CONTRACTS
AEA LORT (D) and SSD&C

Tacoma Actors Guild is defined by its name: our theatre is interested in producing plays which provide actors with challenging roles. Although design support is a consideration, the actor is never relegated to a secondary position—it is the actor through which we reach our audience. We provide Northwest talent with appealing roles, while fulfilling our audiences' expectations of professional productions. Our selections reflect a wide diversity in the canon of dramatic literature. We align ourselves with the established play and mount productions that allow new audiences to experience a play whose title is the only known factor, while giving an older audience the opportunity to rediscover an "old friend." In a period when numerous theatres are turning to modern, smaller-cast productions, TAG seeks to develop a reputation for producing plays from a period of time when larger casts were the rule, rather than the exception.

—William Becvar

Note: During the 1985-86 season, Rick Tutor served as artistic director.

Tacoma Actors Guild. Lynn Tyrrell in *A Christmas Memory*. Photo: Fred Andrews.

PRODUCTIONS 1985–86

The Real Inspector Hound and ***Dogg's Hamlet***, Tom Stoppard; (D) Anne-Denise Ford; (S) Jennifer Lupton; (C) Heidi A. Hermiller; (L) J. Patrick Elmer
A Coupla White Chicks Sitting Around Talking, John Ford Noonan; (D) William Becvar; (S) Jerry S. Hooker; (C) Frances Kenny; (L) J. Patrick Elmer
A Child's Christmas in Wales, Dylan Thomas; (D) Rick Tutor; (S) Richard J. Harris; (C) Anne Thaxter Watson; (L) James Verdery
A Christmas Memory, Truman Capote; (D) Rick Tutor; (S) Richard J. Harris; (C) Anne Thaxter Watson; (L) James Verdery
The Price, Arthur Miller; (D) John Schwab; (S) Jerry S. Hooker; (C) Heidi A. Hermiller; (L) J. Patrick Elmer
Final Passages, Robert Schenkkan; (D) Rick Tutor; (S) Jennifer Lupton; (C) Sarah Campbell; (L) Richard Devin
Home, Samm-Art Williams; (D) Rita Giomi; (S) Richard J. Harris; (C) Heidi A. Hermiller; (L) Richard J. Harris

PRODUCTIONS 1986–87

The Hasty Heart, John Patrick; (D) Rick Tutor; (S) Judith Cullen; (C) Rose Pederson; (L) J. Patrick Elmer
Who's Afraid of Virginia Woolf?, Edward Albee; (D) William Becvar; (S) Jerry S. Hooker; (C) Wendela K. Jones; (L) J. Patrick Elmer
Cowardy Custard, conceived: Gerald Frow, Alan Strachen and Wendy Toye; music and lyrics: Noel Coward; (D) David Ira Goldstein; (S) Bill Forrester; (C) Frances Kenny; (L) Phil Schermer
The Return of Herbert Bracewell, Andrew Johns; (D) Robert Robinson; (S) Judith Cullen; (C) Wendela K. Jones; (L) Richard Devin
The Star-Spangled Girl, Neil Simon; (D) William Becvar; (S) Jerry S. Hooker; (C) Anne Thaxter Watson; (L) J. Patrick Elmer
Sleuth, Anthony Shaffer; (D) Andrew Traister; (S) Everett Chase; (C) Wendela K. Jones; (L) James Verdery

The Theater at Monmouth

RICHARD SEWELL
Artistic Director

MARGARET M. STERLING
Business Manager

Box 385
Monmouth, ME 04259
(207) 933-2952

FOUNDED 1970
Robert Joyce, Richard Sewell

SEASON
May-Sept.

FACILITIES
Cumston Hall

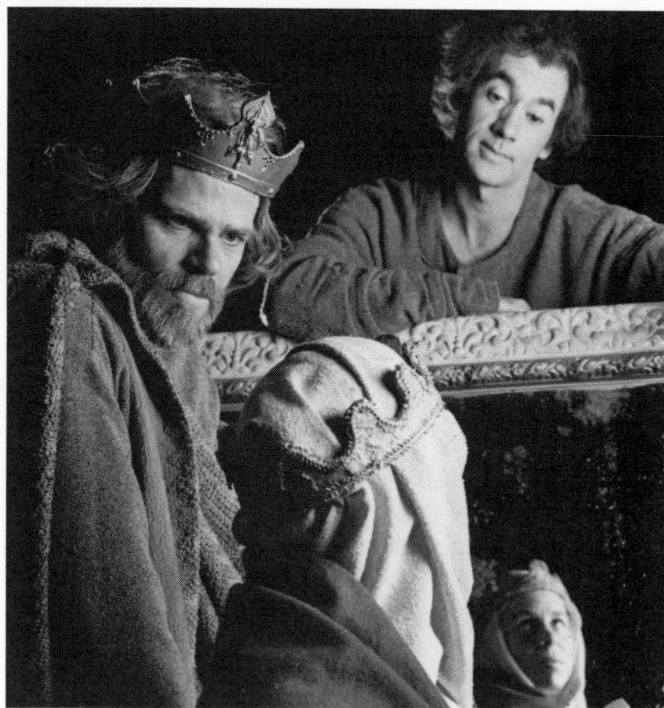

The Theater at Monmouth. Timothy Wheeler, Michael O'Brien and Cecile Mann in *Lion in Winter*. Photo: Susan Mills.

Seating capacity: 275
Stage: thrust

FINANCES
Jan. 1, 1986-Dec. 31, 1986
Expenses: $136,961

CONTRACTS
AEA SPT

The Theater at Monmouth presents classical theatre (in rotating repertory) set in a beautiful Victorian opera house. Our first criterion in play selection is interesting, heightened language. We produce a steady flow of classical productions with a smattering of more recent works. For this artistic mix, we cultivate a core company of performers comfortable with a variety of writing styles and able to convey the meaning of any given text to a variety of audiences. Our high school touring program is designed to introduce young people throughout the state to the works of Shakespeare.

—*Richard Sewell*

PRODUCTIONS 1986

Romeo and Juliet, William Shakespeare; adapt: Richard Sewell; (D) Richard Sewell; (S) Richard Sewell; (C) Deborah O'Brien

The Miser, Molière; adapt: Richard Sewell; (D) Richard Sewell; (S) Richard Sewell; (C) Jane Snider; (L) Patrick Montgomery

The Lion in Winter, James Goldman; (D) Ted Davis; (S) Richard Sewell; (C) Jane Snider; (L) Patrick Montgomery

And a Nightingale Sang, C.P. Taylor; (D) Ted Davis; (S) Richard Sewell; (C) Jane Snider; (L) Patrick Montgomery

The Merry Wives of Windsor, William Shakespeare; (D) Richard Sewell; (S) Richard Sewell; (C) Jane Snider; (L) Patrick Montgomery

PRODUCTIONS 1987

Hamlet, William Shakespeare; adapt: Richard Sewell; (D) Richard Sewell; (S) Richard Sewell; (C) Kim Gordon

The Imaginary Invalid, Molière; trans: Miles Malleson; (D) Richard Sewell; (S) Richard Sewell; (C) Jane Snider; (L) Nina Gooch

Othello, William Shakespeare; (D) Ted Davis; (S) Al Cyrus; (C) Jane Snider; (L) Nina Gooch

Much Ado About Nothing, William Shakespeare; (D) Richard Sewell; (S) Al Cyrus; (C) Jane Snider; (L) Nina Gooch

Uncle Vanya, Anton Chekhov; (D) Ted Davis; (S) Al Cyrus; (C) Jane Snider; (L) Nina Gooch

Theatre de la Jeune Lune

BARBRA BERLOVITZ DESBOIS, VINCENT GRACIEUX, ROBERT ROSEN and DOMINIQUE SERRAND
Artistic Directors

EMILY STEVENS
Business Director

Box 3265
Minneapolis, MN 55403
(612) 332-3968 (bus.)
(612) 333-6200 (b.o.)

FOUNDED 1978
Barbra Berlovitz Desbois, Vincent Gracieux, Dominique Serrand

SEASON
Sept.-May

FACILITIES
Hennepin Center for the Arts
Seating capacity: 385
Stage: thrust

Southern Theatre
Seating capacity: 200
Stage: proscenium

FINANCES
Aug. 1, 1986-July 31, 1987
Expenses: $343,500

Theatre de la Jeune Lune is a theatre of actors. What is important to us is what the actor puts on the stage when the curtain goes up—what happens in front of the audience. With that end result in mind, we enter into each production. There isn't a play we won't do. We could be interested in a classic, a modern work or an original new play. What we do with it is a different matter. We strive to make the play "ours," to bring across, as our audience would agree, our style. Our heart, passions and emotions open the paths to ideas. We create exactly what we want to, within our obvious financial restrictions. Every production is different and each play must be attacked from a new angle with our experience of the past. Pushing ourselves into new areas every year, we want to continue bringing exciting, eventful and important theatre to our community.

—*Barbra Berlovitz Desbois*

PRODUCTIONS 1985–86

The Bourgeois Gentleman, Molière; adapt: Fred S. Tessler; (D) Dominique Serrand; (S) Dominique Serrand and David Coggins; (C) Andrea McCormack; (L) Jeff Bartlett

Christopher Columbus, Michel de Ghelderode; (D) Steven Epp; (S) Vincent Gracieux and Dominique Serrand; (C) Andrea McCormack; (L) Robert Rosen and Dominique Serrand

Theatre de la Jeune Lune. Vincent Gracieux, Robert Rosen and Dominique Serrand in *Yang Zen Froggs in Moon over a Hong Kong Sweatshop*. Photo: F. Desbois.

Yang Zen Froggs in Moon Over a Hong Kong Sweatshop, company-developed; (D) company; (S) company; (C) company; (L) company
Splendid, company; (D) company; (S) Vincent Gracieux and Dominique Serrand; (C) company; (L) Jeff Bartlett
Place de Breteuil, Alain Gautre; trans: Vincent Gracieux and Steven Epp; (D) Vincent Gracieux; (S) Aldo Moroni and Dominique Serrand; (C) Sonya Berlovitz; (L) Jeff Bartlett
August, August, August, Pavel Kohout; trans: Jack Garfein; (D) Barbra Berlovitz Desbois; (S) Dominique Serrand; (C) Sonya Berlovitz; (L) Jeff Bartlett

PRODUCTIONS 1986–87

Circus, company-developed; (D) Robert Rosen; (S) Tom Rose; (C) Sonya Berlovitz; (L) Dominique Serrand
Exit the King, Eugene Ionesco; (D) Vincent Gracieux; (S) Dominique Serrand and Vincent Gracieux; (C) Sonya Berlovitz; (L) Robert Rosen
Yang Zen Froggs in Moon Over a Hong Kong Sweatshop, company-developed; (D) company; (S) company; (C) company; (L) company
Romeo and Juliet, William Shakespeare; (D) Dominique Serrand; (S) Vincent Gracieux and Dominique Serrand; (C) Sonya Berlovitz; (L) Robert Rosen, Fred Desbois and Terry Price
N'Yawk N'Yawk...Who's There?, Marilyn Seven and company; (D) Christopher Bayes; (S) Vincent Gracieux; (C) Sonya Berlovitz; (L) Fred Desbois and Dominique Serrand

Theatre for a New Audience

JEFFREY HOROWITZ
Artistic/Producing Director

26 Grove St., Suite 6G
New York, NY 10014
(212) 505-8345 (bus.)
(212) 505-8346 (b.o.)

FOUNDED 1979
Jeffrey Horowitz

SEASON
Jan.-June

FACILITIES
Triplex, Theatre II
Seating capacity: 199
Stage: thrust

Henry Street Settlement
Seating capacity: 99
Stage: thrust

FINANCES
Sept. 1, 1986-Aug. 31, 1987
Expenses: $340,000

CONTRACTS
AEA letter of agreement and TYA, SSD&C and USA

Theatre for a New Audience presents Shakespeare and contemporary American works on social issues. TFANA relates the arts to individual and social awareness, builds new informed audiences, and educates through performances and workshops. To challenge the young through serious theatre, all productions play both for students, aged 9 to 18, and for general audiences. In productions of Shakespeare, TFANA's goal is to find the relationship between the heightened language of the Elizabethan text and the sensibilities and concerns of today's theatre. For New Voices, TFANA produces plays that explore urgent social issues, and directly involves highly regarded artists in a community in which a problem exists. TFANA's aesthetic combines a respect for the text with a strong directorial sensibility. We produce theatre that is connected to the community, challenges an audience to think critically, excites through its immediacy and theatricality, and, hopefully, provides an understanding of the world about and within us.

—*Jeffrey Horowitz*

PRODUCTIONS 1986

Home Street Home, Phil Bosakowski, Rachel Gewitt and Chris Nowels; music and lyrics: Elliot Goldenthal and Irene Wiley; (D) Liz Diamond; (S) Charles H. McClennahan; (C) Judy Dearing; (L) Jane Reisman
The Tempest, William Shakespeare; (D) Julie Taymor; (S) G.W. Mercier; (C) G.W. Mercier; (L) Ann Wrightson

Theatre for a New Audience. Avery Brooks in *The Tempest*. Photo: Richard Feldman.

PRODUCTIONS 1987

Twelfth Night, William Shakespeare; (D) Mary B. Robinson; (S) Steve Saklad; (C) Gene Lakin; (L) Frances Aronson
The Tempest, William Shakespeare; (D) Julie Taymor; (S) G.W. Mercier; (C) G.W. Mercier; (L) Frances Aronson
Inside Out, Willy Holtzman; (D) John Pynchon Holms; (S) Richard Harmon; (C) Catherine Zuber; (L) Richard Harmon

Theater for the New City

GEORGE BARTENIEFF
CRYSTAL FIELD
Artistic Directors

155 First Ave.
New York, NY 10003
(212) 475-3302 (bus.)
(212) 254-1109 (b.o.)

FOUNDED 1971
Theo Barnes, George Bartenieff, Crystal Field, Larry Kornfeld

SEASON
Year-round

FACILITIES
Seating capacity: 100
Stage: flexible

FINANCES
July 1, 1986-June 30, 1987
Expenses: $450,000

CONTRACTS
AEA Showcase code and letter of agreement

Theater for the New City, now in its 17th season, is a center dedicated to the discovery of relevant new writing and the nurturing of new playwrights. TNC has presented 600 new American plays to more than 750,000 audience members, including the premieres of works by Sam Shepard, Maria Irene Fornes, Harvey Fierstein, Amlin Gray, Jean-Claude van Itallie, Miguel Piñero, Rosalyn Drexler, Robert Patrick—the list is practically endless. TNC has also presented many of America's most important theatre companies and artists, among them Richard Foreman, Mabou Mines, Bread and Puppet Theater, Charles Ludlam, and the Talking Band. TNC's commitment to new artists, lesser-known writers and young performers is evidenced by our New

Theater for the New City. Tom Cayler and Crystal Field in *The Heart That Eats Itself.* Photo: Carol Halebian.

Playwrights Workshop (under the direction of Ms. Fornes, a TNC artist-in-residence), and a Street Theater Performers Workshop (under our direction). We also operate one of the most extensive new play commissioning programs in America. Each year, TNC provides 30,000 free admissions to members of 90 community, senior citizen and youth groups, and we create a free street theatre traveling festival every summer, bringing outdoor performances to New York City's five boroughs. In 1986, after performing in rented spaces, TNC purchased a new home that we're converting into a community-based cultural and performance art center.

—George Bartenieff, Crystal Field

PRODUCTIONS 1985–86

Alex and Joanna, Herb Liebman; (D) Christopher McCann; (S) Mark Lutwak; (C) Nancy Palmatier; (L) Mark Lutwak

And When the Bough Breaks, Jamie Leo; (D) Jamie Leo; (S) Jamie Leo; (C) Jamie Leo; (L) Jamie Leo

Aspersions Cast, Daryl Chin; (D) Daryl Chin and Larry Qualls; (S) Fred Wilson; (C) Fred Wilson; (L) Fred Wilson

Box Plays, Maria Irene Fornes, Lourdes Blanco, Migdalia Cruz, Jose Pelaez, Manuel Pereiras and Ana Maria Simo; (D) Maria Irene Fornes, Ron Orbach and Donald Squires; (S) Ricardo Morin; (L) Craig Kennedy

Crisis of Identity, Robert Heide; (D) Robert Heide; (S) John Eric Broaddus; (L) Michael Warren Powell

Dark Water Closing, Steve Shill; (D) Steve Shill; (S) Suzanne Van Develde; (C) Suzanne Van Develde; (L) Suzanne Van Develde

Casting of Kevin Christian, Stephen Holt; (D) John Margulis; (S) Cecil B. Songco; (C) Natalie Walker; (L) Jeffrey Nash

Cooking with the Elements, Theodora Skipitares; (D) Theodora Skipitares

Daughters of Venus, Howard Zinn; (D) Jeff Zinn; (S) Susan Bolles; (C) Ruth Seidman; (L) Craig Kennedy

Four Leaf Clover Cabins, Sebastian Stuart; (D) Steve Lott; (S) Michael Daughtry; (L) Deborah Constantine

Fulfilling Koch's Postulate, Joan Schenkar; (D) Joan Schenkar; (S) Reagan Cook; (C) Tracey Oleinick; (L) Craig Kennedy

Get It While You Can, Larry Mitchell; (D) Bette Bourne; (S) Paul Shaw; (C) Paul Shaw; (L) Paul Shaw

Green Card Blues, Orlando Dole

Hamletto, Giovanni Testori; (D) Antonio Abujamia; (S) Daniela Thomas; (C) Daniela Thomas

Help Wanted, Franz Xaver Kroetz; (D) JoAnne Akalaitis; (C) Greg Mehrten and Anne Herzog; (L) Jennifer Tipton

Homecoming, Crystal Field and George Bartenieff; (D) Crystal Field; (S) Tony Angel; (C) Animal X and Pamela Mayo

Hoodlum Hearts, Lois Elaine Griffith; (D) Miguel Algarin; (S) Mark Marcante; (C) Robert Jacobson; (L) Jeffrey Nash

I, Walt Whitman, adapt: Daniel Barshay, from Walt Whitman; (D) Daniel Barshay

In the Traffic of a Targetted City, Marc Kaminsky; (D) Arthur Strimling; (S) Alan Glovsky; (C) c. ann pelletier; (L) Craig Kennedy

Living Leg-ends, Bloolips company; (D) Bette Bourne and company; (S) company; (C) company

A Matter of Faith, Maria Irene Fornes; (D) Maria Irene Fornes; (S) Donald Eastman; (C) Tavia Ito; (L) Anne E. Militello

A Matter of Life and Death, Rosalyn Drexler; (D) John Vaccaro; (S) Abe Lubelski; (C) Gabriel Berry; (L) Jeffrey Nash

Fabiola, Eduardo Machado; (D) James Hammerstein; (S) Donald Eastman; (C) Deborah Shaw; (L) Donald Eastman

Notorious Harik Will Kill the Pope, Ronald Tavel; (D) Ronald Tavel; (S) Ronald Kajiwara and Warren Jorgenson; (C) Jane Aire; (L) Craig Kennedy

Off the Cuff, James Camicia; (D) James Camicia; (L) Ken Gray

The Plate, Roy Dobbins; (D) Bette Bourne; (S) Mark Marcante and Jiri Schubert; (L) Janette Kennedy and Nancy Swartz

Pushing the D Train Back to Brooklyn, Leah K. Friedman; (D) Bryna Wortman; (S) John Paino; (C) David C. Woolard; (L) Craig Kennedy

Quartet, Heiner Muller; (D) Gerald Thomas; (S) Daniela Thomas; (C) Daniela Thomas; (L) Gerald Thomas

Salt, Liza Lorwin; (D) Lee Breuer; (S) Julie Archer; (C) Ghretta Hynd; (L) Julie Archer

Solitaire, Ward Oberman; (D) M.A. Hestand; (S) John Paino; (C) David Edwardson

Tail of the Tiger, Ralph Pezzullo; (D) Mark Marcante; (S) John Paino; (C) Mimi Halberstam; (L) David Nelson

Thunderbird American Indian Dancers Pow Wow and Dance Concert, (D) Louis Mofsie

Title: Nietzsche, Larry Myers; (D) Larry Myers; (S) Mark Marcante; (C) Mike Grimes; (L) Vincent Esoldi and Valerie Green

3 Up, 3 Down, Spiderwoman Theatre company-developed; (D) Muriel Miguel; (C) Gloria Miguel and Lisa Mayo

Nails, Patricia Cobey; (D) Patricia Cobey; (S) Jody Pinto; (C) Natalie Walker; (L) David Edwardson

PRODUCTIONS 1986–87

Carrying School Children, Thomas Babe; (D) David Briggs; (S) James Tilton and Mike Boak; (C) Daphne Stevens-Pascucci; (L) Peter West

The Heart That Eats Itself, Rosalyn Drexler; (D) John Vaccaro; (S) Abe Lubelski; (C) Gabriel Berry; (L) Jeff Nash

Family Pride in the 50's, Joan Schenkar; (D) Liz Diamond; (S) Reagan Cook; (C) Tracy Oleinick; (L) Nicole Werner

The Ride That Never Was, Jiri Schubert, Ray Dobbins and Patricia Coleman; (D) Mark Marcante; (S) Walter Gurbo and Tony Angel; (C) Patty Quinn; (L) Zdenek Kriz

Ruzzante Returns from the Wars, Angelo Beolco; (D) Mark Marcante; (S) Tony Angel; (C) Patty Quinn; (L) Zdenek Kriz

An Evening of British Music Hall, various; (D) Mark Marcante; (S) Tony Angel; (C) John Mangano; (L) Zdenek Kriz

Hit the Road or Bummed Out, Crystal Field and George Bartenieff; (D) Crystal Field; (S) Tony Angel; (C) Edmund Felix and Brian Pride

The Hunger Cantata, Peter Schumann; (D) Bread and Puppet Theater company

Space Show, various; (D) George Ferencz; (S) Bill Stabile; (C) Sally Lesser; (L) Blu

Thunderbird American Indian Dance Concert and Pow Wow, (D) Louis Mofsie

The Gay Book of the Dead, Jim Camicia; (D) Jim Camicia; (S) Tony Angel; (L) Jiri Schubert

Great Moments from Science, book: Theodora Skipitares; music: Virgil Moorefield; lyrics: Andrea Balis; (D) Theodora Skipitares; (S) Michael Cummings; (L) Michael Cummings

Time, Place, Language and the Erotic, Stuart Sherman; (D) Stuart Sherman; (S) Stuart Sherman; (C) Stuart Sherman; (L) Stuart Sherman

Experiments in Illusion and Gesture, Alice Farley; (D) Alice Farley; (S) Herbie Leith and Ted Shapiro; (C) Alice Farley

Walks of Indian Women Aztlan to Anahuac, Vira Colorado and Hortensia Colorado; (D) Vira Colorado and Hortensia Colorado; (L) Manny Cavaco

1986 on Parade, NY Street Theatre Caravan; (D) Marketa

Kimbrall; (S) Paul Baker; (L) Manny Cavaco

Second Species, Keith King; (D) Keith King; (S) James Finguerra; (C) Mary Brecht; (L) Ronald M. Katz

Theatre IV

BRUCE MILLER
Artistic Director

PHILIP WHITEWAY
Managing Director

114 West Broad St.
Richmond, VA 23220
(804) 783-1688 (bus.)
(804) 344-8040 (b.o.)

FOUNDED 1975
Bruce Miller, Phil Whiteway

SEASON
Year-round

FACILITIES
Empire Theatre
Seating capacity: 779
Stage: proscenium

Regency Theatre
Seating capacity: 168
Stage: proscenium

FINANCES
July 1, 1986-June 31, 1987
Expenses: $764,500

CONTRACTS
AEA Guest Artist

Theatre IV presents contemporary plays and musicals for adults, and original plays and musicals for young people and their families. In Richmond we are known primarily as an "alternative" theatre. Our productions of such plays as *The Normal Heart*, *Bosoms and Neglect*, *Do Lord Remember Me* and *Fifth of July* represent to our central Virginia audience the "cutting edge" of American drama. Most of our budget is devoted to youth productions which tour extensively throughout our region; we present over 900 performances a year. This is where we earn national recognition. Our original plays *Hugs and Kisses*, *Runners* and *Walking the Line* deal honestly and effectively with the issues of sexual child abuse, runaways, teenage suicide and substance abuse. These plays are a great source of pride to us and to our supporters. Our new homes—the grand Empire and intimate Regency theatres—opened in 1911, and are the oldest theatres in our state.

—Bruce Miller

Theatre IV. ***And a Nightingale Sang.*** Photo: Eric Dobbs.

PRODUCTIONS 1985–86

Scapino!, Jim Dale and Frank Dunlop; (D) Jack Welch; (S) Bruce Miller; (C) Blair Rochester; (L) Bob Minnick

And a Nightingale Sang, C.P. Taylor; (D) Bruce Miller; (S) Terrie Powers; (C) Tom Hammond; (L) Barb McIntire

Nuts, Tom Topor; (D) Gary Hopper; (S) John Glenn; (C) John Glenn; (L) Jean Morris

Quilters, book: Barbara Damashek and Molly Newman; music and lyrics: Barbara Damashek; (D) John Glenn; (S) Terrie Powers; (C) Liz Hopper; (L) Tim Baumgardner

Pinocchio, book adapt and lyrics: Bruce Miller, from Carlo Collodi; music: Rook Strong; (D) Bruce Miller; (S) Terrie Powers; (C) Catherine Szari

Young George Washington, book and lyrics: Douglas Jones; music: Dave Montgomery; (D) John Glenn; (S) Terrie Powers; (C) Tom Hammond

Hugs and Kisses, book and lyrics: Bruce Miller; music: Richard Giersch; (D) Bruce Miller; (S) Terrie Powers; (C) John Glenn

Runners, book and lyrics: Bruce Miller; music: Richard Giersch; (D) Bruce Miller; (S) Terrie Powers; (C) John Glenn

Snow White and the Seven Dwarfs, book and lyrics: Ford Flannagan; music: Dave Montgomery; (D) John Glenn; (S) Terrie Powers; (C) Catherine Szari

Santa's Christmas Miracle, book, lyrics and music: Richard Giersch; (D) Carol Coons; (S) Terrie Powers; (C) Joan U. Brumbach

Babes in Toyland, book: Bruce Miller; lyrics: Glen McDonough; music: Victor Herbert; (D) Bruce Miller; (S) Terrie Powers; (C) Catherine Szari

Santa's Holiday Adventure, book, lyrics and music: Richard Giersch; (D) Ford Flannagan; (S) Terrie Powers; (C) Joan U. Brumbach

The Pied Piper, book and lyrics: Douglas Jones; music: Ron Barnett; (D) John Glenn; (S) Terrie Powers; (C) Tom Hammond

Sleeping Beauty, book, music and lyrics: Richard Giersch; (D) Ford Flannagan; (S) Terrie Powers; (C) Tom Hammond

I Have a Dream, Bruce Miller; (D) Bruce Miller; (S) Bruce Miller; (C) John Glenn

Small Wonders, book and lyrics: Bruce Miller, Kim Strong and Jim Dickerson; music: Rook Strong; (D) Bruce Miller; (S) Terrie Powers; (C) Bruce Miller

PRODUCTIONS 1986–87

Isn't It Romantic, Wendy Wasserstein; (D) John Glenn; (S) Terrie Powers; (C) Jean Morris; (L) Debra C. Marks

The Normal Heart, Larry Kramer; (D) Bruce Miller; (S) company; (C) Ruth Graninger; (L) Donald Printz

Where's Charley?, book: George Abbott; music and lyrics: Frank Loesser; (D) Bruce Miller; (S) Terrie Powers; (C) Sharon Spradlin-Barrett; (L) Terrie Powers

The Cotton Patch Gospel, book: Tom Key and Russell Treyz; music and lyrics: Harry Chapin; (D) Bev Appleton; (S) Terrie Powers; (C) John Glenn; (L) Jeff Lindquist

Rapunzel, book and lyrics: David Crane and Marta Kauffman; music: Michael Skloff; (D) John Glenn; (S) Terrie Powers; (C) Catherine Creager

Young Tom Jefferson, book and lyrics: Bruce Miller; music: Richard Giersch; (D) John Glenn; (S) Terrie Powers; (C) John Glenn

Hugs and Kisses, book and lyrics: Bruce Miller; music: Richard Giersch; (D) Bruce Miller; (S) Terrie Powers; (C) John Glenn

Runners, book and lyrics: Bruce Miller; music: Richard Giersch; (D) Bruce Miller; (S) Terrie Powers; (C) John Glenn

'Twas the Night Before Christmas, book, lyrics and music: Bruce Miller; (D) Bruce Miller; (S) Terrie Powers; (C) John Glenn

Rudolph's Christmas, book, lyrics and music: Jim Dickerson; (D) Ford Flannagan; (S) Terrie Powers; (C) John Glenn

Babes in Toyland, book: Bruce Miller; lyrics: Glen McDonough; music: Victor Herbert; (D) John

Glenn; (s) Terrie Powers; (c) Catherine Szari

I Have a Dream, Bruce Miller; (D) Bruce Miller; (s) Bruce Miller; (c) John Glenn

Puss in Boots, book and lyrics: Douglas Jones; music: Ron Barnett; (D) John Glenn; (s) Terrie Powers; (c) Tom Hammond

The Pied Piper, book and lyrics: Douglas Jones; music: Ron Barnett; (D) John Glenn; (s) Terrie Powers; (c) Tom Hammond

The Little Red Hen, book, lyrics and music: Ford Flannagan; (D) John Glenn; (s) Terrie Powers; (c) John Glenn

Theatre Project

PHILIP ARNOULT
Director

CAROL BAISH
Managing Director

45 West Preston St.
Baltimore, MD 21201
(301) 539-3091 (bus.)
(301) 752-8558 (b.o.)

FOUNDED 1971
Philip Arnoult

SEASON
Year-round

FACILITIES
Seating capacity: 157
Stage: flexible

FINANCES
Jan. 1, 1986-Dec. 31, 1986
Expenses: $501,000

I sit in several hundred theatre seats a year to find work to bring to Theatre Project. I look for work that is small and young—rooted in its own culture, but not bound by it—with a fullness that breaks through the boundaries of language, race, politics. My commitment to these companies is very personal, and it is as much a commitment to an artistic vision as it is to a particular production. My role as a dramaturg, helping a company fine-tune a work for its Off-Off Broadway debut, is a precious one. In my travels everywhere, I see wondrous permutations of the American avant-garde. What is most gratifying is the openness in ourselves and in our theatres to presenting these visions, wherever they come from. I have a kind of romantic belief that this special grace will help keep the planet sane.

—Philip Arnoult

Theatre Project. Jose Martin and Adriana Diaz in Teatro del Sur's *La Pestileria*. Photo: Philip Arnoult.

PRODUCTIONS 1986

Communicado Theatre (Scotland):

The Hunchback of Notre Dame, adapt: Andrew Dallmeyer, from Victor Hugo; (D) Gerry Mulgrew; (s) Cecilia Healy; (c) Cecilia Healy; (L) Colin Salter

Industrial Strength Theatre Company (Baltimore):

My Sad Face, adapt: Mark Redfield, from Heinrich Boll; (D) Mark Redfield

Theatre de Complicite (England):

A Minute Too Late, company-developed; (D) Annabel Arden; (s) company; (c) company; (L) Micheline Vandepoel

¼ Time Productions (England):

Cora, book and lyrics: Julian Slugget and Margaret Hall; music: Alastair Collingwood; (D) Sallie Francis; (s) Raymond Ingram; (L) Raymond Ingram

Spiderwoman Theater (New York):

Sun, Moon, and Feather, company-developed; (D) Muriel Miguel; (s) company; (c) company; (L) company

Grupo Contadoras de Estorias (Brazil):

Mansamente and ***Pas de Deux***, Marcos Ribas and Rachel Ribas; (s) Marcos Ribas and Rachel Ribas; (c) Marcos Ribas and Rachel Ribas; (L) Marcos Ribas and Rachel Ribas

The Ivan Vasov National Theatre (Bulgaria):

Retro, Boris Spirov; (D) Dimitrina Giurova; (s) Atanas Velianov; (L) Petar Dimitrov

Bolek Polivka (Czechoslovakia):

The Jester and the Queen, Bolek Polivka; (D) Bolek Polivka; (s) Dusan Zdmal; (L) Laos Ganicek

Charabanc Theatre Company (Northern Ireland):

Gold in the Streets, Marie Jones; (s) Houston Marshall; (L) Brian Treacy

Inquest for Freddy Chickan, Fred Curchack

You Can't Tell a Book By Looking at Its Cover: Sayings from the Life and Writings of Junebug Jabbo Jones, Part II, John O'Neal, Nayo-Barbara Malcolm Watkins and Steven Kent; (D) Steven Kent; (L) Ken Bowen

Edge of Laughter Series:

Women of Substance, The Thunder Thigh Revue; (D) Joyce J. Scott and Kay Lawal

Janice Perry a.k.a. GAL, Janice Perry; (D) Janice Perry

Selling Out Fast, Kate Lynn Reiter; (D) Warren David Keith

Todd Stockman and Friends, Todd Stockman; (D) Bruce Hopkins

The Kathy and Mo Show, Kathy Najimy and Mo Gaffney; (D) Don Scardino

Man Act, Philip MacKenzie and Simon Thorne

Lyric Stage (Boston):

And a Nightingale Sang, C. P. Taylor; (D) Ron Ritchell; (s) Alexander Okun; (c) Polly Hogan

An Evening with Anne Seagrave and Oscar McLennan, Anne Seagrave and Oscar McLennan; (D) Sophia Caldwell

Anonymous (Quebec):

Li Jus de Robin et Marion, Adam de la Halle; (D) Jean Asselin; (s) Jean Francois Couture and Gilles Dube; (L) Carole Caoette

PRODUCTIONS 1987

Two Ships Passing in the Night, Kathy Najimy and Mo Gaffney; (D) Don Scardino; (L) Joshua Dachs

Teatro del Sur (Argentina):

La Pestileria, Alberto Felix Alberto; (D) Alberto Felix Alberto; (s) Alberto Felix Alberto; (c) Beto Langianni and Deigo Videla Gutierrez; (L) Alberto Felix Alberto

Tmu-Na (Israel):

5 Screams, Nava Zuckerman; (D) Nava Zuckerman and Mendan Koby; (s) Moshe Sternfeld; (L) Judy Kupferman

The Bread and Puppet Theater (Vermont):

The Hunger Project, company-developed; (D) Peter Schumann

The Drawing Legion:

Sistine Floor, Mel Andringa and F. John Herbert; (D) Mel Andringa and F. John Herbert; (S) Mel Andringa and F. John Herbert; (C) Kate Borowski and Anne W. Whitehead; (L) Mel Andringa and F. John Herbert

The Thunder Thigh Revue:

Sticking and Pulling, Joyce J. Scott; (D) John O'Neal and Joyce J. Scott

Women of Substance, company-developed; (D) Joyce J. Scott and Kay Lawal; (L) Eric Morris

Paul B. Davies (England):

The Lost Valet, Paul B. Davies and John Collee; (D) Paul B. Davies; (S) Paul B. Davies; (C) Paul B. Davies; (L) Laura Poehlman

John Sinclair (England):

Lord Buckley's Finest Hour, John Sinclair, Richmond Shepard and Frederick L. Buckley

Bolek Polivka (Czechoslovakia):

The Jester and the Queen, Bolek Polivka; (D) Bolek Polivka; (S) Dusan Zdmal; (L) Laos Ganicek

Kathy Najimy and Mo Gaffney:

Parallel Lives, Kathy Najimy and Mo Gaffney; (D) Don Scardino; (L) Joshua Dachs

Man Act (England):

Man Act II, Philip MacKenzie and Simon Thorne

The Adaptors:

In the Bed, company-developed.

Theatre Project Company

FONTAINE SYER
Artistic Director

DIANE M. HOLT
Managing Director

4219 Laclede Ave.
St. Louis, MO 63108
(314) 531-1301

FOUNDED 1975
Christine E. Smith, Fontaine Syer

SEASON
Sept.-May

FACILITIES
New City School
Seating capacity: 240
Stage: proscenium

FINANCES
July 1, 1986-June 30, 1987
Expenses: $472,640

CONTRACTS
AEA SPT

Theatre Project Company's major areas of work are our mainstage season; our TYA program—The MUNY/Student Theatre Project, that includes touring productions, classes and storytelling for grades K-12; and Backstage/Onstage—our equivalent to a second stage that offers staged readings, workshop productions, the Performers' Festival and experimental programs. In all areas, the company's work is distinguished by emotional intensity, exploration of contemporary values and maximum interaction between the company and the audience. More than 70 percent of our productions are area premieres. The company's core is a group of artists whose collaboration began 10 years ago. We share a common philosophy and commitment. Our process and an open and supportive working environment are as important as the final product. Development of individual artists is also a prime concern. The theatre experience is a journey shared by many people. We are working to make that journey as interesting, as layered, as challenging and as much fun as we can.

—Fontaine Syer

Theatre Project Company. Shawn Tucker and Heidi Thomas in *The Miss Firecracker Contest*. Photo: Sue Greenberg.

PRODUCTIONS 1985–86

Extremities, William Mastrosimone; (D) Fontaine Syer; (S) Bill Schmiel; (C) Laura Hanson; (L) Katherine J. Cardwell

To Kill a Mockingbird, adapt from: Harper Lee; (D) Pamela Sterling; (S) Hunter Crabtree; (C) Joyce L. Kogut; (L) Katherine J. Cardwell

Artichoke, Joanna M. Glass; (D) John Grassilli; (S) Frank Bradley; (C) Caroline Lent DeMoss; (L) Randy Bill Winder

A Delicate Balance, Edward Albee; (D) William Grivna; (S) Mel Dickerson; (C) Laurie J. Trevethan; (L) James J. Burwinkel

A Frog in His Throat, Georges Feydeau; adapt: Eric Conger; (D) Wayne Salomon; (S) Mel Dickerson; (C) Elizabeth Eisloeffel; (L) Glenn Dunn

The Pied Piper of Hamlin, Pamela Sterling; (D) Mark Landis; (S) Jim Walker; (C) Laurie J. Trevethan

What If I Want to Say No?, Pamela Sterling; (D) Fontaine Syer; (S) Jim Walker; (C) Laurie J. Trevethan

The Canterbury Tales, adapt: Pamela Sterling, from Geoffrey Chaucer; (D) Pamela Sterling; (S) Hunter Crabtree; (C) Leo Cortez

PRODUCTIONS 1986–87

The Miss Firecracker Contest, Beth Henley; (D) John Grassilli; (S) Mel Dickerson; (C) Laurie J. Trevethan; (L) Mark Wilson

Mother Hicks, Susan Zeder; (D) Pamela Sterling; (S) James J. Burwinkel; (C) Joyce L. Kogut; (L) Glenn Dunn

Orphans, Lyle Kessler; (D) Wayne Salomon; (S) Bill Schmiel; (C) Elizabeth Eisloeffel; (L) James J. Burwinkel

The Seagull, Anton Chekhov; trans and adapt: Jim Cavanaugh; (D) Mark Landis; (S) Hunter Crabtree; (C) Joyce L. Kogut; (L) Glenn Dunn

Rockaby and ***Footfalls***, Samuel Beckett; (D) Fontaine Syer; (S) Hunter Crabtree; (C) Joyce L. Kogut; (L) Glenn Dunn

The Collection, ***Interview***, ***Applicant*** and ***Trouble in the Works***, Harold Pinter; (D) Wayne Salomon; (S) Hunter Crabtree; (C) Joyce L. Kogut; (L) Glenn Dunn

Glengarry Glen Ross, David Mamet; (D) William Grivna; (S) Hunter Crabtree; (C) Joyce L. Kogut; (L) Glenn Dunn

You Can't Take It with You, Moss Hart and George S. Kaufman; (D) Fontaine Syer; (S) Mel Dickerson; (C) Elizabeth Eisloeffel; (L) Glenn Dunn

The Emperor's New Clothes, adapt: Pamela Sterling, from Hans Christian Andersen; (D) Connie I. Lane; (S) Mel Dickerson; (C) Laurie J. Trevethan

New Kid (New Canadian Kid), Dennis Foon; (D) Pamela Sterling; (S) Mel Dickerson; (C) Laurie J. Trevethan

Scrapbooks, Pamela Sterling; (D) Fontaine Syer; (S) Mel Dickerson; (C) Laurie J. Trevethan

TheatreVirginia. *West Side Story*. Photo: Robert Shelley.

TheatreVirginia

TERRY BURGLER
Artistic Director

EDWARD W. RUCKER
General Manager

Boulevard and Grove Aves.
Richmond, VA 23221
(804) 257-0840 (bus.)
(804) 257-0831 (b.o.)

FOUNDED 1955
Virginia Museum of Fine Arts

SEASON
Sept.-June

FACILITIES
Seating capacity: 500
Stage: proscenium

FINANCES
July 1, 1986-June 30, 1987
Expenses: $1,339,500

CONTRACTS
AEA LORT (C) and SSD&C

The medium is the message. For our theatre to make its maximal cultural and aesthetic contribution, we must remember two things: what makes theatre unique and what makes theatre irresistible. Theatre is not a literal event. Its task is not to create a substantive representation of reality but to transform it by imitation. Neither is theatre essentially a literary event (despite the exquisite literature it may contain). Theatre is a dynamic art which melds the collected imaginations of the creators with the collective imagination of the audience. At the moment those imaginations meet, they transform the world in which we live. The theatre, the theatregoer and our culture all emerge enriched. Theatre is a contact art. It must reach its audience. TheatreVirginia's task is to provide arenas for such meetings of the imagination.

—*Terry Burgler*

PRODUCTIONS 1985–86

Stage Struck, Simon Gray; (D) Terry Burgler; (S) David M. Crank; (C) Barbara Forbes; (L) Lynne M. Hartman
Man of La Mancha, book: Dale Wasserman; music: Mitch Leigh; lyrics: Joe Darion; (D) Terry Burgler; (S) Charles Caldwell; (C) Charles Caldwell; (L) Lynne M. Hartman
A Christmas Carol, adapt: Tom Markus, from Charles Dickens; (D) Bev Appleton; (S) Charles Caldwell; (C) Lana Fritz; (L) Lynne M. Hartman
Agnes of God, John Pielmeier; (D) Dan Hamilton; (S) David M. Crank; (C) David M. Crank; (L) Lynne M. Hartman
True West, Sam Shepard; (D) Bill Gregg; (S) David M. Crank; (C) Catherine Szari; (L) Lynne M. Hartman
The Glass Menagerie, Tennessee Williams; (D) Terry Burgler; (S) Charles Caldwell; (C) David M. Crank; (L) Terry Cermak
Arms and the Man, George Bernard Shaw; (D) Terry Burgler; (S) Charles Caldwell; (C) Susan Tsu; (L) Jackie Manassee
The Foreigner, Larry Shue; (D) Terry Burgler; (S) Charles Caldwell; (C) Susan Griffin; (L) Terry Cermak

PRODUCTIONS 1986–87

West Side Story, book: Arthur Laurents; music: Leonard Bernstein; lyrics: Stephen Sondheim; (D) Terry Burgler; (S) Charles Caldwell; (C) Jordan Ross; (L) Marilyn Rennagel
The School for Wives, Molière; trans: Richard Wilbur; (D) Terry Burgler; (S) Charles Caldwell; (C) Charles Caldwell; (L) Lynne M. Hartman
A Wireless Christmas, book: Terry Burgler and Bo Wilson; music and lyrics: Steve Liebman; (D) Terry Burgler; (S) Roxanne Sherbeck; (C) Marjorie McCown; (L) Lynne M. Hartman
Billy Bishop Goes to War, John Gray and Eric Peterson; (D) Terry Burgler; (S) Charles Caldwell; (C) Julie D. Keen; (L) Lynne M. Hartman
Orphans, Lyle Kessler; (D) Dan Hamilton; (S) Charles Caldwell; (C) Catherine Szari; (L) Terry Cermak
The Amen Corner, James Baldwin; (D) Terry Burgler; (S) David M. Crank; (C) Catherine Szari; (L) Terry Cermak
The Tempest, William Shakespeare; (D) Terry Burgler; (S) David M. Crank; (C) Charles Caldwell; (L) Richard Moore
Pump Boys and Dinettes, John Foley, Mark Hardwick, Debra Monk, Cass Morgan, John Schimmel and Jim Wann; (D) Terry Burgler; (S) David M. Crank; (C) Susan Griffin; (L) Terry Cermak

Theatreworks/USA

JAY HARNICK
Artistic Director

CHARLES HULL
Managing Director

890 Broadway
New York, NY 10003
(212) 677-5959

FOUNDED 1961
Robert K. Adams, Jay Harnick

SEASON
Sept.-June

FACILITIES
Promenade Theatre
Seating capacity: 400
Stage: thrust

Town Hall
Seating capacity: 1,500
Stage: proscenium

FINANCES
Oct. 1, 1985-Sept. 30, 1986
Expenses: $2,088,790

CONTRACTS
AEA TYA

Theatreworks/USA. Gordon Stanley, Colleen Dodson, Greg Zerkle and Glenn Mure in *Sherlock Holmes and the Red-headed League*. Photo: Gerry Goodstein.

As we enter our 27th season of creating theatre for young and family audiences, Theatreworks/USA continues to be inspired by the belief that young people deserve theatre endowed with the richness of content demanded by the most discerning adult audience. To that end, we have commissioned an ever-expanding collection of original works from established playwrights, composers and lyricists. Our creative roster includes Ossie Davis, Charles Strouse, Alice Childress, Joe Raposo, Thomas Babe, Albert Hague, Gary William Friedman, Mary Rodgers, Saul Levitt, John Forster and Leslie Lee. We are also dedicated to the development of fresh voices for the American theatre and encourage emerging playwrights to develop projects about issues that concern them and affect the young audiences they seek to address. We currently give over 1,000 performances annually in a touring radius encompassing 49 of the 50 states.

—Jay Harnick

PRODUCTIONS 1985–86

Look to the Stars, book and lyrics: John Allen; music: Joe Raposo; (D) Jay Harnick; (S) Hal Tine; (C) Carol H. Beule

Play to Win, book and lyrics: James de Jongh and Charles Cleveland; music: Jimi Foster; (D) Regge Life; (S) Tom Barnes; (C) Mary L. Hayes

Rapunzel, book and lyrics: David Crane and Marta Kauffman; music: Michael Skloff; (D) Paul Lazarus; (S) Mavis Smith; (C) Mary L. Hayes

Lady Liberty, book and lyrics: John Allen; music: Joe Raposo; (D) John Henry Davis; (S) Tom Barnes; (C) Martha Hally

When the Cookie Crumbles, You Can Still Pick Up the Pieces, various; (D) Jay Harnick; (S) Tom Barnes; (C) Mary L. Hayes

Babes in Toyland, book: John Peel; lyrics: Glen McDonough; music: Victor Herbert; (D) Paul Hewitt; (S) Jon Talierano; (C) Susan Loughran

PRODUCTIONS 1986–87

Martin Luther King, Jr., book: Leslie Lee; music and lyrics: Charles Strouse; (D) Jeffrey B. Moss; (S) Tom Barnes; (C) Kitty Leech

Sherlock Holmes and the Red-Headed League, book: John Forster, Greer Woodward and Rick Cummins; lyrics: Greer Woodward; music: Rick Cummins; (D) Peter Webb; (S) Bryan Johnson; (C) Kitty Leech

The Emperor's New Clothes, book and lyrics: Lynn Ahrens; music: Stephen Flaherty; (D) Paul Lazarus; (S) Tom Barnes; (C) Kitty Leech

Teddy Roosevelt, book: Jonathan Bolt; music: Thomas Tierney; lyrics: John Forster; (D) Greg Gunning; (S) Philipp Jung; (C) Debra Stein

When the Cookie Crumbles, You Can Still Pick Up the Pieces, various; (D) Jay Harnick; (S) Tom Barnes; (C) Mary L. Hayes

Babes in Toyland, book: John Peel; lyrics: Glen McDonough; music: Victor Herbert; (D) Paul Hewitt; (S) Jon Talierano; (C) Susan Loughran

Lady Liberty, book and lyrics: John Allen; music: Joe Raposo; (D) John Henry Davis; (S) Tom Barnes; (C) Martha Hally

Theatre X

Theatre X. Julia Romanski in *The History of Sexuality: An Investigation*. Photo: Taffnie Bogart.

FLORA COKER
JOHN SCHNEIDER
Associate Artistic Directors

MARC HAUPERT
Managing Director

Box 92206
Milwaukee, WI 53202
(414) 278-0555 (bus.)
(414) 278-0044 (b.o.)

FOUNDED 1969
Conrad Bishop, Linda Bishop, Ron Gural

SEASON
Year-round

FACILITIES
Contemporary Arts Center
Seating capacity: 99
Stage: flexible

FINANCES
Sept. 1, 1986-Aug. 31, 1987
Expenses: $125,000

To examine the construction of theatre is to examine the construction of reality. At Theatre X, it is possible to reconsider every element of theatre production in light

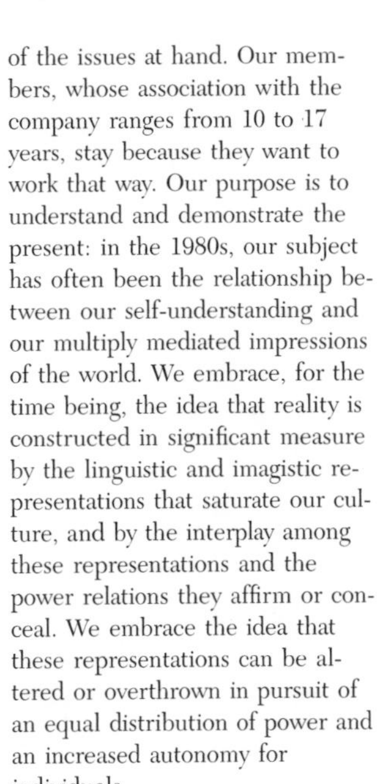

of the issues at hand. Our members, whose association with the company ranges from 10 to 17 years, stay because they want to work that way. Our purpose is to understand and demonstrate the present: in the 1980s, our subject has often been the relationship between our self-understanding and our multiply mediated impressions of the world. We embrace, for the time being, the idea that reality is constructed in significant measure by the linguistic and imagistic representations that saturate our culture, and by the interplay among these representations and the power relations they affirm or conceal. We embrace the idea that these representations can be altered or overthrown in pursuit of an equal distribution of power and an increased autonomy for individuals.

—John Schneider

PRODUCTIONS 1985–86

Rembrandt and Hitler or Me, Ritsaert ten Cate, David Brisban, Deborah J. Clifton, John Kishline, Willem van Toorn and Hanne Tierney; (D) Ritsaert ten Cate; (S) Ritsaert ten Cate

Full Hookup, Conrad Bishop and Elizabeth Fuller; (D) Conrad Bishop; (S) Conrad Bishop and John Story; (C) company; (L) Conrad Bishop and John Kishline

Big and Little, Botho Strauss; (D) John Schneider and Flora Coker; (S) John Story; (C) Sam Fleming

PRODUCTIONS 1986–87

My Werewolf, John Schneider; (D) David Schweizer; (S) Jim Matson; (C) Sam Fleming; (L) Margaret Nelson

A Country Doctor, adapt: Len Jenkin, from Franz Kafka; (D) John Schneider; (S) Jim Matson; (C) Carrie Skoczek; (L) Margaret Nelson

The History of Sexuality: an Investigation, Deborah Clifton, Flora Coker, Mary Ewald, John Kazanjian, John Kishline, Kathy O'Brien, Julia Romanski and John Schneider; (D) company; (S) Jim Matson; (C) company; (L) John Kishline

Second Annual Moving Performance Parade, company-developed

Trinity Repertory Company. Richard Kneeland and Margot Dionne in *The Country Girl*. Photo: Mark Morelli.

Trinity Repertory Company

ADRIAN HALL
Artistic Director

E. TIMOTHY LANGAN
Managing Director

201 Washington St.
Providence, RI 02903
(401) 521-1100 (bus.)
(401) 351-4242 (b.o.)

FOUNDED 1963
Adrian Hall

SEASON
Year-round

FACILITIES
Upstairs Theatre
Seating capacity: 560
Stage: flexible

Downstairs Theatre
Seating capacity: 297
Stage: thrust

FINANCES
July 1, 1986-June 30, 1987
Expenses: $3,300,000

CONTRACTS
AEA LORT (B), (C), SSD&C and USA

Beginning our 24th season, Trinity Repertory Company has earned recognition for its dedication to a resident company of artists, its vigorous ensemble style of production, its long commitment to the development of original works and adaptations, its daring and innovative treatment of world classics and its fresh approach to traditional material. From the beginning, Trinity Rep's two goals have been to provide permanent employment to its resident artists and to engage its audience as participants, rather than spectators, in the theatre experience. The first aim has been supported since we became the first theatre in American history to receive an Ongoing Ensemble grant from the National Endowment for the Arts, enabling us to provide yearly financial security to our artists. The second aim continues to be met with over 20,000 subscribers supporting the company's invigorating theatrical output. Trinity Rep's award-winning humanities program, with essay booklets and post-performance discussions, and the Project Discovery program continue to develop and enhance the audience's theatre experience.

—*Adrian Hall*

PRODUCTIONS 1985–86

Baby, book: Sybille Pearson; music: David Shire; lyrics: Richard Maltby, Jr.; (D) William Damkoehler; (S) Robert D. Soule; (C) William Lane; (L) John F. Custer

Not by Bed Alone, Georges Feydeau; (D) David Wheeler; (S) David A. Rotondo; (C) William Lane; (L) John F. Custer

The Marriage of Bette and Boo, Christopher Durang; (D) Adrian Hall; (S) Eugene Lee; (C) William Lane; (L) John F. Custer

Cat on a Hot Tin Roof, Tennessee Williams; (D) George Martin; (S) Robert D. Soule; (C) William Lane; (L) John F. Custer

The Beauty Part, S.J. Perelman; (D) Philip Minor; (S) Robert D. Soule; (C) William Lane; (L) John F. Custer

A Christmas Carol, adapt: Adrian Hall and Richard Cumming, from Charles Dickens; (D) William Damkoehler; (S) Robert D. Soule; (C) William Lane; (L) John F. Custer

The Crucible, Arthur Miller; (D) Richard Jenkins; (S) Robert D. Soule; (C) William Lane; (L) John F. Custer

Life and Limb, Keith Reddin; (D) Neal Baron; (S) Robert D. Soule; (C) William Lane; (L) John F. Custer

The Tavern, George M. Cohan; (D) Tony Giordano; (S) Robert D. Soule; (C) William Lane; (L) John F. Custer

Pasta, Tom Griffin; (D) David Wheeler; (S) Robert D. Soule; (C) William Lane; (L) John F. Custer

The Country Girl, Clifford Odets; (D) Adrian Hall; (S) Eugene Lee; (C) William Lane; (L) Eugene Lee

PRODUCTIONS 1986–87

Noises Off, Michael Frayn; (D) Tony Giordano; (S) Robert D. Soule; (C) William Lane; (L) John F. Custer

A Funny Thing Happened on the Way to the Forum, book: Burt Shevelove and Larry Gelbart; music and lyrics: Stephen Sondheim; (D) Tony Giordano; (S) Robert D. Soule; (C) William Lane; (L) John F. Custer

The Visit, Friedrich Dürrenmatt; adapt: Maurice Valency; (D) Adrian Hall; (S) Eugene Lee; (C) William Lane; (L) John F. Custer

The Real Thing, Tom Stoppard; (D) Philip Minor; (S) Robert D. Soule; (C) William Lane; (L) John F. Custer

Hurlyburly, David Rabe; (D) David Wheeler; (S) Robert D. Soule; (C) William Lane; (L) John F. Custer

A Christmas Carol, adapt: Adrian Hall and Richard Cumming, from Charles Dickens; (D) Ken Bryant; (S) Robert D. Soule; (C) William Lane; (L) John F. Custer

Our Town, Thornton Wilder; (D) Paul Benedict; (S) Robert D. Soule; (C) William Lane; (L) John F. Custer

Glengarry Glen Ross, David Mamet; (D) Tony Giordano; (S) Robert D. Soule; (C) William Lane; (L) John F. Custer

All the King's Men, Robert Penn Warren; (D) Adrian Hall; (S) Eugene Lee; (C) William Lane; (L) Natasha Katz

Quartermaine's Terms, Simon Gray; (D) Tony Giordano; (S) Robert D. Soule; (C) William Lane; (L) John F. Custer

A Lie of the Mind, Sam Shepard; (D) David Wheeler; (S) Robert D. Soule; (C) William Lane; (L) John F. Custer

Unicorn Theatre

CYNTHIA LEVIN
Artistic Director

JAMES CAIRNS
Executive Director

3820 Main St.
Kansas City, MO 64111
(816) 531-7529 (bus.)
(816) 276-2700 (b.o.)

FOUNDED 1973
James Cairns, Rohn Dennis, Liz Gordon

SEASON
Sept.-June

FACILITIES
Seating capacity: 150
Stage: thrust

FINANCES
July 1, 1986-June 30, 1987
Expenses: $254,000

CONTRACTS
AEA SPT

As the artistic director of Unicorn Theatre, I am dedicated to producing new plays that reflect a social consciousness. I prefer to present works that deal with significant, contemporary issues while creating an intellectual and thought-provoking experience. This includes shows that have not been previously staged in this area as well as world premieres. Two or three of our plays each season are written by lesser-known playwrights. Several of our premieres have been restaged in Chicago, San Diego and Off Broadway. The emphasis at the Unicorn is on the script itself and on the use of local professional artists. The technical aspects of our productions are limited, but we tend to do a lot with very little. Our work is process-centered rather than commercially oriented. Our new space is accessible to the handicapped so we are looking forward to employing disabled artists in the future.

—*Cynthia Levin*

PRODUCTIONS 1985–86

Extremities, William Mastrosimone; (D) Cynthia Levin; (S) Laura Burkhart; (C) Ran Adler; (L) Jazz Jaslow

'night, Mother, Marsha Norman; (D) Peter Bennet; (S) Laura Burkhart; (C) Wendy Harms; (L) Jazz Jaslow

Angels Fall, Lanford Wilson; (D) Jim Tibbs; (S) Chuck Bell; (C) Ran Adler; (L) Art Kent

Never Say Die, Frank Higgins; (D) Chuck Gorden; (S) Chuck Bell; (C) Ran Adler; (L) Art Kent

Painting Churches, Tina Howe; (D) Francis Cullinan; (S) Laura Burkhart; (C) Ran Adler; (L) Jazz Jaslow

Shuffle Off This Mortal Buffalo, Richard Natale; (D) R. Alan Nichols; (S) David Wallace; (C) Nancy Ruark; (L) Art Kent

Still Life, Emily Mann; (D) Cynthia Levin; (C) Wendy Harms; (L) Jazz Jaslow

PRODUCTIONS 1986–87

Heartland, Frank Higgins; (D) Danny Baker; (S) Art Kent; (C) Wendy Harms; (L) Art Kent

Quilters, Molly Newman and Barbara Damashek; music and lyrics: Barbara Damashek; (D) Lamby Hedge; (S) Laura Burkhart and Dan Epley; (C) Wendy Harms; (L) Jazz Jaslow

Expiring Minds Want to Know, Cheryl Benge, Christy Brandt, Rosanna E. Coppedge, Valerie Fagan, Ross Freese, Mark Houston, Sandee Johnson and Peggy Pharr Wilson; music: Mark Houston; (D) Cynthia Levin; (S) Laura Burkhart and Dan Epley; (C) Elizabeth Jenkins; (L) Steven Mark Johnson

Orphans, Lyle Kessler; (D) James Cairns; (S) Randy Cochran; (C) Elizabeth Jenkins; (L) Steve Butler

As Is, William M. Hoffman; (D) David Petrarca; (S) Michael Layton; (C) Ric Thomas Rice; (L) Daniel MacLean Wagner

The Last Good Moment of Lilly Baker, Russell Davis; (D) Toni Dorfman; (S) Laura Burkhart; (C) Ran Adler; (L) Art Kent

Aunt Dan and Lemon, Wallace Shawn; (D) Cynthia Levin; (S) Laura Burkhart; (C) Cheryl Benge; (L) Randy Winder

Unicorn Theatre. Jim Korinke and Lisa Hefley in *Extremities*.

Victory Gardens Theater. Andrew White in *Kids in the Dark*. Photo: Jennifer Girard.

Victory Gardens Theater

DENNIS ZACEK
Artistic Director

MARCELLE MCVAY
Managing Director

2257 North Lincoln Ave.
Chicago , IL 60614
(312) 549-5788 (bus.)
(312) 871-3000 (b.o.)

FOUNDED 1974
Warren Casey, Cordis Fejer, Stuart Gordon, Roberta Maguire, Mac McGinnes, Cecil O'Neal, June Pyskacek, David Rasche

SEASON
Sept.-July

FACILITIES
Mainstage
Seating capacity: 195
Stage: thrust

Studio
Seating capacity: 60
Stage: proscenium

FINANCES
July 1, 1986-June 30, 1987
Expenses: $879,869

CONTRACTS
AEA CAT and USA

Victory Gardens Theater is a developmental theatre that nurtures the Chicago artist, with a special emphasis on the Chicago playwright. The theatre features five basic programs. The mainstage series consists of five productions a year, many of which are world premieres. The studio series presents three productions in our second theatre, focusing on more experimental work. The Readers Theater series presents works-in-progress free of charge to the public on a bimonthly basis. The training center offers classes in all aspects of theatre and serves over 1,000 students a year. The touring program usually features an abbreviated version of one of the mainstage shows, which is seen by more than 10,000 high school students annually. Many participants involved in Victory Gardens may be familiar with only one of these five areas of involvement, but all five areas interact to produce the same result—developmental theatre.

—Dennis Zacek

PRODUCTIONS 1985–86

Wild Indian, Theodore Shank; (D) Dennis Zacek; (S) Rick Paul; (C) Patricia Hart; (L) Chris Phillips

American Dreams, adapt: Peter Frisch, from Studs Terkel; (D) Peter Frisch; (S) Nan Zabriskie; (C) Glenn Billings; (L) Paul Miller

Gentrification, Dean Corrin; (D) Sandy Shinner; (S) Jeff Bauer; (C) Ellen Gross; (L) Rita Pietraszek

Split Second, Dennis McIntyre; (D) Dennis Zacek; (S) Carl Forsberg; (C) Kerry Fleming; (L) Michael Rourke

Mr. 80%, James Sherman; (D) Dennis Zacek; (S) Nels Anderson; (C) Nan Zabriskie; (L) Robert Shook

Tomorrowland, Jeffrey M. Jones; (D) Dennis Zacek; (S) James Dardenne; (C) Kim M. Fenel; (L) Ellen E. Jones

Slumming, Marisha Chamberlain; (D) Sandy Shinner; (S) Eve Cauley; (C) Carol Miller; (L) Howard J. Werner

Penta/Benta, Steven Ivcich; (D) Steven Ivcich; (S) Steven Ivcich; (C) Sheila Myrcik; (L) Barb Reeder

PRODUCTIONS 1986–87

Other Places, Harold Pinter; (D) Dennis Zacek; (S) James Dardenne; (C) John Hancock Brooks, Jr.; (L) Ellen E. Jones

Shoot Me While I'm Happy, book adapt: Steve Carter; conceived: Ronald Stevens and Adjora Stevens; (D) Sydney Daniels; (S) Nan Zabriskie; (C) Kerry Fleming; (L) Barbara Reeder

Eleemosynary, Lee Blessing; (D) Sandy Shinner; (S) Jeff Bauer; (C) Kerry Fleming; (L) Rita Pietraszek

Kids in the Dark, Rick Cleveland and David Breskin; (D) Dennis Zacek; (S) Patrick Kerwin; (C) Maureen Kennedy; (L) Michael Rourke

Play Expo '87:

Gardinia's 'n' Blum, Nicholas A. Patricca; (D) Dennis Zacek; (S) James Dardenne; (C) John Hancock Brooks, Jr.; (L) Robert Shook

In the Service of Others, Valerie Quinney; (D) James O'Reilly; (S) Jeff Bauer; (C) Kerry Fleming; (L) Michael Rourke

Centipede, Rick Cleveland; (D) Sandy Shinner; (S) Jeff Bauer; (C) Kerry Fleming; (L) Michael Rourke

John Wayne Movies, John Logan; (D) Sandy Shinner; (S) Jeff Bauer; (C) Kerry Fleming; (L) Michael Rourke

Mothers and Sons, Lonnie Carter; (D) Sandy Shinner; (S) Jeff Bauer; (C) Kerry Fleming; (L) Michael Rourke

Takunda, Charles Smith; (D) Nick Faust; (S) Jeff Bauer; (C) Kerry Fleming; (L) Michael Rourke

Roof Top Piper, David Hernandez; (D) Chuck Smith; (S) Jeff Bauer; (C) Maureen Kennedy; (L) Michael Rourke

The News from St. Petersburg, Rich Orloff; (D) Chuck Smith; (S) Jeff Bauer; (C) Maureen Kennedy; (L) Michael Rourke

They Even Got the Rienzi, Claudia Allen; (D) Chuck Smith; (S) Jeff Bauer; (C) Maureen Kennedy; (L) Michael Rourke

Floor Above the Roof, Daniel Therriault; (D) Joseph Sadowski; (S) Jeff Bauer; (C) Maureen Kennedy; (L) Michael Rourke

Before I Wake, William J. Norris; (D) Susan Osborne-Mott; (S) James Dardenne; (C) Glenn Billings; (L) Robert Shook

The Figure, Clifton Campbell; (D) Terry McCabe; (S) James Dardenne; (C) Glenn Billings; (L) Robert Shook

Prior Engagements, Frank Manley; (D) Dennis Zacek; (S) James Dardenne; (C) Maureen Kennedy; (L) Ellen E. Jones

Rough and ***Catastrophe***, Samuel Beckett; (D) Bill Payne; (S) Lynn Ziehe; (C) Maureen Kennedy; (L) Barbara Reeder

Naked Zoo, Friends of the Zoo; (D) Steven Ivcich; (S) Mary Griswold; (L) Geoffrey Bushor

Vineyard Theatre

BARBARA ZINN KRIEGER
Executive Director

DOUGLAS AIBEL
Artistic Director, Theatre

GARY P. STEUER
Managing Director

Vineyard Theatre. S. Epatha Merkerson in *Lady Day at Emerson's Bar & Grill.* Photo: Martha Swope Associates/Carol Rosegg.

309 East 26th St.
New York, NY 10010
(212) 832-1002 (bus.)
(212) 683-0696 (b.o.)

FOUNDED 1981
Barbara Zinn Krieger

SEASON
Sept.-July

FACILITIES
Vineyard Theatre at 26th St.
Seating capacity: 65
Stage: thrust

Vineyard Theatre at Union Square
Seating capacity: 150
Stage: flexible

FINANCES
Sept. 1, 1986-Aug. 31, 1987
Expenses: $310,000

CONTRACTS
AEA letter of agreement

The Vineyard Theatre, a multiart chamber theatre, produces new plays and musicals, music-theatre collaborations and revivals of works that have failed in the commercial arena. Our focus has been to provide a supportive and unpressured environment in which playwrights, actors, composers, directors and designers can collaborate, creating work that challenges both themselves and Vineyard's audiences in an intimate 65-seat theatre. While the range of our programming is eclectic, we've been consistently drawn to young writers with a distinctively poetic style and an affinity for adventurous theatrical forms. Because our organization houses an active chamber opera program, as well as an early music and classic jazz series, we have also attempted to explore different ways in which music can enhance and enrich a dramatic text. We look forward to the opening of a large, new, flexible theatre facility, now under construction at Union Square, that will provide us with great artistic and technical possibilities for the future.

—Douglas Aibel

PRODUCTIONS 1985–86

Goblin Market, book adapt: Polly Pen and Peggy Harmon, from Christina Rossetti; music and lyrics: Polly Pen; (D) Andre Ernotte; (S) Bill Barclay; (C) Muriel Stockdale; (L) Phil Monat

Sorrows and Sons, Stephen Metcalfe; (D) Peter Frisch; (S) James Wolk; (C) Jeffrey Ullman; (L) Richard Moore

Lady Day at Emerson's Bar and Grill, Lanie Robertson; (D) Andre Ernotte; (S) Bill Barclay; (C) Muriel Stockdale; (L) Phil Monat

PRODUCTIONS 1986–87

How to Say Goodbye, Mary Gallagher; (D) Liz Diamond; (S) Bill Barclay; (C) Janna Gjesdal; (L) Phil Monat

Songs on a Shipwrecked Sofa, book adapt and lyrics: Polly Pen and James Milton, from Mervyn Peake; music: Polly Pen; (D) Andre Ernotte; (S) Bill Barclay; (C) Muriel Stockdale; (L) Phil Monat

Lady Day at Emerson's Bar and Grill, Lanie Robertson; (D) Andre Ernotte; (S) Bill Barclay; (C) Muriel Stockdale; (L) Phil Monat

Virginia Stage Company

CHARLES TOWERS
Artistic Director

DAN J. MARTIN
Managing Director

Box 3770
Norfolk, VA 23514
(804) 627-6988 (bus.)
(804) 627-1234 (b.o.)

FOUNDED 1979
Community members

SEASON
Oct.-Apr.

FACILITIES
Mainstage
Seating capacity: 675
Stage: proscenium

Second Stage
Seating capacity: 150
Stage: flexible

FINANCES
July 1, 1986-June 30, 1987
Expenses: $1,255,000

CONTRACTS
AEA LORT (D) and SSD&C

The Virginia Stage Company produces a purposefully eclectic mix of plays—classical, contemporary and new. We try at all times to choose plays that we believe in, assuming that an initiating passion is the single most important factor in making a successful creation. The company's artistic character is formed by each group of artists who gather to make a production. The regular return of the finest of these artists means the emergence of an identifiable aesthetic. It is our aim to make theatre that works, that meets our standards for both literary merit and creative production, engages the audience, raises questions and hopefully provides an element of perspective or insight. Theatre that works does not need to be justified by additional programming; it is by itself the very community service we are chartered to provide. Theatre that works confirms the existence of the theatrical form as a genuine alternative to television and film. Theatre that works does not need rhetorical explanation; it just works.

—Charles Towers

PRODUCTIONS 1985–86

The Beastly Beatitudes of Balthazar B, J.P. Donleavy; (D) Charles Towers; (S) John Lee Beatty; (C) Kurt Wilhelm; (L) Roger Morgan

Master Harold... and the boys, Athol Fugard; (D) Alex Dmitriev; (S) Lewis Folden; (C) Candice Cain; (L) Dirk Kuyk

Painting Churches, Tina Howe; (D) Jamie Brown; (S) Michael Miller; (C) Candice Cain; (L) Jim Sale

Wetter than Water, Deborah Pryor; (D) Charles Towers; (S) Michael Miller; (C) Candice Cain; (L) Dirk Kuyk

Jitters, David French; (D) Pamela Berlin; (S) Rick Dennis; (C) Candice Cain; (L) Dirk Kuyk

The Glass Menagerie, Tennessee Williams; (D) Christopher Hanna; (S) Lewis Folden; (C) Candice Cain; (L) Spencer Mosse

Billy Bishop Goes to War, John Gray and Eric Peterson; (D) Mitchell Ivers; (S) Pat Woodbridge; (C) Myra Bumgarner; (L) Jackie Manassee

PRODUCTIONS 1986–87

Cat on a Hot Tin Roof, Tennessee Williams; (D) Charles Towers; (S) Marjorie Bradley Kellogg; (C) Candice Cain; (L) Spencer Mosse

The Frontiers of Farce, adapt: Peter Barnes, from Georges Feydeau and Frank Wedekind; (D) Charles Towers; (S) John Lee Beatty; (C) Martha Kelly; (L) Jackie Manassee

Haut Gout, Allan Havis; (D) Christopher Hanna; (S) Nancy Thun; (C) Candice Cain; (L) Jackie Manassee

The Tempest, William Shakespeare; (D) Charles Towers; (S) Pavel Dobrusky; (C) Candice Cain; (L) Pavel Dobrusky

Virginia Stage Company. Richard Elmore in *The Tempest*. Photo: Mark Atkinson.

The Walnut Street Theatre. Kelly Bishop and Ron Raines in *A Little Night Music*. Photo: Kenneth Kauffman.

The Walnut Street Theatre

BERNARD HAVARD
Executive Director

MARY BENSEL
General Manager

9th and Walnut Sts.
Philadelphia, PA 19107
(215) 574-3550 (bus.)
(215) 574-3586 (b.o.)

FOUNDED 1983
Bernard Havard

SEASON
Oct.-May

FACILITIES
Mainstage
Seating capacity: 1,052
Stage: proscenium

Studio Theatre Three
Seating capacity: 93
Stage: flexible

Studio Theatre Five
Seating capacity: 99
Stage: proscenium

FINANCES
June 1, 1986-May 31, 1987
Expenses: $4,046,071

CONTRACTS
AEA LORT (A), SSD&C and USA

My fundamental commitment is to the continuation and survival of theatre, while creating an environment in which the artist can be nourished temporally and spiritually. I find the model closest to my ideal would be the Old Vic when it was run by Lillian Bayliss. At the Walnut Street Theatre, we have found success in furthering institutional growth while providing a rich setting for theatre professionals. I have a deep interest in new American plays. We currently produce at least one new play each season on our main stage, while our studio series allows us the freedom to produce a whole season of new and developing plays. These studio productions provide the opportunity to explore provocative topics that challenge the audience and the artists, presented in intimate and flexible settings. The Walnut Street Theatre School complements our programming through comprehensive, professional training, as well as providing community outreach pro grams, such as Shakespeare Alive!

—*Bernard Havard*

PRODUCTIONS 1985–86

Isn't It Romantic, Wendy Wasserstein; (D) Tom Markus; (S) Joe Varga; (C) Lana Fritz; (L) Richard Moore

Gypsy, book: Arthur Laurents; music: Jule Styne; lyrics: Stephen Sondheim; (D) Charles Abbott; (S) Mark Morton; (C) Kathleen Blake; (L) Gregg Marriner

The Little Foxes, Lillian Hellman; (D) Josephine Abady; (S) David Potts; (C) Susan Hirschfeld; (L) Jeff Davis

Tomfoolery, adapt: Cameron Mackintosh and Robin Ray; music and lyrics: Tom Lehrer; (D) William Roudebush; (S) James Irwin; (C) Mel Gersney; (L) Jeff Davis

As You Like It, William Shakespeare; (D) Malcolm Black; (S) Paul Wonsek; (C) Kathleen Blake; (L) Paul Wonsek

A Lunacy of Moons, Michael Russell; (D) James Peskin; (S) S. Ian Murray; (C) Pierre DeRagon; (L) Nina Chwast

Oh, Mr. Faulkner, Do You Write?, John Maxwell and Tom Dupree; (D) William Partlan; (S) Jimmy Robertson; (C) Martha Wood; (L) Tina Charney

she also dances, Kenneth Arnold; (D) Charlie Hensley; (C) Pierre DeRagon; (L) Nina Chwast

Salt Water Moon, David French; (D) Andrew Lichtenberg; (S) Nina Chwast; (C) Pierre DeRagon; (L) Nina Chwast

PRODUCTIONS 1986–87

The Prisoner of Second Avenue, Neil Simon; (D) Tom Markus; (S) Joe Varga; (C) Lana Fritz; (L) Richard Moore

A Little Night Music, book: Hugh Wheeler; music and lyrics: Stephen Sondheim; (D) Jack Allison; (S) Fred Kolo; (C) Lewis Rampino; (L) Fred Kolo

The Big Knife, Clifford Odets; (D) Malcolm Black; (S) Paul Wonsek; (C) Kathleen Blake; (L) Paul Wonsek

Dumas, John MacNicholas; (D) Larry Carpenter; (S) John Falabella; (C) Lowell Detweiler; (L) Marcia Maderia

Tintypes, Mary Kyte, Mel Marvin and Gary Pearle; (D) Charles Abbott; (S) Jeffrey Schneider; (C) Barbara Forbes; (L) Clarke W. Thornton

Escoffier: King of Chefs, Owen Rackleff; (D) Laurence Carr; (S) Robert Odorisio; (C) Lynn Fox; (L) Nina Chwast

Eb and Flo, Blake Walton and Amy Whitman; (D) James Bohr; (S) Robert Odorisio; (C) Lynn Fox; (L) Nina Chwast

The Normal Heart, Larry Kramer; (D) Charlie Hensley; (S) Robert Odorisio; (C) Christine Moore; (L) Nina Chwast

One for the Road, ***Applicant***, Harold Pinter; ***Audience***, Vaclav Havel; (D) Andrew Lichtenberg; (C) Christine Moore; (L) Rebecca Klein

Nasty Little Secrets, Lanie Robertson; (D) Stuart Ross; (S) Robert Odorisio; (C) Robert Bevenger; (L) George McMahon

Bubbling Brown Sugar, book: Loften Mitchell; conceived: Rosetta LeNoire; (D) Billy Wilson; (S) Paul Wonsek; (C) Barbara Forbes; (L) Marcia Maderia

Whole Theatre

OLYMPIA DUKAKIS
Producing Artistic Director

KAREN SHAFER
Managing Director

544 Bloomfield Ave.
Montclair, NJ 07042

(201) 744-2996 (bus.)
(201) 744-2989 (b.o.)

FOUNDED 1973

SEASON
Sept.-May

FACILITIES
Seating capacity: 199
Stage: proscenium

FINANCES
July 1, 1986-June 30, 1987
Expenses: $981,588

CONTRACTS
AEA LORT (D) and SSD&C

Whole Theatre. Alexandra Gersten, Susie Jordan, Apollo Dukakis and Joseph Siravo in *We Won't Pay! We Won't Pay!*. Photo: Jeffrey Sestilio.

The Whole Theatre's mainstage season, school and ArtReach residencies strive, in all respects, to reflect the compelling personal statement and teachings of the company's artists and educators. Long-term commitments to playwrights, actors, directors, designers and theatre educators, as well as affiliations with other state arts organizations, educational institutions, community and social agencies, delineate the Whole Theatre signature and institutional identity. Our 200-seat theatre offers a five-play season of new work, hosts "new wave" companies and presents classics uniquely reconceived and staged. Other programs include a humanities series, a women's writing project called "The Gathering," an emerging company of comic writers and comedians, and a developing company modeled after the Living Stage Theatre Company in Washington, D.C. Whole Theatre provides classes for children, teens and adults, and residencies at over 30 sites for groups that include the economically deprived, the disabled, the gifted, the developmentally handicapped, incarcerated women and senior citizens.

—*Olympia Dukakis*

PRODUCTIONS 1985–86

A Midsummer Night's Dream, William Shakespeare; (D) Amy Saltz; (S) Michael Miller; (C) Sigrid Insull; (L) Ann Wrightson

Season's Greetings, Alan Ayckbourn; (D) Kent Thompson; (S) Ricardo Morin; (C) Karen Gerson; (L) Carol Rubenstein

Home, Samm-Art Williams; (D) Billie Allen; (S) Randy Benjamin; (C) Judy Dearing; (L) Richard Moore

Electra: The Legend, Michael Sayers; (D) Austin Pendleton; (S) Michael Miller; (C) Sigrid Insull; (L) Carol Rubenstein

Sand Mountain, Romulus Linney; (D) Romulus Linney; (S) Michael Miller; (C) Sigrid Insull; (L) Richard Moore

PRODUCTIONS 1986–87

Pops, Romulus Linney; (D) Romulus Linney; (S) Michael Miller; (C) Karen Gerson; (L) Rachel Budin

The Seagull, Anton Chekhov; (D) Suzanne Shepherd; (S) Dale Jordan; (C) Sigrid Insull; (L) Ann Wrightson

We Won't Pay! We Won't Pay!, Dario Fo; trans: R.G. Davis; (D) Chris Silva; (S) Lewis Folden; (C) Sigrid Insull; (L) Rachel Budin

Steal Away, Ramona King; (D) Billie Allen; (S) Randy Benjamin; (C) Judy Dearing; (L) Shirley Prendergast
Billy Bishop Goes to War, John Gray and Eric Peterson; (D) Mitchell Ivers; (S) Pat Woodbridge; (L) Jackie Manassee

Williamstown Theatre Festival

NIKOS PSACHAROPOULOS
Artistic/Executive Director

BONNIE J. MONTE
Associate Artistic Director

DEIRDRE MOYNIHAN
General Manager

Box 517
Williamstown, MA 01267
(413) 597-3377 (bus.)
(413) 597-3400 (b.o.)

FOUNDED 1955
Nikos Psacharopoulos, trustees of the Williamstown Theatre Festival

SEASON
June-Aug.

FACILITIES
Mainstage
Seating capacity: 479
Stage: proscenium

Other Stage
Seating capacity: 96
Stage: flexible

Free Theatre
Seating capacity: 000
Stage: flexible

FINANCES
Dec. 1, 1985-Nov. 30, 1986
Expenses: $1,024,298

CONTRACTS
AEA CORST (X), letter of agreement and SSD&C

Since its establishment in 1955, under the leadership of Nikos Psacharopoulos, the Williamstown Theatre Festival has evolved into a major summer theatrical complex encompassing five separate stages. The Equity company performs on the main stage in the 479-seat Adams Memorial Theatre; the Other Stage focuses on new plays in the intimate 96-seat Extension Theatre, where the staged readings series is also held; cabarets are presented at area restaurants; Sunday special events are held at the Clark Art Institute; and a brand new venture—an outdoor free theatre has just been launched. WTF's commitment is twofold—to present important productions of classic works, which because of their scope and complexity are not often seen on the American stage, and to provide a fertile training ground for theatre professionals of the future—actors, directors, designers, stage managers, technicians, administrators and playwrights. Many of WTF's alumni (over 2,000 since 1957) are now well-known theatre professionals and return year after year to enrich the WTF family.

—Bonnie J. Monte

Williamstown Theatre Festival. Christopher Walken and Sigourney Weaver in *A Streetcar Named Desire*. Photo: Bob Marshak.

PRODUCTIONS 1986

Barbarians, Maxim Gorky; trans: Kitty Hunter-Blair, Jeremy Brooks and Michael Weller; (D) Nikos Psacharopoulos; (S) Santo Loquasto; (C) Santo Loquasto; (L) William Armstrong
Sweet Sue, A.R. Gurney, Jr.; (D) John Tillinger; (S) Santo Loquasto; (C) Jess Goldstein; (L) Arden Fingerhut
Summer and Smoke, Tennessee Williams; (D) James Simpson; (S) Santo Loquasto; (C) Claudia Brown; (L) Arden Fingerhut
The School for Scandal, Richard Brinsley Sheridan; (D) Austin Pendleton; (S) Andrew Jackness; (C) David Murin; (L) Roger Meeker
A Streetcar Named Desire, Tennessee Williams; (D) Nikos Psacharopoulos; (S) John Conklin; (C) Jess Goldstein; (L) Pat Collins
The Novelist, Howard Fast; (D) Gregory Boyd; (S) Paul Weimer; (C) Paul Weimer; (L) Christian Epps
Hawthorne Country, adapt: Kenneth Cavander and Lou Berger, from Nathaniel Hawthorne; (D) Kenneth Cavander; (S) Paul Weimer; (C) Paul Weimer; (L) Christian Epps
The Lucky Spot, Beth Henley; (D) Norman Rene; (S) James Youmans; (C) David Murin; (L) Bruce Auerbach
Eleanor, Gretchen Cryer and Nancy Ford; (D) Gretchen Cryer; (S) James Youmans; (C) Claudia Brown; (L) Dale Jordan

PRODUCTIONS 1987

The Crucible, Arthur Miller; (D) Nikos Psacharopoulos; (S) John Arnone; (C) Jess Goldstein; (L) Peter Hunt
The Homecoming, Harold Pinter; (D) James Simpson; (S) James Sandefur; (C) Claudia Brown; (L) Roger Meeker
The Rover, Aphra Behn; (D) John Rubenstein; (S) Paul Steinberg; (C) Pamela Peterson; (L) Dennis Parichy
The Night of the Iguana, Tennessee Williams; (D) Walton Jones and Margaret Booker; (S) Christopher Barreca; (C) Claudia Brown; (L) Stephen Strawbridge
The Three Sisters, Anton Chekhov; (D) Nikos Psacharopoulos; (S) John Conklin; (C) Jess Goldstein; (L) Pat Collins
Dog in Mouth, Morton Lichter; (D) Gordon Rogoff; (S) James Youmans; (C) James Youmans; (L) J.R. Gardner
Campion, Chris Buckley and Jamie MacGuire; (D) Kevin Kelley; (S) Rusty Smith; (C) Rusty Smith; (L) J.R. Gardner
Tuesday's Child, Kate Lock and Terry Johnson; (D) Kay Matschullat; (S) Scott Chambliss; (C) Scott Chambliss; (L) Scott Zilinsky
Moon over Miami, John Guare; (D) Larry Sloan; (S) Scott Chambliss; (C) Candice Donnelley; (L) Roger Meeker
Golden Boy, Clifford Odets; (D) Joanne Woodward; (S) James Youmans; (C) Michelle Matland; (L) Bruce Auerbach
The Emigration of Adam Kurtzik, Ted Herstand; (D) James Simpson; (S) Tim Saternow; (C) Tim Saternow; (L) Bill Berner
A Study in Scarlet, adapt: Steve Lawson, from Arthur Conan Doyle; (D) Kevin Kelley; (S) Michael Dempsey; (C) Rita Watson

The Wilma Theater. John Shepard and June Stoddard in *1984*. Photo: Stan Sadowski.

The Wilma Theater

BLANKA ZIZKA
JIRI ZIZKA
Artistic/Producing Directors

COURTENAY W. WILSON
Managing Director

2030 Sansom St.
Philadelphia, PA 19103
(215) 963-0249 (bus.)
(215) 963-0345 (b.o.)

FOUNDED 1973
Linda Griffith, Liz Stout

SEASON
Oct.-July

FACILITIES
Seating capacity: 106
Stage: proscenium

FINANCES
Sept. 1, 1986-Aug. 31, 1987
Expenses: $629,937

CONTRACTS
AEA letter of agreement

The Wilma Theater presents theatre as an art form that engages both audience and artists in an adventure of aesthetic and philosophical reflection on the complexities of contemporary life. We believe that a fine performance of a great play is one of the most rewarding experiences our culture provides. The Wilma relies on the selection of powerful, compelling scripts, to which mixed media add another dimension, allowing each production to evolve beyond the confines of verbal communication into the world of metaphor and poetic vision. Our productions are a synthesis of many artistic disciplines—visual arts, music, choreography, writing, acting; our challenge lies in finding new connections among these disciplines to illuminate the dramatic essence of the script. Our staging utilizes a succession of impermanent images, cinematic and three-dimensional, to heighten the inner emotional realities of the characters and create a unique scenic rhythm that captures our age of constant speed, surprise and visual stimulation.

—*Blanka Zizka, Jiri Zizka*

PRODUCTIONS 1985–86

Passion, Peter Nichols; (D) Jiri Zizka; (S) Philip Graneto; (C) Diane McNeal; (L) James Leitner
The Fox, adapt: Allan Miller, from D.H. Lawrence; (D) Blanka Zizka; (S) John Musall; (C) John Musall; (L) James Leitner
Childe Byron, Romulus Linney; (D) Blanka Zizka; (S) Philip Graneto; (C) Pamela Keech; (L) James Leitner
1984, adapt: Pavel Kohout, from George Orwell; trans: Jiri Zizka and Michael Ladenson; (D) Jiri Zizka; (S) Philip Graneto and Jeff Brown; (C) Pamela Keech; (L) John Musall

PRODUCTIONS 1986–87

The Sleep of Reason, Antonio Buero Vallejo; trans: Marion Peter Holt; (D) Blanka Zizka; (S) M.R. Daniels and Jeff Brown; (C) Pamela Keech; (L) James Leitner
3 Guys Naked from the Waist Down, book and lyrics: Jerry Colker; music: Michael Rupert; (D) Jiri Zizka; (S) Jiri Zizka; (C) Judy Panetta; (L) Jerald R. Forsyth
Julie, August Strindberg; adapt: Ingmar Bergman; (D) Blanka Zizka; (S) M.R. Daniels; (C) Pamela Keech; (L) James Leitner
Shooting Magda, Joshua Sobol; trans: Miriam Schlesinger; (D) Jiri Zizka; (S) Philip Graneto; (C) Pamela Keech; (L) Jerald R. Forsyth

Wisdom Bridge Theatre

RICHARD E.T. WHITE
Artistic Director

JEFFREY ORTMANN
Executive Director

1559 West Howard St.
Chicago, IL 60626
(312) 743-0486 (bus.)
(312) 743-6000 (b.o.)

FOUNDED 1974
David Beaird

SEASON
Sept.-July

FACILITIES
Wisdom Bridge Theatre
Seating capacity: 196
Stage: proscenium

Civic Theatre for the Performing Arts
Seating capacity: 900
Stage: proscenium

Wisdom Bridge Theatre. Brian Dennehy, James Lancaster and Jim True in *Rat in the Skull*. Photo: Jennifer Girard.

FINANCES
Aug. 1, 1985-July 31, 1986
Expenses: $1,711,142

CONTRACTS
AEA CAT and USA

Wisdom Bridge Theatre is the northernmost of Chicago's thriving Off-Loop theatres, located in Roger's Park, a highly integrated community colonized over this century by successive waves of Eastern European, Hispanic, Caribbean and most recently, Southeast Asian immigrants. Wisdom Bridge is an integral member of that community, deeply involved both in creating new educational and social outreach programs, and in long-range planning. This sense of active social engagement is the focus of Wisdom Bridge's theatrical presentations—current writing that addresses critical issues and bold reinterpretations of classic texts that stress their relevance for contemporary audiences. Our purpose is to create through production that eponymous "bridge" between artists and audiences, to communicate a lively and thoughtful critique of the assumptions we live by, to provide a forum for voices not always heard, and to celebrate the diversity, breadth and excitement of what Brecht called "the theatre whose setting is the street."

—Richard E.T. White

Note: During the 1985-86 season, Robert Falls served as artistic director.

PRODUCTIONS 1985–86

Rat in the Skull, Ron Hutchinson; (D) Steve Robman; (S) Michael S. Philippi; (C) Sara Davidson; (L) Michael S. Philippi

The Middle of Nowhere in the Middle of the Night, adapt: Tracy Friedman; music and lyrics: Randy Newman; (D) Tracy Friedman; (S) Michael S. Philippi; (C) Nanalee Raphael-Schirmer; (L) Michael S. Philippi

'night, Mother, Marsha Norman; (D) Doug Finlayson; (S) Kevin Rigdon; (C) Erin Quigley; (L) Kevin Rigdon

Hamlet, William Shakespeare; (D) Robert Falls; (S) Michael Merritt; (C) John Murbach; (L) Michael Merritt and Michael S. Philippi

Kabuki Faust, Bill Streib and Lou Anne Wright; (D) Shozo Sato; (S) Shozo Sato; (C) Shozo Sato; (L) Michael S. Philippi

The Immigrant: A Hamilton County Album, Mark Harelik; conceived: Randal Myler and Mark Harelik; (D) Doug Finlayson; (S) Russ Borski; (C) Kathryn L. Schimmelpfennig; (L) Michael S. Philippi

PRODUCTIONS 1986–87

Union Boys, James Yoshimura; (D) Jim O'Connor; (S) Michael S. Philippi; (C) Colleen Muscha; (L) Michael S. Philippi

Kabuki Othello, William Shakespeare; adapt: Karen Sunde; (D) Shozo Sato; (S) Shozo Sato; (C) Shozo Sato; (L) Michael S. Philippi

The Voice of the Prairie, John Olive; (D) B.J. Jones; (S) Michael S. Philippi; (C) Jessica Hahn; (L) Michael S. Philippi

Circe & Bravo, Donald Freed; (D) Doug Finlayson; (S) Linda Buchanan; (C) Kaye Nottbusch; (L) Michael S. Philippi

The Wooster Group

The Wooster Group. Spalding Gray, Michael Stumm, Kate Valk and Ron Vawter in *North Atlantic*. Photo: Nancy Campbell.

ELIZABETH LeCOMPTE
Artistic Director

LINDA CHAPMAN
General Manager

Box 654, Canal St. Station
New York, NY 10013
(212) 966-9796 (bus.)
(212) 966-3651 (b.o.)

FOUNDED 1967
Richard Schechner

SEASON
Variable

FACILITIES
The Performing Garage
Seating capacity: 100
Stage: flexible

FINANCES
July 1, 1986-June 30, 1987
Expenses: $640,000

The Wooster Group is a small collective of experimental theatre artists, working together on collaborative projects over long periods of time. The Wooster Group texts stand as an alternative theatre language which redefines the traditional devices of story line, character and theme. Each production reflects a continuing refinement of a nonlinear, abstract aesthetic, which at once subverts and pays homage to modern theatrical "realism." The seven members of the Group are Jim Clayburgh, Willem Dafoe, Spalding Gray, Elizabeth LeCompte, Peyton Smith, Kate Valk and Ron Vawter. Wooster Group Associates include Scott Briendel, Steve Buscemi, Linda Chapman, Dennis Dermody, Norman Frisch, Paula Gordon, Matthew Hansell, Cynthia Hedstrom, Mary Ann Hestand, Jim Johnson, Michael Kirby, Ken Kobland, Anna Kohler, Coco McPherson, Michael Nishball, Nancy Reilly, Elion Sacker, Irma St. Paule, Jim Strahs, Michael Stumm, and Jeff Webster.

—Elizabeth LeCompte

PRODUCTIONS 1985–86

Terrors of Pleasure, Spalding Gray

North Atlantic, Jim Strahs; (D) Elizabeth LeCompte; (S) Elizabeth LeCompte and Jim Clayburgh

The Road to Immortality, Part Two (...Just the High Points), company-developed; (D) Elizabeth LeCompte; (S) Elizabeth LeCompte and Jim Clayburgh

The Road to Immortality, Part Three (Frank Dell's St. Anthony), company-developed; (D) Elizabeth LeCompte and Peter Sellars; (S) Elizabeth LeCompte and Jim Clayburgh

Situations of Confrontation, company-developed; (D) Ron Vawter

PRODUCTIONS 1986–87

The Road to Immortality, Part One (Route 1&9), company-developed; (D) Elizabeth LeCompte; (S) Elizabeth LeCompte and Jim Clayburgh

The Road to Immortality, Part Two (...Just the High Points), company-developed; (D) Elizabeth LeCompte; (S) Elizabeth LeCompte and Jim Clayburgh

Worcester Foothills Theatre Company. Patrick Sweetman and Susan Nest in *Son of a Vandal*. Photo: Lindon E. Rankin.

The Road to Immortality, Part Three (Frank Dell's St. Anthony), company-developed ; (D) Elizabeth LeCompte; (S) Elizabeth LeCompte and Jim Clayburgh
Swimming to Cambodia and ***Terrors of Pleasure***, Spalding Gray

Worcester Foothills Theatre Company

MARC P. SMITH
Artistic Director

BILL JORDAN
General Manager

074 Worcester Center
Worcester, MA 01608
(617) 754-3314 (bus.)
(617) 754-4018 (b.o.)

FOUNDED 1974
Marc P. Smith

SEASON
Oct.-May

FACILITIES
Seating capacity: 349
Stage: proscenium

FINANCES
June 1, 1986-May 31, 1987
Expenses: $133,190

CONTRACTS
AEA Guest Artist

The Worcester Foothills Theatre Company was conceived and realized as an artistic extension of a community that is traditional and pragmatic on the one hand, and innovative and daring on the other. That a theatre company was sustained for a five-year period without a home base, and was then given a multimillion-dollar theatre complex, proves that the mutual commitment between a theatre company and its community works in its own mysterious and wondrous ways. This dialogue now moves back to its rightful space—a stage and an audience. What we create together will be all the more wondrous and mysterious because we are still exploring the source of that magical communion. My guess is that it will be partly traditional, partly experimental, always respectful of our diversity and aware of our unity—a major voice in an outstanding community.

—Marc P. Smith

Note: For the past two seasons, Worcester Foothills primarily presented booked-in events while its new theatre underwent construction.

PRODUCTIONS 1985–86

The Better Half, Jack Neary; (D) Jack Neary; (S) Eric A. Hart; (L) Eric A. Hart
The Son of a Vandal, Stephen Joel Hersh; (D) William A. Kilmer; (S) Eric A. Hart; (L) Eric A. Hart
October Acres, Margorie Lucier; (D) Paul Mayberry; (S) Eric A. Hart; (L) Eric A. Hart

WPA Theatre

KYLE RENICK
Artistic Director

DONNA LIEBERMAN
Managing Director

519 West 23rd St.
New York, NY 10011
(212) 691-2274 (bus.)
(212) 206-0523 (b.o.)

FOUNDED 1977
Howard Ashman, Craig Evans, Edward T. Gianfrancesco, Kyle Renick, Stephen G. Wells, R. Stuart White

SEASON
Sept.-June

FACILITIES
Seating capacity: 122
Stage: proscenium

FINANCES
July 1, 1986-June 30, 1987
Expenses: $500,000

WPA Theatre. John Pankow and Christine Estabrook in *North Shore Fish*. Photo: Martha Swope.

CONTRACTS
AEA letter of agreement

The WPA Theatre (Workshop of the Players Art Foundation, Inc.) is dedicated to the creation of a vital and informed American repertoire based on realistic writing, acting, directing and design. The WPA continues to nurture the new generation of American playwrights, to cherish the American theatrical tradition through the revival of neglected plays that have helped to shape the American realistic style, and to develop and produce new works that grow out of this style. The WPA Theatre is an ongoing celebration of the American theatre.

—*Kyle Renick*

PRODUCTIONS 1985–86

Cruise Control, Kevin Wade; (D) Norman Rene; (S) Edward T. Gianfrancesco; (C) Walker Hicklin; (L) Debra J. Kletter
Fresh Horses, Larry Ketron; (D) Dann Florek; (S) Edward T. Gianfrancesco; (C) Don Newcomb; (L) Phil Monat
Wasted, Fred Gamel; (D) Clinton Turner Davis; (S) Charles H. McClennahan; (C) Don Newcomb; (L) Craig Evans
Trinity Site, Janeice Scarbrough; (D) William Ludel; (S) Edward T. Gianfrancesco; (C) Don Newcomb; (L) Phil Monat

PRODUCTIONS 1986–87

Alterations, Leigh Curran; (D) Austin Pendleton; (S) Edward T. Gianfrancesco; (C) Don Newcomb; (L) Craig Evans
North Shore Fish, Israel Horovitz; (D) Stephen Zuckerman; (S) Edward T. Gianfrancesco; (C) Mimi Maxmen; (L) Craig Evans
Steel Magnolias, Robert Harling; (D) Pamela Berlin; (S) Edward T. Gianfrancesco; (C) Don Newcomb; (L) Craig Evans
Copperhead, Erik Brogger; (D) Mary B. Robinson; (S) Edward T. Gianfrancesco; (C) Mimi Maxmen; (L) Craig Evans

Yale Repertory Theatre

LLOYD RICHARDS
Artistic Director

BENJAMIN MORDECAI
Managing Director

222 York St.
New Haven, CT 06520
(203) 432-1515 (bus.)
(203) 432-1234 (b.o.)

FOUNDED 1966
Robert Brustein

SEASON
Sept.-May

FACILITIES
Mainstage
Seating capacity: 487
Stage: thrust

University Theatre
Seating capacity: 684
Stage: proscenium

FINANCES
July 1, 1986-June 30, 1987
Expenses: $2,225,000

CONTRACTS
AEA LORT (C), SSD&C and USA

Yale Repertory Theatre. James Earl Jones in *Fences*. Photo: William B. Carter.

The Yale Repertory Theatre has centered its artistic mission on the playwright, taking its cue from the beginnings of the Yale School of Drama in 1926. Our program has focused on the development of playwrights and the articulate and dramatic presentation of their work. Yale Rep seeks talented voices from the past, present and from those of the future who have a concern for the quality of human existence and the environment in which it is nurtured. We present their work in a variety of formats. To ensure that there is excellence available for every area of theatre in the future, we provide professional, experimental opportunities for the exceptionally talented students of the Yale School of Drama who are studying and practicing all aspects of theatre. We believe that in every area of our work there should be a consciousness of the multinational, multiethnic, multiracial and religious community in which we live, and that this should be reflected on our stage. We love our work and our audience. We are proud to be one with them.

—*Lloyd Richards*

PRODUCTIONS 1985–86

The Blood Knot, Athol Fugard; (D) Athol Fugard; (S) Rusty Smith; (C) Susan Hilferty; (L) William B. Warfel
Little Eyolf, Henrik Ibsen; trans: Rolf Fjelde; (D) Travis Preston; (S) Elina Katsioula; (C) Arnall Downs; (L) Jennifer Tipton
Marriage, Nikolai Gogol; trans: Barbara Field; (D) Andrei Belgrader; (S) Pamela Peterson; (C) Dunya Ramicova; (L) Danianne Mizzy

Winterfest 6:

A Child's Tale, Carl Capotorto; (D) Dennis Scott; (S) Tim Saternow; (C) Scott Bradley; (L) Donald Holder
Crazy from the Heart, Edit Villarreal; (D) Mark Brokaw; (S) Tina Cantu Navarro; (C) Arnall Downs; (L) Donald Holder
Stitchers and Starlight Talkers, Kathleen Betsko; (D) William Partlan; (S) Michael H. Yeargan; (C) Dunya Ramicova; (L) Michael R. Chybowski
Union Boys, James Yoshimura; (D) Steven Robman; (S) Rosario Provenza; (C) Charles E. McCarry; (L) Michael Giannitti

Othello, William Shakespeare; (D) Dennis Scott; (S) David Peterson; (C) Rusty Smith; (L) Michael R. Chybowski
The Importance of Being Earnest, Oscar Wilde; (D) Alvin Epstein; (S) Charles E. McCarry; (C) Tina Cantu Navarro; (L) Donald Holder
Joe Turner's Come and Gone, August Wilson; (D) Lloyd Richards; (S) Scott Bradley;

(C) Pamela Peterson; (L) Michael Giannitti

PRODUCTIONS 1986–87

Heartbreak House, George Bernard Shaw; (D) Alvin Epstein; (S) Tim Saternow; (C) Dunya Ramicova; (L) William B. Warfel

Neapolitan Ghosts, Eduardo De Filippo; trans: Marguerita Carra and Louise H. Warner; (D) David Chambers; (S) Phillip R. Baldwin; (C) Ellen V. McCartney; (L) Michael R. Chybowski

The Winter's Tale, William Shakespeare; (D) Gitta Honegger; (S) Michael H. Yeargan; (C) Ann Sheffield; (L) Michael Giannitti

Winterfest 7:

Apocalyptic Butterflies, Wendy MacLeod; (D) Richard Hamburger; (S) E. David Cosier, Jr.; (C) Phillip R. Baldwin; (L) Tim Saternow

Exact Change, David Epstein; (D) Jacques Levy; (S) Marina Draghici; (C) Dunya Ramicova; (L) Christopher Akerlind

The Cemetery Club, Ivan Menchell; (D) William Glenn; (S) Tamara Turchetta; (C) Dunya Ramicova; (L) Michael R. Chybowski

The Memento, Wakako Yamauchi; (D) Dennis Scott; (S) George Denes Suhayda; (C) George Denes Suhayda; (L) Michael R. Chybowski

A Walk in the Woods, Lee Blessing; (D) Des McAnuff; (S) Bill Clarke; (C) Ellen V. McCartney; (L) Jennifer Tipton

A Place with the Pigs, Athol Fugard; (D) Athol Fugard; (S) Ann Sheffield; (C) Susan Hilferty; (L) Michael R. Chybowski

Almost by Chance a Woman: Elizabeth, Dario Fo; trans: Ron Jenkins; (D) Anthony Taccone; (S) Tim Saternow; (C) Marina Draghici; (L) Michael Giannitti

East West Players. Shizuko Hoshi in *The Memento*.

THEATRE CHRONOLOGY

The following is a chronological list of founding dates for the theatres included in this book. Years refer to dates of the first public performance or, in a few cases, the company's formal incorporation.

1896

Hudson Guild Theatre

1915

The Cleveland Play House

1925

Goodman Theatre

1928

Berkshire Theatre Festival

1933

Barter Theatre

1934

Paper Mill Playhouse

1935

Oregon Shakespearean Festival

1937

Old Globe Theatre

1946

Stage One: The Louisville Children's Theatre

1947

Alley Theatre
La Jolla Playhouse

1949

Emmy Gifford Children's Theater
New Dramatists
Sacramento Theatre Company

1950

Arena Stage

1951

Circle in the Square Theatre

1954

Milwaukee Repertory Theater
New York Shakespeare Festival

1955

Honolulu Theatre for Youth
TheatreVirginia
Williamstown Theatre Festival

1956

Academy Theatre
Philadelphia Drama Guild

1957

Detroit Repertory Theatre

1959

Dallas Theater Center
San Francisco Mime Troupe
Society Hill Playhouse

1960

Asolo Performing Arts Center
Cincinnati Playhouse in the Park

1961

The Children's Theatre Company
Theatreworks/USA

1962

Great Lakes Theater Festival
Pioneer Theatre Company

1963

The Arkansas Arts Center Children's Theatre
Center Stage
Fulton Opera House
Goodspeed Opera House
The Guthrie Theater
New Jersey Shakespeare Festival
Periwinkle National Theatre for Young Audiences
Seattle Repertory Theatre
Trinity Repertory Company

1964

Actors Theatre of Louisville
The American Place Theatre
Hartford Stage Company
Missouri Repertory Theatre
O'Neill Theater Center
PCPA Theaterfest
South Coast Repertory

1965

A Contemporary Theatre
American Conservatory Theatre
Cumberland County Playhouse
East West Players
Long Wharf Theatre
Looking Glass Theatre
Studio Arena Theatre

1966

Arizona Theatre Company
The Body Politic Theatre
INTAR Hispanic American Arts Center
Living Stage Theatre Company
Marin Theatre Company
New Stage Theatre
The Repertory Theatre of St. Louis
Yale Repertory Theatre

1967

CSC Repertory Ltd.—The Classic Stage Company
Magic Theatre
Mark Taper Forum
National Theatre of the Deaf
Puerto Rican Traveling Theatre
StageWest
The Wooster Group

1968

AMAS Repertory Theatre
Berkeley Repertory Theatre
The Changing Scene
Ford's Theatre
Omaha Magic Theatre
Ontological-Hysteric Theater
Playhouse on the Square
Repertorio Español

1969

Alliance Theatre Company
Circle Repertory Company
Free Street Theater
Odyssey Theatre Ensemble
Organic Theater Company
Shakespeare Theatre at the Folger
Theatre X

1970

American Theatre Company
BoarsHead: Michigan Public Theater
The Empty Space Theatre
Mabou Mines
Manhattan Theatre Club
New Federal Theatre
The Salt Lake Acting Company
The Street Theater
The Theater at Monmouth

1971

The Cricket Theatre
Dell'Arte Players Company
The Ensemble Studio Theatre
Interart Theatre
Jean Cocteau Repertory
Music-Theatre Group
The Old Creamery Theatre Company
The Playwrights' Center
Playwrights Horizons
Theater for the New City
Theatre Project

1972

The Acting Company
Alabama Shakespeare Festival
Eureka Theatre Company
GeVa Theatre
Indiana Repertory Theatre
Intiman Theatre Company
McCarter Theatre
New American Theater
New Playwrights' Theatre
The Open Eye: New Stagings

1973

Bilingual Foundation of the Arts
City Theatre Company
Florida Studio Theatre
FMT
The Hippodrome State Theatre

Unicorn Theatre
Whole Theatre
The Wilma Theater

1974

American Jewish Theatre
At the Foot of the Mountain
Berkeley Shakespeare Festival
Clarence Brown Theatre Company
Creative Arts Team
George Street Playhouse
Germinal Stage Denver
Illusion Theater
The Independent Eye
Jewish Repertory Theatre
L.A. Theatre Works
Northlight Theatre
Oakland Ensemble Theatre
The People's Light and Theatre Company
The Philadelphia Theatre Company
Portland Stage Company
Roadside Theater
Syracuse Stage
Victory Gardens Theater
Wisdom Bridge Theatre
Worcester Foothills Theatre Company

1975

American Stage Festival
Attic Theatre
Caldwell Theatre Company
The Fiji Company
Long Island Stage
Pittsburgh Public Theater
The Road Company
Seattle Children's Theatre
Soho Repertory Theatre
Theatre IV
Theatre Project Company

1976

Alaska Repertory Theatre
Arkansas Repertory Theatre
California Theatre Center
The CAST Theatre
Dorset Theatre Festival
Empire State Institute for the Performing Arts
Great American Children's Theatre Company
Illinois Theatre Center
Mixed Blood Theatre Company
Nebraska Theatre Caravan
One Act Theatre Company of San Francisco
PlayMakers Repertory Company
San Diego Repertory Theatre
Steppenwolf Theatre Company

1977

Actors Theatre of St. Paul
American Players Theatre
Coconut Grove Playhouse
Horse Cave Theatre
Pan Asian Repertory Theatre
Pennsylvania Stage Company
WPA Theatre

1978

A Traveling Jewish Theatre
The Bloomsburg Theatre Ensemble
Center for Puppetry Arts
Crossroads Theatre Company
The Group Theatre Company
Lamb's Players Theatre
Round House Theatre
The Studio Theatre
Tacoma Actors Guild
Theatre de la Jeune Lune

1979

American Repertory Theatre
The American Stage Company
The Back Alley Theatre
Delaware Theatre Company
Grove Theatre Company
Manhattan Punch Line Theatre
Merrimack Repertory Theatre
New York Theatre Workshop
Perseverance Theatre
Remains Theatre
River Arts Repertory
The Second Stage
Stage West
Theatre for a New Audience
Virginia Stage Company

1980

Antenna Theater
The Bathhouse Theatre
Capital Repertory Company
Denver Center Theatre Company
San Jose Repertory Company

1981

The Playmakers
Vineyard Theatre

1982

Heritage Artists, Ltd.
Huntington Theatre Company
Philadelphia Festival Theatre for New Plays

1983

Mirror Repertory Company
Musical Theatre Works
New Mexico Repertory Theatre
Walnut Street Theatre

1984

Center Theater
Lamb's Theatre Company
The Snowmass/Aspen Repertory Theatre

1985

Lincoln Center Theater
Los Angeles Theatre Center

REGIONAL INDEX

INDEX OF NAMES

A

B

C

D

E

F

G

H

I

J

K

L

M

N

O

P

Q

R

S

T

U

V

W

Y

Z

The Acting Company. Mark Moses, Philip Goodwin and Anthony Powell in *Orchards: Seven American Playwrights Present Stories by Chekhov.* Photo: Diane Gorodnitzki.

INDEX OF TITLES

A

B

C

D

E

F

G

H

I

J

K

L

M

ABOUT TCG

Theatre Communications Group is the national organization for the nonprofit professional theatre. Since its founding in 1961, TCG has developed a unique and comprehensive support system that addresses the artistic and management concerns of theatres, as well as institutionally based and freelance artists nationwide.

TCG provides a national forum and communications network for a field that is as aesthetically diverse as it is geographically widespread. Its goals are to foster the cross-fertilization of ideas among the individuals and institutions comprising the profession; to improve the artistic and administrative capabilities of the field; to enhance the visibility and demonstrate the achievements of the American theatre by increasing public awareness of the theatre's role in society; and to encourage the development of a mutually supportive network of professional companies and artists that collectively represent our "national theatre."

TCG's centralized services today encompass some 30 programs, including job referral services, management and research services, publications, literary services, conferences and a wide range of other information and advisory services. These programs facilitate the work of thousands of actors, artistic and managing directors, playwrights, literary managers, directors, designers, trustees and administrative personnel, as well as a constituency of more than 200 theatre institutions across the country.

THEATRE COMMUNICATIONS GROUP

Peter Zeisler, Director
Lindy Zesch and Arthur Bartow
Associate Directors

Board of Directors